DIANE PURKISS is a professor of English literature at Oxford and a fellow of Keble College. She is the author of the much-admired *The Witch in History*, *Troublesome Things* and the acclaimed history *The English Civil War*. She is currently working on a book about the English at sea (William Colli...

WINNER OF THE
FOOD BO...

'*English Food* is an absolute gem … a fabulous read. I devoured it with gusto … my review copy will find a permanent place on my bookshelves … a richly entertaining and enlightening social history of England in its own right. Superb'   *Sunday Times*

'A mouthwatering history … A sumptuous survey of English cuisine that leaves no morsel untasted … liberally seasoned throughout with literary references, from Anglo-Saxon poetry to Michael Ondaatje … fascinating … There's an awful lot of good stuff to get your teeth into here'   *Guardian*

'Every page brings astonishing revelation … She captures the elevating and inspirational rather well … This book is about food, but it's more importantly about how food defines us'   *The Times*

'A fantastic book … Purkiss illustrates how the way we eat is inherently intertwined with notions of class and gender throughout history. Taking us on a journey from the development of the coffee trade to the first breeders of British beef, Purkiss teaches us what it means to eat food in England, and England's historically complicated relationship with the global food market'   *Evening Standard*

'You can't fault this book for detail … Her display of facts and quotations, from hundreds of manuscripts, cookbooks and books on food across the ages, is impressive'   *TLS*

ALSO BY DIANE PURKISS

The English Civil War: A People's History

ENGLISH FOOD

A People's History

DIANE PURKISS

WILLIAM
COLLINS

William Collins
An imprint of HarperCollins*Publishers*
1 London Bridge Street
London SE1 9GF

WilliamCollinsBooks.com

HarperCollins*Publishers*
Macken House, 39/40 Mayor Street Upper,
Dublin 1, D01 C9W8, Ireland

First published in Great Britain in 2022 by William Collins
This William Collins paperback edition published in 2023

2

A catalogue record for this book is
available from the British Library

ISBN 978-0-00-725557-3

Set in Adobe Garamond Pro
Printed and bound in the UK using 100%
renewable electricity at CPI Group (UK) Ltd

For Ivan

CONTENTS

INTRODUCTION

In her long essay *A Room of One's Own*, Virginia Woolf writes of food, and of the way it is both crucial to us and consigned to the margins of our lives: 'It is part of the novelist's convention not to mention soup and salmon and ducklings, as if soup and salmon and ducklings were of no importance whatsoever, as if nobody ever smoked a cigar or drank a glass of wine.' Woolf goes on to defy this convention by describing dinner at a Cambridge college for men, in lavish and seductive detail. The length of the passage elevates the experience of the food to importance. There is sole, under 'a counterpane of the whitest cream, save that it was branded here and there with brown spots like the spots on the flanks of a doe'. There are partridges, with sprouts 'foliated as rosebuds but more succulent'. And lastly, the silent serving man 'set before us, wreathed in napkins, a confection which rose all sugar from the waves'. The effect is powerful, for:

> thus by degrees was lit, half-way down the spine, which is the seat of the soul, not that hard little electric light which we call brilliance, as it pops in and out upon our lips, but the more profound subtle and subterranean glow which is the rich yellow flame of rational intercourse. No need to hurry. No need to sparkle. No need to be anybody but oneself. We are all going to heaven and Vandyck is of the company.[1]

Food, it seems, can be both elevating and inspirational.

But only six pages later, there is a very different dinner in a setting only superficially similar, at a Cambridge *women's* college: 'plain gravy soup. There was nothing to stir the fancy in that' and then 'beef with its attendant greens and potatoes – a homely trinity, suggesting the rumps of cattle in a muddy market, and sprouts curled and yellowed at the edge and bargaining and cheapening, and women with string bags on Monday morning', all of it just too too solid. Last, and worst, are 'prunes and custard', the prunes 'stringy as a miser's heart and exuding a fluid such as might run in misers' veins who have denied themselves wine and warmth for eighty years and yet not given to the poor, then very dry biscuits and cheese. That was all. The meal was over.' The difference between the dinners leads Woolf to decide that 'one cannot think well, love well, sleep well, if one has not dined well'.[2]

As we listen to Woolf, we understand her meaning perfectly because her language is so sensuous. But the foods she describes are likely to be familiar only in theory. Not even school dinners now offer boiled beef, though they don't offer roast partridge either. Woolf's food is both remote and familiar, the food of a past we know *of* without knowing its taste and texture. We can parse it, helped by Woolf, but her appeal to our senses slips past us, catches on no memories. Her argument, however, remains one of the strongest in all food history. Food, in history, is everywhere and nowhere, taken for granted, invisible, yet assumed to be ever-present. If it is not present, all the historian need do is say as much, and move on. Woolf is making an analogy between food – ubiquitous and yet in the background – and women, needed to uphold the ordinary that lies beneath all events, but always pushed into the shadows when those events are recounted. She is also showing how wrong such thinking is, for upon food, she implies, rely the intellectual breakthroughs with which eaters credit themselves. The silence around food in all mainstream history obscures (and even denies) the full identity of the human in all its complexity. For we are not only minds and wills, but also bodies, and as Woolf knows, we are not all united by our bodiliness; rather, even if all of us eat dinner on the same night in the same city, we are deeply divided.

Woolf is focusing on gender, but the difference in the dinners she describes also reflects class; the men's food is upper class and the women's middling. Being a woman at the table means inhabiting a lower class. The women also eat a dinner more redolent of the past. If asked to choose which of these dinners is a typical Victorian meal, most are likely to pick the beef. Woolf's own spotlight, however, also leaves some people, and some foods, in the shadows. What, for example, did the 'silent serving man' eat? And when? And what about the fishmonger who provided the sole, and the fisherman who caught it, and the milkman who brought the ingredients for its sauce, and the sous-chef who watched as it grilled to brown specks, face near a searing grill or salamander all one warm spring evening? Did they have dinner, and if so, what did they eat, what did it mean to them? Most food history offers just a single grim chapter to those below the upper middle classes, the ones who provide the foods. This is not enough, not by half.

And anyway, who chose the menus? Presumably the chefs, but why did they make such different choices? Woolf suggests that the chef of the men's college is responsible, but how did he arrive at a longlist and then a shortlist from which the menu was eventually selected? How did he know about sole? How did he know about sole in a mornay sauce? How did he grasp that there must be fish as well as meat, and that there must then be dessert? And when and where did he learn about the nymph-like, Aphrodite-like dessert? Did he go to culinary training school? If he did, how did the people who instructed him arrive at their knowledge? More importantly, what shaped their tastes and expectations? Was there a chef at the women's college? Could he or she have chosen differently with their limited resources – could everyone, for instance, have eaten a really good single-course meal? They could have raised their own chickens and vegetables. They could have offered wine. And the men's college too could have chosen differently. The sole in white sauce actually sounds fairly pallid in every respect. Perhaps a *truite aux amandes* would have made them burn even more brightly.

The fact is that the diners at these tables no more chose this food than they prepared it. It was, in a sense, pre-chosen for them by an invisible army of architects of huge sweeping historical movements and explorations and invasions, by the men that made snares and bullets, by the inventors of ranges and the makers of pots and pans, by the makers of empires and armies; and then the tastemakers, the chefs that were briefly the fashion, the chefs that aped them, the magazines and newspapers that chose to feature them, to replicate them. The liking for roast partridge is not something Woolf was born with; it is a thing created by culture, by the long chain of choices made by others that give partridge its meaning of rarity, festivity, upper-classness, the countryside, Englishness. Without those meanings, would it taste the same? Food is paradox because it is an idea and a thing; each has a history, and the idea can survive many material changes to the thing. Or the thing can remain stubbornly the same, while the idea shifts and alters. Once – in the Middle Ages – fish meant penance, abstinence. Sometimes, the stories of food feature anonymous people; sometimes too the food itself is the main character, slipping in and out of sight in diverse places. Sometimes foods are remembered, and sometimes they are forgotten so entirely that no government cover-up could work so well.

As well as the invisible menu-creators, there are an equally shadowy army of material creators. Quite apart from the kitchen staff at both colleges, there were the makers of the primary ingredients, the men who cut the hay, and the men who cut the sugar cane halfway across the world, those who brought the coal from the deeps to fire the ranges, and those who smelted the steel for the utensils. Thousands of people made these two dinners, eaten on just one night. And the next day, all of them would begin all over again, because food eaten today does not last.

At the very moment when Woolf's book enjoyed its first printing on 24 October 1929, the interdependence of all things was about to become catastrophically visible. Five days after *A Room of One's Own* was published, the New York stock market broke: not a clean snap, but a frightful fast grinding down into the dust. By 1933, thirty-seven-year-old Englishwoman and mother of seven Annie Weaving had been starving herself to keep her unemployed husband and children alive.

She collapsed and died while bathing her twins.[3] This makes Woolf's need for partridge and £500 a year look rather ambitious. How much, for instance, did these thousands who had provided both dinners get to eat of what the 1930s were to call 'protective foods' – milk, vegetables, meat, fish, fruit – and how far did they simply subsist on potatoes, bread and margarine? As the Depression took hold, both government and charities focused on how the money should be best spent just as Woolf did; what kind of food would be most *enabling*? Such questions might have been a very long way beside the point for families like Annie Weaving's, though this does not make them trivial or unimportant. The divisions made by food matter (food is matter) because of food's capacity to unite. To be left out of the feast is to be left out of society as a whole, left out of ancestry, family, community. Just as professional women's complaints about 'the glass ceiling' should not be dismissed by comparison with the most oppressed women in the developing world, so her views on the semi-deprivation offered by women's college dinners mattered to those women who rightly sought but were excluded from a place at the best tables.

But what is it to be included? Part of eating joyfully is often a refusal to know about the way the food came to be on your plate – the labour that made it, the sweat that went into it, the choices and desires that shaped it. Do we enjoy food most when it seems normal to us? Yet this detached sitting position is, as Woolf shows, a luxury, and a rather complacent and incurious one. Once you begin to think, really think, about the historical forces that have acted directly on the food on your plate, fascinating vertical and horizontal networks of warp and woof spring into view, as your apple links you with the orchard keepers of the monasteries, all the way back to faraway Kazakhstan. Almaty, the former capital of Kazakhstan, and, before that, Samarkand, is a couple of hours' drive north of the Ile-Alatav National Park, where on the northern slopes of the Tien Shan are tangled woods of apple trees: the ancestors of nearly all apples eaten today. Further east, in the mountain forests of the Dzungarian Alps, thousands of acres of wild apples grow. This is the only place in the world where apple trees form forests.[4] Your apple is contingent on so many chances and so many events: on the abrupt opening and closing of mountain passes by snowstorms or by invaders many centuries before you were born, on the dogged determination of many to raise, feed, prune, pick and preserve, on the will to save whole orchards partly lost to time and to the vehement intrusion of wars of religion, on the ambitions of the gardeners of London and Kent, who raised glowing apples for others. Yet most of us will see only the familiar round shiny fruit, will taste the sweetness and enjoy the crunch of it in the mouth.

Yet in a way, all this knowledge about food can seem like clutter if you like to see your intellect as soaring. Poet John Clare, born in 1793, a year of revolution and hunger, could never forget how hunger felt, or whose sweat went into its surcease. Yet both he and Woolf knew that hunger dreams most of easy satiety; that it is the hungry and the sweaty who dream of plenty that appears to drop out of the sky. Just because Clare knew so much anxious poverty, he could write a child's vision of a Sunday feast with no shadow of money or culinary labour:

Sweet candied horehound, cakes, and peppermint.
… Things of all sorts to tempt his eager eye:
Rich sugar-plums in phials shining bright …[5]

Sugar-plums contain no actual plums. They are plum-shaped, and they are dark, but they are all sugar, with a hard outer skin. Horehound, on the other hand, contains no sugarcane. It is a plant which served as the basis for a range of cough remedies packaged as lozenges, loved mainly by the poor.

We are not always free to choose what we eat; perhaps we never are fully free, constrained as we are by cost, labour, commitments, misinformation, habit, and our socially managed expectations. But some of us are freer than others. Clare and Woolf have in common the way their eating was constrained by mental health issues. An oddity of the Woolf dinners is that both are provided by institutions, while Clare's remembered Sunday feast is private and homely. However, both writers came to know a lot about institutional food because of their long stays in lunatic asylums. Both were lucky to be born too late for the era in which lunatics were controlled by vomiting, laxatives and very meagre diets designed to restore the patients' humoral balance; rather, both were if anything fattened up, so that one of Clare's visitors was surprised by how much weight the poet had gained, 'no longer attenuated and pale'.[6] Virginia Woolf, on the other hand, was in the 1920s treated, if that is the right word, by the then recommended regime of complete rest – not even books were allowed, lest they excite the brain – milk, weight gain, fresh air and early nights. One of her doctors, Sir George Savage, was especially keen to treat neurasthenic women by excessive feeding and complete rest. Woolf was given four or five pints of milk every day, half a pint every two hours. After five days of milk on this scale, she was allowed to add a cutlet, malt extract, cod liver oil and beef tea. The rather brainless thinking behind the regime was that since patients like Woolf stopped eating and lost weight when depressed, they could be forced back into wellness by being made to gain weight. Food could be a pacifier, and the people who controlled its supply were the adults, the patients the needy children.[7] Clare too was in a way treated like a child, both by his doctors and by his admirers, and as a child he was fed. So while both Clare and Woolf share treasured memories of the deliciousness of feasting, each had a complex relationship with food choice because of the treatment both were made to undergo. Their tastebuds did not act outside of the culture in which they lived; instead, everything that was eaten was striped with meaning.

The right to control, to make, is important to Woolf. Making butter with her cook Louie is 'a moment of great household triumph', and becomes a source of pride. Her last diary entry in 1940 reads, 'How one enjoys food now. I make up imaginary meals.' Imaginary meals are much easier to prepare than solid recalcitrant material ones. Though, in fact, Woolf does not prepare them in her mind. She stops dead after that sentence. Imagination fails, after all, apparently able to record only the image of the elderly women, 'shabby old maids buying groceries'. Moments of control and delight are very much scarcer for Clare, in part because he can rarely have been able to unknow the complex earthy background of foods, and yet that background was for him, as it was for Woolf, simply enslavement to hard labour. Woolf because she was a woman and Clare because he was a labourer sought to write their way out of the food-making world and into the world of careless, and even feckless consumption. And don't we all? Everyone who has ever eaten in a restaurant has enjoyed being aware of the chasm between what goes into the food – sweat, raw materials – and what comes out – the edible and delectable. When we eat, we remain human beings, not merely animals with bellies, and as human beings we sit down already replete with our identity issues.

In this book, the links between the story of a foodstuff and human beings become clear, in the way Virginia Woolf wanted. By organising the human stories around particular foods, I show how people from different eras pass foodstuffs between them, continually changing the foodstuffs themselves and also their own views of those foodstuffs. The book focuses on the vertical movement of foods down through time, but it also shows the horizontal journey of each foodstuff as it passes through the hands of many makers and users in different parts of England. Yet as the book shows, in food history change and innovation are often complemented by continuity and the longing for food remembered. Paradoxically, it is often immigrants' longing for such remembered things that brings about innovation in the new country.

In making those journeys, across time and across space, we cross class lines and national borders. So, in this book, we learn how and why a fruit from remote Kazakhstan came to seem normal and everyday in England. We pursue the apple through the monastic orchards of the Middle Ages and through the old market gardens of the brisk and business-like times that succeeded the monasteries; we see the apple cooked into green jelly leathers and stiff almond-rich pastes and pottages. In the hands of Victorian country house gardeners, we witness its metamorphosis into prized, rare dessert apples that sat glossy among the crystal decanters of the old dessert course. And we join the old orchardmen in their despair as orchards are lost or destroyed, as 'English' apple dishes are made from apples imported from farther away than their origin in Kazakhstan. Along the way, we meet the makers of the apple, the creators of its culinary uses, and some of those who are the results. And as the weave becomes visible, so too do the people caught in it, the many, many human stories that together make up just one day's meals.

Journeys from Kazakhstan raise an important question: what is 'English' food? Is it food eaten in England? Food eaten by the English? Food the English like? And who are 'the English'? For a big chunk of the Middle Ages, some at least of the English were the French. The English have also sometimes been others who came and settled; the Anglo-Saxons themselves, the Vikings, the Huguenots, the Dutch. And after all, as Kipling said, 'What do we know of England who only England know?' This book looks at the complex way the food of the colonies evolved in those same colonies, and also at the way the colonies 'bite back', creating new ways of eating back in the mother country. All English food – even the earliest we have detailed records of, Roman food – is post-imperial; all of it created from products made to seem natural and normal by our empire, and those of others. So 'the English' are not a single entity. They are riven by class, by geography and by time. They are, however, not the Scots, Welsh or Irish, peoples who have their own food cultures.

Everyone eats. Food is the only subject on which everyone has something to say, a point of view, a knowledge base, an opinion. For that very reason, it can seem too ordinary to be of interest, and too, well, solid, to be important. Until you don't have it any more. Then its ordinariness becomes exquisite, its solidity the only comfort in a world of dead ideas and abstractions.

And our ideas of what is ordinary and what is special have a history. Our ordinary was not always ordinary. It was probably not always ordinary even to us; if you've eaten breakfast today, it likely isn't what you ate for breakfast ten years ago, even if it is what you ate for breakfast yesterday or the day before. This book will ask why you changed and why some things stayed the same. You might have had a fry-up, but only if it was Sunday, while if it was Sunday and you were in Clerkenwell's Fox and Anchor, you might have chosen the City Boy Fry-up, which includes a minute steak, a lamb kidney, calves' liver and a pint of stout. Or perhaps you might have eschewed such things as gendered, macho, old-hat, and instead enjoyed a 'clean' breakfast of carrot and spice-baked oatmeal, because you are modern, twenty-first century?

In the latter case, sorry. Your breakfast is much older than the City Boy Fry-up. Often, when we shake off what those two generations ago thought was normal, we revert unknowingly to what was normal far longer ago. Your medieval ancestors would recognise the general form of the dish, and they would call it pottage. Except … there is one element of your breakfast that is novel, relatively speaking. Your pottage contains an orange carrot. If the carrot were yellow or purple, it could – like the rest of the pottage – be identified as medieval. However, carrots in the early and high Middle Ages were overwhelmingly like parsnips, so much so as to be indistinguishable from them. Recent genetic research shows that the orange carrot was selectively bred from yellow carrots, probably by Dutch farmers in the sixteenth century, possibly to honour their royal family, but more probably because bright colour was prized in food culture.

Most people – even some food historians – write as if there were a period of stability in English food culture, in which the majority of the population was rural, self-sufficient or nearly so, eating the same foods as their immediate forebears because these were the foods available locally. A time without novelty, a time without innovation.

That time never existed.

On breakfast: an essay

'English Civilisation is … bound up with solid
breakfast and gloomy Sundays.'

George Orwell, 'England Your England', in
The Lion and the Unicorn (1941)

If historians and readers think they know exactly when food culture
in England was stable and not subject to the fickle whims of fashion, they tend to finger breakfast as the changeless moment.
Twentieth-century novelist Somerset Maugham said that the best way
to eat in England was to eat breakfast three times a day – meaning not
just any old breakfast, but a full English breakfast. But what *is* a full
English, exactly, and how old is it really? These matters are much more
complex than they appear, and ideas about what a full English is turn
out to be both very vague and fairly recent.

Breakfast is a meal that has shifted often in time and purpose. The
word breakfast differs from the French word, *petit déjeuner*, which
insists that breakfast is a minimal lunch, and German *Frühstuck*,
which stresses that it is both small and early (*Stuck* means 'bit' or
'piece'). The Latin word *ientaculum* means 'a bit while fasting'. In
dropping all direct references to the smallness of the meal, the English
word breakfast allows the possibility that it *can* be big. Yet medieval
and early modern breakfast was more like a mid-morning snack, if it
happened at all – and mostly it didn't. The health guides of the early
modern period recommended breakfast only for children, invalids and

the elderly who had weak digestive systems and had to eat smaller meals.[1]

A medieval labourer left the house to work in the fields or with livestock from first light, returning to the house at mid-morning – or sometimes as late as noon – to break his fast with a warm meal. This meal was called dinner. In the Middle Ages, dinner was in content not entirely unlike breakfast as the English imagination came to envisage it. It began for the better off with pottage, a mixture of grain and herbs, which might be followed by offal – kidneys, perhaps – with some spices. Then might come more meat – such as bacon collops (slices) – and doucet, a sweet custard. The first meal of the day therefore kept its content even as it moved in the diurnal round. With similar slipperiness, the term 'breakfast' arises before the meal is fully established. In Robert Greene's play *Friar Bacon and Friar Bungay* (c.1589), the question 'What have you fit for breakfast?' generates the surprising answer 'Butter and cheese, and umbles of a deer.' A breakfast of preserved dairy and deer offal might strike us as strange, but the reasoning is pragmatic. Cheese is a way of storing milk; umbles are left over after a deer is hung to mature. These are all things that can be grabbed or snatched in haste, in the midst of a day of labour.

There is another reason for the offal, too, and in his post-Reformation way Greene is being clever about what medieval friars were allowed to eat; most orders had rules that forbade eating red meat in the dining room (refectory), but offal didn't count as meat. Yet the friars would have had that kind of fare for dinner at 10 a.m., not for breakfast. (Meals are often about names and times; what you call it affects the idea.) The fast being broken was longer in the Middle Ages, up to seventeen hours, and deemed to be of spiritual merit: 'communion is the best breakfast', hungry young monks were told. Monks rose at about 2 a.m., for Matins, and again at sunrise for Lauds, the hours of darkness and sung prayer. Their early modern descendants rose later – at 7 a.m., like Robert Laneham, who began the day by going to chapel. But then he breakfasted; people had stopped waiting until ten. Laneham ate a portion of bread and drank a bowl of ale. This was standard fare.[2] Most of his contemporaries had something similar –

bread of one kind or another, with beer. The very rich might add a spicy egg dish with sugar and currants, or some preserved ocean fish – pickled herrings or salt cod. Or they might eat a big boiled piece of red meat. In Shakespeare's play *Henry IV Part I*, the gentlemen are said to be 'up already and call for egg and butter'.[3] There was always tension between speed and ease of preparation, and the tradition of a substantial meal.

The move to break the fast earlier was influenced by the godly idea of getting on with the working day that developed following the Reformation.[4] It was also fuelled by the growth of towns and cities, where starting work meant leaving home for the entire day. By the Restoration breakfast was important enough for diarist Samuel Pepys to record what he ate on special occasions. These almost always involved the kind of meat and fish most modern people associate with lunch or dinner, rather than anything that looks like a full English. Among the breakfasts Pepys recorded are a feast of oysters, calves' tongues and anchovies, washed down with wine (1 January 1660), a cold turkey pie and goose (6 January 1660), radishes (5 February 1660), a slice of beef or two and 'too much wine' (9 September 1661), mince pie and a collar of brawn with wine (7 July 1661), bread and butter and sweetmeats (3 August 1662), cold roast beef (13 October 1662), cold chine of pork (29 December 1662), and 'the remains of our supper hashed' (27 July 1663). Only once does he record eggs for breakfast (18 August 1662). But all these notes are complicated by the fact that by breakfast Pepys does not always mean the first meal of a new day, but sometimes a kind of midnight feast after a party, in one case served at 2 a.m.[5]

At the same time, ideas about what breakfast *ought* to be were establishing themselves. Writing in the *Tatler* in 1709, essayist Joseph Addison thought that a traditional English breakfast included beef, and always had:

> The tables of the ancient gentry of this nation were covered
> thrice a day with hot roast beef, and I am credibly informed, by
> an antiquary who has searched the registers in which the bills of

fare of the Court are recorded, that instead of tea and bread and butter, which have prevailed of late years, the maids of honour in Queen Elizabeth's time were allowed three rumps of beef for their breakfast.

Just as we postdate a sumptuous breakfast to the time of Victoria, so Addison credits it to the time of Elizabeth I (actually a time of terrible famine, as we shall see).

Addison's ideal and ours are far from reality; the element of the full English that is most central in the breakfast of the past is toast. Toast is our very own invention, a food we created, as English as the chalk cliffs of the shoreline. No other country does toast. As breakfast settled into its earlier time slot, we can see how very much toast came to matter. In Frances Burney's 1782 novel *Cecilia*, the Harrel family – reckless spendthrifts – eat a breakfast of toast and tea. Toast was a sign that servants could be spared from domestic labour to do nothing but make it and carry it. Moreover, it had to be made from good bread made of fine flour; coarse bread would have fallen apart on the toasting fork. The luxury of toast and tea, praised by Mr Hobson, is contrasted with the gruel of the miserly Mr Briggs, who is hoping to avoid the expense of feeding his servants properly.[6]

While the rich saw toast at breakfast as a pleasant, luxurious feast, warm and labour-intensive, the grain-based breakfasts eaten in institutions were far less appealing, even though they were highly traditional, echoing the pottage and beers enjoyed in medieval households at mid-morning dinner. Such breakfasts *could* be jolly enough; as late as 1731, the children at London's Christ's Hospital had a surprising start – their grain-based liquid was beer, not gruel: 'They have every morning for their breakfast bread and beer.' Much more cheerless is the orphanage in Dickens's *Oliver Twist*: 'the gruel was served out; and a long grace was said over the short commons'.[7] Gruel like Oliver's is at the very bottom of the miserly breakfast menu. It might be made of barley or oats, mixed to a paste, then boiled. Runny, lumpy and flavoured only with salt, it provided few calories and even fewer vitamins or minerals, but it was warm, cheap, and easy for a single cook or maid to manage. What made it worse was its dilution, which was meant to make it easy on the stomach but actually turned it into little more than flavoured water. But while gruel came to suggest the most disgraceful kind of institution to many, some middle-class people such as Charlotte Bronte's Jane Eyre liked its very weakness: 'Hannah had brought me some gruel and dry toast, about, as I supposed, the dinner hour. I had eaten with relish: the food was good.'[8]

Jane is eating her dry (butterless) toast at lunchtime. Toast could also be a teatime food, and then it was more likely that it would be made by those who ate it; in Dorothy L. Sayers' 1935 *Gaudy Night*, Harriet Vane's idyllic day in Oxford begins, apparently breakfastless, with 'mornings in Bodley, … long afternoons, taking an outrigger up the Cher, … then back, with mind relaxed and body stretched and vigorous, to make toast by the fire'. Toast handmade by the fire is all about nostalgia for student days, or perhaps for a certain sort of school days, when toast might be eaten at any time of day:

> Only public school fags can make perfectly golden, perfectly crisp and yet perfectly spongy toast, for the simple reason that they are properly beaten should any one of the eight, pluperfect, decrusted triangles, which constitute a fag-master's traditional portion, evince the slightest sign of scraping, uneven cutting, excessive thickness or imperfect saturation with butter … The public school system seems to me amply vindicated in that it teaches boys to make toast.

This is food writer Morton Shand in 1927.[9] His mild caddishness is traditional; cad and bounder Fred Vincy in *Middlemarch* not only comes late to breakfast but eats mostly toast, having walked round the table 'surveying the ham, potted beef, and other cold remnants, with an air of silent rejection, and polite forbearance from signs of disgust'. And toast remained central even to more lavish breakfasts. At Archdeacon Grantly's, an enormous and heavy buffet is ordered, but novelist Anthony Trollope tells us first about the toast, then other breads: 'there was dry toast and buttered toast, muffins and crumpets;

hot bread and cold bread, white bread and brown bread, homemade bread and bakers' bread, wheaten bread and oaten bread; and if there be other breads than these, they were there'. In *The Warden*, however, there are 'four three-cornered bits of dry toast, and four square bits of buttered toast; there was a loaf of bread, and some oily-looking butter; and on the sideboard there were the remains of a cold shoulder of mutton'. This is 'scanty fare' – there is not enough *toast*.

———

The money involved in serving a lavish breakfast was largely spent on labour as well as ingredients. Victorian housemaids – the solitary maid-of-all-work for modest households, or the cook with helpers for the better-off – faced a morning of vigorous work before food preparation could even begin. One such, Lilian Westall, born in 1893, might when at home in King's Cross nip around to the Salvation Army hostel in Pentonville Road for breakfast – a cup of tea and a big piece of bread and jam. At work in Bletchingley Castle in Surrey, breakfast was very different. The range had to be raked out, and the lumps of still usable coal had to be separated from the ash and put back into the grate; then the stove had to be cleaned with the hideous sticky blacking, wiped clear, and the fire lit. An energetic cook or maid would also clean the stove flues twice a week. And after all that, the real work began, and here the ordeal was all about toast.

An oddity of the meals we associate with the English food of an unidentified past – the roast dinner with veg, the full English – is that they all require several things to be done simultaneously. Gravy has to be made while roast vegetables are turned and boiled vegetables watched. Anyone who has ever made a Christmas dinner singlehanded will understand the difficulty. The Victorian breakfast was similar, made tortuous by the continuing importance of toast. Victorian toast had to be made in front of the range. The bread had to be sliced – thinly, but not so thinly that it would fall apart when stabbed with a toasting fork. If the maid was a perfectionist or had a perfectionist mistress, she could dry out the slices first. Then each slice was speared, and the toasting fork held at just the right distance from embers that were meant to be smokeless. Ideally, the bread would be thin and toasted until dark gold, then a pat of butter placed on it while the maid toasted a new slice. By the time this too was ready, the butter on the first slice was soft enough to spread. While the maid was crouched awkwardly over the embers with her fork, everything else – eggs, bacon, kidneys, mushrooms – was meant to be sizzling away on the range top. (She might have served the porridge already; if not, it too would be bubbling and hissing.) Then the toast had to be brought hot to the table. Some mistresses would also insist that it arrive already buttered, adding to the labour, and increasing the likelihood that it would arrive stone cold. Meanwhile, Lilian's breakfast might be 'bread and dripping. There were often mouse dirts on the dripping to be scraped off first.'[10]

The toaster came like a liberator; first trialled in 1906, it was commercially available from 1909. Before that, every middle- or upper-class slice of toast was the result of anxious, backbreaking labour, sore feet walking fast along long cold halls, tired soap-sore hands carefully holding silver plate dishes weighing upwards of fifty pounds. Obviously, the result was unlikely to be perfect, and the accompanying food too was likely to be cool, and hence greasy. But as nostalgia and cosiness got attached to toast, the idea of it became rigidly traditional. Elizabeth David is contemptuous about the toaster, insisting that only the toasting fork or – in a pinch – the grill pan can create the 'right' texture.[11] David's view is very like that of maid Ilse Lewen's employer in Birmingham during the Second World War; when Ilse's mistress asked her to make toast, she looked for a toaster, but her mistress handed her a fork.[12] Toast was in many respects the food of the privileged, made by the underprivileged, though sometimes you might make it yourself as a game. Biting into your breakfast toast, you could begin the day with the taste of your social class on your tongue.

————

Back in 1775, one Englishman at last sat down to something he liked so much that he said, 'if an epicure could remove by a wish in quest of sensual gratifications wherever he had supped he would breakfast in

… Scotland.' He had tea and coffee, accompanied by butter, marmalade, conserves and honey. The contented man was Samuel Johnson, and he was in the Hebrides. According to his friend and biographer Boswell, Johnson normally partook of tea, rolls and butter for breakfast. What seems to have thrilled him in Scotland were the condiments. And soon the Scots themselves had noticed Johnson's eagerness. In his 1814 novel *Waverley*, Walter Scott wrote:

> Miss Bradwardine presid[ed] over the tea and coffee, the table loaded with warm bread, both of flour, oatmeal, and barleymeal, in the shape of loaves, cakes, biscuits, and other varieties, together with eggs, reindeer ham, mutton and beef ditto, smoked salmon, marmalade, and all the other delicacies which induced even Johnson himself to extol the luxury of a Scotch breakfast above that of all other countries.

Of course, Johnson hadn't actually *mentioned* reindeer ham or smoked salmon. No matter. Scott is now insisting that this elaborate breakfast dates back to Johnson's time, if not time immemorial.[13]

It follows that the Scottish full breakfast precedes the English; I can find no solid and portly evidence of a full English that occurs before *Waverley*, let alone before Johnson. The full English is really an adapted naturalisation of the full Scottish, which in turn was an invention, like the tartan, an assemblage of known foods that said 'Scotland'. And the Victorians *knew* their better breakfasts came from Scotland. Major L. (the pen name of Major James Landon) wrote in 1887 that he could not 'understand why England should be so behindhand in the requirements necessary to the comfort of this meal. In Scotland it is quite a different thing; good breakfasts are the rule, not the exception. Only travel to Scotland, and arrive at Perth station; in the refreshment room you see it at once; excellent fish, excellent meats, and bread and rolls of all sorts.'

Marmalade is central to the breakfast of Johnson's and Scott's dreams. This bitter orange jam is a food everyone knows, if one that has changed beyond all recognition in relatively recent times. It is the fruit of creolisation, initially the uncomfortable melding of cultures in medieval southern Iberia. The Moorish rulers of the kingdom of Al-Andalus brought orange and lemon trees to Europe, along with the irrigation systems needed to sustain them through the long dusty Mediterranean summers. There had been a few orange trees earlier, but their fruits were wizened. The oranges the Moors brought were sour, and when the peel was boiled with sugar, the result fitted with the sweet-and-sour tastes liked by medieval elites. The preservative effect of sugar also let the new fruits travel, first as suckets – sweets. Used to preserved fruit pastes, the English adapted recipes for quinces and apples – both rich in pectin – to the even more pectin-laden Seville oranges. Sir Hugh Plat gives such a recipe in his 1600 *Delightes for Ladies*. However, the result was not much like marmalade as we know it, transparent and glossy, with shreds of peel embedded in it: Plat's was opaque and solid, like the quince paste sold then and now as Spanish membrillo.[14]

There is a dispute about who first created our kind of marmalade; one candidate is Rebecca Price, who wrote out her mother's recipe in 1681. Price lived in Buckinghamshire, and she began her handwritten recipe book that year, just before she married Nehemiah Brandreth. She was twenty-one years old. She went on with her task for the next sixty years, adding recipes, indexing those she had, and in her will she bequeathed her two folio recipe books to her daughter, Alice Brandreth.[15] Rebecca was doing what very many women did: storing up personal culinary lore and tips to pass on to their daughters.

'Recipe' is just a word for how to do something. In the past, such knowledge was probably transmitted orally, but there was good sense in writing recipes down. A woman might keep them on scraps of paper in a 'recipe box', or might open a notebook and transcribe particular recipes, perhaps especially those that were seasonal and easily forgotten. The book might be handed on to a daughter, who might add her own recipes and annotate her mother's. Someone else might add still more notes and recipes. This means that we often know who began a collection and on what date, but we don't always know the date and author of every individual recipe. Such manuscript recipe books were not ousted by the advent of printed cookbooks. They offer a glimpse of personalised food. Mostly, such recipes aim to preserve what the writer knows. Frequently, recipes are added because they are secret or novel. Frequently, too, recipes are transcribed with a pedigree attested: Mrs Bodkin's spice cake, Lady Grantley's bread in the French manner. These notes often point to friendships, social networks; they are records of the closeness between housewives, often crossing class boundaries.

Rebecca Price began her book in 1681, but we can assume her marmalade recipe was added later. How much later? There's no way of knowing; we can't even guess the date by the position of an individual recipe in the book. Very organised recipe books like Rebecca's had sections, and recipes were inserted into the relevant sections. Such books are often bound versions of loose papers written separately from one another; indeed, some recipe collections survive in this form, often massed together and tied with string, or kept in a box. Binding sheets gives them a false sense of unity and an order that may not be part of their original creation. And sometimes a scribe might copy an entire collection afresh and in one go; one reason we know this is that some recipe collections are not books at all, but long continuous rolls or scrolls, like the fourteenth-century manuscript *Forme of Cury*. To complicate things still further, the daughters to whom recipe books are bequeathed often add further recipes, and sometimes do so in the middle of the book. It follows that dating individual recipes is some-thing of a mug's game. So is inferring social class from the original woman's class of origin. However, Rebecca Price's orange marmalade recipe does offer us one small clue: she warns the reader that 'it will not be stiff as other marmelette, to be cut'. This implies that Rebecca was writing for an audience more used to the membrillo kind of fruit paste that the word marmalade had until then connoted.

There is an earlier claim than Rebecca's for the origin of marmalade: the recipe given in a 1584 printed book, Partridge's *Treasury of Commodious Conceits and Hidden Secrets*, reprinted many times.[16] This involves first simmering the thin strips of peel until tender, washing them in three changes of water, and then simmering again until transparent, with syrup 'thin as hony' potted with them. This sounds like marmalade to me. The recipe is part of a book about how to preserve food in ways that will allow it to be used to make 'banqueting stuffe'. The 1573 edition includes a huge number of methods for preserving flowers – roses, violets, succory (chicory) – and even acorns, elecampane root and cherries and barberries. These exotic recipes argue against widespread use of marmalade, and the fact that Partridge thinks his recipe is a secret is also a sign that it was not well known.[17]

Whoever came first, by 1714 orange marmalade appears in Mary Kettilly's *Collection of Above Three Hundred Receipts*; the recipe included the fruits' juice, but it was still a dessert or a subtlety. How and why did its consumption move to breakfast? The Scots, living in a climate too cold for quinces, were working more with imported oranges, which arrived with the sugar shipments from southern Europe and the West Indies; these were destined for the sugar-boiling houses at Glasgow and Leith, set up between 1667 and 1701. Marmalade was seen as warming, and so might replace a hot meal: in 1729, William Macintosh complained that the tea kettle had ousted the big wooden cup of warm ale with toast, while 'marmalet, cream and cold tea' were served.[18] But the orange conserve was already popular enough in Scotland to lead the Dundee-based firm of James Keiller to buy a load of Seville oranges cheaply from a ship that took shelter from a storm in Dundee harbour. His mother Janet made them into marmalade, which sold so well that the business took off.

———

Its warmth, satisfaction and largesse made a cooked breakfast seem desirable to every social class. In Dickens's novels, any hot breakfast, however meagre, becomes a sign of filial love:

'Sit close to the fire, father, dear, while I cook your breakfast. It's all ready for cooking, and only been waiting for you. You must be frozen.'
… 'The meat's ready now, father. Eat it while it's hot and comfortable.' … He looked at her, stirred his tea and took two

or three gulps, then cut at his piece of hot steak with his case-knife.[19]

This is not a rich family, but the breakfast is *steak*. Bacon too – the staple source of protein and fat for the poor – played an increasing part in breakfast, as people began to think that they were meant to eat meat at every meal. So, in *Bleak House*, there is 'a powerful odour of hot rolls and coffee … a rasher of bacon at the fire in the rusty grate'. In *Our Mutual Friend*, 'Present on the table, one scanty pot of tea, one scanty loaf, two scanty pats of butter, two scanty rashers of bacon, two pitiful eggs.' While the steak in *Our Mutual Friend* is a blessing, this full-sounding fry-up is seen as meagre. And not everyone wants it. Mr Skimpole in *Bleak House* opines that 'Some men want legs of beef and mutton for breakfast; I don't. Give me my peach, my cup of coffee and my claret; I am content.'[20] He sounds an ideal husband, though finding or growing the perfect peach is no light task either.

American novelist Henry James describes his first breakfast in Liverpool, in the coffee-rooms of the Old Adelphi Hotel: 'The plate of buttered muffin and its cover were sacredly set upon the slop bowl after hot water had been ingenuously poured into the same … I must have had with my tea and my muffins a boiled egg or two and a dab of marmalade.'[21] Were muffins rather decadent, though? 'Effeminate loungers' indulge in buttered muffins, while a 'hale old gentleman' eats porridge, according to travel writer Thomas Forester in 1850.[22] Much more macho to eat like a Scot! By the turn of the century, Sherlock Holmes's housekeeper Mrs Hudson has 'as good an idea of breakfast as a Scotchwoman' in 'The Naval Treaty', and the male pair – Sherlock and Watson – tuck into ham, eggs and curried chicken.

A burst of cookbooks dedicated to breakfast appeared from the mid-nineteenth century: Georgiana Hill's *The Breakfast Book* in 1865; Mary Hooper's *Handbook for the Breakfast Table* in 1873; M. L. Allen's *Breakfast Dishes for Every Morning of Three Months* in 1884; and Colonel Kenney Herbert's *Fifty Breakfasts* in 1894. Hugely elaborate mixtures of cold meat, hot dishes, drinks, sauces and novelties were on display in all these books as simply normal: snipe on toast, golden eggs

(Scotch eggs without the sausage) in rich sauce, partridge pudding, Russian gallimaufry of cold meat refried with onion, fillet of beef with truffles – all feature in Allen's work, but there are few signs that anyone ate in this way except the very rich. Depicting the breakfast spread in one of England's stately homes, Agatha Christie offers a no-holds-barred mass of food, capriciously picked over by the nobleman:

> 'Omelet,' said Lord Caterham, lifting each lid in turn. 'Eggs and bacon, kidneys, devilled bird, haddock, cold ham, cold pheasant. I don't like any of those things, Tredwell. Ask the cook to poach me an egg, will you?'
>
> 'Very good, my lord.'
>
> Tredwell withdrew. Lord Caterham, in an absent-minded fashion, helped himself plentifully to kidneys and bacon, poured himself out a cup of coffee, and sat down at the long table … With a sad shake of his head, Lord Caterham rose and carved himself a plate of ham … Tredwell reappeared silently with two poached eggs in a little silver dish which he placed in front of Lord Caterham.
>
> 'What's that, Tredwell?'
>
> 'Poached eggs, my lord.'
>
> 'I hate poached eggs,' said Lord Caterham peevishly. 'They're so insipid. I don't like to look at them even. Take them away, will you, Tredwell?'[23]

Christie knew all about country house breakfasts, and so did Daphne Du Maurier, who allotted Maxim de Winter and his shy new wife an equally rich spread. So too did Elizabeth Goudge, who in *The Little White Horse* gave Maria Merryweather a breakfast of vast quantities of porridge, cream, eggs, bacon and mushrooms; even her dyspeptic governess 'ventured on a brown boiled egg'. By now it is all too clear that these enormous meals are enjoyed as memories, reveries of a past of opulence and choice.

That these lavish breakfasts depicted in cookbooks and novels were not what most Victorians actually ate is shown fully in B. Seebohm

Rowntree's 1901 survey. In *Poverty: A Study of Town Life*, even the best-off families – the ones with servants – had more modest ambitions: porridge, fried bacon, eggs, toast and marmalade, and coffee. A full English, in fact![24] Queen Victoria herself generally had only a boiled egg for breakfast, in a gold egg cup, attended by two Indian servants in scarlet and gold uniforms.[25] The English breakfast is therefore a perfect instance of why cookbooks are not the best guide to food history. The gap between the actual food eaten by the majority and the much more lavish spreads in recipe books is notable; most of us nowadays own cookbooks we dig out only on occasion, and only when entertaining. Food in cookbooks is more often a form of what might be than a record of what is. And even more interesting is that the notion of a 'full English' derives not from that lavish cookbook tradition, but from people's humbler adaption of it, the egg and bacon, then toast and marmalade, that people actually ate, not the yards of hot fish and cold game that only a tiny fraction of the population ever enjoyed. It is this real full English that sank deep into our national food consciousness, remaining a longed-for Sunday treat for well over a century. Though the taste for marmalade that accompanied it is now abating, the integers of that breakfast, the breakfast people remember eating, remain.

———

Meanwhile, a new idea of breakfast made its way across the Atlantic: breakfast cereal. Saki, aka Hector Munro, satirised the trend in his story 'Filboid Studge', a cereal advertised with 'one huge sombre poster depict [ing] the Damned in Hell suffering a new torment from their inability to get at the Filboid Studge which elegant young fiends held in transparent bowls just beyond their reach'. Yet the 'studge' ('sludge'?) is presented as an antidote to pleasure. With Filboid Studge, the gloom George Orwell links to breakfast has arrived. Mothers force it on their children *because it is unpalatable*. The mentality is exactly the one memoirist Gwen Raverat depicts from her Cambridge childhood: 'we had porridge for breakfast with salt not sugar; and milk to drink … There was toast and butter, but I never had anything stronger'; 'Jam might have weakened our moral fibre'. Raverat always writes the word jam with a capital J. She also remembers an occasional treat: 'twice a week we had, at the end of breakfast, one piece of toast, spread with a thin layer of that dangerous luxury, Jam. But of course not butter too. Butter and jam on the same bread would have been an unheard of indulgence – a disgraceful orgy.'[26] Yet Raverat found delight nevertheless: she writes, 'the queer thing is that we none of us like it [butter and jam] to this very day. But those two glamorous jam-days have permanently coloured my conception of Sundays and Wednesdays, which are both lovely dark red days.'[27]

The relatively modern breakfast comes to the country house with Jeeves in the works of P. G. Wodehouse. Jeeves has 'the juice of an orange, followed by Cute Crispies – an American cereal – scrambled eggs with a slice of bacon, and toast and marmalade'. But for Bertie Wooster, 'It was the scent of kippered herrings that was now wafted … like a benediction.'[28] Filboid Studge and Cute Crispies take the place of gruel; cereal is good enough for the servants. Food is never just a matter of filling the belly, but of ideas about what will do that best, which is why the starving do not try to eat chair legs but do make toad water (toad water is tea made by burning a lump of bread to cinders and then steeping it in hot water). Toad water *looks* like food. At least expectations can be satisfied, even if bellies stay empty.

To enjoy the full English, we have to see it as a *treat*. No one knew this better than C. S. Lewis:

And immediately, mixed with a sizzling sound, there came to Shasta a simply delightful smell. It was one he had never smelled in his life before, but I hope you have. It was, in fact, the smell of bacon and eggs and mushrooms all frying in a pan … bacon and eggs and mushrooms, and the coffee pot and the hot milk, and the toast.

It was all new and wonderful to Shasta … He didn't even know what the slices of brown stuff were, for he had never seen toast before. He didn't know what the yellow soft thing they smeared on the toast was, because in Calormen you nearly always get oil instead of butter.[29]

This passage asks: what might English breakfast look like to someone from an entirely different food culture, one that sounds very much more urban, sophisticated and cosmopolitan? It would be new, yes, but also 'wonderful'. Shasta is willing to eat things he can't even identify, and it is made to seem natural because the reader knows what toast is and what butter is. Of course, Shasta is really 'something Northern anyhow', a kidnapped prince returning to his true home, his ethnic home, and his breakfast is an initiation rite, a rebaptism. Here, we are forced to side with ourselves.

Bare breakfast tables are not a thing of the past: a 2015 study showed that a quarter of UK secondary school children have no breakfast, according to the British Nutrition Foundation.[30] Some 20 per cent of teachers reported that the number of pupils arriving at school hungry had increased in the previous year, with a majority attributing it to the fact that some families couldn't afford breakfast. But a substantial minority had other explanations, some saying that children were 'increasingly not leaving time in the morning' to have breakfast at home, while others claimed that breakfast was not seen as important by parents or guardians.[31] Breakfast's brief zenith may already be over.

But when breakfast is eaten, in all eras, there is one constant, and that is bread. This central food has shaped who we are, and is in turn reshaped by us and by our changing sense of our place in the landscape, in the year, and in our homes. Our journey into food history will begin with bread, as breakfast begins the day.

Loaves

'Hunger was the inscription on the baker's shelves, written
in every small loaf of his scanty stock of bad bread.'

Charles Dickens, *A Tale of Two Cities*

A baker called George Barlow died in 1584. He knew he was dying; his will had been made the year before, on 26 July 1583. He probably knew because he had a cough that wouldn't go away; he probably knew he had baker's lung, caused by inhaling particles of flour every single day. He would never make old bones; most bakers didn't live long lives. He left few possessions: a bakehouse, a bolting tub, a kneading trough, and other treen ware, literally tools and utensils made from trees. He also had a vital supply of fuel; its importance is shown by its presence in his inventory. He had gorse kindlings, or kiddes, and wood kiddes, turves and coals.[1] George's pathetic inventory shows how hard the life of a baker was, trapped in harsh working conditions. To discover where daily bread came from and what it cost, we must visit the infernal deep of the pre-industrial baker's daily round; for the baker, hours in hell, and for the baker's boy, all night forever, below ground. The history of food should not begin with what is on the table. It should begin with those who make the food.

Baking was for many centuries virtually unchanged. The following description comes from 1805, but the essentials would have been the same 500 or 1,500 years earlier.

Abraham Edlin arrived at his bakery at two in the afternoon, when the nine faggots were put in the oven to dry. At 3 p.m., the bakers began to set the bread sponge; they emptied two sacks of flour into the kneading trough, and then sifted the flour. They made a liquid yeast mixture with six pints of yeast dissolved in water at 29°C. They mixed it into the flour. Now they had dough. They sprinkled flour on the top, to prevent a crust from forming, and wrapped it in two or three sacks to keep it warm. By 6 p.m., the dough had swelled and broken through its floury covering. The bakers stirred in two more pails of liquid yeast, and covered the mass in flour and sacks. At eleven, five more pails of water were added, and 'the whole was intimately blended, and kneaded for upwards of an hour': in the kneading trough, the huge mass of sticky dough slapped again and again against the wooden walls of the trough. (Clothes washing was done in much the same way in the same period.) After that, the dough was cut into pieces with a knife, thrown over the sluicing board and penned to one side of the trough; the bakers sprinkled some dry flour over, and left it to prove till about 3 a.m., when it was again kneaded for the space of half an hour. The dough was then taken out of the trough, put on the lid and cut into pieces, and what stuck to the sides and bottom removed with a scraper.

Then the slow business of weighing required by the law began. Weighing had to be done well and accurately, or a bakery could face closure, or crippling fines, or the pillory. After that, the shaping: quick, delicate, skilled work. The goal of shaping was to create surface tension around the dough, ensuring even baking and a crisp crust. Patting hands, turning hands. Loaves were typically shaped in rounds or ovals because they were baked without the support of tins. Throughout, the fire had to be tended; it was kindled at 2 a.m. and raked out by 4 a.m. The burning wood of the faggots heated the brick walls and floor. Then all fuel was removed painstakingly and the ashes spaded out into the ash-hole, except a few left at one corner, to light the man who set the bread in the oven. The swabber was next used to clean the hot brick further; bakers said bread was best baked in an oaken fire swept out with damp birch twigs.

So, summing up, the bakers began at two in the afternoon, did about forty-five minutes' work, then started again at six. Then they did some more very heavy work at eleven – try kneading five pounds of dough in a washbasin for a sample – and again at three the following morning. The dough also had a sponging period of nine hours before it was even mixed up and kneaded, then a four-hour rise, further kneading, and then proofing. The loaves took three hours to bake in the cooling oven. And finally the bread was ready at 7 a.m., just in time for breakfast.

It sounds artisanal, satisfying. Yet this round-the-clock work was heavy and tiring and not especially profitable. You had to be strong and dumb to be a baker, went an old saying. The baker or his boy had to fetch water, carry wood, weigh the loaves and bolt flour, clean the oven after baking was over and tend the leaven. While the dough took its time, the human beings worked at an exhausting, frenetic pace, as in a top chef's kitchen. It was night all day in the basement bakery, as in a coalpit – most bakeries were located in basements, or in dark front rooms – and dusty, the air filled with flour. The baking cellars were dungeons, often tiny, sometimes with ceilings too low for the men to stand up. Bakers slept in the bakeroom itself, because the stop-start work meant they could never get a full night's rest. 'There are,' reported *Working Men* as late as April 1866, 'many journeymen bakers who have scarcely ever known what it is to sleep in a bed.'

Pre-industrial baking has astonishing continuity, heavy with things; real and recalcitrant things. In the 1823 *Book of English Trades*, there is an unusual image of a baker kneading dough on the lid of the dough trough. The dough is in large lumps in a long column. At the baker's feet are a faggot and an ash-pail; an oven with the door open is visible behind him, showing a fire fuelled by faggots. The room is dark, with only a small window that gives little light; most of the light comes from the fire.

A miniature from a fifteenth-century Franciscan missal is startlingly similar, illustrating the longevity and continuity of the basics of bread-making: mix, wait, knead, wait, shape, wait, bake.[2] The waiting cannot be shown, but the heat and effort burst out of the image like sweat from skin. The bakery's floor is made of red tiles; just twelve tiles across, maybe five metres. The deep room is dominated by the gaping, glowing mouth of the oven. Standing well back, a baker uses a long, flat wooden shovel to spade three pale loaves into the oven's embrace. Just a few metres away, another man leans over a huge wooden chest, a dough trough; his arms have almost vanished into it as he churns and tosses the dough, his braced feet showing the effort he is making. Like a comic strip, the image moves from left to right, showing each stage of bread-making. Shaped loaves wait to be loaded into the fire. Below the oven's glow are the multiple faggots that will be needed to heat the oven tomorrow. Outside, customers queue for the freshly baked loaves.

Other medieval illuminations allow us to see the round loaves, the size of a man's hand; the wooden peel used to deposit them straight onto the oven floor; *couches*, linen cloths that hold the dough while it proves. They show moulds and also shaped breads such as pretzels. We catch a glimpse of a baker forming a *boule* (a round loaf) by rolling it to and fro on a bench with his hand on top. A sixteenth-century engraving shows a baker with hands immersed to the wrists in dough, while the baker's wife carries away the completed loaves in a basket on top of her head, and another half-naked baker uses a peel to load a loaf into the oven to bake.[3] An eighteenth-century decoration on the wall of the Bakers' Hall in the City of London crammed in every stage of bread-making. While two men lift and pummel the dough, others retrieve small loaves from an oven's mouth.[4] A strikingly similar engraving, again from the sixteenth century, depicts a half-naked man holding a peel, taking a loaf from the oven's mouth, while an earlier incarnation of himself is wrist-deep in dough. The room is completely dark except for the light of the fire.[5] Remarkably, an almost identical image to these appears in a third-century Gallo-Roman mosaic from Saint-Roman-en-Gal. The images illustrate a consistent image: the half-naked, sweating baker, snatching bread from the hot mouth of hell. In Pompeii, a grain mill and a mouth-like bread oven survive. The oven is almost identical to one shown in a photograph of an outdoor bread oven taken in Normandy in 1900.[6]

Baking has to be carried out by this process because it is the only way that good bread can be made with the kind of flour produced in northern Europe. Because the climate is damp, the flour contains less gluten than the Canadian and American strong flour with which bread is made nowadays. Gluten makes bread light, the gluten strands forming a network that securely holds bubbles of air. If the flour contains low levels of gluten, these will take a long time in kneading and rising to develop enough strength to make a light loaf. But there are advantages; bread made in this slow way will also develop a more interesting and complex flavour than bread made quickly.

This method accumulated the know-how of generations of bakers. If we go back to Neolithic bread, we can begin to track how that method emerged from the simple need to make grain edible. The oldest bread found in Britain is two small, charred lumps over 5,000 years old, from Yarnton near Oxford. The bread might have burned in a prehistoric cooking accident, or might have been deliberately burned as an offering to the gods. The lumps contain a number of coarsely ground grains, of which only barley can be firmly identified. Tiny samples produced radiocarbon dates of between 3620 and 3350 BC. The pit containing the loaves also contained a large flint knife and other tools, fragments of pottery and charred hazelnuts. These Neolithic breads were hearth breads, a food that to us might look more like naan, crispbread or pitta. They were not fluffy or high, but thin and firm, hard like biscuit. Such unleavened bread was firmly established in Britain; it was the Romans who brought the method and the wheat to make leavened bread.

The wheat was *Triticum aestivum*, often called wheat corn. And the Roman soldiers brought with them their love of labour-intensive fine wheat bread, expensive because so much of the grain was wasted. They brought leaven too; Pliny the Elder says the Romans used for this purpose the froth from brewing beer, by which he probably means what was later called brewer's yeast.[7] The Romans also introduced shallow-lidded pottery dishes for baking, of a kind found at Pompeii with charred bread inside; many have been uncovered at military sites and in major towns dating from the first to the early second century AD. Surprisingly few Roman bread ovens survive, even in London. Because of the danger of fire, bread ovens in Roman forts were built into the backs of ramparts, giving space for any fire to be extinguished before it spread, so the rarity of ovens in towns might be a result of similar precautions. Like those found intact at Pompeii, they were probably almost identical in shape to the Neapolitan pizza oven – only the beginning of our love affair with Italian food.[8]

So, with their wheaten bread, the Romans became the first (of very many) immigrant groups to attempt, with mixed success, to reproduce a food from their parent culture. Like most passionately loved foods brought to new and indifferent lands, it was a childhood favourite: Martial speaks of a Roman morning, when 'already the baker is selling breakfasts to the children'.[9] The Romans installed their preference for white wheat bread, and installed it as a status symbol. In West Yorkshire, sites with more wheat remains also had posher pottery fineware. But the problem for the Romans, and for Roman wannabes, was that their wheat did not grow as well in the damp British Isles as it did in the North African grain basket of the Empire. Wheat harvests in Britain were meagre and of low quality. And yet the Roman elite, like many of their successors, were determined to go on eating the kind of food to which they were accustomed. A Roman-era dough trough found at Poultry in London shows how much they valued labour-intensive wheat bread.

While the Romans saw barley as fit only for horses, there is evidence that it was still popular in some places, partly because Roman garrisons were themselves diverse – the Catterick garrison from the Danube brought a taste for barley and barley bread with them. The South and Midlands also rejected wheat for spelt.[10] But the hard-to-get wheaten loaf left its mark. Even long after the legions had withdrawn, golden-crusted white bread was still an object of desire. The taste for it survives from Romano-British times into the Anglo-Saxon era. And bread remained important symbolically as well as practically. In Anglo-Saxon times, a lord was, literally, a loaf-giver, the one who put bread on the table. The Anglo-Saxon word *hlaford* means loaf-keeper and lord, while *hlæfdige*, lady, is from *hlaibadigon*, bread-kneader.

Archaeology shows that Anglo-Saxon bread often included ground and kneaded barley, rye, oats, buckwheat, dried beans, acorns, hazel and alder seeds, and in particularly lean times, even weed seeds and tree bark, which would have added layers of taste and nutritional value. These extra gluten-free elements could also play a tenderising or scenting role. The idea that impurities in bread helped health had not been unknown to the Romans, whose dieticians supported the consumption of brown bread, and they are also shown to be effective by evidence provided by skeletal remains from the time of the *Domesday Book*, showing no signs of the scurvy and rickets that bedevilled later populations.

But this might have been because porridge had ousted bread. In Saxon times, bread ovens became rarer in new houses. The fiction that the lord gave his people loaves his wife had kneaded might be just that – a fiction. It is also possible that the woods no longer felt safe enough for the gathering of faggots. This might have been pragmatism, but it might also have owed something to Anglo-Saxon Germanic culture, which included an Anglo-Saxon world tree analogous to the Norse Yggdrasill that was subsequently replaced by the cross.[11] Such sacred awe went with healthy fear. As archaeologist Aleks Pluskowski shows, woodlands were the homes of feared wild beasts such as wolves and bears.[12] But it is equally likely that the Anglo-Saxon move away from stone to wooden houses meant that domestic bread baking became unsafe. As we have seen, the bakery is a source of dread because of the extreme heat of bread ovens.

Edward the Confessor created one of England's first food regulation laws, embodied in the *Hlafclaenness Dom*, or Bread Purity Law, in 1047. A description written in the period reads:

King Edward kept Christmas with all due solemnity at York and immediately afterwards set out by the direct road for London. In this journey he found a deficiency in the measures

of bread … He broke some loaves and tasted others, and … he
ordered the bread to be made of fairer ingredients. Henceforth
in the realm bread should be made from only these four things:
fine flour, water, barm [yeast], and salt. And those who broke
this law should be heavily fined.[13]

The Anglo-Saxons were not so much forgetting Rome as trying to
preserve Roman food traditions as best they could.[14] Already, the
pattern of our insular food culture can be seen: its amazing porous-
ness, its food like its language open and hospitable to outside
influences, enriched by them. The Roman liking for bread made with
wheat is retained, and so are grain-based pottages, in harmony with
what the land can give; but the Saxon gifts of beer and mead are bolted
on to this grain culture. 'Without Bread all food turns to loathing,'
said Anglo-Saxon grammarian Abbot Ælfric in his *Colloquy*.[15] For the
majority of people in Anglo-Saxon England, bread was both an
unusual treat, and emotionally and symbolically central; the norm was
porridge, made with rye or barley, and sometimes sweetened with
honey, the only form of sweetening available. Cooking methods were
often very simple: a fire pit in the centre of the room, where smoke
from the burning fuel would escape through a hole in the roof, or just
find its way out through the porous thatch. An alternative was stones
heated on the fire; these were dropped into pots of water or broth to
boil it or reduce cooking times by pre-heating. Such methods were not
likely to keep bread on the menu.

Yet culture and ritual kept loaves in mind, even if they could only
rarely be put on the table. Bread's purity was attested by its use in trials
by ordeal: innocence or guilt was proven by eating it. If the person
died, he was guilty by a 'heavenly judgment'. A tale had it that Edward
the Confessor believed that Earl Godwin had murdered his brother
Alfred, while a court of law had found him innocent. Godwin submit-
ted himself to a trial by ordeal with bread, and died, thus proving his
guilt. It was sacrilege to put impure ingredients into bread used in trial
by ordeal – an attempt to interfere with what should be God's rightful
judgment.

But if the bread was pure, both bakers and millers were still seen as cheats. There were reports of bread with a huge hole in the middle to contain a stone that would make it weigh correctly, of bread that was damp or mouldy or spoiled or underweight or mixed with grit, sand or chalk. In 1327 a fraud was discovered at a public bakehouse where citizens used to take their dough to have it baked. The bakers who ran the place had secret openings made in the moulding boards, and when people's dough was placed on the boards, one of the bakers would secretly pinch off pieces from the uncooked loaves. They were exposed and caught, and sentenced to stand in the pillory with slabs of dough round their necks.

In the fourteenth century, John Lydgate suggested in a short poem entitled 'The Deserts of Thievish Millers and Bakers' that those two groups of men should form a guild and set up a chapel 'under the pillory'.[16] The pillory was a means of turning the baker over to the fury of those he had defrauded. It was not unknown for miscreants to die of the beatings given to them there. The wording of the law makes clear the poetic justice; the pillory was 'the Judgment of the Body', since the baker had left the bodies of others empty.[17] Lydgate's savage satire illustrates the way the malfeasance of millers and bakers was to the paying public a single hideous conspiracy against them.

In fact, however, the miller's rapacity also robbed the baker, who then had little choice but to defraud the public as well. Chaucer's morally dodgy miller is typical:

He was very strong of muscle, and also of bones …
His mouth was as large as a large furnace.
… He well knew how to steal corn and take payment three
    times;
And yet he had a thumb of gold, indeed.

What this means is that he puts his thumb on the scale to make it weigh heavy.

Chaucer's miller is powerful and strong because it required power to lift heavy bags of grain and flour, and to grind grain. As milling increasingly moved from individual households to specialist mills, the powers of wind and falling water, and even tide, were used to drive the heavy stones that crushed the grain. In the earliest Middle Ages, milling – where it was not done by hand using quernstones ('blood-mills', as they were sometimes expressively called) – used either water power or horse-power. Water mills came first, and were in use from the fourth century. Watermills tend to remain on the same site, however often rebuilt; Kipling's mill, which as it runs calls 'Book! Book! Domesday book!', was, he claimed, mentioned in the said book, and is still in operation now.[18] The Domesday Book lists around 6,000 mills in England in 1086. (Blake's 'dark satanic mills' are not flour mills, but cloth mills.)

Windmills appeared in England from around 1180. Fixed mills only worked if the wind blew in the right direction, so the post mill, which could be turned into the wind, was often preferred. They were often sited on high ground or built on a raised mound to catch more wind. A logical development by the end of the Middle Ages was the tower mill. The tower gave height, and only a cap holding the sails revolved. Smock mills, which arrived by the late sixteenth century, are similar, but entirely timber-built, whereas the tower type was built of durable brick or stone, so more tower mills survive. Windmills were favoured in the windy flatlands of East Anglia, watermills in upland areas with fast-running rivers and streams.

Wherever its physical power came from, the mill's financial power was the same. Both mills and bread ovens usually belonged to the local lord, and were a kind of company store to which tenants had to pay a usage fee. Many manors had neither mill nor oven, and in those places people went on grinding their own grain with pestle and mortar, a quern or a hand mill, but it was time-consuming and arduous.

By the late Middle Ages, the city of York ran on bread, mostly bought rather than made at home. York's city council paid special attention to bakers: the locations of all bakeries had to be documented because of the fire hazard they presented. The records of the city of York show that bread was a central component of doles to the poor and the food of prisoners, and also of civic and guild feasts, and funeral meals. Bread could be sold only in the Thursday Market, and not hawked about the city, nor sold by the petty traders, mostly women, who resold 'country bread', brought into the city by outsiders, and bread baked in the city by non-bakers. In 1479, it was said that bakers were passing off their own products as 'country bread', and using traders to sell it. The city wanted to be a closed shop.[19] Despite all the regulations, the bakers were often hard to identify and hence hard to arraign. They overlapped with cooks, innkeepers and millers, all of whom were at various times forbidden to bake bread (which implies that they were doing so). York's housewives could bake flatbread, on bakestones or beneath upturned cooking pots, and might even try to sell it. They could also buy from traders, or possibly from 'regrators', who bought up entire stocks of a commodity to sell at a high price in the resulting scarcity. Like any unregulated buying, the risk was that bread from outside the market would be inferior, underweight, or priced above the assize rate; all of these offences, however, were committed by bakers themselves, many of whom also ran a covert operation outside the rules.[20]

It is easy enough to list medieval bread names, but much more difficult to unravel what kind of bread the names describe. There were regional varieties: York and London had different kinds. Chaucer in the *Canterbury Tales* describes a character that had a face as 'whit [white] ... as paindemain'; he also describes the Prioress feeding her dogs with 'milk and wastelbreed [wastel bread]', which is obviously meant to sound shockingly extravagant; so was wastel bread white too?[21]

In the sixteenth century, William Harrison's *Description of England* arranges a bewilderingly complicated spectrum of breads by social status:

> Of bread made of wheat we have sundry sorts daily brought to
> the table, whereof the first and most excellent is the manchet,
> which we commonly call white bread, in Latin *primarius panis*
> [first bread] ... The second is the cheat or wheaten bread ...
> and out of this is the coarsest of the bran ... taken. The ravelled
> is a kind of cheat bread also, but it retaineth more of the gross,

and less of the pure substance of the wheat; and this, being more slightly wrought up, is used in the halls of the nobility and gentry only … The next sort is named brown bread, of the colour of which we have two sorts: one baked up as it cometh from the mill, so that neither the bran nor the flour are any whit diminished … The other hath little or no flour left therein at all … and it is not only the worst and weakest of all the other sorts, but also appointed in old times for servants, slaves, and the inferior kind of people to feed upon. Hereunto likewise, because it is dry and brickle in the working (for it will hardly be made up handsomely into loaves) some add a portion of rye meal … and then it is named miscelin, that is, bread made of mingled corn.

In hard times, he notes, some people are 'forced to content themselves … with bread made either of beans, peas, or oats, or … acorns', adding that 'of which scourge the poorest do soonest taste, so they are least able to provide themselves of better'.[22]

Harrison's description is lengthy but seems clear, and something like it is often cited by food historians, but on inspection, it presents difficulties and complications. In the light of modern supermarket shelves, interpretation tends to focus on white versus brown. But even if we just *look* at flour, its colour is inaccurate as a representation of what it is. Flour isn't defined by colour – white, brown – but by what a modern baker would call the extraction rate. The extraction rate measures how much of the total wheat berry, or kernel, a kind of flour contains. A whole wheat flour is 100 per cent extraction (that is, nothing is removed: 100 per cent is left after extraction); however, after this, simple percentages do not always tell us *what* has been removed. If you take out both bran – the outer husk – and germ, then you have what in France is called mill flour (*farine de meule*) or Type 85 flour, which shows it is 85 per cent extraction. Because nearly all the hard grains are gone, it has a smooth, creamy mouth texture, but it is not bright white; it is the colour of milky tea. It isn't dazzling. If you want paler flour, you could begin bolting and sieving, using ever-finer meshes. Some particles stay in the sieve, and only the softest inner-most core of the grain, the inner 30 per cent, will fall to the very bottom, and that is what is sold today as cake or pastry flour. There are therefore a number of elements in play: how much bran and germ are removed, how often what is left is sieved, and where in the grain the endosperm (white matter) is from. The innermost section of the endosperm is not only the whitest part of the grain; it is not only the least contaminated by fragments of bran. It is also and very impor-tantly the *weakest*.

We've already seen that the bread-making method used for millen-nia was designed to produce a loaf where good long-term gluten development ensured holes. This, however, is not the same as softness, lightness or airiness. All these are correlated with white bread nowa-days, but it is perfectly possible to make entirely white bread with holes that has a completely different texture. We can find hints of the importance of texture in the earliest surviving recipes. Fifteenth-century cookbooks request 'tendre bread', a designation clearly about texture, not colour. We know the names rather than the natures of many kinds of bread, such as the aforementioned wastel bread (perhaps from the Norman French word *gastel* or cake), which some historians equate with pandemain; or cocket, said by Anne Wilson to be a 'fine white bread' and regarded by others as 'coarse and brown', and possi-bly identical to cockle bread.[23]

Then there is the shape of the bread: the manchets mentioned by Harrison (like cottage loaves) seem to be defined less by their dough content than by their shape. The other frequently neglected criterion for kinds was quantity, often identified by assize criteria, such as 'a penny bread', and also identified as such in household recipe books. These rarely use terms like cheat or pandemain or manchet, but speak instead of 'fair' bread, which may be a reference to colour. 'Fair' bread might just mean not mouldy or spoiled, however, and a penny loaf is not a reliable index of kind or even of size, since the size fluctuated with the price of wheat. York had its own assize of bread, which varied the weights of farthing, ha'penny and penny loaves depending on the price of grain. A penny loaf might expand or shrink according to the success of the harvest. The bread assize also pegged the price of a loaf to the price of wheat in London. You could at least choose how you spent your money. The same farthing could buy you a given amount of finest white wastel loaf, or twice as much brown or treet loaf. It bought you a loaf of cocket a little larger than the finest white wastel or a wholewheat loaf weighing half as much again as the cocket or a loaf of other cereals weighing twice as much as the cocket.[24] In York, the bakers baked four sorts of wheat bread: wastel, simnel (a bread which was boiled, then baked, like a bagel), demesne and cocket. These categories could be further subdivided by names that indicated how often the flour had been bolted. Each baker had his own bolting cloth to sieve the different grades of flour for these varieties. Each had his own sign to mark the bread.[25] In a later city memorandum from the late fourteenth century, bakers are also baking the coarsest bastard wastel and bastard simnel (in France there is still a loaf called the *batard*), and the superior fine white '*payne demayn*'. This last possibly descends from the demesne loaf, with *demesne* reinterpreted as *main* (the word for hand in French). In York this bread was also called *maynebred* – though its precise nature is unknown – and was offered to distinguished visitors at their entry to the city.

To complicate the picture still further, historical change altered the meanings of particular kinds of bread. In York, by the sixteenth century, the old categories of bread – wastel, simnel, pandemayne and cocket – had vanished, and perhaps the kinds of bread went with them, ousted by new varieties. In 1554 there are references to white loaves, white cakes, spice cakes and bolted bread. 'The Cross Loaf' was bread sold at the Cross in Thursday Market. In 1572, the bakers had to bake half 'flat bread' and half 'coppled bread' (bread rising conically to a summit or point), or all flat bread. Ordinances in March 1595/6 told them to bake farthing, ha'penny and penny white loaves, ha'penny and penny wheaten. Bakers also had to make penny and twopenny household bread; the coarser flour could be made into larger loaves. There are hints at an appetite for vast round discs of bread that could feed a family for a week (similar to those still made by some French provincial bakers). Because they were outside the assize, however, they could not be fully regulated. In 1597, the bakers were to bake bolted bread at the special price given to them by the Lord Mayor, or only to bake white bread and rye bread. This suggests that 'white' bread still contained some of the whole grain, and was not so white as that made from finely bolted flour.[26]

Tastes continued to change, and favourite breads continued to vanish. As the sixteenth century progressed, the popularity of the York maynebread presented to visiting dignitaries and served at banquets and feasts declined; by 1552, the bakers had to be ordered to make enough maynebread to serve the city 'according to the Ancient Custom'. The city council became alarmed in 1595 because the baking of maynebread had almost been abandoned, 'which is thought to be by reason that spiced cakes are of late grown into greater use then heretofore hath been which mayne bread as it is reported is not in use nor baked in any other City or place forth of this City in England And hath been used in this City time out of mind of man.' The council commanded that the 'mayne bakers' should make at least ten shillings' worth every Friday, with any remaining at five o'clock to be bought up by the Lord Mayor, aldermen and sheriffs. Despite these efforts, maynebread was not available in 1617 when James I made his second visit to York. He enquired about it, and the Mayor had to explain that spiced cakes were being used instead at banquets. The king then ordered them to bake maynebread, for 'he would not have so ancient a thing to discontinue', and there followed another vain attempt to prohibit spiced cakes. We get a clue about the possible cause of maynebread's decline from a scrap of information: in the 1540s and 1550s, the bakers traditionally contributed a 'shield' and the vintners a 'scallop' of maynebread for the city council's feast during the performance of the Corpus Christi play (York's 'mystery play'). This kind of shaped bread is typically made with very dry dough. Spiced bread, on the other hand, was probably a wetter, softer, enriched dough; sugar was regarded as a spice in the sixteenth century. As sugar began to be imported in greater quantities, and as dental health declined as a result, customers sought out softer bread. Spiced bread created the demand for itself.

To complicate the picture still further, different regions developed different kinds of bread, containing different grains. Some regions planted maslin (a mixture of rye and wheat). Seed was sown in mixed field-crops from Anglo-Saxon times. This is usually explained as a kind of insurance policy, but Thomas Tusser, Elizabethan farming guru, argued that rye tended to swamp the wheat, and that, 'for safety more great', one must make sure one sowed white wheat.[27] Other regions used different grains: rye in Norfolk; barley in north-west England, lowland Scotland, and parts of Wales and Cornwall; oats in upland Wales and the Pennines and Scottish Highlands. So what kind of dark bread you ate depended on where you lived as well as on your social status, and it was not just a matter of bolting wheat flour. The underlying reason for these regional variations was that wheat demanded a longer growing season and better soil than were present in the upland and rocky areas.

In Yorkshire, the best flour was used not for bread, but for pies, and for 'the folks' puddings'. Pie crusts were made of maslin. The defects of barley were well understood; barley is 'so short' and 'will not abide working'.[28] Further south, a Wiltshire shepherd might eat barley bread and nothing else, though not necessarily from choice.[29] A poem of 1635 celebrated the longevity of Thomas Parr of Shropshire, aged over one hundred, who ate nothing but 'coarse maslin bread'.[30] In Cornwall, rye was grown only on ground too infertile for wheat, and the poor in 1602 also used barley, 'grown into great use of late years'; 'and in the dear [famine] season past'. In the warm south-west, barley was especially good because it ripened fast.[31]

Often linked to questions of kinds of loaves is the existence of two bakers' guilds in medieval London, the white bakers and the tourte bakers (in medieval towns and cities, including London, all bakers had to be members of guilds, trade organisations that trained and managed professions). The latter are usually equated with brown bread bakers by historians, but the 1440 Bread Assize Ordinance says 'the white shall bake all manner of brede that they can make of wheat'. It then gives a list, which includes 'cribill [sieve] bread', bread made with the residue left in the sieve, and 'basket bread such as sold in chepe [market] for poor men'. In other words, the white bakers baked many kinds of bread, not just white. It is true that tourte bakers were not allowed to own a sieve, but they may have been defined less by this than by the ability to bake with grains other than wheat. Rye, for example, and barley, are exacting and difficult because they lack gluten, and to this day German rye bakers are specialists and often bake nothing else. It may be that tourte bakers were catering for a different kind of market or taste – or even ethnicity or identity, or regionality. This is reinforced by the fact that tourte bakeries could lend out their ovens, giving them a link with home bread-making.

A resistance to local eating and insistence on 'home' foods is threaded through accounts of regional foods. So it makes sense that Londoners, a mixed bag of regionalities, might have sought to continue to eat their own regional staples. The tourte baker was permitted to bake the dough that people brought to him ready made up, and to make 'horsebread' of peas and beans. In London in 1304 there were thirty-two brown/tourte and twenty-one white bakers. In 1574 there were thirty-six brown and sixty-two white bakers. Tourte bakers may have fallen into a minority because they made some of their income from home bakers, whose numbers may themselves have been in decline, caused by gradual assimilation to a London food culture that saw regional breads as inferior. Meanwhile, the white bakers did everything possible to eliminate the tourte bakers; white bread took over the guild and the markets, and made itself inevitable, made itself the only bread, ousting other varieties.

The picture is complicated yet further by the different role bread played in the diet of different social classes. By around 1300, two societies lived alongside one another. One still ate bread at every meal, but could have dispensed with it in favour of game. The other *needed* bread and ale – both grain products – to make up virtually its entire daily calorie intake. This society was approximately ten times the size of the other. It lived and died by the grain harvest. Its members were also responsible for gathering that harvest, milling it and baking it, though they did not own the land on which the grain grew. England's past is not unlike a developing economy in the twenty-first century, in which the rulers eat the land's resources while the poor are hungry every day. So their stories diverge. The rich – which included the court, nobility and major ecclesiastics – ate a varied diet and observed the church calendar. Among the lower orders, the middling sort – small merchants, prosperous yeomen – ate bread, and in worse times the poor consumed grain as pottage.

The particular crunch time came between late winter – when the last of the pig killed at Martinmas had been eaten (see Pigs) – and the grain harvest in late summer. Piers, the Plowman, is talking to Hunger, in the fourteenth-century poem that bears his name:

> I've no money, said Piers, for chickens, or geese or pork. All I've got is a couple of fresh cheeses, a tiny amount of curds and cream, an oat-cake and a couple of loaves for my children, baked from bean-flour and bran. I give you my solemn word, however, that I don't have the ingredients to fry you a platter of bacon and eggs. All I've got is parsley, leeks, and a huge supply of greens, as well as a cow, a calf, and a mare that pulls my dung-cart in the dry season. You see, that's the sort of food we've got to live on till Lammastide comes, by which time I hope the fields will be ready for harvest. Then I can give you the kind of dinner I'd like to! At this the poor people all went and got their peas, still in their shells, and brought beans and baked apples in their laps, along with spring onions, chervil, and an abundance of ripe cherries. This they presented to Piers to satisfy Hunger. He, however, gobbled it all up, and demanded more. In a panic, then, the poor people set about feeding Hunger, hoping to put an end to him with cabbages and peas. By now, though, harvest-time began to approach, and the new season's corn came to the markets. Then everyone cheered up, and started feeding Hunger with nothing but the best; and taking a leaf out of Glutton's book, they put him to sleep with a draught of good strong ale![32]

You can't cram more food wisdom into two paragraphs than author William Langland manages here. Langland writes as someone who understands hunger, what it is and what it isn't. Hunger is a moral force, warning everyone against excess and destructive waste, but also a terrifying giant who is difficult to appease. He forces the people to pay attention to their bodies. 'Don't eat until you feel a touch of hunger', he suggests, and 'get up from table before you've eaten all you could manage. And don't let Sir Excess Overmuch share your table.' Hunger is envisaged as a squeezing, killing hand, strongly resembling the labour pains with which women are cursed. He makes a careful distinction between the lazy and 'those who've come down in the world through no fault of their own'. The giant urges, 'love them, don't blame them'. But all of them feel the pain he induces.

Hunger rampages down the centuries, alongside his siblings malnutrition and disease. His ravages are increasingly confined to the social group called the meaner sort, but under the Tudors and Stuarts this class expands, swallowing up the previously respectable as wealth is abruptly redistributed upwards. In medieval times, the rich might occasionally have known hunger – real hunger of the kind rarely experienced in the developed world today – in sieges and in warfare. Such experiences became less common, so that eventually, hunger itself was what defined a particular social class. In all eras, the poor regard food as a commodity to sell. They regard it in that light because they have commitments they can only meet by raising money – rent, for example, or shoes, or clothing, or agricultural equipment. Puritan clergyman Richard Baxter noticed that even if a poor man's sow farrowed, he would sell the piglets, along with any chickens, or eggs, or butter or cheese or apples, in order to pay the rent, leaving only skimmed dairy – and, of course, bread – for his family. 'Sell wheat to buy rye', say the bells of Tenbury.[33] The result was a diet where bread alone allowed the poor to stay alive. One schoolboy's meals are on record: 'a little piece of bread … with all the bran in it'. This was sometimes buttered, or eaten with fruit. Dinner was a mess of porridge, and sometimes turnips, kale, wheat and barley, or a 'delicate meat' made of fine white flour and eggs, or, on fish days, skimmed milk, with bread 'put in it', fish, pease or beans – or lupins – and sometimes beer, all with bread. Even this was a more lavish diet than a cottager could expect.[34]

The result is starkly visible in the archaeological record: average male height, having risen from 165cm to 172cm between the Mesolithic and the early medieval period, fell to 171cm; Britons had become taller under Roman occupation, their average height increasing from 167cm to 170cm. This coincided with the Romans' improved water supply and sanitation systems and a more varied diet. Height decreased from 600 AD and then began to climb again, increasing to 173cm in the 1100s, very close to average heights in the twentieth century. But after 1200, men became shorter in stature, and archaeological evidence shows that at this time rural populations were decreasing, farmland had become degraded and there were shortages of crop seeds as temperatures turned colder over the century, with weather becoming far more changeable until the early 1300s. Height decreased again after 1650, reaching just 169cm in the late 1600s – a decline that continued until the early 1800s. Average life expectancy declined too, as infant mortality soared; people born between 1650 and 1750 could expect to live just thirty-five years – down from forty years in the late 1500s.[35]

Reliance on grain also led to vitamin deficiencies. At Poundbury in Dorset, a quarter of Romano-British skeletons showed anaemia and vitamin C and D deficiencies, though more vitamin C had been lost in the Neolithic due to cooking and prolonged storage of food, and even now it is often found to be deficient in infants fed on boiled cow's milk; its lack causes weakness, muscle pain, sores, gum disease and depression.[36] The poor ploughman would probably suffer from protein-fat deficiency, his children would have been swag-bellied and bright-eyed. They might have had marasmus, kwashiorkor, vitamin A deficit, borderline scurvy, pellagra and rickets, iron deficiency. Those disorders might have remitted in good times if they had not gone too far, but the results would have been evident, the damage done. The body created by subsistence is carried around like a broken burden. It has to be made to work, to keep working, hunting, gathering and ploughing. And when the harvest came, and the miller and baker had taken their share, bread would only have met calorific needs, not those for vitamins or minerals or fat or proteins. Ninety per cent or more of the population scraped by from harvest to harvest, with a long and terrible trough between the last bacon and the first bread.

The rich had no such problems. Just as Henry VIII preferred to attend mass from well above the court congregation, so the king had his own personal baker, John Wynkell, who made 'mayne, cheate and payne' for the royal table separately, in the privy bakehouse, as private as the privy chamber or the privy stool. (The fact that Wynkell made cheat as well as mayne for the royal table is evidence of the fallacy of the widespread notion that cheat was only for the labouring classes.) The main bakehouse churned out 200 or more cheat loaves every day, plus 700 manchets, as well as additional bread for the servants who ate at the king's expense.[37]

When great houses built their own bakeries, as Hampton Court did, the large bakehouse was located well away from the palace, among a huddle of outer offices. It baked not only for the king and his household, but also for the army, providing biscuits in July 1544 for the war in France. The bakery's supplies were delivered by cart and barge, and grain and flour were stored in granaries, where they were regularly turned over by the garnetor, to guard against spoiling by mildew or pests, as frequently happened to grain stored in less exalted places. Meal had to be weighed to make sure none had stuck to the miller because the king paid the miller in cash, not kind. The meal was bolted, and the bran sold to the avener, the head of the stables, for feeding the King's horses. The remaining meal was sometimes used to make cheat bread or wheatmeal bread, and could also be further sieved to produce cream flour. But within the bakehouse, the process was exactly the same as it was in any London bakery.

The first printed recipes for bread began to appear during the reign of Elizabeth I. Most cookbooks contained no bread recipes. The very first was in a book called *A Good Huswife's Handmaide for the Kitchen*, in 1594. It was closely followed by Thomas Dawson, in *The Good*

Huswife's Jewell, 1596/7. Read carefully, the *Handmaide*'s recipe confirms the suspicion that Tudor bread was dry and crisp:

> Take half a bushel of fine flour twice bolted, and a gallon of fair lukewarm water, almost a handful of white salt, and almost a pint of yeast, then temper all these together, without any more liquor, as hard as you can handle it: then let it lie half an hour, then take it up, and make your Manchetts, and let them stand almost an hour in the oven.[38]

Apart from measurements, this tells us nothing much of method except the injunction to mix 'as hard as you can handle it'. The recipe seems remarkably dry, too (half a bushel is four gallons, about 90kg), even given that the yeast was in liquid form, so the insistence that it be handled roughly without adding any more liquid is interesting – and puzzling. The bread would have been hard and crisp, like a breadstick or a thin pizza crust. Yet at virtually the same date, Thomas Tusser could write:

> New bread is a divel
> Much crust is an evil
> New bread is a waster, but mouldy is worse
> What that way dog catcheth that loseth the purse.
> Much doughbake I praise not, much crust is as ill,
> The mean is the housewife, say nay if ye will.[39]

He meant that the inside had to be fully baked, not baked so hard or at so high a heat that it was all crust. The problem is that a wood-fired oven could easily be too hot, so that the bread would cook on the outside and be undercooked in the centre. Tusser's reference to new bread as 'a waster' might seem odd to us, since we value very fresh bread. Yet as *The babees book* (a guide for princes, probably written for Edward V and his brother the Duke of York) shows, the principal way in which bread was consumed was as a trencher. At the beginning of the meal, a large slice of bread was cut by each diner to make 'a clean trencher', and when the pottage was brought, or the meat, this could be placed on the trencher, as if the trencher were a plate. The bread for trenchers would have had to be solid and firm. Hence these dryish doughs, baked into a loaf with few large holes.

Gervase Markham's recipe from the beginning of the seventeenth century for manchet makes an interesting comparison: for one thing, he suggests using your feet to knead the dough, or using a device called the brake, a kind of dough hook operated manually. He also insists that manchets be scored about the waist, and slashed across the top, and that they be baked very gently.[40] The precariously genteel Markham was by birth caught up in turbulence. His father had been raised by the notorious Babington family, later involved in a plot to put Mary Queen of Scots on the throne. Markham may have been educated at Cambridge, but he was a jack of all trades – and perhaps master of none; he became a tireless and various writer, penning poems and treatises on horsemanship with equal rapidity. Markham was fifty-two when he wrote this recipe as part of his *vade mecum*, *The English Hus-wife*, though he died poor, despite the perpetual reprinting of his manual for housewives. Like most attempts to urge people to adopt country ways, Markham pretends to describe actual housewives while in fact drawing up rules for them to be entirely self-sufficient in a fashion that was never really possible.[41] Markham does not give a quantity for water, though he is using more liquid yeast than Dawson (eight gallons of flour, three rather than two pints of yeast), but the method is strikingly similar: warm liquid, lots of kneading, a very fast rise and a moderate oven. Manchets made like this would still be crisp and hard, with very little soft crumb.

As a comparison, in the twenty-first century, most bread dough contains far more water than these mixtures; 60–70 per cent of the weight of most modern dough is water. The result is more developed protein, bigger holes, more air and a much darker crust. But these loose, sloppy doughs are all kneaded by machines. The watery doughs called 'artisan' by modern bakers are actually post-industrial; dry dough needs less working. More importantly, it keeps better, as Tusser pointed out. In the damp climate of Britain, drying food out was the best way to ensure it kept well. Dry bread could be soaked in water to make it palatable. Mouldy bread was useless. Surviving images from medieval and early modern texts show pale crusts and solid-looking crumbs with few visible holes, and those holes small.

——————

As we saw in York, there had long been fancy breads associated with festivals; each locality had its own, from the Banbury cake to the Kentish huffkin and Cornish fairing. These were always irregular treats, tending to be served annually on specific holidays. But when reformed Protestantism put paid to the medieval festive calendar, fairings and their like burst out of their festive bounds and invaded the everyday. As competition between bakers in big cities intensified, the attraction of such delectable fare meant that each baker brought regional know-how to the city in the form of a range of rolls and small cakes. The abandonment of licensed periods for gluttony led to an expansion of luxury into an everyday commodity, to be consumed when wealth allowed.

Initially, the mid-seventeenth-century arrival of fancy bread, especially 'whigs' (small, white buns), and the coming of breakfast rolls to go with coffee or chocolate in the early eighteenth century, favoured commercial bakers. But as these new soft and smooth breads became popular, their advent was accompanied by the proliferation in domestic recipe books of many recipes for a sort of bread not included in most previous lists. As we have seen, domestic recipe books were handwritten, and passed down from generation to generation; sometimes a lady might write one for the use of her cook, but more often it was a way of recording families' particular eating pleasures, and each generation might add some extra recipes. Dozens survive from the seventeenth and eighteenth centuries. We can use them to track changes in eating: from around 1660, handwritten recipe books typically contain a recipe for a new kind of bread, often termed 'French' bread. Mary Davies:

FRENCH BREAD

Take half a peck of flour, and half a pint of new ale yeast, a little
salt, 4 whites, 2 yolks of eggs, a quarter of a pint of wine vinegar
make your paste with warm milk make it very soft as puft paste,
do not make it until your oven be almost hot, then make it in
little loaves, bake in an oven that is very quick [hot].[42]

There's a sample of this bread in every recipe book from the seventeenth to the early eighteenth century, and we can also find it in the
main printed cookbooks of the era. This rise of 'French' breads may be
a sign of changing tastes. Reading seventeenth-century recipes, one is
struck by how *dark* people's taste was – dark, slow-cooked meats, especially old meats like mutton, game and offal; rich spicing; heavy wine
and meat-based sauces; relatively few salads or vegetables. They had a
taste for sourness or bitterness, as in the nowadays-none-too-edible
tansies they ate, and the frequent use of vinegar. Palates were really
intense. Added to which, they were drinking a lot of very strong ale
– strong in both senses – and also wine that had been spiced and
sugared.

At some point this fashion for 'dark' tastes began to fade. Venison
was displaced by an urban, feminised, 'civilised' taste for blandness
and whiteness as the acme of *civilité* – not what you put in, but what
you take out, as we will see again when we come to chicken. As pewter
or china replaced the trencher, as teahouses ousted alehouses, so the
bland replaced the tasty, so that white sugared foods became more
desirable than dark, spiced bloody foods. Perhaps, among other
factors, the rise of industry made whiteness more highly valued – by
then, darkness was no longer linked with forests and their denizens,
but with dark mills and soot.

Printed recipe books of the eighteenth century offer the same kind
of formula as the handwritten ones. In the 1769 book by Elizabeth
Raffald, indefatigable mother of six (not sixteen, as often alleged),
there is only one recipe for bread: hers contains butter, milk and egg
white, but her dough has a much longer rest than is specified by the
manuscript recipes, since she advises letting it stand all night then

giving it a further rest of half an hour when divided into pieces –
more an autolyse or pause to allow the gluten to relax than a rise or
proof.[43] The obvious though not the only way to interpret this is that
French bread required a specific technique which had to be recorded,
a possibility which by default might suggest that the main kind of
bread was different. The oddity of all these recipes is a *very* short
rising time. Enrichments such as milk or butter or sugar also disrupt
gluten formation and require a big increase in the amount of yeast
used. The addition of fats and sugar made a far softer crumb and a
darker, more caramel crust. Yet as this recipe was spreading through
the nation's recipe books, there was also a steady decline in home
baking.

There's no reason to imagine that housewives stopped baking
because it was tiring, or boring. The reasons were more likely to be
tightening restrictions on oven hire and bread sales, migration from
the countryside to the towns, and a lack of fuel and other resources,
as well as the erosion of knowledge in newly urban and industrialised
contexts. It is, however, reasonable to suppose that the arrival as a
daily breakfast of what had once been festival treats meant that
people's idea of the delicious left the house and became linked with
what was created by the forces of commerce. One example is the
Chelsea bun.

By the end of James I's reign, bakers were offering little sweet or
spiced cakes as everyday treats. They made an ideal breakfast on the
run, and their attraction was further elevated by the tastes of the new
trade empire, caraway and coriander, along with sugar, in a tender,
rich, brioche-style dough full of eggs and milk. Before the advent of
coffee and tea, they could form a breakfast with ale, and sometimes
with cheese too. They could also be consumed as a snack, and, as we've
seen, in some periods breakfast itself was a snack. The comfort of hot
food and drink was being attached to bread instead of meat.

In the late seventeenth and early eighteenth centuries, many kinds
of buns emerged onto the market as a form of street food, and one
bun house opened on Jew's Row, near Grosvenor Row, by the Ranelagh
Pleasure Gardens in Chelsea, so customers could enjoy a walk and

then buy a bun to break their fast. There is a surviving 1730 Hogarth engraving of the bun house, showing an elegant colonnaded walkway which gave onto the interior, where buns could be enjoyed. Or a bun could be purchased through the window to be eaten during a carriage drive. The house, run by the Hand family, survived into the late nineteenth century on various sites; Richard Hand, 'Captain Bun', was proprietor at the end of the eighteenth century, and always wore a fez and a dressing gown, perhaps trying to assert the Turkish splendour of his wares. For the Chelsea bun of his day was not an ovoid spiral, but a flaky, crunchy, lemon-scented square, structurally like the Breton Kouign-amann, also designed to show butter at its best (Captain Bun's son was famed as a butter seller): 'Fragrant as honey and sweeter in taste!/ As flaky and white as if baked by the light,/ As the flesh of an infant soft, doughy and slight.'[44]

The original bun house's popularity did not long survive the closure of Ranelagh Gardens in 1804, though it had its own garden and grotto, but nearby imitators soon sprang up to fill the void. Henry Mayhew says in *London Labour and the London Poor* that a man with a rich musical voice sold Chelsea buns all year round in Westminster, crying: 'One a penny, two a penny, hot Chelsea buns! Burning hot! Smoking hot! R-r-r-reeking hot! Hot Chelsea buns!'[45]

The 'Chelsea' in the bun was important. Buns began to announce their locality. The Bath bun arrived, not necessarily in Bath, along with its fellow, the Sally Lunn, and its attendant romantic fictions about Huguenot refugees; it was accompanied by the Yorkshire cake, the Eccles cake, the Kentish huffkin and the Goosnargh cake, the Colston bun from Bristol and the Wood Street Cake from the City of London. The last-named, a lightly yeasted fruitcake with rosewater icing, was marketed with a royal story, relating that when in 1648 Lady Anne Halkett helped smuggle the future James II from London into Europe dressed as a woman, she gave him a Wood Street Cake for the journey, for she knew he loved the cakes.[46] The story illustrates the kind of pedigree being claimed for the new baked goods – *old* and *very* posh. Yet the point was also that the bun was grabbed on the run, as a snack for a teenager. Buns had speed in their favour, for consumers and bakers alike. The Bath bun was practical for bakers because it was a fast-rise dough, so bakers could avoid a sleepless night when getting the breakfasts of others ready. The same was true for those who sought to make them at home, using Elizabeth Raffald's recipe of 1760. And it was relatively cheap, as Jane Austen explains in a letter to her sister Cassandra: 'to be sure, the keep of two will be more than of one, I will endeavour to make the difference less by disordering my stomach with Bath buns'.[47] The bun came to represent the delicious (though disorderly) pleasures of urban eating.

Yet urban baking remained a menace. The insecurity of the baker's trade, and the physical, visceral danger of their hell-hot fires, culminated in the Great Fire of London in 1666. The fire gutted a city already ravaged by plague. But was it really the fault of jobbing baker Thomas Farriner, the man traditionally blamed for the disaster? His shop was on Pudding Lane, so called because the Eastcheap butchers had a scalding house for hogs there.[48] Farriner was a little promiscuous with his oven, leasing it out to locals, and he also cooked pies – his own and those of others – for sale. One Saturday evening in September, he shut up shop. It was the end of the day, and his oven should have been all but cold; bakers made the oven hottest at the beginning of the day, and it cooled slowly, passing through a range of temperatures right for various baked goods as it did so, eventually reaching the gentle warmth needed for pies. After these were baked, Thomas filled the bakehouse room with fresh faggots for the morning. His daughter checked at midnight: all was well.

And yet at 1 a.m. the Farriners' servant woke, choked by smoke. She rushed to wake the family, but they all found themselves trapped, and had to climb out through a neighbour's window. Timber and plaster were dry after a hot, rainless summer, and there was a brisk wind. By now, the fire had spread from the bakery to adjacent houses. Around 3 a.m., diarist Samuel Pepys was woken by *his* maid; he looked out, noted the orange glow in the sky, and went back to bed. When he got up the next morning, he climbed the battlements of the Tower of London to see a conflagration swallowing up the whole south-eastern corner of the City. Going down to the river, he hired a boat; from the

Thames, he saw the fire leap to the top of the steeple of St Laurence Pountney. As the fire leapt from house to distant house, rumour too leapt across streets and alleyways. London was full of foreigners, mostly Huguenots or Dutch, asylum seekers, all already resented for taking trade from the native-born, who had become used to throwing dung and old roots at the incomers.[49] Was it the Dutch who started the fire? Did they own the bakery in Pudding Lane? Or was it the French? Soon enough, a foreign baker was found and arrested. By Tuesday, when the residents of Oxford saw an apocalyptic blood-red moon rise, St Paul's Cathedral was on fire. The news swiftly reached the shires, and beyond; Lancashire vicar Ralph Josselin heard that 'a fire began in London in Pudding Lane at a French baker's about one of the clock Sept: 2. being Lords day, and on y* 3 & 4 burnt down almost the whole city but a little quarter from y* tower to Moorgate, and as low as Leadenhall Street.'[50] It wasn't just a baker, but a *French* baker.

Thomas Farriner and his children, keen to avoid blame, signed the bill accusing Frenchman Robert Hubert of starting the fire. Hubert's confession – much too cooperative – was initially of starting a fire in Westminster. On learning that the fire had never reached Westminster, but began in Pudding Lane, Hubert changed tack and claimed to have thrown a crude fire grenade through the open window of Farriner's bakery; he also said accomplices stopped the water cocks to sabotage attempts to put out the fire. Hubert's confessed motive was that he was a French spy and an agent of the Pope. Having never seen the Farriner bakery, he did not know that it had no windows, and he was so severely crippled that it would have been impossible for him to throw the alleged grenade. But a scapegoat was urgently needed; Londoners were whispering that Charles II himself had arranged the fire to punish the people of London for the execution of his father. And Catholics had been favourite suspects since the Reformation. The accusation was added to the Monument put up in 1668: 'the most dreadful Burning of this City; begun and carried on by the treachery and malice of the Popish faction'. Hubert was hanged at Tyburn, and as his body was being handed to the Company of Barber-Surgeons for dissection, it was torn apart by a crowd of Londoners. The Londoners were certain: fire and bakehouses went together, as did fire and Catholics (gunpowder, treason and plot firmly borne in mind).

———————

Alongside fear of the baker and his hellish fires, belief in the supernatural value of bread also persisted. Christian Mass was centred on the sharing of bread, and the belief of the devout that the fragile white wafer became God's own flesh in the Eucharist.[51] The Host, as it was termed, was offered to God as bread, and given back to worshippers as the living body of Christ. Since ordinary lay folk only received the Host once a year, the big event was the elevation of the freshly consecrated Host, held up above the priest's head, so the congregation could see it; real devotees like Henry VIII might celebrate holy days by trying to see five elevations in one day. After every Mass, blessed bread – separate from the consecrated Eucharist – was distributed, and since the Eucharist was set about with rules and restrictions which forbade its reuse, the blessed bread became in its place a reservoir of magic and devotion: the formula for the blessing claimed it offered 'health of body as well as soul'.[52] It could prevent horses from being stolen.[53] Though anathema to some, the magic of bread was so appealing that Protestants had to forbid its use as a lucky charm, and under Edward VI replaced the white wafers with ordinary bread.

In the familiar Grimm tale of Hansel and Gretel, a witch kidnaps two children in order to fatten and eat them after baking them in an oven; in the end she is baked herself. An almost identical tale was told in medieval times, but instead of a witch, the villain of the piece was a Jewish baker. In her book on Jewish child-murder, the blood libel and the Eucharist, Miri Rubin tells the story of a Jewish boy who secretly receives the Eucharist, and is thrown into an oven by his furious father. The Virgin Mary protects the boy in the oven by covering him in her cloak. The boy and his mother convert to Christianity, and the Jewish baker is put in the oven himself.[54] Rubin points out that the boy is a kind of loaf, and a kind of Eucharist, baked in an oven like bread, then reborn from the Virgin.[55]

Bread could reveal occult secrets: if a loaf of bread over-rose and then had many very large holes, it meant the woman of the family was pregnant. Every crumb had to be carefully swept up, and thrown forth as food for some of God's creatures. It was believed that anyone guilty of casting bread into the fire, or in any way destroying it, would sooner or later be hungry. If a young woman was in the habit of burning bread when baking, the saying was: 'Never marry the lass,/ It [that] burns the bread or spills the meal,/ She'll ne'er do well t' child nor chiel [man]'. A woman should not sing while she was baking, or she would shed tears before the bread was eaten.[56]

Because the transformation going on behind the closed oven door remained mysterious, bread-making was itself ritualised. Seventeenth-century folklorist John Aubrey wrote that 'when the Bread was put in the oven, they prayed to God and Saint Stephen, to send them a just batch and even', a prayer that reflects the likelihood that something could go wrong.[57] An understanding of bread as porous to death was manifest in other beliefs: 'Bread will not rise when there is a dead body in the house'; 'A hole in the newly-cut loaf signified a grave'. Bread also had curative and prophylactic properties. Bread hung around a baby's neck was believed to keep the fairies away. Loaves that joined together during baking signified a wedding, and separating them over the head of a tongue-tied child would cure it by sympathetic magic. Barm or liquid yeast was called Goddisgood, yet in folklore such 'good' names are most often ambiguous; it was almost as if a blessing was needed to make it behave, as with the fairies, usually called the good people or the good neighbours to defray any possible wrath. And yet, though bewitchment of ale was common, bread-making was seldom bewitched. Indeed, eating bread could cure bewitchment.

———

Bread remained precious in the countryside because by the end of the eighteenth century it was getting scarcer. Rural England was struggling to find enough wood to fire its bread ovens. In the village of Grovely, Wiltshire, peasants had from medieval times been entitled to snapwood, which meant fallen wood and wood that could be broken off with a hand. This was ideal for bread; snapwood could be tied with furze into quick-burning faggots. Prolific nineteenth-century writer Esther Copley advises that 'The fuel of an oven should be very dry, and such as will heat through quickly. The stalky part of furze, and the brush-wood of faggots answer the purpose best. From one hour to an hour and a half is the time required for heating an oven; nothing but experience can give aptitude and exactness in determining the proper heat.'[58]

In Wiltshire, however, a new law of 1766 made it a crime to take wood, with punishments including flogging. Rights to gather wood were lost.[59] Self-sufficiency was not only a question of access to arable land but also about the right to gather fuel; a major cause of rural misery was that by 1800 most labourers' houses had no fire at all, not even for the provision of light and heat. Yet domestic economists incessantly complained about the failure of cottage wives to bake, without explaining what they were supposed to use to fire their ovens. Early nineteenth-century socialist and author William Cobbett wrote, 'How wasteful and indeed how shameful, for a labourer's wife to go to the baker's shop; and how negligent, how criminally careless of the welfare of his family must the labourer be who permits so scandalous a use of the proceeds of his labour?'[60]

Cobbett – from whom we will hear frequently – was a man whose career spanned a spectrum from loyal defence of the monarchy to radicalism, advocacy of the Reform Act of 1832, and passionate support for Catholic emancipation. Contradictory? No. Cobbett was a man who sought liberty for the people of England in every arena. Influenced by visiting the United States, where he had seen pioneering farmsteads, he sought to create a similar culture of self-sufficiency in England by teaching the rural poor the skills they needed to grow and manage their own food and thus make them independent of landowner and factory-owner alike. He saw that freedom depended on economics, and economics on the belly. He rhapsodised, 'Give me, for a beautiful sight, a neat and smart woman, heating her oven and setting in her bread!'[61] This was all very well, but how was the housewife supposed to heat the oven? Eliza Acton, the daughter of a nineteenth-century brewer, and perhaps the first domestic goddess, in *Modern Cookery for Private Families* contrasted English cottage wives with those of France: 'It might naturally be supposed that the art of preparing bread well, wholesomely, and without waste, would be an object of peculiar household interest to families of every degree throughout the kingdom … Unfortunately, however, this is not the case.'[62]

Esther Copley also stressed the need for virtuous self-sufficiency through bread. In this way, the housewife–baker became a symbol of resistance to manufacturing and consumerism. Yet Acton specifies the need for a fourpenny faggot in the 1857 edition of her book, and adds that this is so only in 'those counties where wood can be obtained at a reasonable price'.[63] This will bake 'eight or nine large loaves'. However, she entirely neglects the question of how the poor can *get* a fourpenny faggot. Fourpence is a lot on a wage of six shillings a week, which in Wiltshire was the average for a labourer, especially since the faggot would not bake enough bread for a week. The right to collect snapwood was crucial.[64] As acre after acre of common land was enclosed, fuel became scarcer and scarcer:

> Where fuel is scarce and dear, poor people find it cheaper to buy the bread of the baker than to bake for themselves … but *where fuel abounds*, and costs only the trouble of cutting and carrying home, there they may save something by baking their own bread.[65]

It follows that where fuel didn't abound, home baking didn't abound either.

In addition, the loaf was from the early eighteenth century poleaxed by a series of disasters that occurred nationally and locally, and eventually made good bread almost extinct. The year 1756, for example, was a bad one for British wheat. Too much violent rain just before harvest levelled the wheat to the ground. The crop was smaller than usual and of much worse quality than the previous year; it wouldn't grind well and the flour produced didn't bake well. In response to the shortage, Parliament authorised a 'standard' bread, stamped with a capital letter S. This was made with more bran than was customary, to extract more nourishment per penny, and it baked up darker than customers liked. It sold for less, too.

People associated dark bread with poverty. They wanted bread that was whiter than white. Painter William Hogarth wrote impatiently in 1753, 'They eat no Bread of Wheat and Rye, but … as white as any Curd.'[66] Meanwhile, a free and rather red-top kind of press gave vent to fresh scandals blaming bakers: 'There is another ingredient, which is more shocking to the heart and if possible more hurtful to the health of mankind' – 'sacks of old ground bones', scavenged from charnel houses. 'Thus the charnel houses of the dead are raked to add filthiness to the food of the living.'[67] Whether true or false, the tale was of a piece with the public's view of bakers. Not only were they incendiary cheats, they were dirty too. In the midst of nineteenth-century progress and economic liberalism, Charles Astridge remembered the bread he and his family were forced to eat: 'We mostly lived on bread, but it wasn't bread like ee [you] get now; twas that heavy and doughy ee could pull long strings of it out of your mouth. They called it gravy bread. But twas fine compared with the porridge we made out of bruised beans.'

And bread was 'that damp you had to dig it out o' the middle with a spoon'. Or as another memoir recalled, in wet summers, 'a slice, when cut, if pulled apart, was as though cobwebby, the colour then black, and it stank'.[68] What was wrong with the bread was rope spores, aka *Bacillus mesenticus* or *pumilus* or *subilis*, a bread spoilage organism which especially affects the bread crumb, particularly at the centre of the loaf, leaving behind a sticky, pasty, stringy mass. It also smells exotically of pineapple. The cause was the wheat becoming wet prior to harvest and/or being harvested in a wet state, a frequent occurrence in wet years. Rope spores survive the baking process, germinate, and make the menacing cobwebs Astridge recalled. Nowadays, nobody in England would eat the horrible result.

This was the era of the Corn Laws. In the early nineteenth century, during the Napoleonic Wars, it had not been possible to import corn from Europe. This led to an expansion of British wheat farming *and* to high grain prices, which led inexorably to high bread prices.

Landowners were encouraged to grow wheat on every tiny scrap of land, under fences and below gates and stiles. It was a boom time for landowners. And like all booms, it had a use-by date. The wars ended with Napoleon's defeat at Waterloo in 1815. Grain could be imported from the Continent once more, and the price of wheat fell sharply, from 126s 6d a quarter (8 bushels) in 1812, to 65s 7d three years later. Landowners applied pressure to Parliament, and Parliament – largely made up of landowners – responded by passing a law permitting the import of foreign wheat free of duty only when the domestic price reached 80s. per quarter. During the passing of this legislation, the Houses of Parliament had to be defended by armed troops against a huge crowd, who knew full well that the law would mean that the staple of their diet, bread, would become unaffordable. With lower prices, farmers planted less wheat. There was a dreadful harvest in 1816. Bread prices shot back up. This was followed by industrial action as workers demanded higher wages in order to pay the increased food prices. As well as strikes, there were food riots all over Britain. Protests against the Corn Laws were one of the objects of a peaceful gathering of workers at a place called St Peter's Field in Manchester on 16 August 1819, leading to the Peterloo massacre.

Poor people in the countryside became reliant on leasings – what was left after gleaning. Leasings were scavenged from the field immediately after the main harvest, with each poor family lined up like runners to secure a good patch, setting off for their chosen area like sprinters. A horn would blow, and the field would be scavenged. Thomas Wrapson's family would boil a little of the grain with a bit of turnip and a pennyworth of milk. If they got more, they took it to the mill to be made into bread. Charles Robinson, a Sussex woodman, recalled the hunger and the scrabbling:

> Crammings was common. It was made of what was left after
> the flour and the bran was taken away, and what was left, mixed
> with a little bread flour, was called crammings … more often
> we made a sort of pudding with it … Many a night it were hard
> work a-getting home, I were that hungry.[69]

But bread had become so essential to every meal that the poor could not imagine any other food. A blind man remarked that 'when I was a child white bread was considered a great luxury … greater than roast beef is today'. 'The principal course at the morning meal … was a small basin of bread soaked in water [salt] occasionally a little skimmed milk, and a small piece of bread tinged with lard in winter … for dinner plain pudding – flour and water – or pork dumpling; sometimes both, with potatoes or onions.'[70]

The appearance of the potato in the diet of the poor resulted from a sustained campaign from above. The potato was urged on rural workers as an alternative to fragile grain crops. It is beloved by nutritional advisers to this day because it provides cheap bulk calories along with a healthy dose of vitamin C. The potato was easy to grow, not subject to problems like pesky old wheat, so very hard to store and so likely to be ruined by bad weather, so likely to run short and provoke social disruption and disorder as a result. The potato was seen as the answer to everything.

Initially the poor hadn't wanted potatoes. When first introduced from the New World, people felt sure potatoes would cause leprosy and wreak poisonous havoc, being a relative of nightshade. But the experts were sure. Potatoes would keep wages from rising, which was good news for landowners. William Cobbett had doubts, and said that in Ireland the bloated tuber had also swelled the population, forcing down wages and allowing the peasant Irish to live in disgusting dugouts, squatting around their potato pots like the American savages from whom the plant derived. For Cobbett, Walter Ralegh was one of the worst villains who ever lived. Thomas Malthus also felt that potatoes were just too easy to eat, a fast food that broke the restraints that kept the population in check. But the potato caught on anyway: nourishing, cheap, easy-to-grow potatoes instead of that silly old convenience food, bread.

Then, in 1845, a disaster crossed the Atlantic: *Phytophthora infestans* came to Europe from America, reversing the journey the potato itself had made. With hideous speed, it sprang spectrally from field to field, destroying the poor family's one reliable source of food. Potatoes turned to black stinking slime in the ground. Overnight, sometimes in just a few hours, apparently sturdy plants would dissolve into a hideous uneatable nauseating substance. We associate the calamity with Ireland, and most readers with an interest in history will know that approximately one million people were killed by this plague directly or indirectly in that country, but the potato blight caused starvation in England too.

Unlike wheat, potatoes do not store well from one year to the next, and it turned out that last year's saved crop could be eaten by the ravaging fungus as easily as this year's. Advice poured from the government, almost all of it useless. Dry your potatoes in the sun. Mix lime with sand and bury the tubers in it. Or burn turf and mix it with sawdust. Grate your rotting potatoes, wash the gratings and dry the pulp. Nothing worked. Going to dig up food and finding rotting stink is depressing even for a twenty-first-century allotment holder. How much worse it was in 1845 when there was absolutely no alternative is unimaginable even for the very poorest allotment holder now.

The failure of the Irish potato crop and the mass starvation that followed forced Sir Robert Peel and his Conservative government to reconsider the wisdom of the Corn Laws. In January 1846 a new Corn Law was passed that reduced the duty on oats, barley and wheat to the insignificant sum of one shilling per quarter. Aware of the recent crisis, the food advice experts stepped up to the plate. Unfamiliar grains and pulses were imported, and recipes for rice bread circulated, while ladies wondered why the cook couldn't make a decent loaf from rice. (The reason is that rice contains no gluten.)

Like the unfortunate potato, rice had been massively promoted for a while; all parochial relief in 1799 was to be via rice, potatoes and soup. Rice was cheap, still cheaper from India via the East India Company than from the recently independent American Carolinas. Rice, said nutritionists, prompted (as they so often are) by the food industry, was just as good as bread. Rice pudding was well known before the era of Napoleon, but was mixed with not only lavish amounts of milk, but also four ounces of mutton suet, six eggs, rosewater and cinnamon; this is how it appears in the receipt book of Martha Washington, wife of the first American president, but probably dating from the late seventeenth century, though modern editor and transcriber Karen Hess turns up her nose at the mutton suet.[71] Not a dish for the poor, with those ingredients. The poor were advised to mix 'a little morsel of Cheshire cheese' with rice to 'greatly improve its flavour'. Rice could be cooked over a very low fire, the experts said, during the working day, but the Manchester cotton workers were unconvinced. The experts felt that drinking too much tea made them demand bread and butter, a convenience food for the idle. Bread, it was opined, was a lazy substitute for cooking, and since the poor could boil a kettle for tea they could have made a pudding with the fuel instead. So in the guise of helping the poor, experts were able to explain that the fault lay with the poor and not with the law.

Even after they had been repealed, the Corn Laws' effects lingered; they had helped to undermine rural self-sufficiency, and as households ceased to be self-sufficient, they had become more subject to the whims of the marketplace. Provincial authorities had no respect for bakers, and great, even inordinate respect for the free market – 'as little skill and no capital are required in the trade of baking, competition will prevent inordinate profit'.[72] Industrialisation and urbanisation also reduced the number of self-sufficient households. True, many cottagers had been forced to depend on the lord's mill and the lord's bread oven, paying exorbitantly for them, and only in a minority of places were the amenities of mill, fuel and oven available, but now the lord was replaced by the more brutal rule of the marketplace as rural–urban drift gathered pace and families left the countryside to search for more reliable employment in towns and cities.

———

Underlying the struggles of the urban poor to feed their families was the abandonment of regulation. The process of dismantling the strict laws on bread began early in the nineteenth century, when supporters of laissez-faire economics convinced themselves that doing nothing was the best thing to do. The market was all-wise, so in 1822, the Assize of Bread and Ale was abolished as archaic; the committee considering the subject declared boldly that 'more benefit is likely to result from the effects of a free competition ... than can be expected to result from any regulations or restrictions under which the bakers could possibly be placed'. The result was to transform baking into an even more precarious trade. Freed from the old guild structure, thousands of new bakers set up shop, and all of them tried to undercut one another. Eliza Acton noted that in 1851 the number of bakers in Paris was limited to 601, which meant that they were all sure to sell plenty of bread, whereas Britain's free trade had pushed the official number of London bakers to 2,286 (the unofficial number may have been as high as 50,000). These bakers may have had commercial liberty but they had no peace of mind. To make a loaf they could sell at a price at which they could find buyers, they were forced to reduce the quality of ingredients to a minimum. A witness to the Committee on Journeymen Bakers commented that 'They [the bakers] only exist now by first defrauding the public, and next getting eighteen hours' work out of the men for the next twelve hours.'[73] The eighteen hours in question were spent in appalling conditions, as we already know.

The indignant Karl Marx wrote in *Das Kapital* that Londoners, 'always well up in the Bible, knew well enough that man is commanded to eat his bread in the sweat of his brow, but they did not know that he had to eat daily in his bread a certain quantity of human perspiration mixed with the discharge of abscesses, cobwebs, dead black-beetles, and putrid German yeast, without counting alum, sand, and other ingredients.' In this last phrase, Marx might have been referring to the fact that there were few baking cellars with toilet facilities, so the bakers tended to use the water pail they would use to moisten the dough to relieve themselves. The abscesses Marx mentions were common among bakers, who worked half-naked in a hot and humid atmosphere full of flour dust. It took its toll: Marx's contemporary, physician Cyrus Edson, reported 'journeymen bakers, suffering from cutaneous diseases, working the dough in the bread trough with naked hands and arms', and reminded the shopper that 'any germs ... on the hands of the baker ... are sure to find their way into the dough, and once there, to find all the conditions necessary for subdivision and growth'.[74] Lung diseases were equally common, including asthma and emphysema from inhaling tiny particles of flour. Eye problems were common too. The royal commission investigating the employment of children and young persons commented in 1863 that journeymen bakers often lay down for naps 'upon the kneading board, which is also the covering of the trough in which the dough is "made"'. After this unrefreshing slumber, the journeymen set out at mid-morning to deliver the bread they had spent the early hours baking.

As baking became more industrialised, all Londoners, not just the rich, demanded whiteness. This might have been because of a decline in dental health, but it might also have been a response to the very idea of urban bread, divested of the darkness of the countryside, clean and modern. It may also have been a result of the way new flours were marketed. By 1813, millers from Abingdon said it was practice to send fine flour to London, keeping back a coarse third to be sold to the poor, as food for country people and their pigs. This can hardly have made it seem desirable. The spread of white bread resulted from improved milling and rolling (commonplace from the 1870s onwards) that removed the germ and bran from the wheat when making flour. This also removed several key nutrients, particularly B vitamins, and the fibre needed for digestive health. Some of the new types of flour – flour that made the whitest of white bread – were whitened further by alum. An enormous amount of nonsense has been written about this, and was also written at the time. Regarded as some kind of deadly toxin, it is toxic in large amounts, but it was added to the bread not to save on costs – alum costs more than flour – but as an early type of dough improver. (Twenty-first-century supermarket bread is packed with dough improvers, from concentrated ascorbic acid – vitamin C – to various enzymes, not to mention added gluten, malt – a natural source of amylase – in various forms, and bleaches to make the flour seem whiter.) Alum worked on weak flour to make its rise faster and bouncier, reducing the time bakers had to spend in the bakery. And alum is unlikely to have been the worst thing the poor found in their bread.

Many dieticians and experts did their best to revive bread-baking in the home, but the results were at best mixed. Charles Elmé Francatelli's attempt to revive domestic baking in his book *A Plain Cookbook for the*

Working Classes, printed in 1852, contains a bread recipe. Cheerily, and crazily, Francatelli tells his readers:

> And now a few words on baking your own bread. I assure you if you would adopt this excellent practice, you would not only effect a great saving in your expenditure, but you would also insure a more substantial and wholesome kind of food; it would be free from potato, rice, bean or pea flour, and alum, all of which substances are objectionable in the composition of bread. The only utensil required for bread-making would be a tub, or trough.

He seems to forget that you also need an oven and fuel to heat it, which would require more than half an hour to fire and rake (and we have already seen how difficult and expensive it could be to get enough fuel). He also neglects to mention the heavy labour involved in kneading a bushel of flour, and the destructive effect of flour on clothing. Small wonder that his words did not find immediate acceptance among those he sought to instruct.

The other great change that guaranteed a taste for complete uniformity and a concomitant loss of skill was the invention of the bread pan or tin. Bread still had to be shaped, but not as much or as skilfully as when baked naked on a stone oven floor. The first mention of a bread tin is in Maria Rundell's second edition of *A New System of Domestic Cookery* (1807), developed for middling families, and intended as a guide for her daughters: 'If baked in tins the crust will be very nice', says Rundell. Elizabeth David notes with some natural regret that 'it is curious to reflect that without those tins we might never have had the sliced wrapped loaf'.[75] Confined within the walls of the tin, the dough could not spread and flatten out, but would spring upwards. Once the tin was in use, bakers no longer needed to understand the dough as intimately as they had in the past; the process could be governed entirely by the clock.

Competition between London bakers intensified still more as fresh immigrants entered the city. Jewish immigrants arrived in Whitechapel in the early 1880s, in flight from the most vicious pogroms Russia had yet seen. They were resented, even dreaded by some of their fellow East Enders, but they settled in and opened the kinds of businesses they had owned in the Russian Pale: tailors' shops and bakeries. The bakers brought with them their levains or starters, cultures of wild yeast formed using rye flour; some could have been as much as a hundred years old. They formed a small union, the Jewish Bakers, Union, the last of its kind in the United Kingdom; once there had been many such unions, ethnic and religious groups, but over time these were subsumed into larger secular organisations. There were bitter divisions between Jewish and non-Jewish bakers over the issue of Sunday baking, and between the journeymen and the masters. Though frequently repudiated by the mainstream of establishment Jewry and sometimes underrated by the British Left, these unions all played their part fighting for justice at home and abroad in the early years of the twentieth century. The Jewish bakers produced a proud banner which showed two bakers shaking hands before a fiercely fired oven; by their feet lay an ear of wheat and a tinned loaf, signs of the work they did.

All bakeries began to replace workers with machines. As always, a reduction in manual work meant a reduction in actual work, and eventually fewer workers. Complaints about unsociable hours and 'hard sweaty work' could be met with new inventions such as the moulding machines, greeted unenthusiastically at first, but eventually ubiquitous. The memoirs of a turn-of-the-century baker in Waltham, Essex, complained that efforts to speed up the bread-making process were counter-productive:

> Basically it had to have a long period of fermentation. It's like wine. You can make wine in a bucket and you can make bread in a short time-process but it is not the same as a long-time dough because the longer the period of fermentation is, the more flavour of the bread.[76]

These intelligent comments illustrate how well experienced bakers – as opposed to bakery owners – understood bread.

But under pressure, bakers moved to embrace industrial processes and to cater to a market interested in hygiene, not taste. Most importantly, and perhaps most fatally, the first industrial bread bakers marketed their products quite specifically as more *sanitary* than bread baked in home kitchens or artisan bakeries. A fear of germs, in conjunction with misinformation about yeast propagated by misguided reformers among the general public, led to a brief craze for bread leavened with the new chemical lighteners – bicarbonate of soda, for instance – instead of yeast.[77] Then the First World War saw bakeries turned over to the production of food for the army; the process was piecemeal, chaotic, and left civilians short of food. One baker, E. H. Gilpin, explained to War Office officials that the old field ovens used in every campaign for half a century and more were tying down men who ought to be fighting, but nobody seemed willing to listen. The army in France continued to rely on field bakeries using ovens known as 'Polly' Perkins. They resembled large metal tanks with a flue, mounted on a wooden wagon base with wooden wheels. Fired by wood, later replaced by oil, poor 'Polly' was finally swept aside in 1939 by the Baker Perkins Standard Army Bread Plant, which was capable of producing over 100,000 rations of bread per day, installed at the base bakeries at Rouen and Boulogne. Baker Perkins became models for civilian bakers too.

Knowledge and pride in bread was soon swept aside. Bakeries used to advertise 'all our bread is baked by hand', but by the 1960s this had become 'all our bread is untouched by hand'.[78] The process of mechanising and speeding up bread-making culminated in the Chorleywood process, demonised by most food historians. Chorleywood was a very fast mixing process that heated the dough rapidly, creating a rise so quick that the whole business took only three hours even with weak flour. Invented in 1961, it made bread softer and more uniform than ever before, and also far cheaper. It uses huge amounts of yeast and some further additives, enzymes to make the bread hold more air, to make it last longer, and bleach to make it whiter. It stays soft for a very long time. Yet few really love the pappy result. A former baker, however, told me he had worked in a bakery since the 1930s: Chorleywood, he said, was salvation. Before it, he said, bread was even worse – even more cottony and adulterated, even more badly made; bakers were lazy and were not well educated and they did not care about the product.

Before Chorleywood, bakeries had already industrialised, had been forced out of city centres by rent hikes and the increased cost of materials. Towards the end of the nineteenth century, on show at the Bakers' and Confectioners' Exhibition at the Royal Agricultural Hall, Islington, in 1897, were the 'Universal' and single blade doughing machines, 'Universal' cake machines, spiral brush sifters, dough trucks, bread racks, water measuring and tempering vessels, dough brakes and dividers, hoists, a Perkins steam-pipe peel oven and a draw-plate oven. The machines made up for ignorance, but made actual knowledge seem redundant, and without that knowledge, the bread was effectively handed over to the devices.

––––––––––

In the popular imagination, sliced bread and the pop-up toaster go hand in hand. In fact, the toaster came first. When toast was made on a toasting fork on the fire, thicker bread was needed, but thick, irregular artisanal bread often threatened to jam toasters and get stuck, inside them. The first electric toaster was invented in 1893, for a British firm called Crompton and Co., and became commercially available from 1909, although the pop-up timer toasters we are used to were not invented until 1919. Again, the idea was to cut preparation time. Since the timer automatically turned off the toaster when the toast was done, and both sides of the bread were toasted simultaneously, it revolutionised the time-consuming chores of watching the toast, and turning it when one side was done.[79] And if the result was less delicious, at least it was clean and easy. The surface of the toast that resulted was so fragile that it had the happy effect of encouraging the use of the new soft spreads, such as margarine.

Sliced bread duly followed. In 1928, the Chillicothe Baking Company of Missouri launched a product called 'Kleen Maid Sliced

Bread'. The name implies that the buyer is used to having servants, but that she is now better served by automation. Taking the humans out of the loop made it clean. Advertised as 'the greatest forward step in the baking industry since bread was wrapped', it was popular. It spread. According to George Ort, manager at H. W. Nevill (aka Sunblest), the first slicing and wrapping machine was installed in the Wonderloaf Bakery in Tottenham in 1937; though its rise to ubiquity was slowed by the war, sliced bread made up 80 per cent of the British market by the 1950s.[80] The new sliced bread did what bread had been meant to do for centuries; it saved the poor from hunger.

————

As we have seen, bread depended on a lot more than just the work of bakers. In the eighteenth century John Locke tried to imagine everything that went into a loaf of bread, a complex chain of very different kinds of activity:

> 'tis not barely the Plough-man's Pains, the Reaper's and
> Thresher's Toil, and the Bakers Sweat, is to be counted unto the
> *Bread* we eat; ... from its being seed to be sown, to its being
> made Bread, must all be *charged on* the account of *Labour*.[81]

Before flour even reached the bakers' door, the grain had already exacted a savage due of toil and sweat from those who had turned the bare brown earth into flour that the baker could use. As well as muscles, minds had to be active: the skills needed to make the earth offer its goodness as bread were formidable, and involved many different experts working together, not always amicably.

The tale of what went on behind the baker begins with a story of enterprise. A recent archaeological discovery reveals that paleolithic Britons imported cereals from Europe long before they turned to growing them themselves. Wheat appeared in the British Isles around two thousand years before farmers began to cultivate it. Although wheat was first farmed in Anatolia about ten thousand years ago, farming it did not reach Britain until some four thousand years later.

However, at Bouldnor Cliff, a site under water just off the Isle of Wight, DNA matching Near Eastern strains of wheat – einkorn – has been recovered. There was no pollen, no implements of cultivation, and the archaeologists concluded the grain probably came from the Balkans or from southern France, and was used to make dough. Ironically, England has *always* preferred to be a trading nation rather than a primary producer. There was never a primal moment of self-sufficiency.

Palaeolithic humans were not solely carnivorous – bones and spears simply leave more marks in archaeological records than grains. Unlike Neolithic humans, who domesticated and cultivated grains such as wheat and barley, hunter-gatherers relied on wild vegetation, but they also traded for grain from farmers, who coexisted with the hunter-gatherers already living in Europe rather than quickly replacing them. Early humans ate ground flour more than twenty thousand years before the dawn of agriculture.

The wheat at Bouldnor Cliff might have been symbolically charged and seen as 'rare, exotic, and valuable,' rather than something to be eaten daily. It was no more a dietary staple than the spices that the English would import centuries later. The sites where grain has been found generally seem to have been used mainly for ritual purposes, and in Britain, on the edge of Europe, grain was grown, or imported, only for ritual purposes. Agricultural implements may also have assumed ritual significance. Practical value followed symbolic and ritual significance, and not vice versa. Grain and agricultural implements have been found at Neolithic sites in Britain, but analysis suggests that not even Neolithic Britons ate a grain-based diet, subsisting mostly on meat and dairy.

The hunter-gatherers of Britain didn't simply crouch in caves; they followed planned movement trails that let them take advantage of seasonal resources. As the boundaries of human settlements pushed outwards, the lives of some animals were diminished: wolves, which possibly clung on in Wales and Scotland; aurochs, which died out in the Bronze Age; beavers, ousted by the Anglo-Saxons; and wild boar, confined to a few hunting reserves by 1250, though kept as a nostalgic curiosity in forests into Tudor times.[82] The red deer that supplied meat to Bronze Age and Neolithic peoples died out, except in parks, by the late fourteenth century; roe deer, once common, were rare by the Middle Ages. 'Wild' animals in England are very often animals that were introduced as game animals. The Normans introduced the fallow deer, and the rabbit, as a food animal, and it established itself well – too well for some.[83]

As animal populations altered, and the human population increased, more land was put under the plough. This wasn't because of hunger, and nor was it straightforwardly about progress; wheat was a cash crop, like coffee in the developing world today. In some places, open-field cultivation was on its way. This meant that all the arable land of a community was divided into strips, which were aggregated into furlongs, and the same crop was grown across the whole furlong. Crops were rotated, with each field ploughed but not sown every third year. By the Middle Ages, the whole field was a small business, and there were regular meetings so that there could be agreement on regulations and practices; any dissidents could be fined. Yet this system, called the open-field system, or champaign country (from French *champ*, field – yes, as in Champagne) was not universal; it was dominant in the Midlands, but everywhere else there were hedged, fenced or walled fields, with small-scale pockets of open-field cultivation.[84] The system was tied to the manorial structure, which wasn't about money, but about service. The king owned all the land, but gave the nobles use of it in return for armed service; the nobles did the same for lesser lords, who did the same for serfs, who served not in the military, but by raising food. They were tied to the land, and they could not leave it. Their bodies and their sweat were their means of payment, because they had nothing else.[85] The champaign fields developed the heavy plough, which needed four teams of oxen to draw it; oxen do not manoeuvre well, which shaped the fields.[86] There were no hedges, no walls. Allotments are 'direct descendants' of medieval strips of land allocated to individuals. Rows about cultivation and boundaries were common; in Langland's *Piers Plowman*, a man records the way the plough could be used to seize the earth of a near neighbour: 'that a foot land or a furrow/ Fetching I would/ of my next neighbour/ And naming of his earth.'

The system was inefficient. Harvests were often thin and poor, frequently failing because of disease and the weather. In order to maximise the availability of food grown (and surviving to maturity) the Anglo-Saxons planted a varied crop each season. They grew a range of hardy cereals, like barley and rye, and other crops such as beans, peas, vetches and 'weeds' (for their animals to eat). The 'weeds' might have been principally an animal crop, but most were fit for human consumption too. If 'corn' (the old word for wheat – not maize, which is a food from the Americas) failed in the fields (and wheat frequently failed in the wetter years) then the Anglo-Saxon farmers grew other foodstuffs to feed them through the year, particularly grains, grasses and beans more tolerant and hardy to the local climate, the soil, and the relief of the land. This also meant, as we have seen, that they added to their bread as a matter of course various ground mixed cereals (not just wheat) and ground dried beans and peas as flour. This made a 'black bread' leavened with beer barm (which was also made with a sourdough or wild yeast starter). Mixed-grain flours never rise as well as wheat-based flours, having less yeast activity, making a firmer, tastier, chewier bread.

The point of grinding grain is to make it more digestible, to release the calories in it. The main cost barrier to grain-only bread was grinding; as we have seen, the mills appearing on the nobleman's estate were not there to help the peasants, but to extract fees from them. In good years, when the cereal grain became fat and the harvest was good, the crop was reaped and used several times. First the cereal grain or 'ears' were harvested to grind into flour, then the long stalks of straw were cut to make ropes, baskets, thatch for houses and the roofs of farm buildings, and 'skeps' for keeping bees. The stubble closest to the ground after both cuttings was kept uncut and used for cattle fodder, and then the pigs and sheep were left to graze over the ground to get the last remaining forage.

Keeping the ears of cereal grains and using them when needed required knowhow. The grains were kept in the driest place in the home, and the grain was left in the husk and in the ear to give further protection, to stop it from sprouting in any damp, or from mouldering. When needed, a handful of stems was taken up, held by the short stalks, and cast into a fire, setting flame to the ears. Then with a stick in the other hand, the ears, now on fire, were beaten just as the husks became burnt. This process, known as 'parching', dries the grain in the husk and frees it, ready for grinding into flour in a hand quorn, a large mortar and pestle. When novelists imagine post-apocalyptic life, they often refer to it as returning to medieval times, but actually, twenty-first-century human beings do not have the skills that medieval people possessed.

To get from bare earth to a sack of flour is a journey as rich as that from idea to book. Ploughing time began on the Monday after Christmastide, but ploughing was not a once-a-year act; the plough-men were out almost every month. Often the land needed several sculptings into ridges and furrows to guarantee drainage; the ridges had to be built up over winter, then levelled down before planting to ensure they retained moisture in summer. Ploughing was also a means of weed control; a wide furrow ensured that weed taproots were disrupted. Weeds in corn were those adapted to frequently turned soil – poppies and corncockle. Ploughing was also part of fertilising; fertilisers included dung, seaweed, silt from rivers, all laid on the land and then ploughed in. In September, the stubble was broken up. Then came the ploughing of the fallow fields, ridging up in the dark days of winter, preparing the ground for peas, beans and oats, then flattening ridges for barley in early April. The only ploughing-free month was August.[87] Patterns of ploughing ensured drainage: furrow and ridge, furrow and ridge.

'Nose to ground, I crawl forward. My nose is the grey enemy of the forest': the riddle in the eleventh-century *Exeter Book* celebrates the cutting tip of the blade of the plough. Saxon ploughs could not turn over and bury the surface – but they could be used even on ground covered with thin snow; and the broken soil would be further cracked by frost. Ploughing was a complex dance between tool, season and terrain. From the eleventh century, a clodhopper's mallet broke down the largest lumps, while a harrower followed the plough, drawn by a horse since the harrow was so heavy an ox would sink. The harrow broke the soil into dust; its destructive force is the origin of our term for emotional turmoil, harrowing: torn up, reduced to tiny pieces.[88] The land was divided by what a plough could do: an acre was originally as much land as a team of oxen could plough in a day, so it differed between hilly and flat lands.[89]

Before sowing, the seeds kept from the previous harvest had to be hand-riddled and hand-picked. The seed might be held in a loose smock fold in front of the body, as illustrated in the *Belles Heures du Duc de Berry* (1405). Sowing, too, was a dance; the sower counted his steps as he moved down the rows, slow, swinging steps along two adjacent plough lines. So many steps to so many handfuls of seed; less for a dry corner, more for a damp section, in even lines to help with weeding later. If rye was sown, it was best done in the dust: 'he drives with drought the dust for to raise', said the fourteenth-century Gawain poet. The harrow might cover the seed, or it might be dressed with urine to make it unappealing to mice. Children scared off crows and pigeons.

Once the sowing was done, the work of cultivation began. Mostly, this was weeding. The weeder walked the rows from April, armed with two hooked sticks, one to pluck the weed from the growing grain without disturbing the roots of the latter, the other to pin the weed's head; the weeder then took a single pace forward, swinging the hooked stick behind him. This slowly created a mulch of decaying weeds alongside the grain crop, perhaps a foot wide. Weeding was rhythmic and enriching, and it never stopped. It also required knowledge. Common darnel looks so much like blades of corn that it was believed Adam's murderous son Cain actually turned corn into darnel. Weeds that could outpace the crop menaced its survival.[90]

After all the cultivation came harvest, a vast, co-operative and usually time-critical task that soaked up everyone able and willing to work. It happened in August, but the exact day depended on the weather. The workers had hand sickles, and they sweated in the hot sun, so tired by midday that the ale-laden break in the fields was often followed by a short nap. It went on then until at least 7pm. Those with gleaning rights went into the fields to pick up what grain they could, and then the community's geese might be let loose.

The harvested corn was threshed only as needed, as it kept better in the ear. It could be done indoors, on the wide threshing floor of a large barn; the floor was earth, beaten flat by the feet of dancers. To thresh, the sheaves were laid in the centre, and the threshers stood around them in a ring, and they did not beat the sheaves so much as force them to vibrate and shake, loosening the grain. The men had to keep perfect time, like bell-ringers, or their flails might hit other threshers. The movements were coordinated by a caller, like a country dance caller. The corn then had to be winnowed, the husk – or chaff – separated from the grain. The heaviest corn was kept for seed.[91]

Those were the pragmatic actions; the centrality of ploughed land and the grain it produced led to a rich symbolic cycle of festivities. When Christmas revelry ended on Twelfth Night (6 January) festivities marking the beginning of ploughing began. Plough lights – candles – were kept burning in many churches, and the ploughs themselves were blessed on Plough Sunday, the first Sunday after Twelfth Night, and in some places the plough and its team were also led around a great fire; both these were rites of exorcism. The next day, Plough Monday, saw the plough dragged along the streets of towns and villages. Then the actual business of ploughing could begin.

The ceremonials could be so elaborate that they were plays. The Willoughton (Lincolnshire) version, called the Plough Jack's Play, was performed by a band of farmworkers parading the streets and calling at each house. The procession took the form of two parallel plough lines. Next came the plough, without wheels and ready for ploughing. At each house they demanded entrance civilly. If allowed in, they performed their play and were rewarded with food and drink. If they were not admitted, then they ploughed up a furrow or two in front of the house. In Northamptonshire the performers were called plough-witches, in Huntingdonshire plough-witchers, and the ceremony plough-witching; this made the magic explicit but also made it a joke.

By far the most common type of play – found in well over a thousand places across Britain – was the St. George Play. Two knights fight; one is killed, but is then healed by a doctor. The plays were not well accepted by Protestants, but churchwardens' accounts show that the custom continued after the Reformation. Full of nonsense words and silly clothes, the plays were not only about merriment but also about ritual: doing and saying things all wrong got the bad luck over with.[92]

The ritual year illustrates the passion and anxiety that went with the grain year, and the need to placate and manage the magic of earth-to-loaf. Just as the plough year began with rites, so the harvest began with Lammas, or loaf-mass, the feast of first fruits. The first ripe corn was reaped and then baked into bread that was that day blessed at church, and later divided into four pieces, each crumbled in the corner of the barn that would eventually hold the grain. This four-corner rite or charm is a bit like the old rhyme, 'Four corners to my bed,/ Four angels round my head'; it creates a safe place, cause for celebration, for a wake, a revel, or at least a fair.

Farmers and labourers believe in magic because they know they are powerless in the face of wind and weather.[93] As Max Weber wrote, 'peasants have been inclined towards magic because their existence is specifically bound to nature'. It was never thought through; bad luck simply existed, and it had to be blocked or appeased. A farmer, they said, must live as if he was going to die tomorrow, and farm as if he was going to live forever. 'Twas done this way since Owd Hinery were an infant', one farmer told George Ewart Evans. A lot of actions were based on the idea that the soil had the same wants and needs as a man; it might like a drop of ale, and a bit of crumbled cake. Other ideas suggest the sensuous closeness of man and land; one old Suffolk farmer judged the land was ready for seed by walking on it, feeling it through his boots. 'If it sing or cry or make any noise under the feet then it is too wet to sow', said an Elizabethan guide. Care in sowing was vital, as 'missed bits', bare patches, foretold a death in the parish. Nothing could be begun on a Friday, except potato sowing and parsley sowing; all seed had to be sown under a waxing moon.[94] Based on observation, predicated on continuity, the folklore of the fields acted as a reminder to each member of the community to do the job properly.

Reading descriptions of the endless round of the grain year, we could imagine it the same since the beginning of farming, with the sun always shining hot on the ripe fields, but this omits the terrifying climate change our ancestors faced; what you have been reading is a depiction of what was supposed to happen, rather than what did happen. The weather in the years from around 900 to 1300 was better than it is today, with temperatures about a degree Celsius higher than in the twentieth century. There were fewer frosts in spring, and fewer winter storms, and it was warm enough for viniculture in southern England.

And then, abruptly, the climate changed radically. Through the 1290s, the winters were cold, and the summers too dry to make for a good harvest. Then, in 1309, it was cold enough for the Thames to freeze in London; even loaves of bread froze solid and had to be warmed before they could be eaten. In autumn 1314 the rain began, and did not stop. The main harvest was in, but it was modest, because the summer had been so dry. The fields turned to muddy soup, and the winter crops of peas and beans, vital proteins for the poor, could not even be planted. When the rains finally stopped, the sodden fields turned to ice. All the people could do was to hole up somewhere and wait for the thaw. And in April the rain began again. They ploughed, and they sowed, but the grain crops rotted in the fields. The harvest was thin and soon the people and animals were thin too; sheep-shearing was cancelled, because it was so cold that the sheep needed their fleece to survive. Violent storms came too; Dunwich in Suffolk was half-destroyed by a huge storm in January 1328. The buildings that slid off the cliff blocked the harbour for twenty years. What use was a church when it was at the bottom of the sea? And then came the diseases, typhus and sheeprot and cattle murrain attacking the half-starved. Eventually, the Black Death came, and finished off a third to a half of the population.

People said this was the end of the world, because they had believed that God kept in being a seasonal cycle of well-being. Now He had apparently changed the rules.[95] A perfect storm of lower solar input, volcanic eruptions creating shrouds that cut off the sun, cold high-pressure systems clamped to Central Asia together made for a Little Ice Age. The Black Death returned in 1361, along with a damaging drought, then a terrible storm in 1362. The population, around five million in 1300, fell to around two and a half million by 1400, and did not reach the levels of 1300 again until the 1630s.[96]

People tried to adapt to what they hoped was a blip. Oats and rye cultivation spread southwards and harvests were later as the grain took longer to ripen, though leaving the crop for too long meant it was vulnerable to winter storms. Whole industries were wiped out. The English wine industry, for example, was now unsustainable.[97] And there were fewer edible birds to hunt, leading the upper classes to tighten sanctions against poaching, as people turned to the food resource of wild game, while predators like wolves and bears emerged to terrorise villagers. The only positive result was the elimination of the malaria mosquito from England, though its power as a disease vector was replaced by the new prevalence of lice and fleas.

In famine, households systematically exhaust their resources; they eat the seed corn, meaning that the next crop will be too small; they kill the heifer; they put themselves at risk by poaching. Even if they downsize their food from wheat to barley, or barley to pea and bran or acorns, they are soon destitute because all resources are gone. The crew of the Tudor warship *Mary Rose* showed in their bones the rickets, scurvy and anaemia acquired during the famine of 1527–9, when they were children.[98]

The events of the calamitous fourteenth and fifteenth centuries reduced the human population and arguably also produced an acute mental climate of fear – fear of hunger, fear of nature itself, and above all fear of those who might control it. Wolfgang Behringer suggests that witchcraft is the Little Ice Age crime par excellence, and certainly the period of the witch craze coincides almost exactly with the period of the Little Ice Age. The problem was that the hunger it created was seen as an *abnormality*. The idea of what was *meant* to happen outlived the era when it was likely. Everyone went on expecting warm springs and the right kind of summers. Consequently, the food culture didn't shift to adapt, not enough, not fully.

Moreover, life expectancy – even for those who survived to five – was much lower for peasants than for yeomen. While a twenty-year-old Worcester yeoman might reasonably expect to see fifty, the poor man next door would be lucky to make it much past forty. Meanwhile, only half the population reached the age of twenty. Hence the population's average age was low, with only five per cent or so over sixty-five, hence the stages of life were truncated – men were in their prime in their twenties, while thirty was worthy solidity, and forty a gathering senescence. Seizing the day meant a lot more when there were fewer days to seize. The agrarian year especially depends on youth, its energy and its hunger. The poor diet also delayed maturation.

Those with plenty of resources – the upper classes – went on insisting on wheat bread while enclosing more and more land for the cash crop wool, and for deer hunting. This process was enabled by the Reformation, itself – among many other things – a result of the idea that humanity had collectively Got It Wrong and needed to behave differently to persuade God to act in their interests once more. The ninety per cent of the population whose lives were more-or-less marginal were in no position to innovate; the harsh times led many to turn against innovation altogether. In 1648, a chronicler reported in London 'the cries and tears of the poor, who profess they are almost ready to famish [die of hunger]', and in Scotland, another remarked that 'poverty and want emasculate the minds of many, and make those who are of dull nature, stupid and indisciplinable', whereas 'those that are of a fiery and active temperament [grow] unquiet, rapacious, frantic, or desperate. *Where there are many poor, the rich cannot be secure in what they have*'.[99]

Each fall in temperature of 0.5°C in the mean summer temperature decreased the number of days on which crops ripened by ten per cent, increasing the risk of a total harvest failure tenfold – or a hundredfold for those trying to grow crops a thousand feet or more above sea level. All the poor could do was migrate to the cities in search of food, in search of work, and the result was the growth of London and its food culture, which became distinct from that of the nation as a whole.

There, innovation could happen, succoured by imports. 'All the country is gotten into London,' James I wrote, 'so, as with time, England will only be London, and the whole country be left waste.'[100]

The Little Ice Age sharpened the edgy difference between rich and poor to a weapon. The rich may have died of disease, but the poor – and in the fifteenth century, the food-insecure made up more than half the population – went hungry every single year between the exhaustion of the winter resources and the grain harvest. Successive poor harvests meant that winter resources grew smaller, to vanishing point. Starving – and the prospect of starving – meant that people became willing to take risks for better prospects; why not, since they were doomed by inaction? Local upheavals were endemic, but the largest was the Peasants' Revolt of June 1381.

The peasants were not revolting because they were hungry *now*; the Black Death's devastating effect on a population depleted by the hunger created by climate change meant that the rich had been obliged to pay workers and give them more freedom. The main issue was the Poll Tax, an effort to fund the neverending wars with France that meant the poorest had to pay 5d each, an excruciating sum. The village of Fobbing in Essex refused to pay, and in May 1381 threw out the tax collector and then the soldiers. Inspired, other villages refused, and the disruption spread to Kent, where the movement found a leader in Wat Tyler. The rebel march on London was a very risky response. Tyler was a hothead, refusing the initial offer of a pardon from the fourteen-year-old Richard II, and rinsing his mouth and spitting at a subsequent meeting with the king, a calculated insult. In the ensuing fracas, Tyler was stabbed, so severely that he fell from his horse. Dragged back to Smithfield, he was beheaded; his followers tried to flee, but many of them were rounded up and executed as well. The revolt had already turned into a riot, as the rebels broke into alcohol stores and drank the contents, enjoying a few simple symbolic revenges as they rebelled. Hungry people don't have good judgement.

Jean Froissart says a lot about what motivated them, recording their claim that 'at the beginning of the world there were no slaves, and that no one ought to be treated as such'; that they were 'men formed after the same likeness with their lords, who treated them as beasts'; 'when Adam delved, and Eve span/ who was then the gentleman?' Froissart reports John Ball as saying:

> They are clothed in velvets and rich stuffs, ornamented with ermine and other furs, while we are forced to wear poor cloth. They have wines, spices, and fine bread, when we have only rye and the refuse of the straw; and if we drink, it must be water. They have handsome seats and manors, when we must brave the wind and rain in our labours in the field; but it is from our labour they have wherewith to support their pomp.

It ended in nothing; in death, in traitors' heads on London Bridge. But the discontent did not end. Jack Cade's rebellion in 1450 expressed similar grievances. Outbreaks of food rioting in the sixteenth and seventeenth centuries were concentrated in the years 1527, 1551, 1586–7, 1594–8, 1605, 1608, 1614, 1622–3, 1629–31, 1647–8, 1662–3, 1674, 1681 and 1693–5. Except for 1605 and 1614, these were times of poor harvests, albeit with differing degrees of scarcity.

Desperate hunger was not the sole motivation; E. P. Thompson suggests that rioters were also moving to enforce a 'moral economy'. For centuries, a rough popular consensus prevailed as to what constituted legitimate practices for the marketing of grain, the milling of grain into flour, and the baking and sale of bread.[101] In Shakespeare's *Coriolanus* the rebels express their sense of wrong:

> What authority surfeits on would relieve us. If they would yield us but the superfluity while it were wholesome, we might guess they relieved us humanely. But they think we are too dear. The leanness that afflict us, the object of our misery is as an inventory to particularize their abundance; our sufferance is a gain to them … The gods know I speak this in hunger for bread, not in thirst for revenge.[102]

Ports that exported grain often saw rioting in times of hunger.

The difficulties of climate change, bad harvests and taxes, were amplified by the Tudor Clearances. Around five hundred years ago, more or less, what are now mounds under thick grass were houses; that long ridge of turf held back the waters of a pond; this hump was once the boundary of an orchard. Harbingers of a world without us, the lost villages vanished not because of plague, but because the people who once lived in them were driven out. The lost villages were homes to workers in fields of cereal crops. Between 1450 and 1550, the owners of the land changed their minds about how to use the land; as the Little Ice Age made cereals chancy, they invested in sheep – using the income from their wool, the owner might build a new manor house, surrounded with parkland in which deer and sheep might graze. He now needed only a shepherd or two, and a game-keeper. The sheep began to overwhelm food crops. By 1500 there were three sheep for every human being in England. The people of villages had no work. They left, or hung on stubbornly and were evicted.

In this way, Oxfordshire alone lost forty-four villages, Asterleigh and Brookend, Cold Norton, Tythley and Wheatfield, and Little Baldons. The shrunken population could put less land under the plough, so open fields began to break up into subdivisions and enclo-sures.[103]

Popular song announced its bitter truth:

> The fault is great in man or woman
> Who steals a goose from off a common,
> But what can plead that man's excuse,
> Who steals a common from a goose.[104]

I focus on Oxfordshire not only because it's where I happen to live, but because of the long-forgotten Oxfordshire Risings of 1549 and 1596, when the rioters cried out:

> We wish the hedges and those who made them in the ditches;
> are there not a hundred good men who will rise and knock
> down the gentlemen and rich men who made corn so dear and
> who took the commons?[105]

In July 1549 the Oxfordshire commons, including several hundred armed participants, marched from the south-east to the north-west of the county, pillaging parks as they went, until eventually retreating into the town of Chipping Norton. As well as food, there was also the question of religion; the hectic pace of Edwardian reform had angered and alarmed the people. In the months immediately before the rising, the introduction of the new 1549 service in early June affected the worship of every parishioner, and a more general resentment of foreign-inspired innovation, such as clerical marriage. In the summer of 1549, the dissolution of parish religious institutions was very recent. This represented not only liturgical change, but also an attack on parish property. The parish of Chipping Norton had been deprived of its three chantries and its Trinity Guild, and cruel punishments were imposed on any who objected: 'dismembered like beasts in the open highway/ Their innards plucked out and hearts where they lay'.

It is difficult to unpick hunger from religion in the rising because of the common belief that a good grain crop was dependent on church magic (the plough plays, the blessing of bread). England was consumed by 'commotions' in 1549.[106] The reason unrest never entirely went away was simple: a labourer's daily wage barely paid for the food he needed, and there were few margins for scarcity or a rise in prices created by it. Moreover, the rich kept trying to grab a little more land, to increase their own margins at the expense of those who had none. A labourer could not earn enough to feed his family as well as himself, let alone pay for clothes and other requirements. Hunger kept reminding the poor of the tradition of food rioting, and kept the idea of rebellion alive. This was so even in good times, but as the climate worsened and the European economy collapsed into hyperinflation and then bankruptcy, prices rose and wages didn't.[107]

The gentry were easy targets, but so too were the merchants. After a poor harvest, prices for all commodities – not just grain – always rose. When two or three harvests failed in succession across the whole country, as they did in the years 1594–7, people starved to death; during this famine one hundred died in Stratford-upon-Avon alone. Conscience didn't prevent their fellow townsmen from exploiting the shortfall: in Stratford in 1597 seventy-five people were found guilty of hoarding corn, including William Shakespeare, who was hanging on to ten quarters of malt. Worse than this, 'engrossers' bought up all the local supply of an important commodity, such as eggs or butter, in order to drive up the price, much like modern commodity speculators. In 1596 wheat hit 170 per cent of its normal price, oats reached 191 per cent and rye had to be imported from Denmark. The fact that underlying food insecurity never went away meant that bad harvests hit even the modestly prosperous.

A surprising amount of political activity is a simple, desperate fight for bread as subsistence against those who see grain as a cash crop to be sold. The Corn Laws may be the most famous site of conflict, but they simply made visible a contradiction written into the whole of English history as the poor fought for bread and the rich for disposable cash. Though food riots might carry the threat of more disturbing disorder, they were predominantly small-scale and highly circumscribed. They were not the stuff of rebellion.[108] The Midland Revolt of 1607 started in Northamptonshire, spreading to Warwickshire and Leicestershire throughout May. It was led by 'Captain Pouch', otherwise known as John Reynolds, a tinker who said he had authority from the King and the Lord of Heaven to destroy enclosures, and promised to protect protesters by the contents of his pouch, which he carried by his side. After he was captured, it was opened and found to contain only green cheese. In early June, a further protest near Kettering, Northamptonshire, against enclosures was put down by local landowners' servants after the local militia refused. Forty to fifty protestors were killed and the leaders of the protest were hanged and quartered.

In Maldon, in 1629, a hundred or so women and children, led by one 'Captain' Ann Carter, the wife of a butcher, boarded a Flemish grain ship and removed some grain in their caps and gowns. A local court lowered corn prices, and Captain Ann toured the area drumming up support among clothing workers. A further riot took place on 22 May, which was taken more seriously by the authorities, and Captain Ann was hanged. The style of Captain was adopted by a number of other activists during the seventeenth century: there was 'Captain' Dorothy Dawson, who organised a protest at Thorpe Moor, and 'Captain' Kate, who was recorded at an election meeting in Coventry.[109] The term 'captain', interestingly, reflects the term for the overseer in charge of the grain harvest, and in some cases the female names were a disguise, like blacking the face, but there is also an echo of the cross-dressed plough plays, where men dressed as women protected the grain.

Discontent did not end there. In the early eighteenth century came the Blacks, groups of men who blacked their faces and then carried out poaching and raiding activities on lands belonging to the wealthy. There were two gangs of so-called Blacks active in 1721–23; one was based in Hampshire, and drew its members chiefly from the Portsmouth area; a second group arose in Windsor Forest. The Hampshire group were led by a king, 'King John'.[110] In response to the gangs, the government introduced the Black Act, which came into force on 27 May 1723. The Black Act made it a hanging crime to hunt in disguise, to poach deer, rabbit or fish. You could and would be put to death for damaging orchards, gardens or cattle, just some of over fifty criminal offences, including being found in a forest while disguised. 'No other single statute passed during the eighteenth century equalled [the Black Act] in severity, and none appointed the punishment of death in so many cases'. It was not repealed until 8 July 1823.

However, severity didn't make the problems vanish, because the hunger that created them remained ever-present. In January 1766, a crowd of some six hundred people gathered at Winchester, threatening to sink corn barges destined for export abroad. From Cornwall to the Midlands and beyond, rioters engaged in direct action. Markets in Truro, Exeter, Bath, Newbury, Lechlade, Stroud, Worcester, Kidderminster and many other towns were subject to scenes of tumult and joy as rioters distributed grain at affordable prices among the least well off. In many cases a loaf of bread was raised on a stick, around which would gather a crowd of protesters. Labourers, colliers, bargemen, skilled craftsmen and other ordinary working people who suddenly found that they could no longer feed their families, took to the streets and market places in a bid to address their situation. It was a short-term fix for a long-term problem.

And the problem worsened. A significant and rapid expansion of enclosure took place in the latter part of the eighteenth and early nineteenth centuries. Enclosure was meant to bring moral as well as economic benefits, by removing the 'attraction' of common land for layabouts.[111] To this day, such august authorities as Wikipedia hail enclosures as a breakthrough in agrarian productivity, sometimes referring to an 'agricultural revolution' which in turn caused the Industrial Revolution. Less is said about the connection between these two events, which is that while it is true that daily calorie intake in Britain increased for the average working man, it did not reach what we now think of as developed-world norms until around 1900.[112] In the meantime, urbanisation and industrialisation guaranteed only the kind of diet that enabled people to stay alive, not the kind that would make them healthy or strong. This was well understood:

> The butchers and the bakers they've come to one decision,
> With the millers and the Quakers on the prices of provision.

> *Chorus*
> There never was such hard times seen in England before.
> The man who speculates in corn will purchase all he can,
> He's nothing but a traitor to the honest working man;
> And I am sure before the poor should have it under price;
> He'd leave it in his granary for all the rats and mice.
> The farmers, millers, bakers too, are plucking up their feathers,
> They are a mob, so help me Bob, of humbugs all together;
> The bounteous gifts of Providence, they do monopolise,
> And rob the poor, I'm certain sure, their guts to gourmandize.

The Cotton Lords of Lancashire, they think it is no more;
The say, bedad, the trade is bad, and they must have short time;
They eat their beef and mutton, aye, and sport about on
    Monday,
But they do not care a button if you eat brick on Sunday.[113]

Nineteenth-century rural poet John Clare's greatest poems are elegies for the commons, protests against the enclosure that he saw as a conqueror:

Inclosure like a Buonaparte let not a thing remain,
It levelled every bush and tree and levelled every hill
And hung the moles for traitors – though the brook is running
    still,
It runs a naked stream, cold and chill.

Clare knew all about hunger, too. His admirers did their clumsy best to provide him with a farmstead so he could be independent and still write poetry. They obtained for him a cottage with enough land with it to be used as a smallholding, but Clare was unwell and a poor businessman. His mental health problems and ever-growing family made it difficult, and he and his wife and children lived on the diet of the poor: bread, potatoes, root vegetables from the garden, tea, ale and tobacco.[114]

Alongside enclosures, other small rights vanished from the agrarian fields, worsening the plight of the very worst off. Until 1788, the tradition of gleaning was taken as a customary right by the poor. In a practice which arguably dates back to biblical times, villagers enjoyed the right to 'glean' the fields after harvest, gathering crops left over. It was a process carried out with ritual and tradition and formed an important feature in the agricultural calendar, and one which, as we have seen, made a significant if meagre contribution to the larders of the poor. Some communities would elect a 'Gleaning Queen' whose job was to oversee the proceedings and ensure that all got an equal share of the pickings. Following the harvest, farmers would carry out a final gathering of their crop as they sought to maximise their yield. Then they would throw open the fields to the village gleaners, more often than not the womenfolk and children of the community. This was a practice governed by the presence of the 'guard sheaf'. This was a single sheaf of corn left standing by the farmer to indicate that he had yet to finish gathering his own crop. Once the guard sheaf was removed, then gleaning could begin. The ringing of the parish church bell, the gleaning bell, was another signal that the fields were open for gleaning. The rewards were bountiful and gleaners could sometimes gather the equivalent of a bushel of corn, enough to make flour and bake bread for the whole family for a fortnight or more.[115]

The legality of gleaning was first challenged in 1786, when a Suffolk farmer, John Worlledge, took action against a shoemaker from the village of Timworth, Benjamin Manning, who had entered Worlledge's fields to glean barley. Two years later, in what became known as the Great Gleaning Case, the Court of Common Pleas gave judgement: 'no person has at common law, the right to glean in the harvest fields'. Despite this, some landlords allowed it, and gleaning went on in a few areas until the 1950s, when it appeared to die out completely due largely to the efficiency of new reaping and crop-gathering machinery leaving little for the village locals.[116]

The first introduction of industrial harvest machinery in the early nineteenth century had led to a new type of protester: 'Captain Swing'. 'Captain Swing' was a pseudonym, a fantasy, a highwayman who aimed at the rich. He was the fictitious instigator of 'a system of intimidation practised in agricultural districts of the South of England in 1830–1, consisting of sending to large-scale farmers and landowners threatening letters over the signature of 'Captain Swing', followed by the incendiary destruction of their ricks and other property.'[117] Swing was used as a violently suggestive metonym, which reflected both the swinging action of a threshing flail, and the much more sinister vision of a body swinging on a gibbet.[118] The Swing Riots' immediate cause was the coming of industrial machinery to the harvest, but were overwhelmingly caused by the result of the progressive impoverishment and dispossession of the English agricultural workforce over the previous fifty years. If the ruling classes had deliberately set out to make life difficult for the rural poor, they could not have done a better job. Before enclosure, the cottager was a labourer with land; after enclosure he was a labourer without land.

In the 1780s workers were employed at annual hiring fairs (called mop fairs), to serve for the whole year. During this period the worker would receive payment in kind and in cash from his employer, would often work at his side, and would commonly share meals at the employer's table. Then the gulf between farmer and employee widened. Workers were hired on stricter cash-only contracts, which ran for increasingly shorter periods, first monthly, then for as little as a week. By the time of the 1830 riots the farm labourer had retained very little of his former status except the right to parish relief, under the old Poor Law system. Once, the medieval monasteries had taken responsibility for the impotent poor, but after their destruction and the resulting land grab in 1536–9, that passed to the parishes. Payments were minimal, and at times degrading conditions were required for their receipt. Let's measure it in bread: three and a half 'one gallon' bread loaves were considered necessary for a man in Berkshire in 1795; provision had fallen to just two similar-sized loaves in 1817 Wiltshire.[119] The way in which Poor Law funds were disbursed led to a further reduction in agricultural wages, since farmers would pay their workers as little as possible, knowing that the parish fund would top up wages to a basic subsistence level.

Farmers could treat the workforce this way because the new machines meant that workers were not as necessary. Horse-powered threshing machines, which could do the work of many men, spread among the farming community, threatening the livelihoods of hundreds of thousands of farmworkers, and the final straw, once more, was terrible harvests, in 1828 and 1829. The government tackled the Swing rioters brutally; nineteen people were executed, four hundred and eighty-one transported to Australia, and more than seven hundred imprisoned.[120]

Agriculture, which *seems* to give human beings greater control of their own lives and fates – allowing them to plan for the future (sowing in order to reap), and creating a surplus production that, in turn, makes possible leisure, the arts, philosophy, religion, and so forth – also made possible social stratification, class struggle, poverty, the whole sordid history of man against man.[121]

And yet, most surprisingly, by 1834 the majority of those convicted for their part in Swing riots were offered a royal pardon. The pardons issued were perhaps riding on the back of the success of those campaigning on behalf of the 'Tolpuddle Martyrs', a group of farm workers in West Dorset who had banded together to form a workers' union. Six of the leaders were sentenced to transportation for seven years following their arrest. The huge public outcry at the time led to a reprieve, and the martyrs returned in triumph to Dorset. Perhaps equally significant was an increase in the allocation of allotments to the landless poor, for the purposes of growing food for their own subsistence. The allotment movement in England originated in 1793, as a counterweight to the rapid expansion of enclosure, but it owed a great deal to the efforts of the Swing riots.[122] By allocating land to labourers on which to grow their own food, reformists and campaigners argued that the poor would be less tied to their wages and less susceptible to fluctuations in food prices, and this might tackle, in part at least, one of the problems that caused people to riot in the first place. In Marlborough and in Church Cowley, near Oxford, the areas of land given over to allotments were given the name 'Van Diemen's Land', or 'Van Diemen's Allotments'. Whether this was a deliberate monument to the toils of the Swing rioters, or the land was named at a later date is difficult to ascertain, but in some ways it sits as a gentle reminder of what the rioters achieved.[123]

In every century, bread came to the table streaked with the sweat of the baker, and of the reapers and harvesters, the ploughmen and millers, and shaped by the skills of all of them and more. The need for bread also marked people's first attempts to speak politically, to protest about the price paid for grain, the price of their aching bellies, and some of them died for their words.

Making food is always in a dance with eating food. To learn how bread was eaten, we can turn to the diarists and novelists who sought to capture the everyday, the working week and the Sunday rest, to see where bread fitted in. William Cobbett pondered as to what would be the requirement for a family of five persons to live well, and decided on five pounds of bread, a pound of mutton, two pounds of bacon, a gallon and a half of beer per day. The reality of the labouring man's diet, as we have seen, was a very different story. Cobbett describes a real income of just nine shillings per week, a mere pittance and certainly not enough to keep the family work-fit.[124] But Richard Jefferies thought that 'The labourer, from so long living upon coarse, ill-cooked food, acquires an artificial taste. Some men eat their bacon raw; others will drink large quantities of vinegar, and well they may need it to correct ... the effects of strong wholesome cabbage'. Faced with raw bacon, bread looks – and is – appealing; it is, among other things, a convenience food. And it always has been: Anglo-Norman knight Walter of Bibbesworth advised:

> If a young child stretches out his hand in the morning towards
>   the bread,
> Give him a lump of it, or a slice if that's all you have.[125]

Urbanisation merely increased bread dependence. After the English Civil War, when London's population surged to 350,000, diarist Samuel Pepys relied on bread for food as he went about his busy urban working day as a navy administrator. Young and energetic, he loved to be out and about, picking up gossip and political news; he did not always want to return home to eat. And he liked bread, though he liked it most in meals. On 2 January 1659/60, Pepys had bread and cheese for dinner 'in the new market'. But for Pepys bread was a baseline, a bare minimum: 'home, there, having not eaten anything but bread and cheese, my wife cut me a slice of brawn ... as good as ever I had any.' Bread was both a convenience and a mark of the ghost of Puritanism that always haunted him: 'I ate some bread and butter, having ate nothing all day, while they were by chance discoursing of

Marriot, the great eater, so that I was, I remember, ashamed to eat what I would have done' (4 February 1659/60). Pepys's modest view of the worth of bread was starkly confirmed when he learned it was the staple of slaves in North Africa (23 January 1660/61). This idea of bread as the food of the poor resurfaces constantly in his diaries. Yet that also makes it comfort food, perhaps the first documented instance of comfort eating in history: 'To bed with the greatest quiet of mind that I have had a great while, having ate nothing but a bit of bread and cheese at Lilly's to-day, and a bit of bread and butter after I was a-bed' (13 July 1660). This combination of bread, cheese and friendliness frequently resurfaces.

Ever observant, Pepys noted that bread was beginning to play a new role at the tables of the great: 'So to White Hall, and saw the King and Queen at dinner; and observed (which I never did before), the formality, but it is but a formality, of putting a bit of bread wiped upon each dish into the mouth of every man that brings a dish; but it should be in the sauce' (8 September 1667). Pepys's interest in bread extended to noting in March 1664/5 'a very particular account of the making of the several sorts of bread in France, which is accounted the best place for bread in the world'. Plus ça change …

In the bright new world of the eighteenth-century novel, bread was foundational. Samuel Richardson's *Pamela* was like bread; it was the first real bestseller, uniting the nation's readers, high and low, in excitement about its servant heroine. Told through her letters, it refers to bread often, as a known basic of life. Writing to her parents, Pamela cries:

> I can be content with Rags and Poverty, and Bread and Water, and will embrace them, rather than forfeit my good Name, let who will be the Tempter.[126]

But when she repeats this, she specifies the *kind* of bread to which she is willing to be reduced, and portrays rye as a part of poverty, like rags and water:

I … think it a less Disgrace to be oblig'd to wear Rags, and live
upon Rye-bread and Water, as I use to do, than to be a Harlot
to the greatest Man in the World …

Bread and Water I can live upon … with Content. Water I
shall get any-where; and if I can't get me Bread, I will live like a
Bird in Winter upon Hips and Haws, and at other times upon
Pignuts and Potatoes or Turneps, or any thing.[127]

To be without bread is to be outside human society, in Pamela's imagination, to be a bird in winter.

Fifty years later, Charles Dickens, too, thought bread was the bare minimum, standing between starvation and life. In *Hard Times*, for instance, 'Stephen came out of the hot mill into the damp wind and cold wet streets, haggard and worn …, taking nothing but a little bread as he walked along'. As always, the portability of bread means it often comes first to hand. Yet the meagre tables are greatly enjoyed:

He … set out his little tea-board, got hot water from below, and
brought in small portions of tea and sugar, a loaf, and some
butter from the nearest shop. The bread was new and crusty,
the butter fresh.[128]

Dickens knew that many criticised the poor for any sign of pleasure in diet; he refutes this firmly. And feasts for Dickens's characters always include bread:

A clear, transparent, juicy ham, garnished with cool green
lettuce-leaves and fragrant cucumber, reposed upon a shady
table, covered with a snow-white cloth; … preserves and jams,
crisp cakes and other pastry, short to eat, with cunning twists,
and cottage loaves, and rolls of bread both white and brown,
were all set forth in rich profusion.[129]

Bread is all that stands between the vulnerable and starvation. Not even Charles Dickens understood just how bad it could really be. At the very bottom of society, a week's food looked like this:

> Fried bacon. Bread. Sugary tea. Cold pork and boiled potatoes for lunch. Bread, butter, and tea. Bread, cheese and a glass of beer.

This diet of a very poor widow in the nineteenth century makes frightening reading. On Tuesday, a treat was in store: afternoon tea consisted of bread and butter, *with jam*. The bread, notably, was eaten fresh on Monday and Tuesday, toasted from Wednesday to Saturday; by then it would have been stale if the widow had bought a single loaf on Monday. But at dinner every day she had bread rather than toast, probably because toast required a fire.[130] Why were Tuesdays her treat days? Did the staling bread by then need jam as a pick-me-up? Did the nameless widow check the bread every day to see if today was the day for jam? Very new bread is too soft for jam; it goes soggy.

Elderly single women were the poorest of the poor. One poor woman in mid-nineteenth century Wiltshire had four gallons of bread, made from the wheat she raised and ground herself, with 1½ lbs cheese, and she looked back on this as the good old days. After her husband died, she and her son had only 1½ gallons of bread, ¼ lb butter, tea, and some sugar. She also had some potatoes. Bread, potatoes and tea dominated the diets of the poor. *Dominated* means that often enough, that was all there was. The food of the poor did vary from place to place; in Lincolnshire it was better than in Wiltshire, and labourers had bacon every day, sugar and treacle. They ate more and more varied vegetables too. Yet even there 'the women say they live on tea; they have tea three times a day, with sop bread, and treacle'.[131]

Husbands and grownup children held mothers to a standard beyond their resources; mothers could only respond by giving their portion to everyone else. On Thursdays and Fridays, even comfortably off mothers ate bread and butter. A Poplar woman ended the week with a kettle bender, a cup of crusts with hot water, pepper, salt and a knob of margarine. Joseph Williamson described his mother:

How my mother existed is a mystery. I am reminded of the
Lord saying 'I have meat ye know not of.' She would sit at table
watching us eat, and she would make little balls of dry bread
and put them in her mouth. One of us would urge her, 'Have
some dinner, Mother,' and she would reply quite cheerfully, 'I'll
have mine presently.'[132]

Women's hunger was unmentionable and self-starvation common. A
Barnsbury couple in 1876 pawned their children's shoes to get Sunday
dinner. The rural poor might by Friday be eating boiled bacon, greens,
potato, apple dumpling (the husband) or bread, butter, cake, hot tea
(mother and child). More recent studies of the British poor show the
same pattern: the one good Sunday dinner, the best food for the male
breadwinner. After 1945, Richard Hoggart reflected on the importance of 'something tasty' in working-class diet as he grew up in
working-class Leeds:

The emphasis on tastiness shows itself most clearly in the need
to provide 'something for tea', at weekends if not each day.
There is a great range of favourite savouries, often by-products –
black-puddings, pig's feet, liver, cow-heel, tripe, polony
[sausage], 'ducks', chitterlings (and for special occasions pork-
pies, which are extremely popular); and the fishmongers'
savouries – shrimps, roe, kippers and mussels. In our house we
lived simply for most of the week; breakfast was usually bread
and beef-dripping, dinner a good simple stew; something tasty
was provided for the workers at tea-time, but nothing costing
more than a few coppers. At the week-end we lived largely,
like everyone else except the very poor, and Sunday tea was
the peak.[133]

Hunger, then, was best appeased by strong flavours, something tasty,
and here Hoggart shows us a working class that had become the repos-
itory of fierce dark flavours of the kind once enjoyed by the middling
and better sort. Could anaemic jelly and custard really compete?

Perhaps not, but cowheel and polony would be ousted by the new tasty fast foods which were to sweep the country with increased prosperity. And bread, made by the Chorleywood method, or the new Milton Keynes process, which allowed supermarkets to claim it was 'freshly baked', became not only a convenience food, but a loss leader, the product that drew customers into the shop to buy other things. Cheap white bread now contains vast quantities of yeast and very little besides white flour and additives to make it bouncy for a long time. While the English have become far more interested in our heritage as bakers, even the most ambitious natural bread companies have to grapple with consumer expectations of mouthfeel and price. While the arduous bakers' day has been shortened by the invention of the proving box, it remains challenging to make a profit from the bread of our ancestors, and even more challenging for the urban poor to find the money for loaves that may retail for £3.50. Bread still indicates social class as reliably as it did in 1300.

When bread is featured on the hit television programme *The Great British Bake Off*, the emphasis is firmly on flavour. However, the flavour in question is extrinsic: sun-dried tomatoes, garlic, spices, herbs, a kind of sandwich filling baked into the loaf. The *Bake Off* and its bakers are strangely innocent of the historic role played by fermentation in adding flavour to food products; fermentation is almost a form of herding, of microbe management that ensures the right bacteria and yeasts turn grape juice into wine, and milk into cheese. In bread, a mixture of different kinds of yeasts and bacteria means that flour, water and salt can be just as strong-tasting as any tomato. But it needs time. Despite the foodie rise of sourdough bread in British bakeries, the *Great British Bake Off* illustrates the way that middle England's bread has yet to grasp the need for slowness, labour and sweat in the creation of bread with taste. If bread is to remain a staple, this lesson needs to be learned. And it may even be that bread with taste is more digestible, since gluten in the wheat is pre-digested in the slow process of fermentation. England needs to revive a taste for real bread. It is the best way to honour our ancestors who fought fiercely for it in the sweat of their brows.

Liquid foods:
beer, coffee, tea, chocolate –
and Madam Genevra

Beer

The word food suggests something solid. However, human beings also need liquid, and liquids have always formed part of our diet. For centuries, beer was prominent in the English diet. The beer of the Anglo-Saxons was a sweet, heavy and dark-coloured drink without hops as a flavouring, also known as ale. When hops were introduced in the fifteenth century, ousting other complex herbal flavourings, beer came to mean specifically the bitter substance they flavoured, with ale retained as a broader category. Beer was consumed at every meal; Elizabeth I drank it for breakfast, and the Earl of Northumberland and his wife drank two pints of beer and wine every day at their first meal. Even the Earl's two young sons were allowed two quarts of beer, though no wine, while his children in the nursery received one quart each. A maid of honour at Henry VIII's court received eight pints of ale at breakfast, dinner and supper every day. It has been suggested that it's impossible to consume this much beer, but there is no evidence that it was wasted. The beer and the ale would have been very alcoholic, much like artisanal beer today; when we think of medieval and early modern foods, it's important to remember that these would have been taken at meals alongside the strong, treacly, and sometimes bitter or sour flavour of real ale. Such tastes primed the nation to enjoy the equally deep and dark flavours of game. Sometimes, ale or beer might be warmed with spices, including sugar. In apple-growing areas, cider too played a role, but this remained mainly local.

Consumption was not moderate; under Edward I, a statute required London taverns to close by curfew, and under the Tudors, increased fears of unrest led in 1552 to the first licensing act (although drunkenness was blamed on riotous soldiers returning from wars in the Low Countries). A visitor to England in 1598 reported that 'beer is the general drink and excellently well tasted, but strong and what soon fuddles'.[1] Many devout Puritans felt that ale distracted people from what really mattered: in 1617, Thomas Young complained angrily about those who 'go 10 times to an alehouse, before they go once to a church'.[2]

Ale played a surprisingly large role in the life of medieval parishes. Instead of having cake sales, parishes raised money through ale sales; like the cakes, the ale was made by the wives of the parish for feast days, which were called church ales. It was these to which later Puritans objected. In general, however, ale-making was a surprisingly respectable way for women to earn a living; because the mastery of ale-making was a key part of the housewife's role, it could be continued into commerce without violating ideas about women's place. As this implies, most ale was made at home, and consumed at home even if purchased elsewhere. There were pubs, but in medieval England these were not as prominent as they were later to become. The Tabard Inn in Chaucer's *Canterbury Tales* is a novelty to the pilgrims;[3] it was more usual for pilgrims to take advantage of monastic obligations to provide hospitality, and of churches' church ales. The alehouse and its predominance are products of the Reformation. Because the monasteries were destroyed, and because church ales were abandoned in many areas due to Puritan opposition, the public house came into existence to replace both, offering accommodation and conviviality in place of the monasteries, and ale in place of church ale sales.[4]

But the heyday of the pub was brief. In the post-Restoration world, it was challenged by other kinds of liquids sold in other kinds of places. In one of the largest changes ever to take place in the English diet, beer was replaced – with remarkable rapidity – by coffee, tea, hot chocolate – and the joker in the pack, gin. Not only was this, in the case of tea and coffee, a shift to a range of stimulants whose principal appeal lay in the caffeine they contained and the sugar used to sweeten them, it was also a shift from local grain to exotic imported substances. Not one of the new beverages was an English invention, not even gin; all of them, however, became essential elements of the English diet, reflecting the growth of England's mercantile trading empire and the criticality of its trade routes.

Coffee

For lo! the Board with Cups and Spoons is crown'd,
The Berries crackle, and the Mill turns round.
On shining Altars of *Japan* they raise
The silver Lamp; the fiery Spirits blaze.
From silver Spouts the grateful Liquors glide,
And *China*'s Earth receives the smoking Tyde.
At once they gratify their Scent and Taste,
While frequent Cups prolong the rich Repast.
… *Coffee*, (which makes the Politician wise,
And see thro' all things with his half shut Eyes)

Anyone who didn't like coffee might be seduced into doing so by these sensuous lines from Alexander Pope's *Rape of the Lock*. They do not confine themselves to stressing the aroma of coffee; they also stress the power of coffee to make the politician wise and far-seeing. Ironically, at the moment when these lines were first printed anonymously in 1712, the craze for coffee and coffeehouses was beginning to wane. The English have had an on-and-off relationship with coffee, deeply in love and then drawing back in horror.

Coffee is native to north-eastern Africa, and was probably first domesticated in the Ethiopian Highlands; the first coffee lovers were the nomadic Oromos, and they didn't drink coffee, but ate it, crushed, mixed with fat, and shaped into treats. As slaves, the Oromos made their way to the Arab markets in the cities, and brought with them their taste for coffee and enough beans to generate new trees.[5] By the fourteenth and fifteenth centuries, the plant was being cultivated around the shores of the Red Sea. From here, it was brought to Europe through Venice, the great commercial gateway from the Middle East. Coffee drinking reached Venice from Constantinople and Cairo early in the seventeenth century, and by 1638, coffee was being sold in Venice at exorbitant prices as a medicinal product imported from Egypt.[6]

Coffee arrived in England from several places in a short space of time. The first coffee drinker in England is supposed to have been a student at Balliol College, Oxford, named Nathaniel Conopios, who brewed coffee in his chambers in 1647, shortly after the end of the Civil War. It was also in Oxford that the earliest English coffeehouse was opened in 1650, by a Jewish entrepreneur: Oliver Cromwell had allowed the Jews to return to England, from whence they had been expelled by Edward I almost four centuries earlier. Most of the returning Jews came from Holland, where coffee and tea drinking had recently become well known thanks to the Dutch trading empire. Two years later, in 1652, the first coffeehouse in London was opened by the Greek servant of an English merchant; the coffee came from Smyrna, in Ottoman Turkey. By 1663, during the early years of the Restoration, there were eighty-two coffeehouses in London, most of them near the Exchange (the association of coffee drinking and business is an old one).

At first, coffee was sold as a health drink: 'it would relieve coughs, headaches, consumption, dropsy, scurvy, the stone, and prevents miscarrying in childbearing women'. But more importantly, it would 'prevent drowsiness and make one fit for business'.[7] Even vegetarian and Puritan Thomas Tryon advocated coffee consumption as a way of balancing sugar in the diet. When William Harvey, discoverer of the circulation of the blood, died in 1657, he left £56 worth of coffee to the London College of Physicians, with the instruction that his colleagues should meet monthly and drink to commemorate his death.[8]

Coffeehouses did not only sell coffee; they also sold chocolate, tea, sherbets, cock ale (boiled ale with pieces of boiled chicken in it), cider, and other drinks according to the season. Coffee became a lifestyle choice. Coffeehouses appealed to the new middle class that had arisen due to the increasing bureaucracy of government, port and banks. An individual might use a specific coffeehouse for breakfast, another for lunch, and yet another for after-dinner refreshment. The Grecian, in Devereux Court, was known as a meeting place for the learned and for people 'adjacent to the law'.[9] Will's was on Russell Street in Covent Garden, and poet John Dryden was a regular visitor. Even more literary was Button's coffeehouse, also on Russell Street, where the stars of literary London would assemble. The coffeehouse turned into a place of wits and satires that was largely attended by poets and playwrights. At Waghorn's and the Parliament coffeehouse in Westminster, politicians were shamed for making tedious or ineffectual speeches; at the Bedford coffeehouse in Covent Garden hung a 'theatrical thermometer' with temperatures ranging from 'excellent' to 'execrable', registering the company's verdicts on the latest plays and performances. At all coffeehouses, men would read political pamphlets and newspapers and discuss them with their friends. In the evenings, literary coffeehouses might host groups of writers; the *Spectator* and the *Tatler* each had their own coffeehouse where men of letters could meet and read early versions of essays and poems. They were the very epitome of civilised urban life.

At first, the only regulation of the coffeehouses was via excise legislation. The Excise Act of 1660, modelled on the system established by Parliament during the Interregnum, extended the excise to coffee. The excise was a tax on articles of English manufacture or consumption, such as beer and cider. Unlike duty, it was not levied by the customs on import but at the point of manufacture, where production was measured by the excise officers. The excise on coffee was set at 4d per gallon in 1660, while tea and chocolate were taxed at 8d; these sums were changed to 6d and 16d respectively in 1670. The nature of coffee preparation made excise checks harder than they were for brewers. So an Additional Excise Act in 1663 required the coffeehouse keepers to pay a bond of security to the Office of Excise, who issued them with a certificate. With this certificate the coffeehouse keeper applied for a licence from the magistrates, without which no 'persons shall be permitted to sell or retail any Coffee, Chocolate, Sherbet or Tea'. The excise certificate cost only 12d, but the fine for each month of trading without a licence was £5.

But as the fashion for coffeehouses became widespread, those in power grew anxious. That coffeehouses were places where literature that was normally subject to censorship was likely to be read was one reason they were considered problematic; in a nutshell, they were rumour mills:

> they [rebels] were ever at Coffee-houses or places of such resort, still listening to every idle Pamphleteer's Discourse, with more Attention than to a Sermon; they could not see a Chimney on Fire, but immediately some Treachery they believ'd was in agitation; and a Drunken Midnight Quarrel in the Streets Alarm'd their Thoughts into the Belief of a Massacre; they had nothing in their Mouths but Plots and Designs; and Holy Writ itself stood upon the same bottom in their Creed with some Witnesses Depositions.[10]

In *A Satyr against Coffee* (1674), black coffee was comically described as a dreadful demon that had possessed the nation: 'Avoid, *Satanick Tipple!* Hence/ Thou Murtherer of Farthings, and of *Pence*;/ And Midwife to all *false Intelligence*!' The satirist was especially anxious about coffee's ability to promote rebellious thoughts: 'The third device of him who first begot/ The Printing Libels, and the Powder-plot'. The same satirist shows a curious knowledge of the origins of coffee in Africa, almost an anxiety about miscegenation: 'The Sweat of *Negroes*, Blood of *Moores*,/ The Blot of *Sign-post*, and the Stain of *doors*'.

A clampdown was proposed in 1666 but nothing was done. Finally, at the Royal Exchange on Wednesday, 29 December 1675, 'A Proclamation for the Suppression of Coffee Houses' was posted. 'The Multitude of Coffee-houses of late years set up within this Kingdom', it declared, were 'the great resort of Idle and disaffected persons' and as such had 'produced very evil and dangerous effects'. More seriously, at their coffeehouse meetings, 'divers False, Malicious and Scandalous Reports are devised and spread abroad, to the Defamation of his Majesties Government, and to the Disturbance of the Peace and Quiet of the Realm'.

To the men of London this was a calamity: a challenge to their liberty of assembly and free speech. Like the gin acts, it was wildly unpopular and impossible to enforce. Almost before any real attempt was made, the king was persuaded to withdraw it.[11]

The activities associated with coffeehouses were indeed ones considered predominantly male at the time: political debates, conversation on newly learned topics, and business transactions – or rather, the way that coffeehouses were conduits for them made sure they remained male. In 1674, a women's petition against coffee alleged that the drink 'makes a man as barren as the deficit out of which this unlucky berry has been imported; that since its coming the offspring of our mighty forefathers is on its way to disappear': the women may have been complaining because they were prohibited from drinking in coffeehouses.

Counting 49 per cent of the population as all that's needed, coffeehouses are still regarded by historians as democratic institutions, open to anyone who could pay a penny or twopence for a cup. Men could stay as long as they wished, meeting friends, talking, reading news sheets or transacting business. The London establishments were spartan in comparison with the rich interiors of Paris cafés and Viennese and Venetian coffeehouses, but they were clean and orderly, and rules and orders posted on the walls demanded that there be no swearing, gambling, quarrelling, dice or card playing, and no shouting all-out disputes. They were places to be intelligent, to be witty. However, intelligence has a double meaning; the coffeehouse acquired a vital role in the government spy network. After 1673's wildly unsuccessful naval campaigns in the Dutch Wars, government spies were posted in coffeehouses to find out how public opinion was receiving the news. Like the internet now, coffeehouses were held responsible for the violence and heat of public debate: 'it was not thus when we drank nothing but sack and claret, or English beer and ale. These sober clubs produce nothing but scandalous and censorious discourses, and at these nobody is spared.'[12]

Their all-male character became a source of a different kind of anxiety. While mixed-sex meetings were often held at inns, clubs and taverns, coffeehouses were not especially mixed, and the result was that male coffeehouse goers were seen as effeminate, foppish, too nice; there were even rumours of homosexual liaisons. The *Tatler* magazine ordered the servants at St James's coffeehouse and White's chocolate house to ensure that 'effeminate pretty fellows' be barred from attending these bastions of polite public sociability and masculinity. Similarly, *The Female Tatler* encouraged all effeminate fops, or those 'impudent beau-Jews', to leave the polite society of the coffeehouse. Some coffeehouses were in fact molly houses, meeting places for gay men. In the *Spectator*, Steele considers how a man who did not feel comfortable in society might find his niche among the company he kept in a coffeehouse: 'It is very natural for a Man who is not turned for Mirthful Meetings of Men, or Assemblies of the fair Sex, to delight in that sort of Conversation which we find in Coffee-houses. Here a Man, of my Temper, is in his Element.'[13] The beginnings of the clubbable bachelor overlap with the beginnings of a safe space for gay men.

The drink itself also began to morph into specific varieties that were the trademark of the different houses. Initially, coffee was typically served black, without milk, cream or sugar, but gradually, different houses began offering a range of additions, including honey, cloves, ginger, cinnamon and spearmint. The main additives were sugar and milk. By the last decade of the seventeenth century, coffee had begun to move into the domestic sphere in aristocratic and wealthy urban households as a drink at breakfast, part of the new lighter meal, and after dinner, though usually in addition to either chocolate or tea.

For about forty years, London and other cities had the kind of coffeehouse culture that was to characterise cities ruled by the Habsburgs. And yet by the 1780s it was all but over. A hardy few houses hung on even into the nineteenth century, but on the whole they were swept aside by regulation, by social exclusiveness which meant that they were transformed into the gentlemen's clubs that continue to this day, and by the spread of alehouses – getting their revenge – and teahouses. In Venice and Vienna, and in Paris, they hung on and flourished. But in London, apart from a very few cafés opened by immigrants from the southern Mediterranean, they disappeared.

———————

Until the espresso revolution of the 1950s which followed the removal of coffee price controls by the Ministry of Food, Italian businessmen who visited Britain were astonished and horrified by the poor quality of the coffee on offer at hotels and restaurants, where it was typically made in vast urns and kept 'hot' for hours. The Gaggia machine came to their rescue. In Frith Street, the Moka bar opened, with a Gaggia and a Formica interior, and it was followed by many others, so that in May 1956 Martha Gellhorn reported that there were 475 espresso bars in London alone, and more than 2,000 around the country. The start-up costs were high, but thereafter the profit margin on each individual cup was impressive. The cappuccino followed, made by using the steam pressure in the espresso machine to heat milk to a creamy foam. Gellhorn thought the coffee was pretty ordinary, weak and lukewarm, but noticed that it appealed to young people, because for the price of a drink they could have company and warmth all day. The espresso bars were opposed by the political left; Richard Hoggart moaned that they were tawdry and gimcrack, inauthentic, not properly working class, and above all American. Others complained that the male patrons had long hair just as their ancestors had worried about gay men in the first coffeehouses. They became associated with teen problems, Teddy boys and skiffle. Those who patronised them might be intellectuals, but they were also angry young men, rebellious and dressed in strangely feminine clothes.

Like the coffeehouses, the espresso bars were short-lived. Soon, England was once more notorious for the dreadful coffee it served. To this day, many workplaces still torture their employees by serving elderly coffee that sits all day in an urn, and tastes poisonous. Rescue, of a kind, was once more at hand. By the mid-1990s, a new coffee-shop revolution was underway with the advent of American chains like Starbucks and their British imitators. Starbucks began as a replica of a coffee bar called Peet's in Berkeley, California; by 1973, it had three cafés, by 1983 it had six. It spread first to the bookish cities – Portland, San Francisco, Los Angeles, Chicago, Denver, New York. By 2003 it was by far the biggest coffee seller in America. Its success in part depended on the so-called Seattle coffee range of lattes and macchiatos, and on the deliberate imitation of an older notion of what a café is – newspapers, armchairs, inoffensive artwork on the wall, classical music, a special jargon or argot to describe the different kinds of coffee. Independent cafés typically failed to compete. It is usual to lament their disappearance, but the sincerity of the lament may depend on memories of just what they were like. My own main memory of London in 1984 was the impossibility of getting a decent cup of coffee anywhere. It is now possible to find a reasonable if not a stellar coffee everywhere – the usual trade-off of globalisation. On the other hand, you don't have to be a purist to ask if the caramel macchiato is a coffee at all, rather than a coffee-flavoured hot milk-shake. Starbucks has produced imitators – Caffé Nero and Costa – but rather than seeing their growth as competition, it would be more accu-rate to view it as the overwhelming supremacy of a certain kind of coffee. And that coffee is as much the product of global capitalism as the seventeenth-century coffeehouse was of mercantile empire. Starbucks claims that all its coffee is ethically sourced, but the mean-ing of the claim has been hotly debated. Coffee is a cash crop grown in the developing world for consumption in richer countries, and that works the way it always has.

If you're thinking of visiting Button's today, brace yourself: it's a Starbucks, one of over 300 clones across the city. The lion has been replaced by the 'Starbucks community notice board' and there is no trace of the literary, convivial atmosphere of Button's. Addison would be appalled.[14]

Tea

It is a tiny silver teapot, holding perhaps enough tea for three small cups. It's one of the few authentic relics of Jane Austen's life at Chawton Cottage in Hampshire. Tea was so precious then that Austen kept the keys to the tea cabinet on a belt around her waist; the cabinet also held sugar. In the novels, characters drink tea often, and it has become so commonplace that no detailed descriptions are offered. Jane Austen and her family were used to drinking tea *after* dinner, once the gentlemen had rejoined the ladies in the drawing room. Friends might come just for evening tea; on 26 November 1815, Jane wrote to her sister Cassandra that two ladies had appeared and 'offered themselves to drink tea' at 8 p.m. At Mansfield Park, 'the solemn procession, of teaboard, and urn, and cake bearers' cheers Fanny, and enables her to escape Henry Crawford as she pours the tea for Lady Bertram. Already, this drink from the east had woven its way into English domestic life.

This did not happen overnight. During the sixteenth century, Europeans could read about tea as a drink in Portuguese and Venetian travel writings, but had little idea of what it was. When an exotic delegation of four young converted samurai was brought to Rome from Japan by the Jesuits in 1585, to be presented to Pope Sixtus V, the Italians witnessed them preparing and drinking their tea, but thought it merely hot water; just another oddity, like seeing them eat their food with ivory sticks. It was the Dutch East India Company that, in 1610, finally imported tea into Europe as a commodity. The first English advertisement for tea appeared on 6 September 1658, the year of Oliver Cromwell's death. But because of its high price, it was sold and used only in very small quantities. On 25 September 1660, Samuel Pepys wrote his diary 'and afterwards did send for a cup of tea (China drink of which I had never drank before)'.

Tea was a luxury in its countries of origin too; in China and Japan, only the elite drank tea. But when it reached London, it appealed to that same new middle class that had taken to coffee, even though it was yet more expensive. Above all, it was regarded as urban and modern. It was certainly modern, though it was traded along the same coasts from which spices and salt had been shipped for centuries. Like coffee, it was hailed as healthy; in 1687, John Jacob Mangetus proclaimed that it was 'moderately hot and dry' and thus good for headaches, colds, asthma, palpitations and gout. He claimed, too, that it prevented drunkenness. Tea was given added glamour by its association with Charles II's Portuguese-born queen, Catherine of Braganza. Even if it is not quite true that Catherine introduced tea to England, as is sometimes claimed, royalist poet Edmund Waller wrote a poem called 'On Tea', in honour of the queen's birthday, that championed the association between 'the best of Queens, and the best of herbs'. Alexander Pope followed suit in *The Rape of the Lock*, when he wrote that Queen Anne, or as he called her 'great Anna', 'whom three realms obey/ Did sometimes council take – and sometimes tea'. Less memorably, James II's queen Mary of Modena was also said to enjoy tea.

The royal associations made tea additionally attractive to middle-class consumers. The Twining family were part of exactly that rural–urban migration that created a rich market for liquid foods. Rural recession drove the family to London in 1684, and nine-year-old Thomas took up an apprenticeship with a London weaver, becoming a Freeman in 1701 at the age of twenty-six; by then he was working for a wealthy merchant at the East India Company, which was importing many exotic new products from Asia, including tea. In 1706, he bought Tom's Coffee House on the Strand and so began his tea business.

In 1707, Twinings Gunpowder Green Tea sold for a price equivalent to around £800 per pound in today's money; rather more than Darjeeling's Makaibari, which in 2014 sold for around $1,850 per kilo, or £670 per pound, and is one of the most expensive teas in the world.[15] The high price of tea in 1707 was due to a punitive system of taxation. The first tax on tea in the leaf, introduced in 1689, was so high at five shillings in the pound that it almost stopped sales. The tax was reduced to one shilling in 1692. By the eighteenth century many Britons wanted to drink tea but could not afford the high prices; smuggling was the result, and was supported by the millions of English tea drinkers who would not have otherwise been able to afford their favourite beverage. What began as a small-time illegal trade, selling a few pounds of tea to personal contacts, developed by the late eighteenth century into an organised crime network importing as much as seven million pounds annually, compared to a legal import of five million. Adulteration also resulted, particularly of smuggled tea. Leaves from other plants, or leaves which had already been brewed and then dried, were added to tea leaves. Sometimes the resulting colour was not convincing enough, so anything from sheep's dung to poisonous copper carbonate was added to make it look more like tea. By 1784, the government realised that enough was enough, and that heavy taxation was creating more problems than it was worth. The new Prime Minister, William Pitt the Younger, slashed the tax from 119 per cent to 12.5 per cent. Suddenly, legal tea was affordable, and smuggling stopped virtually overnight.

Tea was a great commodity, portable and marketable. If its consumers were the English bourgeoisie, its producers and dealers were connected with the growing British mercantile empire. It is well understood that British soldiers in China engaged in outright violence, bribery, drug dealing and theft, and they imprisoned, executed and stole the property of their South Asian allies and employees, all in pursuit of tea. Drinking the product that resulted, the new English bourgeoisie taught respectability and hard work to those below them, creating conditions for an industrial revolution that further spread an empire of trade and commodities around the world.

But was it healthy? Introduced via medical claims that asserted its therapeutic properties, especially for ladies, it was also controversial, like the coffee, sugar and tobacco which accompanied its advent. Some adroit merchants marketed it as close to a health food, but not everyone agreed. Regarded as unhealthy by the medical profession, it was described as 'pernicious to house, obstructing industry, and impoverishing the nation'. Jane Austen herself had little truck with such notions; like most kinds of valetudinarianism, they are relentlessly satirised. One character is horrified by 'two dishes of strong green tea in one evening' and claims that 'it acts on me like poison and would entirely take away the use of my right side before I had swallowed it five minutes'. The heroine is understandably sceptical.

Tea's last great critic was William Cobbett, who condemned it in the 1820s as 'good for nothing … A weaker kind of laudanum … A destroyer of health, an enfeebler of the frame, an engenderer of effeminacy and laziness, a debaucher of youth, and a maker of misery for old age'. However, he was drowned out by the Temperance League's enthusiasm, since it promoted tea as a major ally in its campaign against alcoholic drinks. One of Austen's favourite poets, William Cowper, wrote in 'The Winter Evening':

> while the bubbling and loud-hissing urn
> Throws up a steamy column, and the cups
> That cheer but not inebriate wait on each,
> So let us welcome peaceful evening in.

The emphasis on the power of tea to repel cold and to draw the family together is notable.

Why did the English take to tea rather than to coffee in the manner of virtually every other European country? Its triumph was not certain until the late eighteenth century, when the rates of duty on it were lowered. But this was not the only reason; the coffeehouse had, as we have seen, a masculine and public image, and a controversial one at that, while tea was both domestic and feminine. Moreover, it was more strongly associated with the use of sugar as a sweetener, and the British slave colonies in Barbados, Jamaica and Antigua provided a steady supply of sugar to the English cities. As bread, and every other grain-based food, came under pressure from enclosures and from the Corn Laws, tea and sugar continued to expand as accompaniments to a limited diet, as a source of calories, and as a note of luxury and pleasure amid subsistence. Most importantly of all, it required only limited equipment: a kettle that could hang on the fire, and a teapot. But it could also support elaborate equipment – silver teapots, China tea services – as a family's income improved: for Jane Austen, tea was still a luxury.

The kettle was kept simmering on the hob throughout the day, with more leaves being added as required: in poor houses, spent leaves were carefully dried and reused. And as we have already seen, the poor would sometimes make fake tea, or donkey tea, out of burnt crusts. One sympathetic observer noted that the poor could not afford to make tea very strong.[16] 'Where no tea is used, the bitterest poverty reigns,' said Friedrich Engels.[17]

———————

The tea the Austen family drank would almost certainly have been China tea. Tea was a Chinese monopoly. But the British were not content with being middlemen. Tea cultivation in British India and other colonies exemplifies the way in which cash-cropping fuels capitalism, and capitalism fuels empire. Tea was not grown in India until the British introduced it – because they ruled India but not China. An Indian strain of tea was discovered growing wild in Assam; it was used by the local tribesmen, and given to Major Robert Bruce as a drink sometime in 1823. 'This [people] have known and drank the tea for many years, but they make it in a very different way from what the Chinese do. They pluck the young and tender leaves and dry them in the sun.' Robert Bruce passed this information and the leaves to his brother Charles, and via his senior officer, David Scott, they reached Dr Nathaniel Wallich, who declared it to be 'just another camellia'.[18] The East India Company was preoccupied with China tea, hiring a secret agent called Robert Fortune to take advantage of the chaos of the opium war years in the 1840s to try to steal tea plants for transplantation in the Himalayas. The vast majority of them died on the voyage. Eventually, the company explored the supposed camellia further, and found that it really was a tea plant. Plantations followed, and Assam tea was more palatable in England than its rival from China.[19] The tea workers laboured in appalling conditions for a pittance, and all the profits went back to England – and to Scotland, since the majority of Indian tea planters were Scots. The Indians themselves did not start drinking tea widely until the 1930s.

Though tea was already embedded in domestic life, teashops began to open in the late nineteenth century. Linked to commercial bread companies such as the Aerated Bread Company, which opened its first ABC teashop in 1884, they catered for office workers and also for women shoppers. This obviously meant that they were despised by those who aimed higher: in 'A Cooking Egg', T. S. Eliot wrote: 'over buttered scones and crumpets/ Weeping, weeping multitudes/ Droop in a hundred A.B.C.'s.' The best-known tearoom of them all had its origin in 1894, when the first Lyons teashop opened at 213 Piccadilly, and by 1914 there were two hundred of them in all parts of Britain.

Despite the contempt of the literary aristocracy, tea actually united the nation. A 1936–7 survey showed that the highest tea consumption was still among the wealthiest group of the population, but the poorest drank considerable amounts of it, and drank it at every meal. Tea was rationed in the Second World War to two ounces a week, which given that the national average consumption was four ounces in the 1930s was a challenging reduction. The ration was increased in 1943 to three ounces for people over seventy, and there were additional allowances for merchant seamen, harvesters, blast furnace workers and other essential workers. Large quantities of tea were drunk outside the home in canteens and British restaurants, and during tea breaks in factories, a practice strongly encouraged by Ernest Bevin, Minister of Labour, as an aid to productivity. After the war, rationing continued, until in 1952 the free market returned. The immediate result was that consumption returned to pre-war levels despite sharp price increases. By 1956, 70 per cent of the trade was in the hands of the big four – Brooke Bond, Lyons, Typhoo and the Cooperative Wholesale Society (CWS); in 1987, the four had become Brooke Bond, Typhoo, Lyons and Tetleys, although by the end of the 1980s the last trace of the Lyons teashops had vanished. Tetleys' success was built largely on the teabag, first developed in the United States in the 1920s and introduced to England from the 1930s, and vigorously promoted in the post-war era. Acceptance was slow; teabags occupied only 10 per cent of the market in 1970 but since then they have become dominant.

And now? Tea sales peaked in 2010, and in the decade since have declined by 6 per cent. Sales of ordinary teabags have suffered especially, enduring a 13 per cent decline. Alternative kinds of tea have become more popular: green tea, herbal tea, fruit tea.[20] Just like those of our forebears, our hot drink habits fluctuate according both to fashion and to ideas about what is healthy; the Mintel survey that revealed the decline in ordinary black tea drinking also revealed a faith in the health benefits of more unusual kinds of tea, along with a sense that traditional British tea has a fuddy-duddy image. The success of coffee chains like Starbucks is also credited with depressing the demand for tea. As we move into a globalised food world, our adherence to the food of our parents' generation is wavering, and tea could disappear from our meals as ale did before it. There is one additional factor, however: part of tea's glamour was always its association with empire. It is appropriate that as the empire vanished, tea too faded away. Tea may now occupy a larger place in the nation's imagination than on its tables, and in other countries' idea of us.

Gin

Gin is like beer; it comes from grain, and it is an alcoholic sedative rather than a stimulant. It was an antisocial and rebellious counterblast against tea and coffee, the decorous and bourgeois beverages that were enabling the burgeoning civil service of late seventeenth-century empire to function during long days in the office. And yet, as we shall see, gin eventually acquired its own imperial associations.

In its simplest terms, gin is 'an ardent spirit distilled from grain or malt'. It derives its etymological and chemical origins from the Dutch spirit 'genever': 'a clear alcoholic spirit from Belgium and the Netherlands, distilled from grain and flavoured with juniper'.[21] Although Franciscus de la Boe, a Dutchman, is frequently named as its inventor in the mid-seventeenth century, usage of juniper-based spirits and tonics can be traced back much earlier.[22] Indeed, juniper berries and bark often played a key role in the work of ancient Greek physicians. Medieval and early modern doctors also recommended them. Dutch genever was first produced by distilling wine, which was, however, often burnt in the process. To improve its taste, the spirit needed to be infused with spices and fruits; juniper berries were selected for their historic medicinal properties and the name 'genever' was born.[23]

British soldiers fighting in the Netherlands during the seventeenth century tasted the spirit for the first time, giving rise to the term 'Dutch courage'. Bernard Mandeville in *The Fable of the Bees* (1714) satirically mocked the service of 'genever' for the military, noting that a 'good-humour'd Man' might argue that the social instabilities produced by the consumption of gin in Britain during the 1720s might be a small price to pay 'in the Advantage we received from [gin] abroad, by upholding the Courage of Soldiers, and animating the Sailors to the Combat; and that in the two last Wars no considerable Victory had been obtain'd without'.[24] Mandeville's reference to gin is credited in the *OED* as the first recorded usage. After the English got a taste of gin, imports rose to over 10 million gallons a year in the late 1680s, its heyday the result of being free of duty at a time when French brandy was heavily taxed, and subsequently banned, due to wars with France. The accession of William of Orange in 1688 led to further consumption.[25]

By this time domestic production had begun to take off. Large landowners had a surplus of grain. The answer was distillation. There was virtually no regulation impeding the distilling industry, at a time when the beer industry was increasingly subject to government regulations and also duty. The result was apocalyptic. Distillers sprang up all across London. They produced gin of appallingly low quality, but they produced a lot of it. Distillation is so ridiculously simple that people were able to do it in German prisoner of war camps. Water and alcohol have different boiling points, as do all the other compounds that are generated in the fermentation process. Begin fermentation with anything sugary, like raisins. Then slowly raise the temperature of the liquid, so that different molecules boil off at different temperatures. If you slowly boil your mixture, you can collect the different compounds one at a time by collecting everything that's boiling off at a particular temperature in one tank, everything that boils off later in another tank; and everything that boils off even later (at an even higher temperature) in another tank. The compounds recondense back into liquid form as they cool. As an independent gin distiller explains:

> The stuff that comes off first smells horrible and poisonous, like a combination of nail polish remover, floor varnish, and green apples. This is called the heads and it smells poisonous because it is poisonous … What boils off next we call the hearts, and this is where most of the ethanol – the alcohol we're trying to get – lies. It smells, unsurprisingly, like alcohol. Last comes the tails. Tails aren't poisonous, but they're full of heavier alcohols and oils that are stinky (a combination of barnyard, wet dog, and cardboard).[26]

Purification costs more than serving the liquid without. Flavour could be added later; anything could be used to flavour gin, not only juniper, but also spices, fruits, flowers, or nothing at all. Gin belongs to a large family of flavoured spirits and liqueurs, shaped not by the raw material that they are made from but by supplementary flavours introduced at later stages of production. Any trace of origin is overshadowed by the botanical characteristics of fruit, vegetable, spice, grass or herb. The flavour is produced in a variety of ways: simple maceration, where the flavouring matter is steeped in spirit – usually neutral – to extract its flavour; a distillation, in which the vapours carry only a selected frequency of flavour through from the macerate and no colour what-soever; or the addition of off-the-shelf compounded flavours. It is likely that most of the gin drunk in Hogarth's day was unrefined, and in all likelihood a mix of the tails and the hearts, with more than a dash of the heads. Flavouring would have disguised this. The gin of the eighteenth century was a throat-searing, eye-reddening, vomit-churning hell broth.

Nevertheless, by the 1720s, the consumption of gin had increased sevenfold among the London population. It was associated with promiscuity and with gluttonous self-indulgence. Hence stories such as that of Judith Defour, still 'fresh in every body's Memory … a *Woman* who murdered her own Child, threw it into a Ditch, and strip'd it of the Clothes given that Day by a Charitable Person, to pawn for *nine Penny-worth of Gin*'.[27] There were many pamphleteers for whom her actions came to symbolise the evils of gin and gin drinking.

As slums sprang up and helpless people turned to prostitution or crime as a means of escape from the sheer ugliness of their situation, it was understandable for them to seek oblivion through the widely available gin. By the middle of the eighteenth century every fifth house in London catered to gin in some manner. The famous story of a dram shop with the sign 'drunk for a penny, dead drunk for twopence, clean straw for nothing' was discredited as apocryphal soon after it appeared.[28] But increased death rates and declining birth rates marked gin's progress among London's population of 1½ million. A series of flailing government measures sought to curtail consumption without upsetting the vested interests in wheat. They were ineffectual.

As thousands of men and women began to sell gin without a licence of any kind, a high percentage of gin sellers were to be found in the poorest backstreets, in the twisting lanes, courtyards and alleys of the East End, the areas with the lowest property values, the lowest rents, and the bulk of immigrants. A census taken in 1736 shows that one hundred and sixty-four gin shops were located on lanes in some of the capital's most infamous neighbourhoods, places like Cock Lane, home to many prostitutes. Many of the gin shops were probably pop-ups: gin vendors could set up and move small stalls without taking out a licence. Some didn't even set up a stall; petty hawkers often sold gin by the cupful while wandering the street. They did especially well at public hangings, catering to the watching crowd as well as to the felons en route to the gallows. Sometimes, even the hangman was drunk.[29] Many of these hawkers were older women, the very poorest of the city. The vast majority of gin shops consisted of nothing more than a spare room. They were set out for customers to drink quickly, standing up. The quick cheap service they offered was in keeping with the way the poor ate and drank; without the space to prepare food at home, they often bought ready-made meals from cookshops, and washed them down with gin and water. They drank to get drunk; and it took no fewer than eight Acts of Parliament to bring consumption under control.

The anti-gin campaign quickly became an outlet for attacks on the poor that often involved expressions of disgust about the way they lived. Moralising pamphlets poured from the presses as fast as gin poured from the stills. 'There is such a predominant bewitching of naughtiness in these fiery liquors, as strongly and impetuously carries men on to their certain destruction … To recover him from this condition, he must be, as it were, forced into his liberty and rescued, in some measure, from his own inordinate desires; he must be dealt with like a madman and be bound down to keep him from destroying himself,' wrote the Anglican clergyman and scientist Stephen Hales around the time Judith Defour was hanged.[30] Daniel Defoe said by 1728 that England could now expect 'a fine spindle-shanked' generation because of gin.[31] Thomas Wilson, chaplain to King George II, claimed that female dram drinkers frequently gave birth to children who were 'half burnt up and shrivelled', a description which some have interpreted as an accurate depiction of foetal alcohol syndrome.[32] Wilson was one of the campaigners who brought about the Gin Act of 1736.

What troubled the writers most was the risk that the labouring classes might be rendering themselves incapable of labouring. In 1735, when the London grand jury met at the Old Bailey to protest about public nuisances, the main complaint was that gin was 'robbing the lower kind of people of their will … to labour for an honest livelihood, which is a principal reason of the great increase in the poor'. The real reason that the lower orders had no will to labour, however, was not because gin had made them feeble, but because they were unwilling to work at hazardous jobs for long hours and low pay. Adam Smith noted that even the healthiest carpenters in London did not remain so for more than eight years, and at the height of their earning capacity, scarcely earned enough to buy a newspaper.[33] Arthur Young, a gentleman, admitted that 'nobody but an idiot would expect them to work at such a rate, unless it was their only way of earning a living'.[34]

The situation worsened because of the enclosure of common land, which meant that people left their rural homes for work in cities, especially London; the result was to depress wages, because the newcomers would work for less. Unwilling to work for very little, and left with nothing to do, the lower orders comforted themselves with cheap drams of gin. Gin, moreover, could actually provide calories at a lower cost than bread.

Throughout the 1700s, over 1,120 court cases at the Old Bailey feature crimes in whose commission gin played a central role. Eventually, the justices of Middlesex petitioned Parliament for an Act that would curb consumption, and the result was the Gin Act of 1736, which aimed to stop the supplies of gin to small shop owners through the imposition of relentless duties. Grain farmers tried to force a repeal of the Act, and there was also a pamphlet campaign urging retailers to ignore it. Riots erupted in several parts of London. The Act failed. The law was impossible to enforce; the small dram-shop owners, very poor themselves, did not have the money to buy licences or pay taxes, so that the government could not collect on the money they owed it. And vast and unpopular networks of informers sprang up, only to create further outbreaks of violence. Eventually, the Act was repealed and replaced with another in 1743. Gin sales did then decline, but the respite was brief; an amendment was forced through allowing distillers to sell directly through retail shops for a nugatory licence fee. Gin consumption shot up again.

The anti-gin campaigners hammered the image of the unfit mother: not just those actually hanged for murder such as Judith Defour, but also other 'barbarous mothers' who silenced their charges with 'detestable spirits', an image versified in the anonymous *An elegy on the much lamented death of Madam Geneva*: 'gin's fiery juice the milky streams suppressed,/ And kindly dried the nurse's cumbrous breast'. In the same work, other wet-nurses were accused of neglecting their duties altogether, and of using gin to sedate the infants in their care. In 1753, after the 'gin epidemic' was supposedly over, a certain James Nelson indicates that some mothers and wet nurses were still buying gin and were still in the habit of giving it to infants to keep them quiet: 'There is a practice among the vulgar still more shocking … that of giving drams to the children themselves, even while infants; they … pour the deadly poison down the poor babe's throat even before it can speak.'[35] When these overdosing deaths were investigated, the most common explanation was 'convulsions'.[36] Gin was depicted as destroying babies in many ways. In the anonymous *Elegy*, the poet explains that gin once provided women with the option of abortion:

> In pregnant Dames gin cou'd Abortion cause,
> And supersede prolific Nature's Laws:
> Mothers cou'd make the genial Womb a Grave,
> And anxious Charge of Education save.

Wet-nurses who drank gin were also criticised because their own consumption threatened the health of the baby. 'How many,' exclaimed Thomas Wilson, 'have unhappily drunk this deadly Poison with their Nurse's Milk!'[37] Fielding in his *Enquiry into the Causes of the Late Increase of Robbers* envisioned a dreadful future for the infant 'conceived in *Gin*', poisoned first in the womb and then at the breast.[38]

William Hogarth's engraving *Gin Lane*, printed in 1751, the same year Fielding published his *Enquiry*, is set in the slum district of St Giles Parish, Westminster. The fact that *Gin Lane* and Fielding's book were published the same year is more than a coincidence. Hogarth and Fielding were close friends. The engraving represents almost point for point the issues Fielding raised in his *Enquiry*, and it has been suggested that Fielding had urged Hogarth to provide a graphic representation of his arguments. The focal image in *Gin Lane* is a syphilitic and stupefied hag with the top half of her dress open and an infant tumbling out of her arms. Elsewhere in the engraving, another child weeps, as someone, presumably a parent, is being put into a coffin; another infant is shown skewered on a staff held by a man with a bellows on his head who is presumably senseless because of his drinking; and a baby is being forced to drink gin by a woman pouring the liquid into its mouth. The print was accompanied by a fiery verse from James Townley:

Gin cursed fiend, with fury fraught;
Makes human race a prey;
It enters by a deadly draught;
And steals our life away.

Almost 70 per cent of all those charged under the 1736 Gin Act were women.[39] While women were excluded from many alehouses,[40] gin shops did not have the same gender restrictions. Attitudes regarding the public consumption and sale of gin by females became progressively less permissive as women advanced from marriage to motherhood, and from motherhood to widowhood. As young men and women lived and worked in close proximity, as well as sharing the same social places, the public woman started to transcend traditional notions of female identity.[41] It is significant therefore that the image of the drunken woman forms the centrepiece of all campaigns against the trade and consumption of gin. Ironically, gin drinking and selling were markers of the progress in business of urban women: women could afford to drink gin because of increased wages and could sell the spirit due to the limited start-up costs.[42]

Eager to shake off the image of the dram sold in the street, from the late 1820s gin began to be marketed in elaborately designed emporiums known as gin palaces. Surviving descriptions make them sound like a collage of very bad taste. 'The primary symptoms,' Charles Dickens noted, were 'an inordinate love of plate-glass and a passion for gas-lights and gilding'. Even very tiny gin palaces were divided into separate apartments by ground-glass plates to emphasise their palatial capaciousness. The English language was also ransacked to create names for the new drinks available: 'The Cream of the Valley', 'The Out and Out', 'The No Mistake', 'The Good for Mixing', 'The real Knock-me-down', 'The celebrated Butter Gin', 'The regular Flare-up', and a dozen others. But Dickens also noticed something odd. The glamorous gin palaces, he revealed, rising as they did among the cesspits, 'are invariably numerous and splendid in precise proportion to the dirt and poverty of the surrounding neighbourhood':

All is light and brilliancy. The hum of many voices issues from
that splendid gin-shop which forms the commencement of the
two streets opposite; and the gay building with the fantastically
ornamented parapet, the illuminated clock, the plate-glass
windows surrounded by stucco rosettes, and its profusion of
gas-lights in richly-gilt burners, is perfectly dazzling when
contrasted with the darkness and dirt we have just left. The
interior is even gayer than the exterior.[43]

The customers, however, were much less impressive. The people drinking the gin were the same as the ones Hogarth depicted, even if their
surroundings had changed utterly. Most gin palaces in London were
former taverns, and they aimed to attract all classes. Like the dram
sellers of Hogarth's time, they were the beneficiaries of drastic cuts in
duties and licence fees. The spree did not last; the government reduced
the taxes on beer, and pubs took advantage of the new demand to
renovate themselves in styles borrowed from their old rivals.
Meanwhile, the obvious dependence of their poorer customers on gin
remained a concern for everyone. In particular, writers fretted over the
children, just as they had in Hogarth's day:

Women and children even are coming in with bottles; some
of the latter so little … they are scarcely able to reach up and
place the bottle upon the zinc-covered bar … Even these young
miserable creatures are fond of drink, and may sometimes be
seen slily drawing the cork outside the door, and lifting the
poisonous potion to their white withered lips. They have
already found that gin numbs and destroys for a time the
gnawing pangs of hunger, and they can drink the fiery mixture
in its raw state.[44]

Yet it is difficult to know how seriously we should take this; it is clearly
motivated by the crusading agenda of the Temperance campaigners of
the 1830s, which particularly focused on children.

Of course, no such concerns applied to upper-class drinkers. Nor were they apparently prone to the sexual immorality which gin's opponents ascribed to the gin palace. Indeed, when the British Navy actually introduced a weekly gin ration in 1860, only its officers were paid a portion of their wage in gin. The men were still paid in rum, or grog. Pink gin is widely thought to have been created by members of the Royal Navy. Plymouth gin is a 'sweet' gin, as opposed to London gin which is 'dry', and was added to Angostura bitters to make the consumption of bitters more enjoyable, as they were used as a treatment for seasickness from 1824. Gradually, without anybody appearing to notice, gin became a British drink, making its way back into bars and clubs by the end of the nineteenth century. The navy had already taken to citrus fruits as a way of combating scurvy, and this led more or less directly to the invention of the gimlet, made solely of the juniper spirit and a sweetened lime juice syrup usually known as lime cordial. Gin, originally a foreign product, became a vital munition of empire.

And yet its association with the navy also meant an ongoing connection with foreign parts. Just as gin came from abroad, so too do the favourite English ways to drink it. Gin and tonic was created by the army of the British East India Company. In India, malaria was a persistent problem. Europeans had understood for some time that the bark of the fever tree, or cinchona, could cure or prevent it; the Jesuits imported the bark to treat malaria in Rome from the mid-seventeenth century. By the 1840s, British citizens and soldiers in India were using 700 tons of cinchona bark annually, and they knew it as quinine. Quinine powder kept the troops alive, allowed officials to survive in low-lying and wet regions of India, and ultimately permitted the British to survive in tropical colonies. However, there was a problem; quinine was so bitter that British officials took to mixing the powder with soda and sugar: a lot of sugar. 'Tonic water', of a sort, was born. Erasmus Bond introduced the first commercial tonic water in 1858 – the very same year the British government ousted the East India Company and took over direct control of India, following the 'Mutiny'. As a reliable and palatable source of quinine, it enabled the

British Army to increase its numbers enormously and reduced its reliance on 'native' sepoys. Bond's new tonic was soon followed in 1870 by Schweppes' introduction of 'Indian Quinine Tonic', a product specifically aimed at the growing market of overseas British who had to take a daily preventative dose of quinine. Schweppes and other commercial tonics proliferated both in the colonies and, eventually, back in Britain itself as the soldiers and officials of the empire retired with chronic malaria.

It was only natural that at some point during this time an enterprising colonial official should combine a daily dose of protective quinine tonic with a shot (or two) of gin. Rather than knock back a medicinal glass of tonic in the morning, why not enjoy it in the afternoon with a gin ration?[45] Like curry, the gin and tonic made its way home to Britain from the far-flung lands of empire. And like those foods, it came to count as British because it *had been seen* as British in those foreign lands. A national food that wasn't really national in origin had been created. There would be others.

Chocolate

One more drink made its way into English mouths in the late seventeenth century. Like the others, it was dark and bitter; like the others, the raw materials for it would not grow in England. Slowly but inexorably it would win itself a place like no other in the English diet.

It came from the New World via Spain and Portugal, and was one of the first foods from the Americas 'fill English hearts with joy. It was magic: the Aztecs believed that cacao seeds were the gift of Quetzalcoatl, the god of wisdom, and the seeds had so much value that they were used as a form of currency. Aztec chocolate was served as a bitter, frothy liquid, mixed with spices or corn puree. It was believed to have aphrodisiac powers and to give the drinker strength. The Aztecs gave it to the victims they sacrificed to ease their pain. Christopher Columbus encountered the cacao bean on his fourth voyage to the Americas in 1502, when he and his crew seized a large native canoe that proved to contain cacao beans. None of the men had any idea what they were, but Columbus took them back to Spain. They made no impact, but in 1544 Spanish friars from Mexico introduced chocolate to the Spanish court – with the crucial addition of sugar.

Only the rich and royal could afford it. The drink was time-consuming to make, and its exotic ingredients – cacao, sugar and spices – had to be imported from faraway continents. The additions were vital to the flavour; the beans probably became mildewed and decomposed on the long voyage from the New World. All required large plantations with many slaves. Cromwell's forces seized the island of Jamaica from the Spaniards in 1655; cacao plantations were already flourishing there, and Jamaica became England's main source. By 1657, one entrepreneur was advertising chocolate in an English newspaper. *Mercurius Politicus* of 12–23 June 1659 carried an advertisement: 'Chocolate, an excellent West India drink, sold in Queens Head Alley, in Bishopsgate Street, by a Frenchman … It cures and preserves the body of many diseases.'

By the end of the Commonwealth in 1659, Thomas Rugge, a London diarist, was writing in his journal about coffee, chocolate and tea as new drinks in London, and referring to chocolate as 'a harty drink in every street'. Charles II's physician Henry Stubbe wrote 'The Indian Nectar' in praise of it. Samuel Pepys loved chocolate and mentions it in his diary several times; on 6 January 1663, he says: 'up, and Mr Creed brought a pot of chocolate ready-made for our morning draught'. On 3 May 1664, he 'went by agreement to Mr Bland's and there drank my morning draught in good chocolate, and … sent home for another'. He is clearly more enthusiastic than he is about tea.

The first known English recipe for chocolate appeared slightly earlier, in 1652, and called for sugar, long red pepper, cloves, aniseed, almonds, nuts, orange flower water and, of course, cacao: 'The hotter it is drunk, the better it is'. Unaware of the Aztec custom of drinking it cool, the recipe said that 'being cold it may do harm'.

As with coffee and tea, chocolate was thought to have medicinal value. It was considered nourishing for the sick as well as an aid to digestion and was believed to promote longevity, help lung ailments, energise the body, cure hangovers, suppress coughs and, as mentioned, stimulate the libido. For that reason, the *Virginia Almanac* of 1770 cautioned women against it, warning 'the fair sex to be in a particular manner careful how they meddle with romances, chocolate, novels, and the like', especially in the spring, as those were all 'inflamers' and 'very dangerous'.

During the eighteenth century there was a great increase in European consumption – and so, like tea and coffee, chocolate had duties imposed upon it. All chocolate, at this time made exclusively into drinking chocolate, had to be wrapped in stamped papers supplied by excise men and then sealed proving the tax had been paid. By 1800 the tax was two shillings in the pound on cocoa imported from the British colonies. So its use was restricted to the well-off and chocolate became a feature of the daily life of the smart set. The accounts of Abraham Dent, who kept a shop in Kirkby Stephen (then in the historic county of Westmorland), indicate that chocolate usage in the eighteenth century in the north of England was minimal. Between 1762 and 1765 tea appears often, coffee rarely and chocolate only once. The middle and lower classes had to wait until the twentieth century, when reductions in taxation, large-scale manufacturing, and improvements in processing and transport would finally enable them to enjoy chocolate. Only gin and tea were popular enough for smuggling and lawbreaking to keep them going through periods of high duty.

———

Hans Sloane, Queen Anne's physician, was the first person to try mixing chocolate with milk. This was a closely guarded secret remedy, later sold to an apothecary. The secret was eventually bought in 1824 by the Quaker Cadbury brothers, who successfully mass-marketed it. Sloane had already made himself a considerable fortune, and invested some of it in cocoa plantations in Jamaica, where he had first observed its dramatic effects in reviving sickly babies.

In Jane Austen's unfinished novel *Sanditon* one character comments that 'A large dish of rather weak cocoa every evening agrees with me better than anything'; but, the heroine notes, 'as he poured out this rather weak cocoa, that it came forth in a very fine, dark-coloured stream; and at the same moment, his sisters both crying out, "Oh, Arthur, you get your cocoa stronger and stronger every evening."'

Eventually, chocolate became so strong that it was produced as a solid. In 1828, a Dutch chemist found a way to make powdered chocolate by removing about half the natural fat (cacao butter) from chocolate liquor, pulverising what remained and treating the mixture with alkaline salts to cut the bitter taste. His product became known as 'Dutch cocoa', and it soon led to the creation of solid chocolate. By 1824 the cocoa issue, or CI, was instituted in the Royal Navy, and each man received his daily ration, a one-ounce block of chocolate along with his rum and limes.[46]

Do all these drinks sound diverse? In reality, all of them consist of a strong and bitter substance mixed with sugar. All of them except gin are caffeine in liquid form. Caffeine has permanently changed the sleep cycle of the West. It does not actually prevent tiredness, but it blocks the human ability to sense the build-up of the substance in the blood which suggests that sleep is overdue; this is adenosine, a neuro-chemical that increases in the body throughout the day. As adenosine builds up, we feel sleepier and less alert. Caffeine prevents brain cells from recognising adenosine (but without removing it).

And all the caffeinated drinks drove an increased consumption of sugar. As we have seen, the poorest of the poor drank tea with sugar in it, and ate bread with jam. Sugar was crucial to England's mercantile trading empire and to the Industrial Revolution; as factory owners used the wealth from sugar to fund expansion, the sugar itself fuelled the bodies of the working class that staffed the factories. Slavery and colonialism turned the Caribbean into a cash crop factory for the production of the cheapest carbohydrate of all. The workers for whom this commodity fuelled their economic survival were chained to the invisible mass of slave labourers who produced it, an interdependence among the very worst off, characterising food relations in global capitalism.

The early nineteenth-century essayist Charles Lamb worked for the East India Company, which imported tea, sugar and other colonial luxuries. His friends, the Romantic poets, opposed their novel foreignness, but particularly objected to those commodities grown and harvested by slaves. An anonymous author wrote of sugar: 'Go, guilty, sweet, seducing food/ Tainted by streams of human blood … steeped in a thousand negroes' tears'.[47] Shelley argued that 'on a natural system of diet, we should require … none of these multitudinous articles of luxury for which every corner of the globe is rifled'. He added: 'Let it ever be remembered, that it is the direct influence of commerce to make the interval between the richest and the poorest man wider and more unconquerable.'[48]

But sugar – rather than the drinks that contained it – was viciously addictive, and destined to become the first mass-produced exotic necessity of a proletarian working class. Its power to deform and reshape dietary norms was extraordinary; everything from bread to drinks was dominated by its taste. Without sugar, the diet of the poor even today would mostly be a matter of flavourless bread and water.

Fishes

My home is not silent; I myself am not loud.
The Lord has provided for the pair of us
A joint expedition. I am speedier than he
And sometimes stronger; he stays the course better.
Sometimes I rest, but he runs on.
For as long as I live, I live in him;
If we leave one another it is I who must die.[1]
Anglo-Saxon riddle, a fish in a river

The idea of a fish as part of the river in which it swims in the same way that a thane is part of a war band shows how well fishermen understand their prey. Fish and fishing mean that men – and it is mostly men – must tangle with an element which can kill them in search of food that will keep them alive. To fish is to live not off the land, but in the simplest way off its waters; despite the growth of fish farming in recent years, fish is still understood as the bounty given by river, lake and ocean, the only food for which the eater does not have to wait. Eating fish – and catching it – is therefore especially laden with mythic and even mystical thinking. When we eat fish, we step out of our element and into something else. This is both a wonderful and a terrifying process.

In 'The White Trout Legend', William Butler Yeats retells the story of a beautiful lady promised to a king's son; he is murdered and thrown into the lake, and she understandably goes mad and pines until 'the fairies took her away'.[2] From that day, a white trout is seen in the lake, a ghost fish. Nobody will touch it until one day a wicked newcomer to the area decides to kill it; he duly catches it and puts it in the pan to cook, and it screams. It becomes a beautiful woman, dressed in white, with a gold band on her hair, and blood running down her arm; she says she has to wait for her true love in the lake, but when the remorseful angler throws her back the lake promptly turns red with her blood. This kind of legend, which typically is about refraining from hunting a wild animal, is common in the annals of hunting and clearly links the trout to other quest beasts such as deer and boar.[3] But a trout?

Yes. In ancient Europe, trout enjoyed cult status – a cult that persisted as a relic of mysterious, water-related beliefs long after the arrival of Christianity. Traces of these beliefs remain in the form of sacred fishes present in holy wells.[4] In one Welsh village, rickets and scrofula could be cured if one of the well's resident trout came out of hiding in the presence of the sick person. Prehistoric monuments are frequently linked to wells and springs and to rivers. Silbury Hill, Britain's largest prehistoric mound, was built at the spring head of the clear, bright chalk stream the River Kennet, and it has been suggested that Stonehenge was part of a much larger ritual complex centred on the headwaters of another chalk-fed river, the Avon. These two rivers are prized for their trout, and the fish might have been seen as the embodiment of guardian spirits of pure, constant waters that rose almost magically from the earth.[5] Fish wove a watery way through the landscape, and through the imaginations as well as the bodies of the human beings that ate it.

Some think that eating fish helped our ancestors to gain the edge over Europe's native cavemen, the Neanderthals. Isotope analysis of fossil skeletons from the time when modern humans colonised Europe indicates that – as revealed by the presence of high levels of nitrogen – freshwater fish formed a crucial part of their diet, but Neanderthals clung to the diminishing herds of reindeer and mammoths.[6] It takes imagination and intelligence to think of eating creatures that look very different from us: Samuel Johnson rightly said that it was a bold man who first ate an oyster.

In 9000 BC, most of the population of these islands lived on the now-drowned low-lying plains of Doggerland, rich in fish and game. The hunter-gatherers of Britain didn't simply crouch in caves; they followed planned movement trails that let them take advantage of seasonal resources. As Doggerland sank slowly under the North Sea, finally succumbing to one last storm surge, its people moved to the mainland, taking with them their knowledge of both land and water prey. But they also linked that netherworld of fish with death itself; where fish could breathe, men would drown. To go fishing was to dice with death, to play with death by water.

When the Romans came to this fish-eating world, they brought with them a passion for fish which they had partly inherited from the ancient Greeks. In the ancient Mediterranean, fish was both a staple of the everyday and a special feasting dish. The pre-Christian Romans already thought of fish as an appropriate dish for funerals and as food for the dead. The singer Orpheus was called a fisher of men in the fourth century BC, and in other Near Eastern religions only priests could eat fish. This association between fish-eating and dealings with the dead was then fed by Christian stories of the risen Christ appearing and eating fish with the apostles. Some early Christians even portrayed Christ himself as a fish, roasted on the cross on Good Friday. The medieval connection between fish and Fridays might have less to do with fasting than with the symbolic connection between fish and the dead.

The Romans were among the first to try to preserve fish for later consumption by salting: their fish sauce, called *garum*, was so popular and so fundamental to their food that many recipes survive. (As we shall see, these frequently resemble the methods used for preserving herring in the Middle Ages.) Small fish were covered with salt, spread out in the sun and turned from time to time. When completely fermented they were scooped into a fine-meshed basket hanging in a vase. The liquid that seeped into the vase was *liquamen*. The very best garum, according to the tenth-century Byzantine compilation *Geoponica*, was called *haimatum*. It was made solely with the innards of the tuna, including blood and gills, put in a pot with salt. Such fermented food is a normal part of many cultures; Korean kimchi and German sauerkraut, like Roman garum, use fermentation to begin the digestive process. Garum is not unlike nam pla, the Indonesian sauce made from fermented fish.[7]

Medical theory also made fish popular. Galenic medicine insisted that it was vital to avoid the consumption of semen-producing foods, since these meant a constant search for release through sexual intercourse. Without that release, headaches and emaciation were sure to follow, as the semen ate into the flesh. Later dietaries recommended fish as cool and thus chaste; it became part of fasting regimens because of its power to make those who ate it pure, all but immune to carnal desires. Eating meat, by contrast, inflamed desire, to a point where even those committed to a life of celibacy might be overcome by sudden surges of lust. Christian thinkers, such as Augustine of Hippo, argued that reversing the effects of the fall of man depended on bringing the body under control; if the faithful could subdue their bodies, they could hope to live in paradise. Fish was cooling, calming, and had been eaten by the resurrected Christ. Yet fish did not feature in early guides to Christian fasting. When ideas about abstinence and asceticism were formalised in the monastic rule of Saint Benedict in around 530 AD, fish was not a fasting food, but a delicacy. Monastic rules insisted that fish was not suitable for fasting except as an extra treat at the midday meal, and abstaining from fish as well as white meats and cheese, eggs, butter and wine, was especially virtuous in Lent. Fast days for ordinary people involved bread, water and greens. So the often-repeated idea that Christianity meant huge demand for fish because of fast days is misleading. If anything, demand for fish was reduced when the Roman Empire fell; fish became far more expensive and scarce, in part because the collapse of Rome impaired travel. The only exceptions were coastal villages, and habitations near rivers or lakes.

———

Anglo-Saxon fish consumption never matched the enormous middens of bones found at Roman sites. Anglo-Saxons ate freshwater and migrating fish. Written sources say little about sea fishing, and archaeology confirms that before AD 1000 there was little consumption of marine fish. Abbot Ælfric's Latin teaching dialogue depicts a river fisherman using a net, and a hook and line. Ælfric's fisherman is expert in catching inshore and freshwater fish, but the ocean terrifies him. He is contented with the resources nearby. River fisheries are documented in the Domesday Book; there were many hundreds of weirs and traps in rivers or mill ponds.[8] Domesday also recorded fishing boats and almost 100 fishermen, but much smaller numbers of sea fisheries. Virtually no cod was consumed before around 1000, and what there was would have been from inshore catches; but from the eleventh and twelfth centuries more cod and herring appeared in refuse heap bone samples. This sudden enthusiasm for ocean fish may have been sharpened by the declining availability of freshwater fish due to the growth of mills and dams, which created obstacles to fishing on rivers. The increased consumption of fish was the result not of fasting rules, but of the taste for it formed by the upper classes, which they partially justified by consuming it only on fast days.

According to the poem *The Seafarer*, Anglo-Saxons did not venture onto the open ocean until after the first cuckoo of early summer. Severe gales are eight times more frequent in these waters during winter than in summer, with rough seas at least every fourth winter day.[9] Ælfric's fisherman has only a small boat. The very oldest fishing boats were simple: a raft, a dugout canoe, or a coracle covered in hide or bark. They were little more than flotation aids; far from shore, in seas of any size, they were useless. But they were a beginning, and the hope of going out further and coming back faster than others was a spur to innovation. Sails made of skins caught the wind and harnessed it; oars were added, more than one set, and in Scandinavia the innovation of segmented whole compartments allowed far bigger ships; a crew of two dozen men paddled the clinker-built Hjort spring boat. This was no fishing boat; it was a warship, the precursor of the Viking longship, slender and quick. But the Viking fishing fleet was not entirely dissimilar; the Orkney yole, a clinker-built boat used for fishing and powered by sail and oars, is its lineal descendant.

The ocean fish eaten from the Norman Conquest onwards still came for the most part from inshore fishing. England has a very long coastline; the British Isles sit amid a broad expanse of shallow continental shelf stretching from Scandinavia far into the Atlantic. Every winter, storms mix nutrients from the seabed with surface water so that in spring, when the days lengthen and sunshine warms the sea, there is explosive plankton growth. This rich plankton soup nourishes the immense schools of fish upon which the larger predators fall in endless pursuit. Along the coastline, there were hundreds of villages huddled around small harbours, facing the sea and turning their backs on the fields and hills.

The largest commercial fisheries in medieval Europe were in the western Baltic: herring and cod, centring on Danish ports and on Lübeck. Twelfth-century chronicler Saxo Grammaticus said herring was so densely packed in the Danish sound that it was hard to row a boat, and easier to catch them with bare hands than with the net. From the tenth century onwards, inshore herring fisheries had been established on the east coast of England, supplying the local monasteries but also producing herring for market, responding to consumer demand from increasing urbanisation. In Essex every tide left a cartload of fish to be collected, a marketable surplus. There were estuary fisheries on the Severn as well as unrecorded coastal fisheries and probably many small weirs. The eel that mysteriously appeared in springtime, swarming in rivers by the thousands, became so valuable that in the fens of East Anglia, monasteries tried to control the whole fenland, while Glastonbury Abbey owned a local fishery along the River Axe in the Somerset Levels, which yielded as many as 16,000 eels every year. The fatty flesh of eels could be boiled or dried, or smoked.[10]

The Normans took to the larger fish available in the sea in part because of the Norman tradition of wanting to share a single beast between diners, a kind of union through flesh. In the medieval city of York, well-preserved fish bones indicate heavy consumption of cod (in the years 1020 to 1120) and haddock (1200 to 1260), as well as large numbers of sturgeon, Atlantic herring, pike and whiting. This confirms the shift in emphasis from freshwater fish to ocean fish, and the percentage of sea fish in the total kept increasing, most of it caught in the relatively local waters of the North Sea. Archaeology shows that bishops ate much more fish than others in the same locales. Medieval peasants did not eat much fish because it was expensive. The monarchy and the nobility now owned all the freshwater fishing grounds, and could also pay high prices for ocean fish. Even salted herring was a luxury to the poor. As feudalism spread, the type of fish people ate – if they ate it at all – depended heavily on their social class.

By 1300, a network of increasingly specialised fisheries had spread along the east coast of England; the main inshore fishing centred on cod, because as they spawned the fish moved slowly south in summer and autumn. In the early fourteenth century, Yarmouth fishermen went out only for two nights, and they usually landed at seasonal stations so that their catch could be salted; but as the century wore on, many fishing boats went out to less well-known grounds. By 1383, East Anglian doggers were fishing off Denmark and Norway, and by 1408 off Iceland too. Hull men had also made it to Iceland by 1421, getting into fights there. Records in Scarborough show that in winter, the herring fishermen sought inshore fish with the odd lobster to add to the catch; in Lent, there was fishing from larger boats; in summer, there was coastal herring fishing, and also cod fishing in the North Sea; then in late summer, the shoals came again, predictable as wheat – that is, not particularly. The seasonality of fish was well understood by writers like Thomas Tusser. For instance, he speaks of mackerel as a late-spring fish: 'when mackerel ceases from the seas/ John Baptist brings grass beef and peas'. But much piscine seasonality was very local.

In western England, inshore fishing meant lookout men perched on rocks to watch for approaching shoals. At their signal the fishing fleet headed out, and then the lords moved in on one-third of the catch. Some also invested in the industry, funding seine and drift nets. Drift nets enabled big catches of herring from deeper waters. There were also a few sea weirs, large fixed structures – underwater stone walls in which were set wooden stakes connected by a kind of screen formed

Reaping, carrying and carting scene from the *Luttrell Psalter*,
illumination, *c.* 1300–1340.

Roman baker putting bread into the oven,
mosaic, third century.

Farm worker (centre) explaining to a clergyman how he has set fire to a
hay-rick in protest at being evicted from both his farm and cottage, print, 1830.

Country people leaving a village due to enclosures,
illustration, eighteenth century.

Medieval fishermen draw in their nets, print, fifteenth century.

River fishing, wood engraving, sixteenth century.

'The Virgin and Child Under an Apple Tree' by Lucas Cranach the Elder, oil on canvas, 1530s.

A girl gathering berries on the Yorkshire moors, 'The Costume of Yorkshire' by George Walker, colour engraving, 1815.

'Gin Lane' by William Hogarth, print, 1751.

from woven branches and twigs. The walls converged to form an angle facing the sea, with nets stretched across the neck of the weir. As the tide ebbed, fish were left stranded in the staked enclosure. Such weirs cost a lot to build and maintain, the goal being to catch as many fish as possible for the least possible trouble. This was no longer a subsistence but a commercial model.

Most fishermen did not get to eat the fish they caught. They took risks to provide pleasure for others. The banqueting fare of the Middle Ages included ostentatious meals of fish on Fridays, which could be replicas of meat-based banquets. In the fourteenth-century poem *Sir Gawain and the Green Knight* we hear of fish 'baked in bread, some broiled on the coals, some seethed, some in gravy savoured with spices'.[11] High-status consumers sought variety, but access to variety was the direct result of the exchange of gifts between people of the same social class, typically nobles and the greater gentry. Turbot (ocean fish) and whole salmon (from the rivers) were the most prestigious. Rich medieval diners might enjoy salmon grilled before it was poached, then garnished with small sprigs of parsley, or a caudal of salmon with leek, almond milk, saffron and salt.[12]

Food historian Peter Brears thinks that the whole fish served at medieval banquets would not have been filleted, but only gutted; but the textural experience of finding fishbones in your mouth and the spectacle of diners choking on fishbones is not recorded, and labour was relatively cheap. There is, however, the story of the German bishop Blasius, who achieved fame by saving a little boy who had a fishbone stuck in his throat; Saint Blaise, who becomes the patron saint of throats, saves a child from a similar fate.[13] These tales suggest that fishbones were a source of anxiety for parents, as they still are, and this in turn suggests that fish was not always filleted, or that the filleting process was not perfect.

The closer an estate was to the sea, the greater the variety of fish available. But luxury could be bought. Fresh fish were transported in baskets on the back of pack horses; large households had wet larders with a water source or well, located in cool basement rooms: York Place had a fish house with fresh running water. Fish could be kept alive until needed, or could be transported cooked in pastry coffins. A separate larder for preserved fish had to be kept dry; preserved fish were usually held in barrels, while stockfish – fish preserved by simply drying in air – might be kept on dry straw. The latter was for the servants. Herring was cheaper in autumn, so might be bought then in bulk for consumption during Advent and Lent. Other fish were considered such a delicacy and had seasons so short that they were almost always eaten fresh; mackerel, for example, was enjoyed during May and June. As with forest and field game, the elite appreciated the rarity of certain fish. Fresh fish, like other fresh fare, was comparatively more expensive than preserved fish.[14]

For prosperous gentry families in the Middle Ages, one rare delicacy was salted whale meat, or *craspois*, which attracted a duty so heavy that it was clearly seen as a luxury. The Bishop of Salisbury, meanwhile, dined on porpoise in February 1407. A surviving recipe for frumenty with porpoise is striking because it combines two feasting dishes. Brears says that it was 'one of the highest status fish dishes'. The fish (not really a fish, of course, but a cetacean) was boiled, and then served in a dish half-filled with hot water, accompanied by a dish of hot frumenty, the milk-boiled and spiced-wheat grain mixture associated with festivities in the medieval period. The carver would cut the porpoise into pieces for the lord as he dined.[15] Oddly, porpoise was apparently still being eaten even after the First World War: Virginia Woolf saw porpoise for sale on a fishmonger's slab at Christmas in 1925.[16] The point was its size. Augustine called all fish an allegory of Christ: just as they could remain alive in the sea, so Christ could live in the deeps of death and then rise again, as the porpoise did. Having a choice large fish on the feasting table was a way of illustrating religious devotion and imitating Christ and the apostles. In 1257, King Henry III and his court celebrated Saint Edward's Day by dining on 300 pike, in addition to 250 bream and 15,000 eels, transported from all over England.[17]

But the common people had to make do with portions of red cod or salted herring. The culture of fast days encouraged cooks and diners to see fish as a substitute for meat in a dish, often a straight substitute.

For example, a recipe for 'fish chewets for fast days' follows almost exactly the recipe for meat chewets, a dish including very finely chopped meat which could be cooked in a variety of ways (rissoles or pies). It doesn't even matter what kind of fish is used: haddock or salmon, plus dates, raisins, pine kernels, ginger, cinnamon and salt: poach the fish and dates for ten minutes, drain, grind, and mix with the remaining ingredients; pack a pie case with the mixture and bake.[18]

The timing of Advent and Lent meant that demand for fish peaked at exactly the time of year when marine fishing was most difficult and dangerous. Winter also closed off international shipping; this was a factor in the heavy dependence on preserved fish. Harvest workers in thirteenth-century Norfolk ate herring, salted or dried cod, and cheese, while workers at Wilton Abbey were rewarded for carrying dung with salted mackerel. Two surviving sets of accounts vividly portray the contrast between what fish meant to the elite and what it meant to the ordinary citizen. The English garrisons in Scotland in 1300 had 122 fish days per year, but the only fish given to them were stockfish and herring, with an allocation of half a stockfish each; on fast days, bread and beer provided more calories than the fish did. By contrast, monks at Westminster Abbey were given about two pounds of fish per head at dinner during fasting seasons.

When fish did establish itself as a Lenten meat, it lost its luxury status and became a despised necessity. In one of Erasmus's colloquies this is noted by a fishmonger: 'Fishmonger: When they may eat anything they like, many men will abstain from meat. As among the ancients, there will be no fine dinner without fish. And so I'm glad the eating of flesh is permitted. I only wish the eating of fish were forbidden. People would eat it the more eagerly.[19]

———

'I'd rather eat a cabbage stalk than a herring,' thought one hungry schoolboy.[20]

Preserved herring remained the fish of the poor, in Lent and out. Herring hide in the ocean depths in winter, but in spring they rise and swim, sometimes thousands of miles, to their coastal spawning grounds. The phenomenon takes place from the Russian and Scandinavian Baltic across the North Sea, as far south as northern France, and across the Atlantic from Newfoundland to Chesapeake Bay: 'a whole living world rises from the depths to the surface, following the call of warmth, desire, and the light'.[21] A herring shoal consists of thousands of fish and, once located, provides an ample catch. Herring feed by gulping in seawater as they swim and filtering out minuscule zooplankton. They spend their lives searching for these drifting beds of food. When their food is exhausted, a spot that had always been teeming with herring may suddenly be empty. The loss of the herring, the suddenly bare sea, was a catastrophe, often blamed on the sins of the fishing community.

Salted herring was a living for the fishermen. It was a low-end product. Cured herring had even lower status than salted cod, and it was hated by many poor people who had nothing else to eat for holy days. Smoking was a northern solution to the lack of salt; while salt is necessary for smoking, it's only required in small quantities because the smoking aids preservation. Nobody knows who invented the method, though the Romans smoked cheeses and hams. Red herring, a famous export from East Anglia, was soaked in brine of salt and saltpetre and then smoked over oak and turf. The discovery of red herring was described by a native East Anglian, the pamphleteer Thomas Nashe, in 1567. He claimed that it came about after fishermen with an unusually large catch hung the surplus herrings on a rafter, and by chance the room had a particularly smoky fire. Imagine their surprise the next day when the white-fleshed fish had turned as red as a lobster. (But satirist Nashe is an unreliable witness.) The results must have been very smelly, because the term red herring for a distraction originates from hunting; a red herring will throw the hounds off the scent.

By the sixteenth century, if not earlier, Scandinavian peoples had developed a number of ways of preserving herring, but these never caught on in English-speaking lands. The taste is too strong. The smell is too powerful. The whole thing is, well, too fishy. English lack of interest in preserved fish meant that they struggled to develop a palatable form of it, with a very few exceptions – kippers, bloaters – which remained strictly regional and mostly working-class delicacies. The Cley smokehouse in East Anglia is trying to revive the bloater tradition, offering 'succulent whole herring to produce a less salty and less intensely flavoured fish than our Kippers with a slightly gamey flavour'. But the bloater – a cold smoked and ungutted herring – can only be presented as a kind of kipper. Unlabelled, undefined cured fish is of course widely available as smoked haddock or smoked mackerel, and there are still traces of the fish pastes that were once an alternative method of preservation; their best survivor is probably the potted shrimp. The vast majority of English people avoid such medieval staple foods now. Only smoked salmon – a river fish from Scotland – retains its place as one of the foods of the better-off. When it comes to fish, the English still see fresh as better. Whether via quick cart transport from the south coast to Billingsgate, or through keeping fish alive for as long as possible, the nation swerved away from preserved fish, and has done so consistently over a very long period.

Alongside preserved fish, the other cheap and easily accessible kind of fish was shellfish. Thirteenth-century market regulations show an understanding that shellfish must be fresh, specifying that shellfish had to be on sale for only two tides going out and one coming in. Archaeological sites show that medieval people ate a huge number of oysters, which were regarded as food for the poor. There were also cockles, whelks and mussels, which were added to monastic diets in Lent precisely because they were poor-people's food. 'Fridays and fast days a farthing's worth of mussels\ Or as many cockles would be a feast for such folks', records the fourteenth-century allegorical poem *Piers Plowman*.[22]

––––––––

Since preserved fish were never as prestigious as fresh, rich people kept fish alive for eating in natural or man-made ponds. Saltwater fish were trapped in wooden cages. It is common knowledge that monasteries had fishponds in which they raised carp; it's a lot more complicated than that, however. Fishponds came about because of the increased use of watermills on the Thames and other rivers. To turn the increasing harvest of grain into food required mills, usually watermills, each with a reservoir of still water made by damming a river or making a weir. Fishing weirs, too, slowed the passage of water, so that fish like salmon that depend on fast, clear streams became scarcer. The result was to create a shortfall that was also a business opportunity – at a price. The first pond built after the Norman conquest of England, the 'King's Pool' at York, required the flooding of farmland, taking down mills, changing the run of roads. Fishponds were proof that you were separate from ordinary people, which is why they were so often built at the edge of an estate or just within the fences and walls.[23]

Nor were all the ponds for carp. Bream was by far the most popular freshwater fish on the royal table in the thirteenth century, followed by pike and tench. Pike required a separate pond. Even if isolated from other fish, pike can very quickly learn to prey on one another. The Bishop of Lincoln had a sizeable pike pond by the side of his other fishponds at Lyddington, which showed that he could command this very special fish, one that carried on its body the marks of Christ's Passion: the marks of nails, whip, cross and thorns. To eat it was not only a status symbol; it showed that the bishop himself had been chosen by Christ to speak about him, as the fish had.

Instruction manuals were printed to support the construction of new fishponds, made by channelling a small brook or rill into a valley. They advised adding the fish during cold weather, to ensure that they did not become unwell on the journey, and also advised keeping predatory fish away from fish that fed mostly on seeds, roots and worms. And they reminded readers about the pike and its voracity: 'he may be eighteen or twenty inches before Hollantide, at what time he will eat more fish every day, then will suffice a man, and will feed only of Carpe before any other fish, if there be Carpe fry in the pond'. Both carp and eel might be raised in other ponds to feed the pike.[24]

The Bishop would never have deigned to catch his own fish. The ponds of great estates were drained every three years or so, and then the dying fish were gathered. This system was designed to produce a feast, but most fishponds were not even that useful. The ponds were signs of wealth, like modern swimming pools or designer kitchens.

The bishops of Winchester had four hundred acres of ponds but used barely a tenth of the fish they could produce. The fishponds and their inhabitants were for show, like their deer, and in fact much like the carp in the ponds of twenty-first-century parks and gardens. English monarchs did not aim for self-sufficiency in fish even at feasts, buying freshwater fish to eat despite all the fish stock in their fishponds: the show of the feasts and the show of the new landscape were entirely different things. Showing off could extend to giving fish away to a monastery in return for prayers; this happened often enough for monks to have gained a quite unjustified reputation as pioneers of fish farming. While in the past historians always associated the carp with monasticism, the presence of carp bones on monastic sites are evidence of gifts from nobles.

One reason that fishponds were not a prime source of fresh fish is that freshwater pond fish are often unappealing in flavour and texture; bream and pike, sometimes perch, often tench, roach and dace are bony, slow-growing, muddy-tasting fish. So is carp, but at first it was a novelty, and initially it arrived alive in barrels, probably by boat from Flanders. Fast-growing carp were ready to harvest in three years, instead of the eight it took to raise bream; carp could be encouraged to grow by a diet of grain, blood and chicken guts. By the time of the first major treatises on fish-keeping in the sixteenth and seventeenth centuries, carp was in the ascendancy.[25] Carp is one of the most important food fish in the world, and are traditionally part of Christmas dinner in many parts of Europe. But in England, it never became central either to banqueting or to everyday eating. Carp remained an interesting, exotic and fundamentally foreign fish, even if it came from a fishpond just up the road.

An entire class existed that supplied freshwater fish for the market; these fishermen were concentrated in areas of large natural fisheries, like the Fens, which in the twelfth century were fished day and night throughout the year but still abounded in fish. The estates of Cambridgeshire's Ramsey Abbey in the fifteenth century recorded the considerable income derived from their fisheries. This usually came from rents and leases; it was not general practice for such establishments to be involved in the direct sale of the produce. (Such status consciousness meant the medieval economy was full of middlemen.) When Henry III needed extra freshwater fish, he asked the sheriff of Cambridge and Huntingdonshire to get them. The greater aristocracy seemed uninterested in making profits from their own fishponds beyond meagre rents. Religious houses also asked only for very low rent.

So the gentry often bought fish when a dinner party was planned. A comfortably-off family like the Tudor Willoughbys in the Midlands sought out fresh fish supplies for banquets, even though Francis Willoughby also had fishing rights on the Trent. The bulk of he household's fish fish was bought, not raised in their own fishponds or fished from rivers where they had the exclusive right of access. Great households bought fish fresh from local suppliers, and many ocean fish were available to families like the Willoughbys; they included not only skate but also shellfish, including oysters and shrimp. Some families enjoyed mackerel and pilchards, but these were from Channel coast catch, and Nottinghamshire was too far for even the quickest supplier to reach with such delicacies intact.[26]

And yet the ideal still persisted that fish should be obtained for free. Jesus's apostles had been fishermen, and for that reason, fish was as close as one could get on Earth to the food on the menu in heaven. Plus, in the feeding of the five thousand, Jesus had divided loaves and fishes between the multitude, and on the road to Emmaus, the resurrected Christ had offered fish to his disciples.[27]

The amount of fish eaten started to decline from the fifteenth century; aristocratic households spent less on herring and stockfish than in previous centuries. Perhaps they were no longer feeding the lowlier members of their household on fast days, or perhaps they no longer cared about the church calendar. The decline in fish consumption across the board was not caused by the Reformation, but was rather a natural process of decline that occurred for unknown reasons. Problems transporting sea fish inland may have decreased their popularity and the notoriously muddy pond fish were no substitute. Dried salt fish, once another staple, also fell out of favour. The number of fish days mandated for English troops guarding the Scottish border was reduced; they were encouraged in fierceness by being held to only thirty-three fish days a year and they never had to withstand the horror of the hated red herrings. And yet, as the population grew and fisheries close to the shore were fished out, the inshore fishing fleets expanded, men resorting to fishing because other livelihoods had been taken from them. A vicious circle developed and churned: when fishermen started heading far out into the North Sea, to the Dogger Bank that lies between Jutland and England, they needed more capital for stronger, larger ships. To get the money, they ran up debts with the fish merchants in town, and quite often they could not pay and they lost their ships; or else they had to take jobs on other ships owned by the merchants.

And yet the fishing fleet was also the nation's first line of defence. In 1588, it was a fishing boat – a humble fishing ketch – that brought Drake word that the Spanish Armada was on its way, and the skills of fishermen were a vital strategic resource that the navy could call up and call on in times of national emergency.[28]

In Shakespeare's time most ships were steered simply by means of a long pole that controlled the rudder from the deck. Holding the rudder steady in heavy seas was difficult to the point of impossibility.[29] While pilots knew the ports and headlands, the currents and the phases of the moon and the tides, they were familiar only with inshore waters. A pilot might use a compass and a plumbline, and of course his eyes, but if you were in a fishing boat trying to reach Newfoundland, these tools would not do the job. How could any ship's captain maintain a steady course when the wind and the currents kept him even from reckoning his whereabouts?

They managed. It required complicated mathematics, instruments such as the astrolabe and the quadrant, and a knowledge of the stars. You might also have a chart, and you might know about Richard Eden's book *The Art of Navigation translated out of Spanish into English*, printed in 1561, or William Bourne's *Regiment for the Sea* (1574). Bourne's book includes tables on calculating tides and latitude by means of the stars. By the time of *Certain errors in navigation* (1599) by Edward Wright, the idea of adapting the Mercator projection to plot an exact course across the oceans had begun to take hold. Any straight line on a Mercator projection map is a line of constant true bearing that allows a navigator to plot a straight course. The technique relies on a method first developed by Thomas Harriott, a man so clever that many believed he had magic at his disposal. Such developments in navigation gave the English access to new territories and new fisheries. But every fishing trip remained dangerous and exacting.

The fishing grounds within 5,000 miles of Britain include the Greenland coast, Iceland, Bear Island and Spitsbergen, the Barents Sea, the Faroes, the Baltic and the Bay of Biscay. By the end of the reign of Elizabeth I, English fishing fleets were travelling to all of them. It is obvious that others wanted to fish in the same areas, and they wanted the same fish too; they wanted the herring, usually taken in the spawning season, and they wanted the cod, which could be caught all year round, but was best in the winter months. Bottom-dwelling fish were caught with long lines, while shallow-swimming fish were caught with nets. At least until the advent of the dragnet trawler: a petition addressed to Edward III in 1376 survives, complaining about a device called a wondyrechaun:

> upon which instrument is attached a net so close meshed that no fish, be it ever so small, that enters there in can escape, but must stay and be taken, and that the great and long iron of the wondyrechaun runs so heavily and hardly over the ground when fishing that it destroys the flowers of the land below water there and also the sprat of oysters, mussels and other fish upon which the great fish are accustomed to be fed and nourished.[30]

Not unreasonably, the fishermen complained that this meant that fish were taken in infancy and were never given a chance to grow to maturity. Catches were impoverished.

The main problem with 'fresh' fish was that it could and often did spoil before it reached those who wanted to eat it. Compared with meat, eggs, and cheese or butter, fish keeps very badly. We might expect the nose to have been the ultimate organ for detecting the bad, and sayings testify to the stench of putrid fish – 'fresh fish and new guests spoil, by the time they are three days old'. Erasmus's butcher, denouncing his rival the fishmonger, makes it plain that diners in earlier periods found the smell of fish disgusting even when it was fresh: 'A fish always smells like a fish, though you smear it with sweet ointments … Meat pickled in brine keeps for many years … Smoked meat acquires a not unpleasant odour. If you treat fish in just the same way, it will still smell like nothing but fish. That no stench can be compared with the rottenness of fish, infer from the fact that salt itself – which is given by Nature to protect things from spoiling … – is rotted by fish.'[31] Both medieval and Renaissance doctors believed that bad smells could themselves cause serious illnesses. Fish did not enjoy a long shelf life – 'daughters, and dead fish, are no keeping wares'. We sometimes imagine that people in earlier periods were insensitive to smells of decay; in fact, just the opposite was true, because they strongly believed that the smells themselves were unhealthy and even deadly. In an era before refrigeration, smell was also an important indicator of freshness. Shakespeare's contemporary Richard Braithwaite warned that the stench of rotting fish was not for queasy stomachs. Samuel Pepys's stomach turned at the spectacle of a dish of sturgeon on which he saw 'very many little worms creeping', and cases of rotten and stinking fish and seafood were presented periodically to the courts.

The punishments for selling bad fish could be extreme; the vendor could be pilloried, with the foul-smelling lump of fish tied in front of his face. The point of the pillory was not only to humiliate; it was up to the crowd that assembled to decide on how severely they wanted to treat the prisoner, and as a result the pillory was so savage that it could even substitute for the usual punishment for treason, which was hanging, drawing and quartering. The punishment for selling bad fish could be the same as the punishment for trying to poison an employer, or for the treason of slandering Queen Elizabeth by claiming she had

had children by the Earl of Leicester, or for homosexual love. Virtually every small local court might have access to a pillory; the court leet in a manor, or even the hundred court, and almost every town and parish had a pillory set up near the church, or in the marketplace, connecting the crime with the place where it had been committed.[32]

Despite these hazards, the sea was and is astoundingly generous in comparison with arable land. Whereas until the modern era a wheat farmer could expect only one crop per year, at least one stock of Atlantic herring spawns every month. Each spawns at a different time and place (spring, summer, autumn and winter). This means that herring is locally seasonal, but that it is also possible for the fishing fleet to move from one spawning centre to another. The herring shoals reached the coast of Britain in a series of waves, coming later in the year the further south you went. The first spring schools appeared in the northerly Shetland Islands around April. They came inshore at Wick and northern Scotland a month later, arriving in northern England in July/August, before finally the great schools of East Anglia arrived in October. The herring shoals finally reached the south coast, and were fished off Sussex, at the same time as the Cornish welcomed their pilchards.[33] The very name 'herring' is thought to come from the German *heer*, meaning 'army':[34]

> When the main body is arrived, its breadth and depth is such as to alter the very appearance of the ocean. It is divided into distinct columns, of five or six miles in length, and three or four broad; while the water before them curls up, as if forced out of its bed. Sometimes they sink for the space of ten or fifteen minutes, then rise again to the surface; and, in bright weather, reflect a variety of splendid colours, like a field bespangled with purple, gold and azure … The whole water seems alive; and is seen so black with them to a great distance, that the number seems inexhaustible … By these enemies the herrings are cooped up into so close a body, that a shovel or any hollow vessel put into the water, takes them up without farther trouble.[35]

Fishing fleets had to be willing to travel, and grew used to doing so. In spring, the North Sea fleet set out to catch haddock and cod on their spawning grounds east of Dogger Bank; when the herring moved on, the fleets did too, seeking skate, while others headed for Iceland to take more cod. They *could* wait for the herring, but often enough the fleet moved out in pursuit of the silver darlings.[36] Increasingly accustomed to going far, the fishing fleets of the North Sea ports and the West Country made their way to the Iceland cod fisheries, and then to Greenland. Some sailors made Iceland many times a year. Cornish fishermen even reached Finnmark on the Norwegian north coast. The West Country fishing fleet's drive and expertise in navigation made the exploration and settlement of the New World both possible and thinkable, and it is no coincidence that Francis Drake and Walter Ralegh were both from the West Country.[37]

The fishing fleets were full of courage and even derring-do. But it's easy to be sentimental about the old days of herring fishing. As with other industries that filled the tables of past centuries, there is a beauty and stability about it that seems enviable. However, depictions of the quayside 'once thronged by the herring fleet' obscures the dangers those who worked on it had to face. For Virginia Woolf, the lights of the inshore herring fishers marked the boundary between the known waters and the deep ocean: in *The Waves*, Rhoda imagines herself launching a garland of flowers beyond the lights of the herring fleet.[38] On the boats, men were cutting their hands to the bone hauling lines.

Each skipper would tack up and down on the wind, searching for signs of herring before shooting the nets and letting the herring and the tides do the rest. The skills involved were enormous, the spectacle extraordinary:

Surrounding us on all sides was … a moving world of boats; many with their sails down, their nets floating in the water, and their crews at rest … Others were still flitting uneasily about … the sucker goes splash into the water; the 'dog', a large inflated bladder to mark the far end of the train, is heaved overboard, and the nets, breadth after breadth, follow as fast as the men

can pay them out, each division being marked by a large,
painted bladder, till the immense train is all in the water,
forming a perforated wall a mile long and many feet in depth;
the 'dog' and the marking-bladders floating and dipping in a
long zigzag line, reminding one of the imaginary coils of the
great sea-serpent.[39]

The herring fair at Great Yarmouth was an enormous multinational event. Sixteenth-century historian Thomas Damet wrote of the presence of 'great numbers of the fishermen of France, Flanders and of Holland, Zealand and all the low countries yearly, from the feast of Saint Michael the Archangel, until the feast of Saint Martin, about the taking, selling and buying of herrings'. The gathering developed into Yarmouth's Free Herring Fair, where there was freedom for all to catch, sell and buy herrings. Visiting fishermen lodged with families or merchants in the town who undertook to sell their catches, fixing prices and taking profits.

In their many different forms, herring formed a critical part of the year of many regions. In the West Country, it was pilchards. A pilchard is a sardine, but a mature one, and sardines are really a subset of herring. Bloaters and kippers are also herrings, but identified by method of preservation. The name sardine probably derives from Sardinia, but nobody knows the origins of the term pilchard. What is clear is that the pilchard is regional. Pilchards are shoaling fish, and they swim at around 40 metres below the surface by day and 25 metres by night. Their shoals, too, could be enormous. They were called 'fair maids' because of their timidity and shyness: there is a moving account of their desertion of the south coast of Ireland due to the cannon fire from the wars of 1688. Often, the fishermen found the shoals at night by hammering or stamping on the bottom of the boat: the noise induced the pilchards to jump, thus causing a brilliant phosphorescence in the water.[40]

In Cornwall, the pilchard season began about August or September, and sometimes lasted until December. It was seasonal work. Those who were to net the pilchards – the seiners – were 'put into pay', and then as the season approached, the huers were called up to watch for the shoals from the clifftops, from a hut. The huer would stand where he had a clear sight of the sea and the coast. He would hold a furze bush in each hand to guide the boats below. Some huers even had a purpose-built tower such as the one at Newquay. The huers watched for the coming of the pilchards between the harvest and All Hallows (September to 1 November). Offshore, the small boats were waiting with their seine nets ready. When the fish came, they were like a great red stain spreading over the sea – fish by the millions. During his journey through England and Wales in the 1720s, Daniel Defoe had noted the delight of fishermen on the River Dart upon spotting a school of pilchards; the man cried out loudly 'a school a school', and 'the word was taken to the shore as hastily as it would have been on land if he had cried fire … By the time we reached the quays, the town was all in a kind of uproar.' In 1818 the *West Briton* enthused, 'The refulgent appearance of the scaly tribe, struggling, springing and gleaming in every direction; the busy and contented hum of the fishermen, together with the plashing of the frequent-plying oar, altogether form a picture to which language is incapable of doing justice.'[41]

The 'silly small fish' were 'greatest for gain' and 'most in number' but were available only for very short periods; as with the grain harvest, the work was all-absorbing and incredibly exhausting, and enough labour had to remain on call for processing at the right time of year. In season, the villagers reeked of fish, but they called it 'the smell of money'; in St Ives, they said, the smell was so bad it stopped the church clock.

The fish were pressed using 'pressing poles' and 'pressing stones'. The pilchards were laid out on raised slabs and covered in salt: a layer of pilchards, then a layer of salt, then a layer of pilchards, till a vast mound was formed, which was then left for a month or more. Gutters below the slabs carried away the brine and oil, which was later sold to the carriers. As the livers were squeezed they yielded train oil, used for cooking and lighting. Once the salting was complete, the pilchards were packed in hogsheads for export to Mediterranean countries: Italy,

France and Spain. In 1871, an excellent year, 45,000 hogsheads were exported, amounting to some 135 million fish. More usually, exports ranged from 15,000 to 30,000 hogsheads.

1871 was the peak. Then the shoals started to get smaller. When monster shoals did appear, they were greeted ecstatically: at St Ives on 2 September 1905, a large number of visitors 'witnessed the busy scene with the keenest interest – a sight they will not soon forget. One great reservoir of fish, the water literally boiling with pilchards – a teeming, convulsed mass of shining, glancing, silvery scales – one compact mass of thousands upon thousands of fish.' This apparently good news quickly had a downside, as the huge catch flooded the market and depressed prices from 11s to 7s 6d per thousand. But the overall decline continued. The pilchard fishery employed 6,000 fishers and twice as many women and children in good years. The last factory to pack the pilchards into wooden boxes closed in 2005, because of falling demand in Italy, where they had for many years been a favourite of poorer Italians.

As well as the more familiar canned variety, the Cornish also cooked pilchards fresh, splitting each fish and peppering it, then placing one fresh fish flat on another, backs outside, and roasting them on a gridiron, a process known as scrowling. Another Cornish tradition is dippie, made by cooking potatoes and fresh pilchards in thin cream.[42] The most celebrated destination for the pilchard is stargazey pie, mythologised as commemorating the bravery of a particular Mousehole fisherman, Tom Bawcock. Stargazey pie bears all the hallmarks of a fairing, too, a dish made to mark a special event. Alan Davidson investigated the rationale for the heads sticking out of the pie; one hypothesis was that it saved the oil in the fish heads by having it drip down into the pie. To have the heads poking out is part of an upper-class pie tradition, where birds' heads also poke decoratively from their pastry coffin. Modern sensibilities are offended by the sight of fish heads, but the tradition belongs to the idea of pies as a dish containing an exciting surprise. There is also something local about it; eaters of the pie already knew what pilchards looked like, so it was a test of how Cornish you were, a test outsiders were bound to fail.

(Cornish particularity is just as powerful as that of the other Celtic-language regions of the British Isles.)[43]

Cornish fishing fleets also sought mackerel. For this catch they had to compete with fishermen from East Anglia, and resentments ran high. In May 1896 there were riots as the people of Newlyn marched down the quay, boarded the Lowestoft boats, and threw 100,000 mackerel into the sea. The bulk of the St Ives fleet was in the Scilly Islands at the time, but hearing of the fracas, they promptly set sail for Newlyn to help. It took three hundred and fifteen soldiers of the Berkshire Regiment, rushed to Penzance by train and marched into Newlyn with fixed bayonets, to restore order. While the ringleaders were punished, the conflicts continued, as the Lowestoft crews went on fishing on a Sunday and claiming more of the catch.[44] The Cornish fished for herring along their rocky north coast, hard fishing and ancient on a coastline with no safe harbours. They soon began pursuing the herring out into the Irish Sea despite a glut that caused a fall in prices, then chasing other fish along the North Sea coast, and sending out long-lining boats in summertime onto inshore fishing grounds for more mackerel. There was a short-lived boom in crabbing from the late nineteenth century onwards, though Cornish crabbers were forced to compete with the Breton crabbing fleet, which began to encroach on their fishing grounds from around 1902. These different kinds of Cornish fishermen also disputed with one another; as territorial as alley cats, the far-faring western Cornishmen referred to east Cornishmen as 'mere Fishers in their own puddle'. To this day, the big Cornish trawlers that go far out into the Atlantic inspire a pride which belies the appalling working conditions on board.

————

Harvests from the sea could fail inexplicably, just like those on land. The fishermen did not understand why fish stocks suddenly crashed in areas where fish had recently been plentiful. They tended to blame bad luck, and competition from other fishing fleets, and the remedy was to go further and find new fishing grounds. This could be a question of a few fishing boats heading out in the general direction of away, but was more often a question of carefully financed voyages, based on reports and keen observations of currents and the movements of fish and waters. In 1480, a wealthy customs official, Thomas Croft, and a Bristol merchant named John Jay sent a ship in search of Hy-Brasil (a phantom island in the Atlantic) as a potential base for cod fishing. The following year, Jay dispatched a further two ships from Bristol, the *Trinity* and the *George*. The ships returned with so much cod that the city told the Hanseatic League that it was not interested in negotiations to reopen the Icelandic fishery.[45]

In 1497, five years after Christopher Columbus landed in the Bahamas, the Venetian seaman Giovanni Caboto (otherwise called John Cabot) sailed westward from Bristol. Cabot was gentle, temperate, not the kind of man you imagine as a fearless mariner. As a Venetian, he came from a place where ships and trade routes were everything, where men lived as far as men could live in and off the sea. Like Columbus, he wasn't looking for fishing grounds; he was looking for a north-west or north-east passage to the Indies, to Japan, and his plan was to make England the maritime centre of a trade in spices.

Abruptly, in mid-ocean, his crew noticed something extraordinary. The water under the keel had become shallower. They were moving over undersea mountains – and with them were fish. The crew stopped to catch provisions. The undersea mountains that Cabot's crew had noticed were the Grand Banks, where warmer water flowing north from Florida collides with cold water travelling south from Labrador. The Banks extend for hundreds of miles. Cabot was much less interested in the Grand Banks than in the dream of a passage to the land where 'all the spices of the world, as well as the jewels, can be found'. That land would give him incalculable wealth. And Cabot needed money; he'd come to London to hide from his creditors. But he didn't understand the money he was seeing. Fortunately, his crew was from Bristol, and the men in it understood that a rich catch of fish was wealth indeed. And these fish were enormous, numerous, heavy. A little further to the west they came across land, steep hills, covered in trees. Cabot thought it was Asia, the home of 'the great Khan', now claimed for England. So, in hope, they followed the long coast south, searching for the great island of Japan, but eventually they turned back, having seen no signs of habitation except a few notches in the trees.

Cabot announced that he had found a new land – a new-found land. He felt sure that somehow there would be a way to Asia. But it was his crew's discovery of the silvery riches of the Grand Banks that was to fuel both economic and naval greatness in the years to come.[46] A letter written by an Italian visiting London, who heard tales of Cabot's voyage, recounts how 'the Sea there is swarming with fish which can be taken not only with the net but in baskets let down with a stone, so that it sinks in the water'. The Bristol men aboard Cabot's ship the *Matthew* returned certain that their ships would 'bring so many fish that this kingdom would have no further need of Iceland'.[47] By 1500, huge fishing and whaling fleets sailed every year for the Grand Banks.

So our national love affair with flaky white fish, ideally served plain and simple, was the direct result of our longer love affair with spices, with cinnamon and galangal (a kind of ginger used in the modern world mostly in Thai cooking), nutmeg and mace. On the maps – even the increasingly sophisticated maps of the fifteenth century – it looked so straightforward. There *had* to be a short route westward to the spice lands of Ind and Cathay. The reason it looked likely was because of the fundamental mistake that most expedition leaders made: they believed the globe was far smaller than it actually is. Men like Cabot set out under a misapprehension; they thought what they wanted was quite close, and they weren't willing to learn that an entire continent stood in the way.

Cabot tried again a year later. No one knows what happened to him. He may have returned and died in England, or he may have foundered somewhere in the icy waters that kept men like him from the rich, warm paradises they craved. Rumours began to circulate that Cabot had been murdered by the Spaniards in the New World for his maps. His son, Sebastian (1474–1557), followed in his footsteps, exploring various parts of the world for England and Spain. It was Sebastian who, in 1494, described the land his father had found:

'There are a lot of white bears and very big deers, big as horses, and many other animals. As well there are infinite fish: plaices, salmons, very long soles, 1 yard long and many other varieties of fish. Most of them are called cod.'

The vagueness with which the fish are identified is telling. The Cabots just didn't care. Again it was the ordinary sailors on their ships who recognised this silver-backed treasure. The younger Cabot may have made it to Hudson Bay; eventually, however, Henry VIII cut off his funding and he moved first to Spain and then to Venice, and then back to Spain. Here he was paid to convey colonists to the Moluccas. The romance of seeking the lands of the east was by now a cover story for less exalted kinds of colonialism. Cabot's expedition floundered and he returned to Spain with only one ship to face disciplinary charges. He still had his maps, however, which allowed him to wriggle off the hook – so to speak – and in later life he assured everyone that he and he alone had led the great expedition that found and claimed Newfoundland and discovered the Banks.[48]

Henry VIII was reluctant to fund trade voyages, but enthusiastic about battleships. During his reign, the English navy expanded, both to defend and to extend the rule of England. Not only was the navy manned by seamen from the fishing fleets, and sometimes even by fishing boats, but the cod of the Grand Banks gradually became a small but crucial part of naval supplies. Henry's great ship the *Mary Rose* was stocked with salt cod. Each group or mess's ration was boiled in its own bag, and then served to the men, without any additional seasoning to make it palatable. Dried cod was a staple; it still came mostly from the North Sea and around Iceland, but one of the cod served to the crew of the *Mary Rose* on that morning in July came from the north-east coast of the Americas, from Newfoundland.[49] It is possible to exaggerate the significance of this; only one sample was *probably* sourced from even more distant fishing grounds off the North American coast. But we can easily imagine the link between Newfoundland cod, caught by an English boat, its usefulness to Henry's burgeoning navy, and investment in North American fisheries.

In order to transport the cod back to England, they had first to be dried, salted, or smoked. This required at least temporary land settlements, and ultimately cod did make a contribution to the North American settler colonies. However, it is just as likely that the single American cod on the *Mary Rose* was imported from the Netherlands with cod from other Baltic or Hanseatic fisheries, as well as the many other cod on the *Mary Rose* that have been traced to those places. Always very eager to buy food rather than to catch or grow it, the English Tudors in all likelihood were perfectly willing to pay cash for fish, just as they were willing to sell fish for cash.[50] Rather than seeing the presence of Newfoundland cod as proof of English commitment to colonisation, we could actually take it as proof of the characteristic English interest in shopkeeping. Cabot had only found the cod because he was looking for commodities to sell. His crew understood that cod was valuable merchandise. If this is the beginnings of empire, it is the beginnings of an empire of mercantilism; the English empire was all about trade, and about controlling trade routes.

But there was an overlap between the control of trade routes and the control of fishing waters. We think of the Cod Wars as a phenomenon of the 1960s, when actually they originate in Tudor times. Already, the English fishing fleets had managed to set up camps in Iceland, and their competition for cod with the Icelandic fishing fleet had become increasingly ferocious. They did not see such camps as homes or settlements. They saw them as a temporary necessity.

The wars were not always with Icelandic fleets. By the early fifteenth century, fishing fleets of two- and three-masted ketches with rudders were used to sailing far from the coast of Europe. Every codfish had to be stolen from waters that the Icelanders reasonably thought were theirs and that other fleets also aspired to exploit. Extending the range of the English fleet from Iceland and the Faroes to the Americas was a response to violent incidents such as the murder of Englishman John the Broad at Grindavik in Iceland in 1532. His killers were not Icelandic, but members of the Hanseatic League.[51] And the fishing fleets that made it to Newfoundland began to ply a trade as lucrative as the spice trade Cabot had longed for.

So the fishing fleet began to set up larger settlements in Newfoundland in order to salt and dry the cod. Like many other private ventures, this was at least in part the result of government sponsorship and government contracts. Cod was salted and dried on the shore on huge wooden racks; first gutted and decapitated, it was then split in half and salted. It was vital to get the level of salt right; too much would make the fish unpalatable, and too little meant it turned red when dried. In inclement weather it was sometimes dried in smokehouses, but more often it was simply spread out in the sun. When ready it was piled into the ship and taken back to England. But as England gained ascendancy in the naval wars with Spain and Portugal, the fishing fleet began to head south with cargoes to sell to the Basques, who had themselves once fished the Newfoundland coast and had developed a taste for salt cod. The English could trade their salt cod for characteristically Mediterranean products such as wine and olive oil, to be sold in England. The fleet helped to turn England into a nation of shopkeepers. It also began the long-standing triangular trade between the west coast ports of England and the Americas, with ports on the southern Atlantic coast making the third leg of the triangle; ultimately, this would lead to the slave trade.[52]

Investment was required to obtain salt. England is relatively short of salt. Many English towns with a name ending in '-wich', derived from an Old English word for a shallow bay or salt spring, were at one time salt producers. But there was never enough of it. So cod fishing depended on salt from France and North Africa. The air in England had never been dry enough to allow the production of stockfish. The English created a summer-cured salted dried fish which they called Poor John, a fish so notoriously stinky that the monster Caliban in Shakespeare's thoroughly seagoing play The Tempest is said to reek of it.[53]

Poor John was not especially appealing. Like John Barleycorn, he needed to be beaten before he could be eaten; according to John Collins, writing in 1682, he had to be beaten with a mallet for half an hour or more, then soaked for three days, then boiled for an hour, and finally cooked with butter and eggs. Even this elaborate treatment may not have made him tasty. Later cooks like eighteenth-century cook-book writer Hannah Glasse suggested soaking Poor John in milk and warm water.[54] Much later, the flushing toilet has sometimes been suggested as the best way to manage salt fish. It's unpromising.

Salt mattered in England because it preserved many kinds of flesh, not just fish. Salt was regarded as of strategic importance because salt cod and corned beef formed the rations of the British navy. Because of its apparent power to prevent corruption, salt also possessed powerful magical significance. In the rite of baptism, a dab of salt on the baby's tongue was meant to exorcise demons.[55] The use of salt to preserve cod was merely an adaptation of its use in the thirteenth and fourteenth centuries to preserve herring. While the British and French navies used salt cod, Dutch ships, both for war and commerce, continued to be provisioned with salt-cured herring.

———————

At the opposite end of the scale of courage, the angler is a central figure in the English landscape of small quiet rivers. Picture the calm of the fisherman, line cast in the river, waiting. The most primitive way of getting food. The line between land and water is the ultimate boundary, one that is dangerous to cross. Rivers, like oceans, often mark boundaries; many old county boundaries simply followed the lines of rivers, as do many national boundaries to this day. Crossing running water is still seen as a significant act, a commitment. Crossing the Rubicon; one more river to cross and that's the river of Jordan. In the water, everything is different.

Thinking about river fishing involves a critical distinction or two; one is the distinction between coarse fish and game fish. Game fish includes salmon, trout and char; everything else is a coarse fish, although there is some dispute about grayling. Essentially, game fish are caught with a fly, while coarse fish are caught with bait. The distinction is not really about zoology but social class; game fish are the preserve of the aristocracy and gentry, while lesser mortals have to make do with fish like chub. I asked the lock-keeper at Buscot, the last-but-one lock on the Upper Thames, about chub; he said people often get chub in Buscot, but it's full of little bones, and honestly it's easier to go to Tesco if you want fish. Fishermen and women also have to observe the game season. This is different for every river, but in general the seasons for both salmon and trout begin in spring; the salmon season ends around Halloween, while the trout season ends a little sooner, in early autumn. Many river fish have at one time or another been food, but salmon and trout dominate the English imagination.

In most nations around the world, rivers are public property: if you can get onto the river from the road or elsewhere it is yours to enjoy. English rivers are different. The rivers, access to them and the right to fish them are in private ownership. Every inch of bank and every square foot of fishing rights from the moment the water emerges from the ground to the tidal estuary is owned by someone, enshrined in ancient statute, and if you are one of those lucky few, you have the right to call yourself a riparian owner.[56] So important are riparian rights and the right to erect fish weirs that they are referenced in both Magna Carta in 1215 and the Grand Remonstrance in 1641.

Fish connected the people with the waterways of their islands. To fish is to observe. It is to own the countryside with your eyes. Those who fish come to a detailed knowledge of the animals and plants that intersect with the river and the fish who live in it, and who may compete with anglers for prey. In his book *Waterside Companions*, angler Tag Barnes gives us elegant vignettes of *Wind in the Willows* riverbankers; a stoat, fighting a rat for its life; a robin 'executioner', whose beak ends in a deadly spike, so he can kill with a single blow behind the head where it meets the neck vertebra. The robin preys delightedly on the fishermen's maggots. Barnes sees the robin's voraciousness as a hidden truth that parallels the angler's own devouring passion. Bats, especially pipistrelles, turn out to take fishing flies as if they were real flies. They get entangled in the line and have to be rescued. Barnes particularly hates swans. For him, they deserve 'both barrels of a 12 bore shotgun'.[57]

Those who fish the rivers of England generally come to know and understand the unique bounty of chalk streams. Down in their clear waters, where the temperature barely changes from winter to summer, the nymphs, shrimps, snails and young fish multiply. In other kinds of rivers, swollen and dirty with winter rains, they might be having a hard time, but here they thrive. The yearling brown trout is small but perfectly formed, about the size of a finger. Most baby trout are devoured before they have a chance to grow and mature, but the successful ones carve out a river territory, a space no more than a few feet square, with a feeding spot and a resting spot. That feeding spot in gravel shallows is what fishermen try to find.[58] Chalk-stream fish have been sought for centuries, but nothing substantial was written on the subject until the 1486 *Book of St Albans*, in which Dame Juliana Berners wrote a calendar of appropriate flies for use in particular months, replicating the behaviour of insects.

The preparation of her fishing tackle involved much effort and skill. She began by cutting a staff a fathom and a half long, of hazel, willow or aspen. It had to be cut between Michaelmas and Candlemas (the end of September and the beginning of February). The fishing line was made using high-quality long hairs from the tail of a white horse; later, people were advised to choose a stallion or gelding, as mares urinate on their own tails and weaken the hairs. The hairs were dyed so that different hairs could be selected for different times of year or for different water – brown for dark and sluggish water, for example. The individual hairs had to be plaited and twisted together to make links of sufficient strength. There were no fishing reels; the line was attached directly to a loop at the end of the rod. Making hooks involved heating a needle in a fire to render it workable, raising a barb, filing the point, tempering the needle again in the fire before bending it to shape, and then hammering the tail of the hook flat and filing it. Finally the hook was heated red hot and then quenched in water to make it hard and strong. The level of ingenuity involved is startling.[59]

Walter Scott once said that 'angling alone offers to man the degree of half business, half idleness, which the fair sex find in their needlework or knitting, which, employing the hands, leaves the mind at liberty and occupying the attention so far as is necessary to remove the painful sense of the vacuity, yet yields room for contemplation, whether upon things heavenly or earthly, cheerful or melancholy'. One such man was the gentle fisherman philosopher of the seventeenth century, Izaak Walton, who said that 'God did never make a more calm, quiet, innocent recreation than angling.' But the calm that rises from the pages of his evergreen book *The Compleat Angler* is forced. An unswerving Royalist, the defeat his side suffered in the Civil War taught him that all beauty was vulnerable; he reacted by going fishing. For him, angling was Anglicanism. His biblical epigraph from 1 Thessalonians, 'Study to be quiet', links the pastoral calm of the angler with silent prayer and contemplation. Walton's angler reflected on a fractured world by celebrating (and recommending) a natural order that is secret, silent, subtle, like God himself. Like the waters it wanders, into sidestreams and deep still pools.

The book is in the form of a dialogue between the fisherman Piscator and the huntsman Venator. Venator disdains the humble chub as 'the worst fish that swims', but Piscator promises to make it a good fish by dressing it. Venator is duly delighted by the chub, so Piscator explains his method, giving us a detailed sense of what seventeenth-century diners wanted from a fish. The chub, he says, is 'full of small forked bones, dispersed through all his body' and 'the flesh of him is not firm, but short and tasteless'. He explains that providing the chub is carefully gutted and cleaned of weeds and grass it may be dressed with 'some sweet herbs' in its belly, tied to a spit and roasted, basted often with vinegar or with 'verjuice and butter, with good store of salt mixed with it'. Or, he suggests, 'broil him on charcoal, or wood coal, that are free from smoke; and all the time he is a-broiling, baste him with the best sweet butter, and good store of salt mixed with it. And, to this, add a little thyme cut exceedingly small.' He concludes that 'a Chub newly taken and newly dressed, is so much better than a Chub of a day's keeping after he is dead, that I can compare him to nothing so fitly as to cherries newly gathered from a tree, and others that have been bruised and lain a day or two in water'.

Walton greatly understood and admired bait animals. On worms, he writes, 'of these there be very many sorts, some bred only in the earth, as the earthworm; others of or amongst plants, as the dug worm, and others bred either out of excrement's, or in the bodies of living creatures, as in the horns of sheep or dear, or some of dead flesh as the magnet'.[60] Lovingly, he alludes to the preferences of his favourite fish: 'for the trout, the dew worm which some also called the lob worm and the brandling are the chief and especially the first for a great trout and the latter for the less'. Walton makes notes on worm husbandry; he urges helping them recover by putting milk or cream into them by drops or with beaten egg; and yet this fattening leads but to the hook. Caterpillar and worm husbandry are part of the angler's skills.[61]

Walton's favourite fish was the trout, 'a generous fish ... a fish that feeds clean and purely, in the swiftest streams', best for 'daintiness of taste'. It reads as though the writer spent every day outdoors by a chalk stream. In fact, Walton's book is drawn from other books, rather than being the fruit of natural observation.[62] And this is part and parcel of Walton's sense of angling as a practice outside time, not subject to the vagaries of men's lives. He assumes that the angler owns the waters he fishes, and depicts Piscator eating his catch. His work is about the way the gentry saw themselves, rather than the way they actually behaved; a book stream of book fish and book recipes.

The problems inherent in this approach were not lost on one reader: Richard Franck in his own book *Northern Memoirs* (1694) attacked Walton for historical and technical inaccuracy. Franck fished for Scottish salmon, not Staffordshire trout, and had served under Cromwell, so it is hardly surprising that in their only meeting Walton 'huffed away'.[63] Franck, too, couches his book as a dialogue, and so this most solitary of pursuits becomes conversational. Franck also saw the countryside as the embodiment of classical pastoral. Yet his advice was often detailed and practical: like Walton, he was interested in suiting baits to the fish hunted. There was also a lyricism in his writing, an imaginative curiosity about water and its inhabitants:

> We begin to discover those silent and solitary deeps, those rapid and swift falls of water, besides those stiff and strong streams, that invite us to treat the family of fish. So that I conceive it is almost impossible to direct a line, and miss a reward: And the

bottom, if you please, let us examine that with ground-bait, to prove the effects of our art and skill, to summons contribution from so generous an adventure.[64]

Most medieval fishermen, however, had chosen simpler methods: unauthorised traps, tucked away on inconspicuous stretches of water. While poaching was a crime, the laws against fish poaching were far less savage than those against the poaching of furred game. One man caught in the act of grabbing a tench from a pond explained that 'my dear wife had lain a bed a right full month and for the great desire she had to eat tench I went to the bank of the pond to take just one tench, and never other fish from the pond did I take'.[65]

Poachers need to know even more than anglers, in order to outwit both the fish and the legitimate fisherman. Poaching was just as addictive and exciting as legitimate angling. It wasn't because the poachers loved the taste of fish, and it wasn't always about the need for food; it was the sport they enjoyed. One poacher, a blacksmith, 'could hardly keep his tools in his hands on certain days when the trout were in the pool below the bridge, often went angling. When he deserted the smithy he would leave a note on the door for any farmer. It would state briefly, "up the water" or "down the water", and the caller would either go away or go up-and-down the water to find the smith.'[66] Poaching was often less active than this; it could involve leaving lines for fish in the river to be checked later. A poacher might set two to three dozen lines on a particularly favourable bit of stream. The dangerous moment came when checking the lines. That was when the poacher had to watch for the gamekeeper. However remote the stream, the right to fish in it was owned by somebody, however little sense that made. 'Can a man own the clouds, the rain, the streams that trickle over the rocks? Can he own what the herring takes from the pool without permission, what the otter carries in his whiskered mouth?'[67] Alas, he can. But the poacher could still take his share.

Fishing sounds cruel. Yes, fish are cold, and unlike us. As Keith Thomas shows in *Man and the Natural World*,[68] the creatures that excite most sympathy are mammals. Fish did not cry out or change expression, which enabled angling to retain its reputation as a philosophical, contemplative, innocent pastime, one given impeccable ancestry by the New Testament and particularly suitable for clergymen. Fishing, unlike hunting, had never been forbidden to clerics by the medieval church; and in the sixteenth and seventeenth centuries it was the favourite recreation of many who thundered against other animal sports. Commentators objected to some details, like the use of live bait or the practice of spearing fish, but they seldom attacked the sport itself.

Yet before the nineteenth century, fishing too was sometimes attacked because it inflicted pain. In 1799, Charles Lamb described anglers as 'patient tyrants, weak inflicters of pangs intolerable, cool Devils'; whilst to Byron angling was 'that solitary vice': 'whatever Izaak Walton sings or says:/ The quaint, old, cruel coxcomb, in his gullet/ Should have a hook, and a small trout to pull it.'[69] Eighteenth-century satirist John Wolcot or 'Peter Pindar' had also sided with the hunted fish:

Enjoy thy stream, O harmless fish;
And when an angler for his dish,
Through gluttony's vile sin,
Attempts, a wretch, to pull thee out,
God give thee strength, O gentle trout,
To pull the raskall in![70]

The Romantics were right: modern research suggests that fish are not robotic sensory apparatuses, but rather that they have a consciousness like our own. Fish can, for example, be tricked by visual illusions just as human beings can.[71]

Yet the most serious danger to fish has never been from hook and worm, but from industry. Pollution of the rivers even in George III's day began to reduce the numbers of barbel, trout, bream, dace, gudgeon, flounder and other fish which had in Elizabethan times swum in the London Thames, just as it would reduce the thirty different kinds of fish found in the Trent in the Stuart era. The overall effect of human action, whether deliberate or inadvertent, was to bring about a dramatic reduction in the wildlife with which England, its rivers and seas had once teemed, at exactly the moment both where the population was climbing, the Corn Laws and bad harvests made grain crops expensive, and enclosures made ordinary land unavailable to ordinary people. The increasing numbers forced to move into the towns could expect to find there only preserved fish, or none. Food historians sometimes behave as if everybody in a vanished past had access to foods that were, in fact, always for the few. Probably, had many been able to eat fresh perch, there would be even fewer left today. The inconvenient truth is that only industrial fishing and fish processing has ever made fish available to the vast majority of people.

———

Once, the Thames offered many fishy delights. Juliana Berners had praised the Thames angler: 'he hath his wholesome walk … a sweet air at the sweet savour of the meadow flowers that may kiss him hungry'. William Harrison noted salmon and other fish on the Thames in the sixteenth century with delight:

> What should I speak of the fat and sweet salmons, daily taken in this stream, and that in such plenty (after the time of the smelt be past) as no river in Europe is able to exceed it? What store also of barbels, trout, chevins [chub], perches, smelts, breams, roaches, daces, gudgeons, flounders, shrimps etc., are commonly to be had therein.

However, Harrison deplores 'the insatiable avarice of the fishermen', and exclaims, 'oh that this river might be spared even one year from nets, etc.! But alas then should many a poor man be undone.'[72]

By the eighteenth century, fishermen had colonised most stretches of the riverbank in the immediate vicinity of the markets of London.

By 1798, some four hundred earned their living between Deptford and London Bridge. One of the most ancient trades on the river was that of the eel boatmen, who would search for eels buried in the mud and sell them at the eel market on Blackfriars Stairs on Sunday mornings. Many people hated eel, because they thought it came from the decomposing remains of an animal, or from mud; others believed it was created when a horse hair was suspended in the water. Roach were believed to be most easily caught in autumn when the water of the river was coloured by rain; and it was said in the early nineteenth century that you could catch haddock in your hand at London Bridge because the fish were so blinded by the spray of the fast water, the rapids of the bridge, that they could not see where they were going.

By the second half of the nineteenth century, fishing in the tidal river – the river below Teddington – came almost to an end, with just a few whitebait and shrimp being caught. The middle and upper waters still had perch and roach, carp and chub, barbel and bream, but the tidal river died in a flood of pollution. The salmon vanished. The lobsters disappeared. The flounder was extinct. The shad was gone. At the height of the river's pollution in the late nineteenth century there was a sad warning in Richard Jefferies' 1885 novel *After London* that the Thames would become a vast stagnant swamp. So desperate did the situation remain that, even in the 1960s, there was the case of a famous angler and columnist for a national newspaper painting spots on a salmon and claiming it was a Thames brown trout. He almost got away with it.

———

Despite the claims of William Harrison, the Thames had never been a great river for salmon. Salmon must return to the river from which they set out as smolts to mature, and nobody really knows why or how, but from early times people noticed the phenomenon, and understood the fish to have magical properties. Since there were early salmon fisheries on the Tay, the Spey, the Tweed and the Dee, the salmon became associated with Scotland. There are salmon in English streams too, but not in such abundance. Their life cycle is extraordinary. The salmon's first return occurs after only a year at sea; they are then called grilse. Others stay at sea and grow; they are fattest when they have come straight from the ocean. Most shoot out their milt over the eggs and then die of exhaustion, but a few survive to reach the sea once more.[73]

In spite of their modern troubles, salmon still carry a shimmer of power. Such animals were once seen as powerful spiritual beings; Celtic mythology links the salmon with knowledge, and with prophecy and inspiration, because of the fish's ability to return to its birthplace. The most famous role for the salmon of knowledge is in the legend of Finn McCool, the most renowned of Ireland's early semi-mythical heroes, a peerless warrior, poet and seer. As a child, Finn settled down to study with an old druid poet and seer, who lived near a sacred pool of wisdom because he planned to catch its resident salmon of knowledge. When the druid finally caught the fish, Finn was instructed to cook it for his master but warned not to partake of it himself. However, while turning the roasting fish on a spit, Finn burned his thumb by bursting a blister that rose up on the salmon's skin, and put the burned thumb in his mouth. On being served the fish, his master asked, 'Did you eat of the flesh?' Once he had been told the truth, the druid offered Finn the whole fish, from which he gained all of the salmon's knowledge. Ever afterwards, when Finn sucked his thumb, he could prophesy the future.

Careful note was taken of salmon assets; the Domesday Book listed England's salmon fisheries in its natural resource indices. These were trade and commodity resources, and were not to feed the local population. The Romans had shipped salted salmon home from Gaul, and long-distance trade really picked up in the medieval era. Consumption of salmon shifted from fresh local fish to preserved fish transported by sea. Glasgow merchants in the fifteenth century dispatched salted salmon to Flanders, France and Holland. Salmon rubbed with salt and pepper was smoked with peat and shipped in a wooden barrel; leathery and very salty, it bore little resemblance to today's soft, mildly smoked strips. Scottish pickled salmon eventually replaced salted and kippered. Boiled in salt, and packed with a topping of brown vinegar, sometimes with added spices, Aberdeen's fish merchants exported to Bilbao, Marseille and Venice, and also to London. Before the Industrial Revolution, Newcastle was famous for salmon, where it was pickled with West Indian allspice, black pepper and vinegar. Berwick-on-Tweed shipped the fresh article to London aboard sailing ships; with a stiff north wind, the journey from Perth in the 1760s could take just sixty hours. If the prevailing winds were in the wrong direction, though, the catch was unloaded, boiled, pickled and stored, and set off again when the winds were favourable. In the 1780s, Perth merchants shipped the first salmon packed in ice to London's Billingsgate fish market. In this way, Scottish salmon could become an English way of eating.

In Scotland, Daniel Defoe found salmon 'in such plenty as is scarce credible, and so cheap, that to those who have any substance to buy with, it is not worth their while to catch it themselves'; this was in Sutherland, in northern Scotland. But then fishing for salmon in Scotland became a popular recreation for the rich. The most accessible Scottish river, the Tweed, was a particularly valued destination. By the 1850s, the locals who fished for a living or to supplement their protein supply could no longer afford the rents the English gentry and industrialists were prepared to pay. Local fishing for the table was pushed out.

In London, salmon was and is a luxury food. Outside Scotland, the solution seemed simple: tinned salmon. In the British general election of December 1923, fought principally over the incumbent Conservative Party's plans to solve unemployment with tariff reform, Liberal Party campaign materials featured tinned salmon, described as 'the people's food'; in reply to encouragement to eat more salmon, the voice of the people replied, 'We Can't, We Can't, the Conservatives are going to put a tax on it and make it cost us more.'[74] The proposed tariff, the Liberals explained, applied only to tinned salmon, fresh salmon being the food of 'well-to-do people'. An advertisement for John West tinned salmon from 1938 depicts a mother and child crouched over the tin:

'Daddy will be glad it's salmon, won't he?'

The first plump flesh of a noble salmon, cooked to such tenderness that it melts in your mouth. 'You were right when you said we have something tasty tonight.' Sealed in its own rich natural oils – that's the goodness of John West's middle cut. 'Anyone would think that boy never saw food before'; a juicy red slice of salmon is a full-sized meal for a hungry man. 'Well, I feel fine after that!'

Further images beside the text show a man sitting opposite a woman; the table bears a tablecloth and elaborate cutlery and china. Also on show is a stove in which the salmon has been warmed through in its tin.[75]

————

On the coasts, the fishing fleets had developed cultures and lifestyles of their own over the centuries. Fishing was a man's job, but every stage of it employed people, including those who made the means to catch; the ships, the dories, the nets, lines, poles and spears, but just as much those making salt, or barrels and carts, those hawking in the fishing markets and streets, and, ultimately, the cooks. The oddity of sea fishing was that fishermen and their support staff had to be mobile. They had to move to follow the fish. Women and children prepared bait, repaired gear and sold the catch, while men concentrated on catching fish. In small communities, fishing *was* the community.

Fishing villages were as subject to boom and bust as gold-mining towns. In the seventeenth century, the Lowestoft herring industry expanded enormously. The decline caused by the three Dutch wars, which came immediately after the English Civil War, was reversed, and by 1690 the industry reached its zenith. In the busy autumn season, almost three-quarters of the town's male population were fishing or handling and processing fish. Women and children also helped in the processing, and in the maintenance of fishing gear. The herring fleet brought its catch into Scarborough, and groups of women, some from as far afield as Scotland, came to meet it. They were ready to clean, salt, pickle and barrel the catch.[76]

The fisherfolk of Yorkshire had their own special festivals, notably Staithes Fair, at which joints of beef and ham were roasted – anything but fish – for it was a time of reunion and open house. Staithes Fair had its serious purpose too; it was where crews were rearranged, half-yearly accounts settled, quarrels resolved and matrimonial matches made. It was a kind of reaffirmation and renewal of community. As the fishing declined at Staithes, so did the fair. Eventually, it degenerated into little more than an annual funfair, but by then the fishing had ended too. It is now an Arts and Heritage Festival.

While fishermen could earn more money than was possible for those in rural communities, their work was seasonal and often involved harsh physical suffering. There was no unemployment benefit; the families of fishermen were often forced to undertake other forms of seasonal labour to make ends meet, such as potato picking. Pheasant shooting, blackberry picking and hawthorn gathering also helped keep the families going; at brambling time the children could make up to two shillings, picking the blackberries not as food for themselves, but to sell.[77] The margin between sufficiency and want was so fine that few fisherfolk could put money by as an insurance against illness or bad weather, even though they knew that both might happen.[78]

If the men's lives were hard, the women's could be harder. In northeast England in 1858, an observer noticed tall stalwart sunburnt women in middle age, wearing old wood bonnets, tattered bed gown skirts, stockings without feet, and old shoes, carrying their shrimping nets on their shoulders. They had been fishing five miles from home; the sand and mud on Teesside is so broad many ranged through it for two hours before they came to water at low tide. In their skirts, the fisherwomen often waded up to their waists, fishing for shrimps. There were many dangerous holes, but pushing the net before you acted as a safety measure. Some women shrimped at Redcar itself: nineteenth-century observers reported that there were as many as forty nets at once, all women. At home, the fishermen's wives had plenty of other work to do. Because of the rough sea, the men were sometimes ashore larking about in the street in crowds, playing pickaback, while the women were indoors mending the nets or baiting long lines. Using unopened mussels that they'd gathered themselves, a long line could take hours to bait. Other kinds of bait also had to be gathered. The women did it every day. It was mucky, smelly, laborious, repetitive and time-consuming, but for at least six months in every year it was part of daily work – and sometimes in winter the mussels were frozen and they cut your hands. 'They find work when we have none,' said the men.

Whitby, now associated with only a single ship, the one that brought Dracula to England, was in Victorian times far richer in marine associations. The Whitby fishing fleet pursued many different kinds of prey, but the big prize was whales. Whale meat did not feature often on English tables, but the whale fish, as it was incorrectly known, had many commodities to offer. William Scoresby – father and son – became famous for their extraordinary feats of whaling. They were not searching for food, of course, but then, as we have seen, few commercial fishermen were. They were searching for something to sell, and the whale fitted the bill.[79] Whaling became a vital source of maritime experience and mercantile speculation. Every April, as the weather softened, Whitby ships set out for Greenland, the chief whale fishery. They brought back chunks of blubber that had to be rendered. The process turned Whitby into a stinking town, but the whaling captains lived well above the reek, in Georgian houses overlooking the harbour. The town below was made of whale. Whalebones were used as timbers for roofs and walls, and whole houses and workshops were made from giant ribs and jaws. William Scoresby senior took his pet polar bear on a leash to Whitby harbour to fish for his lunch every day. Scoresby had an almost religious faith in whaling. He saw it as a tribute to man's ingenuity and God's grace, given the disparate size of hunter and prey. For him the whale was 'a marvellous enterprise', a kind of immense undiscovered country to be claimed by man. His son William Scoresby junior was a scientist, and an acquaintance of naturalist Joseph Banks, who accompanied fellow Whitby townsman James Cook on his voyages to the Pacific.

'The Greenland Whale Fishery' is a song about the Spitsbergen right whale fishing in the 1720s. It appeared on a broadside around 1725, shortly after the South Sea Company decided to resuscitate the then moribund whaling industry by sending a dozen large ships to Spitsbergen and the Greenland Sea. The song went on being sung for many years, with small changes all the time to bring it up to date. In earlier versions, the whale is a right whale, but over time it becomes a sperm whale. Either way, the ballad is a comment on the callousness of the skipper, who calmly watches his men die but lowers the flag to half mast over the loss of the whale, which gets away. Greenland is a land of death:

> Now, Greenland is a horrid place,
> Where our fisher lads have to go,
> Where the rose and the lily never bloom in spring;
> No there's only ice and snow.

While the words apply strictly to whaling, they could serve as a lament for the dead of the whole English fishing fleet, pushed into extreme conditions by competition and commerce.

The archive of World War II memories gathered by the BBC has an account of an encounter with whale meat in the Second World War:

> It had been soaked overnight, steam-cooked, and soaked again, then blanketed with a sauce, but still it tasted exactly what it sounds like – tough meat with a distinctly fishy flavour, ugh. Just this once the next-door's cat ate it!
>
>   Yes, we laugh about it all now, yet after all these years I still cannot bear to see good food wasted or thrown away – but I think I could make an exception with whale meat.[80]

A distinctly fishy flavour! That's the last thing an English diner wants from their seafood. I once ate whale meat myself at a conference banquet in Vardø, where thin carpaccio slices were served. If nobody had told me it was whale meat, I would have taken it for tuna carpaccio; a little gelatinous, rich, deep pink, tender, almost sweet. It sounds to me as though the Second World War speaker overcooked the whale, perhaps in sheer horror at its oddity.

––––––––––

For oceanographer Callum Roberts, fishing itself fundamentally and disastrously alters the life of fish as a species: successful fishing destroys its own future. The lives of fishermen too have become very much harder. In the past, fishermen could at least hope for a good catch as a result of their labours. From 1889, the mass deployment of bottom trawlers led to ever-increasing catches – in that year, more than twice as many bottom-feeding fish such as cod, haddock and plaice were caught in British waters as we catch today. The peak came in 1938, when the fishing fleet landed over five times more fish than we do now. For every hour spent fishing today in boats bristling with the latest fish-finding electronics, fishermen land just 6 per cent of what they did 120 years ago. The reason for this is the effect of fishing on fish size. As Roberts explains, when you exploit a population, the average size of the animals gets smaller. Most fishing methods are size selective, choosing animals that have bodies or mounds larger than most. Over time, therefore, fishing alters the balance between large and small, and young and old, in a population.[81]

This was always the case. In the ancient shell middens of California, where mussels were found to have decreased in size by over 40 per cent during a period of more than 9,000 years, we see the same picture. While the risk of death from fishing increases as an animal grows, evolution favours those that grow slowly, mature younger and smaller, and reproduce earlier, which is exactly what we now see in the wild. Young fish produce many times fewer eggs than older large-bodied ones, and many industrial fisheries are now so efficient that few animals survive more than a year. The loss of larger animals and smaller species usually leads the fishing fleet to change to a different kind of fish. This fish stock then undergoes the same changes.

––––––––––

Fishing, then, is always a trade of exploration and innovation; it has to be. But the eating of fish is often highly conventional. One reason for the continuing preference for fresh fish was the custom of sending presents of fish to friends; it did not die out during the Middle Ages. Before the coming of the railway, it was still quite usual for those living by the sea to send gifts of fresh fish to their acquaintances inland. In February 1808, Jane Austen sent 'four pairs of small soles' to Kintbury Rectory in Berkshire, with a note hoping they would arrive while still fresh. Mrs Bennet, in *Pride and Prejudice*, is horrified to find that there is no fish to be had on a Monday, when Mr Bingley is coming to dinner, because there has been no catch on the previous day, a Sunday.[82] As improved methods of transport brought fish of all kinds to inland markets, the fish from ponds, on which some rural communities had formerly depended, began to fall out of favour because of their muddy taste. At Donwell Abbey in *Emma*, too, 'the old Abbey fishponds' are still in existence, though they are viewed as a curiosity rather than as a source of fish.[83] However, a recipe for a sauce for carp does appear in a collection associated with the Austen family. Maria Rundell offers two recipes for carp in her *New System of Domestic Cookery*, published in 1805, though these are very extensively sauced, one with black and Jamaican pepper, as well as cloves, onion and beef gravy, anchovies, mustard, walnut ketchup and butter, and its own fried roe. The other includes bay leaves, parsley, basil, thyme, both sorts of marjoram, port wine and anchovies, with a final dusting of cayenne and a squeeze of lemon. It seems unlikely that any flavour from the fish would survive, but perhaps that was the point.

The multi-course meal of middle-class Victorian dining ensured fish a place at the tables of the prosperous. In the 1861 edition of Isabella Beeton's *Household Management*, the fishes of the season are carefully listed. For June, the list includes carp, crayfish, herring, lobster, mackerel, mullet, pike, prawns, salmon, sole, tench, trout and turbot, and for December, the list is barbel, brill, carp, cod, crab, eels, dace, gudgeon, haddock, herring, lobster, oysters, porch, pike, shrimps, skate, sprats, sole, tench, thornback, turbot and whiting. Yet the very fact that such a list was needed implies that Beeton's readers were increasingly out of touch with their fishmongers, let alone with what the waters were likely to give them.

Beeton's words do, however, make every effort to widen the range of fish the English can eat. Consider, for example, her description of the barbel:

> This fish takes its name from the barbs or wattels at its mouth; and, in England, is esteemed as one of the worst of the fresh-water fish. It was, however, formerly, if not now, a favourite with the Jews, excellent cookers of fish. Others would boil with it a piece of bacon, that it might have a relish. It is to be met with from two to three or four feet long, and is said to live to a great age. From Putney upwards, in the Thames, some are found of large size; but they are valued only as affording sport to the brethren of the angle.[84]

Such eager enthusiasm for unfamiliar fish is very unusual in England. It is the fish course that usually lays bare our reluctance to try something new. But for one brief shining moment, the Victorians were willing to experiment with the likes of barbel – even though, like many foods, it had only recently become unfamiliar as a result of its decline in the Thames.

The increased demand for fresh fish to supply the new middle-class fish course helped to power the biggest change in fishing, a tragic breakthrough. Once ships were powered by steam engines, the bottom trawler was created, and in the course of Victoria's reign they began working the North Sea, where a fishing ground called the Silver Pits, just south of Dogger Bank, had been discovered; Hull and Grimsby became major trawling ports. As a result, the size of the English trawling fleet expanded from around 130 boats in the early 1840s to over 800 by 1860, helped by the advent of steam-powered railways in getting the fish quickly inland, before the ice packed around it had melted.

The expansion was an unwelcome development to the many thousands of fishers using lines, nets and traps. Increasingly, the trawlers came into conflict with other fishers, and trouble erupted.[85] In the 1850s there were violent protests in Ireland and parts of Britain, with nets burned and trawlermen driven away by intimidation. Like their fourteenth-century predecessors, the fishers complained that trawlers were wiping out fish stocks, especially by destroying fish spawn and immature fish. They argued that trawls cleared the bottom and ruined their bait beds, such that longliners could not get enough mussels and whelks to bait their hooks. Trawlers swept away their drift nets, longlines and crab pots, and crab populations were imperilled by soft crabs being crushed when shedding their shells. Pilchard and herring fishers also claimed that trawls broke up and dispersed schools of fish, driving them away. With the fishing industry at boiling point, the British government appointed a royal commission in 1863 to inquire into the complaints against trawling and investigate other grievances. Their terms were to investigate 'firstly, whether the supply of fish is increasing, stationary, or diminishing; secondly, whether any modes of fishing … are wasteful, or otherwise injurious to the supply of fish; and thirdly, whether the said fisheries are injuriously affected by any legislative restrictions'. The three members of the commission toured the nation, visiting eighty-six fishing communities and taking over a thousand pages of evidence from many hundreds of witnesses. One of the commissioners was the zoologist Thomas Henry Huxley, then only thirty-eight years old but already well known for his robust defence of Charles Darwin's theory of evolution by natural selection. Three years later, the commission concluded that 'fishermen, as a class, are exceedingly unobservant of anything about fish that is not absolutely forced upon them by their daily avocations', and insisted that any technology which increased the size of catches was all to the good.

Perhaps predictably, the lot of fishermen did not improve greatly with these technological advances. After the introduction of steam, many boats were no longer owned by their skippers. Initially, boats often belonged to retired fishermen with links to the local community, but by the later nineteenth century most boats were the property of very much richer men, men who had never been at sea on a fishing boat themselves, men who devoted themselves to golf and billiards, gardens and housebuilding. They might have been highly moral pillars of their local communities, but they knew little about the ordinary men who worked on the trawlers, particularly after the huge growth in fishing pulled in a larger workforce from around 1910 onwards. The shortage of labour meant short-term wage rises for the ordinary fishermen, but there was increasing pressure on skippers, boats and fleets to perform with vast catches. As market prices for fish fell, secrecy enveloped each boat and its skipper, and unsuccessful skippers were very often sacked. Company policies, set by men who had never worked on a fishing boat, also meant that maintenance was neglected. Old boats were often described as insanitary and rat infested, and one observer described a fishing fleet as 'like a set of dented, rusting seagoing dustbins'.[86] Competition also meant that boats had to move further out and further north, so that men were often working on an open deck that jolted and bucked with the sea, with no more than a low rail protecting them from being swept overboard, and machinery that they had to tend in darkness on an icy deck. While steam power had originally made fishing safer, competition made it more and more dangerous.

There had been a tradition whereby trawlermen were given fresh fish for their families at the end of a trip, while skippers gave a few fish to boys from poor families on the quayside, which the boys would then sell. Sometimes, too, a skipper would empty his fish boxes on the floor and invite bystanders to help themselves – the recipients usually being unemployed fishermen who could in this way give their children 'a decent meal once a day'.[87] But the owners disapproved. They prosecuted generous skippers whenever the opportunity arose, turning traditions of charity and sharing into a crime. The trawling industry sucked men into a system that transformed a skilled, satisfying and knowledgeable way of life into a form of paid labour bondage that broke family ties, assaulted moral values, and paid its employees with drink. Like other heavy industries, the steam trawlers used child labour; in Grimsby, orphans and foundlings escaped the miseries of the workhouse by going to sea as apprentices on board the fishing boats. The earliest known fisher lad went to sea in the early nineteenth century and the system continued until the First World War. For more than a century young boys – some only eight years old – went to sea in the traditional sailing boats that braved the North Sea to bring back the fish that kept Grimsby prosperous. It was a brutal life. The same took place in Hull.[88] The scheme was not abandoned until the boats became unprofitable.

But trawler development continued. In 1881, a shipyard in Hull built a steam-powered trawler named the *Zodiac*. It was equipped with a net kept wide open horizontally by doors and heavily armoured planks on either side. For fish, it was the beginning of the end. What did improve were the boat owners' profits.

Trawling and the railways in effect brought a surplus of fish to London, a glut which as Henry Mayhew noted turned it into the staple food of the working classes, with food prices in the 1870s falling in relation to wages.[89] So popular was fish in Victorian times that a series of fish taverns opened in London; the best known was Lovegroves, at Blackwall, which specialised in whitebait. Their preparation is described in detail in a Victorian periodical:

> The fish should be cooked within an hour after being caught,
> or they are apt to cling together. They are cooked in water in a
> pan, from which they are removed as required by a skimmer.
> They are then thrown on a stratum of flour, contained in a large
> napkin, until completely enveloped in flour. In this state they
> are placed in a cullender, and all the superfluous flour removed
> by sifting. They are next thrown into hot melted lard, contained
> in a copper cauldron, or stew vessel, placed over a charcoal fire
> … in about ten minutes they are removed by a fine skimmer,
> thrown into a cullender to drain, and then served up quite hot.
> At table they are flavoured with cayenne and lemon juice and
> eaten with brown bread and butter; iced punch being the
> favourite accompanying beverage.[90]

Whitebait was also the basis of a dinner held every year to celebrate the end of the parliamentary session, a custom introduced by the younger William Pitt at the end of the eighteenth century, and a major factor in establishing the standing of the river taverns.[91]

The most elaborate kinds of fish taverns were those that served turtle soup, which was highly elaborate and difficult to prepare. As we saw from Mrs Beeton, an enormous diversity of fish shoaled through Georgian, Victorian and Edwardian meals. A well-heeled gentleman might eat fish at every meal – breakfast, lunch, tea and dinner. (At tea, he might enjoy bloater cream sandwiches, egg and anchovy sandwiches, or potted salmon sandwiches.)[92] He might come to eat fish during more than one course at lunch or dinner, savouring an hors d'oeuvre made of fresh caviar or pickled oysters, followed by turtle soup for the soup course, before the fish course proper, after which came a savoury known as Scotch Woodcock, scrambled eggs on toast spread with anchovy paste. (This enthusiasm led to the use of separate silver- or silver-plate fish knives and forks; in earlier periods, fish had been eaten with a silver fork and a piece of bread.) Middling families could breakfast on fish – kedgeree, smoked haddock or salmon, oysters or even caviar, while in Blackpool, sea bream or haddock was baked in bacon rashers like game.[93] A working-class Victorian might eat kippers for breakfast, shellfish for supper and snacks, and plaice, mackerel, sprats, fresh herrings, even sole for dinner. No wonder, then, that a cookbook devoted entirely to fish cookery was published in 1883 by Isabella Thwaites.

Posh dinner parties were not the only thing that kept the market going; the newly urban poor were also experimenting with fish. From Roman times, fish had been used to flavour otherwise dull carbohydrates – grain, roots or bread. In an unlikely fashion, the stinky Roman fish sauce survived as a component of the Victorian working-class tea, in the form of the kipper and the herring. Working-class people enjoyed the strong flavour. The word relish appears frequently. George Sala described dockworkers enjoying an evening meal of 'a mess of potatoes, with one solitary red herring smashed up therein "to give it a relish"'.[94] The herring the Victorian poor used as a relish would have come mostly from Great Yarmouth, where the catch was harvested and cured in autumn, or from Northumberland, where it was harvested and cured in the spring – or, of course, from the Netherlands. The Victorian working class especially enjoyed the bloater, with its silvery gold skin and dark translucent flesh, and with a gamy, smoky flavour. It was a treat, and when the salt tax was abolished in 1825, the herring became much cheaper. 'Three a penny, Yarmouth bloaters … come and look at! Here is toasters!' bellowed a fishmonger, with the Yarmouth bloater stuck on a toasting fork. Three bloaters for a penny was a splurge for Saturday night tea.

Working-class people were also very willing to eat fresh shellfish, especially oysters, which were very cheap, harvested very close to London, and easily transported. When oyster beds were developed off the coasts of Sussex, the price fell even further – but the new beds were soon exhausted, and a combination of disease and bad weather soon made what had been a limitless food very rare. Almost overnight, in the 1860s, oysters became the food of the wealthy, along with lobster and salmon.[95] It was a warning that the sea's seemingly inexhaustible riches could be destroyed in a generation or two, but the warning was not heeded; instead, shortages spurred the search to find new resources, which were soon exhausted too.

———

The multiplicity of marine sources and species gave rise to one of the great and memorable sights of Victorian London:

Four o'clock in the morning. The deep bass voice of Paul's … has growlingly proclaimed the fact. Bow church confirms the information in a respectable baritone. St. Clement Danes has sung forth acquiescence with the well-known chest-note of his tenor voice … At five it is high market at Billingsgate. To that great piscatorial Bourse … Great creels and hampers are there too, full of mussels and periwinkles, and myriads of dried sprats and cured pilchards – shrunken, piscatorial anatomies, their once burnished green and yellow panoplies now blurred and tarnished. On the whole, each dried-fish shop is a most thirst-provoking emporium, and I cannot wonder much if the blue-aproned fishmongers occasionally sally forth from the midst of their fishy mummy pits and make short darts 'round the corner' to certain houses of entertainment, kept open, it would seem, chiefly for their accommodation, and where the favourite morning beverage is, I am given to understand, gin mingled with milk.[96]

It's worth quoting this passage at length for its rolling sentences; the amplitude of the prose allows us to sense the wonders on sale. From the time of Edward III, fish was sold on this site in enormous quantities, though Billingsgate did not become exclusively fish market until the sixteenth century. The fishmongers sold every kind of fish imaginable, though there were many little quirks and oddities; in 1699, the sale of eels was restricted to Dutch fishermen whose boats were moored in the Thames, because they had helped feed the people of London during the Great Fire. One side of the market was set apart for shellfish, with whelks, 'curling out like corkscrews'. A long row of oyster boats were moored close along the wharf at Billingsgate, and the costermongers called it Oyster Street. Each boat had a signboard and a salesman. The holds were full of oysters in a grey mass of sand and shell.

In the nineteenth century around 500 tons of fish were sold in the market each day, even on Sundays, when mackerel could be put on sale before the hours of divine service. It was famous enough to attract American writer Nathaniel Hawthorne, who described it as 'a dirty, evil-smelling, crowded precinct, thronged with people carrying fish on their heads, and lined with fish-shops and fish-stalls, and pervaded with a fishy odour'.[97] It was a place apart, in an atmosphere of reeking fish, with fish scales underfoot and 'a shallow lake of mud' all around.

Work began at 5 a.m. The porters carried the fresh fish ashore. It was said that a Billingsgate porter probably made more money in less time than any unskilled labourer in Europe. Once the fish was displayed, the hubbub began. Henry Mayhew best documented the sheer noise of Billingsgate:

'Ha-a-ansome cod! best in the market! All alive! alive! alive O!'
'Ye-o-o! Ye-o-o! here's your fine Yarmouth bloaters! Who's the
buyer?' 'Here you are, governor, splendid whiting! some of the
right sort!' 'Turbot! turbot! all alive! turbot!' ... 'Here you are at
your own price! Fine soles, O!' 'Oy! oy! oy! Now's your time!
fine grizzling sprats! all large and no small!' 'Hullo! hullo here!
beautiful lobsters! good and cheap! fine cock crabs all alive O!'
'Five brill and one turbot – have that lot for a pound! Come
and look at 'em, governor; you won't see a better sample in the
market.' 'Here, this way! this way for splendid skate! skate O!
skate O!' 'Had-had-had-had-haddick! all fresh and good!' ...
'Eels O! eels O! Alive! alive O!'[98]

It's an aural record of what was on offer in 1850 or so. The shouting
was famous. Above all, there were the wives of Billingsgate, the original fishwives. They dressed like fishermen's wives. They smoked small
pipes of tobacco, took snuff, drank gin, and were known for their
colourful language. A Billingsgate wife was defined by a dictionary of
1736 as 'a scolding impudent slut'.[99]

Like the fishing villages, Billingsgate had its own festive
calendar. There was the harvest of the sea at St Mary-at-Hill
Church in London's Lovat Lane, every October on the second Sunday
of the month. The church was decorated for the occasion with nets
and other seagoing paraphernalia, and housed an intricate design
made from a variety of fresh fish and seafood, supplied by the
Billingsgate traders.[100]

And yet the dominance of Billingsgate made consumers less rather
than more likely to get hold of spanking fresh fish. People visiting
coastal holiday resorts were often surprised to find that fish was just as
expensive as it was in London, and sometimes unavailable altogether.
Large local catches were sent up to Billingsgate to be sold (where they
might be bought by coastal fishmongers, unable or unwilling to deal
directly with the local fishermen). So, for instance, a whole salmon
became easier to obtain in London than in the places where the fish
were caught.

At Billingsgate, cod, turbot, salmon, skate, halibut, mullet and sole were 'prime' fish; plaice and haddock were ranked as offal. In the deep dungeon-like basement below the market, shellfish was sold, hundreds of bushels of crabs and lobsters, prawns and shrimps, cockles, mussels, whelks and winkles 'under the flaring gas-jets'. In a side chamber on this floor was the boiling establishment, where the shellfish were prepared for consumption. Very few shrimps or prawns, however, found their way to the Billingsgate boiling-house; most were boiled on their way to the market on board the fishing smacks.[101]

Billingsgate Market still exists, but on a different site. It is now in Poplar, in the East End; Canary Wharf, even. It is still big. It still opens early – earlier, actually, at 4 a.m. It has its own training school. It offers 140 to 150 fish products. But like Covent Garden Market, it has been exiled from the city, made invisible. Nobody goes there after a night clubbing, as they might to Borough Market, as they used to before the Second World War, because there would be food and coffee available for the stallholders. Abstracted from the life of the city, the market no longer links what is seen on the plate with those who supply it.

In India, the English struggled with the unfamiliar fish and the heat. Fish were constantly compared to the equivalent ones at home. The Indian seer was thought to be like salmon, though it was white – some thought it tasted like cod. An Edwardian edition of *Mrs Beeton* claims that the hilsa is 'almost identical with' the mackerel, while the mango fish was likened to whitebait, and the Calcutta bectie fish was compared with cod, as was the gole fish, favoured by the British for the glutinous properties of its head. Small fish were often likened to herring or sardines.[102]

Then there was the Bombay duck, also called the bummalo. This was a small gelatinous fish, preserved by pegging up by the head to dry on huge racks on the beaches of fishing villages, and famous for its powerful aroma. After drying, it was dusted with asafoetida. The crispy fried fish crumbled over plates of curry and rice was a desirable adjunct to a curry tiffin in the club or the officers' mess. In Framji's *Indian Cookery for Young Housekeepers*, they are cut into chips and added as an accompaniment to a dried fish stew.[103] Nobody knows how it came by its name, though a variety of none too credible theories connected with Bombay as a railway centre have been suggested. Its aroma means that it has to travel in sealed containers. The fish itself, however, can be cooked and served fresh in India.

The British did enjoy eels from the deltas of large rivers, and they introduced crab and lobster pots. Around Bombay, so-called lobster – really crayfish – became popular, along with prawn and shrimp. The British also took to Indian oysters, though they were 'small, beardy, and protected by great uncouth shells', or so said Anglo-Indian writer Edmund Hull. When the railways came, the oyster even found its way as far north as Simla. Mrs Bartley's oyster stew involved cooking them for thirty minutes.[104] The British also happily ate the green turtle of the Indian sea, along with its eggs, though they rejected the river turtle.[105]

Echoing centuries of earlier worries in England, Flora Annie Steel wrote that stale fish was 'perhaps the most dangerous of all foods'.[106] Stale fish was 'rank poison',[107] but despite her doubts, Steel does recommend Indian fish for the table, though she cooks them very plainly, using Harvey's sauce and béchamel sauce. It is true that in the 'hot weather' of India, fish could go off in just a few hours: it was cooked as soon as it arrived home in order to extend its shelf life, so the Raj cooks created many ways to use cold fish – such as fish balls mixed with nutmeg, Worcester sauce and an egg, fried in oil, and in fish pudding made with a lot of butter. There were also tinned imports; Steel recommends a dish called Dublin lawyer: one tin of lobster, heated in a silver dish with sherry, butter and a squeeze of lemon.

The most famous use of cold fish was in kedgeree. There are early references to *kitjiri* as a dish for elephants from 1443, but this was a vegan mix of beans and rice, still made and served thus. According to 'Wyvern', aka Colonel A. R. Kenney-Herbert, who wrote on cookery in the second half of the nineteenth century, it was the English who added cold minced fish and a lump of fresh butter with minced garden herbs. The Indian cooks added turmeric to turn the rice a pale yellow colour, and instead of garden herbs they added thin strips of chilli and green ginger. They called it breakfast rice. It had some affinities with the favoured Eastern rice-based breakfast of congee. The addition of fish and eggs brought the rice dish into line with the English upper-class taste for a protein-rich breakfast. Sometimes the fish incorporated into the kedgeree wasn't even local; the Raj also enjoyed kippers in kedgeree, brought out from England on the slow ships at enormous expense.[108] Steel's kedgeree is devoid of any curious foreign spices; it is simply flaked fish, boiled rice, salt and hard-boiled egg.

The meals that resulted must have been a disappointment to everyone, a constant reminder of something else that couldn't be obtained. The underlying assumption was that such fare was temporary, pending the diners' return to England or the natives' adoption of more fully English ways. It may have been exactly this way of thinking which ensured that the British were indifferent to the subtle Indian understanding of local differences in cooking and eating. The British had only the most general sense of how food operated to define regions.

———

The golden age of fish and fishing is now a very long time ago. The First World War crushed the herring industry because it was no longer possible to export herring to Europe. Fishing was always dependent on the existence of a market for the catch, and this was often in Europe rather than England. The practice of fishing has always been a weird mixture of finicky skills, local knowledge, affinity with water, and often fierce danger from sea and sky. Savage injuries were endured to produce the feast of a moment. In the post-war world, more and more men risked their lives in deep and stormy waters to capture the feast. Huge factory ship trawlers required investors; it was no longer a question of one man and a boat, or even a crew of men and a boat. Each vessel was a factory, a factory of death – death for fish, and death for men. As super-trawlers began to conquer the fishing grounds, both the fish and the communities it supported began to die out.

The new factory trawlers were not just bottom-sweeping nets; they also contained a processing plant on board. Frozen fish could go straight from ship to shop. You could buy frozen fish anywhere. As more and bigger factory ships were launched, scouring every scrap of life from the ocean floor, few fish of any size could survive. Millions of unwanted fish – called bycatch, a euphemism for unwanted species, undersized fish, fish that exceeded the quota, fish with a low market price – would be tossed overboard, already dead. The vast factory ships required no knowledge of the sea. The old fishing fleets that launched from the West Country or from the North Sea ports had to know sea and sky in order to survive, let alone flourish. Canny dory captains might search the horizon for a cloud of seabirds that showed baby fish in flight from big underwater predators like cod. Such methods were made obsolete by the coming of the factory ships, as was knowledge of the weather and the waves. The use of sonar or spotter aircraft was meant to take the uncertainty out of fishing, and in a way it did. But at a terrible price. Working conditions on the factory ships were no better; they were worse. The men needed fewer skills, so they were easier to replace. As in other factories, injuries were common. Inspection was more difficult. Profit was the only god. The men paid the price. So did the oceans.

And our model for our favourite kind of fish is the fish we do not cook ourselves: fish and chips. Fish and chips is perhaps the ultimate expression of fish as convenience food prepared outside the house, as food of the poor, as food to be relished, as fish flesh mingled with vinegar and salt and leavened with carbohydrate. Like other simple foods, fish and chips can be wonderful or terrible. There are various reasons why it is more likely to be terrible than wonderful, but the main one is the effort made to save money on frying fat, and on fuel for reheating. As most Brits now know, chips must be twice or even three times cooked; they must be lifted from the oil so that it can regain a high temperature before they are lowered back into it again.

So popular were fish and chip shops at the beginning of the twenti-eth century that Alice Foley's family in Bolton ate battered fish for breakfast.[109] At their peak, in 1927, there were as many as 35,000 fish and chip shops in the UK. Today, there are around ten and a half thousand. The nation eats 382 million portions of fish and chips every year, spending around £1.2 billion on them. In London, there are many fish and chip shops that date back before the Second World War, including Rock and Soul Plaice, in Covent Garden, opened in 1871. At the D-Day landings, British soldiers identified each other by calling out 'fish', to which the response was 'chips'.[110]

Yet like most other 'English' foods, fish and chips come from immigrant communities. Their exact origins as a combination are disputed, and it is not clear which area of the country and still less which individuals deserve the credit of bringing about the momentous marriage: it may have been in the textile manufacturing towns around Oldham, Lancashire, that somebody first put fried fish and chips together, or it might have been in London. Separately, however, hot fish was sold in London from the Middle Ages. London cookshops, which sold hot food to the poor, were selling fish from as early as 1170;[111] fried fish came from the rise of London street food sellers in the nineteenth century, who typically sold ethnic food to their own communities at first, but were then patronised by others. Fried fish was street food for the Jewish communities of London, both Sephardic and Ashkenazi. They joined forces to create a particular way of frying fish in batter; this was a legacy of the Portuguese Marranos, who came to England as refugees in the sixteenth century. The fish was drenched in flour, dipped in egg and breadcrumbs and fried in olive oil. Recipes were included by Hannah Glasse in the mid-eighteenth century (using batter and beef dripping, or hog's lard) and Eliza Acton in 1845, and there is a reference to a fried fish warehouse in Charles Dickens's *Oliver Twist*, at the beginning of Victoria's reign.[112]

It was, however, eaten cold. Henry Mayhew claimed there were over three hundred fish fryers and street sellers in mid-nineteenth-century London. They fried fishmonger's leftovers that were distributed by costermongers, and were located in three places: the streets around the Inns of Court, the fringes of the East End in the Bishopsgate area, and the Borough district just south of the Thames near London Bridge. From the 1850s and 1860s, substantial and permanent fish shops spread throughout London. The biographer and celebrity chef Alexis Soyer, writing in 1859, took it for granted that fried fish was readily obtainable in the Soho area. In the meantime, the chip trade was growing apace in northern England, and it is in northern cities on both sides of the Pennines, like Oldham and Bradford, that we first find chips collocated with fried fish.[113] Once fish and chips were combined, they became central to the growth and transformation of the British fishing industry, fuelling the demand for fish which led to the creation of the great steam trawlers. Demand for potatoes expanded too. Specialist engineering and hardware industries sprang up, and the market was stimulated for oils and fats, paper, fuel, salt, vinegar.[114] Wet fish alone could have been supplied by the smaller kinds of trawler, and the smaller fishing ports. But the fish of fish and chips was responsible for the concentration of the fishing industry into a few large ports, and the decline of smaller fisheries.

Inexorably, fish and chips made eating food cooked outside the home completely normal. They came to be almost ubiquitous in industrial Britain by the early twentieth century. By 1905 there were, on one calculation, fewer than 400 people per fish and chip shop in Oldham and Leeds and only about 600 in Bolton and St Helens.[115] And like all massively popular street food – like ice cream, like pies – fish and chips soon acquired a connection with rubbish, fraud and sickness. A combination of appalling smells from unrefined frying media and primitive technology, with visibly defective hygiene, and occasional well-publicised prosecutions for the sale of fish which was nasty as well as cheap, made such a perception understandable. Alongside gut scraping and tallow melting, fish and chips was seen as an offensive trade, a designation that persisted officially until 1940. In 1917, the interior of a fish and chip shop in South Shields was described as follows:

> Only three teeny little boilers no proper pans or fryers or
> anything tater peelings all over the floor. Two cats squabbling
> over some fish at the back. No vinegar or pickles to be seen. The
> holes was closed up with grease, and it was empty into the

bargain. Mice almost certainly; dead flies like blackberry jam in the little cracked window which was steamed up, and the flypaper hanging over the fire had too many flies in it. The counter was greasy and scruffy and surely the walls weren't really yellow?[116]

Critics alleged that fish and chips was indigestible, expensive and unwholesome. Like eating bread and jam, it was seen as an aspect of the 'secondary poverty' that arose from the incompetent or immoral misapplication of resources that would otherwise have been sufficient to sustain an adequate standard of living. This miserable way of thinking is still common.

And yet a fish and chip shop, or chippy, is in some ways a model small business.[117] The fish and chip trade is overwhelmingly composed of single-family businesses. It requires a lot of basic labour of a light and repetitive kind, as well as a great deal of hard manual work, in its preparation processes. The fryer's children were a labour resource that could not be ignored, especially but not exclusively in the strenuous years before the First World War. It was also a perfect model of capitalist competition. In most towns of any size and even in some villages the fish and chip trade was highly competitive. These values coexisted uneasily with the traditions of craft solidarity and trade union consciousness from which many fryers were recruited; they also cut across expectations of solidarity and mutual aid in working-class neighbourhoods.

The outbreak of the First World War led to the use of ling, then catfish, sold under the euphemism Scotch hake. Then coalfish, although it was disliked for its dark colour as well as its name. At the end of 1917, there was even talk of frying sprats. One vendor said, 'You don't tell the customer it's dogfish; he won't know.' These expedients were tolerated during wartime, but when rising fish prices and lower customer incomes forced north-eastern fryers to abandon haddock in the early 1930s, there was fierce consumer resistance. Mr Barrett told the Sea Fish Commission in 1935: 'Two years ago if you had asked me to cook slices of black jack [coalfish] I would have cursed you. Today I cannot afford to buy anything else. My customers do not like it, but I have to tell them that I cannot afford to buy anything else, and they have to have that or nothing.'[118]

This is hardly likely to have endeared the fish to customers, yet they went on putting up with it because the crispy batter made it bearable.

If you associate fish and chips with summer holidays, you are not alone. One of the problems faced by fryers is that fish and chips is a seasonal trade: most had to make their profits during the summer months, in the hope that this would tide them through the high fish prices and depressed demand of the winter.[119] In some areas, however, fish and chips became part of many families' regular diet, often alternating with more traditional local fare, as shown by contemporary food research. In Lancashire, many families ate fish and chips once a week alongside rural, homemade delights such as soup, vegetables, home baking, and foraged nuts and blackberries. In Grimsby, Mrs Vincent, a brewer's daughter, ate fish and chips regularly along with sheep's head broth, shin beef, and the produce from her father's allotment – which included peas, beans, lettuce, celery and tomatoes. A Preston cardroom worker had fish and chips two or three times a week, but also enjoyed tripe, and cow heel, stewed with an appetising mixture of vegetables. Another textile-manufacturing family ate Sunday roasts with vegetables as well as stews and hotpots, while paying regular visits to the fish and chip shop. Bolton families also consumed fish and chips alongside homemade bread, cakes, soups and stews, even in households where great pride was taken in the mother's domestic skills and the wholesomeness of her cooking. Housewives in Bolton revealed strong prejudices against cheap frozen meat – women who purchased it were the butts of gossip – brown sugar (it was for poor people because it was a lot cheaper) and tinned food (people who had to use it weren't very good housekeepers), but there were no such comments about fish and chips.

Throughout the 1930s, the government, keen to blame the poor for their diets, steadfastly denied that nutrition was a matter of food intake, or that it could be clinically tested. Officials maintained that there was no connection between low income and malnutrition; if 'sections of the population were malnourished, then the fault lay with individual idiosyncrasies or ignorant housewives'. In 1938, experts pronounced on 'the poverty of fish – on the whole, fish are very expensive as a means of purchasing calories, the only real exception being the herring. The fact is, fish are a poor source of almost everything except protein and iodine, and might well be banished from the poor man's table.'[120]

Then came Clarence Birdseye. Birdseye believed that he could improve frozen food technology with his 1946 quick-drying program process. Crucially, he incorporated filleting into his fish processing; this in itself overcame at least part of the abhorrence that fish induced in British diners. In a further development, the Birds Eye company was to popularise a new form of battered fish, a convenience food that resembled but did not completely replicate the pleasures of fish and chips. Once people got used to eating fish that had once been frozen, the cooking methods used began to adapt to the looser, damper flesh. The fish market was now being driven by what consumers wanted. And what they wanted was white, soft, textureless, boneless, tasteless flesh, but with a crisp outer casing. And for a very low price.

It is a commonplace of English food history to complain that the English do not really like fish. In her book *English Food*, Jane Grigson remarks that 'fish is the great scandal of English eating, and of English cooking. We live in islands surrounded by a sea that teems with fish, yet we eat fewer and fewer kinds, and those not always the best, even allowing for different judgements in matters of taste.'[121] Unhelpfully, Grigson blames the fishing trade, which she describes as 'very poorly organised' and 'run by people without ambition or desire to improve things'. She complains especially about consumers' reluctance to buy fish imported from the Seychelles 'at a reasonable price'. She describes the fish as 'glorious rainbow creatures of bright turquoise and red and gold'. We neglect pike, one of the best for firm sweetness, she complains. You never see pike on sale, they are 'just left on the bank to die'. She fails to mention what a bony fish it is, and how much labour is involved in filleting it. Grigson does, however, stand up for undyed kippers and bloaters. We have not been greatly given to salting fish, she says, adding that she does not know why. (The reason is the lack of a reliable supply of salt near the great fishing ports.)

Her jeremiad, like most of its kind, is based on the underlying assumption that there is something intrinsically the matter with the way the English approach food; it also shows a profound lack of interest in the sweat, ingenuity and hardships endured by those who craft and shape the kinds of food we eat. One thing she omits almost entirely is that mackerel has a season, one that coincides completely with the season for gooseberries, which explains the brilliance of serving the two together – and, as Auguste Escoffier knew, the combination is an English invention (for more on Escoffier, see the chapter on Chicken); on the other hand, she does know that elvers – tiny eels – have a season and she knows that that season is spring. What she doesn't appear to know is that eel are far less common than they once were, exactly like oysters, and for that matter like inshore cod and herring.

But she is certainly not alone in seeing fish as the nadir of the English diet. In Virginia Woolf's novel *The Years* (1937) Eleanor goes to a London restaurant, where she eats 'white fish with pink blobs on it'.[122] Woolf presents the fish and its sauce only in terms of colour; it has no taste, no smell. Eleanor does not identify it, or the pink blobs that adorn it. Eventually, she 'began to eat her fish ... It was an insipid fish, watery, and full of bones.' Earlier, the hors d'oeuvre consisted of 'little pink strips of fish'. The hateful fish that Eleanor has to endure is only one part of the picture, however. While Woolf wrote joyful letters about the delicious food she ate in France, and enjoyed cooking, she scorned what she saw as the typical miserable middle-class food of the England of her day. By contrast, she revelled in better English food, using almost mythological terms to evoke Cambridge college lunch, as we saw in the Introduction, the sole 'branded here and there with brown spots like the spots on the flanks of a doe'.[123] In 1907 she wrote to Nelly Cecil, 'Why is there nothing written about food – only so much thought? I think a new school might arise, with new adjectives and new epithets, and a strange beautiful sensation, all new to print.'[124]

And the English are not completely alone: worldwide, many people greatly dislike fish. When asked the reason, they often cite its strong smell, the fact that it is difficult to cook properly, and its texture – slippery, woolly, oily or shuddery, or tickly. But most often cited is an early encounter with a fishbone. This might be why those who say they dislike fish will often happily eat fish fingers, tinned tuna and salmon fishcakes, or fish pie. Chef Nathan Outlaw, whose restaurant on the Cornish coast has two Michelin stars, reckons 'anything coated with crumbs', such as sole goujons, is a winner. 'The schoolkids I work with will even eat oysters if they're dipped in breadcrumbs and deep-fried.' The most-consumed fish in the US are tuna and salmon, 'unfishy' fish with a meaty texture and flavour. In fact, I frequently hear people say that they don't like 'fishy' fish, which means that they don't much like fish.

Seventy-seven per cent of adults never eat oily fish, which is regarded as 'fishier' than white fish. Regardless of smell, all seafood has a bigger, louder taste than meat, from the concentrated amino acids that fish produce to maintain fluid balance with the water. As is well understood, much of taste is actually smell. Ocean creatures must fill their cells with amino acids and amines to counter the saltiness of seawater. Ocean fish tend to rely on trimethylamine oxide (TMAO) for this purpose. The smell arises when fish are killed and bacteria and fish enzymes convert TMAO into trimethylamine (TMA), which gives off the characteristic fishy odour. This chemical is especially common in the flesh of cold-water surface-dwelling fish like cod. In fact, it is the presence of trimethylamine that is used as an indicator of how fresh a fish is.

Freshwater fish generally do not accumulate TMAO because their environment is less salty than their cells. As a result their flesh tends to be milder, and they get less 'fishy' than ocean fish. However, freshwater fish sometimes suffer from an unpleasant 'muddy' aroma (distinct from any 'muddy' taste). This often occurs in bottom-feeders such as catfish; the smell comes from blue-green algae eaten by the fish and concentrated in the skin. This is one reason that fish recipes often include acidic elements such as vinegar and lemon juice, which break down the compounds that produce the muddy smell.[125] Treating ocean fish with acidic ingredients such as lemon, vinegar or tomato can also cause TMA to bind to water and become less volatile so the odour compounds do not reach the nose.

As ocean fish stocks have been depleted by trawler fishing and drag nets, as well as by the factory boats that produce fish fingers, virtually all fish sold as ocean fish in Britain is now frozen. Even freshwater fish is likely to have been frozen, though here there are greater opportunities for eating trout or salmon, at least, completely fresh. The gourmet delights of pike, deriving especially from the French haute cuisine *quenelles de brochet*, seem almost completely over. Instead, the upmarket English fish of the early twenty-first century is very much inspired by Mediterranean cooking, with a scattering of nursery food and street food, and a bit of Far Eastern. The trouble is that Mediterranean cooks understand the need for the fish to be entirely fresh, and British cooks don't, or if they do have few opportunities to take advantage of the understanding. On Crete, I have been to a restaurant so small that it didn't even have signs, where we were invited to choose the fish we wanted to eat from the morning's catch; the sole chef then simply put the cleaned fish on the grill over a clear wood fire, and served it with no accompaniments. It was the best fish I've ever had; a close second, however, was the turbot in Pascale Barbot's *menu degustation* at L'Astrance in Paris, which doubtless required an entire brigade to replicate the effect of simplicity.

On lunch: an essay

As we saw with breakfast, mealtimes are suspended between natural and human time, between the hours the sun marks in the sky and the human use of those hours. And lunch is especially arbitrary and liable to be forgotten due to the pressure of work and other events. Human beings are part of a capricious and sometimes unjust nature, as a result of which they once had to work for food by the sweat of their brows. Farmers had to understand the seeding, growth and ripeness of plants and the effect of weather. All of us act as though these natural timings are far more predictable than they really are. We desperately impose the structure of the seasons on the variability of weather. In the same way, our mealtimes are an effort to manage and control the day, and the way our bodies move through that day, and we tend to do it by means of time, In the Middle Ages, monastic communities had two meals a day, one in late morning and the second at dusk. These were timed by the sun's movements; in the modern world, we use clocks, computers or mobile phones.

Five hours is about the optimal time for human being to do without food while awake. To take meals at an appointed time is a relatively recent luxury, and has only been available for the top 10 per cent for about a hundred years. For the other 90 per cent, the timing of meals across the centuries was – and is – determined by things other than the needs of their own bodies: the factory whistle, the confines of the office day, the need to work as a group, the welfare of animals from milch cows to sheep. Mealtimes are complex: a class-based sifting of time, nomenclature, and practical issues ranging from

the availability of artificial light and the other events exerting pressure
on the timetable from working hours to naval watches. Some meals
were meant to be flexible rather than fixed. Yet there are consistent
elements, too. There is always one main meal in the day, and this is
always called dinner. Breakfast is always a wake-up call; lunch is
always a snack to keep you going. Everything else is superfluous. As
wealth increases, superfluity also increases. And from excess, lunch
was born.

Lunch only became firmly moored to the meal in the middle of the
day after dinner began to move. In the seventeenth century, it was
normal for dinner, the main meal, to begin at 1 p.m., but during the
eighteenth century it began to drift, first until 2 p.m., then until 3,
and finally until 4 or 5 p.m. So lunch is an interloper. It is recent.
Once, it was faddish, pretentious and a bit, well, girly. It implied
weakness and decadence, since it was only taken by those who dined
late. But by the same token, it implied prestige.

Ominously, the word *lunch* originally meant the sound made by the
fall of a soft heavy body. This interpretation alternated with an equally
unappealing meaning: 'A piece, a thick piece; a hunch or hunk',
usually applied to bacon or bread or cheese. Bread or bacon might be
cut into 'little lunches'. From this came the original meaning of lunch
as 'a slight repast taken between two of the ordinary meal-times, *esp.*
between breakfast and mid-day dinner'. The word lunch was stigma-
tised as vulgar, and perhaps it does sound clumsy and clunky, with its
awkward associations with chunks and tumbles. Confusingly, people
also referred to lunchings as snacks between meals.

Before there was lunch, there was *nuncheon*, a word that meant
'noon drink', rhyming with puncheon. Bread and ale were issued to
the workmen at King's Hall in Cambridge in 1342, and to workers at
the convent in Abingdon in 1375. The word was originally *nonesuch*,
meaning incomparably good. Another forgotten word for such a meal
was the *bever*, pronounced the same way as the animal, from the
French word for drink; when the drink was ale, this was itself a nourishing interlude. Such small repasts could also be called nuncheons
and *noonings*. Noonings were first recorded in the 1650s; the term

went on being used occasionally until the middle of the nineteenth century.

Jane Austen called the midday meal noonshine from time to time, such as when Lydia and Kitty Bennet, waiting to meet their two older sisters at the coaching inn, eat 'such cold meat as an inn larder usually affords', along with salad and cucumber, which comprises 'the nicest cold luncheon in the world'. Coaching inns and pastry shops provided food while one was out of the house, which might still be called nuncheon. In Austen's *Sense and Sensibility*, nuncheon is a rough and hasty meal consumed by a horseman at an inn on the road. In jagged, uneven lurches, *luncheon* became the word that most people used, though initially it was regarded with disdain by some, such as the members of Almack's club, who in 1829 said that 'luncheon is avoided as unsuitable to the polished societies there exhibited'.

Gradually, the midday meal expanded. In the eighteenth century, offered to morning callers between 11 a.m. and 3 p.m., it might include cold meat sandwiches, cake or preserved fruits. By 1815, in London, fashionable people had begun to drop into coffeehouses or pastry cooks between noon and 1 p.m., and in the country even when a vast breakfast ended at 11 a.m., cold mutton and sherry was felt to be needed by one o'clock. Similarly, Jane Austen in her 1814 novel *Mansfield Park* portrayed a small group travelling ten miles after breakfast and eagerly eating a cold collation on arrival. In her diary in 1823, novelist Maria Edgeworth described a lunch with 'a cold first course, consisting of ham, pickled salmon, boiled round, then a hot course of little trout from the river, with new potatoes, and then a custard pudding, and a gooseberry tart and cream'. The simplicity and freshness of the food exemplify what diners began to seek from this particular repast.

So, with the pushing back of dinner, it became a sign that you were posh not to eat heartily at noon. In 1822, Dr William Kitchener suggested that by noon, the appetite would be craving a luncheon of roasted poultry, a basin of good beef tea, or eggs poached or boiled in the shell, a sandwich made with stale bread and half a pint of home-brewed beer, or toast and water. (Toast and water was made by pouring boiling water over a slice of toasted bread, leaving it to infuse until cool, then straining off the liquid. It was a dish that aroused passions: some favoured blackened toast, and others pale brown.) Kitchener explained that 'the solidity of the lunch should be proportionate to the time it is intended to enable you to wait for your dinner'. He assumed that dinner would happen at around 5 p.m.

It was always the ladies who lunched. Men were resistant to the idea of luncheon. Charlotte Brontë's heroine Shirley offered callers in the middle of the day an 'impromptu regale' of cold chicken, ham and tarts to make up 'a neat luncheon'. Anne Brontë depicted lunch as a regular item in the ladies' day in her 1848 novel *The Tenant of Wildfell Hall*; when a man joins the luncheon party, there is a sense of a *faux pas*. However, businessmen like Charles Dickens's Ralph Nickleby began to use lunch at 1.30 p.m. as a way of continuing rather than interrupting business. Ralph saw lunch as rather like a drink: a form of refreshment which men could either accept or decline. City gentlemen often took a sherry with a rock cake standing at the counter. White-collar workers in the nineteenth century, clerks like Bob Cratchit, did not go home for a midday meal; they had a hearty breakfast, and perhaps a drink and a few biscuits during working hours. Similarly, curate Frances Kilvert carried his lunch with him whenever he was out visiting parishioners, and it was simply a handful of biscuits, an apple and a flask of wine.[1] At home, women and children might eat a few leftovers from dinner the night before – cold meat, game, soup, mashed potatoes and perhaps even a pudding. Ragout and hash were especially suitable for lunch.

To try to make sense of these divergent practices, etiquette guides attempted to resolve the dilemma of when to eat. *The Family Friend* of 1853 thought lunch 'admissible' only when the interval between breakfast and dinner was unusually prolonged. Yet individual households were settling into their own routines. In Charlotte Yonge's 1853 sensation novel *The Heir of Redclyffe*, and in the novels of Trollope, lunch at one o'clock is a solid and unquestioned custom; just as, according to his daughter Mamie, it was for Charles Dickens in the last decade of his life. Dickens had his midday meal with his family.

He didn't care what food was on offer. His daughter remembered that 'he would come in, take something to eat in a mechanical way – he never ate but a small luncheon – and would return to his study to finish the work he had left, scarcely having spoken a word in all this time'.[2]

Clerks in the city might not be able to afford lunch unless they brought a packet of sandwiches from home, or were able to commission the office boy to buy ginger nuts for the scrivener to munch, as Herman Melville's Bartleby the scrivener does. Their betters began enjoying a midday break from their ever longer day labours. As artificial light improved, members of Parliament and barristers, as well as journalists, stayed longer and longer in the office. Bankers, senior accountants, merchants and businessmen often had lunch catered for, so that, as for Ralph Nickleby, eating and meetings went on simultaneously. There is a superficial resemblance between the snacking Austen heroine and a Dickens attorney at the insolvency court in Portugal Street 'regaling himself, business being rather slack, with a cold collation of an Abernethy biscuit and a saveloy'.[3] Sausages often turn up in Dickens's midday repasts. When Meg brings her father his midday meal in a basket, she tries to make him guess from the smell what is inside: it is notable that all the guesses involve processed meat or offal.

And so it came about that *lunch* happened between 12.30 and 2 p.m., though in great houses it was complicated because the servants had *dinner* while the family had *lunch*, and a third, separate meal was produced for the children, usually also called *dinner* (but sometimes *tea*). Men grew more resigned to luncheons when these included the elaborate hunt lunches, catered for by special hunting luncheon cases that had a division for a pie, or cold cutlets, and another for bread, cake or plum pudding. Increasingly, it became fashionable to invite friends to lunch rather than dinner. At Glamis Castle, the menu book shows that luncheon parties in the summer of 1866 outnumbered dinner parties, with some luncheon parties involving twenty-two guests. Middle-class enthusiasm for luncheon was fuelled by the use of leftovers. Yet at the same time, many working families continued to eat a full meal at midday, though not servants – some household manuals insisted that 'it is usual for servants to have lunch, either bread and cheese or a piece of cake, about 11 o'clock; but they should not be allowed to sit down to it, as the morning hours are too precious.'[4]

———

The ultimate lunch is Christmas dinner; it is still called that, and still takes place in the middle of the day. Perhaps it is really the last, stubborn survivor of the old midday dinner. Dickens is responsible for a lot of what we call Christmas tradition. When the Spirit of Christmas Present arrives at Scrooge's room, he brings with him greenery and a mighty fire, and also 'heaped up on the floor, to form a kind of throne … turkeys, geese, game, poultry, brawn, great joints of meat, sucking pigs, long wreaths of sausages, mince pies, plum puddings, barrels of oysters, red hot chestnuts, cherry cheeked apples, juicy oranges, luscious pears, immense twelfth cakes, and seething bowls of punch'. As Scrooge and the ghost venture out into the street, they see an equally impressive plethora of food:

> The poulterers' shops was still half open, and the fruiterers were radiant in their glory. There were great, round, potbellied baskets of chestnuts, shaped like the waistcoats of jolly old gentleman. There were ruddy, brown faced, broadgirthed Spanish onions, shining in the fatness of their growth like Spanish Friars. There were pears and apples, clustered high in blooming pyramids; there were bunches of grapes, piles of filberts, mossy and brown … And the grocers! Oh the grocers! Nearly closed, with perhaps two shutters down … but giving the air around the blended scents of tea and coffee so grateful to the nose.

Sunday dinner was like Christmas dinner in little. Families would splurge to buy the breadwinner a bit of meat with potatoes, the best and largest joint the housewife could afford so that the remains of it could form midday lunches in the week.

For most, the Victorian midday meal was anything but elegant. It usually consisted of leftover roast meat, beef or mutton, eked out with potatoes, plain bread, and sometimes a pudding. Children's midday meal was especially dull, for it was economically sensible as well as nutritionally wise to take the dinner leftovers, cook them again, and serve them in the nursery. This led to some cute names like bubble and squeak, toad in the hole and eggs in the nest, but the results were fatty and almost unbearably solid. Plain and wholesome food was understood as easier to digest, especially for children, whose digestions could be ruined, Victorians felt, by too many condiments, and also by fresh fruit rather than stewed. Neither were servants allowed to eat game, entrées or sweets: these would make them irritable because they would be unable to digest the rarefied food, thought Mrs Eliot James in *Our Servants*. They could, however, be permitted to share the same joint of meat as their masters.

Lunching led to a volley of recipes that dressed up the previous night's roast. It was an opportunity to show ingenuity with leftovers, and this new kind of knowledge ousted some of the older rural know-how with ox heart or sheep's head. Moralists claimed that many middle-class families were in debt because Victorian gentlewomen didn't know how to instruct their servants, and servants, increasingly, came from the town rather than from the large rural families where they had helped their mothers cook and preserve foods. A rough girl from the workhouse, Cassell's *Book of the Household* warned, would be likely to waste the family's money.[5] And without the family pig, nobody knew what to do with scraps such as vegetable parings or gristle from meat. In reality, hard-pressed servants worked as best they could to serve apparently luxurious food on a modest budget.

The idea of lunch enormously benefited the rise of London clubs as they took over from coffeehouses during the nineteenth century. Depending on his profession, a gentleman could apply for membership of one of more than thirty clubs in the West End; at the Reform Club, lunch might be prepared or created by Alexis Soyer or Charles Francatelli. Such lunches could be very grand and lengthy. For those who could not afford a club, the next step down in the social hierarchy were the chop houses. Strikingly, diners at such premises had to provide their own meat bought at a butcher to be cooked on site; it was then served at a long communal table. There was also a kind of set lunch menu. The Cheshire Cheese and Simpson's in the Strand became successful examples. At the Cheshire Cheese, a man might eat rump steak pudding, stewed cheese and vegetables, along with complimentary beer. The Cheshire Cheese was especially popular with the press men, editors and literary men of Fleet Street. Simpson's was originally a smoking house, but expanded into food provision. Many professionals did not have time for this kind of lunch, but sandwich shops sprang up to cater for them; one such, Garraway's, produced huge trays of ham, beef and tongue sandwiches, placed on the bar, a grander form of what the lower-middle-class clerk had probably brought from home, which might be a herring sandwich, or a slice of cheese and bread. There were also dining rooms and eating houses, providing soup and bread that cost from 4d to 6d, and the names at least were grand – His Lordship's Larder at Cheapside, for example. Still lower down the social scale, no lunch break at all was scheduled for builders or factory workers. In the countryside, the noonday dinner in the fields was a tin bottle of cold tea with bread and cold bacon, a small cube of bacon on the top or bottom of a cottage loaf, or for the less fortunate, bread and lard or bread and a morsel of cheese, or the end of a cold pudding with treacle.[6]

By the late Victorian period, even fewer adults were at home for a midday meal, as middle-class women began entering the workforce in larger numbers as typists, telephone operators, teachers, nurses, bookkeepers and sales assistants in department stores. The word 'lunch' began to push out the posh luncheon and the rural dinner, while women began to found clubs of their own, and also to enjoy restaurants designed for them, many run by Temperance Leagues to keep people out of gin palaces and alehouses. Lyons Corner House had 250 teashops and three restaurants by 1918, as well as their more exclusive restaurant, the Trocadero. The most popular dish at lunchtime for Lyons customers was roast beef and two vegetables for 10d, or you could have the day's set menu for 1s 6d.

Station buffets were opened on the Metropolitan Railway line, and special halts were made by long-distance trains to allow the passengers to eat. Passengers on the Leicester to Trent service could also buy a refreshment basket, which contained half a cold chicken, ham, bread, butter, cheese and a pint of claret or stout, all for 3s. The first-class dining car, between Leeds and London, began running in 1879.[7] In 1903 a railway timetable reassured travellers that 'luncheon-baskets may be obtained at the principal stations'. Passengers could wire ahead for these and collect them to be eaten on the journey.

When John Betjeman wrote that 'life was luncheons, luncheons all the way' – of course, Betjeman couldn't bring himself to say the dreaded word 'lunch' – equating the midday meal with elegance and sophistication, he was marking a distinction between post-war Oxford and the Victorian era that in other ways he so revered. 'Open, swing doors, upon the lighted "George"/ And whiff of *vol-au-vent*!'[8] Like the crisp layers of puff pastry, the Betjeman lunch was a sign of freedom, sitting lightly to life, having time to spare, and avoiding a solidity understood as old-fashioned, rural, even backward. The journey to a life of lunches was a long and halting one, and only the top 10 per cent ever reached Betjeman's destination.

One result of the invention of 'lunch' as the name for the midday meal is that it has come to symbolise the class divisions that still riddle our society. Those who eat dinner in the middle of the day are deemed less sophisticated than those who eat lunch or luncheon. If there was a single person who created food snobbery as a middle-class value, it was outlying Bloomsbury Circle member Elizabeth David. Not only were David's recipes mostly about light lunchtime food, but even her dinners were luncheon-like in their emphasis on ease and freshness. The idea that such food involves great discrimination but little labour fitted perfectly with lunching as an expression of wealth and leisure.

To this day, it is routinely assumed that David and David alone saved the British from their own dreadful post-war food. 'When Elizabeth David began writing in the 1950s, the British scarcely noticed what was on their plates at all, which was perhaps just as well,' says Artemis Cooper, summing up the received wisdom. But like all myths, this one is only partly true. In fact, David discriminated between kinds of English food. One of the groups she spoke for was ladies who lunch, those who disliked the stolid dinners enjoyed by the less posh, and the solid food served at them. Her preference for an omelette and a glass of wine as Christmas dinner exemplified what she represented: lightness, ease, elegance, and a firm rejection of Dickens and his Christmas cornucopia. She also opposed elaborate haute cuisine in favour of what she took to be the bourgeois food of Italy and France.

David's first book, which had been turned down by every publisher in London, owed its existence not to foodies, but to Bloomsbury. On first looking at the manuscript of David's *Mediterranean Food* (1950), Bloomsbury publisher John Lehmann asked Julia Strachey to report on it. She thought that it was a masterpiece. As the niece of Lytton Strachey, one of the central figures of the Bloomsbury group, Julia had been nourished on ideas of sensuality, freedom from repression, and desire for the Mediterranean and its hot sun – as opposed to Britain, a nation that David felt produced food 'with a kind of bleak triumph which amounted to a hatred of humanity and humanity's needs'.[9] Like most masterpieces and most bestsellers, the lines of David's thought had already been very thoroughly tried out by the Bloomsbury writers and their imitators.

David changed the meaning of the words 'French cooking' from posh upper-class hotel food of seven courses to lorry-stop food, *auberge* food – lunch food. She made it simple. She discovered a way to reconcile middling aspiration with practicality in the post-war servantless family. In Virginia Woolf's 1927 *To the Lighthouse*, Mildred, Mrs Ramsay's cook, spends three days preparing her *boeuf en daube*, to a recipe from Mrs Ramsay's French grandmother. However, in David's hands, French food stopped being something you told your cook to do, and became something you could do yourself for a quick lunch: *cuisine bourgeoise, cuisine bonne femme*. In reality David's recipes were as impracticable as any other musings by a posh hostess. They transform us into people with a venerable *grandmère*. They transform us into peasants from *la France profonde*, shrewd and full to the brim with *joie de vivre*. But David's *joie de vivre* pretended to an egalitarianism it did not in fact embrace.

She saved English food, but she did it by killing the Englishness of it. Her writing was given animation in part by venom. Let's take a leaf out of one of David's books:

> Provence is a country to which I am always returning, next week, next year, any day now, as soon as I can get on to a train. Here in London it is an effort of will to believe in the existence of such a place at all. But now and again the vision of golden tiles on a round southern roof, or of some warm, stony, herb-scented hillside will rise out of my stew. The picture flickers into focus again. Ford Madox Ford's words come back, 'somewhere between Vienne and Valence, below Lyons on the Rhone, the sun is shining … There, there is no more any evil, for there the apple will not flourish and the Brussels sprout will not grow at all.'[10]

Ford's faith in the near-religious power of the southern sun is a summation of David's food writing. Provence is the promised land because there are no Brussels sprouts or apples; no need then to bother learning how to cook those local ingredients properly. Like Ford, David depicts the transformation of conventional English people by encounters with the warmth of the Mediterranean, which awakens excitement, vitality and sensuousness. In 1950, when *Mediterranean Food* was first published, rationing meant that the likelihood of recreating one of David's meals was slim, but she did not expect her readers in a time of scarcity to stuff a whole sheep, or roast 'a couple of lobsters' with 'a bottle of champagne' and '2 lbs. truffles'; such recipes were included for reading pleasure and for a glimpse of another world. David acknowledged this fantasy element of the book in the preface to the second edition in 1955: 'even if people could not very often make the dishes here described, it was stimulating to think about them; to escape from the deadly boredom of queueing and the frustration of buying the weekly rations'. For David, food writing was about the creation of a Lawrentian myth of escape, redemption and sensual awakening, a myth she told and retold to delighted middle-class audiences suffering from years of Lenten privation, and derived from her reading of the writers of the first decades of the twentieth century and an affinity with the ideas of the high modernists.

David's descriptions of Mediterranean food are artistically filled with vibrant colours ('shiny fish, silver, vermilion or tiger-striped') and strong smells ('aromatic perfume of rosemary, wild marjoram and basil').[11] Eunice Frost (the Penguin director responsible for publishing *Mediterranean Food* in paperback) revealed to Artemis Cooper that:

> *I am not a cook, then no more than now.* I read it as an artist, and I felt ravished. It was so visually exciting, so illuminating, with such a sense of purpose and place – it was like finding yourself in an oasis filled with beautiful and delicious things, and it made one realise what one had missed all through the war. [emphasis mine]

But clearly it didn't lead her to don an apron.

David is often wrongly credited with introducing English cooks to olive oil. However, as well as the numerous seventeenth- and eighteenth-century recipes in which it was an ingredient, we might note that Woolf's *daube* includes a clear reference to olive oil. Even Victorian cookery writer 'Tabitha Tickletooth' recommends it.

Long before Elizabeth David, Ambrose Heath – referencing *To the Lighthouse* – provides a recipe for *daube* in his 1932 book, drawn from an even earlier source (Escoffier).[12] He uses a cheaper cut of meat than David does; in *French Provincial Cooking* she (scandalously and absurdly) uses top rump for a *daube*, and omits the marinade, and in

French Country Cooking she uses leg meat, and also omits the marinade. It is one thing to talk about the food of the French peasant in rapturous tones; it is another to understand that meat which is to be cooked long and languorously must begin by being tough, or it will fall tastelessly apart. David did understand this, hence the reduced cooking time, but she didn't explain her choice, and why she felt that her natural (upper-middle-class) audience would be attracted to, and expect, rump steak as an ingredient.

David claimed Mediterranean food 'had always had some sort of life, colour, guts, stimulus, there had always been bite, flavour and inviting smells … elements totally absent from English meals'.[13] She contrasted such glamours with 'things like powdered soups and packets of dehydrated egg' in England, and saw her 'empty cupboard' as 'an advantage'.[14] She claims that 'I sat down and … started to work … out of a furious revolt against that terrible, cheerless, heartless food by writing down descriptions of Mediterranean and Middle Eastern cooking. Even to write words like apricot, olives and butter, rice and lemons, oils and almonds, produced assuagement.'[15]

But she seems to need English food to be and to have always been unremittingly dreadful. In *Mediterranean Food* she writes almost in erotic terms of 'the Florentine, or sweet fennel, much cultivated in southern Europe for its thick and fleshy leaf stalks, as distinct from the common fennel, which will spread like a weed in any English garden'.[16] Sternly, she writes that 'a genuine cassoulet is not … a cheap dish … and it should be remembered that tinned beans and sausages served in an earthenware casserole do not, alas, constitute a cassoulet.'[17] This quick right-and-left is typical – not only do we lack a peasant dish as authentic as cassoulet, but we make a mess of theirs because we are cheapskates. But we learn nothing here, except that *we are inferior*.

The notion that Elizabeth David revolutionised post-war British cuisine has taken on a mythic quality of its own. Katharine Whitehorn exemplifies the hyperbole surrounding David when she writes, 'David completely opened up the insularity of British cooking. Food was just grey and awful and lifeless and across those awful grey mud flats, Elizabeth David burst like a sunrise, gilding pale Spam with heavenly alchemy.'[18] (Whitehorn was at boarding school when *A Book of Mediterranean Food* came out, so she is unlikely to remember the alchemy personally.) Claire Tomalin claims that 'Elizabeth David made us nostalgic for worlds most of us could not possibly know … she turned our faces away from England … encouraging whole worlds of fantasy about food.'[19] Turning our faces away from England sounds profoundly unhelpful, as does encouraging whole worlds of fantasy. Good food is at least in part about specific knowledge and technique, not fantasy.

And David may have misdiagnosed the problem in shunning English food. English food was less awful than English efforts to imitate the food of France for half the price; this went along with waiters who pretended to be French and menus that pretended to be in French. By contrast, reading Richard Llewellyn's *How Green Was My Valley* (1939) shows an idealised but very Welsh set of foods that make the mouth water just as much as David does, without the sneering. It is with a similarly averted head that David remarks that if she is going to have plates and glasses at a picnic, then she 'will have china plates and glass glasses' for all food and drink is spoilt when forced to use a 'brightly coloured composition mug'.[20] What David did supremely was to turn the nation's middle classes from despising the cook and the scullery maid to the greater and ultimately more comforting task of despising other food eaters and makers, tapping into a powerful and rather intoxicating vein of self-definition through food that had already been apparent before the war. It was David more than anyone else who made being very picky about food into a marker of class. It was she who ensured that a week-old imported boule of *pain Poilane* was a status symbol.

One difference between French cooks and English cooks after the war can be exemplified by Michel Roux's mother. When eggs were scarce, she made crêpes that were mostly flour and water, but as eggs became more readily available and milk became cheaper, she increased the quantity of these ingredients until the crêpes were light and lace-like. For this to happen, she must have retained a memory of what good crêpes were like. Her English counterparts might have struggled to do so precisely because the Depression was so very bad for the English urban poor, associated with a hunger assuaged only by potatoes and rice pudding, soaked bread and the occasional piece of cheese. That moment of division between rich and poor, in which the better off went on eating as they chose, meant that interwar English cuisine could not survive wartime rationing as French cuisine did. It had nothing to do with the sunshine – and everything to do with class.

So when John Betjeman says that 'life was luncheons, luncheons all the way' and when modern journalists referred to 'ladies who lunch', they are also seeing perfection in food as an identity that includes some but vehemently excludes others. Why else should there be lunch, after all? To enable Betjeman to say 'no wonder, looking back, I never worked.' He never took his Oxford degree, even after he had downgraded it from an honours degree to a pass degree. As he heads off to another lunch, at the Liberal Club, women students pass him, their bicycle baskets heavy with books on Middle English. Betjeman runs away.[21]

Foraging

The year was 1632, and a ten-year-old servant boy called Edmund Robinson was hungry. He had been sent out to the hedgerows to forage. It was late autumn, the feast of All Saints – the last quarter day, when rents were due – and he knew what kinds of pickings were likely to be left on the hedgerows so late in the year, if the first frosts would have wiped out the berries but improved the hips and the haws. 'Upon All Saints' Day last past, he being with one Henry Parker … desired the said Parker to give him leave to gather some bulloes [bullaces] which he did; in gathering which he saw two grey hounds.'[1]

The reason we have Edmund's account is that these were not ordinary dogs, as he was later to testify. They were transformed witches, recognisable as two of his Lancashire neighbours.[2]

A date of 1 November does not fit very well with the natural history of the bullace, which is normally ripe in late July or August, and is very unlikely to be still sitting on hedges so late in the year. The divergence cannot entirely be explained with reference to the Little Ice Age or the Julian Calendar Reform, both of which would have made 1 November more reconcilable with finding a few bullaces than it might seem at first glance. Uncertainty – ours, not Edmund's – about what exactly a bullace was complicates matters. Bullaces are often confused with damsons because both are plums that benefit from cooking rather than eating in hand. But bullace, *Prunus insititia*, still comes in several varieties – Shepherd's Bullace, which is pale green, and the much more ancient Small Black Bullace, actually blue and about the size of a sloe, the most ancient kind still in cultivation, and which, like hips and haws, improved and sweetened by the first frosts.

It might seem odd to regard Edmund as a reliable source of information on foraging after hearing about the magic dogs he saw, and learning that this story is part of an accusation of witchcraft. Stories about witches, however, are intimately bound up with the dreadful, gnawing food hunger of the poor. Witches are often met with during food preparation, or during food consumption. Witches were people who disrupted such work, people summoned out of some great and terrible world-cavern of hunger and need. This ever-present maelstrom of hunger and fear has been reduced like a *jus* by folklorists to the notion that it is unlucky to pick or eat hedgerow fruits after a certain date, often specified as Michaelmas (29 September), because the devil puts his cloven hoof on them, as if getting his revenge on St Michael, who normally crushes *him* underfoot. As with a *jus*, some of the nuances of the original ingredients are lost in the reduction. Like blackberries, common bullaces are black and bitter, showing the devil's role in their begetting. The devil has terrible manners, too, and is inclined to spit on the berries on a particular date – 10 October, in one nineteenth-century account – to ensure that they become poisonous or at least unlucky. In protecting the berries, the devil is behaving like any other landowner.[3]

The wild fruits of the hedgerows were snack foods, dietary supplements, flavourings. You couldn't live exclusively on them – you would have been very short of fat and protein. At the witch feast to which Edmund was magicked, there was meat, butter and milk. A young woman gave him meat and bread on a trencher. Dairy and meat: both were symbolic of the gap between what you could find and what would keep you alive.

'We ate sorrel, beech leaves, briar tops,' remembered an old man who grew up near Farnborough, in Kent. Briar tops, gathered on the way home from school, with skin or bark peeled off, were 'sweet and juicy'. My own daughter foraged happily for the sweet nectar of dead nettle flowers on her way home, to the amazement of her classmates, who assumed all wild plants were deadly poisonous. I remember foraging for mulberries, and also for honeysuckle dew: you pull the stamen back and a bead of translucent liquid forms at its end, sweet as sugar. Others snacked on 'bread and cheese'. Usually this means haws – the berries of the hawthorn, wrapped in a fresh hawthorn leaf. The berries do look like a very small Gouda cheese. Eaten raw and ripe, they have a taste faintly reminiscent of a very mild starchy cheese of that kind. But for other children, 'bread and cheese' meant silverweed, for example, or bent grass, or wood sorrel.[4]

Alongside the loss of more obvious expertise in traditional cheese- and bread-making, knowledge of hawthorns too has been lost, and even food-savvy people are amazed that their fruits are edible. In this area there is a slow attrition of knowledge, so that we as a society are now in danger of dying – not of calorie deficit, but of taste deficit – in the midst of a plenty of wild tastes. We have long since lost our sense that we are part of a landscape of plants and earth. Food comes to us from shops, in detached packages.

———

It is impossible to be historically specific about foraged foods in the way we can about fruit or even vegetables. Much foraging is secret, transgressive of ownership rights – poaching. Much is also common-place, so ordinary as to pass without record. One source for foraged foods is the foods of the herb and flower garden. Endlessly enacting the transition from gathering to farming, foragers came to collect and to plant in their gardens the wild food plants on which they had relied. The converse process also occurred. Some 'wild' foods were once cultivated foods; it has been suggested that many 'weeds', such as ground elder and nettle, were introduced to the British Isles as salad and greens. They were certainly low maintenance, and the nitrogen-fixing powers of nettle as a fertiliser were well understood by seventeenth-century gardener John Gerard.[5]

Foraging may be the oldest way of eating on record. The perfectly preserved bog bodies of Europe show last meals consisting of a mix of local grains and local herbs. The Danish Tollund Man's belly contained linseed and barley, with a lot of knotweed and many different examples of the weeds which follow the plough.[6] Cheshire bog bodies, Lindow Man (or Pete Marsh) and Lindow III, also had last meals of grains, but remarkably various grains: bran, wheat, rye, emmer and spelt (*Triticum spelta*), along with the seeds of several weeds of cultivation. Ingested earlier, before the final meal, had been traces of sphagnum moss, knotgrass, fat hen, black bindweed and oat. It has been suggested that all was eaten in the form of a small griddle cake. Lindow III had also eaten hazelnuts.[7] What – if anything – is clear is that the bog people ate what they found. The pollen in his stomach indicates that Lindow Man died in around March or April, the famine time of spring.

Most attempts to make a synthesis of the evidence for the foragings and gatherings of our Palaeolithic ancestors assume that biology is king. But even Neanderthals might have had food knowledge passed down through the generations. So too must the hunter-gathering hominids who succeeded them. And arguably the most catastrophic loss of food knowledge in human history is not our own, but that endured by our ancestors in these isles around 10,000 years ago. They introduced agriculture. Tragically, some progress is regress. In every inhabited landscape a turning point came when human beings no longer expected to live on what they found and hunted and trapped and caught, but on what they grew. For each group there might have been no obvious moment of decision. Mobile groups move when a food source is depleted, by seasonal change or by exploitation. But what if it is not depleted? Or what if the new food source for which the move was made is already exhausted, by disease or by another group or by something harder to know and define? Why not retreat to that trout stream and live off fish supplemented by the seasonal plants? And then, if the fish grow a bit scarce, why not think of helping some of the plants that provide food by clearing the land around them?

This seems like the sensible choice. But the fossil record tells the tragic story of the disaster. The turn to settlements meant that people had enough to eat, could meet their daily calorie needs. But they paid a high price. The Palaeolithic diet consisted of big servings of lean meat, venison and boar and bird meat, and long hungry days and nights with nothing but grains, berries, nuts, a few eggs and greens. There was probably a moment when people learned to cook the meat they gathered. Richard Wrangham argues that this is crucial for survival; healthy eaters of raw food struggle to make enough calories available to their bodies, hence the popularity of the diet with celebrities.[8] He does not take account of the old notion of leaving meat to age, however. Wait for the first maggots, runs an old freegan saying about roadkill, something that might once have come about naturally and simply because of the sheer slog of transporting a heavy animal carcass. Cooked meat makes many more calories and nutrients available, although others are destroyed in the process, notably vitamin C: eating cooked meat made midwinter scurvy likely. We don't know when cooking began in the British Isles. Human beings needed to have control of fire first, something that happened at least 200,000 years ago; the Beeches Pit site in Suffolk shows fire being used to make tools 400,000 years ago. Tooth size then changes at about 150,000 years, suggesting a softer source of food that required less chewing. Reproduction begins earlier when dietary needs are met – the average age of menarche, the first menstrual period, has been dropping since the Second World War, pointing to a much more adequate general diet. Menarche happens when body weight reaches 100 lb. Over the past two centuries the average age at which a typical British girl starts puberty has fallen from around fourteen to closer to ten. Most of that change is due to better health and improved diet and living conditions, but over the past twenty years the trend has accelerated, thanks in the main to burgeoning levels of childhood obesity – overweight girls tend to mature faster.[9]

The changes in tooth size and age of fertility were not the only ones. As human calorie intake expanded, diseases ravaged the now-settled race. Flukes appeared, and tapeworms; as populations settled, water sources doubtless became polluted with parasites which had been less easily transmitted in a mobile life. As humans made the slow, jerky transition from deer hunting to farming, their bodies bore the marks of the change. Even by the late Mesolithic, people were two inches shorter than their Palaeolithic ancestors. There were dramatic increases in arthritis and fractures were much more common. Farmed grain provided calories, but not much protein, vitamins or minerals. It was a hollow plenty. Rickets, anaemia and bacterial bone infections increased as the ability to metabolise iron declined. People domesticated more animals, exposing themselves further to new diseases: humans and their animals lived under the same roof, swapping pathogens and parasites. Despite this, populations soared, and they cleared land to create space for more crops, meeting new wild animals and new diseases. People became even shorter. As the population succumbed to diseases, scrub spread across the cleared lands, bringing with it rickettsial diseases such as typhus which live in such habitats. Diets worsened, and 'herd' diseases developed. The disaster of having enough had overtaken the people of Europe. Slowly, over millennia, sustaining seasonal variety in foods was replaced by the mirage of contentment.

———

This is a choice we make over and over again. We choose sugar over a complexity of spices. We choose trans fats over fresh dairy. Why? Because it's secure, or because it seems secure. All eating choices are a trade-off between the longing for novelty and the urge to eat the safe, affordable, known same-thing. In order to understand why we don't eat exactly what our grandparents ate, we need to understand that trade-off and how it works. It can't altogether be a matter of evolutionary biology, though clearly there are advantages in a willingness to try and eat new foods, because then you won't starve to death if the wheat crop fails, or if McVitie's stop making chocolate digestives.[10] (There's a disadvantage too, because if you try a handful of sweet-tasting yew berries you will die.)

Before the sugar trade, longings for sweetness must have centred on foraging – berries, autumn fruits, and at other times the excitement of discovering honey. In the New Testament, honey-sweetness is the gift of God; not made by man, it signifies grace and bounty. In reality, honey is anything but divine. Bees' spit splits sucrose into its two constituent sugars, dextrose and fructose. This is the basis of nectar, which in the hive turns into honey by evaporation. The resulting substance is complex, containing both sugars but also pollen, wax, pigment, enzymes, vitamins and minerals, and it is these impurities that give it different tastes and colours beyond those of sugar syrup.[11] The flavour is volatile and easily destroyed by heating. Perhaps because honey was found in vast amounts when found at all, it programmed us to gorge. In Palaeolithic times, it must have provided a near-miraculous calorie boost. Kept in cool dark conditions, honey has a shelf life measured in centuries.

Foraging is all very well, but you can't live solely on its products without a life of calorie deprivation, intermittent or permanent. Greg Critser has suggested that obesity is the result of starvation in a life prior to our own, our mothers' or grandmothers' deprivation, and evolutionarists claim that we are programmed to eat and eat.[12] The mothers who resisted Jamie Oliver's dogged reform of school dinners were criticised relentlessly, but their words revealed a forager mentality: they and the school dinner ladies alike were afraid that the children would simply go hungry, be forced to endure no food at all. What if they refused Jamie's courgette pizza and had no lunch? What about eating enough to live? They sought to defend children from their own hungers.

One aspect of the loss of forms of knowledge like foraging is the lost awareness of seasonality, in which the appearance of one plant quietly heralds the search for another. This should not necessarily be an object of nostalgia; our urban obliviousness to seasons is an outcome of plenty. Once, seasonality was impossible to ignore: it beat in the belly as hunger. In northern Europe, there are two main seasons for foraging, located on either side of the peak grain harvest like bookends. One is in spring, before the green wheat is certain to survive; the other is in autumn, after the harvest has been gathered in, the time for hedgerow fruit and mushrooms. Historians who describe pottage-based diets as dreary or monotonous know nothing of foraging and its power to infuse the grain or pulse with colour and scent and variety – and vitamins and minerals too. A pearl barley soup with some meat stock or a few morsels of bacon, or plain water, using a bit of lard or bacon fat to fry up an onion, with whatever greens you find. Any kind of pottage (aka risotto), or any egg dish (nettle frittata, or soufflé), and also burdock, chickweed and good king Henry (which has no claim on our attention as a comment on Henry VIII, but is so-called simply to distinguish it from *bad* king Henry, which is poisonous), cow parsley, hairy bittercress (handily on a six-week growth cycle), horseradish, land cress, pennywort, ground elder, dead nettle, white yarrow: they add colour, taste, vitamins, minerals and freshness. Anyone who assumes the diet of the poor was a mush of tasteless grains should head out into a hedgerow or neglected garden in early April with a basket and a pair of scissors.

Spring was famine time, because last harvest's grain had been eaten and the pig had been eaten and there was nothing left, except for dairy and spring greens, until harvest time came round again. Hunger for foraged plants in spring accompanies their abrupt growth.[13] As well as pottage, soup and salad, there was dock pudding. 'Dock' could mean the green plant that we know as a cure for nettle stings, but in dock pudding it sometimes meant bistort, mixed with oatmeal or other grain, sometimes an onion, all boiled together. Left to cool, it turned firm, like polenta, and then it could be sliced and fried in bacon fat; the bacon taste drowns out that of the dock, while performing the vital role of fat in transmitting vitamins to the body. It was not an everyday food, but specifically a food of the pre-Easter season. The various names of bistort – Easter ledges, passion leaves – denote its role in this fasting cake, the deliberate antithesis of the various Easter foods.[14]

Old ways of eating include many foods now almost wholly forgotten. Unless you are a very curious vegetarian you may well not have thought about where vegetarian rennet comes from. Animal rennet comes from the lining of a calf's stomach, but vegetarian rennet comes from thistles, or members of that botanical family, such as cardoons. Older herbals frequently mention drying thistles, and in the late seventeenth century, John Evelyn in a letter mentions cardoons: 'I know not whether they serve themselves in Spain with the purple beards of the thistle, when it is in flower, for the curdling of milk, which it performs much better than rennet, and is far sweeter in the dairy than that liquor, which is apt to putrefy.'[15] Jane Grigson notes that the French continue to make a cheese called *caillebotte au char-donette*, using cardoons as rennet.[16] You place the thistle flower in a muslin bag and steep it in the milk. It works much better in goat's or sheep's milk than it does in cow's milk; my one effort to use it to make curds in very fresh raw cow milk was a failure. But it still represents a plant most of us see as a mere nuisance. Perhaps a good definition of nuisance is something whose use we've forgotten.

Tansy, too, is an unfamiliar dish, though every manuscript and printed recipe book from the medieval and early modern periods will contain a recipe: a mixture of eggs, sometimes a spice including sugar, and the plant itself, often with other plants. (Modern versions usually reduce the amount of tansy to a bare minimum.) A tansy came to mean something very close to a frittata – not an omelette, as is sometimes averred, as a tansy is set firm. The herb itself is very strongly flavoured, even bitter, too much for most modern palates, but medieval tansies are very strongly flavoured with it.[17] By the seventeenth century, recipes advised cooks to use it only sparingly, and to colour the dish with spinach instead; the goal was to create a vivid green omelette, but tansies did still contain the bitter herb, because bitterness tends to intensify sweetness on the palate; tansy is molecular gastronomy.[18]

Another forgotten treasure are the berries of the service tree. Known to prehistory, they fade away from reports and recipes in medieval and early modern times.[19] The market sellers in Paris cried them in the Middle Ages, along with sorb apples and medlars.[20] Among early modern writers, Andrew Boorde commends them alongside wild strawberries and medlars as a healthy dietary item.[21] They are in the main a fruit of the south, of Kent and Sussex and the Isle of Wight, and their wild form is smaller, stronger and sharper than the domestic kind. Children picked them on the Isle of Wight as late as the 1850s.[22] The trees live in ancient woodlands; the fruit is red-brown and unremarkable – and inedible when first formed. But the fruit is gorgeously sweet – like a dried mango, or a toffee – when bletted (left to ripen virtually to the point of rottenness). To save the fruit from birds and squirrels, those living near a service tree would pick it before bletting, and hang the branches inside the house. The fruits were then picked off when ready. The season to forage was therefore not the same as the season to eat: what was picked in August might not be edible until just in time for Christmas.[23]

A close relative of the rowan, the service tree also protected against the attacks of witches, and its supernatural powers perhaps kept it in circulation long after knowledge of its taste was gone. Another name for it is the chequer tree, one source of the common pub name, later rationalised as the board game. The Chequers in Smarden, West Kent, boasted a huge service tree in its grounds, and while the current sign features a chequerboard, in 1925 an old man recalled that in his childhood the inn sign would be garlanded with the service fruit. The fruit was an occasional flavouring for ale prior to the advent of the hop, and hence a sign of ale nouveau. Or perhaps the inn was worried by local witches.[24]

Even when the poor gathered food, it was often enough just to sell, as we have seen with fishing communities, whether seashells, samphire, wildflowers, blackberries or mushrooms. In *The Country Housewife's Book*, Lucy Yates offers Depression-era housewives advice in a manner that also lets us see what people found to forage for in the years immediately before the Second World War: she urged cowslip wine, elderberry wine, and the preservation of small amounts of unexpectedly ripe fruit as pulp.[25] A hundred years before, Esther Copley had offered the same advice.[26] But unless you are sitting on a truffling oak or a morel-laden wood, it is hard to make much of a living from gathering wild produce. Part of the poverty of foraging is that it takes time. And then, too, human beings compete with squirrels, who always get to the cobnuts first, and birds, who are first to the berries. Climbing for the fruits others haven't reached is productive mostly of accidents.

Coastal foraging was the most dangerous of all. Drownings have happened during winkle picking, even from the gathering of samphire.

The Chinese immigrants drowned by the Morecambe Bay tidal bore in 2004 while collecting cockles were not making much of a living out of their labours.[27] Foragers have to contend with tides, waves and cliffs. The rewards are potentially lavish – not only oysters, but cockles, limpets, whelks, winkles and clams, as well as seaweeds like laver and samphire, dulse and carrageen, babberlocks and tangle – but modern foragers should beware, as sea creatures take in heavy metals from polluted water. The tidal estuaries of rivers are also longstanding sites for foraging. On the Thames, as we have seen, oysters once kept the poor in London on a high-protein diet, until they vanished. More even than hedgerows, foraging from river and sea requires exact and seasonal knowledge, and diurnal knowledge of the signs of a rising tide.

Sterner ways do exist. On St Kilda, until the populace abandoned their traditional and extremely taxing lifestyle in 1930, the islanders' meagre potato and oat crops were supplemented by sheep's milk cheeses, but also and crucially by the flesh and eggs of the seabirds who nested and still nest on the islands. Gannets, fulmar and puffin eggs and young birds were eaten – and had been for a very long time. An 1877 excavation of the *Taigh an t-Sithiche* (the house of the fairies) unearthed the remains of gannet, sheep, cattle and limpets. The building is between 1,700 and 2,500 years old, which suggests that the St Kildan diet had changed little over millennia.[28] To obtain the seabirds, however, the islanders had to climb precipitous and often slippery cliffs, rock stacks and 'chimneys', which took strength and sense in equal measure. What drove them was necessity, a harsh mistress.

———

Necessity paid the whole nation a visit in the war years. There were also guides. 'Never touch deadly nightshade berries,' writes the Vicomte de Mauduit, insouciantly.[29] He had written a number of successful cookbooks between the wars, but in 1940 he turned to foraging as the only way to survive the onset of rationing. 'The aim of this book,' he began, 'is to show where to seek and how to use Nature's larder, which in time of peace and plenty people overlook or ignore.'

The French Vicomte urged upon the struggling English more and more daring foraging. Samphire. Squirrels. Nettle soup, nettle cake and nettle toast, herb soup. Or perhaps roast sparrows or roast starling? 'Far from despicable,' says the Vicomte. Roast cygnet, or ptarmigan? Red beet port wine? But a fantasy element enters with beech nut toffee, which requires a pound of sugar.

By 1941 the government had taken up foraging with zeal. Government departments tried to organise local foraging parties. People were guided by experienced foragers to the hedgerows to seek brambles, crab apples, haws, rosehips, elderberries, rowanberries, sloes and cranberries. The notion was to preserve the hedgerow pickings as jams, chutneys and ketchup, the homemade and free versions of which had been rendered obsolete by the availability of cheap bottled products. Blackberries too were gathered. School pupils helped with the collection, and were remunerated for their efforts. Schools also made jam. Some food was simply incorporated into the domestic supply, but bramble jam went to the hungry cities. As often with wartime food policy, it must have been annoying for those who had, with sturdy independence, used their own individual knowledge over the pre-war years.[30]

The Ministry of Food was galvanised in part by a very poor fruit harvest in 1940 and a worse one in 1941. From 1941 to 1950 wild fruits were gathered systematically across the countryside, and there was also a scheme to forage for and gather medicinal plants, including foxgloves, sphagnum, nettle, dandelion, raspberry, elder, fern, valerian, burdock and rosehip. This is an interesting list because all the plants except foxgloves are foods, and it implies government concern about the risk of scurvy. But the medicalisation of food was the whole problem with rationing in the first place. It was truly efficient compared with the disastrous collapse in the food supply during the First World War, but it was also the dream of the interwar nutritionists. Whole grains and vegetables and wholemeal bread. Lots of wonderful boiled potatoes and carrots. No slices of bread and jam or scrape (bread with a cheap form of fat: margarine or dripping), or not many. Not much bacon. Not much tea. Not much sugar. Often presented as a glorious triumph in which the poor were at last forced to eat in the way the rich had always thought best for them, it would be more accurate to say that the middling sort had now been compelled to eat in the way they had always claimed would be very good for the poor.[31]

The variety that foraged foods might have brought to the diet was offset by the government's decision to restrict foraging to a much smaller range of plants. From 1943, only rosehips and foxgloves were gathered, and after the war only rosehips for vitamin C. Like many hedgerow berries, rosehips are not an especially interesting food before frost has shrivelled them; after that they become sweet, tangy rather than mouth-puckering. Understandably, the government did not give priority to considerations of taste: the rosehips were most often distilled into rosehip syrup, given to babies and young children. But the result might have been not to pass on to the foraging parties the kind of local knowledge that would lead them out to the hedgerows after the war, but actively to stifle such knowledge in favour of a much duller 'scientific' notion of nutritional measures. To cite another wartime staple, if cod liver oil were to be declared a gourmet food, people would rejoice over its deep gold colour and powerful scent. But as it is, they don't. They murmur about vitamin D and omega 3, words to sound the death knell of any food pleasure. Ironically, if people really allowed their tastebuds free rein to make decisions, and chose to eat food as close as possible to the land from which it comes, season-ally, the result would probably be a healthy diet. Admittedly it would also and at some times of year and in some places be uncomfortably at the lower end of human calorie needs.

———

In the past, and particularly before the twentieth century, the middling and upper middling sort probably ate a far greater range of local and seasonal foods than we do now, including parts of the animal, kinds of plant, and parts of the plant available at different times of year. Flowers were chosen across the centuries for scent and colour.[32] Broadly, edible flowers can be sorted into three categories: garden flowers, herb garden flowers, and wild flowers. However, these categories are not historically stable. Some herb garden flowers originally grown for their medicinal value have now been relegated to garden or hedgerow. One of the most popular flowers of the early modern period was the clove dianthus or gillyvor, also called July flowers and pinks (not because of their colour, but because of the serrated edges of the petals). They smell like cloves, were used to flavour syrup and as a flavouring for wine, hence their name 'sops-in-wine'. And while William Lawson in his 1618 *Country Housewife's Garden* treats them principally as ornamental, in 1650 John Murrell – the doyen of seventeenth-century French-style food in England – has a salad of rosebuds and clove gillyflowers. Pick rosebuds, he advises, and 'put them in an earthen pipkin, with white wine vinegar, and sugar; so may you use cowslips, violets or rosemary flowers. From this you concoct a dressing.'[33]

Cowslips grow in vast swathes in England's regions of chalky soil, but they are now officially endangered. Izaak Walton favoured what he called minnow tansies to use up the tiny fish caught on an expedition, fried in egg yolk, the flowers of cowslips and of primroses, and a little tansy.[34] Others made Paigle pudding, dried cowslip petals mixed with flour, or cowslip cream: 'Bruise in a mortar, and to a handful put [add] a quart of cream, a blade of mace, fine sugar and orange-flower water, the yolks of 2 or 3 eggs to draw it up, garnish with flowers.'[35] Honeycomb cakes of cowslips, boiled sugar with petals, cowslip cake, and primrose cake testify to the mental link between nectar and the sweet. Cowslips were also used to make wine, tea, vinegar, confits and sweets, and cowslip mead.

Hawthorn flowers are spring incarnate. A fifteenth-century recipe used spinette (hawthorn), red rose, primrose and violet to make a pottage – though violets and red roses are not usually in flower together – with almond milk, honey and amydon, a smooth starch which operated much like cornflour or potato flour but was made from tapioca.[36] Heather too can be used to scent and flavour drink; Irish and Scottish tradition records that the Danes and the Picts made a sweet beer from heather flowers.[37]

There are disappointingly few old recipes for lavender, though they abound from the last twenty years. It was used in gardens, and as its name implies was a cleansing agent. John Gerard mentions it very cautiously; it was thought to be hot and thus enflaming, but the blue part mixed and made into powder with cinnamon and cloves was thought to help against the passion of the heart, while confits made of lavender could protect against palsy and the racing heart. He also suggests an infusion of olive oil and lavender.[38]

Genial early modern eccentric Kenelm Digby liked marigolds with beef, while the mid-eighteenth century *Country Houswife's Companion* (1750) uses them as a flavouring for cheese. Hannah Glasse has recipes for salmagundi with nasturtiums, and says you can use borage or violets instead.[39] Syrup of peach blossom emulates the hawthorn syrup with an orchard flower, while the fifteenth-century cookbook preserved in the Harleian manuscript collection has a mix of rice flour, almonds, honey, saffron, and ground primrose flowers tempered up with the milk of almonds, and then a sprinkle of powdered ginger. This is a fairly humble sweet, using honey rather than sugar. Roses were loved too, but mainly for scent rather than taste; they could however be central to a certain sort of dish, Crusader cooking, like the chicken b'stilla-type dish described in a later chapter.

Violets were rushed into London with the dew still on them from their Devon gardens. Most ways with them were pretty, to use and bring out their myrrh-like taste – syrup, jam, candied. But Escoffier's violet ice, with a violet syrup, is interesting and intense.[40] And all flowers could also be infused into teas or cordials or tisanes – camomile flowers, violet blossoms, roses, borage flowers, orange flowers, mallow flowers, elder flowers, marigold flowers, woodruff.

Most tree lovers will recognise ash trees in autumn by their keys, the twirling seed cases they send spinning to the ground, but these too can be eaten, though pickled rather than fresh; Murrell has a recipe:

To pickle green ashen keys, elder buds, broom buds, or as ye like

Put in linen bags and let them lay in vinegar and salt 8 or 9 days, and then set them in a pot of water close covered on a gentle fire till they look green, which will not be under a day or

two greening; and when they are cold put them in the pickle,
the vinegar and salt in which they were steeped very well
boiled.[41]

Some flowers can be substituted for other, scarcer ingredients. Broom
can be pickled in place of capers, which are themselves flowers. Broom
buds are almond-flavoured. Peas, nasturtium seeds and buds, and
many kinds of unripe berries may also be substituted, as may barberries. Solomon's seal and butcher's broom were used as substitutes for
asparagus, as were the young shoots of burdock, willow herb, elder,
and garden goat's beard, and the flowering stalks of turnips. Other
flowers were incorporated into meat cookery. Sweet basil, Florence
White noted in the 1930s, does not grow wild in England, but was
used as a seasoning in the sausages for which Fetter Lane was once
famous, and was also used to flavour mock turtle soup (a cheaper
imitation of expensive turtle soup, using beef).[42]

Sometimes a herb kept in the kitchen for medicinal use could then
be used for other purposes. Borage, according to Francis Bacon, could
be used to repress 'the fuliginous vapours of dusky melancholy and so
cure madness'.[43] The following is a sixteenth-century tart recipe: 'Take
borage flowers, and parboil them tender, then stain them with the
yolks of three or four eggs, and sweet curds, or else take three or four
apples and parboil withal and strain them with sweet butter and a little
mace and so bake it.'[44] They can also be dropped fresh and blue into
lemonade or Pimm's, giving a beautiful cucumber taste. The slice of
cucumber in a Pimm's is probably a substitute for borage.

Garden plant lore is, however, particularly subject to anachronistic
food fictionalisation – or fakelore. Take this passage, often cited as Sir
Thomas More's view of his own herb garden. I keep the original olde
spellyinge for a reason:

There is manie a plant I entertain in my Garden and paddock
which the fastidious would caste forthe. I like to teach my
children the uses of common things, to know, for instance,
the uses of the flowers and weeds that grow in our fields and

hedges. Manie a poor knave's pottage would be improved were
he but skilled in the properties of burdock, of purple orchis,
Lady's Smock and Brooklime, and of Poor man's pepper.

Resonant wisdom from the past? Well, no. This is as splendid an example of foodie fakelore as I have discovered. Relentlessly recirculated on
internet websites, it derives from a late Victorian novel, Anne
Manning's *The Household of Sir Thomas More*, 1896 edition.[45]

Other flowers were used as vegetables. Cardoons, for example, in
addition to their use as rennet, could be boiled as pease or as asparagus, or:

> Stew them until they are tender, put in a piece of butter rolled
> in flour, and when of a proper thickness, pour them into a dish;
> squeeze the juice of an orange into the sauce, and scrape over
> them some Parmesan or Cheshire cheese, and then brown them
> with a cheese-iron, but not of too high a colour.[46]

Or a ragout of cardoons, from 1744: boil, then toss with veal gravy, a
teaspoon of lemon pickle, a large spoonful of mushroom catsup,
pepper and salt; thicken with flour and butter.[47] As late as 1920,
Escoffier has heart of cardoon, with buttered meat glaze, as a good
garnish for tournedos and sautéed chickens.[48]

Salad greens were widely sought, and John Evelyn had a complex
system for understanding their health benefits. In *Acetaria*, he writes
of 'Clary, *Horminum*, when tender not to be rejected, and in Omlets,
made up with Cream, fried in sweet Butter, are eaten with Sugar, Juice
of Orange, or Limon' and 'Clavers, Aparine; the tender Winders, with
young Nettle-Tops, are us'd in Lenten Pottages'. For him, the countryside is a source of little-known foods: he describes 'Earth-Nuts,
Bulbo-Castanum; (found in divers places of Surry, near Kingston, and
other parts) the Rind par'd off, are eaten crude by Rustics, with a little
Pepper; but are best boil'd like other Roots, or in Pottage rather, and
are sweet and nourishing.' These are probably the pignuts which
Shakespeare's Caliban offers to dig for the marooned drunkards in *The*

Tempest. Similarly, he reports that 'Jack-by-the-Hedge, Alliaria, or Sauce-alone; has many Medicinal Properties, and is eaten as other Sallets, especially by Country People, growing wild under their Banks and Hedges'.[49]

––––––––

Many people long for what Evelyn also craved – slow food, seasonal food, the gentle amble across pretty country in search of that which is known to be there. Oddly, the foods deemed edible now, in the twenty-first century, may actually embrace some that our ancestors would have regarded as animal feed. Beech nuts, chestnuts, acorns – eaten at need, perhaps, but not in preference to a solid loaf of bread. Conversely, our ancestors ate things we regard as inedible, such as brooklime (*Veronica beccabunga*), which has edible leaves somewhat reminiscent of a bitter watercress. It can be used in place of watercress, more sparingly. Hartshorn could be made from the shavings of stag's antlers, and then used to set a jelly or raise a cake. Between them, Roger Phillips, Richard Mabey and David Clement-Davies have eaten just about everything that grows and is not poisonous.[50]

Medieval historian Piero Camporesi believes that once upon a time, a combination of hunger, perpetual deficiency, and hallucinogenic plants would have ensured that not many people were sane.[51] For Camporesi, people were not knowingly eating – say – ergot-contaminated rye or hallucinogenic mushrooms for their potent chemicals, but were unknowingly eating things that made you hallucinate before they killed you; that is, he makes the good point that most hallucinogens are poisons in large-enough doses. To complicate things further, some items are edible with enough cooking, but deadly with inadequate preparation. *Amanita muscaria*, commonly known as fly agaric, is the toadstool of nineteenth-century children's books, a large white-gilled, white-spotted, usually deep red mushroom. Although generally considered poisonous, deaths are extremely rare, and it has been consumed as a food in parts of Europe, Asia and North America after parboiling in plentiful water. However, *Amanita muscaria* is now primarily famed for its hallucinogenic properties, though only in

Siberia is there any solid evidence of frequent use for such purposes.[52]

For some freegans and holidaymakers, foraging is now a fad:

> At the moment look out for giant puffballs, bristly ox-tongue
> and rocket, the latter often found in the cracks between walls
> and paths in cities. If you need any more excuse to hit the coast,
> now is the perfect time to collect seaweed. The real beauty of
> wild food is not only that it's highly nutritious and ecologically
> sound, but that picking it is also a fantastic excuse to go
> adventuring with friends.[53]

It sounds idyllic. And yet it must be obvious that if everybody on British beaches began searching for seaweed and shellfish, supplies would quickly be exhausted. By contrast, waste ground – brownfields, the neglected bit of your garden – contains lots of very nourishing weeds – if you haven't been spraying them with glyphosate, of course; and if you have perhaps it will be all right, since the wheat that went into your bread was more than likely sprayed with it too. And of course if the brownfield site isn't further contaminated by lead from passing cars or from decaying buildings.[54] As long as you avoid big umbellifers, and pretty flowering plants like columbines and sweet peas, and the leaves of some edible plants such as rhubarb and tomatoes, and as long as you cook stinging plants like nettles and other plants with visible surface hairs like cleavers, or goose grass, which is perfectly edible as long as it is boiled, and of course steer clear of any evergreens, which are a common source of poison … oh, forget it.

Caution about their lack of knowledge is one of the main reasons modern people do not forage. And that lack shouldn't be underestimated. On a farm tour, the farmer pointed to a rosemary bush, and asked the kids if anyone knew what it was. After twenty seconds, one twelve-year-old raised his hand and proclaimed it to be 'corned beef'. Worse still, none of the others laughed.[55] Stories like this abound. Jamie Oliver showed everyone a bunch of working-class kids failing to recognise vegetables.[56] I had a friend who worked in a day nursery and said there were three-year-olds who didn't know what an apple was and wouldn't touch it when told.

You can walk past people's gardens and allotments in spring and almost weep for the waste. A 2005 report announced that 'the British may waste more food than any other nation, throwing out 30–40% of all the produce they buy and grow each year'. Modern food production methods may appear efficient, but large-scale manufacturing and rigid supply chains can be incredibly wasteful. Restaurants throw out perfectly good food and so do supermarkets: Sainsbury's, which distributes surplus food to more than 400 charities, says it also sent 91,000 tonnes to landfill, of which at least 70,000 tonnes is believed to be waste food.[57] But it's not just the supermarkets: all over the countryside, blackberries rot on the hedgerows, and crab apples, plums and even apple cultivars lie in the wet grass because taste and habit have turned against them.[58]

Meanwhile the former foods of poverty are now prestige foods as the former foods of the wealthy make way for the intensely-flavoured and time-expensive cheap meat cuts served at St John, and the foraged food served at Le Champignon Sauvage. Interestingly these trends do not so much appeal to, as artificially instil, a sense of the food past. They are like Philip K. Dick's Rekall, offering the pleasure of remembering something never actually experienced. They play with the prestige of the real precisely as a reaction to tinned asparagus and salmon and new potatoes.[59]

They have something else going for them too, and that is that all gourmet and prestige food is at least partly about overcoming a fear of dirt, or a reflexive disgust. Posh food often involves eating what others cannot 'swallow' – fish eggs, or goose liver, or other transformed offal, or well-hung game, close to 'off', or stinky cheese that smells like old running shoes, or even Bordeaux that smells of rot and manure and mildew. Posh diners both want and don't want those things; they want enough, but not too much contact with the exotica of death and decay and disgust. Hence the restaurant can offer to perform the labour of immediate interaction with the unprocessed disgusting. You can feel authentic as you eat the duck hearts, without having to tear them from the carcass yourself. But are you really eating them because they are traditional, and do we know what is traditional anyway? Lavender was really not a culinary herb in the past, however many lavender short-breads and sorbets and crème brulées and roast lamb rubs are now eaten containing it. Conversely, you still don't see much in the way of sheep's head or cleavers or the sheep's feet that used to be a London street food.

Why would we want authenticity anyway? Authenticity is two boys coming home from school and eating bramble tops because they can't be sure of anything to eat when they arrive.

Apples

It is one aspect of the love of apples that they are insular, a word which means both 'a. of the islands' (the British Isles) and hence 'b. circumscribed and detached in outlook and experience; narrow or provincial'.[1] Apples, we think, or we like to think, are *du terroir*, of us; seasonal. True, an apple can be understood as dull, conservative in taste, a timid choice, the bland vanilla of fruit. This does little justice to the truth about apples and apple-eating; first, it ignores the enormously neglected and in some cases actively destroyed variety of apples, and second, the apple even in these isles has a spooky Celtic otherworld resonance. But in the twenty-first century, the idea of apples as English is a myth. The supermarkets are full of Pink Ladies and Galas and Granny Smiths and other varieties which will not even fruit in England. At farmers' markets the old varieties can still be obtained, but buyers need to understand that many are not bred to keep for six weeks in supermarket storage. The mango is now a more familiar pleasure than Ashmead's Kernel or Devonshire Quarrenden. The once-exotic fruits of empire have become the familiar fruits of home. And our homeland's fruit has been made exotic.

It is a story of accidental loss. Ronald Blythe's 1969 book *Akenfield*, and the subsequent 1974 film, presented an elegiac snapshot of the changes in a particular Suffolk village. Malcolm Peck, Akenfield orchardman, speaking in the early 1990s, remembered:

There used to be 140 acres of apples and pears. Now I reckon we've got about twenty-five acres of them; fifteen acres of Coxes, six or seven acres of Bramleys, some James Grieves and about five acres of Conference pears … All our Bramleys go for what we call peeling. They're peeled and put into Mr Kipling pies and things like that. For the peeling machine you have to have an apple between seventy and 100 millimetres, anything over that is too big. So you just can't sell the big apples … big beautiful apples … you just see them all wasted … All the apples the supermarkets want now are Coxes and Bramleys. We used to have Worcesters and they were lovely and sweet, a real tasting apple … We used to have George Caves, Scarlet Pimpernels, Laxton's, but we haven't got them any more. The Coxes have size restrictions too. We don't pick Coxes over eighty millimetres to sell in the supermarkets. You don't see apples like that in the supermarket because they don't sell them … They have to be a perfect colour too. Years ago they used to pick everything. The orchard was picked clean, and they used to pick the ones off the floor – those were used for cider. But no-one wants them now.[2]

The old orchards at Akenfield used to be a seasonal rainbow of variety and beauty. The season began with the early apples on 15 August, George Cave, Scarlet Pimpernel (which had themselves driven out Beauty of Bath and were now being displaced by Discovery). Then on 1 September came Worcester Pearmain, the Grenadiers that were the first cooking apples, and afterwards Lord Lambdon. Next, on 20 September, came Egremont Russet, Laxton's Superb, Cox's Orange Pippin, and on 1 October Bramley, Newton Wonder – a cooker till Christmas, an eater afterwards – and Blenheim Orange. Finally, on 25 October, came William Crump.[3]

What is Newton Wonder? Introduced in the 1870s, found by a Mr Taylor, this apple may be the answer to Elizabeth David's question: what apples did people use to make apple purée before Bramleys were invented? (She probably knew the answer, but it is pleasurable to

embark on answering a question she left unanswered.) The finding of
Newton Wonder is worth thinking about; Taylor was an innkeeper,
and he found the new variety growing in the thatch of his pub, the
Hardinge Arms in King's Newton, Derbyshire. New apple varieties are
often a result of luck, of somebody spotting a wilding and trying it,
and being enraptured. Apples do not breed true from seed; each seed
is unique, so the apple core you threw away yesterday might have
contained a gorgeous new early fruiting variety. Conversely, apple trees
do come true from suckers, just like other trees – elm, for example –
and buds from the base of branches will take root, while what looks
like a stand of trees may actually all be the one tree. But their variability from pips also means that we don't know where old apples go.
Once, every orchardman in England planted a kind of apple called
Redstreak, a cider apple. Now not a single example survives.

Chasing the parentage of any forgotten variety is an endless task.
Newton Wonder is probably the child of Dumelow's Seedling and
Blenheim Orange. Dumelow's Seedling was the top Victorian cooker,
still found in some gardens, and it cooks to a strong-tasting foam,
paler and more golden than Bramley. Dumelow's is not really suitable
as a dessert apple because of its acidity. But it's a good keeper; it can
keep until April. It probably derives from Norfolk Greening, which
might be the Green Roland, from east Norfolk in the 1800s, recorded
in gardens but not in orchards and known locally as Norfolk Green
Queen, its skin a dull green colour with an occasional pinkish-brown
flush, which cooks to a firm puree needing little sugar. But some
record that Roland is recent, even post-war. And Norfolk Greening
may not be a variety at all, but a state of ripeness; it may be a Norfolk
Beauty or Beefing or Royal or Royal Russet, but still green and unripe.
Or it might just possibly be the Northern Greening, a cooker also
described as cooking to a foam. But nothing is known of its parentage.
So we lose the lineage hereabouts, and with it the seductive ability to
trace the Akenfield apples back through their kin, as if they were some
great noble family.

At first, life in Akenfield in 1966–7 looks wonderful. But it doesn't
take much reading to discover that the worm was already in the apple.

Alan Mitton, the orchardman, was giving way, slowly but inexorably, to the demands of the supermarkets that were to overwhelm his successors, expanding the Coxes, and leaving the James Grieves merely to pollinate them. All the apples went into cold storage to ripen.[4] This well-intentioned, practical, highly skilled man was presiding over a behemoth of destruction that he could not even see, and which was not confined to East Anglia.[5] Of 157 recorded Gloucestershire apple varieties, only 86 are still known to be in existence.[6]

———————

Looking at apples, there are five overlapping traditions: we can classify by use, so cookers, eaters, dual purpose, dessert apples, etc.; or by growth, so codlings were immature green apples (though this might be a cooking category after all) and pippins were grown from a pip or seed; or by colour – red, russet, golden; or appearance more generally – scabbies – or by size. Codlings are big apples which hold their shape after cooking, apples for coddling (gentle cooking). But this is not at all the same kind of classification as the russet or leathercoat, a classification which refers to appearance.[7]

Originally, there appear to have been just two main kinds: codlings and pippins. The codlin or codling might have been the first apple we know about which cooks to a puree, and yet some authorities say codlings don't cook to a foam, in fact that a codlin is precisely that which does *not* collapse. It may originally have meant a small immature apple which would retain its form when cooked, so it could be served as codlin and cream. This was so familiar that 'codlins and cream' became a nickname for edible bay willow herb. The Kentish Codling is mentioned in botanist John Parkinson's 1629 *Paradisi in sole paradisus terrestris* as 'a fair great greenish apple, very good to eat when it is ripe, but the best to coddle of all the other apples'.[8] Seventeenth-century food historian William Rabisha mentions codlings, too. The etymology is disputed, with the *OED* stoutly denying any connection with coddling, in the sense of gentle cooking. The point agreed upon is less about what it cooks to than about the need to cook it at all; a codling is, literally, *not* a dessert apple. This might imply a cider apple that needed pounding: 'Take a very fine young Codling heire and pound him as small as you can … then you must cozen him.'[9] Later the term codling was applied to apples of an elongated shape. For Shakespeare, a codling – as the suffix '-ing' implies – is a young apple, either small or unripe or both: 'As a squash is before tis a pescod, or a Codling when tis almost an Apple.' And young apples needed cooking, or coddling.[10]

The pippin is a mystery like the codling, though you can often find authorities saying that a pippin is an apple that grows from a pip – except that the most famous pippin, the Cox's Orange Pippin, can't: notoriously, if you plant a Cox seed, the very last thing you get is a Cox. Probably it simply derives from a Romance base meaning 'small', from which we also get Spanish *pepita*, seed. The botanical longing to array and classify and structure knowledge of plants is at strife with the grower's knowledge of the tree at the edge of his own field, the cook's knowledge of the apples in the village. Taste, eat, cook, learn what can and can't be done.

The oldest variety on record is the pearmain; it needs to be eaten at once, like the strawberry its flavour recalls. People loved the red skin and strawberry taste of Worcester Pearmain; John Gerard records two kinds, a summer and a winter, although by that he might have meant not two different varieties, but two different stages of the same variety. By 1754, the variety's texture was a subject of complaint: 'The summer pearmain is an oblong fruit, striped with red next to the sun; the flesh is soft, and in a short time mealy', 'so that is not greatly esteemed', though some still loved it.[11]

The Romans liked apples. Their goddess Pomona, whose name comes from the word for fruit, is the source of the French word *pomme*. Yet the Latin word for apple is *malus*, which is also the word for evil, and this is one reason why the fruit of Eden is often assumed to be an apple. The goddess Pomona was green and chaste until one day a god saw her. That god was Vertumnus, his name an enchanting portmanteau word in which spring (*ver*) meets autumn (*autumnus*). He is the god of the changing year, or more accurately, the god who *forces* things to change – bud, blossom, ripen, decay. He sees the virgin goddess, and she flees from him – the fruit does not *want* to ripen. He overwhelms the goddess, ravishes her, and the fruit becomes ripe and delicious. We probably don't feel comfortable with the myth, but the Romans knew the apparent reluctance of fruit to ripen as a stubborn force which had to be almost furiously overwhelmed by the hot sun, and they also knew that yesterday's greening is suddenly today's ripe treat – and tomorrow's wasp-ridden wreck. Many orchard skills are Roman; the Romans, with their billhook, could do budding and grafting, and pruning. Since grafting is the most reliable way to reproduce varieties in all plants related to the rose, as apples are, it was essential for husbandry to prosper.

In Britain, Roman knowledge encountered the mythology of the indigenous inhabitants. In Celtic myth, the hero Connla was sustained by a single bite of an apple which kept him alive for a month without need for food or drink. Connla's fairy lover gave it to him, but the apple also bound him to her, made him long for her and for her country. Druid wands were made of apple wood. For the Romans' successors, the Anglo-Saxons, apples represented youth: in Norse legend, the apples of the goddess Iduna keep the Norse gods young. When she is stolen from them, they grow old swiftly.

The Bardsey apple – perhaps the rarest now in cultivation – is found solely on the Welsh isle of Bardsey, home to a monastery. The monastic day was structured, and regular, and dedicated to preserving knowledge and transmitting it to the next generation. Monks of the Benedictine order had some botanical knowledge, and would have noticed wildings and sports, and used them to improve the apple stock they had; abbots also travelled to other monasteries of the order, and could thus pass on both skills and plants to other houses. It was part of the order's charism to grow food for itself rather than simply to beg it, and though as the Middle Ages wore on most houses did gather in goods from the countryside, the ideal of island self-sufficiency was maintained even if the actuality was a thing of the past – until Henry VIII's men destroyed the monastic foundations, scattering their libraries of knowledge and breaking a tradition that stretched back for hundreds of years. The trees were left to grow wild in a shattered landscape. Their seasons of pruning and bearing might not have been well understood even by the lay servants that the great monasteries accumulated, and the locals were probably all too used to seeing the apple as belonging to someone else.

The value of medieval orchards can be discerned from records of theft and damage. In 1366 Bedfordshire, John de Mowbray complained that Elizabeth, his father's widow, had destroyed the orchards that should have been his. She had 'committed waste by destroying the trees, digging up the land and allowing the buildings to fall to decay'. The complaint also enumerates some thousands of trees, including hazels, apple trees, pear trees, plum trees and cherry trees. Elizabeth replied that one dwelling was pulled down because it was unsafe and the other was blown down in a gale, while the cottages were pulled down because the tenants had died of the plague (probably the plague of 1362, which was felt severely in Bedfordshire), but she did not explain about the trees. Such complaints seem to have been not uncommon. Similarly, in 1370, Alice, widow of Thomas Francis, was alleged to have dismantled and sold the timbers of a hall and inner court, valued in all at more than £250, in a kind of cash-stripping exercise, and to have destroyed oak, apple and pear trees.[12]

Apples could be a rent currency for monastic and other tenants, a typical annual rent being an apple every Michaelmas. A trace of such 'rents' may survive in a later custom. On the first day of the year the shepherds in North Yorkshire appeared at the court of the manor and did fealty 'by bringing up to the court a large apple pie and a twopenny sweet cake'.[13]

Just as Roman Vertumnus had to force Pomona to ripen, so too earlier peoples saw their role as to compel nature to behave in civilised ways.

A custom still prevails of what was called in ancient times 'wassailing the apple-trees'. This custom was accompanied by the superstitious belief, in the words of an old poet,

'That more or less fruit they will bring,
As you do give them wassailing.'
This ceremony at some places is performed on Christmas-
eve; in others, on Twelfth-day Eve. It consists in drinking a
health to one of the apple-trees, with wishes for its good
bearing.[14]

Although this is a Victorian report, wassail just means 'cheers'; it was
the English way of saying *prost* or *le chaim*, and it is noted as such by
the Normans. The wassail bowl contained spiced ale or cider – sometimes with apples floating in it, as in the Cotswolds, when it was called
lambswool and might for that reason have also been connected with
the fertility of the flocks. Wassailing probably made more sense as part
of the vanished ecclesiastical calendar that created apples such as
Margarets, Joanings and Johns.

Orchardmen's knowledge was so blended with supernatural and
saintly beliefs that it was difficult to disentangle from them. As late as
1940, the superstition was repeated that late sun on the apples on
Christmas Day would mean a good crop the next year. Each new apple
crop was blessed on St James's Day, 25 July.[15] Then there had to be rain
on St Swithin's Day, 15 July, to allow for keeping apples through the
winter.

The risks associated with the beauty of apples found their way into
folktales. Orchards had a guardian spirit called Awd Goggie, a giant
caterpillar-like gnome who protected the green gooseberries and apples
from the eager hands of foraging and scrumping children. There was
also Lazy Laurence, who haunted orchards. Lazy Laurence took the
form of a colt, a bit like the Scottish water kelpie, but he could also
cause a disabling illness for anyone who had stolen an apple. These
have become nursery bogies, intended as Awful Warnings to scrumping children who might ordinarily be expected to steal fruit.

Remember the apple given to Snow White by the disguised step-
mother-witch in the Grimms' fairytale? In 1579 or thereabouts, an
Essex witch called Elizabeth Lord gave a piece of apple cake to Joan
Roberts, a servant-girl who fell sick after receiving the gift. The story

illustrates not only the diabolical power of apples, but also the existence of apple cake at an early period. Most 'traditional' apple cakes, of
course, predate the invention of chemical raising agents in the nineteenth century, and usually apple was not used in fairing cakes, as
preserved fruits of other kinds were preferred, particularly raisins,
currants and citrus. The witch in the Grimms' 'Hansel and Gretel' also
gives apples mixed with a cake, in her case pancakes, something that
could be cooked on a griddle. Another suspect in a real trial gave children gifts of an apple and a piece of bread and butter. When Jane
Watson gave Jonas Cudworth's child an apple, he lost the power of
speech and lay 'in great torment and pain', and half the apple 'was
found at the bedfoot'.[16] In these stories, expressive of the fears of a
rural land-hugging class who could no longer rely on the magic of the
old church to safeguard them, suspected witches used a gift of food to
take control of a child. Apples could be innocent-seeming Trojan
horses through which the power of the witch could enter the defended
citadel of the body.

In medieval romances, apples are equally linked with enchantment.
Thomas of Erceldoune is taken by the queen of the fairies from under
an apple tree. The round ripeness of apples can symbolise the world
and its flesh – or the opposite, as expressed in a modern poem by Anne
Sexton called 'Jesus Suckles', where Jesus thanks God for Mary's 'white
apples', her breasts.[17] Perhaps this resemblance to the maternal breast
helped make apples easy for witches to enchant. Many scholars believe
that witches were most often annoying beggars who asked for food,
but there are just as many cases involving witches who *give* food to
those they wish to bewitch, and those foods are often apples, or
apple-related foods.

———

Apples were of course a seasonal pleasure. However, no medieval cookbook or inventory records their use raw, and many diet books record
the notion that raw fruit could cause wind. Should this really lead us
to conclude that people never ate raw apples, or that apples were really
too sour to be enjoyable, as apple expert Joan Morgan suggests?[18]

Looking at foraging, we saw that people seem routinely to have eaten much sourer and more bitter flavours than an ancient apple would provide; we must not underestimate how our palates have altered in the direction of the sweet. The uses that arose from raw and sometimes even unripe apples are also more often misunderstood than recorded accurately. It's understandable that there are no recipes for raw apples, but there are also no recipes containing raw apple. As little as a hundred years ago, raw apples were seen as all but indigestible in any quantity; it may be that longer ago people simply didn't find raw fruit palatable because of the texture. Very little was eaten in the pre-industrial era that was hard and crisp. Hard, crisp things were more difficult to eat in a period where sugar had rotted teeth, but it might also be that earlier eras correlated them not with freshness, but with staleness – stale bread is crisp, and pre-industrial people often didn't eat the pastry cases of pies. A crisp apple might *feel* like something unprepared; twenty-first-century people don't eat raw potatoes, for example. Until the rise of the dessert apple, the best-known apple was the cooked apple. It is possible to lay out a series of transitions – cider gives way to cooker, cooker to dessert apples, and just of late, dessert apples to juicers – but this is and must always be an oversimplification. The apples of medieval England *were* sometimes used for cooking; it is food fakelore that they were only used for cider.

In many of the Anglo-Norman and Old and Middle French texts it is unclear whether the fruit referred to is a variety of apple or pear. Terminology is against us; the language overlaps. The Anglo-Saxons liked apple dumplings, the same size as the little bun-like griddle cakes of the era. In the Middle Ages, the 1390 household manual *Menagier de Paris* is exemplary in showing how apples might have served as part of the vast main meal of the day; while it would be an error to assert that all medieval cookery is somehow the same, the medieval editor of the *Menagier* is plainly selecting menus that were understood in common ways. For example:

FISH DINNER FOR LENT
First service and platter. Cooked apples, large roasted Provence figs with laurel leaves [bay leaves] on them, cress and sorrel with vinegar, strained peas, salted eels, white herring, sauce over a grill of saltwater and freshwater fish.

And also:

ANOTHER MEAT DISH
Third service. Frumenty, venison, browned apples and Spanish peas and young lampreys, roast of fish, jelly, lampreys, congers and turbot with green sauce, bream in verjuice, fried bread slices, meat tarts and a large side-dish.[19]

Apples here are to be eaten with meat as a relish, a flavour-enhancement, as we might eat chutney. This is another illustration of the almost Chinese need to balance flavours – sweet and sour, rich and acidic, dark and hot or spicy. It is in these food contexts that we can understand the English medieval recipes for apple pie of almost the same moment. There is a fourteenth-century recipe for apple pie in *Diversa Servisia*:

FOR TO MAKE TARTYS IN APPLIS
Take good Apples and good spices and figs and raisins and perrys [pears – but here the origin of the word perry is very obvious] and when they are well beaten colour with Saffron well and do it in a coffin and do it forth to bake well.[20]

Which spices? How much of them? How many apples? What kind of pastry? How hot should the oven be? Nothing is specified. This is a naked signpost to a known food which simply reminds you of what you are assumed to know well already. But you would never gather from these curt notes that all the ingredients are meant to be diced small, as for mincemeat, as another and very similar recipe suggests. The Laud Manuscript has a recipe for 'Pomesmoille': 'Take rice, and bray him in a mortar, temper him with almond milk, and boil them. Take apples, and carve them small as dust, cast them in after the boiling, and sugar, and colour it with saffron, cast thereto good powder, and serve it forth.'[21]

The Forme of Cury from around 1390 also has a pudding of rice tempered with almond milk boiled with apples cut very small, and sugar: a kind of apple rice pudding with almonds, the sort of food the Middle Ages liked more than we do, but which with its galangal might not taste out of place as a dessert at an Asian restaurant.[22] Another popular use of apples was apple moy, moyle, or in modern English, apple softness, or mush. (Or, we might say, apple sauce.) A typical recipe contains almonds, honey and saffron, thickened with rice flour.[23]

The other way fruit could be served in the Middle Ages was as a fritter. An apple and parsnip fritter shows how far our own ideas of 'fruit' and 'vegetable' are historically specific. A tart apple and a sweet parsnip may be of equivalent sweetness. Apple fritters, made with wheat flour, zest, ale, saffron and salt, are recorded in a fifteenth-century manuscript; the instruction is to cut the apples as thin as *obleies*, or communion wafers.[24]

The monastic orchards were often intended for cider. At Glastonbury, cider was the staple drink, and cider spread across the western counties of England with the development of the cider press. Before its advent, cider apples had to be crushed in a pestle and mortar, or by rolling a stone wheel in a log. But with presses the apples could be crushed much more easily, while techniques of distillation also improved. Later, John Gerard reported of Herefordshire having 'so many trees of all sorts that the servants drink for the most part no other drinks but that which is made of apples'.[25] Surprisingly, the apple was seen as much more virtuous by Puritans than the rye and wheat which could be used to make ale. Part of its virtue was its humble usefulness: it could be eaten, drunk, dried, preserved and made into vinegar, and a few trees were within the reach of anyone. Its prunings made ideal faggots for the bread oven or kindling for the fire. Orchards also supported pigs: there was an ideal symmetry in the relation between apple tree and pig. The pig fed off the windfalls, and it fertilised the ground around the tree as it did so.

Growers' reliance on grafting for apple cultivation meant that this could be a basis for exchange and gift-giving, for building an impressive tree collection, and for laying hold of new varieties before competitors did. A surviving letter of 1539 shows that James Hurst, curate of Essenden in Hertfordshire, sent grafts of pear and apple trees to Lord Burleigh, who had almost certainly asked for them.[26] Burleigh was clearly revitalising an old orchard with new grafts, but that meant that whatever old varieties it contained would be overwritten by new ones. In Elizabeth's reign, orchard husbandry was a fashionable preoccupation. Sir Thomas Smith wrote to his wife on 10 January 1571, 'I would ... that a little bank might run to the cross wall which divides Nanes park, set with apple and pear trees, and roses or gooseberries betwixt them.'[27] The letter envisages a garden coloured like a popular dessert: apple compotes and jellies with layers of rose petals to enhance redness rather than greenness.

The Reformation saw the arrival of the first refugees in England's history, the French and Flemish Huguenots, and they brought with them new knowledge about apple growing. This is probably why Hugh Plat in 1608 recommends the new espaliers, dwarf apple trees trained horizontally to maximise fruiting. The seventeenth-century gardens of the rich contained a fruit wall, only eight or nine feet high. Apples were dwarfed by grafting them a few inches from the ground to the Gennetmoil, or Joanetmoil, and to slower-growing French paradise apples.

William Lawson's *A New Orchard and Garden* of 1618 credited Henry VIII's fruiterer Richard Harris with bringing the first pippins to England from France.[28] In Kent, soon to become London's giant allotment, Harris had noticed that the apples brought over by our Norman ancestors 'had lost their native excellence by length of time, and that we were served from foreign parts with these fruits on that account'. In 1533, he imported new varieties: the sweet cherry, henceforth usually called the Kentish cherry; the temperate pippin 'hence for the like reason called the Kentish pippin'; and the golden renate, or reinette. Even in Victorian times, Harris's chronicler is already lamenting a lost variety: 'but the Kentish pippin is now hardly to be met with'.[29]

William Lawson was the doyen of the new orchards. He described what could be grown in the north of England, complaining that most growers' manuals were borrowed from texts written for the Mediterranean:

> Fruit-trees most common, and meetest for our Northern Countries: (as Apples, Pears, Cherries, Filberts, red and white Plums, Damsons, and Bullaces) for we meddle not with Apricots nor Peaches, nor scarcely with Quinces, which will not like in our cold parts, unless they be helped with some reflex of Sun, or other like meanes, nor with bushes, bearing berries, as Barberies, Goose-berries, or Grosers, Raspe-berries, and such like, though the Barbery be wholesome, and the tree may be made great: doe require (as all other trees doe) a blacke, fat, mellow, cleane and well tempered soyle, wherein they may gather plenty of good sap.[30]

Unsurprisingly, apple culture was disrupted by the horror of the English Civil War and the famine it induced. Across the west, where the war was mostly fought, trees were chopped down by troops desperate for firewood. The bleak landscapes that resulted horrified John Evelyn, not due to any humanitarian impulse, but because he saw England weakened, and dependent on foreign imports. In his magisterial *Pomona*, printed in 1664 as a supplement to his tree-planting manual *Silva*, Evelyn urged the nation to abandon sweet imported Canary wine for the healthy, local and patriotic drink of cider. But he also had much of interest to say about eating apples, commenting, albeit in a puzzled manner, on varieties: 'Some Apples are call'd Rose-Apples, Rosemary-Apples, Gillyflower-Apples, Orange-Apples, with several other adjuncts, denominating them, from what Reason I know not.'

It is hard not to empathise with Evelyn's praise of orchards. For him, they are a specifically English remedy for specifically English problems, gloom and spleen and winter winds.[31]

———————

The Redstreak apple was especially vital to cider-making, and a small orchard could make a big profit, or so the experts said. Like cash-croppers in a developing country, the nation's landowners rushed to cash in, enclosing more common lands, and forcing tenants to plant more Redstreak trees in hedgerows, on the edges of fields and on arable fields. Fruit from these trees, designed for cider, might not have filtered into the diet of those who planted and tended them. The small-field orchard, with trees in rows, is also a development of this era of cider-making. But the trees themselves were subject to a kind of entropy. There are no Redstreaks now in England or anywhere else because the variety was weakened by viral disease – as happens to all plants raised in large concentrations. The bugs, as a rose grower friend remarked, eventually find you. Diseases develop. Old stock is grubbed up and replaced with new stock, which in turn becomes subject to a new disease. So the historical continuity of varieties is at war with nature itself, which regardless of consumers seeks constant change and renewal through evolution. One of the problems with the food mono-cultures loved by the retailers and agribusinesses is that they want more guarantees and continuities than is natural or even feasible.

All this new knowledge had at first little impact on the way in which apples were cooked. People went on in the old medieval manner, and no recipes specify new varieties of fruit. Dishes of cooked apple puree (moyle, moye, moise, mush) span the social scale from solid middle-class to posh banqueting stuff; a recipe might simply offer a way to reduce apples to a pulp and then thicken them with eggs, or it might advise on how to turn this apparently humble dish into a display item, as Thomas Dawson did in 1597.[32] No varieties for making the mush are specified. As we've already seen, recipes are not the same as what people eat, but are sometimes guides not to eating but to aspiration, to social networking, to who people thought they were and who they wanted to be, to the anticipated or imagined or recollected rather than the actual pleasures of food. The frequency with which recipes occur may or may not tell us about how apples were cooked or eaten. It may be that most people ate apple mush, because they could cook it in a single pot, and it also had many uses. A kitchen staple, it could go with meat, go in pottage, become a pudding-type accompaniment, with the addition of almonds or rice flour. Diluted, it could be a drink, and thickened it could become a cake, a dough moistener and enrichment.

Apple moyse or moise was still included in Robert May's cookbook of 1661 – in a way. There is no recipe, but May expected his readers to know what it was. It is a yardstick for thickness in making almond blancmange with chicken stock and fine manchet. Apple codlings or quodlings – with the meaning of an apple too green to eat – feature in May's work, boiled and shaped into little cakes held together with egg, and with biscuit and breadcrumbs. At once influenced by the France of his day – especially by François Pierre La Varenne's *Le Cuisinier françois* (1651), much of which he simply translates – and eager to recover a pre-Civil War England of peace and plenty, May is both innovator and recorder. His apple recipes are heavy with verjuice and vinegar, especially his ways with crab apples, and so they begin a kind of approach to chutney, with preservative sourness and sweetness together, crucial to the strong sweet-sour taste of most dishes.[33]

May's real love is barberries, which were a delight to his school of cooking because of the way they coloured the food. Colour and beauty were important, and May advises the cook to make red tarts of barberries or red gooseberries to accompany the green tart coloured by codlings (or by grapes, green plums, green apricots); a yellow tart could be a custard of egg yolks turned yellower with mace, while a white tart could be made from egg whites and cream, or from almonds and cream. Living in a world of artificial colour in food, and aniline dye in our homes, we do not altogether understand the delight in pure colour experienced by our ancestors. Quinces were especially valued because by cooking them to different degrees, a rainbow of colours from yellow through pink to deep red could be obtained. Gervase

Markham also has recipes where the point is to create a spread of tarts with fillings in different colours – red, green, white, yellow. He advises on how to make the best use of colour to make something beautiful.[34]

As well as colour, cooks began to play with texture. Time works not only on stored apples, safe on their straw-lined slats, but even on preserves. Keep apple butter for long enough, or apple marmalade, and it becomes stiffer, even chewy. At an earlier stage it can be incorporated into apple fritters in a batter composed of egg white, cream and flour. Or sliced fresh apple could become a fritter in a batter made principally of ale, spiced, then fried in beef fat.

The first windfalls, or greenings, unripe apples easily detached by wind or heavy rain, had specific uses. Greenings made a fine clear preserve, fresh and bright. Apples no bigger than walnuts can be scalded in boiling water, then peeled, and boiled again in the scalding water till they turn green – about fifteen minutes, though no older recipe gives a time. Then you drain them, keep the water and add a little of it to them, about a cupful, with their own weight in sugar, and boil together until it gels; the results are a little reminiscent of membrillo in texture. In her recipe book, early modern cookery writer Elinor Fettiplace says to pick greenings about five weeks before the usual harvest.[35] The scalding is to extract and retain as much of the green colour as possible. It's laborious, but it's also an illustration of how as well as being divided horizontally by type or variety, apples are also divided vertically by ripeness, and unripe does not mean useless.

Kenelm Digby tells the readers of his cookbook that 'my Lady Paget's' apples in jelly are done best when pippins are 'in their prime for quickness, which is in November'. He adds, 'I conceive Apple-Johns instead of pippins will do better, both for the jelly and the syrup; especially at the latter end of the year; and I like them thin sliced, rather than whole; and the orange peels scattered among them in little pieces or chips.'[36] William Rabisha suggests that the apples should be boiled 'until they are as tender as codlings'. For Rabisha the word codling seems to mean both the process, and the kind of apple that can be boiled till tender, or that is soft from the tree. We also learn from him of the value of clarity – 'as clear as christall', he boasts, of his jelly, 'as green'. It sounds gem-like in its intensity.[37] Rabisha was himself a cook to the exiled Charles II. But he magisterially disproves Karen Hess's generally acute remark that scholars don't cook and cooks are not scholars.[38] Rabisha was *interested* in food history. He dug out a piece of it himself, a feast given by George Neville, Archbishop of York (and brother of Warwick the Kingmaker) in 1467, which has excited food historians ever since. Like all such historians, he was quick to conclude that things had really been better in the past. Among the hundreds of diners was Richard, Duke of Gloucester, then about fourteen years old, later to become Richard III. The food served included plover and egret and bittern, porpoise and seal meat, and the meat of wild cattle, and plain and 'parted' jellies; just as we saw in the *Menagier de Paris*, cooked apples were accompaniments to meat, fish and poultry. Some of the 4,000 jellies served were doubtless apple jellies, red and green and white, and Rabisha helped to keep alive the idea of this preserve.

In 1675, Hannah Woolley – also a cook – is less interested in brilliant colour, and more interested in preservation. 'Let them boil leisurely', she stresses, and that single adverb takes us back, back to a kitchen full of the sweet tart smell of apples cooking long and slow.[39] In this genre of forgotten recipes is 'To Make Any Green Paste', in the Martha Washington receipt book brilliantly transcribed and annotated by Karen Hess: 'Set them by a soft fire for 3 hours and make them ready to boil and the heat of the water will draw out all redness and sappiness of them.' They are then sieved and reboiled with sugar.[40] Elizabeth Raffald in the eighteenth century also gives a recipe for codling jelly 'to preserve green codlings', which starts: 'Take codlings about the size of a walnut with the stalks and a leaf or two on.'[41] It is nearly identical to the Elizabethan recipe for greenings, but there is a different ingredient: rock alum. Alum, demonised by every panicking food writer in the Victorian era (see Bread), is in small quantities a preservative which maintains the crispness of fruit and vegetables, and can also substitute for cream of tartar as the acidic component of baking powder. In the modern world it is mostly used in preserved fruit. If you've ever eaten a maraschino cherry, the kind you get on skewers in resort drinks, you've probably eaten alum, so it is likely that Raffald's apples would have had the same stiff texture. Such new gelling agents substituted for the natural pectin in fruit, and may have inclined cooks to begin to slight the pectin-rich greening.

Some sinister misreadings have attached themselves to green apple jelly. Food historian C. Anne Wilson thinks the green colour was created by the interaction between the copper or brass pan and the acidity of the greenings; she adds that vine leaves were included to enhance the colour, which is probably true. But since none of the recipes specify what kind of pan should be used, this hypothesis seems hard to substantiate. Wilson cites Elizabeth Raffald as a source for the story about the poison green of the pot, but Raffald also gives two recipes for the green jelly, so perhaps she is merely inveighing against making a dye of too deep a green. We are always rather prone to jump to the conclusion that in the past people ate poison all day long, unlike our wise selves.[42]

Plenty of cooking pots were made of material other than bronze: earthenware, iron, tinware (increasingly from the eighteenth century), and it is hard to believe early modern cooks would have failed to notice verdigris forming, since it would corrode an expensive piece of kitchen equipment. And verdigris was in any case a valued mordant (fixative) in dyeing, and also used as a pigment. It seems clear that it isn't the copper that is making the green colour so much as the apples themselves.

The early nineteenth century minded less about jewel colours and clarity. Maria Rundell is a fan of jelly, but as an invalid food, not for banquets.[43] Eliza Acton has a crab-apple jelly where crab apples are playing the role that would once have been played by greenings; as often, her recipe is exact and sensible, giving the user crucial advice about not allowing the apples to fall apart. Unlike Rundell, she stresses both clarity and colour (though she was almost certainly not using unlined copper):

JELLY OF SIBERIAN CRABS

This fruit makes a jelly of beautiful colour, and of pleasant flavour also; it may be stored in small moulds of ornamental shape, and turned out for a dessert dish. Take off the stalks, weigh, and wash the crabs; then, to each pound and a half, add a pint of water, and boil them gently until they are broken, but do not allow them to fall to a pulp. Pour the whole into a jelly-bag, and when the juice is quite transparent, weigh it, put it into a clean preserving-pan, boil it quickly for ten minutes, take it from the fire, and stir in it, till dissolved, ten ounces of fine sugar roughly powdered, to each pound of the juice; boil the jelly from twelve to fifteen minutes, skim it very clean, and pour it into the mould. Should the quantity be large, a few additional minutes boiling must be given to the juice before the sugar is added. To each 1½ lb. of crabs; water, 1 pint: 12 to 18 minutes. Juice to be boiled fast, 10 minutes; sugar, to each pound, 10 ozs.: 12 to 15 minutes.[44]

Florence White, who records the recipe, adds that 'this seems to be own sister to damson cheese', a remark that could apply to all these apple jellies. They are wonderful with cheese, and delicious with sausages, ham, game – dark, flavoured meats.

––––––––––

As well as jelly, there are recipes for apple pie from the seventeenth century onwards. Gervase Markham in 1615 has a pippin pie, where whole pippins are peeled, cored, and put into the pastry coffin with a clove or two stuffed into the core space; 'then break in whole sticks of cinnamon', he adds exuberantly, 'and orange peel, and dates, and on top of every pippin a little piece of sweet butter', the whole covered with sugar and baked. His Warden Pie (pear pie) suggests you reproduce the spicing for apples. Strong flavours were added to autumn fruit; quinces and apples were both preserved with wort, the liquid obtained by infusing malt in water, a beer-making preparation, and Hugh Plat also says quinces can be preserved in ale if the ale is changed every ten to twelve days.[45] This produces another dark, sweet-sour taste range.

The following apple pie recipe from the end of the seventeenth century clearly demands collapsed apples:

> Take 19 or 20 large codlings or pippins coddle them very soft over a slow fire, squeeze them through a colander, put to it six eggs half the whites beaten, and strain. Add six ounces of butter melted, half a pound of sugar, the juice and rind of 2 lemons one ounce and a half of candied orange peel, half an ounce of candied lemon peel, and orange flower water to the paste, and bake it in puff paste in a dish.[46]

The filling is essentially apple moyle, but it has lost its almond thickening. Twenty-first-century gourmets will be familiar with almond as a thickener from recipes from the Indian subcontinent – again, it's hard not to note the overlap between English food before 1700 and foods we would see as 'Asian'. But the 'white gazpacho' of Spain is also thickened with almond, and in English recipes, almonds are nearly always a sign of southern, Moorish influence in cooking. In Europe they were popular as a substitute for both meat and dairy in Lent; in England, with the demise of Lenten fasting and the ongoing wars with Spain, they declined too.

Jane Austen mentions apple tart often in her books, and the recipe book used by her cook-housekeeper is kept at her house at Chawton. It records a careful recipe for apple pie, though Austen herself complained that the pastry was not well made. The original recipe does not specify either pastry or an apple variety (in updating it, cookery writer Maggie Black anachronistically insists on Bramleys, not introduced to a nursery catalogue until 1865). Apple pies were quite often made with suet crust or with the various kinds of puff, including a kind of layered, enriched bread dough.[47]

Apple recipes Jane Austen and her cook could have known come from Maria Rundell's *A New System of Domestic Cookery*. She has apple puffs, trifle, fool, marmalade, jelly for the table, apple and rice soufflé, apple pie, and a sauce for goose or pork, along with methods to scald codlings, to keep codlings for several months, and stewed golden pippins. The apple trifle, recently tweaked by Fergus Henderson, uses no cake, only apples or gooseberries: their interchangeability suggests that tartness was the desired quality. Pippins are preferred for the cooked apple recipes. The recipe for keeping codlings involves picking them very early, at midsummer.[48]

Only a little later, Eliza Acton, in addition to her apple tart recipe, conducted her own survey of apple tart forms, and suggested that 'The cover divided into triangular sippets, was formerly stuck round the inside of the tart, but ornamental leaves of pale puff-paste have a better effect.'[49] She calls this the old-fashioned way, but it is clearly not the oldest way. Its strongly dairy ingredients would have been novel in the eighteenth century, and would have been themselves a substitute for almonds and sugar, and then for sugar and eggs.

———

The relation between cook and orchard was to change gradually with the coming of a new trend: the dessert apple, bred to be eaten raw. In her book on British food, Jane Grigson punctiliously deploys the following, most of which you will not find at Tesco even in October: 'Arbroath Pippin, Beauty of Kent, Blenheim, Claygate Pearmain, James Grieve, Cox's Pomona, Mank's Codling, Margil, Norfolk beefans [used for drying, says Elizabeth David, chiming in], White Melrose (a dual apple from Scotland, cooking early and eating later), and the Ribston Pippin'.[50]

These apples are all products of the Victorian dessert course, the poshest course of all, the one that required back-breaking labour and astonishing know-how from gardeners, none of which was visible across the polished mahogany table. It was also ragingly competitive, with head gardeners seeking pay rises through the creation or mastery of exotics, the creation of new varieties of the familiar, just as chefs experimented in kitchens. You could cook with many, perhaps even most of them, but that is not what they were bred for.

What is or was dessert? Now it is a word for pudding or sweets, a bit of a restaurant word. However, it also has another meaning, a meaning to do with fruit. In odd, backward places like Oxbridge colleges and London clubs, they still have dessert in the archaic manner: after eating pudding, you get up from the table and progress to another room with a new seating partner, and there a new table has been laid, without a cloth. In the centre of it is a mound of fresh fruit. Next to your elbow are a variety of glasses, and at the head of the table are an array of decanters to match the glasses – whisky, port, madeira, claret, or any number from two to five of these. The host passes them by pushing them to the person on his left, who fills a glass, then rolls the decanter on, without commenting or ceasing to attend to conversation with his neighbour. You are only supposed to use one of the glasses, though a friend of mine once filled all four and then bolted them, in dread that someone had seen her do it. In front of you there is a plate, and a silver knife and fork. You take a piece of fruit as that too is passed around – there are special silver scissors for cutting a bunch of grapes – and you are supposed to eat the fruit with a knife and fork, though it's quite common to see people using their fingers. Only men used to eat and drink this kind of dessert, and it makes a kind of insane game out of eating and drinking. And it is for this stiff, sometimes somewhat drunken event that most heritage apples were created.

Outside this dessert competition, the mid-nineteenth century was already beginning to narrow towards a few well-marketed varieties. Isabella Beeton is careful to be explicit about the kind of apples she wants to use, in a list that appears to be sourced from Scottish botanist John Loudon's 1825 *Encyclopedia of Agriculture*. Loudon recommends rathripes or Margarets for earliest use, juneating, pomeroy, summer pearmain and Kentish codling for summer use, and for autumn the Downton, the pippins – especially ribston pippin and nonpareil – and other small russets.[51]

When I visited the wonderful apple stall at Stroud Farmers' Market, it had enormous pale lime-green Reverend Wilks, some divine candy-striped Worcester Pearmains in perfect condition, stripier Laxton's

Fortune, the tiny, early eighteenth-century Miller's Seedling, red sour Sunset, the miraculous Ten Commandments, with its ten tiny red core spots to justify the ways of God to man, and vivid Tydeman's Early Worcester, plus a big, hearty Howgate Wonder. A stunning dessert platter, like a cheese platter, could be assembled from these, judiciously tasted in thin elegant slices. But this would be a celebration of only a fraction of apple history. They are nearly all dessert apples, introduced from 1848 to 1918. Only one dates from before Victoria's reign. They are none the worse for that, but in preserving them and them alone, we have already lost another range of possibilities.

———————

Part of us longs for food that's always there. Throw yourself on the mercy of nature and uncontrollability enters in, like a pagan energy that simply can't be managed or harnessed. The apple has been subject to time in another way, too; it was once haloed with the crackle and energy which spoke of its magical and paradisal origins. When Glyndebourne staged Engelbert Humperdinck's opera *Hansel and Gretel* in 2010, it replaced the traditional figure of the witch and her apple pancakes and gingerbread house with the cereal aisle at a local supermarket, presided over by an enormous obese witch. This intelligent reimagining rightly located sugar rather than apples as the fearsome substance, though the attentive reader of the recipes above will probably have noticed the growing role of sugar in preparing the fruit. In our imagination, it is sweets that occupy the magical and seductive place once held by the apple. And like some of the liquid foods discussed earlier, sugar cannot be grown here; it is a food of empire. The cheap explosive pleasure of sugar means a lack of interest in the slower, local flavour of apples, however sophisticated their breeding.

Perhaps the country house dessert apple was the beginning of a trend where people ignored the food they could grow for themselves in favour of food wrung hard from afar, food that showed their command of the whole globe. Classical Pomona has metamorphosed into beautiful, deadly, fascinating and Coca-Cola-loving siren Mami

Wata; Mami Wata, Nigerian and also Caribbean, no longer longs for fruit, but for Coke, but lacks the wealth or access to the world's wealth that would enable Africans to participate in that system.[52] She is oddly like the apple-loving fairy queen who seduces Thomas the Rhymer into being her lover; Nigerian novelist Chinua Achebe says 'they are beautiful with a beauty that is too perfect and too cold'. Both Pomona and Mami Wata *are* the foods they crave; the seasonal apple and the white, cold magic of sugar, careless of the lives it costs, slave lives and consumer lives.

Pigs

An angry and an untamed beast, and is very cursed when he companyeth with the sow ... the wild boar is commonly black and he sticketh with his long crooked teeth as hard and sharp as it were iron ... Without doubt he will put the hunter in jeopardy of his life except he be nigh to a tree that he may climb upon for his succour.[1]

The story of the pig is the tale of how this wild, fearsome and energetic beast is tamed by culture, by industry, and by urban taste. During the process, he plays a cruel, unintended role in a famous massacre, and is many times massacred himself. And yet he is a staple food that comes to characterise English meat, even more than the roast beef celebrated by the upper echelons of society.

There might have been a single moment of pig domestication, in Turkey, but DNA suggests many other moments, all independent and springing from the wild. The first farmed pigs took a long time to appear, perhaps 2,000 years after domestication. Probably, scavenging pigs were attracted to human settlements, seeking food; when hunting failed, they would have been scavenged themselves. They could also have helped the community's health by eating human faeces; some parts of India still have pig toilets, in which styed pigs are deliberately stationed under a human latrine. These casual human–pig relations continued for some time before domestication proper began. Then the rich, fatty meat became an object of the kind of passionate desire we largely associate with sweets.

In ancient times our difficult relationship with pigs was addressed through stories which mixed appetite, envy and dismay, though languages generally denote the wild boar by a different word from that meaning the domesticated pig. The boar was found all over Europe in early times and was, along with the bear, the most ferocious and aggressive animal likely to be encountered. The boar was the best animal to hunt, admired both for its physical strength and for its heroic defence when cornered. Its flesh was fit for heroes. In Gaelic Scotland the boar's skin was thought an appropriate dress for a warrior. Greek historian and geographer Strabo comments on the large fierce boar to be found in Celtic lands and on the people's fondness for fresh and salted pork. Competition for the champion's portion of the feast is evident in the eighth-century story of Bricriu's Feast. The antiquity of this tradition is attested by Posidonius, who during the first century BC said that in earlier times the bravest hero at a feast was given the thigh. This is the part of the pig that is nowadays used for ham, still a prestige cut.

Pigs also developed dark, sinister associations. The Celtic Lord of the Otherworld carried a roast pig on his back; he was companion to the dreaded death-goddess Badb, and was a man with one eye, one hand and one leg. The pig he carried was always still screaming, neither alive nor dead; it represented the endless regeneration of animals – they are hunted, killed, eaten, and yet there are always more of them. Pigs' role in digging, eating carrion, and generating fertile soil also stirred a range of legends which connected them with burial. Pigs in pre-Roman Britain were sometimes buried with the dead, and therefore acted as feasts in the underworld.[2] There, pigs were slaughtered and eaten every day, only to be reborn by magic and consumed afresh. Not only were sides of pork buried alongside the dead, but pork was also buried in the fields, or mixed with seed before sowing, to make the soil fertile, to bring the dead to life. Many gods also required a pork sacrifice. Pigs could consume the powers of the woods in the form of acorns, and then themselves be consumed. By eating acorns, they partook of the sacral status of the oak tree in druidical lore. Swineherds also had folk-loric power, just like the pigs they guarded. The swineherd could cross from this world to the world of the dead, and come back with magical knowledge. In Welsh traditions, there were Three Powerful Swineherds of Britain, all with quasi-magical powers.

The domestic pig alternated with his wild cousin as a food source, just as he does today. Slaying a wild pig single-handed may have been a rite of passage. Finn, the heroic mythological leader of the Fianna, was magically bound to complete the single-handed slaying of a boar. Pigs, either wild or domestic, were major components of the rewards due to lords from their clients at Samhain (the season of Halloween) and at festivals held later in the year. Just prior to Samhain, cattle, women and children returned from the upland pastures and the domestic pigs which had been turned loose to forage in the oak forests were rounded up. Both the wild pig and the domestic pig were at their best during the Samhain season, having fattened themselves on the wild acorn crop, and were slaughtered for storage and rendering to the lord during this season.

———————

In ancient times, all farming was mixed, which limited the spread of disease and ensured against single-crop failures. Young pigs were kept near the farm until the beginning of August; in the late summer or early autumn the piglets were strong enough to survive the rigours of the woods. Pigs from a variety of owners were often herded together and minded by a single swineherd or by a young slave. If the pigs foraged far from home, the swineherd camped with them.

Pigs' association with rootling to make fields fertile tied them into the agrarian economy: their role was always the same, ploughing and turning the earth, foraging, fattening, and then keeping a family in fat and protein between harvests, though the breed changed and developed with new waves of invaders. The Romans in Britain ate pork and liked both suckling pig and well-fed pig, as well as boar. At a dinner party recorded by the Roman author Athenaeus towards the end of the second century, a single roast pig is served entire on a platter.

The Anglo-Saxon pig was a primitive breed known as the prick-eared pig.

The Anglo-Saxons' pig ate herbage in spring and summer, and was sometimes turned into the fields after the harvest to scavenge up any remaining greenery or grain. Scavenging pigs could be a nuisance, and the classic piggy ring through the nose was intended to stop pigs eating foliage destined for human tables. The pig could be the beast of non-arable land, and the creature of the smallholder with his limited or non-existent pasture; this pig ate human leftovers.

Conversely, and more classically, there was also the wood pig, or pannage pig. The pig was perhaps the most important of the animals that some tenants had permission to release into forested areas so that they could eat the fallen fruits – acorns, nuts and roots (the very best bacon was produced from pigs fed on acorns and mast); this right was known as pannage. In wood pasture, the pigs grazed among the trees with other animals, often including geese, sometimes even rabbits. Threatened from Neolithic times with clearance, wood pasture was nobody's priority – farmers always wanted to clear it for arable crops, and nobles always wanted it to become a game preserve. After the Romans spread out over the whole land, there were fewer woods than there are now, patches of wood and farm. There is dispute over whether there was a reversion to woodlands after the 'fall' of Rome – not much woodland is recorded in the Domesday Book – but the existence of woodland does make sense with the pig. A domestic version of the same pig might live in an orchard, snuffling for windfalls. They could also feed on the smallholders' waste products – buttermilk, whey, beans, peas and scraps, and could be turned out among pea ricks in the fields, near furrows, in open field systems. If there was an idyllic pastoral era in England, it was probably the age of the pannage pig. Pigs are efficient at turning vegetables into meat. A piglet gains a pound for every three to five pounds it eats; a calf needs to eat ten pounds for the same weight gain.

The pig would also root around, turning over the soil and helping to maintain the forest. This sounds idyllic, though a surviving manuscript illumination from the reign of Mary Tudor shows a pig being accompanied into the woods by men who beat the trees so that they release nuts and acorns, rather than leaving the pig to his own devices.

Another problem was that before the acorns and mast were ready and ripe, the pannage pig still needed to eat. Frequent disputes arose as hungry, unringed pigs broke into pastures and gardens and devoured the food of equally hungry humans.

The crucial right to allow a village pig to forage in the woods was vital to the peasant diet, since the pig carried on his sturdy body the protein and fat required for that diet to work. It is necessary to take in adequate fat for the successful absorption of vitamins and minerals from vegetables, and the pig's body thus lent crucial support to the vegetable patch – when he was not alive and eating it up himself, that is. Wood pannage could be a village right, or could be paid for by individual fees. The season for pannage in all periods and over all woodland areas was limited to prevent damage to young trees, but the limits varied over time, and across different demesnes. In the New Forest, the Court of Verderers decided – and to this date, still decides – when animals might be allowed into the wood to feed; on other manorial estates, the reeve or estate manager might make the decision. Medieval pannage usually began on or around 29 August, and ended on 31 December.

Driving swine to forests was thus especially associated with early autumn. The swineherd – who would often be sleeping in the pigsty – would collect the pigs for the entire village. It was not a high-status job, obviously, especially since the swineherd didn't own the pigs himself. However, he got a payment of one suckling a year, the entrails of those killed, and the tails of all pigs slaughtered.

Forests had many more oaks in Saxon times than they do now. In the fifteenth century, when the growth of forests had been deliberately encouraged, parts of England must have seemed one vast forest, an almost unbroken sea of treetops with a few thin blue spirals of smoke rising at long intervals. Each of those smoking fires – hamlets, villages, single steadings – would have had a pig on which its owners depended. Whatever the region, people could keep pigs on scraps, even in places like Cornwall where grain crops were difficult to grow. In Lincolnshire, where in medieval and early modern times labourers were mostly fed by landlords, pigs were vital. Their meat brought savour to everything, even to rooks, thrushes and blackbirds eaten with hard-boiled egg and bacon in a pie.[3] The pig gave his unctuous fat to everyone who couldn't afford to keep a cow for butter – which meant most people.

Pig numbers (as a proportion of the human population) probably peaked in the years following the Norman Conquest, because after that nobles did their best to prevent pigs from dominating forest hunting preserves. Nobles wanted to keep the poor and their pigs out of the forests altogether, and so gradually reduced the time allowed for pannage, eventually bringing it down to an impractical end date of Michaelmas (29 September). All pannage pigs were affected by the decline in woodlands. If anything lowered the rate of pig consumption over the centuries it was the same old story: a decline in the available environment, and a careless upper-class lack of realisation that animals and people depended on it. As lords began to annex their woods, and peasants charged a fee to let pigs forage in the stubble of their vegetable gardens, the pannage pig was doomed, elbowed to the margins of a food culture that still needed him but could no longer support him.

At the same time, pigs could be a simple currency item. Like apples and chickens, pigs could be used as rent. 'Adam de Werberton holds the land of Robert de Wodeford; rent 5s. and one customary pig every year at Martinmas. 5s. 0d. Sydde Mervyn holds by charter the moiety of all the land of Badecok; rent 2s. 6d. and half a customary pig at Martinmas. 2s. 6d.' Note the timing. The 11 November (Martinmas) date shows us the pig gorged on the fruit of the autumn wood.[4] The tenants of the Chapel of Wolverhampton had to give their best pig every year at pannage time.[5] As late as the Victorian period, the manor at Chichester in Sussex was charged with handing over at Christmas a pig and two trees to the hospital of St James outside the town, and a 'second best' pig and a tree to the hospital of Lodesdon in Westhampnett.[6] Pigs were especially associated with tithes. 'And sometime comes she with a tithe-pig's tail/ Tickling a parson's nose as a' lies asleep,/ Then dreams he of another benefice'. So said Mercutio, very drily. Tithes were originally a tax of one-tenth of all produce, payable to the local clergyman by his parishioners. They were payable in kind – one sack of wheat for every ten sacks produced, a pig for every ten pigs.[7] A tenth of a pig was less easy to collect, so clergymen began instead to demand cash from the poor.

As people began to drift into larger settlements, pigs came with them. An asset in the forests, the village and town pig was a constant challenge to order. Despite living in close proximity to people, pigs sometimes behaved like wild animals, and attempts to fit them into medieval village settings often foundered on neighbourly disputes. In some areas, the pig's nose ring was enforced by law.[8] The general stink of piggeries was a recurring issue. Communities sometimes appointed pig police to manage the animals. In Feltham, Middlesex, one of their duties was to give warning to the owners of every 'un-ringed' hog or pig they found in the commons or fields; if after two days the warning was still disregarded, they were entitled to 4d for each hog and 2d for each pig over and above the amount of the fine paid by the owner to the lord of the manor.[9]

Other parishes appointed pig collectors to pick up the often noisome dead pigs. London tried a belt-and-braces strategy. Its ordinance of the thirteenth century announced that 'no pig be henceforth found by the streets or lanes of the City or suburb, nor in the ditches of the City; and if found they shall be killed by whoever finds them, and the killer shall have them without challenge or redemption for 4 pence from the owner'. This created an incentive for the poor to round up and slaughter any straying animals on the spot. London also tried to control pigswill aromas: 'Whoever wishes to feed his pigs, let him feed them in the open away from the King's highway [or] in his house, under heavy penalty.'[10]

However, any pig that was considered by the supervisor of the London market unfit to be killed for food had a bell attached to it by a proctor of St Anthony's Hospital, and was then free to roam the streets to pick up what it could. These were St Anthony's pigs. It was a good deed to feed them, and they often throve. Pork was a feature of the menu on St Anthony's Day, 17 January (a good day for pig-eating, well within the seasonal norm).[11] The St Anthony pig was often a runt. Some sources say they belonged to medieval friars, whose pigs were allowed to roam in the streets. The privilege seems to have been abused, for in 1311 Roger de Wynchester promised the City of London authorities that he would not claim pigs found wandering about the City, nor put bells on any swine but those given in charity to the hospital. In any case, the 'Tantony pig' became a symbol of the poor.

The relationship between the very poor and their pigs was often uncomfortably close.[12] So crucial was the pig's flesh to their food economy that really horrible scavenging of pig parts occurs. In 1353, a man with the sinister name Richard Quelhogge had 'bought a pig that had been lying by the water-side of the Thames, putrid and stinking, of one Richard Stevenache, porter, for 4 pence'. Quelhogge did not waste the trove; he 'from the same had cut two gammons for sale, and had sold part thereof, in deceit of the people'.[13]

Medieval calendars show that the pannage pig was usually slaughtered in December, but pig killing might occasionally begin at All Hallows (31 October) or on the feast of St Martin (11 November), to provide protein and fat over the winter months, continuing until Ladymass (25 March). The pig killer was as vital as the ploughman. Illuminations in medieval manuscripts depict him as a man with an axe and a live, unblemished pig; the axe was used to stun the pig, and then to cut its throat and drain its blood. Later illustrators focus on the act of throat slitting and the collecting of blood in a basin.[14] Pigs had to be killed gently, without fright. First, the pig was simply stunned with a blow to the head. While knocked out, it was bled, and the blood collected for black puddings. Slowly, it died, all the while unconscious. (This was the ideal, but there are many anecdotal accounts of squealing pigs.) In Coventry, impromptu garden pig-slaying was banned, and all pigs had to be killed at the slaughterhouse. A further issue arose with the preparation of the carcass by scalding; in Coventry, this was carried out next to the river, so that scalding water, mixed with blood and hair, was ejected into a ditch and then infected the river too. Understandably, the mixture smelt foul. Other town ordinances insisted that slaughterhouses keep their doors clean from blood and other filth.

From medieval times pig was above all the meat of the poor. When fourteenth-century Piers the Plowman confesses that he no longer has bacon left to make collops, he is saying that he will be hungry and even malnourished.[15] The Irish peasantry, who lived in a subsistence fashion for longer, called June and July the hunger months; the pig meat was all eaten and the potatoes and grain not ready.[16] Pig was a staple but also a yummy treat; when gossips met in a tavern for a chat in the London of Shakespeare and Jonson, they might bring morsels of pork to share.

––––––––––

There was a kind of class hierarchy written on the pig's thick and flexible skin. The parts that looked the least piggy were the poshest in all pre-industrial eras (except for the head of the wild pig, though this was more a display item than a food); the piggiest and the darkest parts were the least posh. Yet a number of foods arose from the entrails, in the form of andouille-like sausages; or the offal could simply be eaten at once. Neighbours killed their pigs at intervals so they could share the perishable offal, which was a treat. Then preservation work – bacon and salt pork – began, as we shall see later.

In some places in Europe, pigs instead of the more usual lambs were especially fattened for Easter. The smallest pig might be reserved for it. Ham is the particular Easter dish of Burgundy and northern France. In Paris there was a 'ham fair' on Good Friday, to allow housewives to stock up for Sunday. The sudden devouring of fresh pork and lard celebrated Christian non-Jewishness – 'the more we enjoy the piglet/ The better Catholics we become', says one frank song from Burgundy. Monastic records suggest this also happened in England. Under Abbot Geoffrey at St Paul's Walden (1119–46), the Hertfordshire villages of Codicote and Walden were obliged between them to supply a pig at Christmas and at Easter.[17] In the same century the village of

Rickmansworth supplied, along with hens and eggs, one pig at Christmas and one pig at Easter.[18]

Not everybody loved the sweet and fatty pig's meat. For the Jewish communities of medieval Europe, such meat was not a feast, but was strictly forbidden by their religion. The Jewish dietary restriction on eating pig meat was noted as early as ancient Rome; gourmand Roman writer Petronius Arbiter in a poetic fragment misunderstood this as the Jews' reverence for a porcine deity.[19] The same restrictions were true of any visiting Muslims; Christian awareness of this difference probably grew during the Crusades. The realisation that the Jews did not share Christian delight in pig meat marked them as outside the eating norms of society. This in turn laid them open to suspicions of other and more terrifying transgressions. If the Jews refused to eat delicious pig and tasty bacon, then what did they want? Terrible rumours grew and circulated.

On 25 March 1144, a boy's corpse showing signs of a violent death was found in Thorpe Wood near Norwich. The day was Holy Saturday, the day before Easter. The body was not touched until Easter Monday, when it was buried where it lay. Local Jews were suspected of the murder on account of the nature of the boy's wounds, which were supposedly like the wounds of the crucified Jesus. The body was that of William, a tanner's apprentice. It was said that William had been in the habit of frequenting Jewish houses. On Fig Monday (Monday of Holy Week), William had been decoyed away from his mother, and was seen to enter a Jew's house; this was the last time he was seen alive. On Spy Wednesday, after a service in the synagogue, the Jews allegedly lacerated his head with thorns, crucified him and pierced his side; a Christian serving-woman, with one eye only, caught sight through a crack in a door of a boy fastened to a post as she was bringing hot water at her master's order. On Good Friday, the Jew Eleazar and another supposedly carried the corpse in a sack to the wood. A Jewish convert claimed that 'in the ancient writings of his Fathers it was written that the Jews, without the shedding of human blood, could neither obtain their freedom, nor could they ever return to their fatherland. Hence ... every year they must sacrifice a Christian in some part of the world.' In 1144 it had been the turn of the Jews of Norwich.

This was the first recorded case in England of what came to be known as the blood libel. The story crystallised Christian preoccupations with the Jews' alleged guilt for the death of Jesus Christ (this was focused especially on the phrase in Matthew's gospel in which the Jewish priests present at the trial of Jesus say, 'his blood be upon our heads and upon those of our children'). The Jewish refusal of pork was linked to the blood guilt that also led them to torture and murder Christian children in imitation of Jesus' Passion. The fiction persisted with slight variations throughout the twelfth century (it is recorded in Gloucester in 1168, Blois in 1171 and Saragossa in 1182), and was repeated in many libels of the thirteenth century. In the case of Little Saint Hugh of Lincoln, the link between child murder and food was only too obvious: 'the Child was first fattened for ten days with white bread and milk [like a pig] and then … almost all the Jews of England were invited to the crucifixion.' The story was designed to arouse fury and dread, and its spread meant that anti-Semitism took more and more violent forms.

To the motifs of crucifixion, sadism, hatred of the innocent and of Christianity, and the unnaturalness of the Jews, there were added from time to time the ingredients of sorcery, perversity, and a kind of blind obedience to a cruel tradition. Even the commonly expressed link between Jewishness and red hair became a sign of the Jews' blood lust and blood needs. This bloodiness also linked them to pigs, because pigs too were believed to be bursting with blood, a belief connected with the fact that they were usually killed by having their throats slit and their bodies drained of blood, a method of slaughter that – oddly – comes close to kosher killing.

More educated Christians knew that the Jews abhorred blood; the Emperor Frederick's synod of converts (in about 1243) stated: 'There is not to be found, either in the Old or the New Testament, that the Jews are desirous of human blood. On the contrary, they avoid contamination with any kind of blood.' A few years later, in 1247, Pope Innocent IV wrote: 'Christians charge falsely … that [the Jews] hold a communion rite … with the heart of a murdered child.' Yet these words did not stop the libel. Perhaps Christians were constantly reminded by what they saw as the peculiarities of the Jewish diet. Pigs kept cropping up in the blood libel stories, condensing the Jews' supposed crimes into a single symbol. Some blood libel folktales depicted Jews who, trying to buy the heart of a Christian child to eat as communion, were fobbed off with the heart of a pig instead.[20] Similarly, a Jew seeking the milk of a Christian wet-nurse was tricked with sow's milk. In another tale, a Jew soaked the head of a hanged man in sow's milk, bribing a Christian to help him, and the next day all the local pigs gathered at the spot and killed one another.[21]

Violent tales led to violence. Trouble often began at carnival time, with the Jews' failure to share in the giant pig meat feast of Mardi Gras (Fat Tuesday). A massacre of Jews at Stamford in Lincolnshire took place at the Lent Fair itself, on 7 March 1190, and another massacre at Bury St Edmunds in Suffolk on Palm Sunday, 19 March 1190.[22] Food was so much a part of both festivals, Passover and Easter, that it made the cultural and religious disparity particularly visible.[23] Beginning on Ash Wednesday, medieval Christians began to eat almost like Jews, forced to avoid all pig flesh – along with other flesh, to be sure, but there was a curious emphasis on pig flesh in depictions of the *gras* to which everyone was saying farewell. Pots and pans were scoured, rubbed with ash, and all pork was encased in cloth wraps, sausages stored out of sight or scent, and fat pots sealed off. Their many roles in cooking were replaced by oil, herring, cod and herbs. Chickpeas, pulses and peas also came into use, and these too were associated with folktales which pitted the Jews against Christ. (Chickpeas helped Jesus hide from the Jews by growing miraculously.) The church calendar reminded Christians at every turn of the Jews living among them.

In 1190, events came to a head in York on Shabbat Ha-Gadol, the Sabbath before Passover begins, the day on which pious Jews would obtain their perfect lamb. For urban Jews, this may have involved trading with the Christian community, and thus inadvertently reminding them of their supposed blood guilt. As Passover neared, the Jewish community in York did what other Jewish communities had been forced to do: they threw themselves into the hands of law and order. Their leader Josce asked the warden of York Castle to receive them with their wives and children, and they were accepted into Clifford's Tower. At once the tower was besieged by a mob, demanding that the Jews convert to Christianity. Trapped in the castle, the Jews were advised by their religious leader, Rabbi Yom Tov of Joigny, to kill themselves rather than convert. Josce began by killing his wife and children, and then he himself was killed by Yom Tov. The father of each family killed his wife and children, and then Yom Tov stabbed the men before killing himself. A handful of Jews who had not killed themselves surrendered at daybreak on 17 March, leaving the castle on a promise that they would not be harmed. That promise was not kept, and they were murdered. In the aftermath the wooden tower was burnt down. William of Newburgh, our best contemporary source, is sure that local nobles and gentry who owed the Jews money exploited the crowd hysteria, much as modern looters might exploit political protests, but such cold pragmatism did not cause the violence, though it may have exploited it. The marking of holidays by communal feasting meant that anyone who failed to join in was marked out.

The links between the Jews, pigs and pig-feasts were part of the reason for the horrific massacre of the Jews of York. The English are les rosbifs, the French are frogs, and the Piedmontese are polenta eaters. They are what they eat. But the Jews are what they *don't* eat. They are defined by refusal. Food history tends to deal with populations as if they were a single mouth and a single belly. In reality, even the foodstuffs most privileged by one dominant segment of society may be rejected by others.

———————

One reason, perhaps, for the pig's centrality to identity is that the pig is the boundary between human and animal. Pigs are like humans in a way that other animals are not. Like humans, they seem naked, their fur fine, their skin visible, pink or black. Like humans, they are omnivores. Like humans, they are keen problem-solvers. Caring for a piglet is like caring for a baby. Fed like us, on our food, the pig is troublingly like us. And as he accompanied us through history, he became more like us, and therefore he troubled us more and more, at least until the modern day.

Even more than other animals, the hairless pig defined what counts as human. Pigs were a summation of what is basic and banal in the human. The equation between pigs and people reached an apogee with the appearance of some freaks. In the 1630s, one 'pig-faced lady' came from Holland to London, seeking a husband. She was called Tannakin, and had been brought up very carefully at home, always wearing a veil. What had caused her to have a pig face? Tannakin's mother remembered that while she was pregnant, an old woman had come to the door begging for coin. Tannakin's mother turned her away with rough words, and the old woman was heard to mutter to herself the devil's Paternoster. Even at the stake, the old woman refused to reverse the spell. Tannakin ate from a silver trough, but could speak only in squeaks and grunts. Finally, a magician called Vandermist suggested she be married off to cure her, and the parents offered a gigantic dowry to help matters along. Venal suitors duly appeared, but none could bring themselves actually to marry the swine-faced lady, despite her wealth.

Thomas Grenville collected pamphlets about the pig-faced woman. Later he had them attractively bound, in pigskin. Samuel Pepys was interested, too, keeping a copy of the ballad about her, 'A Monstrous Shape'. As time went on, fake pig-faced ladies began to be manufactured as entertainments. Such tales of pig-faced girls were another aspect of the anti-Semitism that defined Christianity in opposition to Judaism. In medieval folktales, the pig-faced girl was the daughter of a man who had converted from Christianity to Judaism. His daughter was born with a pig's head, but she was restored to beauty when the man reconverted to Christianity. The difference between pig and human is no greater than that between Christian and Jew, the story suggests. To live surrounded by wealth, but to live ugly and alone, an outsider unable to share the feast ...

And yet the pig's closeness to the human could also create soothing dreams, such as the popular medieval dream of the land of Cockaigne.

This was a realm where you could eat whatever you wanted, whenever you wanted it. No heart attack. No weight gain. No reproach. No expense. No indigestion. And absolutely no shopping or preparation. The food drops into your hands, or into your mouth, like a kiss from God. Such food was *holiday* food. Most people probably know that the very word holiday derives from the term holy day, a day set aside for feasting. The medieval calendar alternated between periods of normality, periods of fasting, and periods of highly specialised excess. Still well-known is the fast of Shrove Tuesday, or Mardi Gras. Pancakes might be the norm now in England, but the point of them was to use up the householder's supply of forbidden Lent foods: animal (especially pig) fat, typically lard (still used in Brittany), once used to grease the griddle and also included in the recipe, butter, eggs. As we have seen, Shrove, or shrive, Tuesday was a kind of Christian version of the great clearing out that accompanies Jewish Passover. It was mainly about saying goodbye to meat, because meat was hot and dry, and liable to make the eater hot and dry too, angry and sinful and sexual. In renouncing it, the penitent was also saying goodbye to his own carnal nature (from Latin *carnis*, meat, the flesh of animals). So it is not surprising that meat, *lots* of meat, was the object of passionate, even crazy fantasy. The chronically hungry in particular fantasised about meat, for meat contained the protein and fat they craved. Fasting is compensated by bingeing. Oddly, the dieter's cycle of near-fast followed by enormous brownie pig-out – note that term well – is a private secular version of what was once a religious festival.

So it was that fasting and privation – voluntary and involuntary – were accompanied by dreams of the land of Cockaigne, a land where cheeses fell from the sky, roast geese flew directly into the mouths of the recumbent gluttons, and the houses were made of barley sugar and pancakes, like the witch's house in 'Hansel and Gretel'. Other Cockaigne houses had paling fences made of sausages; the streets were paved with pastry, and the shops supplied goods for nothing. Best of all, roasted pigs wandered about with knives in their backs to make carving easy and guilt-free, rather like the magic pudding in Norman Lindsay's book of that name, or the suicidal cakes in *Alice's Adventures in Wonderland* which beg 'Eat me'. The suicidal roast meats not only reflect laziness, but also a kind of guilt about the carnage which would otherwise be involved in a meat orgy.[24]

The closest to these orgiastic spectacles in real life were fairs and feasts, also depicted satirically by those who disapproved of them. In his 1614 play *Bartholomew Fair*, Ben Jonson – who worried constantly about his own porkiness – seems to think we are what we eat. His riotous Fair is a haven of the flesh, where those interested in the spirit are rebuked. The roast pig on sale is itself an object of the unnatural longing of pregnant Win-the-fight (a Puritan name). The 'fleshly motion of Pig' is 'the Tempter' and Win must resist it. But she must also indulge her longing for the sake of her baby; it was believed that pregnant women's cravings represented their babies' needs. The cure for Win's sickness is a roast pig pig-out. Win's pregnant pigginess is echoed by Puritan minister Zeal-of-the-Land Busy's greed: Busy has already eaten a turkey pie and drunk a glass of malmsey while hidden in a cupboard, but he finds the roast pig very hard to resist. Fairground pigs seem to flow into the characters and reveal their animal natures. The porky ruling spirit is Ursula the pigwoman, whose immensity makes everyone who sees her think of unmanageable flesh: 'she's mother o' the pigs ... some walking sow of tallow'.[25] After burning her leg by getting into a fight while carrying a fat-pan, Ursula exclaims 'Run for some cream and salad oil, quickly!', as if she herself were now an edible dish (incidentally, it also shows that a *salade aux lardons* was both imaginable and edible). The nausea thus induced is meant to indicate the dismay of indulgence. In a similar vein, Shakespeare calls fat Falstaff 'thou whoreson little tidy Bartholomew bore-pig'.[26]

The pig-eating at Bartholomew Fair is a remnant of the much older Easter traditions described above, of pig giving and pig sharing as the foundation of social relations, even though St Bartholomew's Day is 24 August, opposite Easter on the wheel of the year, ending summer rather than launching it. Puritans felt as exiled from this as Jews. Bartholomew Fair, first licensed in the fourteenth century, lasted a full two weeks and covered four parishes; it was famous for public drunkenness and disorder. Ursula's pigs were also famous, pigs of excess, pigs whose dumb, succulent flesh contrasted with the busy, mobile grounds of the fair and seemed redolent of a more indulgent past. But in Jonson's play, the pig is eventually accepted by Busy just because of anti-Semitism: he proclaims 'there may be a good use made of it, too, now I think of it: by the public eating of Swines' flesh, to profess our hate, and loathing of Judaism, whereof the brethren stand taxed. I will therefore eat, yea, I will eat exceedingly.' Clearly this is an excuse, but it is a telling one, and it is picked up eagerly by others: 'I' faith, I will eat heartily too, because I will be no Jew, I could never away with that stiffnecked generation: and truly, I hope my little one will be like me, that cries for Pig so, in the mother's belly.' The point about pig meat is that it was impossible to disguise. The fair's gingerbread, on the other hand, is suspect: 'stale bread, rotten eggs, musty ginger, and dead honey'.[27]

At festival time, dietary taboos are publicly and spectacularly broken. Frantic bingeing results from the effort to scarf down the food while the feast lasts. Prohibitions must occur to make such eating more fun; the whole point of festive food is to crave it in advance, and that requires that it can be envisaged, as exactly as possible, and that the appetitive person expects it to be identical each year. If you long for Bartholomew pig, then it must be the same pig every year. If Ursula failed to appear, or if she ran out of pork, it would cast a cloud over expectation for ever. (Convenience food merchants underestimate the public's appetite for the same old thing in their pursuit of a greater market share.) The fairground's roast pork transcended social class and emulsified it, but only for a few days, and only by inviting the better off to pretend to be peasants in autumn.

———

Outside such festivals, the rich ate relatively little pork. The Willoughbys of Wollaton Hall, a gentry family, ate much more beef than anything else, and so too did the Pagets of Beaudesert, Staffordshire, in 1576. Mutton came next, pushing pork out of second place sometime in the fourteenth century; archaeological evidence from Lincoln shows a fall in the number of discarded pig bones found.

Pigs were reared in great houses in association with the dairy, because they could be fed on whey and other dairying by-products, as well as on waste grain from brewing. At Wollaton, pigs also ate bought pease.[28]

Pork, bacon and brawn were all associated with late autumn, winter and early spring. All the bacon or brawn was home-produced. Brawn was a delicacy for Yuletide; the rolled, soused meat of a wild boar was a noble meat. William Rabisha uses the word 'brawn' for the edible flesh of *any* beast, any part that looks like meat but is not offal. William Harrison comments on the English delight in it, as prepared by their French cooks. Thomas Tusser also has it on the Christmas table: 'he that can rear up a pig in his house,/ Hath cheaper his bacon, and sweeter his souse.'[29] The staple pig at Wollaton was the porker: according to the OED 'a young pig raised and fattened for food, esp. one raised for uncured pork rather than bacon; (also more generally) a pig'. Originally the porker was a better class of pig, but like most words linked to pigs, it became an insult. The porker, with his refined diet, his hefty fattened body, became a metaphor for greed, and slow-witted greed at that: 'thou dunder-headed English porker'.[30]

———

Second-century medical writer Galen had praised pork's healthy qualities, and many later medieval and Renaissance dietary advisers agreed.[31] Other dieticians, however, said pork was mainly appealing to wantons – a lust for flesh – and still others likened pig-eating to cannibalism. The taste of pork 'has such likeness to man's flesh, both in savour and taste, that some have eaten man's flesh instead of pork,' thought Thomas Cogan in 1636.[32] Pork offal was reckoned delicious, but not to be indulged in often. Pork, thought Thomas Moffett, 'is sweet, luscious, and pleasant to wantons … it was the bane of my own Mother'. Other dietaries were troubled by God's prohibition on swine flesh in the Old Testament, and spent considerable energy defending the pig: 'Almighty God, did prohibit the Jews to eat swine's flesh: it was a figure to abstain from unclean things, which I leave to the divines.' Bullein a Puritan physician, continues with a robust account of blood sausages: 'The Blood of Swine doth nourish much, as is seen in Puddings, made with great Oatmeal, Pepper, sweet suet, and Fennel, or Aniseeds. Young Pigs be very moist, therefore Sage. Pepper and Salt doth dry up the superfluous humours of them when they be roasted.'

He also expresses enthusiasm for boar: 'boar's flesh is proved in the time of Pestilence, to break a plague sore. Boar's grease, and his stones, or any part of them stamped together and warm applied to the same sore, worketh that effect.' Health foods in this period were always considered to work homeopathically – that is, a small amount of whatever poison was killing you would draw out the rest, so the plague-relieving power of boar might not be as comfortable a prospect as it seems at first glance. This discomfort with the pig is reaffirmed when Bullein writes, in apparent relief, 'and thus I do end of Swine, which in their lives be most vile, noisome, and never good until they die'.[33] Similarly, pig fat was seen as medicinal precisely because of its uncleanness. Fulke Greville's physicians treated his wounds by filling them with pig fat rather than disinfecting them. The pig fat turned rancid and infected the wounds, and he died in agony four weeks after the attack.[34]

We are perhaps oddly susceptible to stories which show us pigs' capabilities. In his book *The Pig Who Sang to the Moon*, Jeffrey Masson uses the story of the eponymous musical pig, and assumes this will keep us from pork, bacon and sausages.[35] But my paternal grandmother had a hand-reared runt pigling with a passion for music. He always crept into the room to listen, ears raised and head cocked, whenever she played the piano. My father recalled that despite this pig's elevated sensibility, they ate him as usual. Evidently, my father's entire family failed entirely to grasp the pig's human-like consciousness. Something about the pig prompts such stories of the wanton destruction of such a life, a life of known sensibility – an ensouled life? *Charlotte's Web*, *Babe*, *Betty Blue-Eyes* – all are stories of pigs, menaced by the knife. Why pigs and not sheep or cows? Because sheep or cows have other purposes, perhaps? Or because pink, clean piglets look very like human babies, as Lewis Carroll observes in *Alice's Adventures in Wonderland*, where Alice warns the baby that she will have nothing more to do with him if he turns into a pig?

In his satire 'A Modest Proposal', Jonathan Swift suggested controlling Irish poverty by encouraging the Irish to sell their babies as meat for wealthy gourmets. While writing of children, he is clearly thinking about pigs and their treatment. Part of the discomfort he intends to create in the reader depends on the resemblance between child and pig:

> the addition of some thousand carcasses in our exportation
> of barrelled beef; the propagation of swine's flesh and
> improvement in the art of making good bacon, so much
> wanted among us by the great destruction of pigs, too frequent
> at our tables, which are no way comparable in taste, or
> magnificence to a well-grown, fat yearling child, which roasted
> whole will make a considerable figure at a Lord Mayor's feast or
> any other public entertainment.[36]

Swift's very sharp point is that gluttony in England is devouring the Irish already. The uncomfortable sense of eating something that looks quite like a human baby leads on to a willingness to recognise that human babies are dying as a result of gluttonous eating.

The pig's interest in humans and his sensitivity to feelings are well documented, but find little fictional outlet until the 1950s, when a batch of children's books such as *Charlotte's Web* seek to offer a gentler pig. In E. B. White's novel, the distance between the farmyard and the urban readership the book solicits has become a gentle occasion for sentiment. White had previously published 'Death of a Pig', an equivocal tale of his own experience with a sick pig, and his dislike of becoming the pig's doctor and advocate when he all along intended to kill it: 'I wanted no interruption in the regularity of feeding, the steadiness of growth, the even succession of days. I wanted no interruption, wanted no oil, no deviation. I just wanted to keep on raising a pig, full meal after full meal, spring into summer into fall.'[37]

For White, the pig is somehow imbued with the same vitality that the ancient Celts sought to ingest in the wild boar feasts: 'From the lustiness of a healthy pig a man derives a feeling of personal lustiness; the stuff that goes into the trough and is received with such enthusiasm is an earnest of some later feast of his own, and when this suddenly comes to an end and the food lies stale and untouched, souring in the sun, the pig's imbalance becomes the man's.' This atavistic identification oddly roots the regret for the pig's illness entirely in what that illness symbolises for the man who wants to eat him. White's story further undermines Masson's argument. Our ancestors might prefer disgust as a weapon, but whatever is chosen to divide us from our pigs can be overcome by fresh efforts to make the animal's death seem justified.

Pigs have long presented a particular category problem. We can think of the interchangeability of humans and pigs as appealing rather than as demonic and dreadful, as it is in George Orwell's *Animal Farm*. Our difficulty with categories is exemplified by our very affection for the pig we eat, versus the dog we will not eat. 'Pigs', we say, 'are intelligent, sensitive animals', and there are a number of heart-wrenching tales of pig emotionality to back this up. In 1847, William Youatt had noted that:

> In their native state swine seem by no means destitute of natural affections; they are gregarious, assemble together for warmth, and appear to have feelings in common. How often among the peasantry, where the pig is, in a manner of speaking, one of the family, may this animal be seen following his master from place to place, and grunting his recognition to his protectors.[38]

But the term 'protectors' is odd here, as is the idea of the pig as a family member, when the family is planning to eat it. If someone is a family member, they should not be eaten. And yet the sympathetic pig exists only to be eaten by the villagers who succour him.

Pigs remained both rural creatures, fed on acorns and berries, and urban, fed on brewing waste. At the very moment in the early seventeenth century when cities were trying to exile shambles and tanneries from their centres to make for cleanness and order, some of their citizens sought to bring the pig back to town. Ambulatory livestock like hens and pigs continued to be a problem. Because pigs are omnivores, as we have seen, they were also urban foragers, rooting in dunghills and middens. Towns passed further ordinances and laws to control them. In 1664, keepers of pigs in Liverpool were forced to house them in backyards, not in the streets – roaming pigs were to be given to the injured party, a proviso which illustrates the expectation that there would *be* an injured party. In other towns, there were complaints about dead pigs clogging the streets, and owners were required to bury them, but these were evidently pannage pigs from the countryside, not sty pigs, whose owners were treating the town streets as an impromptu and unlicensed pannage site. This was practical in a world of pannage charges, increased restrictions on access to forests, and the obvious difficulty of driving pigs from the town to distant woodlands. Eventually, a kind of pig clamping scheme was introduced – owners had to pay to get their pig back.

Towns made further desperate efforts to control slaughterhouse waste. In Cambridge people had to take to the pudding pits beyond Castle Hill the paunches, guts, filth, entrails and blood of all beasts. In Southampton a group of butchers were fined in the first year of James I's reign for creating very bad smells, while another Southampton butcher was given to fly-tipping waste into the back gardens of his neighbours, which was not appreciated. The huge piggery on Tottenham Court Road in London also aroused many complaints. Neighbours complained that their servants got sick because the smell 'drives through walls'.[39] Similarly, the smells around the Smithfield slaughterhouses aroused real distaste. To try to make use of the mess, offal in London was collected to feed the dogs of the common hunt. However, many were not reconciled; the streets were 'infested with this shameful practice [slaughter]; the offensive smells, the disagreeable Objects of bleeding heads, entrails of beasts, offals, raw hides, and the kennels flowing with blood and nastiness'. When manners and gentility come into play, the process of food production becomes problematic. Though there were also complaints about unswept vegetable markets.

As London and other towns began to win the war against stinking tanneries and obnoxious slaughterhouses, people were able to be 'nicer', more squeamish and mannerly; their distance from the smelly source of food increased, and was further widened by the distance they wished to put between themselves and the servants who prepared their food. The vastness of London ensured that nobody needed look the pig they were about to eat in the eye before dining on it. They needed no longer even look the pig's killer in the eye. They didn't know about its innards, its ears, its tail.

As the sense of discernment and discrimination increased, it began to make an impact on nose-to-tail pig eating. Class-based discrimination between parts of the pig increased. Tender single joints, later steaks, become valued meats and correspondingly expensive. Odd bits, blood and organs, became devalued, except for an eccentric taste for tripe or pig's ears. Sausages were especially feared because nobody knew what ended up in them; pork pie was doubtful too. But even the freshest pork became suspect. When low fat became equated with health, fatty pig meat lost its status. Still useful for the poor, it was no longer satisfying for the elite.

Why do people's food tastes *ever* change? Most studies of 'taste' are static. They trace the 'development' of tastes, but not how or why they altered. Often, key assumptions are simply reiterated: babies seek sweetness, all people seek a return to childhood tastes and are impeded only by lack of availability of their childhood favourites, more 'sophisticated' tastes can be 'acquired'. But the overfed inhabitants of both developed and emerging economies are constantly bombarded with 'new' foods, or more commonly with new ways to present old foods, searches for novelty *and* familiarity as the safest bets. Most research on the subject has been done by food marketers, with academics loping lamely behind. Marketers also know that setting influences flavour; there is no naked palate. So taste happens not just in the palate, but also in the mind. And yet in England few of us eat as our parents did. Was it really just astute marketing that changed our tastes so radically?

If any man knew the value of the pig, it was William Cobbett. His rules for pig-keeping are so detailed that they could be used as guidelines even now. But they are descriptions as well as prescriptions. He urges that 'the cottager's pig should be bought in the spring, or late in winter; and being then four months old, he will be a year old before killing time', and goes on to insist – just as a modern foodie might – that mature meat is far better than young meat:

> The flesh is more solid and more nutritious than that of a young hog, much in the same degree that the mutton of a full-mouthed wether is better than that of a younger wether. The pork or bacon of young hogs, even if fatted on corn, is very apt to *boil out*, as they call it; that is to say, come out of the pot smaller in bulk than it goes in.

He also insists that the pig's fat is the best part of the beast:

> Lean bacon is the most wasteful thing that any family can use. In short, it is uneatable, except by drunkards, who want something to stimulate their sickly appetite. The man who cannot live on *solid fat* bacon, well-fed and well-cured, wants the sweet sauce of labour, or is fit for the hospital.

And he urges cottagers not to waste the drawn innards: 'Here, in the mere offal, in the mere garbage, there is food, and delicate food too, for a large family for a week; and hog's puddings for the children, and some for neighbours' children, who come to play with them ...' His joyful account of the pig's carcass – 'then the house is *filled with meat!* Souse, griskins, blade-bones, thigh-bones, spare-ribs, chines, belly-pieces, cheeks' – is full and greedy.

In *Rural Rides*, Cobbett meets a labourer hoeing turnips. 'I was glad to see his food consisted of a good lump of household bread and not a very small piece [i.e. a large piece] of bacon.'[40] Cobbett 'saw, with great

delight, a pig at almost every labourer's house'. The houses had 'a pig
in almost every cottage sty, and that is the infallible mark of a happy
people'.[41] This is naïve of him; Wiltshire was poor and dependent on
the pig cash crop, so it's likely that the pigs were simply raised for sale.
His love affair with pigs defines centuries of rural masculinity. It was a
man's job to butcher, perhaps even to smoke or salt-cure. And it was
men who ate the products, because the fat they contained would allow
men to keep working.

———————

The modern world is very used to meat in ready-prepared portions.
But such portioning is relatively recent; our fathers (let alone our forefathers) were once required to carve a joint or a whole bird at the table,
a display of prowess (or the lack of it) with the knife that itself was also
a display of generosity and hospitality, and which could be correlated
with status and even with sexuality (as in Alfred Hitchcock's joke line
for Cary Grant and Grace Kelly – 'breast, or leg?'). However, apart
from suckling pig, the pig was not usually experienced in this way;
pork butchery involved the creation of pig products which were not
even spoken of as such – brawn, headcheese, bacon, ham, pork,
gammon, pudding, lard – as if to disguise their piggy origins, so that
the word 'pig' could be left to accumulate associations of dirt and
greed which did not contaminate or only lightly contaminated the
meat. A whole pig at a feast might well have been an unusual, perhaps
even a transgressive or upsetting sight, recalling the body of a child in
its slender nakedness. But the suckling pig, that decadent luxury …
served with the head attached, the eyes in place. Whole enough to
imagine in life. A gourmet dish, and that means food which hovers on
the edge of what we find comfortable.

When was the middling urban gourmand born? We might identify
Charles Lamb as the first of them. Lamb was a close friend of leading
Romantic poets Wordsworth and Coleridge, a writer whose essays
were popular in his lifetime and adored afterwards by the Victorians
for their kindly thoughts. Lamb loved the grimy metropolis, and felt
he could almost taste it. For Lamb, the London fog itself had a flavour,

'something between egg flip and omelette soufflé, but much more digestible than either'. When asked about the Lake District, he said he was obliged 'to think of the Ham and Beef shop near St Martin's Lane'; he also characterised London by 'steams of soups from kitchens'.[42]

Lamb's friend Shelley denounced 'the hypocritical sensualist at the Lord Mayor's Feast' who declaimed against the pleasures of the table, while eating roast pig. To be a flesh eater was only a step from being a cannibal: 'those accustomed to eat the brute, shall not long abstain from eating the man', said vegetarian Joseph Ritson; 'when toasted or broil'd on the altar, the appearance, favour, and taste of both would be nearly, if not entirely, the same.' But Lamb became the champion of 'the indulgence of the immoderate pleasures of the palate'. Against Coleridge's honeydew and milk of paradise, he set the taste of roast pig and crackling. Lamb's fictional essay character Edax insisted that man was naturally carnivorous, while society's reformers saw consumer culture exemplified by luxury and overindulgence in flesh-eating.[43]

Edax's large-scale eating was contrasted with another Lamb character, Elia, more judicious in his gourmandising, less interested in quantity than in quality. Elia, however, was the one who feasted on the most delicate taste of all, roast pig. Ritson tried to deter people by portraying the pig made to suffer by being pierced by red-hot spikes. But Elia described the pig as the triumph of a civilisation over the barbarism of raw meat. Depicting a nauseating devouring of raw flesh, Lamb's essay went on to tell a folktale of the discovery of the joy of cooking. A young boy in China sets fire to his father's hut by accident, thus incinerating his herd of pigs. In a strange echo of Finn and the Salmon of Knowledge, the horrified boy, feeling a pig's carcass for signs of life, burns his fingers, and applies his burnt fingers to his mouth. He thus discovers burnt flesh, and in particular the pleasures of '*crackling*!' The boy is so delighted that he tears up handfuls of scorched flesh. The father arrives home to a smoking ruin and a boy gorging on pig flesh. He too is instantly converted by the unforgettably wonderful taste. The family are found devouring dead pig and are put on trial, but eventually the whole jury are likewise converted.

Lamb presented this as a tale about the irresistible pleasure of roast pig. A single taste, a mere lick of the fingers, prompts near-ferocious, unstoppable conversion and gorging. As a narrative about changes in taste, however, it says nothing. The story takes it for granted that the taste itself will convert the unwilling, even those who see eating flesh as disgusting or sacrilegious.[44]

Ritson himself used the story, which originates in third-century philosopher Porphyry's 'Essay on the Abstinence from Animal Flesh', as a disgusting parable of gluttonous loss of control, animalistic tearing at bodies.[45] Lamb simply reversed the meaning, rhapsodising over the 'crisp, tawny, well-watched, not over-roasted crackling', the 'teeth overcoming the coy, brittle resistance' (note the sexual language), with 'the adhesive oleaginous – O call it not fat – but an indefinable sweetness growing up to it – the tender blossoming of fat – fat cropped in the bud –' The dashes seem like gasps of pleasure, as if Lamb is in erotic love with the pig he eats.

In Lamb's imagination, the piglet almost enjoyed the warmth of the oven: 'Behold him, while he is doing – it seemeth rather a refreshing warmth, than a scorching heat, that he is so passive to. How equably he twirleth round the string! – Now he is just done.' This may be fantasy, but it becomes more disturbing when Lamb imagines in lyrical and even miraculous terms the piglet's eyes bursting in the heat of roasting: 'To see the extreme sensibility of that tender age, he hath wept out his pretty eyes – radiant jellies – shooting stars – See him in the dish, his second cradle, how meek he lieth! –' The pigling, he explains, was not really slaughtered, but saved from the fate which awaits the older pig, a fate of degradation, the 'grossness and indocility' of maturity – and being eaten as sausages by a 'coalheaver'.[46]

The suckling was thus saved from a precipitous descent of the class ladder by being killed before his time. In a letter to Coleridge, Lamb also delights in 'brain sauce', crackling 'the colour of the ripe pomegranate', and praises brawn – produced, Shelley said, by 'cruelly keeping the pig upright to make his flesh hard'.[47] For Shelley, animal rights were set against urban commerce, which was understood as callous and rapacious. Lamb however trumped mere commerce with his gastronomic sensitivity and rapture. Feasting on a suckling pig represented both a trembling sin and a shivering delight: 'A young and tender suckling – under a moon old – guiltless as yet of the sty – his voice as yet not broken, but somewhere between a childish treble and a grumble – the mild forerunner, or praeludium, of a grunt.'[48]

Lamb wrote as if the pig were still alive. And Lamb's pig is *lucky* to be eaten … The brutality of the pig industry that produced him takes some believing. Pigs were whipped to death to improve their flavour. Lamb, though, simply regarded the piglet as edible baroque. Even the most tough-minded gastronome must recoil a trifle at Lamb's relish at consuming the small and vulnerable baby. But the babylike flesh is the subject of desire just because it is so different from the tough, rotten, elderly swine flesh gobbled by the poor.

Not everyone agreed with Lamb. Suckling pig, wrote twentieth-century teacher, florist and cook Constance Spry, 'is undoubtedly pork in its most delicate form; unfortunately, served in the traditional way it can look unpleasantly realistic, and to children in particular may be almost horrifying'.[49] She concluded that it was better for the suckling to be 'carved out of sight, so that I may never see it whole as a dish'. But even today, the suckling pig is served in excess, with head and trotters firmly attached: suckling pig for fourteen to sixteen diners is a speciality of Fergus Henderson's St John Restaurant, and it is served with a knife sticking out of its head, alone and entire.

When the family of Lamb's more modest contemporary, Jane Austen, moved abruptly to Bath, in 1801, they lost access to their dairy, poultry yard, brewery and beehives, so they had to shop for more of their food, and pay for it with money, too. In their previous home at Steventon, they had been able to live off their family glebe lands and the rented Cheesedown farm – and together these supplied pork, mutton, wheat, peas, barley and hops. As soon as they moved again – to Southampton – they developed their small terrace garden into a vegetable patch. Expensive commodities had to be bought – chocolate, sugar, tea, coffee, wine and spices. Austen's brothers were in the navy. Just as food circulated among friendly households – a glut of apples, but also a glut of pork meat when a pig was butchered – so Austen's brothers took pork cured at home with them on long sea voyages, perhaps as modern students returning to university might take boxes of biscuits.

Making a present of pork to your nearest and dearest was probably less odd when the pig himself lived in close proximity to those who were to eat him. Even quite modest landholders could have a large stock of pigs, and the Austens had over twenty. Their pigs were killed in November, and it was quite an event. 'We are to kill a pig soon,' Jane wrote, and this pig was probably the one cured for Charles Austen. Jane Austen never lost the awareness of economy that her limited circumstances imposed, but this also involved sharing and gift exchange. Miss Bates in *Emma* also wants to share her gifts of pork and apples with her neighbours. Pork was a breakfast meat in *Mansfield Park*, eaten with mustard; this might be preserved pork, because most of a freshly killed pig went into bacon, ham, and brawn in pork jelly. Pigs intended to be eaten as pork, rather than preserved, were known as 'porkers', and were much smaller animals, less burly, and more likely to have been confined. This kind of pork made a luxury gift, as when Emma Woodhouse thinks of sending a hindquarter of pork to her former governess, who proposes to roast it, and to salt the leg for later consumption.[50] Such knowledge of how to eat pork was crucial to an economy of meat exchange. At Chawton Cottage, to which they moved in 1809, the Austens had homegrown fruit and vegetables, bees, and the ability to make bread, but neither a cow nor pigs. Reduced circumstances indeed.

———

Imagine it. The pig killer has done his job. You now have a whole, dead pig. What you do with it will depend on what kind of pig it is; it will have been reared with particular purposes in mind, perhaps. But if it is just an ordinary trotter, your course of action will be entirely determined by your nationality. Every nation in Europe will look at the hind legs and think of ham. Every nation around the world except those who don't eat pig at all will think of blood puddings in one form or another. But only the people of north-western Europe will think of bacon. Bacon is ours. And only the people of Britain will think much more of fresh sausages than of smoked, dried or cured sausages. Yes, Bavaria has Weisswurst, so fresh that they have to be eaten the same day as they are made, but in most places fresh sausages are a sideline to the real, preserved, preservable deal. Not in the insular countries and civilisations.

Compared with the historical variations in fruits and dairying, the sturdy continuity of pig foods is astounding. We can, as we will see, record and understand changing food tastes through changing tastes for chicken. A history of pork cookery, however, does not mark a variable or even fickle set of tastes, but an absolute determination to adhere to what is known. The recipes cannot be synchronised with the historical narrative. All that really changes is industrialisation, which allows some tinkering with methods to achieve what is supposed to be the same effect.

Gervase Markham had recipes for both black and white puddings. His white pudding contained a lot of suet, and a lot of dried fruit too, but no meat. His blood/black pudding recipe involved steeping oatmeal grits in pig's blood 'while it is warm' (presumably from the just-killed animal); the grits were then drained, mixed with cream and a lot of very finely chopped herbs (thyme, parsley, spinach, succory, endive, sorrel, strawberry leaves), and some chopped suet and spices. Along with a much more familiar recipe for link sausages, with sage and pork chine, Markham offers a recipe for hog's liver puddings, itself close to what we could call sausage:

> take the liver of a very fat hog and parboil it, then shred it
> small, and after, beat it in a mortar very fine, then mix it with
> the thickest and sweetest cream, strain it, add two egg whites
> and six yolks, grated crumb of a penny loaf, currants, dates,
> cloves, mace, sugar, saffron, salt, and the best swine suet, or
> beef suet, and after it has stood a while, fill it into the farmes
> [cleaned intestines], boil them, then lay them on a gridiron
> over the coals, and broil them gently.[51]

The word sausage relates to the word salted, denoting their role in preservation. It contains the bits people don't want to eat by themselves: small scraps, offal, including tripe (intestines), blood, morsels of fat, lungs. The *OED* says that originally a sausage was 'A quantity of finely chopped pork, beef, or other meat, spiced and flavoured, enclosed in a short length of the intestine of some animal, so as to form a cylindrical roll (usually, one of the "links" formed by tying the containing intestine at regular intervals); later also, in generalised sense, meat thus prepared.' Then it adds, rather disapprovingly, 'since the 19th cent., the application of the word has been greatly extended'. It's probably not referring to the problem of the modern sausage, which is to do with the proportion of meat to other, cheaper ingredients. As with bacon, sausages are often mostly water. You don't want a sausage that's all meat: they are dry, hard, unpalatable, and so too are sausages made only with lean meat. But you want pork intestine casings, not cheap polymers. And you don't want polyphosphates that allow the sausages to be bulked out with water, or soya bulk, or monosodium glutamate.

A recipe from the seventeenth-century, for instance, says: 'You must take beef fat, lean pork, mutton, bacon, pigeon or any sort of fowl stewed in white wine vinegar, herbs, mace, onions ['a good handful'] marygolds, 2 or 3 anchovy, carrots, turnips, and a few green beans or collyflowers and any greens.'[52]

Sausages deserve a whole volume to themselves. British sausages are the island equivalent of cheeses in France. They mark regions, especially in England. They vary locally, and they are named for their locale. They are *du terroir*. Oxford kates are caseless sausages – kates here just means cakes, as it often does: pork, beef suet, cloves, mace, salt and sage, mixed and bound with egg, shaped into fingers, fried in boiling hot butter, and served with the pan juices deglazed with mustard. Hannah Glasse substituted breadcrumbs for egg, which might reflect an economical turn for the sausage, though it represents the entry of the devil for some.

Unlike sausages from other food cultures, sausages in England always contain raw meat. They themselves are not cured or smoked;

they must be cooked before they can be eaten. The cheaper modern sausage may in particular contain mechanically recovered meat or meat slurry. This kind of unpleasant product could not be made before the industrial era, but earlier pig butchers and sausage makers were still notorious for filling casings with the cheapest possible content. It was the poor that benefited from eating the frugally prepared and unlovely remnants of a carcass from which the richer pickings had already been snaffled by the better off, who expected to see the whole animal, or large recognisable pieces of it, such as the leg.

The only British sausage to escape the raw meat rule is the Boloney sausage, its name strongly suggesting an association with Italy, but beloved by Charles Dickens, beef guts filled with minced pork, flavoured with caraway and laced with saltpetre. They are smoked, dried, and stored in wood ash. William Rabisha knew about them in the mid-seventeenth century, and writes of using very thin slices of them served with olive oil and vinegar, like a salade lyonnaise.

———————

Roasting and baking are among the pig's common fates, though Robert May was unusual in suggesting roasting the pig with the hair still on. The drawn pig, with feet cut off, and trussed, is spitted and laid close to the fire, though May advised that you 'be careful not to scorch him.' When one-quarter roasted,

> the skin will rise up in blisters from the flesh; then with your
> knife or hands pull off the skin and hair, and being clean flayed,
> cut slashes down to the bones, baste it with butter and cream,
> being but warm, then bread it with grated white bread,
> currants, sugar, and salt mixed together, and thus apply basting
> … till the body be covered an inch thick; then the meat being
> thoroughly roasted, draw it and serve it up whole, with sauce
> made of wine vinegar, whole cloves, cinnamon, and sugar
> boiled to a syrup.[53]

May also suggested making a pudding (a sausage/forcemeat) in the belly, with grated bread and 'some sweet herbs minced small, beef suet, raw egg yolks, nutmeg, ginger, currants, cream, salt and pepper'. The pig can also be trussed so his head is looking over his back, with a bellyful of creamy bread, and a sauce made of tart vinegar and meat juices. May had roasted pork, but also pork broiled and grilled in crumbs, breaded with mustard and vinegar, or he suggested that it be coated in apples, boiled in beer and beaten to a mash with butter. Pork was combined with green sauce, cinnamon and sugar.[54]

Pork's natural companions are warm golden spices and tart sweetnesses, plums or apples, cinnamon or saffron. Thomas Dawson's stuffing was white wine, sweet broth, nutmegs in quarters, rosemary, bay, thyme and sweet marjoram.[55] There are fifteenth-century recipes for pork balls fried in sage leaves, dumplings in broth, or roast loin of pork in boar's tail sauce, or roasted with coriander and caraway sauce.[56] Then there is the venerable pork pie, leg of pork larded with bacon and seasoned with cloves and mace, soaked in verjuice, and coloured with sandalwood or blood.[57]

Even the pig's bladder had multiple uses. Elinor Fettiplace gives a recipe for cleaning it, poking sugar with a hollow quill into it, then blowing it up like a balloon, adding a chicken, and suspending by a thread 'over a very soft fire' all day.[58] Contemporary York chef Josh Overington at Le Cochon Aveugle uses exactly that recipe to slow-roast a guinea fowl. It is apt that pig recipes are most likely to return in triumph if they have temporarily been mislaid or submerged. Later cookery writers offered extra advice on using up your pig bits. In the eighteenth century, Hannah Glasse has a variety of pork pies, including a Cheshire pork pie which contains apples and white wine as well as pork loin, and ham is central to many of her dishes, not least to her ragouts, or ragoos. She has brawn, too, though by that she means both the preserved flesh of a wild boar, and on another page the fatty foreparts of a tame pig.[59]

As we have seen, the pig was slaughtered in late autumn to provide fat and protein for those who had raised him throughout the winter months; much pig food is therefore about preservation. Before refrigeration, methods of preservation involved the use of materials which slowed or prevented the decomposition of the valued flesh. Bacon is cured meat. The *Oxford English Dictionary*'s timeline of the usage of the word bacon shows that it peaks in 1300 to 1350, and again in 1600 to 1650; both these are half centuries of hunger for the ordinary people living on the land. The word comes from old French, and from the word for back, but bacon did not always preserve a particular part of the pig.

The bacon cure could be done with smoke or with salt alone, depending on what was most readily available in a particular area. Once pigs were bred especially for bacon, they were fattened more than other pigs, because the fat took salt so well, tasting of it only mildly, while the lean tasted of it far more. Bacon-making is oddly like cheese-making (hence bacon is often sold by cheese shops rather than butchers). Like bread and beer, bacon was once made on a very small scale, even a household scale, though London bacon was made from Wiltshire pigs. The standard British bacon is still the Wiltshire cure. Originally a dry cure, this involved covering the pig's legs with salt. Stacked skin side down, the flesh began to turn pink. After a fortnight the salt was brushed off and the sides matured for a further week. This dry cure was – well, let's be kind, adapted – by the replacement of salt with brine, injected into the sides, or made into a bath in which the meat could be soaked; here saltpetre and sugar were often added. The big smoke-rooms that developed in London could produce a flitch of bacon in as little as eight days, but it was not properly preserved; real bacon took six to eight weeks of salting and smoking. Pigs also helped to feed the English navy. Samuel Pepys assigned pigs to the boats that went out to fight against the Dutch – salt meat could include pork, usually brined, but sometimes dry-cured with a spice rub. Some sailors, though, were superstitious about pigs, replacing the word 'pig' with euphemisms like 'grunter' or 'porker'. A few would not even allow pork or bacon on board, possibly because of the Gadarene swine and a belief that pigs could not swim.

The arrival of liquid on the bacon-making scene happened in the early modern period: Kenelm Digby gives a German recipe for a partially liquid curing method in 1669. The animal is rubbed with salt, laid in a tub for seven days, and wiped dry. Digby stresses that the whole point is to force the beast to exude water, which will run off it and dissolve the salt. The modern industrial rasher, on the other hand, is injected with phosphates to force it to take in water. This boosts the meat's weight, but it is a cheat. As the bacon rasher is fried, it will exude a milky liquid, and the bacon will also hang on to a very high level of salt.

William Cobbett, as we have seen, wrote extensively about Wiltshire bacon in the early nineteenth century. He gave a detailed account of how to make it:

> The two sides that remain, and that are called *flitches*, are to be cured for *bacon*. They are first rubbed with salt on their insides, or flesh sides, then placed, one on the other, the flesh sides uppermost, in a salting trough which has a gutter round its edges to drain away the *brine*; for, to have sweet and fine bacon, the flitches must not lie sopping in brine.

He conceded that using more salt is more expensive (because of the salt tax).

Cobbett credited bacon with the power to right every wrong: '*Some* other meat you may have; but, bacon is the great thing. It is always ready; as good cold as hot; goes to the field or the coppice conveniently; in harvest, and other busy times, demands the pot to be boiled only on a Sunday; has twice as much strength in it as any other thing of the same weight.'[60]

After salt curing, the bacon can also be smoked over oak or pine sawdust. Digby's Frankfurt cure suggests lying the carcass on hay and then hanging it up again in September, implying a surprisingly early date of death for the animal, though after the weather has grown cooler, since making the carcass too warm might lead to decomposition or infestation by parasites. You must, he says, cut away 'a little piece of flesh within, called in Dutch the mouse; for if that remain in it, the bacon will grow resty [off]'.

Bacon curer Maynard Davies gives a recipe for a ham he believes is Roman – it uses salt, but also coriander, red wine and honey, with white wine vinegar. The exotics are painted on the outside. Other recipes give similar additions: coriander, sweet pepper, nutmeg, mace. Preparation was regional, too – apple juice or cider could be incorporated in the West, juniper berries in Derbyshire. As Maynard Davies says, 'These days, curing is not carried out simply to prolong the shelf-life of meat. It has become a specialist procedure used to greatly enhance the taste of pork, infusing it with subtle blends of flavours and using delicate or robust smokes to make a bacon that is now savoured worldwide.' Parma ham, prosciutto and Serrano ham have broken foodies in to the idea of the high-end pork product; few would think these a horrible waste of something that could have been eaten as a suckling. But English bacon makers seem to have held on to their simple knowledge more stoutly than cheese-makers or bakers. Yes, most bacon is now fake-on, but traditional bacon has never disappeared – perhaps because it is so loved, and perhaps because it is so simple.

Bacon came in collops (slices), which were probably thicker than today's rashers, as they are now called. It could be bought in pieces, too, to be boiled with vegetables to make pottage or soup more nourishing. But even Gervase Markham has a recipe for collops and eggs, in which the bacon is carefully desalted, as one might with an anchovy now, and the eggs are fried with vinegar. Recipe books also refer to smoked meat. Smoking is – obviously – an art dependent on access to wood or to sawdust. In the eighteenth century, York ham was still cured the traditional way by salting and smoking. Sometime in the eighteenth century, pickling was introduced, perhaps by the immigrant Dutch or Huguenots, and spread fast in some regions, where it was seen as preferable to dried bacon and ham, cheaper and more reliable. However it is processed, the flavour will still to some extent depend on what the pig has eaten. As we have seen, the pannage pig ate acorns and other foraged food in the forest. When the pig moved to town, his diet became noticeably duller. The traditional pig food still deployed is Greenwich Gold, the leftovers from gin making, the mash. Gin and bacon, strong-tasting bedfellows, both might be flavoured with juniper.

Pigs could also be used as banqueting food, cooked or dressed up to taste or look other than they were. In Tudor times, A. W. described how to treat pig like a young deer:

> To bake a Pig like a Fawn. Flay him when he is in the hair, season it with pepper and salt, Cloves and mace, take Claret wine, Verjus, Rosewater, Sinamon, Ginger and Sugar, boil them togither, laye your Pig flat like a Fawn or a Kid, and put your syrup unto it and sweet butter, and so bake it leisurely.

A. W. does not say whether you should serve the pig as if it really *is* a fawn. But how about using your pig to make a fake monster? Fancy a cokagryce? Just join the upper half of a cockerel to the lower half of a piglet. Or why not present the cockerel mounted on the pig's back; give it a lance to wield, and a paper helmet. Petronius, similarly, fantasised about a rabbit dressed to appear as Pegasus.[61] What about a fire-breathing piglet leaning from the battlements of a fake castle?

Fillet of pork endored, or goldened, was a pre-industrial manor house feasting dish, spit-roasted before – not *over* but *before* – an open fire, the juice carefully collected. A thick paste of ginger, saffron and black pepper mixed with water was painted over the meat, which was then returned to the heat until set. More layers were added and coated until the batter was used up. The simpler, unspiced roast suckling adored, even worshipped, by Charles Lamb was itself an emulation of this method. The medieval cormarye – heart of Mary – turned the pig deep red by marinading in red wine, then spit-roasting it. Later country house cooking offered chopped pig's ears and trotters – sometimes entrails too – served with salt, vinegar and herbs, or pig's fry: heart, liver, lights and sweetbreads of pig, served with onion and tomato gravy or apple sauce.[62]

Compiled from the early nineteenth century, Esther Copley's recipes preserve the prosperous householder's ways to preserve pig meat. After hair removal, 'the pig is hung up till the next day, when it is cut up, and the other parts being taken away, the two sides, or flitches, are to be cured for bacon.' Piles of flitch were to be placed on 'a bacon trough or tray' with 'a gutter round its edges, to drain off the brine, which would otherwise soak in, and spoil the meat'. She gave a very few variations – for her, bacon was so simple and so good that it didn't need much. 'Some people add, for each hog, half a pound of bay salt, a quarter of a pound of *saltpetre*, and one pound of very coarse sugar or treacle; but this is not necessary. Very capital bacon may be made with common salt alone, provided it be well rubbed in, and changed sufficiently often.' She suggested reusing the run-off brine. She also advocated smoking bacon – 'much better than merely drying it', and says a month will do, and the smoke must not be from deal or fir.

Copley also discusses lard – preserved meat just as bacon and ham are – and pig skin, 'crittens', which can be chopped up and used in a pie with apples and raisins. She uses everything but the squeak: liver and craw (throat) can be family dinner on pig-killing day, and haslet is made from anything left over:

> The lights, melt, sweetbread, any liver and crow [sic] that may remain, and any other little trimming bits that happen in cutting up the pig, make a fine dish, seasoned with pepper and salt, and sage and onions. They may be baked in a stewpot, with a quart of water, and some sliced potatoes; or covered with a pie crust, or a batter pudding. You will have plenty of bits of fat to chop up for puddings and pies as good as the best of suet.[63]

As I read this, I'm lost in the nostalgia Copley herself wanted to evoke. It's the hope of utter and entire self-sufficiency which is not selfish but generous and frugal at once. A more didactic version of Copley's sentiments were provided by Charles Francatelli's patronising cookbook *A Plain Cookery Book for the Working Classes*. Like Copley, it gave detailed instructions on how to make the most of the pig, including: how to singe off the bristles; gutting; hanging up the pluck (the heart and lungs – hence courage); and splitting in halves. It assumed legs would be cured as hams.[64] It contained some very encouraging recipes for piggy foods: smoked ham, black pudding, sausages, pluck fry-up, what to do with trotters, and a spiced confection of pluck called Italian cheese.

Copley was consciously an evangelist, writing to encourage the use of bits of the pig that had fallen out of favour by her day. She wanted her readers to use tripe, or chitterlings, and she complained that others neglected them. From her writings on pigs, you form a powerful sense of how precious every scrap of meat was. She offered a method for black or hog puddings, made with cold blood, not the warm blood others suggested. The warm blood was mixed with salt until cold – this stopped it from coagulating – and she suggested that this was a suitable job for a child. In the meantime, casings were prepared from the guts. Her puddings were deeply savoury, with flavourings including 'a little sage, winter savoury, or marjoram and thyme; some add a leek or two, finely shred; mix as much pepper, salt, allspice, and ginger, as will season the whole. If you intend them for sale, grate in a small nutmeg.' The mixture is completed with pig fat pieces. The 'for sale' reference is interesting: 'A cottager's wife, who is known to be a thoroughly nice clean woman, may be sure to find a customer for these among her richer neighbours, who like such a thing if sure that it is nicely done; but seldom like the trouble of doing it at home, even if they kill their own pigs.'[65]

Similarly she urged the manufacture of sausages for resale, since 'nicely made sausage meat is sure to find a ready market, and fetch a good price.' She includes a recipe for Oxford sausages:

> one pound of lean pork, one pound of fat, and one pound of lean veal, all carefully cleared of skin and sinews, shred as fine as possible, or beat with the lard beater, one pound of crumbs of bread, about thirty leaves of sage, shred very small, (some add also, a little parsley and thyme – others a little garlic, shallots, or leek); mix it well together; season with pepper, salt, and nutmeg; beat separately the yolks and whites of four eggs; mix in the yolks, and as much of the whites as is necessary just to make it thoroughly adhere. These sausages are to be fried; each

pound should be divided into eighteen equal parts, and a very
small dust of flour shaken over them; they will require no fat in
the pan; but must be done over a clear fire, and the pan shaken
the whole time; after they are done, there will be fat enough
remaining in the pan to fry a slice or two of bread, or some
sliced potatoes, which are generally liked to eat with the
sausages.[66]

She also has a recipe for 'Epping sausages', 'mostly used about London':
'Chop equal parts of fat and lean pork very fine, season it with sage,
pepper, and salt, and half fill hog's guts that have been made extremely
clean, in the same way as directed for hog puddings.' Interestingly,
modern recipes for 'traditional' Epping sausages are for a skinless
sausage, and give nutmeg and lemon as key flavourings.

We shouldn't be surprised by these disagreements, since the Epping
sausage is also linked with fraud. The fraudulent Victorian sausage was
a confirmation of the dark suspicions always entertained by pie-eaters
and sausage consumers, by consumers of pork in any form, 'an uncomfortable suspicion respecting the bona fides of the veiled delicacy'. The
most suspect were the sausages found in 'poor neighbourhoods', especially the kind known as best beef and sold at fourpence or fivepence
a pound. There were, however, 'fastidious folk' who turned in dismay
from the 'veiled mysteries' and 'marvelled how it was that their unre-
strained consumption was not signalized by a marked increase in the
death rate in those localities where the demand for them was greatest'.
Even such fastidious people accepted sausages from Epping, however,
believing that 'the villainous devices of the unscrupulous skin-stuffers
of the slums of London' were unknown in such rural climes, where
pigs fed on beech mast from the trees. Sent to London daily by waggon
– a broad-wheeled waggon, with a russet-coloured awning, a pair of
farm horses in the shafts, and for a teamster a pippin-faced country-
man, in a snowy smock-frock, and with turnpike tickets stuck in the
band of his battered old beaver hat – a select quantity of just seven or
eight hundredweight. Alas, it occurred to 'an individual of an inquir-
ing turn of mind' to go down to Epping and view the famous and

extensive factory from which the sausages came, and he found that no one in the village could give him any information on the subject; the village pork butcher was in the habit of making a few pounds twice a week, but they were commonplace, mottled-looking affairs, and no more to be compared with the delicate dainties forwarded to London daily by the waggon than chalk is like cheese.

It was a mystery, and the man with the enquiring mind resolved to sift it. He took lodgings within a mile or so of rural Epping and waited for the waggon. At last it appeared, pippin-faced teamster, russet awning and all, jogging Londonward; but when the inquisitive journalist peeped in over the tailboard, the vehicle was empty! He kept it in sight for a few miles, until it halted at a wayside inn where there was a stable-yard, and already there was a London cart, harnessed to which was a good horse that looked as though it had made a long journey and drawn a heavy load. There was the load in the cart, packed in scrupulously clean wicker baskets, each one lettered on the lid 'Warranted genuine Epping sausages'.[67] While the waggoner and the cart-driver were busy transferring the freight from one vehicle to the other, the enquirer glanced at the name on the shaft of the London cart, and made it out to be that of a notorious cheap sausage-maker whose business premises were situated in Smithfield.

Obviously this discovery was unfortunate for the makers of 'real Epping sausages'. Rumours of sausages containing horsemeat or dog meat or rat meat continued to vex the sausage trade. Actually, cheap sausage contained very little meat of any kind:

> I was coolly told that 'anyhow, all the actual meat there was in say half a pound of cheap German sausage, couldn't do any one much harm if it was ever so 'dicky.' "Tain't as though it was all meat. Only enough meat is used to give the stuff a foundation,' explained a hoary-headed 'machine-man' of many years' experience. 'There's lots of things besides meat – meal and all manner, and then there's the "colouring" and the spice.'[68]

Before we condemn the past, we could remind ourselves of the Swaddles organic scam (see Chicken). The pippin-faced man in the cart could probably sell a few local and traditional products nowadays too, judging by the number of images of cheery harvesters on packets of flour (mostly imported from the American wheat belt) and happy cows on packets of butter. 'Natural' is widely used to sell products. In the article 'Packaging as a Vehicle for Mythologizing the Brand', researchers explore the connotations of 'natural' in contemporary culture and the ways in which these connotations are exploited to sell products. Marketers of organic products depict the modern world as a deeply distorted reflection of what it originally was – the garden inhabited by, let's say, pigs wandering under shady trees – before agro-chemical technology. While the values of the past include family, tradition, authenticity, peace and simplicity, the current era is associated with broken family ties that need to be restored, scientific 'advances' that pose threats, constant pressure on the well-being of humans, and unnecessary complexity in everyday life. Naturalness appears as a rich emotional word that connects with positive contemporary images of nature.[69]

Consumers routinely obsess about insignificant health risks that have never even been shown to occur (pesticides, hormones) and routinely ignore large health risks (foodborne illness caused by bacteria like *E. coli* and salmonella in the animal waste used as fertiliser) that have been associated with widespread outbreaks of illness and even death. David Ropeik discusses the causes of misperception of risk in his article 'The Consequences of Fear'. Two factors, control and origin, are especially relevant for understanding the (mis)perception of food risks. Risks over which we *feel* as though we exercise control are routinely perceived to be smaller than risks that are imposed from outside. Few people dread travelling in cars in comparison with those who fear flying, even though car journeys are more likely to be deadly than plane journeys. This is because we have a sense of control when we are behind the wheel, and the risk of crashing is both familiar and chronic, factors that make risks seem less threatening. Similarly, consumers of organic food tolerate the real and substantial risk of illness from pathogens in manure, but fear the effects of pesticides. The risks of technology are widely perceived to be greater than those from nature, neatly dovetailing with the cultural mythology surrounding nature.

Ultimately, these myths are joined in service of the overarching myth, that of the 'empowered' consumer. All eating involves risk assessment. Apple-cheeked wagon drivers inspire more trust than London butchers, and we know that the less we trust, the more afraid we will be. The more we trust, the less fear we feel. We all know that nature can kill, but the deaths it causes don't scare us as much as the cancer we dread, which we imagine might be caused by pesticides or irradiated foods. It is a *comfort* to return to sausages, a nursery food though fatty and deadly.

Modern foods often achieve through science a distance from the smelly and the bodily, foods that don't seem ever to have been alive. 'Food becomes so brittle it's like glass', says one modernist exultantly on the effects of carbon dioxide, and the Pacojet, the centrifuge, the vacuum sealer and CO_2 are as likely to revolutionise cooking as did once the freezer, the blender and the domestic oven. All cooking is about denaturing, and the current molecular or modernist gastronomic idea of bringing science into the kitchen is simply another way of advertising that one has the income and the ability to do such denaturing. We do not need to tear at a piece of meat; we can afford to wait. And yet the greed so easily implied by such banqueting frills is, as we all know, piggy. Nobody needs to eat a piece of glass, and nobody needs a hall fire to roast a pig. Piglike: resembling or suggestive of a pig; unpleasant; stubborn, greedy, unattractive, dirty. Somehow, it is the pig who is piggy, and not us, for eating so much of him down the years.

In the twenty-first century, mass-farmed pigs are a skinny lot; pigs that produce supermarket pork are bred for lean meat, fast growth and docile behaviour, and almost never for flavour. Older breeds, on the other hand, take longer to grow to killing weight, have more fat, produce tastier meat and, depending on the breed, can be very active and even aggressive. Our own beloved and seemingly traditional pigs – as depicted in the nursery – probably owe their snubby brachyce-phalic heads to an imported Chinese pig breed, dating from relatively recent times. Pig breeds were always unstable because of cross-breed-ing with wild pigs in forests, but like apple varieties, breeds are constantly threatened and pushed around by the demands of indus-trial farming. The Lincolnshire curly coat pig had a soft fleece, like a lamb: no more. We have also lost the Cumberland, the Dorset Gold Tip, the Yorkshire Blue and White, and the Essex and the Wessex Saddleback. The current list of British rare breeds is still a found poem: Berkshire, British Lop, British Saddleback, Gloucestershire Old Spot, Large Black, Middle White, Tamworth and Welsh. Not only their names but the animals themselves are beautiful and various. Tamworth pigs, for example, are not pink or black, but a golden caramel brown; they do not look like farmyard pigs, but more like muntjac deer. Peppa Pig, pink and squishy, is not the only kind of pig.

Just as well, because little pink Peppa carries with her the difficult obligation of looking rather too human. As we have seen, the pig in all eras carries a troubling charge of being easily deployed as a symbol of whatever we humans don't like about ourselves – plumpness, greed, aggression, stink – but also a puzzling and anxious kind of attraction. At the very moment of domestication, it may be that our ancestors were learning to displace the oldest and most worrying eating taboo onto the pig. We have seen that Irish heroes could be too much like the pig for comfort – but so say all of us. The pig-meat feast announces that we have decided not to eat one another. The very existence of cannibals is controversial: some anthropologists state that the location of cannibals at the far side of the world is just folklore. But others believe, and so any group that is socially excluded is likely to be perceived as violating this most sacred of all taboos. There is the idea that human flesh is called 'long pig' by those who consume it. In the film *Long Pig* (2010), the cannibals are not Palaeolithic peoples, but 'the powerful, the wealthy, and the elite … They feed upon those whom they deem will add to their power … In darkness they hunt. In blood they feed.' Part of the horror is that people are prey, mere consumables, like pigs.

The pig flirts with such myths, especially when served entire, as a baby. Pigs look disturbingly like us, naked and pink. The film *Delicatessen* (1991), which also featured cannibalism, showed a pig on its poster. We have already touched on *Animal Farm*, where the pigs lead and therefore exploit the other animals – and become human in the final scene. The political allegory does not entirely push out the queasy transformation of the edible into the eater – indeed, it depends on the idea that the piggy prey becomes the human predator. Working alongside the farmer to plough and civilise the land, the pig was so like the farmer. He lived on the same greens, and he ate the farmer's leftovers.

On tea: an essay

L ike lunch and dinner, the word *tea* means different things to different people when used as a word for a meal. For some it refers to the
evening meal; for others, it refers to an elegant leisured repast taken
between midday and evening, typically between 4 and 5.30 p.m. This
latter meal in its brief heyday was enjoyed mostly by the upper classes.
It was one of a series of markers in the day that allowed for an elaborate
and expensive change of clothes while enjoying a sense of having nothing better to do. Therefore it was decidedly low to refer to the meal as
'afternoon tea'; if you were upper class, afternoon tea was the only tea.

Elsewhere, especially in the north, people might have thought of tea
as a far heartier and more extensive meal to be taken rather later, and
this eventually became known to some as 'high tea'. At this meal, eaten
around 6 p.m., kippers might jostle with teacakes. The term is sometimes misunderstood by visitors to Britain as posh when it is in fact
exactly the opposite. There was also nursery tea, when children had
their main meal in the middle of the day, and I have on occasion been
a guest at a uniquely English hybrid meal called bread and butter tea,
which embraced sliced bread and butter, a variety of spreads put on
the table in their jars, a block of cheese, a bowl of tomatoes, and often
a fruitcake, but lacking the hot food of high tea. The numerous books
on tea taken at 4 p.m. tend to confuse matters still further by offering
recipes and advice for high tea mixed in with recipes and advice for tea
as it was taken by the leisured elite.

To resolve such confusions, there is no better guide than
Oscar Wilde, who always knew the English better than they knew

themselves. Here is *The Importance of Being Earnest* from 1895 on the vital issue of cucumber sandwiches, treating the trivial as momentous:

Algernon: Please don't touch the cucumber sandwiches. They are ordered specially for Aunt Augusta. [Takes one and eats it.]

Jack: Well, you have been eating them all the time.

Algernon: That is quite a different matter. She is my aunt. [Takes plate from below.] Have some bread and butter. The bread and butter is for Gwendolen. Gwendolen is devoted to bread and butter.

Jack: [Advancing to table and helping himself.] And very good bread and butter it is too.

Algernon: Well, my dear fellow, you need not eat as if you were going to eat it all.

Note that the tea table is all about allowing each person to indulge an individual passion. Yet it is also about delicacy. Cucumber sandwiches contrast with the hearty salt beef sandwiches named after (though probably not invented by) John Montague, fourth Earl of Sandwich, said to require nourishment during his long nights of gambling. By contrast, tea sandwiches are unnecessary delights and also rarities. Ironically, in Wilde's play, emotions and identities are expressed throughout in terms of tea:

Cecily: May I offer you some tea, Miss Fairfax?

Gwendolen: [With elaborate politeness.] Thank you. [Aside.] Detestable girl! But I require tea!

Cecily: [Sweetly.] Sugar?

Gwendolen: [Superciliously.] No, thank you. Sugar is not fashionable any more. [Cecily looks angrily at her, takes up the tongs and puts four lumps of sugar into the cup.]

Cecily: [Severely.] Cake or bread and butter?

Gwendolen: [In a bored manner.] Bread and butter, please. Cake is rarely seen at the best houses nowadays.

The joke here is the momentous triviality of preference. Everyone concerned regards tea as an opportunity to express absolute truths about the order of eating, a kind of domineering identity politics that insists angrily on its own rectitude. It's a mock epic on the scale of Pope's *Rape of the Lock*. Later, Algernon's ability to eat muffins calmly despite emotional turmoil is understood as an aesthetic preference:

> **Jack:** How you can sit there, calmly eating muffins when we are
>   in this horrible trouble, I can't make out. You seem to me to
>   be perfectly heartless.
> **Algernon:** Well, I can't eat muffins in an agitated manner. The
>   butter would probably get on my cuffs.

It follows that when Algernon's manservant Lane has been unable to obtain cucumbers 'even for ready money', both Algernon and his aunt are livid. In these delicately worked examples, Wilde's choice of food tells us very clearly that we are among the upper crust. It's important that Gwendolen chooses bread and butter above cake, and declines sugar in her tea; Jack and Algernon's focus on the savoury aspects of tea – cucumber sandwiches and buttered muffins – is also a sign of their social supremacy.[1]

It is often claimed that this kind of tea food was introduced in England by Anna, seventh Duchess of Bedford, in 1840. The story is that the duchess would become hungry around four o'clock in the afternoon. The evening meal in her household was served fashionably late at eight, thus leaving a hungry gap between lunch and dinner. So the duchess asked that a tray of tea, bread and butter and cake be brought to her room during the late afternoon. This became a habit of hers and she began inviting friends to join her.[2]

This story of the invention of 'le 4 o'clock' is only partly true. A possible seventeenth-century reference to the custom of afternoon tea is suggested by some lines in Thomas Southerne's play *The Wife's Excuse* (1692), inviting the ladies to drink their tea; there is also a reference in one of Mme de Sévigné's letters to *thé de cinq heures*. William Congreve has the ladies retire for tea and scandal in his 1693 play *The Double*

Dealer, while Alexander Pope in 1712 says of Queen Anne herself, 'great Anna! whom three realms obey,/ Dost sometimes counsel take – and sometimes tea', when the sun is shooting his ray 'obliquely'. However, these *could* all refer only to the drink.[3]

By the 1740s 'afternoon tea was an important meal in England, the Netherlands, and English America'.[4] Women monopolised and presided over the tea ritual, which brought families together and provided opportunities to teach children good manners and demonstrate the decorum and respectability that were essential to status. The *OED*'s first usage of the noun to mean a meal dates from 1738, well before the Duchess of Bedford, and it is repeated in 1778 and 1789.[5] More interestingly, it has also been suggested that the duchess's elegant tea parties borrowed from the bluestocking ladies of forty years earlier. The Blue Stocking Society was founded in the early 1750s by Elizabeth Montagu, Elizabeth Vesey and their friends as a women's literary discussion group, a revolutionary step away from traditional, non-intellectual, women's activities. They invited various people (both women and men) to attend. Tea and refreshments were served; alcohol was forbidden. One of the bluestockings, Hannah More, celebrated tea in her poem 'Bas Bleu: Or, Conversation' as the intersection between tea, conversation and wit, the focus being still on the drink:

> Rise, incense pure from fragrant Tea,
> Delicious incense, worthy Thee!
> Hail, Conversation, heav'nly fair,
> Thou bliss of life, and balm of care,
> Still may thy gentle reign extend,
> And taste with wit and science blend![6]

Other evidence suggests that tea might have emerged as a new way of eating out. The tea garden began in the reign of Charles II; both John Evelyn and Samuel Pepys recorded visits to the New Spring Garden (also called Vauxhall) on 2 July 1661 and 29 May 1662 respectively. A polite, feminine alternative to the coffeehouse (from which, as we have seen, women were generally barred), the tea garden allowed ladies and gentlemen to take their tea out of doors surrounded by orchestras, hidden arbours, flowered walks, bowling greens, concerts and gambling, or at night by fireworks. The tea garden reached the height of its popularity in the eighteenth century. A newspaper advertisement from the *Bath Chronicle and Weekly Gazette* of 10 April 1766 advertises both 'breakfasting and afternoon tea' in the newly reopened Spring Gardens.[7] The famous tea gardens were not only places to see and be seen, but also places with windings and turnings in which young ladies could temporarily evade the gaze of their mothers.

However, the custom of eating with tea took some time to spread to the private home. Georgiana Sitwell wrote categorically of the 1830s:

> There was no gathering for five o'clock afternoon tea in those days, but most ladies took an hour's rest in their rooms before the six or seven o'clock dinner … It was not till about 1849 or 50 … that five o'clock tea in the drawing room was made an institution, and then only in a few fashionable houses where the dinner hour was as late as half past seven or eight o'clock.[8]

Mrs Beeton wrote, 'A pretty little afternoon tea service is placed upon a small table and there are plates of rolled bread-and-butter, as well as biscuits and cake.'[9] The advised time was 4 p.m., just before the fashionable promenade in Hyde Park. From the 1840s these teas became grand enough for a buffet table to be set up with refreshments. Cakes, thin bread and butter, fancy biscuits, ices, fruits and sandwiches comprised the food, while big silver urns dispensed tea, coffee, wine, claret cup, sherry and champagne cup. Initially, sandwiches were made only with ham, tongue or beef. It wasn't until the 1870s that cucumber sandwiches were being served regularly. Oscar Wilde's cucumber sandwiches were a sudden fashion, like avocado toast today.

Manners of Modern Society, written in 1872, still needed to describe the way in which afternoon tea had gradually become an established event. 'Little Teas,' it explained, 'take place in the afternoon' and were so called because of the small amount of food served and the neatness and elegance of the meal. They were also known as 'Low Teas', because guests were seated in low armchairs with low side-tables on which to place their cups and saucers; 'Handed Teas', since the hostess handed round the cups; and 'Kettledrums', presumably because the kettle was a vital piece of equipment involved in the ceremony. But *Manners* also claimed that the meal was a revival: 'Now that dinners are so late … the want is felt of the old-fashioned meal at five, and so it has been reinstated, though not quite in the same form as before.' Afternoon tea provided a meal suitable for children.[10]

As Marie Bayard wrote in 1884 in *Hints on Etiquette*, tea was 'not supposed to be a substantial meal, merely light refreshment'. Mrs Beeton (herself deceased, but still the figurehead) 'told' readers in 1892 that sandwiches 'intended for afternoon tea are dainty trifles, pleasing to the eye and palate, but too flimsy to allay hunger where it exists'. The ritual of English teatime was perfected and all but sanctified in the early twentieth century by Queen Mary; desperately shy, she liked the comfort of tea.[11] By now, tea was beginning to be liked across the class spectrum. In *Lark Rise to Candleford*, Flora Thompson's tea included china 'with a fat pink rose on the side of each cup; hearts of lettuce, thin bread and butter, and the crisp little cakes that had been baked in readiness that morning'.[12]

The production of tea sets also supports an eighteenth-century origin. The new china makers in the Potteries started to produce porcelain tea services to supplement those imported from China. In 1765 Queen Charlotte commissioned Josiah Wedgwood to create a tea service made from his quality cream-coloured earthenware, which he named Queen's ware. From that moment on he was the Queen's potter. Wedgwood's creamware was thin, attractive and durable, and it quickly became popular. By 1775 other manufacturers, including those on the Continent, had widely copied Wedgwood, imitating Queen's ware and creating increasingly fanciful teapots.

The fragile femininity of decorated porcelain predicted and may actually have contributed to the superfluity of the meal. Yet bone china was really made of ground bone. The first development of what would become known as bone china was made by Thomas Frye in a factory in Bow, in 1748. His factory was located very close to the cattle markets and slaughterhouses of Essex, and hence had easy access to animal bones. Frye used up to 45 per cent of bone ash in his formulation to create what he called 'fine porcelain'. There was something extravagant and terrible about eating from bone rather than eating bone.

————

The whole point of this fantasy afternoon tea is that it was meant to be over-the-top and extravagant. At the time when it was first created, therefore, the foods involved were expensive, elaborate, and often involved hothouse rarities such as strawberries and cucumber alongside puff pastry, thinly sliced bread, and sponge cake, which might take up to an hour of a servant's time to make on its own. Some of these foods no longer seem like luxuries to us, and so other luxuries now tend to be included at the posh hotels in London that continue to cater for those who expect a four o'clock luxury meal on a visit to England. Champagne is often served alongside tea, and smoked salmon and even caviar alongside brioche and other special breads. The Oscar Wilde Lounge at the Café Royal, which has some claim to have been visited by Wilde himself (along with a horde of rent boys), serves a range of foods and luxuries which he might not recognise: Atlantic prawn cocktail muffin, Truffle Burford Brown egg sandwiches, and a range of luxury patisserie such as Earl Grey and bergamot choux, quince, apple and vanilla tart, mint chocolate brownie, lavender lemon cake and raspberry lychee rose choux. The emphasis on summer fruits reflects a connection between afternoon tea and the London Season, the heyday of the elite's ritual year of celebrating itself (and now perhaps the more mundane tourist season). Strawberries at Wimbledon show how mid-afternoon delight is still dominated by these choices. The Season follows the seasons – spring and summer – and so its foods and meals also offer a kind of endless summer, when there is always – in the words of Cambridge aesthete Rupert Brooke – honey still for tea.

————

The cucumber sandwich may be part of this delicate world of subtle and unnecessary pleasure, but while some were worshipping them, others were enjoying a light evening meal after eating the main meal of the day around noon, a meal variously called tea or supper. Among them was the young Charles Dickens, who had half an hour for tea: 'When I had money enough, I used to go to a coffee-shop, and have half a pint of coffee, and a slice of bread-and-butter. When I had no money, I took a turn in Covent Garden market, and stared at the pine-apples.' If anyone gave him money he spent it on food.

Mealtimes are really just an idea to the very poorest; you eat when you can. A modest tea could be luxury: 'A small tray of tea things was arranged on the table, a plate of hot buttered toast was gently simmering before the fire, and the red-nosed man himself was busily engaged in converting a large slice of bread into the same agreeable edible, though the instrumentality of a long brass toasting fork.'[13]

Bread: as we have seen, both convenience food and delight. Even in the Marshalsea prison with Little Dorrit there was tea: 'Mr Dorrit gives his old pensioner a tea of teacakes, fresh butter, eggs, cold ham, and shrimps,' while John Chivery gives Arthur Clennam fresh butter in a cabbage leaf, slices of boiled ham in another cabbage leaf, and a little basket of watercresses and salad herbs.

Afternoon tea was the missing puzzle piece that allowed the life of the top 10 per cent to take the form we nowadays associate with unspecific olden days, spent in a country house. Lunch was always at one o'clock unless it was Sunday, and sometime between three and five there was formal tea with cake, hot dishes, small trays, and perhaps even musicians to entertain the guests. A modest tea might be very thin bread and butter, and Madeira, seed or Dundee cake. A more extravagant tea might include cucumber sandwiches in summer and buttered toast in winter, or perhaps muffins or scones. By the time Daphne Du Maurier wrote *Rebecca*, in 1937, tea had come to represent the enviable sumptuousness of country house life:

I think of half-past four at Manderley, and the table drawn
before the library fire ... Those dripping crumpets ... Tiny crisp
wedges of toast, and piping-hot, floury scones. Sandwiches of
unknown nature, mysteriously flavoured and quite delectable,
and that very special gingerbread. Angel cake, that melted in
the mouth, and his rather stodgier companion, bursting with
peel and raisins. There was enough food there to keep a starving
family for a week. I never knew what happened to it all, and the
waste used to worry me sometimes.[14]

Tea must always be in the past, seen nostalgically, and also with an
edge of guilt: did we really lay out so much food? Du Maurier is especially vague about the sandwiches. We can learn more from Lady
Sysonby: Victoria Lily Hegan Ponsonby (née Kennard), one of the last
generation of *châtelaines* of English country houses like Manderley.
This is her cookbook, printed in 1935:

The ideal tea table should include some sort of hot buttered
toast or scone, one or two sorts of sandwiches, a plate of small
light cakes, and our friend the luncheon cake. Add a pot of jam
or honey, and a plate of brown and white bread and butter,
which I implore my readers not to cut too thin, and every eye
will sparkle.

Tea should never be served in the dining room, but in the drawing
room or the library (as at Manderley). People sat on small chairs, and
ideally there would be two teapots, offering guests a choice of China
or Indian. The mainstay was country house sandwiches filled with a
mixture of things chopped very fine: hard-boiled eggs with mayonnaise, or mango chutney; cream cheese with nuts and apricots:
smoked salmon with anchovy butter or minced lobster or rose petals.
Of Lady Sysonby's own recipes that for brown bread sandwiches, with
a filling of toasted oatmeal sprinkled on honey, is a standout. It
sounds like health food. Cakes for tea are on the whole unexotic; the
pound cake iced with lemon, the ginger cake or Madeira cake plain

and bolstering. Seed cake is the same plain butter cake scented with caraway.

How did those glory days come to an end? With a whimper which recalled their delights, a wisp of memory; here is a wartime recipe for cake:

> 1 egg or 1tb dried egg
> 2 oz fat
> 2 oz sugar
> 4 oz national flour
> ½ tsp baking powder
> Milk or household milk
> Beat the egg. Cream the fat and sugar, add egg and then the
>   flour mixed with the baking powder. Spread in a tin and bake
>   for fifteen minutes, or steam in a basin for 1 hour. Four
>   helpings.

Four very small helpings of heavy cake. But the allegiance to the *symbol* of cake is apparent in the pathetic attempt. A luminous instance of the way preference for a certain kind of food trumps innovation to an extent where even the most ersatz and nearly inedible version of that food continues to be served and eaten. This food conservatism is a widely known phenomenon, which often derails schemes to help the poor eat healthily and sometimes even makes food provision during famine difficult. Here, the contents of the cake are – roughly – those of a Victoria sponge, and the proportions are – again roughly – correct. But wartime cake is not a Victoria sponge, but a representation of one. In wartime America, some such tiny cakes were actually served inside the larger and entirely fake cardboard shell of a large or great cake. It may be wrong to say this, but perhaps cakes, more than anything, are often the representation of a cake, and the point is not to eat them, but to see them, cut them, and note their marking of a calendrical feast, as we shall see in the chapter on Cake. People in the Anglophone world are still very unwilling to draw back from foods they 'know' and proclaim them inedible, however badly made they are. Paving – pun intended – the way for the world of post-war convenience foods, the war cake told people that cake was a name rather than a texture or a taste.

––––––––

Once rationing was safely over, a fresh burst of enthusiasm for tea and cake occurred, under the authority of Constance Spry. She had put her shoulder pluckily to the wheel during the war, teaching the nation how to manage on rationed foods, but when she published *The Constance Spry Cookery Book* in 1956, she caught the nostalgia of the feast perfectly. She wrote amiably that 'the disposition of women's time made teatime possible, and the taste for, shall I say, the cosier figure, gave no cause for apprehension'. Yet she is clearly harking nostalgically back, in a similar fashion to Du Maurier. She urges quality, not quantity:

> It was not then considered good taste to have too many small things – one good plum cake, one light cake, perhaps of the sponge or sponge-sandwich variety, or an orange cake, iced, might appear, and a hot dish of crumpets or buttered toast, anchovy toast or hot teacakes, and in particular that admirable hot cake described as Irish Sally Lunn. A country tea might also include radishes, a loaf of home-made bread, a pat of butter, and watercress, and if you were hungry from exercise, a boiled egg.

Other tea possibilities – but not all at once – include homemade crumpets and muffins, and other old kinds of cake – already, the revival of forgotten delicacies was becoming desirable – such as Selkirk bannock, Singin' Hinnies and potato cakes. There could be rock, bath and Chelsea buns for schoolroom tea (and 'match teas' made famous by Enid Blyton's school stories), and the plainer cakes raised with yeast – bun loaf, Gugelhupf (yeast-raised cake, usually with fruit), Sally Lunns, Galette de Savennières (yeast-raised cake, slightly enriched with egg) – but there were also the new cakes: plain sponge cake with a crusty top, orange cake, rich chocolate cake, and sponge sandwich with rose-petal jam filling, this last again carrying with it a nostalgia for the past. The cakes are, note, now much more important than sandwiches.

Tea still happens at hotels and tearooms pitched largely at tourists. While few families now sit down to sandwiches, muffins and cakes at all, the meal is still known and understood as an occasional feast, a celebration, like that other very English treat, the 'full English' breakfast. So the normality of such meals is gone, but the foods themselves survive, all but embalmed.

Milk

Milk is not an inevitable part of the human diet. Far Eastern cultures and the native cultures of the Americas and of parts of Africa never use milk. Many Asians actually have lactose intolerance, rare in northern Europeans. The Hong Kong Chinese say that Westerners smell disgusting because of their dairy diet. Milk easily putrefies, and yet its English heyday began before the great age of refrigeration, before even the icehouse was more than an occasional curiosity. Like many English food trends, the sudden passion for dairy foods that overtook England in the seventeenth century was a fashion for food from the Continent, brought back by travellers; the exile of the monarchy and the court during the English Civil War coincided with the rise of French *haute cuisine*, a mode of eating that involves the ingestion of vast quantities of butter and cream, and a sudden enthusiasm for their unctuous softness on the palate. When the court returned to London, they brought their enthusiasm for cream and butter with them.

This was a complete upending of the hierarchy of food prior to the Restoration. Even more than foraged foods, milk was regarded as a desperation food of the very poor. There were, of course, cows before the real fashion for dairy, and many medieval villagers kept one, often on wood pasture that might also support pigs, geese and sheep. Because the fourteenth century saw a scarcity of labour for intensive cultivation, grazing expanded instead. In Chaucer's *Nun's Priest's Tale*, Chanticleer the rooster belongs to a poor widow who has three large sows, three cows, and a sheep called Mall. The widow has meals of milk, brown bread and sometimes bacon. Because the cows provide a steady supply of milk, one cow can also be allowed to calve and then its calf sold, as could any butter or cheese. Such cows provided the 'white meat' of the poor, a food of last resort.

The story of dairy begins with butter. Butter may be the oldest dairy product in the British Isles. Our ancestors buried butter in bogs, possibly for the dead, or alternatively in times of war or insecurity for later retrieval, a treasure of animal fat. Milk and its products were the main food source of the Gaelic Irish until the enforced collapse of cattle farming in around 1700. Bog butter is usually a hard, yellowish-white substance. It was offered for sale in Tralee as late as 1853; the flavour was described as *an-ghoirt*, very salty, a taste said to appeal to the early Irish.

Butter was common throughout northern Europe, and Pliny comments on its making. Romans made and understood cheese, but the ancient Greeks actually called the Thracians *boutyrophagi*, butter-eaters, and thought it made them smelly. Some thought people in northern countries rubbed themselves with butter instead of oil to wash themselves. The Latin word for butter, *butyrum*, means 'cow cheese'.

Like soft-rinded cheese, butter is seasonal – sweetest in June and September because this is when grass is fresh. For centuries, it was made with the wooden plunge churn. That meant long, heavy work; at first the dash – the wooden plunger – moves easily, but it gets heavier and heavier as the butter forms. Butter does not become firm in the churn; it has to be retrieved, rinsed, kneaded like dough and shaped with wooden bats. Seventeenth-century Gervase Markham says butter 'only proceedeth from cream', and despite social and food historian Dorothy Hartley's claims, I have had no success making it from raw unhomogenised milk.[1] Markham more accurately portrays a process of fleeting, analogous to threshing, the first stage in the butter-making process: 'Fleeting cream comes first, morning milk you shall with a fine thin shallow dish take off the cream about five in the evening;

evening milk fleeted at 5 am, put in a clean, sweet and well leaded earthen pot close covered, and set in a cool place.'[2]

The fleeted cream keeps for about two days in summer, four in winter. Since none of the cream was pasteurised or cultured, it would have made a stronger-tasting butter than we are used to, more like 'raw' butter, *beurre cru*. In all eras before refrigeration, finished butter was preserved with added salt, packed into earthenware pots or wooden tubs, and sold at markets.

Yet butter was still something of a mystery. As a result, it was enmeshed in ideas about magic; since cream entered the churn liquid and left it solid, was this not magic? And if it was magic, could it be undone by *bad* magic? Butter-making was a long and laborious process, fraught with anxiety. Fear of witches and demons led to countermagic. Thomas Ady, writing in 1655, reports the following charm used during churning:

> Come, Butter, come,
> Come, Butter, come,
> *Peter* stands at the Gate
> Waiting for a buttered Cake.
> Come, Butter, come.[3]

Butter charms are tributes to the apparent magic of a natural process, the capricious magic of dairy. For example, butcher Nicholas Strickland's wife was making a breakfast partially of scalded milk for his workers. Something went wrong: the milk 'stank and was bitter'. After that, his wife 'went to churn her cream that she had gathered' – which she might have skimmed off the milk – 'and she was from the morning until ten of the clock in the night a-churning, and could have no butter'.[4]

Throughout the Middle Ages, demons were thought to love milk and cream.[5] In story after story, demons and fairies were fed on milk. The child of an accused witch described the rite of feeding the familiar demons: 'they stood in her chamber by her bedside, and saith, that she hath seen her mother to feed them with milk'.[6] Brownies and hobs had to have regular feeds of cream; any attempt to substitute skimmed milk aroused their wrath. Cows are tricky, and dairying especially vulnerable to dirt, but those explanations do not seem entirely to justify the devil's role in the dairy. Demons were also eager to suckle from witches – in England they were more interested in feeding on witches than in having sex with them – and witchcraft yellow-press tales gave an unhealthy emphasis to the location of witchmarks or devil's teats on the anus or vulva. A moment's thought shows that such an uncomfortable and even disgusting arrangement is the norm for obtaining milk, which requires that the milker sit almost under the milch animal's belly, pulling on an area below it; the idea that the result is a food is odd, since human beings normally shun the products of the lower body. Early modern medicine knew from Aristotle that milk was a blood product, and saw it as purified by the action of the heartfires of maternal love. Once people notice the oddity of drinking a blood product they draw back in some dismay. All that saves milk from this revelation is its pure white colour. White was in heraldry the colour of purity and perfection, which would later be associated with the Grail Knights.[7] Pure white milk is excrement in redeemed form.

Butter was a booming new industry in the early modern period. To cope with the increasing trade, towns built stone butter markets. Butter wasn't initially spread on bread, but added to sauces. The idea of butter as a thickening came from the French *haute cuisine* tradition. Cream also had clabbering (curdling) and thickening qualities, probably well understood from the butter-making process.

As dairy ascended, it elbowed out its older white enriching cousin, the almond. Earlier recipe books had at least one or two recipes for almond dishes. But by the mid-eighteenth century, almonds were *out*. As we have already seen, the sudden onset of 'French' – dairy-enriched – bread reflects an increasing use of dairy, and the abolition of the long 'black fast' of Lent also allowed dairy to take up the place once held by vegan almonds. Together with the interruption of supply through intermittent wars with Spain, the destruction of Lent in its traditional form more or less did away with the almond-led fasts and dishes of the Middle Ages; they died hard, but their demise left cooks searching for alternative ways of thickening, drying and raising, and they turned increasingly to butter and eggs, and also to the widening variety of stale baked goods – cake crumbs, biscuit crumbs – to do the thickening and drying that almonds had once performed. Without the subtle almond flavour, cooks added other flavourings, especially orange water, lemon and spices, and particularly sugar, and in so doing they discovered sugar's adhesive powers. Almonds thus found themselves banished from the main course with the sweet-savoury dishes they had accompanied.

The seventeenth century substituted homemade vinegar and imported lemons for other spices; galangal, though still known, was in decline, and, as we have seen, was for the most part displaced by ginger powder, while mace and nutmeg elbowed out sandal and even cinnamon. As cream and butter sauces gradually replaced the integral jus of the meat itself, the goal came to be the thick smooth emulsion, which required a little acidity to maximise the absorption of fat. But increasingly the acid used was white wine, and cooking was on its way to a French-style sauce.

By the early nineteenth century, butter had risen up the social scale to become 'nice'. Nice did not mean pleasant, but over-fussy. William Cobbett regarded it as a spoiling food: 'Country children are badly brought up if they do not like sweet lard spread upon bread, as we spread butter … now-a-days, the labourers, and especially the female part of them, have fallen into the taste of *niceness* in food and *finery in dress*.'

Victorian recipes swam in butter. Take Eliza Acton's fish sauce:

RICH MELTED BUTTER

Mix to a very smooth batter a dessertspoonful of flour, a half-saltspoonful of salt, and half a pint of cold water; put these into a delicately clean saucepan, with from *four to six ounces of wellflavoured butter*, cut into small bits, and shake the sauce strongly round, almost without cessation, until the ingredients are perfectly blended, and it is on the point of boiling.

This is vaguely like *beurre blanc*, without the emulsifying effect of the acid base, but with stabilising flour; it is also like a béchamel without milk but with a large butter enrichment. Acton also has a recipe for 'French Melted Butter', which is a hollandaise, and the one following it in the book is a *beurre blanc* without the acidic element. Every dish must have been swimming in one butter emulsion or another. Acton knew well that the dullest sauce could be improved by adding a lot of butter to it. She also has burnt butter, telling us that 'in France, this is a favourite sauce with boiled skate, which is served with plenty of crisped parsley, in addition, strewed over it'. French cooking is again the model. Despite the diversity of the sauces, butter would have been the dominant flavour in all of them.

'At each end of the Mall there are stands of cows, from whence the company at small expence may be supplied with warm milk.'[8] A French visitor to London in the seventeenth century described the scene: 'The cows are driven about noon and evening to the gate which leads from the Park to the quarter of Whitehall … [T]heir milk, which is being drawn from their udders on the spot [and which] is served with all the cleanliness peculiar to the English, in little mugs at the rate of 1d per mug.'[9]

The cows were part of a collection of animals – spotted deer, antelopes, an elk, two pelicans and a crane with a wooden leg; William III built himself a birdwatching hut on an island. Other kinds of wild life were on display, too, especially prostitutes. Not far away was Green Park, with its Restoration icehouse for cooling drinks in summer.[10]

It was sensible Elizabeth Cromwell, wife of Oliver, who installed cows in St James's Park, but the restored court gave it a huge boost after 1660. The taste for dairy was not a simple result of snobbery and imitation. New consumers have to learn to love new foods, and the process is often fraught with difficulty. The radical new mouth feel of cream, bland, soft, unctuous, was not just a new desire, but a new kind of desire. A desire to be soothed. A desire to ingest not strength and primal energy, but civilisation and sweetness. Some food historians think that this taste was already addressed by the medieval passion for almonds and almond sweets. However, almonds always have a hint of bitterness, and commonly a hint of grit too. And even the richest almond milk is nothing like as unctuous as cream.

The best-loved Restoration sweet was syllabub. Charles II, it is claimed, liked syllabub's combination of the unctuous with the sweet. As opposed to modern syllabub, usually a sherry cream, set firm, like a cheesecake filling without the base, Restoration syllabub was essentially a lemon- or beer- or wine-flavoured whipped cream, exciting because whipping and aerating were themselves novel. Whisking had only just been discovered. The syllabub, and its trifling, aerated cousins the flim flam and the whim wham, were desserts that appealed largely because they used the new skill.

The cows in St James's that provided warm milk for syllabub were still flourishing in the nineteenth century, at the time of the Great Exhibition. Henry Mayhew reported that 'The chief customers are infants, and adults, and others, of a delicate constitution, who have been recommended to take new milk. On a wet day scarcely any milk can be disposed of. Soldiers are occasional customers.'[11]

One of the sellers told Mayhew that 'People drink new milk for their health … They're mostly young women, I think, that's delicate, and makes the most of it.' Earlier eras had noticed the health benefits: 'Children in Dairy Countries doe wax more tall, than where they feed more upon Bread, and Flesh.'[12] Surprisingly, milk was also a dating drink (for 'servant-gals out for the day'), and generally a drink of the young: 'Very few elderly people drink new milk. It's mostly the young.'

Both the luxury syllabub and the health/dating drink used the freshness and warmth of very new milk, and before pasteurisation and refrigeration such a treat was always bracketed by experiences that were less than ideal. But such fresh, new milk could form a powerful symbol of love, beauty and nature, much as flowers might today. Mayhew also said young men might treat a young woman to curds:

> The preparations of milk which comprise the street-trade, are
> curds and whey and rice-milk … The one is a summer, and the
> other a winter traffic, and both are exclusively in the hands of
> the same middle-aged and elderly women. The vendors prepare
> the curds and whey in all cases themselves.

Dairy products were in a minority, dwarfed by savoury cooked foods
– fried fish, sheep trotters, and pea soup and hot eels. Still, Mayhew
described the method of curd-making, reminiscent of yoghurt-
making:

> The milk is first 'scalded,' the pan containing it being closely
> watched, in order that the contents may not boil. The scalding
> occupies 10 or 15 minutes, and it is then 'cooled' until it attains
> the lukewarmness of new milk. Half a pound of sugar is
> then dissolved in the milk, and a tea-spoonful of rennet is
> introduced, which is sufficient to 'turn' a gallon. In an hour, or
> in some cases two, the milk is curded, and is ready for use.

A woman who had sold 'cruds' – as the street people usually called it
– for eighteen years described them as an acquired taste. They were a
treat for what she called 'quiet working people' and 'street boys'. The
personal festive pleasure had displaced the religious festival.

———————

Shakespeare's Henry V envied the peasant, with his empty head and
full belly, but Elizabeth I had wanted to be a dairymaid.[13] 'They are
not troubled with fears and cares, but sing sweetly all the day and sleep
securely all the night.' This was because she did not know about the
heavy yoke they carried on their shoulders, a full pail on either side. In
May, Elizabeth thought them especially enviable; they garlanded their
pails with flowers and bore silver dippers for the milk. They would
dance along the streets on May Day, accompanied by a fiddler … Of
course, a good deal was hidden from the queen. The pure milk was
sometimes diluted with water from the pump, or perhaps the horse

trough; the milk was left to stand overnight, with its cream skimmed off in the morning, then sold in the street as 'new milk'.

Because milkmaids had to look clean – had to *be* clean – as part of their work, as part of their sales techniques, they were attractive objects of desire, and the attraction spilled over, so to speak, into the products they sold. They were the best advertisements for their own wares. So toothsome was the milkmaid that some customers saw her as the product, as the song 'Pretty Bessy Milkmaid' suggests. Bessy is courted by a squire, attracted by her cry of 'Do you want any new milk?'[14] All ends well – in a way. The squire is forced to marry Bessy, who bears him two children and is last seen cuddling them. Perhaps the sauciest of these songs is 'A-rolling in the dew makes the milk maid so fair', which also envisages sex with a milkmaid in a pastoral setting.[15] We can think, too, of Tess of the D'Urbervilles, pretty milkmaid. The prettiness of milkmaids was in part due to the cowpox that made them immune to smallpox scarring (was this why Elizabeth I wished to be a milkmaid?), but there is a sensuousness about cream itself that attracted. Cream … Devon dairymaids up to the shoulder stirring what was to be clotted cream, slowly, arms bare, silken in the cream. Less seductively, clotted cream was also made over slow peat fires in earthenware pots.[16] For a long, halcyon period, the dairymaid's fresh body and her fresh wares were deliciously and scandalously entangled.

Calves had to be pastured where their mothers could neither see nor hear them; then their mothers could give their milk to humans. The milkmaid was nursemaid to the calf, feeding the calf three times a day according to Tusser. Calves had to be fed from above by encouraging them to suck the milkmaid's fingers.

What would the milkmaid say if she could speak? Poet Ann Yearsley, herself a milkmaid in the eighteenth century, pointed out the discomfort that came with the job: 'half sunk in snow,/ Lactilla, shivering, tends her fav'rite cow'.[17] Milk was hard to transport to the hungry cities by means of the slow carts required for a heavy load; it would spoil before it reached its destination. Jolting it on horseback led to butter. Instead, it was cows that were transported and milked at the door; some families in towns kept a cow or a goat, and there was a city cow byre on the Mile End Road near Aldgate pump, at almost the opposite end of London from St James's. The prominence of the milk-maid in the national imagination reflects the new predominance of dairy foods in the diet, and particularly the door-to-door sale of milk in big cities.

Milk and other dairy products came to household kitchens in waves of sound, so singsong that like advertising jingles they could be imitated by young children:

> Milk below, maids!
> Strawberrys, scarlet strawberrys!
> Two bundles a penny, primroses, two bundles a penny!
> Round and sound, fivepence a pound, Duke cherries!
> Sweet China oranges!
> Hot spiced gingerbread, smoking hot!
> A new love song, only a halfpenny apiece!

Primroses and milk, and a new love song too. Here dairy comes into focus as an instant food, a treat.

From the Restoration, and well into the Victorian period, increasing numbers of enterprising families set up 'milking parlours' throughout the city, including one in the Strand where the cows were lowered into a cellar to be kept and milked for a time, before being sent back to the pastures to the north and the next shift of cows brought in. Then the milk pans were handed over to the milkmaids who hawked them door-to-door. One milkmaid recorded her daily route, which extended for nineteen miles. As milk delivery was a daily occurrence, many milkmaids ran slates for their customers, proving they were literate and numerate – and also hard enough to call in a debt.

Milkmaids and dairymaids needed a number of highly specialised technical skills. They were highly manual. As late as the twentieth century, Florence White reported a woman in Devon who made butter by beating it with her bare hand, and women also stirred clotted cream with bare arms, while the gentle slow heat turned it to rippling clots.

Andrew Boorde's *Dyetary* of 1545 mentioned clotted cream, and Hannah Woolley at the end of the seventeenth century gave a method, clabbered with rosewater apparently: new milk was mixed with cream and stood on a low fire for a day and a night, then it was skimmed, and Woolley warned 'let there be no milk in it'; it was served in a cream dish with scraped sugar. More remarkably she had what she calls cabbage cream, which contained no cabbage; milk was heated to boiling point, then poured into 'earthenware bowls as fast as is possible without frothing; then when they are a little cold, gather the cream on the top with your hand, rumpling it together, and lay it on a flat dish; when you have laid three or four layers [presumably gathered successively] one on another, wet a feather in rosewater and musk, and stroke over it, then grated nutmeg and fine sugar, then add more layers, season as before', then boil the milk again and repeat the whole process, 'that it may lie round and high like a cabbage'. Woolley instructed keeping back one of the first poured bowls until the rest of the process was completed, 'that the cream may be thick and crumpled'.[18]

Woolley's recipes give the lie to ideas that milk from city cows was dreadful. Urban milk was gloomily described by novelist Tobias Smollett as full of cabbage leaf feed and fouled by tobacco quids, but there is no strong evidence for this beyond the regular food scares that always pursue dairying (and indeed most types of food production). It may be true that the urban cow's lot was unhappy; as cities grew the only feed available was limited, and cows were probably fed on brewer's waste and hay, and tethered in small dark stalls. Urban cow milk was called blue milk; this might have been because it had been skimmed, or because it had little cream content to skim off in the first place. But some cows remained the transport vehicles for their own milk; walked along the streets, they were milked directly into the consumer's receptacle. The poshest milk came from the Lactarian in St James's Park, which retained its cows and its royal associations.[19]

The reliable way to preserve milk and have it for ever was cheese, 'immortal milk'. The ancient Romans supplied their armies with cheeses, and the basic military diet for the Romans stationed in Britain consisted of cereals, bacon, cheese and perhaps a few vegetables. Cheese-making equipment and technology came with them, and Roman ceramic cheese moulds have been found.[20] As the Roman Empire began to collapse, the number of slaves available to perform the labour of dairying shrank, and with their departure went the vast landed estates of empire. As land was re-divided into smaller units, cheese-making and dairying began to reflect the smaller dairy herds and reduced labour available, bringing cheese into what is called manorial cheese-making. However, the methods being used were no different to those described by the first-century Roman author Columella: add rennet to fresh warm milk to induce coagulation, ladle the curd into small draining forms such as wicker vessels or baskets, allow the curds to drain and mat together, and press the cheese with a small stone or other weight to hasten draining. Then rub the compact cheese with dry salt or submerge it in a salt brine solution. Not only was this method the basis for medieval English cheese-making, it was also the norm for the evolution of the famous French rinded and washed cheeses, though the exact moment when ordinary cheese-making led to the manufacture of Brie has not been fully determined. One issue for English and French cheese-makers alike was that typically they could only use one milking a day, and the small amount of milk obtained must at times have seemed hardly worth the effort needed to make cheese. However, a practice may have evolved whereby that small amount of milk was kept until a second milking could be added to it, resulting in a different kind of product than that made using only fresh milk.

Andrew Boorde lists four kinds of cheese in the early sixteenth century: green cheese, soft cheese, hard cheese and spermyse. Green, he explains, is not green in colour, but only in newness – probably like Caerphilly; spermyse is made with herbs, a bit like Sage Derby, and hard cheese was made with skimmed milk, so it was very hard and tough, much harder than any modern cheese, and eaten mainly by the poor. These hard cheeses could be so solid that they were impossible to bite. To preserve it for winter, cheese was dried and salted, as with butter. It was also pressed, and cured with rennet, as such cheeses keep rather better than acid-cured cheeses. Whey cheese – cheese made only from whey – was hard, bitter, but protein-rich. Salt was used so extensively that Thomas Tusser warned his dairymaids that it could cause 'the stone' (kidney stones). Soft cheese was a bit like gouda: still firm, waxy, but much softer than hard cheese. As well as calf's stomach rennet, medieval cheese-makers used lady's bedstraw, or *Galium verum*. Some, as we have seen, also used thistles and cardoons. Flowers, too, were used in cheese manufacture and, in Gloucestershire, to colour Double Gloucester cheese.

With the so-called dissolution of the monasteries by Henry VIII went the demesne cheese-makers, often dairymaids, who had been employed to help the monks create dairy products, for use in Lent as well as for sale. While it may be that some of these dairymaids managed to transmit their knowledge to the yeoman and greater gentry families that took over the land, knowledge – and certainly some history – was lost, in particular the history of varieties of cheese. Dairymaids tended to guard their knowledge as a trade secret to be handed down from mother to daughter, from mistress to servant, not to be shared with their competitors. In gentry and German households, the housewife typically supervised the dairymaids at work, and passed her knowledge on to the next generation.

As London's population grew, East Anglia came to have a virtual monopoly on the London market for cheese and butter, and it also exported cheese and butter to northern France and supplied cheese to the English army and the navy.[21] Churning and cheese-making were not only traditional activities; they were associated with a new kind of commercial farming, farming for sale and not just for subsistence, and therefore farming in direct competition with other dairy creators.

To resolve problems of storage, there was an incentive to make cheeses larger and larger. They had less surface area in relation to volume, leading to a lower rate of evaporation, so that they also lost less weight in storage; the weight of a typical Cheshire cheese grew from 10–12 lb in the mid-seventeenth century to around 24 lb by the start of the eighteenth century. Production often required expensive equipment and new methodologies; the salt rub became more important, since the new thicker cheeses took longer to diffuse the salt, leading to the risk of rotting from the inside. Nevertheless, the number of cheeses continued to grow and diversify across the different counties of England, and eventually, acidic cheeses were especially in demand, particularly the much-acclaimed Stilton cheese, which first became popular in the mid-eighteenth century. Like other cheese-makers, Stilton cheese-makers pre-salted the curd before pressing, but they did not press the cheese as hard as Cheshire cheese-makers. As the cheese increased in size, it became an open-textured, high-moisture, acidic cheese, that when aged in a cool and moist environment would support appropriate mould growth. It was so moist and so soft that it had to be wrapped in bandages to prevent the cylindrical form from slumping and becoming misshapen during ageing.[22]

———————

This was a dairy Garden of Eden for prosperous consumers, who were able to enjoy a great range of new and regional cheeses. Paxton and Whitfield opened a market stall in Aldwych in 1742, and moved to luxury premises in St James's in the last decade of the eighteenth century. They are still trading. On the Thames, the Buscot cheese wharf near Lechlade in Gloucestershire was one of many sending cheeses by river to the south and to London. Like all businesses built on the desires of the City, this one was subject to changes in fashion. Established in the Middle Ages, the cheese wharf sent at its nineteenth-century peak some two or three thousand tons of cheese annually down the Thames – though in the same year, 1813, dairymen complained that they could not sell their cheese.[23]

But a serpent was about to arrive, one that would sting diners as well as makers: imports of American factory-made cheese during the second half of the nineteenth century, after the first US cheese-making factory was launched in 1851. The English population was growing, while England had also lowered tariffs on food to encourage imports, and it was at this time that American 'Cheddar' cheese began to appear in English shops. It was cheap because it was made in a factory, and it drove down the price of all cheese. English cheese-makers were forced to act. Some switched to producing milk for the growing liquid milk markets of London, a process helped enormously by the coming of the railways; many farmhouse cheese-makers stopped making cheese altogether, and simply sold their milk. Other cheese-makers tried to establish factories of their own, and the first English factory began operations in 1870. Dairying regions resisted the move to factory manufacture, and factory cheeses were correctly seen as inferior. Nevertheless, their low price, and the arrival of fresh imports from Canada and New Zealand, meant that by the mid-1920s more than 70 per cent of the cheese consumed in England was imported – although at the same date, of the cheese consumed that was still made in England, farmhouse cheese accounted for an impressive 75 per cent of domestic production.[24] Progressive artisan cheese-makers cultivated a growing luxury market. Unfortunately, the crisis of the Great Depression and then the Second World War put an end to this resurgence. The wartime ration was two ounces a week; this was composed of Government Cheddar, factory-made. In particular, wartime policy insisted that farmhouse cheese-making should be replaced by factory production of a few high-priority hard cheeses. When wartime controls were lifted in the early 1950s farm-based cheese-making failed to recover, and by the late 1950s around 95 per cent of total domestic production consisted of factory-made cheese. There have been revivals, but the market is still dominated by industrially produced cheeses that crushed craft.

During its heyday, cheese, and especially high-quality cheese, was a masculine pleasure. By contrast, sweetened dairy treats consumed on dates, in individual servings, prompted innovation, and merchants produced and then distributed new versions of the basic idea. The most exciting and most novel of these was ice cream. Ice cream was a taste we had to acquire. Like many foods we now consider a familiar part of our diet, ice cream was invented somewhere else, distributed by immigrants in big cities in both an elite and a low-level popular form, and required imported ingredients to flavour it, including sugar, chocolate and vanilla.

The ice was the apotheosis of the new creamy taste. Dairy plus sugar plus eggs = ice cream. Plus cold … the freezing is based on the addition of mineral salts to water to lower its freezing point. Normally, containers of liquid would simply cool rather than freeze. The icehouse craze, in which an underground bunker was filled with ice and used to cool foods, began under James I, perhaps influenced by Italians at court, but early icehouses were not cold enough to do more than preserve some freshness. Naples, the European centre for ices, began its freezing with efforts to reproduce oriental sherbets, basically lemon with other flavourings such as ambergris and musk added after freezing, but it was still water and fruit ice. A very early ice *cream* recipe comes from Ann Fanshawe's manuscript recipe book; Ann was living in exile during the years of the Republic and the Protectorate, with her husband Sir Richard Fanshawe. She does not concern herself with the freezing process, any more than she bothers about how to supply firewood for the baking oven, but this kind of lack of detail is normal for seventeenth-century recipes:

> Take three pints of the best cream, boil it with a blade of mace, or else perfume it with orange flower water, or amber[gris], sweeten the cream with sugar, let it stand till it is quite cold, then put it into boxes, either of silver or tin, then take ice chopped into small pieces and putt it into a tub and sop the boxes in the ice covering them all over, and let them stand in the Ice two hours, and the Cream will come to be ice in the boxes, then turn them out into a salver with some of the same seasoned cream, so serve it up to the table.

The ambergris flavouring is a Restoration item; Charles II is said to have loved eggs with ambergris.[25] Ambergris might have matured to a sweet, alcohol flavour, compatible with eggs as Marsala is, custardy and strong. In 1718, Mary Eales had a recipe that does give the exact freezing process:

> To six Pots you must allow eighteen or twenty Pound of Ice, breaking the Ice very small; there will be some great Pieces, which lay at the Bottom and Top: You must have a Pail, and lay some Straw at the Bottom; then lay in your Ice, and put in amongst it a Pound of Bay-Salt; set in your Pots of Cream, and lay Ice and Salt between every Pot, that they may not touch; but the Ice must lie round them on every Side; lay a good deal of Ice on the Top, cover the Pail with Straw, set it in a Cellar where no Sun or Light comes, it will be froze in four Hours, but it may stand longer.

Later in the eighteenth century both Elizabeth Raffald and Hannah Glasse gave recipes for ice cream.[26]

However, ice cream for centuries remained something that only the very rich could afford to try. What changed all that was the coming of Italian immigrants in the early nineteenth century, bringing with them the knowledge required to make a product that could be sold in the street.

At first, ice cream was a minority taste, an oddity. Not only was it very different from the way most people expected to consume milk, it was also a radical departure from the norms of street food. Henry Mayhew said in 1851 that there were only twenty ice-cream sellers on the London streets, compared with 300 sellers of cooked sheep's trotters. So different was the food from what customers were expecting that Mayhew told the mournful tale of two failed ice entrepreneurs, and attributed the failure to the fact that the buyers 'had but a confused notion how the ice was to be swallowed'. The trouble was that they were used to gulping down dairy curds. One seller also told Mayhew that even when the customers had worked out how to eat them, something less than rapture resulted:

Yes, sir, I mind very well the first time as I ever sold ices.
I don't think they'll ever take greatly in the streets, but there's
no saying. Lord! how I've seen the people splutter when they've
tasted them for the first time. I did as much myself. They
get among the teeth and make you feel as if you tooth-ached
all over.

In an age when tooth decay and weakness were more prevalent, the
likelihood that ice would hurt was far higher. So great was the challenge of this kind of food that the vendor claimed that the trade was
most successful with 'servant maids that gulped them on the sly'.[27]

Gradually, ice cream settled in. Mayhew pointed out that many
street foods were seasonal, and among the most seasonal were the
ice-cream sellers:

Parti-coloured Neapolitan ices, vended by unmistakable natives
of Whitechapel or the New Cut, whose curious cry of "Okey
Pokey" originated no one knows how, have lately appeared in
the streets. Hokey Pokey is of a firmer make and probably stiffer
material than the penny ice of the Italians, which it rivals in
public favour; and it is built up of variously flavoured layers.
Sold in halfpenny and also penny paper-covered squares, kept
dreadfully sweet, dreadfully cold, and hard as a brick. It is
whispered that the not unwholesome Swede turnip, crushed
into pulp, has been known to form its base, in lieu of more
expensive supplies from the cow.[28]

The hokey pokey sellers lived huddled together, mostly in the poorer
quarters of the town, where lodgings were cheap and sanitary conditions primitive, forced to make long journeys to get ice and salt cheap
in the early hours of the morning, made to freeze the ice cream under
the 'most revolting' sanitary conditions, either in badly ventilated
sheds or on the pavements themselves, and then drag their heavy
barrows, on an empty stomach, to distant pitches in the town where
the boys and hooligans of the neighbourhood annoyed them, broke

their glasses, threw dirty matter in their freezers, and sent them home in tears without any money.[29] Ethnic prejudice played a role; some worried about 'the swarthy sons of Italy, who annually visit us with their gaudily-painted barrows and questionable ices'.[30]

While some eaters declared the cold would kill them, others were literally killed by the bacteria they ingested. Sir Robert Baden-Powell opined about 'the awful hokey-pokey of the Italian ice-cream vendor at street corners, the delight of the street Arab, and the horror of the microbe and bacillus hunter'. Bigoted though he was, he had a point about standards of cleanliness. Penny licks were ice creams in thick glasses. When the ice cream had been licked off, the glass would be rinsed in a pail of water and wiped. In 1899, scientists analysed samples of water used to wash the glasses. Their findings confirmed everyone's worst imaginings: they saw 'an evil-smelling, thickish and slimy liquid, full of bacteria and sediments, including, of course, saliva from the many mouths that had touched the glasses during the day'. One batch of ice cream examined under a microscope turned out to contain bed bugs, bugs' legs, fleas, bed straw, human hair, cats' and dogs' hairs, coal dust, woollen and linen fibre, tobacco, dry skin and muscular tissue.[31] One campaigner joked that 'the cream, of course, must be held blameless, for this ingredient occurs in such small proportions that we may neglect it.'[32] As late as 1946, the Ministry of Health was still keen to intervene to ensure all egg used in ice cream was dried.[33]

As often with dairy foods, efforts to prevent the manufacture of genuinely horrible cheap products acted against the top end of the market. At the same time that hokey pokey was full of bedbugs, Gunter was the king of ice. Gunter's Tea Shop was famous, located in Berkeley Square, founded by Domenico Negri; he kept his recipes a secret, and attracted rich and mighty patrons. Ladies would sit in their carriages while the waiters rushed across with their orders. The ice cream tearoom closed only in 1956. Elizabeth David remembered Gunter's before the war, 'slightly crunchy, grainy, bisquecoloured brown bread ice' and 'rich, creamy, pale pink strawberry ice cream'. She herself called this recollection 'absurdly idealistic', and she went on to describe with horror her tea at Gunter's after it had moved to Curzon Street, after the war.[34] David promptly set about attempting to make the remembered delights using William Jarrin's recipes, published alongside Gunter's.[35] But David didn't actually like Jarrin's recipes, and halved the number of egg yolks – with the result that she failed to replicate what she said she was seeking, appearing to miss the point that the omitted egg yolks would have altered the texture of the ice. She reduced their number further for a recipe given in *House and Garden* in July 1959 – long after rationing had ended – increasing the amount of dairy liquid. She thought you need not stir the ice 'depending on your refrigerator'.[36]

Egg yolks act as an emulsifier, keeping ice crystals small even at relatively low milk-fat levels; Italian gelato typically contains much butterfat, and was probably the basis for the ices at Gunter's. The absence of eggs, or the reduction in their amount, has an effect not unlike their absence or reduction from mayonnaise. The fat in ice cream – in cream – is held in suspension within the larger embrace of the egg yolk emulsifier, held in tiny droplets. Many modern ices are much richer even than Gunter's, and David's food history here suggests the astounding difficulty of bending the mind to reproduce the past exactly. Her alterations mirror those which typically accompany books with titles such as *Food in Medieval England*. Like works of art, classic dishes require tireless reinvention in order not to disappear altogether.

Apart from Gunter, the other big name in nineteenth-century ice cream was Mrs A. B. Marshall, a self-promoter who could have induced envy in Martha Stewart. Her name was on the door of her large cooking school and employment agency on Mortimer Street. She also wrote for culinary magazines, and had product lines of cooking utensils and food products; she gave lectures and wrote cookbooks. She held live demonstrations, attracting huge Saturday crowds. Her cookbook, *Fancy Ices*, is still cited and approved by Heston Blumenthal; she designed a fast ice-cream machine (patented by her husband), and in 1888 suggested putting ice cream in an edible cornet or cone of ground almonds (like a tuile), a practice previously thought to have originated in the USA.[37]

Later associated with the USA was the ice cream sundae, and in particular the knickerbocker glory. Nobody is sure why it is called the 'knickerbocker' – was it just the resemblance of a tall sundae glass to the inverted leg of a knickerbocker, with the accompanying whiff of naughtiness? Chocolate syrup, vanilla ice cream, crushed raspberry, ice cream, pineapple, ice cream, whipped cream, and a glacé cherry: for the ordinary person, this was accessible profusion. It was a cornucopia, a symbol of urban abundance.

———————

Ice cream was mostly not made during the war, but an ice cream substitute – called, ominously, hokey pokey – was served. It was made with parsnips. The post-war ice cream trade became much more concentrated in the hands of a few manufacturers – Lyons, Wall's and Eldorado, while regulations designed to safeguard the public against bugs in ice cream – one case of typhoid in 1948 meant the closure of many small businesses – alongside discomfort with genuinely rich foods, were the gateway to cheap and clean ice cream laden with additives. Wall's was a sausage-maker until 1922, when it began making ices in a factory at Acton, importing the method from the USA. The Lyons ice cream parlours began making their own ices at the same time. They both used ice cream powder, which only needed milk or water to be churned into ice cream; the first ices made from it were also probably the first to be based on emulsified fats.

Cheap ice cream labelled simply 'ice cream', without the word 'dairy', can be made from refined vegetable oil, mostly palm oil, sugar, and methyl ethyl cellulose (manufactured from algae or woodchips, initially an off-white powder). So-called 'soft-serve' is not actually ice cream in the traditional sense. Squirted out of a nozzle to make the cones you buy from an ice cream van, it used to contain pig fat or lard. Now its ingredients are corn syrup, whey, monoglycerides and diglycerides (emulsifiers), artificial flavours, guar gum, calcium sulfate, cellulose gum, polysorbates 65 and 80 (emulsifiers), carrageenan, magnesium hydroxide and air pumped into the mixture as it crystallises.

Virtually all basic supermarket lines from own-brand soft scoop to Carte d'Or rely heavily on vegetable oil – usually palm oil. Anything labelled simply 'ice cream' is only required to contain 2.5 per cent milk protein and 5 per cent of any kind of fat. This rarely comes from any fresh ingredient. Partially reconstituted skimmed milk is one source. Another is whey solids, produced in vast quantities by the dairy industry and sold in dried form as a muscle-building agent. All of these vegetable fats and milk-based products are what the industry refers to as 'bulking agents' or 'fillers', 'cheap ways of adding volume but not cost to the ice cream'. There is of course the cheapest bulking agent: air. Ice cream is sold by volume, not weight, so a way of making it go further is to whip as much air into the mixture as possible before freezing it into plastic tubs. More additives are then required to turn all this into something that might remind people of frozen egg custard. Yellow colouring is a must. Emulsifiers such as 'diglycerides of fatty acids' prevent the fat and water content separating into a greasy puddle. Alginates enable manufacturers to inflate it ad infinitum.[38]

Eventually, the United States reintroduced England to 'premium' ice cream. Haagen-Dazs, for example, was started in 1959, but didn't achieve supermarket distribution until the mid-1970s. Ben & Jerry's was founded as a small artisanal outlet, but also became a worldwide brand, playing on its vaguely hippy image with flavour names like Cherry Garcia. Originality was all. This is also the goal of Gelupo, the Soho gelateria, whose ice cream menu includes:

FRESH MINT STRACCIATELLA (a beautiful, fresh mint
   gelato, flecked with dark chocolate)
HAZELNUT (With lightly-roasted hazelnuts from Piedmonte)
PISTACHIO (With lightly-roasted Bronte pistachios from
   Sicilia)
RICOTTA & SOUR CHERRY RIPPLE (A light, sheep's milk
   ricotta gelato swirled with sour cherries)
SUMMER PUDDING GELATO (a blend of blackberry,
   raspberry, strawberry and fragola grape sorbetti, marbled
   with a vodka & mulberry soaked sponge)

Yet it's hard to ignore the fact that this is fundamentally an un-English menu; despite recent efforts, English ice-cream manufacturers will still be associated with artificial additives rather than with top-quality ingredients. Of a list of ten top ice-cream manufacturers in England, six are Italian.[39] Some of the exceptions have somehow survived legislative onslaughts, and consumers' demand for lower-cost products. Like English cheese-makers and English butter-makers, these makers connect the land with those who live on it. But for how much longer?

———————

Tastes are undergoing another revolution, against the one that brought dairy to the fore in the seventeenth century and with it the food of France. If the times they are a changin' once more, this is in keeping with the current mood in which French dominance of the food high ground is coming under renewed scrutiny and criticism. French haute cuisine has held its buttery, creamy top slot on the basis largely of the emulsive softness of dairy. But if that sweetness and richness ceases to be pleasurable, then France will continue to lose its food position to harder, rougher flavours: North African spices, Eastern mouth explosions, Italian pepper oils, all of which have been used to pep up ice cream and make it new. Something larger might be in motion. Writing on the crisis of French haute cuisine, Steven Shapin cites *Distinction*, in which Pierre Bourdieu notes that 'Your food is supposed to get lighter as you move up in the world.' That is the case now, but once it was supposed to get bloodier and darker. Then it was supposed to get whiter and richer. Thanks to misguided campaigns to reduce fat intake, the idea of riches meaning richness has been on the back burner for fifty years. The rules are made up, and then adhered to like a religion.[40]

Cake

When a modern eater visualises cake, what will first come to mind is perhaps a puffy golden Victoria sponge, or a flourless chocolate cake like a giant truffle. Yet these are of relatively recent date. The 'heritage' Victoria sponge depends on a series of innovations not available to earlier bakers, and the chocolate torte depends on chocolate, only occasionally used in baking before the First World War. What are now designated 'cakes' are products of the eighteenth century's idea that beaten eggs can leaven through trapped air, and of the nineteenth century's equally momentous discovery of non-yeast raising agents – baking powder, but first ammonia, and cream of tartar and soda. The only cake still in wide circulation that bears a superficial resemblance to the great cake of the Middle Ages is the fruit cake made for ceremonial occasions, weddings and Christmas and birthdays.

The first reference to the 'traditional' English fruit cake is from seventeenth-century vegetarian Thomas Tryon: 'Observe the composition of Cakes, which are frequently eaten … In them there are commonly Flour, Butter, Eggs, Milk, Fruit, Spice, Sugar, Sack, Rose-Water and Sweet-Meats, as Citron, or the like.'[1] Such great cakes were seasonal, part of a church calendar of festivity. Cakes now linked with specific locales were once calendrically indexed, and associated with the feasts of particular saints or with holy days, especially Christmas and Easter. Most of us still think of cake as festive, but the festivities involved are the secular ones of birthday and wedding. These still retain a trace of cake's association with the sacred, an association that caused problems for Protestants when they abandoned the idea of physical worship as uncomfortably pagan. Thomas Cranmer had, after all, condemned the Catholics and their 'cakey god' the Eucharist in an anti-sacramental outburst. There were many saint-related cakes for Puritans to fear and despise. Madling cakes (containing mutton suet, flour and yeast) probably commemorated the feast of Mary Magdalene in late July. They represented the jar of precious spices with which Mary Magdalene anointed Jesus: two layers of the cake were separated by a layer of currants 'so that none can be seen till the Cake is broke'.[2] A madling cake might eventually have become a Madeleine, the very cake whose taste led Proust back to a moment of childhood. Cake is often seen as offering a window to a more stable past. But they were also a way of making holiness delicious. Before the Reformation, you ate religion, in the form of cakes, and reformers never quite succeeded in breaking the pattern.

———————

A homemade cake before 1500 was mostly, though not invariably, something baked on a griddle – hence the term girdle cake – rather than in an oven.[3] A cake is therefore not a substantively different but simply a differently *cooked* product, so that 'cake' is a term analogous to 'fry-up': 'Some brede is bake and tornyd and wende at fyre and is callyd a cake.'[4] Cakes of this kind were a grilled mass of dough, dry, flat and entirely unleavened and unsweetened, made with grains and mixed with water; the result would have been very like what is now still called an oatcake. Such cakes, sometimes called bannocks, were just oatmeal and water and salt, baked on a heated bakestone. A thin oatcake might also contain meat fat, like lard. Cakes of this type could also be made of wheat flour, rye meal, or even peasemeal.[5] Surprisingly, cakes very like the Roman placenta and the Anglo-Saxon oatcake are still baked today and still known, though they have been pushed into the background by the advent of chemical leavens, mechanical whisks, and above all the coming of chocolate as the hallmark of baked goods' flavour and savour.

Oatcakes too were once part of a particular set of calendrical festivals. Soul Mass cakes or soul cakes were a type of oatcake made in

Lancashire and Herefordshire.[6] Parties of children went 'souling', going round soliciting doles on or about All Souls' Day. John Aubrey notes a custom in Shropshire for a 'high heap of soul cakes' to be set on a household table – visitors would take one while saying the rhyme 'a soul-cake, a soul cake, have mercy on all Christian souls for a soul cake'.[7] A well-known version of the song goes:

A soul, a soul, a soul cake
Please, good missus, a soul cake
An apple, a pear, a plum or a cherry
Any good thing to make us all merry
One for Peter, two for Paul
Three for Him who made us all

The interweaving of bodily sense and material world with ecclesiastical matters was rejected firmly by Protestants, especially when it became clear that the gift of a cake bought a blessing, including perhaps animal reproductivity or fertility:

God bless the master of this house, the mistress also
And all the little children who around your table grow
Likewise your men and maidens, your cattle and your store
And all that dwells within your gates
We wish you ten times more.

This festive begging is closely related to wassailing (see Apples), but the cake gifts have older and much darker origins which explain their links with All Souls Day. Originally, soul cakes were not given to the living, however needy; they were for the dead. A soul cake was left for the spirits that departed their graves on Samhain (Halloween) and did not return until 2 November, All Souls' Day. The old churning rhyme 'St Peter stands at the gate/ Waiting for a butter cake' is sometimes recorded as 'waiting for a soul cake', as if this is a payment for a soul's entry to heaven. In Carnaerfon the custom of feeding the dead became a gift of bread and cheese for the dead, 'food of the letting loose of the dead'. The soul cake might also be connected with the oddly named teen-lay, a kind of outdoor bonfire lit with straw over which cakes could have been cooked.

Fairy cakes take on a sinister new meaning when we learn that they could be used ritually as an offering to real fairies: 'I know not why,' says eighteenth-century folklorist John Brand, 'but they [fairies] are reported to have been particularly fond of making cakes, and to have been very noisy during the operation.'[8] Brand also has this story: 'In Ireland they [the fairies] frequently lay bannocks, a kind of oaten cakes, in the way of travellers over the mountains: and if they do not accept of the intended favour, they seldom escape a hearty beating or something worse.'

Once, then, there were *real* fairy cakes, spread out for the godmother, the fairy. A teen cake might be a cake offered to the fairies as a tithe, a kind of rent.

Teen cakes and soul cakes were not the only cakes which linked the supernatural and the dead to humanity. It would be more accurate to say that *all* cakes had ritual links than to try to single out those for which the links were especially strong.

'Rock-Monday, and the wake in summer, shrovings, the wakeful catches on Christmas Eve, the hoky or seed-cake, these he yearly keeps, yet holds them no relics of Popery.'[9] This is Jacobean essayist (and famous murder victim) Sir Thomas Overbury's characterisation of a franklin (a landowner without a noble title), who is perhaps influenced by his tenants. The seed cake or hoky cake is mysterious, and might be a fertility cake, or even a Beltane Cake, a plain oat bannock made with water, but that was what a Beltane or May Day cake was, an act of faith that there would be grain again, and a sacrifice to unnamed beings. It's worth noting that all these cake rituals are linked to agriculture, in which from the dark unseen space below the tilled field comes new life and food. They are all fertility rites.

It followed that as the darkness gathered, it was better to give cakes away than to guzzle whole plates of them alone. The gift itself ensured that the darkness of the year was somehow appeased; it redistributed hope. 'We Wish You a Merry Christmas' is a popular sixteenth-century English carol from the West Country.[10] It is still well known:

> Good tidings we bring for you and your kin,
> We wish you a Merry Christmas and a Happy New Year.
> Now bring us some figgy pudding (x3)
> and bring some out here.

The structural similarity between this and the soul-cake song is notable – give cake and get a blessing. The singers stand outside the home and the food must be brought to them.[11]

The tradition of cake- or pudding-begging at Christmastide, and its extensions into the Twelve Days, of which more later, may also be a way of ensuring the flow of hospitality that wards off the terror of the Wild Hunt. The New Year feast included children arriving at each doorstep, exchanging their gifts for reward. One early Christian complained:

> This festival teaches even the little children, artless and simple,
> to be greedy, and accustoms them to go from house to house
> and to offer novel gifts, fruits covered with silver tinsel. For
> these they receive, in return, gifts double their value, and thus
> the tender minds of the young begin to be impressed with that
> which is commercial and sordid.[12]

Children do the begging. They represented the Christ Child, of course, but also the darker powers that the cake ritual was supposed to defeat. Unbaptised infants were especially likely to become inhabitants of the dark Otherworld of the fairy realm. The mischievous Yule demons who returned to the house as 'trowies' (northern British fairies) at Yule to steal or spoil food were simply lonely and shut out. They could be appeased, or at least driven back, by the cakey sharing they missed in life.

The flat oatcake was transfigured with the arrival of the waffle iron, recorded in the twelfth century by John de Garland. In addition to their festive and gift-giving associations, the Middle Ages saw wafers and waffles as the snack of choice; they could be spiced, sweet or savoury, and they were supposed to be crisp, fresh and hot. There was something in their hot instantaneousness that suggested love and courtship. Wafers were a love-gift, or a dating gift. Chaucer's unsuccessful courtly lover Absolon sends Alisoun 'wafers, piping hot out of the glede [waffle iron]' in 'The Miller's Tale', while the poet Hoccleve liked to buy 'wafers thick' for the girls at the nearby Paul's Head tavern. Wafers were easy to make with just irons, a charcoal brazier and a bowl of batter; as they didn't require an oven, wafer makers could be mobile, trundling from place to place. Like modern crepe sellers in Paris, the wafer makers congregated around churches on feast days or wedding days. There were rules regarding the placement of stands at a minimum distance from each other, to reduce the danger of fire.[13] Some of these crisp, flat cakes became central to the medieval church's practices. Circular wafers were made of white flour and stamped with a cross, an Agnus Dei – a holy lamb carrying a crusader flag – or the letters IHS, prepared for consecration in the celebration of the Eucharist; these waffles became the prototype for the Host, which was also called the obley, or oblation, an offering, sacrifice.[14]

In the post-Reformation seventeenth century, holy cakes were reinvented and renamed as regional specialities, pruned of their hallowed associations. Take the Banbury cake, for instance; it is indeed an ideal sample, since structurally it strongly resembles other 'local specialities', and also the more controversial mince pies. Folded layers of pastry hold in place a sweet, dark, sticky, spicy filling composed of dried fruit and sugar and spices. Banbury cakes have origins which go back to medieval pies and pasties, and yet the first reference to the name is very late: Banbury, says Addison in the early eighteenth century, 'was a Place famous for Cakes and Zeal'.[15] This reference is interesting because it suggests the possibility of a coexistence between cakes and the godly, though that coexistence was bought at the price of a stern name-change.

Many holy cakes did not survive. Once there was the *manus Christi*, the hand of Christ; this is Thomas Dawson's recipe:

> Take five spoonfuls of rosewater, and grains of ambergrease, and four grains of pearl, beaten very fine … Then take four ounces of a very fine sugar, and beat it small … Then take a little earthen pot, glazed, and put into it a spoonful of sugar, and a quarter of a spoonful of rose water, and let the sugar and rose water boil together softly till it do rise and fall again three times. Then take fine rye flour and sift it on a smooth board. And with a spoon take of the sugar and the rose water, and first make it all into a round cake and then into little cakes. When they be half cold, wet them over with some rose water, and then lay on your gold. And so you shall make very good *manus christi*.[16]

Nobody has eaten these for hundreds of years.

Stripped of its religious connotations, cake became simply a snack food, one Samuel Pepys relished: 'Met with Mr. Woodfine, who took me to an alehouse in Drury Lane, and we sat and drank together, and ate toasted cakes which were very good, and we had a great deal of mirth with the mistress of the house about them.' These toasted cakes might have been more like oatcakes or English muffins than a modern idea of a cake.

Many cake-related activities with pagan origins survived, in part because they were strongly tied in to fertility. In the late seventeenth century, John Aubrey said there are 'cakes at Twelftide when they wassail the Oxen',[17] while John Brand reported that in Herefordshire 'the large cake is produced, and, with much ceremony, put on the horn of the first ox … The ox is then tickled, to make him toss his head: if he throws the cake behind, then it is the mistress's perquisite; if before the bailiff himself claims the prize.' The cake-tossing reuses many of the symbols we have seen circulating around the cake: the overturning of authority and its replacement by chance, the grain cake as symbol of fertility, the uproar, drinking, singing and bad behaviour. Other versions of this rite included one in which thirteen fires were lit in the cornfields, said to represent the twelve apostles and the Virgin Mary; the farmhands retired to a shed where they led in a cow on whose horns a plum cake had been impaled. A bucket of cider was flung in the cow's face, with the wish that the animals might be fertile in the year to come. There is something very rebellious about these customs, something of an unleashed anger and incautious joy in overturning the order of things, even if only for one evening.[18] Moreover, such rites used cakes as cement, attaching one person to another; this social glue sometimes defended real and vital economic rights, especially to wood commons and to areas where firewood could be gathered, and to orchards where fruit might be obtained. When thinking about food, we must always remember the basic folkloric truth: the rite comes first, and later the story that explains it.

The Twelve Days of Christmas encoded an implicit agreement: the labouring poor got to share the life of the lords for whom they worked, in exchange for quiescence the rest of the year. The very last night of Christmas, Twelfth Night, was especially associated with disorder and misrule through the lottery of the Twelfth Night cake. The cake itself contained expensive spices; a 1620 Geneva tract gives (in shocked tones) a recipe with honey, ginger and pepper.[19] Many English readers might never have eaten a true Twelfth Night cake, though these are still common in European countries. Epiphany commemorates the arrival of the Three Wise Men or kings from the east; they give gifts to the infant Jesus of gold, frankincense and myrrh. The themes are the arrival of the precious and exotic in poor circumstances, the bowing of secular power to the sacred power of a baby. Those themes are carried forward in the tradition of the Twelfth Night Cake, a lottery you can eat. It is still served and the lottery still played out in many countries, using cakes that show an affinity with the flat offering cake we have been encountering. The northern French galette also bears a passing resemblance to the Roman placenta cake, since it comprises two pastry discs holding between them a layer of almond cream. The Provençal galette is made of a disc of enriched bread dough with dried fruit and nuts pressed into it.

While Twelfth Night customs were subject to numerous variations, one element transcended virtually every culture that observed the holiday: the choice of a mock king for the occasion. 'The way he was chosen might vary,' Bridget Henisch explains, 'but it was always a matter of chance and good fortune: lots could be drawn or, in the most widespread convention, a cake would be divided. The person who found a bean, or a coin, in his piece was the lucky king for the night.'[20] Such cakes were usually large, intended as the centrepiece of a feast. It was important that the king be chosen solely by luck. He *had* to be lucky in order to confer luck on others for the year ahead. The temporary change in status was sustained with ceremony: the king was given a crown, the authority to call the toasts and lead the drinking and, sometimes, the more dubious privilege of paying the bill on the morning after. The lucky cake with its bean and pea were symbols of fertility, symbols of the harvest, health and prosperity. All households needed luck at such a time; the king's reign spanned the dark turn from one year to the next.[21]

Twelfth Night rites flicker across locales, bringing together harvest fertility rites, cake distribution, cake begging, drinking (cakes and ale) and the dominance of misrule:

> Sometimes a penny was put in the cake, and the person who
> obtained it, becoming king, crossed all the beams and rafters
> of the house against devils. A chafing dish with burning
> frankincense was also lit, and the odour snuffed up by the
> whole family, to keep off disease for the year. After this,
> the master and mistress went round the house with the pan,
> a taper, and a loaf, against witchcraft.[22]

They embraced the great; an Elizabethan court letter from 15 January 1563 mentions that Lady Flemyng was 'Queen of the *Beene*' on Twelfth Night that year.[23] In Ben Jonson's *Masque of Christmas*, Babycake, one of the characters, is attended by 'an Usher, bearing a great cake with a bean and a pease'.

John Brand quotes the same 1620 Genevan tract as evidence that the ancient Twelfth Night cake was composed of flour, honey, ginger and pepper, highlighting its similarity to gingerbread, like an import from the German states. He goes on to describe an anonymous 1623 pamphlet, *Vox Graculi*, which alludes to special Twelfth Night delicacies: 'this day, about the hours of 5, 6, 7, 8, 9, and 10, yea, in some places till midnight well nigh, will be such a massacre of spice-bread, that, ere the next day at noon, a two-penny brown loaf will set twenty poor folks' teeth on edge'.[24] When baked, the cake was divided into as many parts as there were persons in the family, and each had a share. Portions of it were also assigned to Christ, the Virgin and the three Magi, and were given in alms. The cakes themselves sound like the recipes for a Great Cake in Kenelm Digby's book, large dryish fruit cakes: Digby had one recipe for cake involving eight quarts of flour, a pound of loaf sugar, an ounce of mace, thirty eggs plus fifteen whites, and a quart of ale-yeast, scented with rosewater, musk and ambergris cream. His cake also had icing.[25]

Other such Great Cakes are iced *before* they are baked. All Digby's Great Cakes are raised with yeast, and all contain exotic flavourings and fruits. The oldest versions use almonds; not only is almond paste/marzipan one of the oldest luxury delicacies, gracing many medieval feasts, but the French version might once have been a taffety tart, from which evolved the very English Bakewell tart or pudding, a flagrantly secular name, so much so that it cannot be very old, though the foodstuff itself may well be much older. A taffety tart was simply a tart with a transparent, coloured filling. Food historian Karen Hess suggests that the term 'taffety' derives from the silk fabrics of Twelfth Night costumes. And Shakespeare speaks of 'changeable taffeta' in *Twelfth Night*, a play concerned with bewildering changes of station and identity. Change is indeed the theme of Twelfth Night, the last night of Christmas feasting.

Further evidence of the fears aroused by Twelfth Night and the role of cake in annealing them comes from Barnabe Googe, aka Naogeorgus, in *The Popish Kingdome* of 1570, who described with true Protestant disgust a dreadful spendthrift feast of Twelfth Night among the evil superstitious Catholic peoples of the Middle Ages, who sound as if they are having far too good a time:

> Then also every householder, to his ability,
> Doth make a mighty Cake, that may suffice his company:
> Herein a penny doth he put, before it come to fire, …
> But who so chanceth on the piece wherein the money lies,
> Is counted king amongst them all, and is with shouts and cries
> Exalted to the heavens up, who taking chalk in hand,
> Doth make a cross on every beam, and rafters as they stand:
> Great force and power have these against all injuries and harms
> Of cursed devils, sprites, and bugs, of conjurings and charms.[26]

This is much earlier than most accounts of an English king-cake; clearly, the cake is not a French import in a post-Restoration world, but an older rite with strong associations with driving back the occult powers of the dark of winter.

Other Christmas baking traditions illustrate the perseverance of the very themes that Puritans found most distressing. One obscure but fascinating local cake is the yule-doo (or Yule dough?), 'a kind of baby, or image of paste, which our Bakers used formerly to bake at this [Christmas] Season, and present it to their customers'. 'Perhaps … intended for an image of the child Jesus, with the Virgin Mary', adds John Brand. Like soul cakes, yule-doos are cakes for dependents and inferiors, and were sweetened, and enriched with fruit, so that they were sometimes called currantydoos.[27] Other archaic Christian seasonal cakes included the pop- or pope-lady, a diminutive figure of the Virgin Mary, or possibly of Pope Joan, still being turned out by a St Albans bakery even when the baker no longer had any idea what they were supposed to mean. But the Enlightenment Twelfth-cake enjoyed by Pepys and his household was urbane, apparently devoid of arcana: 'We had a brave cake brought us, and in the choosing, Pall was Queen and Mr. Stradwick was King.'[28]

The King and the Queen sound rather less comfortably secular after we have understood their context in Christmas baking; a secularisation perhaps still troubled by their pre-Reformation antecedents. Pepys's later account, on 6 January 1669, illustrated that the custom was in the process of changing: 'In the evening I did bring out my cake, a noble cake, and there cut it into pieces, with wine and good drink; and after a new fashion, *to prevent spoiling the cake*, did put so many titles into a hat, and so drew cuts; and I was the queen; and Theophila Turner, King.'

So as cake decorations became more important, and perhaps as the Twelfth Night Cake became more a keeping cake and less something to be shared among a large group, the lottery began to be independent of the cake, though like all food changes this one was not instantaneous. Twelfth Night had been generally linked with games of change and chance. A wager in a game of dice or a seasonal hand of cards even for those who did not normally play could symbolise the greatest change of state of all, the incarnation of the Son of God as a poor child cradled in a manger, but visited by kings, and the gifts – cakes or presents – allotted to children commemorated the gifts given by the kings to the baby Jesus.

The festive climate in a mid-Victorian bakery on the eve of Twelfth Night is reported by early nineteenth-century journalist and author, William Hone:

> Countless cakes of all prices and dimensions … all are
> decorated with all imaginable images of things animate and
> inanimate. Stars, castles, kings, cottages, dragons, trees, fish,
> palaces, cats, dogs, churches, lions, milkmaids, knights,
> serpents, and innumerable other forms in snow-white
> confectionary, painted with variegated colours.

Loving descriptions of the cake emphasise its perennial Christmas content:

I love to see an acre of cake spread out – the sweet frost covering the rich earth below – studded all over with glittering flowers, like ice-plants, red and green knots of sweetmeat, and hollow yellow encrusted crowns, and kings and queens, and their paraphernalia. I delight to see a score of happy children sitting huddled all round the dainty fare, eyeing the cake and each other, with faces sunny enough to thaw the white snow.[29]

Historians, and food historians in particular, tend to assume too easily that food choices are dictated mostly by necessity, by hunger, by 'innate' taste, but often enough they are dictated by custom. Cakes and the rites associated with them kept traces of paganism alive for far longer than burrowing antiquarians or scurrying patissiers. Cake is still understood to be ceremonial; and to reflect luck, money and the general goodness of life. Because of this, the overall nature and structure of ceremonial cake has been preserved.

———

Much of what the Twelfth Night cake used to represent has been transferred to the Christmas pudding, which still bears the charms to foretell a fortune for the year, if not for the feast. And not the charms alone; the pudding is still supposed to be set ablaze, delightfully transgressing all norms of domestic cooking, its blue fire in a dark room dimly waving across the centuries at the oaten cakes and burning straw which once held back the dark and ensured fertility. So certain were the Victorians of the efficacy of such a rite that they added a related one, the Snapdragon, where you set light to liquor-drenched raisins, and guests have to snatch them from the blue fires with bare hands. The unnatural blue fire of burning alcohol, spectacular in a darkened room, offers a blessing from the beyond:

A stout servant staggers in with a gigantic pudding, with a sprig of holly on the top, there is such a laughing and shouting and clapping of little chubby hands and kicking up of fat dumpy legs as can only be equalled by the applause with which the astonishing feat of pouring lighted brandy into minced pies is received by the younger visitors.

This is Dickens, of course, in 1837, and it is all a matter of tradition – except it isn't. Dickens is writing on the cusp of – and in part creating – a great movement of the feast to a central position in the calendar, the place it has occupied ever since. To take up the place of winter festival, Christmas had to elbow out the ghost of the past, the ghost in fact, of the wilder and more dubious Twelfth Night. It was helped, as food revolutions often are, by developments in commerce and technology. Dried fruit, for example, though eaten at Christmas as early as the seventeenth century, became much cheaper with the advent of railways and steamships.

The pudding does not, of course, derive directly from the Twelfth cake, though its charms and threepences do. It comes from plum pottage. Medieval plum pottage was actually porridge, enriched with bone marrow or beef broth, and containing wine, spices, sugar and dried fruit. Plum porridge in turn came from frumenty. This early version of pudding worked compatibly with the Twelfth cake, neither overshadowing the other. But gradually frumenty gave way to the simpler and more commercial pudding.

———————

Every rite of passage was marked by cakes, from cradle through wedding to grave. Childbirth involved cake exchanges and sharing. John Brand reported the following:

> AGAINST the time of the good wife's delivery, it has been everywhere the custom for the husband to provide a large cheese and a cake. These, from time immemorial, have been the objects of ancient superstition. It was not unusual to preserve for many years, I know not for what superstitious intent, pieces of 'the Groaning Cake.'[30]

Despite the sinister name, groaning cake seemed connected with the life of the child, perhaps also with the life of the woman. A French traveller in England said: 'The custom here is not to make great feasts at the birth of their children; they drink a glass of wine, and eat a bit of a certain cake, which is seldom made but upon these occasions.'[31]

This was a keeping-cake rite. Christening cakes too can be keepers. And, stretching forward into the future, cake can foretell the child's future. More importantly, the luck of gift-giving staves off the bad luck attendant upon opening the world to an unchristened child, or chrism child:

> At Burcester [Bicester], in Oxfordshire, at a christening, the women bring everyone a cake, and present one first to the minister, if present. At Wendlebury, and other places, they bring their cakes at a gossiping, and give a large cake to the father of the child, which they call a rocking cake.[32]

Exchanges of blessings and cakes were also common in many areas, but such rites may have been misunderstood, too, as many accused witches were reported to have offered cake to their young victims. Some of the women accused of witchcraft may have been following this practice:

> It was a good old custom for godfathers and godmothers, every time their godchildren asked them blessing, to give them a cake, which was a *gods-kichell*; it is still a proverbial saying in some countries, 'Ask me a blessing, and I will give you some plum-cake.' A cake called a God's kichell, because godfathers and godmothers used commonly to give one of them to their godchildren, when they asked a blessing.[33]

One reason then for the ceremonial cake was that it carried a blessing. The ceremony used at the solemnisation of a marriage was called *confarreation*, and involved a cake of wheat or barley.[34] Aubrey says:

When I was a little boy (before the civil wars), I have seen,
according to the custom then, the bride and bridegroom kiss
over the bridecakes at the table. It was about the latter end of
dinner; and the cakes were laid one upon another, like the
picture of the shewbread in the old Bibles.[35]

The tiered cakes sound remarkably like a modern wedding cake. In the
eighteenth century, pieces of cake, or wafers, were immersed in wine
at wedding feasts. They were properly called sops, and doubtless gave
name to the flower termed Sops-in-wine (a variety of dianthus, or
pink). Cakes could also be a method of fortune-telling in love:

The Maids in Oxfordshire have a way of foreseeing their
Sweethearts by making a dumb cake; that is, on some Friday
night, … every one makes the cake, and lays it on the gridiron,
and every one turns it, and when baked enough every one
breaks a piece, and eats one part, and lays the other part under
their pillow to dream of the persons they will marry. But all this
is to be done in serious silence without one word or one smile,
or else the cake loses the name, and the virtue.[36]

Just as the year died with cake, so did the individual. Chestings – a
funeral feast served from the deceased's coffin – featured cakes and
ale. This was overtly about the dead offering a last treat to the living,
but there could be an even stranger, darker reason behind such apparent geniality. Aubrey describes a 'sin eater' in Hereford, taking on all
the sins of the dead to prevent them from 'walking' again; Kennett
added this note to Aubrey's manuscript: 'It seems a remainder of this
custom which lately obtained at Amersden, in the county of Oxford,
where, at the burial of every corpse, one cake and one flagon of ale,
just after the interment, were brought to the minister in the church-
porch.'

Cakes could be funeral gifts, too, from the deceased to the community, as in the case of a London woman who died during the reign of
Edward I, leaving money to pay for cakes to be distributed 'for the

good of her soul'. Her name was Flaoner, and a 'Flaoner' was a maker of flans or flauns, a light cake not unlike a pancake.[37]

Cakes, of course, have changed in content as well as function. We can trace the evolution of the cake as we know it across the anonymous manuscript recipe books of the seventeenth and then the eighteenth century:

POUNDS CAKE

Take eight eggs, then take a pound of fresh butter that has lain in rose water, then beat up your eggs with a little brandy, a little sack, a grated lemon, a chean [china] orange rind shred in, mix your butter well with your eggs till your butter have taken up all your eggs and put in a pound of loaf sugar and a pound of currants, very well washed picked dried and plumped by the fire and mix it very well and mix in by degrees a pound of fine flower and beat it well put in an ounce of candied lemon and an ounce of candied orange so beat it well and butter your garth [girth] and bake it.[38]

The raising agent here is eggs, and the cake is stiff with fruit. The mixing method is very unlikely to beat in the maximum amount of air. The result is heavy by modern standards, but lightness may not have been the desired aim; richness may have been the goal. Strong tastes may have been the main point of such cakes. Nowadays, pound cakes are plain. The same manuscript has a recipe for a fierce 'White Seed Cake', again a mix of eggs beaten with wine and brandy, rosewater and loaf sugar: 'When you see it look very white [a sign of eggs beaten well enough to hold air] then put in an ounce and a half of caraway seeds.'[39] In comparison with modern recipes (such as those of Florence White and Fergus Henderson), this cake is bursting with caraway seeds.[40] Similarly, an early recipe for Ginger Bread cakes is strongly spiced, with 'one pennyworth of ginger', cloves, mace, nutmeg and coriander seeds.[41]

Appearance mattered. Even leavened cakes were sometimes stamped or printed in early modern kitchens and bakeries; one recipe actually adds 'forget not to print them'. Gingerbread, made of breadcrumbs, was powerfully spiced and scented, and also moulded like a fruit paste:

> Take a quart of honey and seethe it and skim it clean; take
> Saffron, powdered Pepper and throw thereon; take grated
> Bread and make it so charged that it will be leached; then take
> powdered canelle [cinnamon] and strew thereon enough;
> then make it square, like as thou would leach it; take when
> thou leachest it, and cast Box leaves about it, and stick
> thereon cloves.[42]

Hester Denbigh's seventeenth-century recipe is very similar, but without the breadcrumbs:

> Take 2 pounds of treacle a pound of butter melt these together
> then put it in a pan and put to it 2 ounces and a quarter of
> beaten ginger and 2 ounces of beaten caraway seeds then mix it
> with flour till it becomes a paste then make it into cakes and
> bake it in a slack oven till it is hard.[43]

Such bread cakes would always be flat and heavy, more like a biscuit.

Even cheesecakes were strong and rich. One eighteenth-century cheesecake is filled with something very like crème patissière; it begins with a mixture of eggs and grated bread, then cream and butter are boiled together and added, along with sugar, salt, cinnamon, currants and/or almonds. The result – which contains no cheese – was cooked in a pastry case. Abigail Rand's recipe from the late seventeenth century, headed 'Shrowsberry cake', is reminiscent of the fairing of that name, showing the way such cakes moved from fairs into private households: it contains flour, sugar, cinnamon, butter, two or three eggs, sack and rosewater.[44]

As the price of sugar fell steeply from the beginning of the eighteenth century, it no longer conferred prestige; on the other hand, it was now cheap enough to be used not as a spice, but as a main ingredient. At the same moment, baking was becoming ever more urbanised and professionalised. Cakes were now differentiated not by taste, or even rise, but by appearance. Not only did the making of cakes for special occasions became more professional, but small cakes in particular were increasingly made industrially rather than at home. As balls and assemblies displaced country house feasting, so small delicate cakes became staple fare. Ratafia biscuits and other *petits fours* suitable for dances and parties, assemblies and balls, were dominant, and were also feminised. Balls in fashionable Bath in the late eighteenth century involved sending to London for the delicacies; the anxiety must have been agonising as hostesses awaited their arrival.

Decoration, already growing in importance, now began to eclipse all other concerns, including flavour. Elizabeth Raffald favoured gold and silver webs of spun sugar to cover dishes of sweetmeats and a variety of decorative jellies, a Solomon's Temple of flummery. The ne plus ultra of decoration were the *pièces montées* of French pâtissier Marie-Antoine Carême, who worked for Talleyrand in Paris, and the Prince Regent in London. Not really English, but English by adoption, the *pièce montée* was barely edible, though it was made of food. It was food there to show the diners were not hungry enough to eat it. Like the show-stopping Union Jack cake in *The Great British Bake Off*, they teetered on the edge of being Regrettable Food, where the illusion of sculpture ousts the food too effectively. Those with a strong stomach can visit the Cake Wrecks website for the ultimate modern examples.[45]

Raffald's longing to achieve rise plainly involved a lot of beating. In a recipe for plum cake, she writes: 'First work the butter with your hand to a cream, then beat in your sugar a quarter of an hour. Beat the whites of your eggs to a very strong froth, mix with your sugar and butter.' Such cakes had begun to push out the old heavy plum cakes. The cake in Raffald's book that is most like a modern sponge cake is probably the Prussian cake; it is also quite like a Savoy cake, or fatless sponge.[46]

From the mid-Victorian era, cakes were progressively if unevenly detached from the communal sacred and the ritual, and instead yoked firmly to the individual's rites of passage. Such cakes were close to an ersatz, commercialised substitute for the efficacious rites of the past; commerce now took over from religion the task of managing and ensuring the festive calendar, communal and also individual, and individual festivities multiplied because they could then be tied to products.

The mistress of the New Cake was Eliza Acton. Her cookbook *Modern Cookery for Private Families*, first published in 1845, was an immediate and lasting success, establishing her as the first modern cookery writer. She wrote with great charm and clarity, but what marked the book as innovative was her original plan of listing, very exactly, the ingredients, the time taken, and all the possible pitfalls for the inexperienced cook. Sensible advice abounded: currants should be very nicely washed, dried in a cloth and then set before the fire. Before they were added, 'a dust of dry flour should be thrown among them, and a shake given to them, which causes the thing they are put to, to be lighter'. 'Eggs should be very long beaten, whites and yolks apart, and always strained'; sugar should be rubbed to a powder on a clean board, and 'sifted through a very fine hair-lawn sieve'. The heat of the oven 'is of great importance for cakes, especially those that are large'.

So successful was Acton that Isabella Beeton reproduced her advice almost without emendation. Acton's methods allowed domestic cooks to imitate the effects of commercial bakeries. Cakes were traditional in conception, but in the industrial era they became a site of innovative gadget-creation. Cake textures were improved by better ways of keeping flour dry, as damp flour will never produce a good or even rise; better sieves allowed finer-textured flour and hence finer-textured cakes; and cheaper and ready-ground sugar of better quality replaced sugar that had to be pounded or shaved (Beeton still has loaf sugar, insisting that it be finely grated). Raising was improved first by the discovery of eggs' ability to hold air in suspension, through the coagulation of egg proteins into solid filaments when heated, adding structure to baked food. Without the support given by egg protein, the puffed-up shapes of unyeasted baked goods would collapse. Made possible by the hybridisation of chickens, the increased size of eggs also became a factor. Next came chemical leavens: bicarbonate of soda was introduced in the 1840s, and then combined with a mild acid to make baking powder. Before that there was ammonium bicarbonate, also called hartshorn, which left a residual flavour.

Making a cake with a wooden spoon took hours. As a result, make-shift whisks were constructed by taking two forks and placing them together so the tines interlocked and made a cage – far more effective than a single fork at incorporating air into a mixture. Whisks might also have been made from twigs. The first whisk in frequent use was the chocolate mill, and inventive households might have turned it to cake-making. The biggest breakthrough was, of course, the machine mixer. These replaced both servants in the home and underlings in the bakery. In 1908 Herbert Johnson, an engineer for the Hobart Manufacturing Company, invented an electric standing mixer. Bakeries still use the Hobart. In 1919 Hobart introduced the KitchenAid Food Preparer for the home. In 1930, the Sunbeam MixMaster was introduced, selling at a fraction of the KitchenAid's price. It was these machines – my mother and grandmother were among their owners – which made ordinary women without servants into bakers.

Recipes with exact directions, probably modelled on the emerging precise recipes for confectionery, which dealt at length with the behaviour of sugar, were essential for inexperienced home cooks. And cake baking in particular was helped by the development of cake rings or rounds for giving shape to baked goods; once wooden hoops had been used, but metal is a better conductor of heat, though it can rust. Home bakers also benefited from the increasing availability of ovens with fuel on tap and reliable temperature controls. My grandmother claimed that gas ovens were best for meat, but that nothing beat an old wood-fired range for baking. She tested its readiness with a piece of paper; she put it in the oven, and watched for how quickly it went brown.

She didn't have any way of timing it, though, and inattention or incorrect estimates might have spelled ruin.

And then there was cake mix. Launched in the 1940s, cake mixes made cake achievable for all women, including the poor. It is sometimes claimed that they failed to sell in quantity until manufacturers removed dried egg and replaced it with the demand that women add a real egg. This is untrue. What actually ensured their success was the idea of making a novelty cake, a Humpty Dumpty cake or a football cake, to satisfy ever more elaborate ambitions for children's birthdays.

(The birthday cake, whose status is signified by the many little fires that accompany it … one for each year. Nothing pagan about that, is there? And our tendency to set fire to the Christmas pudding just as the year begins to turn back towards the light. Cake in all eras is still connected with ritual, however modern our equipment.)

Cakes also tend to be seen as feminine. Cupcake bakeries often have girls' names, like Lola's or Ruby's. As does one of England's most celebrated kinds of cake, the Victoria sponge. True, Queen Victoria did *like* cake; there was a cake called the Queen's Own cake, made for Victoria's wedding breakfast after her marriage to Albert.[47] According to a frank biography of Victoria composed by 'a member of the Royal household',[48] she was particularly fond of 'chocolate sponges, plain sponges, wafers of two or three different shapes, langues de chat, biscuits and drop cakes of all kinds, tablets, petit fours, princess and rice cakes, pralines, almond sweets, and a large variety of mixed sweets' ('She is more like a barrel than anything else', observed one doctor in the 1840s).[49] The cake that bears the name of the queen is a version of the quatre-quarts, a cake well known in Austria and France, using the same weight of eggs (in their shells), butter, caster sugar and flour. The method used by Constance Spry in 1956 is the creaming method that suits the advent of the domestic stand mixer, though the main method of aeration is the use of baking powder.[50] The cake has to be sandwiched together with jam and dusted with icing sugar; in the modern world of heavy frosting, it looks quite modest.

There are plenty of recipe sites online but bakeries are more elusive, confirming the view that British cakes come from home and that bakeries make more exotic fare. The traybake and the lemon drizzle cake and Victoria sponge are about home baking and National Trust tearooms, and tearooms with Royal Albert china in heritage areas like Budleigh Salterton in Devon, which has about five such. And there are other pressures on home baking. American baked goods are elbowing out British teatime fare. Brownies trump biscuits, and American blueberry muffins oust English griddle-baked muffins. Cupcakes see off teacakes. The rise of commercial baked goods has always been a menace to the indigenous traditions sustained by home baking. Urban people long for a fast dirty shot of flavour, and some at least of them probably also yearn for the very revulsion that makes them put the cake down. To be eaten in solitude, perhaps even in secret like a whole tray of brownies in American teen fantasies, the baked goods of today are at their lowest ebb; once they were festive, but now their bedizened surfaces say 'Keep out. All mine.' The saints may weep.

On dinner: an essay

'"How good to eat!"
(The gipsies have no word for "beautiful".
This is the nearest.)'

Virginia Woolf, *Orlando* (1928)

Whatever its timing, whether eaten at 10 a.m. or 8 p.m., dinner is the name given to the main meal of the day. There was a steady tendency for dinner to be eaten later and later as the early modern period became the industrial era. At the beginning of the sixteenth century, dinner was taken at 10 a.m.; by the mid-seventeenth century, it had moved to 1 p.m., and by the early eighteenth century had made its way to 2 p.m. By 1750, dinner could be eaten at any time between 3 and 5 p.m.; morning lasted until dinnertime, whatever time that was. As a result, late-eighteenth-century 'morning' calls could be made as late as mid-afternoon. When Lord Orville plans a meeting between Evelina and her half-brother, he asks 'shall you be at home tomorrow morning?', in order to arrange a call for 'about three o'clock.'[1] But such timing was never observed by everybody.

When dinner was truly spectacular, it became a banquet, and the whole point of banquets was to impress. As has been mentioned previously, one of the most famous banquets in English history was that held at Cawood Castle near York to celebrate the enthronement of George Neville as Archbishop of York in September 1465. Neville was the brother of the most powerful man in England, the Earl of Warwick, known as the Kingmaker and at the height of his power. Historians disagree about how long the feast lasted and also about how many people were there, but the food showed all the guests his status. There were subtleties, mysteries, designed to offer something never seen before. It included:

A Great custard, planted
Chestons ryall [royal]
Chambiet viander;
A Dolphin in foil
And a hart.
And a Tart;
Leche Damask
Sampion
A suttletie of Saint William, with his coate armour betwixt his
    hands
Gilt leche Lumbert
A coloured jelly.[2]

A cheston is a species of plum, so called because it resembles a chestnut. A 'leche' is food that can be sliced, not quite a cake as we know such a thing now, but something heavier and denser, like gingerbread. Dulce de leche, for example, is thickened milk. Damask is Damascus, probably a spice blend.

But the guests did not survive on subtleties alone. Here is a list of the animals used to provide meat for the feast:

Oxen 104, Wild bulls 6, Muttons 1,000, Veals 304, Swans 400,
Kids 204, Cranes 204, Chickens 2,000, Conies [rabbits] 4,000,
Bittens 204, Heronshears [Young herons] 400, Pheasants 200,
Partridges 500, Woodcocks 400, Curlews 100, Capons 1,000,
Pigs 2,000, Plovers 400, Quails 1, 200, Rees [female
sandpipers] 2,400, Peacocks 104, Mallards and Teals 4,000,
Stags, buck and does 500, Egrets 1,000, Porpoises and seals 12.

And that was just the meat. The dinner also used up 300 quarters of wheat, 300 tons of ale, 100 tons of wine, one pipe of Hippocratic, 4,000 cold venison pasties, 1,000 parted dishes of jellies, 3,000 plain dishes of jellies, a further 1,500 hot venison pasties, and hot custards, sugared delicates and wafers.[3]

It was not a typical banquet. It was intended to be, and was, exceptional – as exceptional as God's creation of the world in the book of Genesis. The point was to show supreme mastery of land and sea, river and mountain. We know a little about one guest who was present: the future Richard III. Because of the recent discovery of his skeleton, we have a good idea of how often he ate this kind of food. Richard had a protein-rich diet, perhaps a quarter of which derived from seafood, a typical diet for a late medieval nobleman who could afford to consume plenty of expensive foods like meat and fish. When he became king, his diet became even richer and more exceptional, far richer than that of other equivalent high-status individuals in the late medieval period. At the end of his life it was dominated by luxury foods that were typical of banqueting feasts at that time, such as fresh fish and wild birds, likely to include egrets, peacocks and swans – exactly the kinds of things on the menu at the feast, in fact; eating like a king was an important part of being one. And dinner for a king was a public meal, held in daylight (lighting was difficult and expensive) so that everybody could see exactly what luxuries were consumed. For a king, the everyday was exceptional, showing his mastery, letting the nobles see the difference between him and them.

Tudor aristocrats might have their main meal at ten in the morning. Seating was viciously hierarchical. At one end of the dining hall, the top table was set up on a raised dais, as is the case in Oxford and Cambridge colleges to this day. A mass of servants was assembled, ready to provide everything needed throughout the meal. The meal was preceded by the saying of grace, emphasising that food came from God. At the top table, a mixture of elaborate dishes created by professional cooks would have been served: dishes such as a fillet of pork beaten with a piece of veal, bound by egg, seasoned with ground cloves and pepper, coloured with saffron, boiled in a broth, and served with ground almonds, soup, prunes, currants, and a seasoning of mace and ginger – not unlike cold almond soups from Iberia today, often garnished with fresh grapes. But whereas in Spain almonds are a local ingredient, in Tudor England they had to be imported, along with the currants and all the spices, as well as the prunes which would have come from France. This dish would probably have cost about a week's wages for a labourer.

That was Tudor dinner for the rich; we know far less about dinner for the rest of society. When the *Mary Rose* sank in the Battle of the Solent in 1545, her cooks were preparing midday dinner. While the officers might have hoped to enjoy the kind of expensive game that had been served to Henry VIII himself on the nearby *Henry Grace a Dieu* the day before, the men had a weekly ration which consisted mostly of meat extended with grain and biscuit. The meat had been preserved by salting, and had to be soaked in order to be edible; it was then boiled, sometimes with crumbled biscuit, sometimes with flavourings such as hops and pepper, which were also found on board. It was probably not very appealing food, and it was certainly not nutritionally balanced, but it was better than the average seaman might have enjoyed in his home village.[4]

In the mid-seventeenth century, we can see from Pepys's diary that he was still eating the main meal at midday, even though many of his acquaintances were dining later. This entry from Thursday 22 November 1660 reveals the disparity: 'Dinner being done, we went to Mr. Fox's again, where many gentlemen dined with us, and most princely dinner, all provided for me and my friends, but I bringing none but myself and wife, he did call the company to help to eat up so much good victuals.'

So, having had dinner, Pepys goes to dinner. What kind of food was served? On Saturday 8 June 1667 'we all sat all the morning, and then home to dinner, where our dinner a ham of French bacon, boiled with pigeons, an excellent dish', and he recalls on 2 February 1667/8 'a very good dinner we had, of a powdered leg of pork and a loin of lamb roasted', additionally lavish because it was Sunday. He also records dining with friends at midday on Saturday 2 August

1662: 'we had a plain, good dinner, and I see they do live very frugally.' Clearly, he meant it when he wrote on 9 November 1665, 'Strange to see how a good dinner and feasting reconciles everybody.'[5]

Richard Steele, the essayist, complained in 1729 that in his memory the timing of dinner had crept from noon to three in the afternoon.[6] Alexander Pope's friend Lady Suffolk scandalised him because by the 1740s, she was serving dinner as late as four. Pope declined to attend. He was fifty years old and in poor health, and he liked to have his dinner at two. Every single retreat in dinner time was met by complaints from the old guard. French visitor de la Rochefoucauld thought English dinners intolerable because they lasted so long. Dinners begun at 4 p.m. might last until midnight. Sometimes an earlier dinner might merge indistinguishably into supper: parson James Woodforde recorded in the mid-eighteenth century that he ate a four o'clock dinner of ham, tench, boiled fowl, plum pudding and apple tart, and then at six moved on to hashed fowl, duck, eggs and potatoes, and supped on them with his guests till ten.[7]

Pepys's confidence in the solid worth of dinner, and his sense that it was the answer to everything, were to be more fully realised with Samuel Johnson. Despite his genial demeanour, Johnson suffered from what he himself called black dog, bouts of depression and melancholy.[8] He might have been the first man to do comfort eating and really to equate food choice with his personality. His biographer and fan James Boswell reported him saying: 'Some people have a foolish way of not minding, or pretending not to mind, what they eat. For my part, I mind my belly very studiously, and very carefully; for I look upon it, that he who does not mind his belly, will hardly mind anything else.' He relished good food as if it were religion: 'we could not have had a better dinner had there been a *Synod of Cooks*.'[9] He also loathed bad food. Boswell reports that 'At the inn where we stopped he was exceedingly dissatisfied with some roast mutton we had for dinner … "It is as bad as bad can be: it is ill-fed, ill-killed, ill-kept, and ill-drest."'[10] He also scoffed at doctors who advocated healthy foods, because he was sure that taste mattered more.[11]

At the beginning of the nineteenth century, the Wordsworth family were a complete contrast, living frugally and eating a simple diet. Sir Walter Scott, after a visit to Dove Cottage, recalled 'three meals a day – two of which were porridge'; William Wordsworth preferred to see it as a domestic life characterised by 'plain living and high thinking'.[12] Mealtimes were not fixed; they tended to drift around or disappear altogether. On one occasion, Dorothy Wordsworth recorded, 'we had ate up the cold turkey before we walked so we cooked no dinner' (27 January 1802). Another time she wrote, 'we got no dinner but Gooseberry pie to our tea' (12 June 1802). A typical day from Dorothy's journal has them eating a bowl of mutton broth for breakfast with bread and butter, and at their midday dinner, a savoury pie filled with veal, rabbit, mutton, giblets or leftovers. Supper was broth again. On their travels, she recorded, 'We dined at the public-house on porridge, with a second course of Christmas pies.' A dish of bread soaked in milk was the Wordsworths' usual family supper – it was soothing to the digestion and a way of making stale bread palatable.[13]

Yet the Wordsworths' diet was not necessarily typical, and far better food was available nearby. Joseph Budworth in the first published walking tour of the Lake District, *A Fortnight's Ramble in the Lakes* (1792), sang the praises of Robert Newton's, and went on to reproduce the entire menu for dinner for two people at tenpence a head: 'Roast pike, boiled fowl, veal-cutlets and ham, beans and bacon, cabbage, pease and potatoes, anchovy sauce, parsley and butter, plain butter, butter and cheese, wheat bread and oat cake, three cups of preserved gooseberries, with a bowl of rich cream in the centre.'[14]

Lurching between the borderline malnutrition typical of Dorothy Wordsworth and excess characterised dinner in the nineteenth century: what had once been two meals had become three, and the ever-expanding middle classes were trying to work out how to use them for entertaining. In Wordsworth's and Jane Austen's day, the word *course* at a middle-class dinner meant something very different from what it means in the twenty-first century. The dinner table was covered with separate dishes of every kind of food, all available at once – soup, fish, meat, game, poultry, pie, vegetables, sweet and savoury puddings – arranged symmetrically around the centre dish. This buffet-like spread was a course. Nobody expected any diner to eat everything; each person chose two or three of the items they wanted. Once everyone had nibbled their selection, an intermediate course of cheese, salad, raw celery and other fresh finger food was served while the table was cleared. Then another equal quantity of different dishes, still a mixture of savoury and sweet, was brought in, and as before each diner chose from the available selection. The table was cleared again, and the dessert course was set out – nuts and fruits, perhaps ice creams, and often sweet wine.

A typical course – also sometimes called a remove – might involve the following: curry of rabbit soup, open tart syllabub, macaroni, pastry baskets, salmon trout, sole, vegetable pudding, muffin pudding, larded sweetbreads, raised giblet pie, a preserve of olives and a haunch of venison, and buttered lobster. At the centre would be a showpiece, something like bombarded veal, a boned fillet stuffed with a forcemeat of bacon, cream and egg, crammed into slits in the meat. There were 'Rules for a Good Dinner':

> There should be always two soups, white and brown, two fish, dressed and undressed; a bouilli and petits-pates; and on the sideboard a plain roast joint, besides many savoury articles, such as hung beef, Bologna sausages, pickles, cold ham, cold pie, &c. some or all of these according to the number of guests, the names of which the head-servant ought to whisper about to the company, occasionally offering them. He should likewise carry about all the side-dishes or entrées, after the soups are taken away in rotation … Beware of letting the table appear loaded; neither should it be too bare. The soups and fish should be dispatched before the rest of the dinner is set on; but, lest any of the guests eat of neither, two small dishes of patés should be on the table. Of course, the meats and vegetables and fruits which compose these dinners must be varied according to the season, the number of guests, and the tastes of the host and

hostess. It is also needless to add that without iced champagne and Roman punch a dinner is not called a dinner.[15]

In 1815, the timing of dinner was still variable. Thomas de Quincey claimed that 'a large part of London' still took one meal at two o'clock and another at seven or eight, 'but now the late meal is the main one'; he blames the move on the increase in business 'that boils along the tortured streets', so that the evening meal becomes something to look forward to.[16] In Charlotte Brontë's 1847 novel *Jane Eyre*, dinner at the Reeds is over by 3 p.m., though in the same period the increasingly conservative William Wordsworth still dined at one o'clock at his house Rydal Mount, with tea at six and then a light supper at bedtime.[17] From 1815, there is some evidence of ordinary middling people having a meal called dinner at six in the evening, even though most people stuck to 4.30. Supper was still an important feature of the evening, especially after some kind of entertainment – cards, a ball or the theatre. As a result, some families now ate four meals a day. In 1835, a Londoner might dine at any time between 1 p.m. and 8 p.m. Those who dined at one o'clock would have supper at eight; those who dined at eight would have lunch at one. This did not make the two kinds of meals interchangeable: dinner was always heavy and sustaining, and the others – lunch or supper, early or late – light and dependent on novelty. However, heavy and sustaining did not necessarily mean multiple courses; in Thackeray's *Book of Snobs*, gentlemen were happy with a joint and half a pint of sherry.

As dinner moved into the night, it became more of an event, with elaborate menus, multiple plates, removes. The middle and upper-middle classes engaged in competitive dining, eager to show off their wealth, class and knowledge. Dinner parties could last for hours. In the perfect Victorian country house day, dinner would be served at 8 p.m., and guests would enjoy seven courses; if there was no company, the family might have five. Either way, dinner would be served à la Russe; that is, plates would be removed between courses. Courses would usually be confined to soup, fish, an entrée, pudding, and a savoury or a fruit and port dessert.

Charles Dickens's great-grandson Cedric Dickens, noting the change in eating times, says that his great-grandfather dined at 5 p.m. when his career first began, but by the time he was writing *Our Mutual Friend*, wrote that – as Mr Podsnap puts it – the world got up at 8 a.m., shaved close at quarter past, breakfasted at nine, went to the city at ten, came home at half past five, and dined at seven.[18] In *Martin Chuzzlewit*, Tom Pinch and John Westlock walk through the snow to a Salisbury inn, where the hall is 'a very grove of dead game, and dangling joints of mutton; and in one corner an illustrious larder, with glass doors, developing cold fowls and noble joints, and tarts wherein the raspberry jam coyly withdrew itself, as such a precious creature should, behind a latticework of pastry'. 'It's like a dream,' says John, but the narrator interjects:

> nobody ever dreamed such soup as was put on the table directly
> afterwards, or such fish, or such side dishes, or such a course of
> birds and sweets, or in short anything approaching the reality
> of that entertainment at 10 and sixpence a head, exclusive of
> wines.[19]

Note that the food is perceived as kinds of meat, much as it was at George Neville's banquet.

As we have seen, there is an astonishing amount of food in Dickens's novels. Dickens's workers and travellers very often eat out, in pubs and inns, in chop shops and pie shops. In *Bleak House*, Mr Guppy and his friends Mr Smallweed and Mr Jobling delight in eating out at a grand dining house that actually has a menu. They are treating Mr Jobling, who has lost his job, and he eats ale, veal and ham, French beans, summer cabbage and marrow pudding, and reaches the stage of Cheshire cheese. When the three of them have finished, 'then I'll pay,' says Mr Guppy. Mr Smallweed, compelling the attendance of the waitress with one hitch of his eyelash, instantly replies as follows:

Four veal and hams is three, and four potatoes is three and four, and one summer cabbage is three and six, and three marrows is four and six, and six breads is five, and three Cheshires is five and three, and four pints of half and half is six and three, and four small rums is eight and three, and three Pollys [a King Polly is a cigar 'that talks to itself'] is eight and six. Eight and six in half a sovereign, and eighteenpence out![20]

This sounds like madness, but it shows how well Dickens understood the delights available to the less well-off, and how meticulously they had to be measured.

The social ups and downs of dinner mattered to the middle-class readers who gobbled up every word Dickens wrote. Dickens himself very much liked elaborate meals. In the introduction to *What Shall We Have for Dinner?*, the book of recipes published by his wife Catherine, with an introduction written under the pseudonym Lady Maria Clutterbuck, he wrote: 'Daily life is embittered by the consciousness that a delicacy is forgotten or misapplied; a surplusage of cold mutton or a redundancy of chops; are gradually making the Club more attractive than the Home.'[21] So Catherine struggled to attract him with menus balanced between colours and scents, maybe turbot with lobster sauce and cucumbers in one course, or potent oyster curry and an unexpected soft grenadine of veal. Not everyone loved the extra touches. Jane Carlyle waspishly said that the Dickenses' dinner parties with their 'quantities of artificial flowers' and 'overloaded dessert' were too grand for a 'literary man'. She worked herself to a pitch of excitement because 'the very candles rose each out of an artificial rose! Good God!'[22]

What Shall We Have for Dinner? outlined menus served to the great man and his friends, offering an uncomfortably voyeuristic glimpse of celebrity dining along with the assurance that the middle class was holding firm to its values. Yet its paean to Dickensian domesticity was a mirage. The book was produced among the emotional rollercoaster of marriage to a nervy icon with a recurrent interest in young and pretty actresses. Prepared and published at the very centre of the nineteenth century, 1850–1, the menu book stabilised and bolstered a family stretched thin by the manic energy of its patriarch, who was always 'used up' and morose at the end of his own enormous creative labours.

The menus, like the entertainments that Dickens loved to host, were window displays of what middling people wanted. A linchpin was soup. The soup prepared for Dickens was based on stock from the white and brown stockpots constantly kept at the back of the range and into which chicken or beef bones could be thrown. These stocks could be further boiled down to make a glaze that set like a jelly into sausages, so that a slice could be added to pots of soup, stew or sauce; this is what is called a meat *jus* on today's menus. Nor was the fat wasted. Any skimmed fat from the pot was melted and cooked (rendered) until pure lard that could be used in pastry was created.[23]

A typical dinner menu might embrace mutton broth, cold beef, minced beef with bacon, mashed and fried potatoes, salad, marrow pudding and bloaters; or in a different season filleted sole, shrimp sauce, roasted and stuffed leg of mutton, French beans, potatoes, greengage tartlet and macaroni – even though Dickens himself had complained that the British didn't know how to cook pasta. Dickens's own favourite dinner course was toasted cheese. Cheese was mixed with porter, and sometimes butter, and served on toast with a salad of watercress.

The dinner party by that time had become a vital form of social cement. Hosts and hostesses selected their guests to be of comparable rank and status. The size of the guest list varied depending on the status and wealth of the hosts. Usually, guests arrived at about 7 p.m. and were shown into the drawing room, which was always upstairs. They were given no drinks and no food on arrival. A servant would then announce dinner, and couples in order of status preceded down to the dining room and sat down following a carefully designed seating plan that reflected the status of each individual guest. A full dinner might involve:

a delicate soup and turtle, turbot with lobster and Dutch sauces, a portion of red mullet with cardinal sauce, flying dishes like oyster or marrow pate to follow the fish … Supreme chicken with truffles, a sweetbread au jus, land cutlet with asparagus and peas, a fricandeau of *oseille* (veal cooked with sorrel) … either venison, roast saddle of mutton, or stewed beef a la jardinière, with salad, beetroot, vegetables, French and English mustard. A turkey poult, duckling, or green goose commenced the second course, with peas and asparagus, plovers' eggs in aspic jelly, a mayonnaise of fowl, then a macedoine of fruit, meringues *à la creme*, a marosquino jelly, a chocolate cream, then a savoury of sardines, salad, beetroot, celery, anchovies, plain butter and cheese, 'for those who are Gothic enough to eat it,' and then to ices, Cherry water and pineapple cream, with the fruit of the season.[24]

Just as in Austen's day, the guest was not meant to ingest everything offered. As with a modern buffet table, he or she was supposed to take a small helping of a single offered part of the course.

'Thackeray,' said Ruskin, 'settled like a meat-fly on whatever one had got for dinner, and made one sick of it.'[25] In his short story 'A Little Dinner at Timmins's', Thackeray portrays the disaster of middle-class pretensions to fine dining in the over-elaborate menu which drives the young hosts into debt:

DINER POUR 16 PERSONNES
Potage (clair) a la Rigodon.
Do. a la Prince de Tombuctou.
Deux Poissons.
Saumon de Severne Rougets Gratines
a la Boadicee. a la Cleopatre.
Deux Releves.
Le Chapeau-a-trois-cornes farci a la Robespierre.
Le Tire-botte a l'Odalisque.
Six Entrees.

Saute de Hannetons a l'Epingliere.

Cotelettes a la Megatherium.

Bourrasque de Veau a la Palsambleu.

Laitances de Carpe en goguette a la Reine Pomare.

Turban de Volaille a l'Archeveque de Cantorbery.'

And so on with the entremets, and hors d'oeuvres, and the
  rotis, and the releves.

'Madame will see that the dinners are quite simple,' said
  M. Cavalcadour.

'Oh, quite!' said Rosa, dreadfully puzzled.[26]

Thackeray revels in the pretentious nonsense of the menu; it probably doesn't need adding that no nineteenth-century couple would really have sat down to a dinner of dinosaur cutlets. After this ill-fated meal, the couple's life gets worse in every possible way. The cook becomes discontented, their jeering and snobbish relatives and neighbours snub them, true friendships are ruined, and the Timminses' debt mounts to sky-high proportions – and all they achieve is exactly the same dinner party as everybody else. Luxury food is a natural symbol for evanescence, and therefore for waste; it is not properly bourgeois because it vanishes, becoming only a memory. And nothing fostered memory and nostalgia so strongly as reminiscences about dinner. After the carnage of the Western Front, those seeking the pleasures of the table came to see in it an exciting and even adventurous realm of the senses, to be relished without control. Eating the best food became a lifestyle choice that illustrated an elevated sensibility and refined taste.

Virginia Woolf wrote that 'A good dinner is of great importance to good talk. One cannot think well, love well, sleep well, if one has not dined well.'[27] She reached this conclusion after the two very different dining experiences at Cambridge colleges with which this book opened, both eloquently described, one representing the pinnacle of middle- and even upper-class food, and the other representing the same at its lowest possible ebb. The kind of dinner that went with real privilege could be enjoyed by a lucky few at the ancient universities. John Betjeman particularly relished dinner with Maurice Bowra, 'high up in Wadham's hospitable quad', where the guests ate oysters and drank 'a dryish hock', followed by claret and tournedos and a bombe surprise (a moulded sphere of ice cream containing a sphere of different flavoured ice cream in the centre). Over dinner, the guests were told how to think about literature and about the University in 'scathing epigrams'. Betjeman clearly saw the delicious food as fundamentally connected with the growth of taste and certainty. Less kind readers might think of entitlement. It's a private dinner in Bowra's own rooms, and the chefs and even the waiters have vanished completely from the scene. The 'evenings dining with the Georgeoisie' reek of the same pleasure in ruling a world of luxury.[28]

By contrast, Woolf understood the amount of headspace that food takes up in the minds of women; the coordination of material resources required to make a dinner party happen is the opening story of *Mrs Dalloway*. Clarissa announces that she intends to buy the flowers herself because she recognises that her maid, Lucy, 'had her work cut out for her'. Among other things, Lucy is expecting 'Rumpelmayer's men', perhaps to install 'the most tempting array imaginable of little individual, one- or two-mouthful teacakes' as pudding. As Clarissa's thoughts dart to and fro, across provisions and social pleasures, glancing at other dinner parties that compete with her own, where 'films of brown cream mask turbot; in casseroles severed chickens swim', it is the cook who focuses on the food that is actually going to be served today:

> Next morning they would go over the dishes – the soup, the
> salmon; the salmon, Mrs. Walker knew, as usual underdone, for
> she always got nervous about the pudding and left it to Jenny;
> so it happened, the salmon was always underdone. But some
> lady with fair hair and silver ornaments had said, Lucy said,
> about the entrée, was it really made at home? But it was the
> salmon that bothered Mrs. Walker, as she spun the plates round
> and round, and pulled in dampers and pulled out dampers; and
> there came a burst of laughter from the dining-room; a voice
> speaking; then another burst of laughter – the gentlemen
> enjoying themselves when the ladies had gone.[29]

Seeing a dinner like Bowra's, but at a distance, and as a series of anxious tasks, restores perspective. Dinner does not materialise with the wave of a magic wand. Mrs Walker has to wrangle the stove and manage the dampers. Woolf is consciously restoring something she saw as absent. The careful elaboration of dinner was women's work, from the kitchen to the dining room, securing food supplies and managing guests. Woolf's friend Mary Hutchinson gave a dinner that included 'an enormous earthenware dish ... garnished with every vegetable, in January – peas, greens, mushrooms, potatoes; and in the middle the tenderest cutlets, all brewed in a sweet stinging aphrodisiac sauce'.[30] The description is just as careful as the cooking. There is a trace of conscious transgression here. Could such pleasure really be permissible?

Awkwardly, it was bad food – even the underdone salmon – which suggested that somebody had to make it, suggested buying and labour and even animals that once carried the meat around. The people the food conjures up are poor people. Woolf subtly hints at the reason; it is, she suggests, because people refuse to admit that food is important to them, insist that they can manage without it, that there is something virtuous about simply eating what is put in front of you, that complaining is unjust. Low expectations breed lower outcomes. Yet the indulgence of appetite and excess could come to seem not so much licensed as horrifying. When should dinner ever stop? Bowra was known for his obesity as well as for his savage wit. Contemporary with Bowra and Betjeman was the most expensive dining society in history, the Railway Club, bankrolled by John Sutro and enjoyed by Evelyn Waugh. Members of the club delighted in luxury dinners of fillet of sole, roast chicken, apple tart, raspberry mousse, on board specially chartered trains bound for Leicester or other more faraway destinations before being returned to Oxford in time for bed. Club members boasted of out-drinking, out-eating, and outspending their predecessors. Dining had become another ruthless, exhausting competition for a few, served by the invisible and perhaps uncomprehending labour of the many.[31]

The widening split was to be enormously exacerbated first by the Depression, and then by the war and rationing. The prune-eating class enlarged enormously, and probably had some right to congratulate itself on its abstemiousness. In more modest households, dinner had always been curtailed, with high tea at 6 p.m. or 6.30 and a supper of tea with cakes and sandwiches three hours later.[32]

The Depression itself and the government's mismanagement of the economy and lack of interest in the suffering of the unemployed assembled a formidable death toll by the mid-1930s. For many women, dinner did not exist. John McNamara, an out-of-work factory hand from Lancashire, testified:

> It was a common thing for a housewife and a mother to sacrifice herself. Unbeknownst to hubby. Unbeknownst to kiddies. 'Oh, I've had mine,' they'd say [of dinner], but they hadn't had a bite. A good mother went without many a meal. Kids come first. And husband. She was last, though she worked harder than anyone. But you didn't find out till it was too late.

In 1933, the BBC commissioned seventeen talks on the 'human face' of unemployment after sending a journalist to the country's unemployment black spots. These are a few of the voices they heard:

> 'The staple ingredients [of all meals] are bread and butter and tea and cocoa and cheese.'
>   'Dinner is two slices of bread and about 2oz cheese. Tea two boiled eggs, or tomatoes, or a tin of baked beans.'
>   'I have not tasted meat, potatoes or vegetables for over 12 months.'

One unemployed house painter was married with six children; an inspector described him and his family as not in need of assistance. Their chief food source was bread and margarine, tea with sweetened condensed milk, fresh meat on Fridays and Saturdays, and some fresh vegetables with cheap sausages.[33]

The complexities of life during the Depression are difficult to grasp and the ingenuity required to feed a family remarkable. One miner's wife got a pig and built herself a pigsty with the help of her two young sons, even ensuring that the sow was put to a boar so she farrowed. She carried bracken to the pigsty for bedding. Her initiative came about because the soup kitchens provided for miners during strikes didn't offer any meat; the plain but good food was cocoa, and then potatoes, greens and rice pudding for dinner.[34] And yet in the 1930s, in the midst of the Depression, Viscountess Hambledon was hosting dinners at her country house outside Henley that involved either thick or clear soup, followed by fish, followed by chicken or quails as the entrée, then saddle of lamb or beef, pudding, savoury, and then fruit.[35]

The ruling classes dined on. Churchill's cook, Georgina Landemare, named the wartime leader's favourite recipes; among them were Sole Champeaux (sole with a creamy white wine sauce with prawns) and Tournedos Montpensier (eye fillet with foie gras and black truffles). Churchill liked chicken Maryland, lobster, dressed crab, jugged hare and tinned orange slices, but didn't like tripe, currant cake, marmalade, stew, hotpot, Chinese food or boiled eggs. He also could not stand corned beef, lemon curd, pickled onions and black pudding: the things he liked were much more expensive than the things he didn't like. At Chequers during the war, dinner started with champagne at about 8.30 p.m. The menu was always clear soup, perhaps turtle soup or consommé, then roast chicken or game if it were in season. Pudding was ice cream, with a little chocolate sauce, and after that, a pear and some Stilton cheese, which he loved.

Like everyone else the Churchill family were required to use a ration book, but Chartwell with its large estate and farm supplied them with eggs, milk, cream, chicken, pork, fruit and vegetables, most of which were out of reach of ordinary folk. (Was this what was meant to happen? Almost certainly not.)[36] When shown a plate of everyday rations permitted to the average adult, Churchill mumbled that it was 'not a bad meal' and was shocked to learn that he was being shown the basic rations for a whole week, rather than a day.

For other people, food rationing began on 8 January 1940, four months after the outbreak of war, and *pace* Chartwell, it reduced some of the differences between rich and poor for the first time in the history of England. Yes, there was a black market, and yes, London clubs and restaurants still used its produce to keep their moneyed clientele. However, rationing was a great leveller. Limits were imposed on the sale of bacon, butter and sugar. On 11 March 1940 all meat was rationed. The nation was taught how to make the best of what food could be grown in Britain. Soup and vegetable stew were recommended by the government. Most famous, for reasons which can only be guessed, was Woolton pie, named rather ironically for the Minister for Food. The recipe involved dicing and cooking potatoes (or parsnips), cauliflower, swede, carrots and possibly turnip. Other vegetables were added where available. Rolled oats and chopped spring onions were added to the thickened vegetable water which was poured over the vegetables themselves. The dish was topped with potato pastry and grated cheese and served with vegetable gravy. The content of the pie filling could easily be altered to include whatever vegetables were in season at the time.

In 1947, Gallup asked the British public what their no-expense-spared fantasy meal would be. The answer was humble, even boring: 'Sherry, tomato soup, sole, roast chicken with roast potatoes, peas and sprouts, trifle and cream, cheese and biscuits and coffee.'[37] The war and post-war rationing had made this dull food into a luxury, lowering people's expectations. Rationing restrictions were gradually lifted, starting with flour on 25 July 1948, but not until 4 July 1954 did meat and all other food rationing end in Britain.

Lord Woolton had undoubtedly saved the nation from starvation, and for many poor people, the diet imposed by rationing was far better than their pre-war diet had been. In these circumstances, just having enough to eat was a luxury for most. There was, however, a noticeable scarring of the nation's collective food psyche. It had become patriotic not to care what you ate. The dinners of debutantes in the 1950s show a notable falling off in culinary ambition from even the wartime dinners at Chequers, and perhaps this allows us to see the long-term effect of rationing even on upper-class food culture. A ball was almost always preceded in the debutante era of the 1950s by a dinner party held somewhere else in London in a private house, a restaurant or hotel. Hotel menus in those days were still unreconstructed and high society expected an anglicised version of elegant French food. A typical pre-dance menu served in 1958 at the Hyde Park Hotel comprised the following: 'Prawn cocktail, Noisettes d'agneau Zingara, Haricots verts au beurre, Pommes nouvelles persillées, Fraises refraiches, Crème Chantilly, Café moka.'

Prawn cocktail, one deb recorded, was a silver cup of shredded lettuce, peeled prawns in mayonnaise combined with Heinz tomato ketchup and Tabasco, with a few prawns in their shells sitting on top for garnish. What was Zingara? The word means gypsy woman. Zingara is a garnish or sauce consisting of chopped ham, tongue, mushrooms and truffles combined with tomato sauce, tarragon and sometimes Madeira. Commercial varieties used fewer ingredients, leaning on tomato paste, paprika, bell peppers and sometimes onion. In the post-war atmosphere, some replication of the commercial variety seems likely.[38]

At home matters were little better. In the *Tatler*, the following menu was suggested as ideal for a pre-dance dinner: consommé Olga (beef consommé made with mince), crepes de crème de volaille (chicken in béchamel), pilaff de riz, salade de fruits au Kirsch.[39] Luckily, many of the attendees would have been to a cocktail party in advance, where they would have been plied with sticky gin and orange and canapés on silver platters: little squares of cheese and pineapple on cocktail sticks; miniature sausages, warmed up and slightly charred; tiny chicken vol-au-vents; twirls of smoked salmon in brown bread; and a horrible invention of the period, the dip, a cream cheese mix the consistency of porridge into which you dunked a strip of raw carrot or a stick of celery.[40] Everything would have tasted bland, floury, dulling the palate. One reason it's so ghastly is that it's aimed at women. In every social class, men eat better.

Indeed, if there is a transhistorical British food not subject to the whims of history, still eaten with magnificent and oblivious continuity, it is the food of the 10,000, of the club, of the top (male) people. It saw off the short-lived fashion for dairy and egg-based *haute cuisine française* in the seventeenth century. Club food was over its 300-year history forced into a few redoubts, where it survived almost intact; for example, among the old-fashioned rural upper classes, now increasingly separate from their urban selves. When those 'country' people came to town, they created and inhabited gentleman's clubs like White's, and kindred sites could be enumerated: old-style restaurants, richer Oxbridge colleges, the few remaining chop houses like the Guinea Grill, and their imitators like St John's, where they celebrated the game seasons. The dark, rich, salty, vinegary, heavy taste in question can be found in the following foods, which are still eaten and will still be recognisable to most readers. Not all were eaten in the eighteenth century, but all reflect the tastes of *gentle*men of that era: well-hung game, especially grouse, pork pies, sausages, and also forcemeat stuffings, especially with sage and onion, gentlemen's savouries, such as anchovy toast/*patum peperium*, Marmite/Bovril, steak and kidney pudding/pie, Stilton, old-fashioned claret/chewy Bordeaux/vintage port, fish and chips with malt vinegar, marmalade, real ale, eel pie, pie and mash, mushy peas, black pudding, vindaloo and baked beans on toast.

Predominant are game, offal, fat, salt, vinegar, hot pepper. So potted shrimps, melting over hot toast, or a roast grouse, with bread sauce and game chips followed by a savoury of Scotch Woodcock or Welsh Rarebit sloshed with Worcestershire sauce. The chef at White's says, 'They [club members] love smoked eel and a lovely Lincolnshire smoked trout that I find, and we pot 9kg of shrimps a week.' This food is still a recognisable *kind* of food, and despite the evident surges and ebbs in popularity, most of its elements are still in circulation. But the intrinsic Britishness of it lies in its darkness, its strong flavours.

And yet all this was diluted by rationing and fading memories into a kind of parody of itself, at least for most people. The war left its mark even on those born long before – a timidity … Take C. S. Lewis. His taste in food was for the plain, the solid and the traditional:

He liked roast meat of any sort, hot or cold, served with the
conventional trimmings … He took no interest in vegetables
apart from new potatoes, in puddings, or in fruit, but he
enjoyed cheese, especially ripe Stilton or Cheddar. What made
him a difficult guest at the dinner table was the tremendous
speed at which he ate … Once he began to eat, his main ideas
seem to be to finish the meal so he could smoke a cigarette.[41]

Even Lewis's friends saw his taste as dull. Yet the likings expressed here
probably typify the favourite food of a generation of English middle-
class people who had never been abroad, and had few expectations
beyond meat and two veg and a pint. Tastes like this go with traditional mealtimes in the same way that a taste for tapas and small plates
goes with our current disdain for them. Like the clothes fashions of
the previous generation, the food fashions that immediately precede us
always look unbearable, unambitious or plain weird. But it's worth
reminding ourselves that unless we are among the 10,000 mostly male
club members, there's every chance that we will look just as bizarre to
our grandchildren.

Chicken, and a few rarer birds

If this book were being written in 1930, this chapter would be about beef. But chicken is now the dominant meat in Great Britain, as it is across the globe. This chapter tells the story of how a small forest bird became the country's chief source of protein, and how in Britain it pushed out other meats that had once been preferred to it.

Nothing is as global as chicken. Chickens are the world's most common farmed animal. There are more than 20 billion chickens on Earth, three for every human being. Chicken is the favoured source of food of most human beings. One reason for their success is that they provide both meat and eggs. They require little space, though they like to roam freely and widely. The industrialised modern chicken farm allots each chicken less than 12 square inches; consumers embrace the cheap meat and cheaper eggs that result. The meat is easy and quick to prepare. And it makes ideal fast food for the new megacities that replicate London and its dominance over the surrounding countryside.[1] Yet because there is also still expensive, hand-reared chicken and eggs, the bird has retained some at least of its prestige. It features on top restaurant menus; it is a desirable Sunday lunch, even if its place as Christmas dinner has been ousted by the larger but otherwise very similar turkey. The old way for the chicken was a few years of egg laying, then into the pot. But the new way is a few weeks of misery, then into the abattoir.

As we have just seen, in 1947, the British fantasy meal was centred on roast chicken. Gallup's respondents probably saw themselves as selecting a very British and very traditional meal. However, chicken is a relatively recent favourite. To be sure, it has long been known on English tables; like so many foods, it was introduced to Britain by a Roman elite culinary culture. But the bird itself comes from very far afield, and so do the recipes which brought it to earlier generations of diners. Moreover, and shockingly, chicken ousted the much more traditional and much more lauded festive meat long associated with Englishness, which was roast beef.

Before festive chicken came Martinmas beef, eaten on the feast of Saint Martin, 11 November. Martinmas was a date when pigs and oxen too were slaughtered; this was the reason the month of November was called Blood Month or Slaughter Month in both Anglo-Saxon and Welsh. The lord was meant to host a special dinner for the workers of a spiced ox. Martinmas was the last great feast before the Advent fast began.

From the Middle Ages until the middle of the nineteenth century, Christmas dinner meant roast beef. Isabella Beeton noted that whenever a songwriter wished to account for the valour displayed by Englishmen at sea or on land he referred to the roast beef of old England. It was roasted extremely simply, and not until the 1800s did anyone bother to write down a recipe. The point was to maintain a fragment of the tradition of Yuletide hospitality, provided by the lord of the manor and enjoyed by all the tenants, and maintained in urban settings. As late as 1808, the Duke of Buckingham served beef as one of the removes for his Christmas dinner. Even in the workhouses that offered Christmas dinner, such as the Kensington workhouse in 1859, each of the 300 inmates was allowed twelve ounces of beef, a pound of pudding and a pint of porter, along with currants.

Chicken's role, ironically, was as an advance payment for the beef. At Christmas on many great estates it was the custom for each tenant to give to the lord a hen (partly as payment for being allowed to keep poultry), or sometimes grain, which was brewed into ale. Sometimes the custom said explicitly that the lord had to give a Christmas meal because the tenant had given him the food. In at least one instance the value of the food to be provided by the lord was to be the same value as that given by the tenant. The role of the lord in this case appears to have been merely to organise the village Christmas dinner.[2]

Beef was once so foundational to national identity that it had a political face. The beefsteak clubs exemplified English conceptions of liberty – male, red-blooded, jolly, given to jokes and japes. The first was founded early in the eighteenth century to be a meeting place for actors and politicians. When it failed, it was replaced by the Sublime Society of Beef Steaks, established in 1735, which was to number Samuel Johnson and the Prince of Wales among its members. Members wore bright blue coats and buff waistcoats with brass buttons, sporting a gridiron motif and the words 'Beef and liberty'. They celebrated the beefsteak as a symbol of liberty and prosperity. A 'Rump-Steak or Liberty Club' (also called 'The Patriots Club') of London was in existence in 1733–4. It was revived in 1966 and meets annually at White's Club in St James's, where its members are able to dine at the earlier society's nineteenth-century table and where it also keeps the original 'President's Chair', which Queen Elizabeth II gave to the current society in 1969.[3]

———

There is no logical reason why chicken should be a softer option, a reduction in masculinity. In the ancient world, chickens were mainly reared for cock-fighting, a vicious betting game which relied on their extreme rage when roused. The winning and therefore reproducing birds were easily infuriated, especially by anything coloured red. From this, cocks acquired their reputation for, well, cockiness. Their ferocity could frighten ghosts away. They were loved by all gods of light. The main use of chicken in pre-industrial times was as alarm clocks; the Greek word is *alektryones* – awakener – while geese were principally understood as watch animals. The modern domestic chicken is descended from a jungle fowl, a territorial ground-dwelling non-migratory bird. Powerful short-range flyers, they roosted in trees to escape predators at night, and modern domestic chickens still urgently need to roost as the sun goes down. Chickens in the Near East had a role in Egyptian religion, as common sacrificial birds and as markers of time. Roman knowledge of chicken-rearing probably derived from Egypt; fourth-century BC Greek records state that the Egyptians had mastered both poultry husbandry and the artificial incubation of chicks: their incubators were capable of hatching up to 15,000 eggs at a time. Historically, there is no doubt that the egg came before the chicken as a food for human beings. Doubtless, however, common sense meant that hens too old to lay were eaten, along with roosters too old to do their jobs.

However, while this pattern does persist historically, birds reared for the table and not for egg-laying appeared surprisingly early in the ancient world. The place where chickens were first raised for meat was the city of Maresha, which flourished in the Hellenistic period from 400 to 200 BC on a trade route between Jerusalem and Egypt. Where it stood, archaeologists have unearthed more than a thousand chicken bones. There are twice as many bones from female birds as male, so these were not being raised for cockfighting – and knife marks were visible on the bones. These chickens were being raised for their meat. After Maresha, chicken eating spread: an extensive survey of animal remains from 234 sites shows a sharp increase in finds of chicken during the Hellenistic period. As Roman power expanded, so did chicken-eating.

Chicken was a luxury food, consumed by the Roman upper classes. But chicken was almost certainly not straightforwardly secular. The cock was seen as an emblem of the god Mercury, and some evidence from temples suggests that chickens were rotisseried as sacrificial animals rather than as a source of food. And those who worshipped Mithras consumed cocks as part of his worship, because of their association with the dawn and that of Mithras with the sun. In 162 BC, to conserve grain rations, the Lex Faunia forbade the fattening of hens, a situation which was to find an echo in Second World War England. The regulation was renewed a number of times, but does not seem to have been successful. Fattening chickens with bread soaked in milk was thought to give especially delicious results.

The Roman compilation attributed to Apicius offers seventeen recipes for chicken, mainly variations on boiled chicken with a sauce. Roman banqueting culture may well tell us something of what was enjoyed in Roman Britain. All parts of the animal were used, including the gizzard, liver, testicles and the tail (sometimes called the parson's nose in England). Columella gives advice on chicken breeding in his treatise, *De Re Rustica* (On Rural Business). For farming, native (Roman) chickens were preferred, or a cross between native hens and Greek cocks. The ideal flock consisted of 200 birds, which could be supervised by one person if someone was watching for stray animals. One cock should be kept for every five hens. Columella also stated that chicken coops should face south-east and lie adjacent to the kitchen, as smoke was beneficial for the animals and 'poultry never thrive so well as in warmth and smoke'. Dry dust or ash should be provided for dust-baths.[4]

The conquering Romans brought their methods of poultry rearing to Britain. Julius Caesar said that the Britons reared fowls and geese, like hares, for pleasure and amusement, but that there was a taboo against eating them, though this is contradicted by archaeological finds.[5] Household accounts from the Batavians stationed at Vindolanda in AD 104 mention the supply of chickens for banquets. Another letter from Vindolanda contains a shopping list for twenty chickens and several hundred eggs.[6] Eggs have been found in graves in Colchester and York, where they were included as funerary offerings for the dead and the gods of the underworld. They were both a food and a symbol of regeneration. The Romans also kept doves, especially in winter, and game birds, especially pheasant, wood pigeon, pigeon and partridge have been found at Roman sites. In Colchester, the bones of mallard, teal, tufted duck, woodcock, swan and crane have been found; the Romans feasted on them all.[7] The elaborate eating of game we associate with medieval banqueting appears to have begun with the Romans.

It seems likely that birds were cooked whole rather than jointed, with the wingtips and feet removed. A senior officer at the fortress of Caerleon left clear evidence of chicken eating in his kitchen waste. As residences grew in status, the amount of poultry eaten also increased.[8]

At a Colchester church and its associated cemetery founded c. 330, when most of the population were Christian, large quantities of animal bone indicate that funerary meals were consumed in the church building; this suggests a communal feast of mourning, at which large chicken and young pig were especially favoured.[9] Already we can see the two great communal feasting meats – pig and fowl – emerging. This sideways glance at the exceptional occasion of the funeral feast shows us chicken had a place as a desired meat, a feast to be shared on the special occasions when people did not dine alone or *en famille*, but with others.

———

People ate chicken in a variety of ways, but all recipes across every culture and era repeat two elements: something to sharpen the flavour, and something to enrich it. A modern version of Apicius's recipe shows the elements that bring chicken to life:

PULLUM FRONTONIANUM (Chicken a la Fronto)

Ingredients:
1 fresh chicken, Oil, Liquamen (salty fish sauce, reminiscent of
    nam pla), or 200ml wine + 2 tsp salt, leek, fresh dill, saturei
    (summer savory), coriander, pepper to taste.
A little bit of Defritum (fig syrup)

Instructions:
Start to fry chicken and season with a mixture of Liquamen
    and oil, together with bunches of dill, leek, saturei and fresh
    coriander. Then cook approximately 1 hour (at 220°C) in
    the oven. When the chicken is done, moisten a plate with
    Defritum, put chicken on it, sprinkle pepper on it, and
    serve.[10]

This very ancient gourmet recipe adheres to the standard formula: fat plus cutting ingredient. Here, the oil is the fat, the fish sauce and herbs the cutting ingredients; they outweigh the fat, so the impact is modulated by the fig syrup. Other recipes from the same source offer a similar structure of flavours. There is something Roman in the way the quantity of cutting ingredients outweighs the emollients: what does this tell us? What does a strong palate tell us about a culture, a society, a civilisation? The basic materials are the same, but the proportions differ. In part, Romans saw strong dark tastes – *umami* flavours – as healthy because masculine, though only in proportion.

As gourmets, perhaps the first such to leave records, the Romans wanted a mix of novelty, showmanship and constant stimulation. A hungry diner might gulp down plain meat. A replete gourmet needed the excitement of a strong taste. In Petronius's satire *Satyricon*, the *nouveau riche* Trimalchio serves a dinner full of bling to bored gourmandisers:

> Slaves bring out a live hen, and as the orchestra plays a tune,
> two slaves search in the straw for eggs. It is not normal hens'
> eggs that are found, but pea hens' eggs – this is another example
> of food looking like one thing and being another. The eggs turn
> out to be covered in pastry. Encolpius finds that his egg in fact
> does have a half-formed chicken in it and nearly throws it away
> until another guest proclaims that this in fact is the point of the
> dish and eats the tiny hedge bird inside.

The trickery is itself a sign of excess; it takes enormous effort to conceal and disguise the original foodstuff. Trick food makes repeated appearances in Western culture, including the regrettable dishes of the late 1950s, where for example meatloaf was disguised as cake, and is reprised in the modernist food of the twenty-first century.

The Roman gourmet Marcus Gavius Apicius squandered a hundred million sesterces and became overwhelmed with debt. He killed himself when he realised that his remaining wealth was not enough for even one more good banquet.[11] He did, however, have disciples, undeterred by his example or trying to outdo him in strangeness. The Roman emperor Elagabalus ate camel heels, the tongues of peacocks and nightingales, the brains of flamingos and thrushes, partridge eggs, the heads of parrots and pheasants, and the beards of mullets 'in imitation of Apicius'. He also ate cockscombs, which have had a revival lately in keeping with nose-to-tail eating trends.[12] Like other animals, chickens come with numerous odd bits – not only cockscombs but feet and wingtips and bones and livers, and roosters' testicles. With a texture often likened to gummy candy, cockscombs don't carry much flavour, but they have been used of late in desserts; this tiny Apician amuse-bouche involves serious hard work in the kitchen to skin and braise. Generally, discarded bits of an animal will include food visible as organ or appendage; what disqualifies the combs is that they look like combs. As we have seen, there is a long-standing link in all eras between gourmet food and that which is not eaten by the majority. Foods can be rebracketed from disgusting to exciting for those seeking novelty.

'Apicius' was writing as and for the bored, rich gourmet seeking a novelty which shocks and questions. It is however impossible to infer the norm from these texts: were Apicius's flavours exaggerations or clean breaks with what was more generally liked? We can't tell. We know, for example, that the Romans linked fish sauce with the spread of their culture, so that might be a norm, but it might also have been the ancient world's Marmite, loved and hated in equal measure. Historians of food in the ancient world, such as John Wilkins, say that the Romans relished fish for its strong taste, but that is what makes it repugnant to others. Chicken, on the other hand, has far less flavour, so more people tend to like it.

———

Medieval chicken followed the Apician pattern, more or less: salt and sour. But the saltiness decreases, and the spicing level rises. Recipes in the *Menagier de Paris* include chicken ambrogino with fruit, and chicken limonia with lemon and pomegranate juice. These are powerful tastes, but sourness has begun to oust the more straightforward saltiness. The most loved chicken in England was Arab chicken. It brought together spices and fruits with nuts in new ways that added richness. Take 'Saracen chicken', with its almonds, prunes, raisins and dates. This style of cooking brings out the sweetness in chicken by pairing it with other sweet tastes. But the principle is not as dissimilar as it might appear. Sweetness can cut across the palate and refresh it. One incarnation of this kind of medieval/Arab-inflected dish brings chicken together with sugar and roses:

FOR TO MAKE ROSEE

Take the flowers of roses, and wash them well in water, and afterwards pound them in a mortar and then take almonds and temper them and seethe them, and afterwards take the flesh of capons or of hens, and hack it small and then pound it in a mortar and add it to the rose so that the flesh accord with the milk and so the meat be charged [so the meat absorbs the almond milk] and after do it to the fire to boil, and add sugar, and saffron, so that it be well coloured and rosy of leaves [petals] and of the foresaid flowers and serve it forth.[13]

A scented rose-petalled boudin blanc or weisswurst with no casing emerges. This kind of dish was often enjoyed even by middling families, made with their own *rosa gallica*. Then there was blancmange: chicken and pork, poached in wine flavoured with spices, including cloves and toasted almonds, and thickened with more almonds, ground, and sweetened just a little, sometimes with rosewater. The cook could add red colouring, and the whole could acquire a pastry carapace. The mixture could be made into balls or into more elaborate shapes. If this were served today, you would swear it was Indian; it also strongly resembles chicken bstilla, a Moroccan dish which includes light pastry over a kind of blancmange of chicken and almonds. Medieval cooks understood chicken as white meat, and so to them it went naturally with both almonds – themselves white, and remarkably like cream when crushed to pulp and left in water – and also, paradoxically, with the scents and colours of spices and aromatic flowers or leaves. It was the basis for exotic flavouring. But it was a relatively minor delicacy; they would be amazed by our endless appetite for it.

Walter of Bibbesworth, a thirteenth-century Hertfordshire gentleman, wrote a treatise for his neighbour Denise and her children. For him, eggs were more important than meat.[14] In winter, slaughtered chickens might be dampened and then placed for six days in ice, and in summer chickens smothered under a mattress might be put to cook in water and with bacon 'to give appetite'. (Clearly, the chicken itself wasn't seen as a delight.) The cook might add parsley, sage and hyssop, a little verjuice to sharpen it, and a very little ginger, and saffron to add colour. Saffron too can be a cutting taste; it is not sweet and edges bitter and sour.

A recipe for 'white elder' brings together scalded chickens, stewed in almond milk thickened with egg yolk, then flavoured with the ground-up dried flowers mixed with salt.[15] It does not sound terribly abstemious, but because chicken was white meat, it counted as suitable for fast days, enhancing its popularity. This might seem surprising, because for us, chicken is just as much meat as a steak or hamburger. In the Middle Ages, though, as we have seen, fasting was about the regulation of diet and particularly about reducing the quantity of red meat eaten because it was associated with the power to arouse violent passions, including sexual desires. A hangover from ancient Hebrew law also meant that meat with a reddish colour was seen as more blood-filled than white meat.

In one fifteenth-century treatise on food, John Russell proposed a feast for a franklin. This began with grapes and cherries, and was followed by several separate servings of a multiplicity of dishes. The banquet included brawn and mustard, bacon and peas, stewed beef, boiled chicken, roast pork, goose, baked meat, and chicken in a custard. Boiling a chicken with eggs and cream when both were available was doubly rich. After that came a subtlety, an elaborate sugar representation of the Annunciation. Then there were two more smorgasbords, and the feast ended with fritters, jellies, wafers and cheese. Chicken played an important role, but never stood alone.[16] At banquets, few foods did.

Russell's modest franklin's feast also features capons, '*capon agréable*'. We often assume people in the past were at ease with food-rearing methods which we find distasteful. But in the case of capon-cramming, the process aroused considerable disquiet. A capon was a castrated rooster that was fattened by force-feeding. Capons were made peaceable and fat by castration, and they became symbols of cowardice, impotence, idiocy, overindulgence, obesity and emasculation. William Cobbett's early nineteenth-century description of the moment of the rooster's castration – and by a woman – is one of the few to survive; reading it, one can see why:

> To cut them, the cock must lie on its back, and held fast, while with a very sharp knife she cuts him only skin-deep about an inch in length, between the rump and the end of the breast-bone, where the flesh is thinnest; next she makes use of a large needle to raise the flesh, for her safer cutting through it to avoid the guts, and making a cut here big enough to put her finger in, which she thrusts under the guts, and with it rakes or tears out the stone that lies nearest to it. This done, she performs the very same operation on the other side of the cock's body, and there takes out the other stone; then she stitches up the wounds, and lets the fowl go about as at other times, till the capon is fatted in a coop, which is commonly done from Christmas to Candlemas, and after.

'Capon' became an insult for the stupid and privileged. In *As You Like It*, the middle-aged justice's worldliness is compared to the capon: 'The Justice in fair round belly, with good capon lined'.[17] Not only the capon but being crammed – and especially with capons, crammed with the crammed – is suspect, even worryingly sexual.

The fatty whiteness called for coloration:

> Take a capon and scald him, roast him, then take thick almond milk, temper it with white and red; take a little saunders and a little saffron, and make it a marble clear, and so at the dresser

> throw on him in the kitchen, and throw the milk above, and
> that is most comely, and serve it fresh.

'Saunders', or sanders, is sandalwood, also a colouring agent. The idea
was to swirl the sauce to create a marble effect; the sandalwood was
red, and the result like porphyry.[18] A different recipe from another
medieval collection has capons stuffed with parsley, sage, hyssop, rosemary and thyme, coloured with saffron and placed in an earthenware
crock; carefully splinted away from the sides, the capon is doused with
wine and more herbs, the pot set on a charcoal fire, and then the
capon extracted on a spike, and served with a sauce of raisins, wine,
sugar and powdered ginger.[19]

With this small, fatty, hand-reared bird available, the problem of
dry meat was resolved in the poultry yard rather than in the kitchen.
When old boilers were killed, their flesh was a kind of waste product
to be used up sensibly in the pot, where they could – like bacon –
impart taste to other things: vegetables, grains, legumes. Eventually,
and not coincidentally shortly before the demise of castrato singing
stars, the capon simply became too embarrassing and too expensive to
rear, and it disappeared; with it went the knowledge of how to castrate
a young male bird without killing it. Its place was then hastily taken
by the larger, weightier and slightly more multipurpose hen.

––––––––

In 1545, when the English sought to cut off food imports to France, a
letter preserved among Henry VIII's state papers stated that the fron-
tier officers 'will not suffer so much as an egg, a chicken or a sparrow
to come hither'.[20] This chicken is understood not as ample, but as
meagre, the very smallest allowable thing, on a par with an egg or a
sparrow, so minor that its insignificance is used to indicate the severity
of the ban. Chicken is still essentially a skinny shrubland fowl. Fifteen
years later, the English and French captains met for dinner, each bringing the food he had: the English brought beef, bacon, capon, chicken,
wine, and the French brought a 'cold capon roast, a pasty of a baked
horse, and 6 rats well roasted', telling them that was the best fresh food

they had.[21] So horse, rat and chicken are cosily coupled; all are seen as the food of desperation. Horse and chicken are alike in leanness. Rat and wild chicken look alike: skinny, agile, lean bodies. They have similar habits, too. Yet we normally eat just one of those meats with enthusiasm, and this is clearly true of the English by 1560.

In most of Europe, the horse is eaten, though rarely with eager enthusiasm, But in Britain, the taboo dates back to before the Tudors, and has strengthened over the years. Horsemeat is a choice only if the alternative is starvation. Horse was sold and eaten in wartime, for example.[22] Usually this repugnance is explained in terms of the idea of the horse as pet, but it is quite ordinary in rural life to eat – for example – chickens, pigs and cows that have been given names. As for rats, the main objection is that they are rodents, but we eat other, larger rodents, such as rabbits. If the horse or pony is too near to us, the rat is perhaps too far away to make it to the table. Yet the eminently edible chicken shares many of the characteristics and behaviours that deter the British from eating horses and rats. On the horse side, the chicken can be a pet, and on the rat side, the chicken is an omnivorous scavenger. Perhaps if we were used to breeding for the table, rat might become a delicacy, like rabbits and hens.

Our wish to know, understand and thus control what we put into our mouths and take into our bodies has ancient roots. As we have seen, witches could afflict cattle and dairying, but witches and chickens are also though less frequently linked, and especially in relation to both the strangeness of chicken feet and the extreme oddity of eggs. In stories of early modern witches, told at their trials, witches were often linked with food, and some foods were especially viewed with suspicion, even dislike, because they were seen as especially permeable to bewitchment.

One dark night in 1670, a group of witches in Lancashire and the North were enjoying a feast of food, according to a girl called Anne Armstrong, probably a teenager, almost certainly someone who had listened to fireside stories about the great Lancashire witch trial of 1612, which featured the first descriptions of a witches' sabbath in English trial records. When Anne described the food, she did so in real, even overwhelming detail; it attracts by far the most careful description in all her testimony. For a second, we glimpse a meal longed for and desired, a meal worth someone's soul:

> Lucy wished that a boiled capon … might come down to her
> and the rest … which capon Lucy set before the rest of the
> company, whereof the devil … was their chief, sitting in a chair
> like unto bright gold. And the said Lucy further did swing, and
> demanded the plum broth which the capon was boiled in,
> and thereupon it did immediately come down in a dish.

Others also wished for and received luxury foods: a cheese, a beaker of wheat flour, half a quarter of butter 'to knead the said flour withal; they having no power to get water'.[23] The diabolical luxury specifically included the capon, acme of leisure and decadence. It also reflected luxury tastes in bread and pastry. What the witches are described making was the bread of the rich: wheaten bread, moistened with dairy and not mere water. Food they had seen, but had never been allowed to eat; food that was not for the likes of them.

It is clear that these witches were performing on a grand scale the pettier larcenies enacted by most witches when they stole milk or butter. The capon was an exquisitely labour-intensive food. In Anne's times, all labour came from the servants, who did not eat the result. A kind of food apartheid characterised the servants' hall, where servants ate markedly cheaper and inferior versions of dishes they themselves had sent up to the master's dining table.

We tend to see 'fast food' as modern, but medieval and early modern food sometimes had to be fast too. Not everyone could afford the kitchen facilities to make their own meals. Public eating houses, one kind called ordinaries, supplied those in London who were forced to eat out. Servants went off to such places for snacks and for booze when off duty. For John Stow, the Eastcheap streets rang with cries that asked the customer to pay attention mostly to food, and especially to pies, in a sharp contrast to the Westcheap streets, where the cries were about clothing.[24]

In the fourteenth century, a man called Henry Pecche bought a fast-food chicken pasty – containing two baked capons – and a tale of nightmare unfolded, the usual tale of finding half a worm in an apple:

Being hungry, [Henry] did not perceive that one of the said two capons was putrid and stinking, until they had eaten almost the whole thereof; whereupon they opened the second capon, which he produced here in Court, and found it to be putrid and stinking, and an abomination to mankind.

The cook who sold them, also called Henry, said the capon was fine, but the poulterers who tested it agreed that it was horrible. The cook was sentenced to the pillory, with the capon to be carried before him on his way there.[25]

Unsurprisingly, there was an upsurge of interest in discerning freshness via sensory tests, beginning with Thomas Tryon, who wrote enthusiastically of digging in with knives and prodding with a finger, sniffing, and holding up to the light. White bread, clear liquid, white meat – all those came into their own in an era of sensory checking. The hen was especially fit for the new and much larger city of London. A man might come round with wicker baskets strapped to a big sturdy pole; in each would be one or more chickens. 'Buy my fat chickens,' he might cry. The purchaser might buy a small chicken and fatten it for later eating, or might buy a bird ready for the knife. One cookbook advised the wife to avoid purchasing live chickens stuffed into small baskets. A bird slaughtered all too long ago might also be available; the age of the corpse could be detected from its sunken eyes and hardened feet.[26]

One way we can track the growth of chicken eating is through the use of chickens and eggs as rental currency; like apples, they show us how widespread the fowl were. On one Oxfordshire manor, rent was 'a chicken at Christmas and ten eggs at Easter'.[27] Similarly, in Kent, rents were payable in many portable materials: 'Hay, calves, *chicken*, lambs, pigs, geese, *hens*, *eggs*, ducks, pigeons, bees, honey, wax, swans, wool, milkmeats, pasture, flax, hemp, garden-herbs, apples, vetches … and all manner of small tithes arising from all things whatsoever.'[28]

In a town with a name that sounds like clucking hens, Cucklington, most rentholders also paid eggs or chickens at Easter along with small quantities of wheat and oats.[29] Tithe reports from most London parishes include both chickens and eggs. A steady chicken and egg supply marked the round of the year.

As chicken moved away from being seen as specifically festive, its association with ideas of goodness and simplicity – and secular ideals of health – came to the fore. Chicken was a food for invalids from an early period, in particular chicken broth – light and golden, subtle and transparent, infusing health and warmth into the sick, comfort into the glum.

The chicken's own diet didn't agree with the idea that they were not really meat. Hen-keepers were advised to put a dung heap near the henhouse which could be watered with blood so that maggots formed for the hens to eat. The goal was to keep hens laying through the winter, and the role of carnivore food in doing this had begun to be acknowledged.[30] But few such grisly tips survive, because this was women's work, and as such rarely written down.

At the same time, there was an evolving regionalisation. Hertfordshire hens were fed on beans and hempseed, and were cried up by sellers for their superior eggs.[31] East Anglian birds were given buckwheat. Later, the Dorking chicken came to connote special chicken, reared with extra care. As banqueting stuff appeared, the sugar feast-after-the-feast, so eggs became more important. The methods of poulterers came to matter more; one London poultry-keeper in 1699 fed his hens on toast dipped in ale – invalid food – and boiled barley, an improvement on hens who merely scratched up what they could.

Cookbook writer Thomas Dawson shows the repertoire of early modern chicken usages. He had a recipe to boil chickens with grapes and mutton, and to garnish with green herbs – a bunch of hyssop, rosemary, thyme, savory and marjoram. Chickens needed a stuffing to moisten them – parsley and butter, verjuice and pepper. Another recipe had chickens, mutton and dried fruit boiled together with pepper, lemon and an egg yolk liaison. Fried chicken which 'you must not let … brown' gives us an indication that what was valued about chicken was white softness, not crispness; in fact, the textures sought are always soft and juicy, though often with tart flavourings. Dawson wrote his works for the new London of the last years of Elizabeth I: a world of merchants and aspirant sellers that sought genteel credentials and gave dinner parties to guests and business contacts; people who had servants, but not great households. Thomas Dawson might have been one of them; a gardener perhaps, since he was the first to publish a recipe for sweet potatoes, months before John Gerard did.

Gervase Markham was a product of the same world. He was an eager supporter of Robert Devereux, Earl of Essex, the nobleman who made a bid for the throne on the grounds of traditional aristocratic values, the old link between nobles and their lands. There is a shadowy link between Essex's ideal England and that ideal portrayed by Markham, where fowl wander joyfully around the feet of henwives; his is perhaps a littler and more down-to-earth vision of Essex's noble ideals. However, the utter failure of Essex's rebellion left his supporters stranded, and Markham took up farming for a few years. This period probably inspired him to write *The English Housewife*, printed in 1615, and revised and reprinted many times. Some of it is unoriginal, but it is remarkable in evoking and championing the ideal of the self-sufficient household. Markham himself remained eccentric and short of money.

He was interested in pies, the portable food of the era, and his interest reflects the growing pie market in London. Markham showed the use of chicken as a pie filling; his recipes included a chewet pie, containing shredded roast chicken brawn and wing meat with fine mutton, and a sweet spice mix of cinnamon, clove, mace, sugar and salt, all in a pastry coffin; a chicken pie with trussed chickens, their bones broken, laid with their bodies full of butter in a pastry dish, then on top of them layers of dried fruit, the same sweet spices, more butter, then white wine and rosewater, with the yolks of three eggs poured in around and over them.[32] Markham's book draws heavily on the cookbooks published by John Murrell, and Murrell too has many chicken recipes. Despite his advocacy of contemporary French-style food, his recipe for capon is strikingly like the old medieval ways; he nonetheless announces it as 'the newest and most commendable fashion' and as 'the French fashion':

> Scald your Capon, and take a little dusty Oatmeal to make it boil white. Then take two or three ladlefuls of Mutton broth, a Faggot of sweet Herbs, two or three Dates, cut in long pieces, a few parboiled Currants, a little whole Pepper, a piece of whole Mace, and one Nutmeg. Thicken it with Almonds. Season it with [ambergris], Sugar, and a little sweet Butter. Then take up your Capon, and lard it very thick with a preserved Lemon. Then lay your Capon in a deep Meat-dish for boiled meats, and pour the broth upon it. Garnish your Dish with Suckets and preserved Barberries.[33]

This mix of fruit, spice, sour and enrichment is only 'French' because of the butter in the sauce, and because the bird is served coated in the sauce in a single dish. Otherwise, Murrell is adhering firmly to a fairly traditional set of medieval tastes and textures.

Markham hailed chicken as meat which traverses the social spectrum: boiled, they 'feed the poor as well as the rich'. He suggests stuffing them with parsley and nothing else; then you add the removed parsley – now steeped in juices – to verjuice, butter and salt to make a sauce; he also has sorrel and sugar, or sops soaked in mace and ginger. Markham has no interest in roasting chicken: his long section on roasting contains many small animals like rabbits, but he may have thought chicken too dry to be roasted; the recipes cited above are all about moisture.[34]

As well as printed cookbooks, manuscript books also illustrate the uses of chicken. Elinor Fettiplace has a classic chicken and almond dish, analogous to the kind of soup served today in some parts of Spain, and apparently surviving with little change from the Middle Ages, and she also has two near-Roman recipes of chicken boiled with egg and verjuice, and chicken boiled with herb and gooseberry sauce, or spinach sauce. All these dishes followed the Roman approach of sharp flavours to cut the emollience of the chicken.

Fettiplace also uses chicken as the basis for a classic, presentational recipe:

> Take a good pullet and cut his throat hard by the head, and make it but a little hole. Then scald him clean, and take out of the small hole his crop. So done, take a quill and blow into the same hole, for to make the skin rise up from the flesh. Then break the wing bones, and the bones hard by the knee. Then cut the neck hard by the body, then cut off the rump … mince the flesh with sheep's suet, grated bread, and three hardboiled egg yolks, bind with raw egg yolks, barberries, and season with clove, mace, ginger, pepper and salt, and saffron. Then stuff your pullet's skin with it … make it after the proportion of an eagle in every part, having his head to be cleft asunder and laid in two parts like an eagle's head.[35]

The goal here is the delight of fakery, seen in chicken from very early.

For food historian Stephen Mennell, the publication of *Le Cuisinier françois* (1651) by François Pierre La Varenne is the key event in European food history. We have already seen his influence on Robert May, in the chapter on Apples. Preserved food was replaced by fresh food. Herbs ousted spices, dairy pushed out nuts, and sweet and savoury were rigorously separated – an odd development, which became one of the distinguishing marks of Western as opposed to Eastern and Far Eastern cuisine. These changes can be seen most clearly with chicken. Replacing butter with almonds had an immediate and dramatic effect: chicken came to seem fresh and French, part of the La Varenne trend of whiteness and purity and simplicity. Eggs, too, were a key ingredient in forming liaisons. Mennell associates with this the decline in use of exotic birds, the lighter, less mixed spicing, the use of reduced consommés, and the creation of meat that tasted like itself.

Yet important though all this was, the chicken and capon recipes in the 1654 English translation of La Varenne are very much like Gervase Markham's. For example: a capon stuffed with oysters soaked in wine vinegar, mixed with breadcrumbs, mace, onion, salt and nutmeg, and four eggs. Essentially, this adds onion and substitutes oysters for parsley. Another capon recipe puts the parsley back, and adds a novelty: some fennel, though mace is still the main spice. What has gone is the verjuice. Sauced capon is more radical, acquiring a more gelatinous sauce from the addition of a calf's foot, but still amply acidulated with lemons. Bashed chicken or rabbit is a boiled chicken layered with turnip, but still spiced with ginger and sauced with egg yolk and butter and cream. Sauces are, however, made with butter, a bundle of unspecified herbs, mushrooms, onion, and flour to thicken. In the same period, William Rabisha published many boiled fowl recipes, all, like his predecessors', finished with barberries, or grapes, or gooseberries, or lemon, but often – like La Varenne – with butter rather than almonds.[36]

In England, it was Robert May who seems to some food historians to have offered new, innovative and inventive ways with food. Take his peeping chickens, à la mode; as the name implies, looks are all. You scraped the crumb out of manchet boules, cut a hole in the top, mixed the crumb with the meat of a roast capon, added marchpane paste [marzipan], egg yolks, sugar, sweet herbs, cinnamon, saffron and currants, and refilled the breads with the mixture, boiled them in mutton or capon broth, and topped with sweetbreads. This elegantly preserved the medieval flavour range, while also offering a way to protect the chicken's delicate flesh from direct heat.

However, May's list of carving verbs draws attention to how many different kinds of animal might form part of a feast:

> Break that deer, leach that brawn, rear that goose, lift that swan,
> sauce that capon, spoil that hen, frust that chicken, unbrace
> that mallard, unlace that coney, dismember that her[o]n,
> display that crane, disfigure that peacock, unjoint that bittern,
> untach that curlew, allay that pheasant, wing that partridge,
> wing that quail, mince that plover, thigh that pigeon, thigh that
> woodcock.[37]

Radical? Not exactly. This entire list is transcribed from *The Book of Kervynge*, printed by Wynkyn de Worde in 1508. May does not even bother to reorder the ingredients. This is explicable in a number of ways. Writing and publishing just after the cataclysm of the English Civil War, May was above all eager to restore and revive the arts of aristocratic living that he feared were endangered by that revolutionary ferment. The whole purpose of providing these learning lists was to encourage traditional life – leisurely, hunting and feasting life – to resume.

Chicken became all things to all men: ersatz game, healthy whiteness, delicious and digestible succulence. Its ascent coincided with the Reformation, and also with urbanisation and in particular the explosive growth of London. Chickens were portable and more easily urbanised than pigs. For the slightly less elevated, the good life had begun to include roast chicken, and Lady Anne Blencowe's personal recipe book shows this. Her compilation dates from the late seventeenth and early eighteenth centuries, and included one of the earliest recipes for roast chickens, 'Sir Thomas Perkingses way':

> You may roast the fowl with about fifteen middling sized raw
> Oysters in each fowl, with a Scotch Onion or two. Run two
> or three spoonful of cloves thro them when drawn in the dish.
> Roast them by a brisk fire even to crisp the feet, which must
> be laid flat backwards towards the rump for their being easier
> carved; but roast not the bodies of the fowl too much, that
> the gravy may be in them.[38]

Blencowe is worried about losing the gravy or juice. Her recipe was written after the La Varenne cookbook had changed the emphasis from visual artifice to simplicity. And it's very simple.

Chicken is beginning its journey to whiteness and ease; May's efforts to preserve medieval food had failed, swept aside by La Varenne. Why? One simple reason might be the loss of equipment in the English Civil War. The loss of hunting lands, too, and revenues, the growth of London as the setting for eating, the development of food in small dainty portions rather than in huge spreads: all helped to boost the ideas of La Varenne and the chicken with him. In 1760 Elizabeth Raffald had a recipe for roast chicken, basted with butter, coated with more butter and parsley. No oysters, though, and no mutton broth to add flavour; her chicken by now is a recognisably modern roast, perhaps the first.[39] Otherwise, she has only boiling chicken, fricassee of chicken – a new kind of technique, used for all meats – and broth, all recipes in part dictated by the age of the available bird.

As chickens became more popular, science tried to provide more of them. Nathaniel Matson petitioned William III to support an invention 'for producing all sorts of fowle out of their eggs, by artificial heat'; which invention was proposed 'to furnish the town with chicken in winter, when they are not otherwise to be had, but at great rates, and with partridge and pheasants, in summer, whereby the game within 50 miles of London may be better preserved'.[40] Chickens were scarce in wintertime, so scarce that they were expensive – but demand was high. Similarly, game birds were scarce in summer. This particular enterprise did not succeed, though the value of heat and darkness were soon widely understood. But Matson's experiment shows us how the rise in chicken's popularity and its growing centrality at the table.

More chicken recipes began to circulate, and chicken assumed a more and more prominent place in recipe books. Martha Washington took chicken into her book as a 'frykecy', but despite the new-fangled name, the dish reproduced flavours which would have been familiar in the fifteenth century. Her chicken was fried in browned butter with bones broken, then water added to deglaze the pan, then parsley, onion; then egg yolks, wine vinegar or lemon juice to finish. The eighteenth century often added flour to stabilise the egg liaison – Hannah Glasse uses *beurre manié*, a paste of flour and butter. But other Washington recipes were still seasoning with nutmeg, pepper and clove, and adding vinegar, while yet others exploited new ingredients to create old effects: for example, sugared gooseberries, either in the sauce or as a garnish. Hen sauce was hardboiled egg, mutton gravy and mustard – this seems less of a surge towards French taste and more a forerunner of the much more muddled and ponderous Victorian palate. Moreover, the loss of a simple egg-yolk liaison and its replacement by flour implies deskilling and almost certainly produced a worse outcome. You could say the same about Washington's alternative sauce, based around red wine (claret) and an anchovy. Sauces were by the mid-eighteenth century thickened *only* with flour – no egg and butter liaisons. Flour-based sauces are a great culinary devil on our backs that we have just managed to shake off in the twenty-first century. The effect of the flour is to dull the taste, to replace cleanness with a muddy ease, a sludgy slide of thickness. The light, fresh *jus* or the sensuous egg and butter liaison becomes something that will turn forbiddingly solid at low temperatures.

Because chicken was still seen as a light and digestible invalid food, it is a staple of suppers at Hartfield in Jane Austen's *Emma*, where Mr Woodhouse's digestion must not be assailed by the toasted cheese which was Austen's own favourite. Lady Lucas regales herself with a supper of ham and chicken. Some of Austen's characters are also poultry raisers: 'Lady Lucas was enquiring of Maria, across the table, after the welfare and poultry of her eldest daughter.' Austen's irony here skewers the triviality of the poultry. For Lizzy Bennet, Charlotte's domestic interest in her hens is a gloomy sign of the limitations of her life:

> Poor Charlotte! it was melancholy to leave her to such society! But she had chosen it with her eyes open; and though evidently regretting that her visitors were to go, she did not seem to ask for compassion. Her home and her housekeeping, her parish

and her poultry, and all their dependent concerns, had not yet
lost their charms.[41]

Clearly, Lizzy thinks that they will nevertheless lose appeal. The poultry merits another slice of irony via the tirelessly rude Lady Catherine
de Bourgh:

> She [Lady Catherine] … told her how everything ought to be
> regulated in so small a family as her's, and instructed her as to
> the care of her cows and her poultry. Elizabeth found that
> nothing was beneath this great Lady's attention, which could
> furnish her with an occasion of dictating to others.[42]

To Austen, poultry is paltry even when a lady speaks about it. The
Austens were more interested in pigs and in tea.

———————

Clearly, many people in the class to which Austen assigned Charlotte
were keeping a few hens, but the tradition of smallholding as a means
of defying the crushing might of industrialisation emanated in part
from the powerful pen of William Cobbett, who bought a farm in
Hampshire to practise what he advocated himself.[43] Cobbett recorded
that fowls are kept equally for meat and eggs by the end of the eighteenth century. Virtually everything he said of them is remarkably
sensible, and could be of use to any free-range chicken keeper in the
twenty-first century: 'The dry cold, even in the severest cold, if *dry*, is
less injurious than even a little *wet* in winter-time. If the feathers get
wet, in our climate, in winter, or in short days, they do not get dry for
a long time; and this it is that spoils and kills many of our fowls.' He
advocates the French diet for chickens, especially:

> curds, *buck-wheat*, (which, I believe, is the best thing of all
> except curds;) parsley and other herbs chopped fine; leeks
> chopped in the same way; also apples and pears chopped very
> fine; oats and wheat cribbled; and sometimes they give them

hemp-seed, and the seed of nettles; or dried nettles, harvested in summer, and boiled in the winter. Some give them ordinary food, and, once a day, toasted bread sopped in wine.

Note Cobbett's reuse of household scraps, though he (still) sounds very much like a rich man telling the poor how to live. In the hungry years of the Corn Laws, a poor family would have been eating any leftovers themselves.

The task of teaching the English housewife how to cook a chicken was taken up by others. The simplicity of chicken needed a cook of the genius of Eliza Acton to bring it out. She provided a recipe for a white sauce that refined the flour-thickened roux, and the first fully detailed printed recipe for roast chicken. It took preparation to a level that most readers would not have understood or known:

> Strip off the feathers, and carefully pick every stump from the skin … Take off the head and neck close to the body, but leave sufficient of the skin to tie over the part that is cut. In drawing the bird, do not open it more than is needful, and use great precaution to avoid breaking the gall-bladder. Hold the legs in boiling water for two or three minutes that the skin may be peeled from them easily; cut the claws, and then … singe off the hairs without blackening the fowl. Wash, and wipe it afterwards very dry … Truss and spit it firmly; flour it well when first laid to the fire, baste it frequently with butter, and when it is done draw out the skewers, dish it, pour a little good gravy over, and send it to table with bread, mushroom, egg, chestnut, or olive sauce. A buttered paper should be fastened over the breast, and removed about fifteen minutes before the fowl is served: this will prevent its taking too much colour.

Acton also boiled, grilled, 'bashed', minced and fried her chickens. She was among the first to celebrate the grouse, as a posher form of chicken, but most importantly, she gave real directions that could be followed to the letter. Cooking was becoming a literate art. Chicken was ready to take its place as a festive bird.

———————

However, it had a rival. Once, a goose was the family Christmas dinner all across Europe, in urban settings especially; the old estates and nobles might still serve boar or even beef, but in the towns, poultry began to predominate. Then, in the latter half of the nineteenth century, the English began to substitute turkeys for geese. This in itself seems to have been part of the adaptation of Christmas dinner to an ideal of amplitude, and the man to blame is probably Charles Dickens. In 1843's *A Christmas Carol* the Cratchits' goose comes home cooked from the baker's, but Dickens shows its meagreness:

> There never was such a goose. Bob said he didn't believe there ever was such a goose cooked. Its tenderness and flavour, size and cheapness, were the themes of universal admiration. Eked out by apple-sauce and mashed potatoes, it was a sufficient dinner for the whole family; indeed, as Mrs Cratchit said with great delight (surveying one small atom of a bone upon the dish), they hadn't ate it all at last. Yet every one had had enough, and the youngest Cratchits in particular, were steeped in sage and onion to the eyebrows.

The family's delight is implicitly disproportionate to the goose itself. When Scrooge repents, much more stress falls on the immensity of the bird he buys:

> 'Do you know whether they've sold the prize Turkey that was hanging up there – Not the little prize Turkey: the big one?'
>   'What, the one as big as me?' returned the boy.

Interestingly, it is never clear how or by whom the monster bird is cooked or eaten. Cooking a turkey this size on a small domestic range would have taken at least four to five hours, even after the range had been fired up. It seems unlikely that either the Cratchits or Scrooge would have had the equipment necessary for so large a bird; it would have needed a big, powerful spit, or a large range oven, a rarity at the time the book is set – which is why the Cratchits' own goose has been taken to the bakery to be cooked in the bread oven. The point of the prize turkey is its sheer size, which represents the scale of Scrooge's repentance and munificence. Generosity seems to matter more in repentance than the actual practicalities of cooking and eating. The point about a feast is the excess, the overspill, the over-catering, the appearance of surplus. This became central to the Victorian idea of Christmas as a medieval feast.

And yet until fairly recently, the turkey was still a rich man's bird. Before the rise of the battery hen in the early 1960s, even a chicken was still a luxury, enough of a luxury for Christmas. As numbers attending Christmas dinner dropped, a small family might well make do with one, and did up until the Second World War.

A feast in Mary Elizabeth Braddon's 1864 sensation fiction *The Doctor's Wife* offered chicken as the pinnacle of riches: 'There were flowers upon the table, and a faint odour of orange blossoms and apricots pervaded the atmosphere … Mr Lansdell put some creamy white compound on her plate, which might or might not have been chicken … there was a dream-like flavour to everything.'[44]

Like mythical King Midas, we want to eat our gold, our money. This unidentified creamy chicken tastes of class. Not even money – class. Its purity can ennoble and enrich. Transform. Is it even chicken? If it cannot be called chicken, perhaps it cannot be called meat. Perhaps no living thing had to die so that humans might eat it. This meal is a denial of materiality. It partakes of an overall disdain for food that is almost anorexic in its anxiety about ingestion. Foams occupy this place in modern cuisine, including chicken foams, perhaps. It is a substance that doesn't need chewing, an edible that is not food. A dream-like flavour implies an exquisite subtlety, requiring an equally exquisite palate for appreciation. The growth of the notion that subtle senses, sensitive senses, are more important than robust ones helped to elevate the starry pallor of chicken. What made us long for whiteness

Pannage: men knocking down acorns to feed their pigs on a calendar page for November, *Queen Mary Psalter*, illumination, fourteenth century.

Saint Anthony with a pig and a bell from *The Book of Hours* W.719, Master of Ghent Privileges and associates, illumination, *c.* 1450.

'A Family of Three at Tea' by Richard Collins, oil painting on canvas, 1727.

An illustration from the book 'The Black Man's Lament,
or, How to Make Sugar' by Amelia Opie, 1826.

Waitresses, or 'nippys' as they were called, running in a tea-tray race at a Lyons sports meet held at Sudbury, photograph, 1936.

HER MAJESTY'S BRIDAL CAKE.

The cake made for the wedding of Queen Victoria and Prince Albert, drawing, 1840.

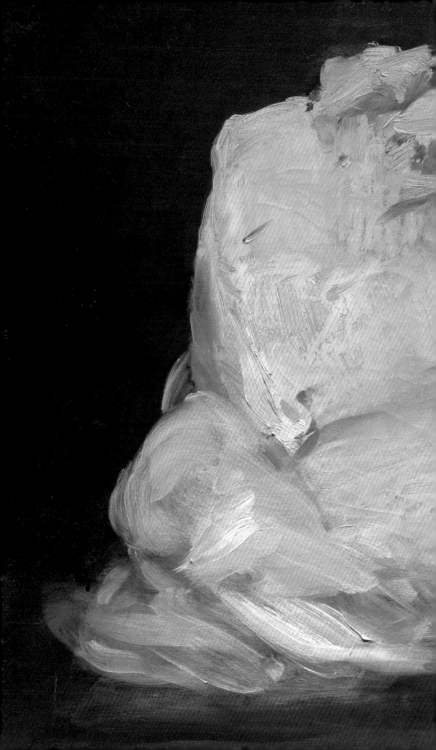

'Mound of Butter' by Antoine Vollon, painting, 1875–85.

Depiction of a village woman churning butter with the devil, medieval fresco.

'Milk Below Maids' ('Cries of London') made by Luigi Schiavonetti
after a painting by Francis Wheatley, engraving, 1793.

Poultry merchants, Caledonian Market, London, photograph, 1926–1927.

Three female workers preparing cans of fruit and vegetables in giant metal crates for labelling at a canning factory, photograph, 20th March 1940.

and purity in our meat, for meat with no trace of blood? The bland palate introduced by a particular and odd version of French cuisine, one where dairy – butter and cream – replaced verjuice, vinegar and citrus as the main sauce ingredients? The wars of the last century? The vegetarian movement? The wish to have meat which is not meat, which is close to industrial? Our guilt about higher animals? Or troubling masculine associations with red meat – the very associations identified by Roland Barthes – with masculinity and proletarian body shaping? Chicken, the ladies' choice? Symbolic of the longing not to eat at all? The chicken's golden auras of posh, moneyed food for all?

Chicken meets all our needs; it radiates a virtue that other, redder meats lack. The structural simplicity of it defeats misconstruction. Food was always layered socially; in the Middle Ages and the early modern period, the upper classes ate more meat than vegetables, and pure white eggs, not brown; as we have seen, their taste was either for the rich and dark – venison, game birds – or for the white and pure – almonds, sugar. When parishes began to serve communion wine to the laity, the rich had malmsey, while the poor were fobbed off with claret.

Whiteness was part of the allure of chicken from early times, though; we have seen blancmange, literally 'eat white'. White food is pure, mother's milk. Innocent food. The semiotics are so powerful that even knowing about chickens' lifestyles, chicken slaughter, does nothing to dent them. Eating lightly, with refined tastes, often involves eating whiteness. A cooked chicken ranges from white to gold, denoting its own status. It gleams. 'Skin gold-embroidered like a chasuble', said Marcel Proust. (Jane Grigson points out that Proust's golden chicken would not have had white flesh, but would have been pale gold all through, fattened on maize.)

————

As innovation in food became a critical part of Victorian middle-class dinner parties, designed to impress, cooks sought to sound like chefs, and hostesses tried to impress guests with upward-looking meals. An example is Chicken Marengo, which allegedly commemorated

Napoleon's victory at the battle of Marengo, without butter, but with oil and mushrooms, and white wine, using the basic structure of Chicken Provençal.[45] When Europe went mad for Napoleon, English cooks too were willing to take up dishes that celebrated his triumphs. This is Isabella Beeton's way:

> Cut the fowl into 8 or 10 pieces; put them with the oil into a stewpan, and brown them over a moderate fire; then pour in the stock or water – simmer for rather more than ½ an hour, skim off the fat; add the mushrooms; season with salt, pepper, garlic and sugar, remove the meat, and reduce the sauce.[46]

This is a fricassee, but the stewing time is beginning to creep up. Was this the result of people's teeth getting worse? With the flood of cheap West Indian sugar, and perhaps with increased longevity and diets based on white flour, the answer is likely to be yes. George Washington had a denture made of the tusks of a hippopotamus, and there are earlier examples, but it was when porcelain front teeth came in that dentures became affordable. Affordable, but not actionable: the dentures were purely for show, and were too loose-fitting for any actual chewing.

Chewing itself had become an issue. By 1890, everyone was supposed 'to eat slowly and masticate the food properly, then they will always feel at their ease at the grandest tables in the land'.[47] New social codes drew people away from animality; they were to show no eagerness for food, and no preference for a particular food item, while their actual eating was to be both invisible and inaudible. To prevent 'loud' and 'fast' chewing, and to allow for the very slow, silent chewing considered healthy, all food was cooked to a softness difficult for us to like or approve. Rotten teeth could split on biting into rare meat or crisp fruit, and so such things were shunned and also understood as unhealthy. Because chicken meat was very often boiled, or fricasseed and then boiled, it was very soft and therefore thought to be healthy. This anxiety about chewing is part of a more general Victorian trend, the search for rules and certitude in all things. 'Do not use your knife to carry food to your mouth or put your knife into your mouth', advised one etiquette guide. Another urged: 'The mouth should always be kept closed in eating, both eating and drinking should be noiseless', and 'Vegetables [and cheese] are eaten with a fork.'[48] Everything is about quiet.

As England expanded its trading empire in India, English people were exposed to new modes of cooking and eating which became hugely influential. Perhaps there has never been a greater change or challenge to English ways of eating than the coming of the foods of the Indian subcontinent to England. In exploring their emergence here, under the heading of chicken, I draw attention deliberately to the fact that this part of history has no obvious or single place as part of our mealtimes or our kinds of food. Instead, Indian food is always experienced in England as an exciting eruption into a less interesting norm, a breath of otherness redolent with spice and risk. The apparent commonality of the place of chicken in Indian food and in English food creates a false pontoon bridge that draws attention to the gulf it spans.

David Gilmour recorded the 1689 experience of dining with East India Company merchants at the factory in Surat, and eating a meal cooked by three cooks, Indian, English and Portuguese, producing 'the most common Indian dish', a palau with boiled rice, boiled fowl and spices intermixed; on Sundays, these entertainments were made more large and splendid with the addition of 'Peacock, Antelope, and Persian fruits such as pistachios, plums, and apricots'.[49]

Interestingly, the first curry recipe printed in English is for chicken or rabbit curry; Hannah Glasse, writing in 1747, gives this 'to make a currey the India way':

Take two Fowls or Rabbits, cut them into small pieces, and three or four small Onions, peeled and cut very small, thirty Pepper corns, and a large spoon full of rice, Brown some Coriander seeds over the fire, in a clear [clean] shovel, and beat them to a Powder, take a Tea spoonful of Salt, and mix all well

together with the Meat, put all together into a Sauce Pan or
Stew Pan, with a pint of water, let it stew softly till the meat is
enough, then put in a piece of fresh Butter, about as big as a
large walnut, shake it well together, and when it is smooth and
of a fine Thickness, dish it up, and send it to Table; if the sauce
be too thick, add a little more Water before it is done, and more
Salt if it wants it. You are to observe the sauce must be pretty
thick.[50]

From the mid-eighteenth century, India was commercially positioned
to dominate the British table, larder and sense of self.[51] And yet the
dish above is almost indistinguishable from many others diners would
have known well. It is in essence a fricassee. The Middle Ages would
have recognised it too, though they would have thought Glasse's hand
much too light with the spices, and would probably have wanted to
add sugar and ginger.

In her colonial cookbook *The Virginia Housewife* (1824), Mary
Randolph gives a more sophisticated recipe for curry powder than did
Glasse:

CURRY POWDER
One ounce turmeric, one do. coriander seed, one do. cumin
seed, one do. white ginger, one of nutmeg, one of mace, and
one of Cayenne pepper; pound all together, and pass them
through a fine sieve; bottle and cork it well – one tea-spoonful
is sufficient to season any dish …

TO MAKE A DISH OF CURRY AFTER THE EAST
INDIAN MANNER
Cut two chickens as for fricassee, wash them clean, and put
them in a stew pan with as much water as will cover them;
sprinkle them with a large spoonful of salt, and let them boil till
tender, covered close all the time, and skim them well. When
boiled enough, take up the chickens, and put the liquor of
them into a pan, then put half a pound of fresh butter in the

pan, and brown it a little; put in two cloves of garlic, and a large onion sliced, and let these all fry till brown, often shaking the pan; then put in the chickens, and sprinkle over them two or three spoonsful of curry powder; then cover the pan close, and let the chicken do till brown, often shaking the pan; then put in the liquor the chickens were boiled in, and let all stew till tender; if acid is agreeable, squeeze the juice of a lemon or orange in it.[52]

In general, however, the spicing of curry became more routine as it became more familiar. William Makepeace Thackeray's chortling poem lays all bare most succinctly:

Poem to Curry
What's next my dexterous little girl will do?
She pops the meat into the savoury stew,
With curry-powder table-spoonfuls three,
And milk a pint (the richest that may be),
And, when the dish has stewed for half an hour,
A lemon's ready juice she'll o'er it pour.
… PS – Beef, mutton, rabbit, if you wish,
Lobsters, or prawns, or any kind fish,
Are fit to make a CURRY.[53]

Note that chicken is not included as even a possibility. The recipe is also very buttery, and in Thackeray's time English people complained that curry was rich, oily or greasy. He is unspecific indeed about the curry powder itself. Small wonder, when the authority of Isabella Beeton endorsed the packaged product. Beeton said that 'some persons prefer to make it [curry powder] at home, but that purchased at any reputable shop is, generally speaking, far superior, and … more economical'. She uses it in mulligatawny soup, curried beef (with beer), mutton, and rabbit, all ways of using up leftovers.[54] Note the association with leftovers: is this the source of the old canard that spices hide rotting meat?

While recipes dated from 1747, curry had been available in restaurants from the late eighteenth century; its first appearance on a menu was at the Coffee House in Norris Street, Haymarket, London, in 1773, but the first establishment dedicated to Indian cuisine was the Hindostanee Coffee House at 34 George Street, Portman Square, in 1809, as recorded in *The Epicure's Almanack*. It was opened by Dean Mahomet (from Patna, Bihar, India, via Cork in Ireland). He offered a house 'for the Nobility and Gentry where they might enjoy the Hookha with real Chilm tobacco and Indian dishes of the highest perfection'. The decor was very colonial, with bamboo chairs. Like many 'coffeehouses', it did not serve coffee, but was simply cashing in on a popular name of the time. It was not a success; Mahomet had to file for bankruptcy in 1812, although the restaurant did carry on without him in some form until 1833.[55]

And yet curry – from the English point of view – may be one of the first examples of what Jeremy MacClancy calls eating the other.[56] Ordinarily, human beings are resistant to novelty, but by the coming of the East India Company, London consumers at least were encouraged to value the exotic. The adoption of both tea and coffee fostered the same ideas. It is not surprising that shortly afterwards curry and curry-related recipes began to find their way into English recipe books. Of course, curry is not really an Indian dish at all, and its story in England is about the re-creation of small elements of Indian spicing in terms that could be understood by English diners. The word curry had been first used in English during the reign of Elizabeth I; according to the *OED* the word comes from the Tamil *kari* sauce, a relish for rice, whence comes Portuguese *caril*.

From the mid-eighteenth century, the interchanges of names and tastes in England were driven more and more by the widening empire. Increasingly, the English of all classes visited places like India, not as tourists, but as part of the staff of empire. Young and posh youths might have been in the Indian Civil Service in the Punjab, meeting their wives out there and settling, while middling boys might have been in the army, first as lieutenants and later with the rank of major. The working classes, meanwhile, would have had their first chance to be waited on by others as their scions became first privates and then sergeants in the army, marrying, then moving to a bungalow on the hot plains.

At first, there was an adaptation process, because the Indian cooks and servants only knew how to prepare Indian food. The English gentry families attended the occasional Maharajah feast, but even their everyday fare had to shift. Beef and pork were often unobtainable because of the respective religious restrictions of Hindus and Muslims. 'The result was that we had to fall back on mutton, usually very tough, or the equally tough chicken which was the staple diet of many of us in India.'[57]

When the army and civil service wives, the memsahibs, took charge, adaptation was largely abandoned. Most of them had no wish to adapt to or understand Indian cuisine. We can learn a lot about the Raj household from the books of advice they consulted, such as Flora Annie Steel and Grace Gardiner's book *The Complete Indian Housekeeper and Cook*, first published in 1888. Steel and Gardiner listed huge numbers of desirable foods, all crazily English, and all difficult to make or source in India, and then, very grudgingly, eight 'native dishes', with the warning that 'most native recipes are inordinately greasy and sweet' but 'your native cooks invariably know how to make them fairly well'.[58] The recipes included Burtas, which were 'useful in using up the remains' of vegetables served in very English ways; a vegetable curry, dal and dal pooree, dumpoke – boned chicken with a forcemeat made from boiled rice, herbs and hard-boiled eggs: 'stuff chicken with this, and braise it gently'. Also included were mutton curry, with curry powder – the idea of freshly ground spices was alien to Steel and Gardiner – and kidgeree and pilau. The idea that there was not one single 'native' cuisine, but many, had yet to dawn. All Indians were 'natives', and 'native cooks' were portrayed throughout as profoundly uncooperative. Chicken was present as a fricassee: the only style of cooking that Steel and Gardiner liked besides English was French.

'Indian cooks put ground almonds in the sauce,' said Steel and Gardiner. 'This is a mistake.' Note the entire lack of compromise. It was a mistake. It just was, even though the memsahibs' medieval ancestors had also used almonds to thicken sauces. 'The milk in which the bird has been boiled will of course make the sauce.'[59] Clearly, the 'native' wanted to thicken the sauce with almond rather than milk precisely because almond was safer in heat and also had more flavour. Never mind that the milk wouldn't thicken the sauce the way almond would. Chicken rolls consisted of boned chicken squares filled with rice, breadcrumbs and chopped bacon. These were then stewed in milk, later reduced to make a velouté; flavourless, heavy, dull and dry.

The memsahibs may have thought they should extend their civilisation to the natives; colonial subjects feel it incumbent upon them to repeat and maintain the norms of 'home' far more diligently than those actually at home do. In India it was the privileged, isolated women who created ludicrously inappropriate menus. They were often young, and very homesick. Their husbands were constantly away. And so they planned dinner parties that tried very hard to bring 'home' to life around them like a protective shield against the local culture.

In her magisterial history of curry, Lizzie Collingham suggests that English disdain for Indian food was due to the desire to keep up 'with fashions back home'. What she doesn't say is *why* food in India became an act of placation of unseen forces 'back home' or why the usual defensive reactions of the exiled colonial subject came suddenly into play. The cause is almost certainly the events of 1857–8, often known as the Indian Mutiny, sometimes as the Rising or as the First War of Indian Independence, an event in which clashing food cultures were enmeshed from the very beginning.

The rebellion was triggered by rumours about food differences: allegedly, the British had put pork fat and tallow on cartridges, forcing their loyal sepoys to violate their religious dietary taboos in biting off the cartridge paper. The sepoys and their communities may have responded in kind. British officials in the northern parts of India were repeatedly sent chapattis; to this day, nobody knows exactly why, but it has been suggested that they acted like chain letters, with each community feeling obliged to send them on to its own British garrison lest they be left 'holding' cholera; this practice, *chalauwa*, could even be read as a mild form of bioterrorism.[60] Some merchants also alleg-edly sold hugely underpriced flour, or *atta*, which turned out to be ground pig and cow bones. What little commensality and gastronomic trust there was between the two sides collapsed. Physical differences and the dread of 'going native' were a part of Raj culture; particularly troubling were the 'Eurasian women' with whom husbands consorted while their wives were in the hills for the hot weather, and children raised by nurses, ayahs, who waited on them hand and foot.

Food was also a flashpoint in towns under siege. The townspeople refused to sell food to the Europeans at Cawnpore, though the rebel leader in the area – Nana Sahib, or Dhondu Pant – allegedly had a larder stuffed with goodies from Fortnum & Mason.[61] Cawnpore was a trading city, with many day labourers and artisans, and it was also a meeting and clashing point of cultures. The siege of Cawnpore was marked by lack of access to water. Harrowing tales were told of women and children without water in 120-degree heat, and their sorties to the water wells, the sick with blackened tongues and the children sucking on empty goatskins.[62] Having starved and parched, the survivors were then attacked by cleaver-wielding butchers, and the bodies thrown down the dry well. The rebels' crime was avenged by acts of eating. Rebels confessing to or believed to be involved in the massacre were forced to lick the clotted blood from the floor and walls of the Bibighar compound, where the women and children had been held and killed, while being whipped. The sepoys were then religiously disgraced by being forced to eat (or force fed) beef (if Hindu) or pork (if Muslim). The Muslim sepoys were sewn into pig skins before being hanged, and low-caste Hindu street sweepers were employed to execute the high-caste Brahmin rebels to add additional religious disgrace and pollution to their punishment.[63]

After the rebellion had been crushed, the Raj formally took over India, moving the British presence in India from uneasy alliance to occupation. This meant that the British lived more with one another than with the maharajahs, fortifying the new sense of ethnic and hier-archical distinction. The cholera epidemics which coincided with the rebellion made the British even more uncomfortable with the heat, the

Indians and the local food. So the rebellion and its atrocities, the sense of betrayal that it engendered, the onward march of technology allowing access to tinned food, the growth of theories of racial difference and hierarchy, the cholera pandemics, and finally the way in which this pressure made the officers and men huddle together in compounds rather than mingling with the Indians … all these led directly, as we shall see in the next chapter, to the predominance of new and hideous tinned dinners.

Sometimes Indian men would dine English-style, but their wives would maintain Indian ways. But on the whole the Indian middle classes felt no urge to eat with the English, in part because the Hindu caste system meant they were impure. Orthodox Brahmins had to bathe after contact with Europeans. Muslims were sometimes more flexible, as long as no pork was served. Vegetarianism among Hindus was also a problem. The royal families of India carried their own food on trains; the cooks prepared 'tiffin carrriers', holding curries, rice, lentils, curds and sweets. But after this first meal, you were in the hands of railway caterers, and it was in this way that Gayatri Devi met with the dull meals called 'curry' by the occupying power. These were sold at stations, and called 'railway curries', 'no beef, forbidden to Hindus, no pork, forbidden to Muslims', so lamb or chicken curries, and vegetables. The value of chicken in India was that it was forbidden to nobody. Like many creolised meals, these curries represented a lowest common denominator, easy to read as a betrayal by both sides.

The elaborate cooked breakfasts of Victorian great houses were a feature of the height of the Raj, and yet Victorian Britishness came to seem dated even in India after the First World War. In 1856, breakfast at Government House in Calcutta might include fish, meat, eggs, fresh fruit and dessert, with hot chocolate to drink; yet in 1893, Steel and Gardner complain that breakfasts 'are for the most part horrible meals'. But after the war, Jennifer Brennan says her family had fresh yoghurt in little pottery containers, silky and delicious, and piles of hot chapattis, with freshly churned butter and whisky marmalade, all served on white and blue Minton china. In the cold weather, the hunting season, there were just a few thin fingers of toast, then the hunt breakfast after a few jackals had been dispatched. Hunt breakfasts were hearty, consisting of mixed grills and egg dishes, and a hunt cup. Yet how creolised is this food? Devilled eggs, for example, are an English club food pushed into India, not a true hybrid, even when further hybridised with the addition of a spoonful of mango chutney. Eggs feature strongly. Before the Mutiny, Harriet Tytler could write that 'an omelette is never cooked to such perfection anywhere as by an Indian cook', and this respect and affection was retrieved for the most part after 1920.[64] Soon kedgeree came into play (though there had been many dishes of moderately similar names from the fourteenth century onwards): 'Wyvern' explains that kedgeree 'of the English type' omits the turmeric, though he also uses strips of green ginger, crisply fried onions and thin slices of chilli, while Brennan's recipe restores the chilli, but not the ginger or turmeric.

Some successful hybrid dishes take in the difference of India. The best known was Country Captain. According to David Burton, the 'country' just means 'Indian' (as with 'country parsley', coriander), and the captain is one in charge of sepoys, so the name suggests a truly colonial dish. (It might, however, refer to the captain of a ship.) The chicken is flavoured with chilli and turmeric, fried in a pan in ghee. Some recipes add onion, some add garlic. Simla chicken, which also speaks of the Raj and of the hills, had a sauce of whipped cream flavoured with ginger, mustard and Worcester sauce. Anglo-Indian recipes are often for jointed chicken, the quick cooking answerable to the leathery flesh of the local birds.[65] In Rudyard Kipling's novel *Kim*, 'rice and good curry, cakes all warm and well scented with *hing* (asafoetida), curds and sugar' exemplify Kim's own status as the colonial child, hybrid and interracial.[66] All such food involves negotiation and compromise, in which each culture gives up something and takes on something else.

When the English returned to England, a culture shock awaited them. They had often longed for 'home' and retirement, but once there they struggled, plagued by their comparative insignificance in 'the busy world of England'. In Alice Perrin's 1912 novel *The Anglo-Indians*, the Fleetwood family's life in India involves a large bungalow surrounded by an orange grove, where they employ thirty servants and live lavishly and generously, enjoying hunting, riding and entertaining. After retirement, they are mystified by the fact that everyone in a large crowd is white, and feel themselves to be suddenly and unfairly invisible. Higher prices were another hurdle. So too were the staff, paid decent wages but condemned in the same terms as the Indians had been; 'the modern maid will leave a gas-jet burning in one room while she sits in another'.[67] Clubs were a help, especially the East India Club in St James's. India-sick homecomers began to look for curry.

In 1897 Indian G. B. Pillai published *London and Paris through Indian Spectacles*. 'Once on board the steamer you begin to eat English dinners', he noted disconsolately. He, too, sought out curry in England. The curry houses, he thought, were horrifying. Whole toasted spice had been bastardised into powder mixes. The places where he ate decent curry were socially marginal – lascar cafés on docksides in London and Bristol. There is a marvellous lost story here, of perhaps the first unadulterated ethnic restaurants in England, dockside dives run by sailors for other sailors, where the spices were fresh off the boats. If only we knew what had been on the menu. The lascar seamen, as they were called, were actually the key makers of the curry house; few of them would have prepared home-cooked meals back home, and in England they were forced to adapt as the English had been forced – or refused – to alter in India. Veeraswamy began at the British Empire Exhibition in 1924; it was really just for the Anglo-Indian community.[68] It was opened in Regent Street in 1926 by Edward Palmer, the great-grandson of an English soldier and an Indian princess. In its early years, Veeraswamy served Anglo-Indian cuisine, the food of the British Raj, not the food of India, mulligatawny soup and 'curry'.[69] It is still open.

Modern Indians living in Britain have also created their own creolised cuisine. *Cooking like Mummyji: Real British Asian Cooking* is the latest testament to the angular marriage of British and Indian food. Vicky Bhogal's book offers a Punjabi-English crossover diet. It might not appeal strongly to everyone, but it represents a tranche of the British middle-class diet not usually discussed. Her recipe for Tandoori

Chicken is, she says, a dish usually eaten only at parties and weddings. There is also the homier Thariwala Chicken, where four eat from two chicken legs, and the clubbable-sounding 'devilish butter chicken', fast and rich, with chicken breasts, butter, and the kind of coloration Indian chefs offered the Raj, here provided by red food colouring.[70] Canned tomatoes feature often; so does garam masala. She offers her own history, or testimony, of how this style of cooking came into being.

Immigrant lines of identity are drawn, but are also rubbed out. 'We don't use measurements. That's for English people. If you stand here long enough, and cook it over and over again, you will soon learn how much salt to put in.' For Vicky, English teen identity is at stake: 'I just wanted to know how to make it, not move permanently into the kitchen at the sacrifice of *Top of the Pops*.' Later, however, when it can be regarded with nostalgia, as is the way with all food, it becomes important. '[This is] not just for other British Asians … I have often thought it such a shame that the Western world is not let in on the secret of real Indian home cooking, as though it is a sort of long-standing trick, our last remaining jewel.' She sees other Asian cookbooks as 'geared towards the British curry-house fan', full of dishes 'no self-respecting Indian would ever cook or eat at home (and tend to be written by non-Asians) or … highly stylised and often complicated'.[71] She reminds us that when we ask about English food, we need to ask not only about the ethnic English. What are the Chatterjis eating? And the Lis? And the others – the Woiczinskis, the Biarams? What about the Greens, from Barbados?

Is English food just a question of going for a curry now? (Or a cheeky Nando's, of South African origin?) There's no denying that those choices are shaped, sometimes inexorably, by large global forces. The British Empire was not just a matter of wetter curries with fewer spices. It was a vast series of commercial enterprises that united in deploying a metaphor of sameness in difference. Indian tea and Australian dried fruit *were* British. The global reach of the empire on which the sun never set meant that in daily life the English could celebrate their own centrality to that world by eating breakfast brought from thousands of miles distant. What the Empire meant was that the produce of the world was raised for English tables (counting the other nations of the UK as part of the Empire).

———————

Oddly, most of the population of England in 1900 would have found fresh eggs as unfamiliar as curry. At the beginning of the twentieth century, few people had even tasted one freshly laid egg in their lives.[72]

In the medieval monastic diet, eggs had formed an important element. They were a substitute for meat for the poor, and observant and devout monks could imitate the poor by choosing to eat eggs as well as fish on fast days.[73] The tendency to substitute these foods for meat had the paradoxical effect of enhancing their status, making them appear more desirable as a form of the food of the rich. A diet of fish, cheese, eggs and vegetables became an increasingly common feature of most people's lives. To give up meat was no longer a gastronomic humiliation, but often a sign of identification with a specific religious community. And eggs, despite their lowly status, were a fresh food, and thus had a rich image; the food of the poor tended to be durable, dried meat, preserved dairy, grains and legumes and nuts.

But by the nineteenth century, and despite their vagaries, and the impossibility of ensuring their freshness at the moment they were bought, eggs became more and more popular, and by the First World War, they were a common sight in spring. Hens evidently stopped laying in midsummer as eggs became scarce between early August and the end of February, giving meaning to the idea of an Easter egg.[74] Older eggs were preserved by pickling and boiling. Even so, they were too expensive for most ordinary people. It follows that many baked goods associated with fresh eggs could not be widely made until the egg trade had matured, which in some areas happened only after the Second World War. Fresh eggs became associated with breakfast because hens mostly lay in the morning. In her recipe book *The Country Housewife's Book*, Lucy Yates wrote in 1934 about the importance of preserving and pickling eggs. Her methods were designed to ensure that the plentiful egg supply of spring and early summer was stored for use in winter. Each egg could be rubbed with a greasy rag, or painted with water glass (isinglass, a collagen gel). She insisted that the laid egg must be cold before it was preserved, but also that an egg more than twenty-four hours old should not be preserved, so the window was small. Once preserved, the eggs should be kept in a cool cellar. She also recommended pickled eggs and lemon curd as a way of preservation. The egg shortages were eventually resolved by improved breeds. Chickens in the wild may lay as few as thirty eggs a year. By contrast, the best modern layer is the white Leghorn, who will lay between 230 and 300 eggs during her most fertile two-year laying period.

The favourite food of the First World War soldier was egg and chips. Perhaps because many Tommies came from very poor backgrounds, in which eggs had been a treat, the men were overjoyed when local French couples managed to set up egg and chip shops. Many officers commented on the amazing number of eggs that the men could eat at once. Partly this was because the incessant preserved beef got boring. But it was also because eating eggs in a café or eating house had been a pre-war treat. Eggs were plain, easily digestible, tasty, unthreatening.[75] They were not a regular part of the ration, but they were fed to sick and wounded men as part of an invalid diet in military hospitals. A surviving letter from a nurse reassured a soldier's mother that her boy was 'very fond of a little champagne and an egg with his tea'.[76] Eggs were reliable because you could easily tell if they had gone bad, unlike meat products. It's also possible that the egg represented a cosy feminine and maternal comfort, further symbolised by the French women who took on the job of feeding the hungry troops. One soldier remarked that 'these French women know how to cook!' By which he meant that he had had a 'ripping fine egg and chips'. In contrast, the French were unable to satisfy the alien appetites for a suet pudding and treacle, though one hungry soldier who asked for it got a jam omelette instead.[77]

Some families did try sending live chickens to the trenches because they were so popular; the meat was more manageable, although at least one soldier had to throw away a chicken because it had been on the road too long by the time he received it.[78] One ingenious mother packed so brilliantly that she was able to send fresh eggs. Chicken became popular because, like eggs, it was not included in the soldiers' rations. Officers could order a hamper for themselves from Fortnum & Mason or Harrods. One regiment enjoyed a Harrods hamper every week.[79] One posh captain demanded a brace of partridges be sent each week from the family estate, and complained about the quality of the Fortnum's parcels. Other officers received special parcels from their estates; Douglas Gillespie received a brace of grouse, sent from Scotland by his parents, which his servants left on the side of a trench for a day and a half in the sun. They were ruined.[80] At Courcelles, Graham Greenwell was shelled for thirty-six hours, but recovered 'after a really excellent English breakfast of porridge, kippers, and eggs and bacon'. Those who were servants to the officers commented wryly that you couldn't expect them to do without the good food to which they were accustomed.

Rationing in the Second World War meant that eggs became something of an obsession on the Home Front. Without fat and animal protein, virtually all wartime diets led to a nagging sensation of hunger even if in theory daily calorie needs were being met.[81] That nagging sensation could easily become a craving. It followed that the food you couldn't have was the food for which you longed: eggs. In 1940, millions of commercially farmed hens had to be killed and sold off as food, as there was a shortage of feed. This led to an egg shortage, and rationing of one egg per person per week. Expectant mothers and vegetarians were allowed two eggs a week. Eggs could be kept fresher for a bit longer by rubbing them with lard to seal the pores, or for longer periods, by storing them in crocks under water with isinglass or waterglass mixed in (as in the method recommended by Yates, mentioned above), or by turning them into pickled eggs.

Consequently, some people started keeping chickens in their back gardens, because that meant you had unrationed eggs. The catch was that you had to give up your egg ration, but you were entitled to grain rations instead for your chickens. The Savoy Hotel in London had its own chicken farm, set up by Hugh Wontner, managing director of the hotel from 1941 to 1979. This supplied the Savoy with its own unrationed source of chicken and eggs. (They were still required to ration them on their restaurant menus to customers, however.) In theory, rationing applied to the royal family as well – even they were issued ration books, and had to register at merchants to use them. Ingenious people found ways to feed their new flocks, including National Flour, officially called 'wheatmeal'. While not quite whole wheat flour (in order to be a bit of a compromise), all the bran was left in it. It was greyish in colour. Some women in desperation would sift it through their nylon stockings (if they had them) to get white flour; if you kept chickens, the bran sifted out could go to make a ration-free chicken mash.

America produced huge quantities of powdered egg, which the British never liked but had to eat because it was often all there was. Everybody hated dried egg. It existed because the egg was concentrated and took up only 20 per cent of the shipping space required for fresh eggs. From July 1942 onwards – courtesy of America – there was National Dried Egg. Every four weeks, each British household received a packet of dried egg supposedly equivalent to a dozen fresh eggs. Egg powder was used to make omelettes and scrambled eggs. But it didn't behave like egg. However much it was whipped into a froth it didn't aerate anything. Jill Beattie remembered a breakfast of 'a 2 inch block of hard scrambled egg oozing with water which saturated the half slice of so-called toast beneath it. And the taste – ugh.'[82]

Guidance was provided on how to use dried and powdered egg. A farmhouse scramble meant adding water to dried egg with some mixed cooked vegetables. In theory, carefully reconstituted eggs could be turned into a boiled egg by being poured into a small greased ramekin and then set in a pan with a little boiling water. Egg Champ could be made using leftover green vegetables and potatoes. 'If you've never made custard with dried eggs, you've no idea how easy it is,' screamed an advertisement. You made it with water … and a teaspoon of sugar. Dried egg powder was used as a raising agent in cakes too, and this same dried egg could be reconstituted and fried, yielding a dull, yellow, rubbery-like apology for the light and fluffy real thing. Dehydrated eggs were known as 'dreggs' by the British soldier. The fraudulent, well-intentioned, nutritional recipes of the war were designed to discourage people from noticing what they were eating, in case it was horrible, as it often was. This was also the era that popularised Bird's Custard, a completely egg-free compound invented for a woman with an egg allergy.

One Mass Observation diary keeper living in London, a housewife and voluntary worker, clearly middle class because she has maids in the plural, illustrates the anxiety provoked by food shortages. What worried her most was shortages of eggs. She was well educated, and understood that her three- and two-year-old children needed fat and protein in their diets to thrive. 'The egg shortage seems to be getting a bit serious. I've heard of one or two people who have had difficulty in getting any eggs at all. It looks as though [those of us who] did not lay any eggs down are going to suffer for our folly.' She took up the subject with her egg supplier, a Kent farmer who came up to London every Friday. He assured her that she could rely on him 'letting us have whatever eggs he could every week'. On 17 July, however: 'Eggs are still more or less unobtainable … Eggs are an important food especially when meat and fats are short.' The next day, she took decisive action: 'I've actually managed to collect three dozen eggs, mostly in threes from each shop … What a triumph! … They should see the children through the winter all right.' She preserved them in isinglass, and added that 'the local delicatessen informs me I can have a dozen eggs from there if I don't mind paying four shillings'. She was aware that this was illegal, and that the government price was 2s 9d. But she reassured herself with tales of other people's cheating, and blaming the government, since the egg shortage was caused by a shortage of chicken feed. This in turn was caused by the government's failure to store maize for food, and exacerbated by its drive to encourage everyone to keep backyard hens. As a result, she argued, feed was squandered on local, inexpert poultry keepers. Meanwhile, expert poultry keepers could sell their eggs locally for the maximum legal price, and therefore had nothing to gain by sending them to the towns – all stemming from the government's decision that eggs were not an essential food.[83]

All of which illustrates the fact that the generally accepted history of rationing needs qualification. We were not all in it together, not really. Most tried their utmost to get out of being all in it together. Part of the rosy way in which rationing is presented has to do with the far less successful effort at rationing during the First World War, in which at one point the country was a week away from running out of food. Rationing plans for war were made as early as 1936. As international relations worsened, women's magazines began to provide more advice on emergency preparation, urging housewives to add a tin to the larder every week. As soon as war broke out, the government set up the Ministry of Food, and to prevent profiteering the prices of the most important foods were controlled. One of the foods with a fixed price was eggs, and another was butter. (Where there were no price controls, prices rose very sharply; a pineapple in 1944 cost five guineas.) The Ministry of Food also took control of all food imports, and initially tried to introduce standard brands of margarine and tea, but there was an outcry and soon commercial brands were back. The Ministry of Food was not only keen to manage the nation's food supply so as to prevent civil unrest and pressure for peace, it was also eager to reform the nation's diet. When sugar was rationed, the Ministry pointed out that its carbohydrates could be easily obtained from vegetables, or oatmeal, along with nutrients that sugar lacked.

In June 1941 eggs in the shell were further rationed to one egg as often as supplies permitted. This worked out at about three per month. Children, expecting mothers and invalids got more. Rationing something made its arrival seem more valuable. Allegedly, the Royal Air Force during the war had a standing joke: 'if you don't come back, can I have your egg?' Alongside all this, the black market flourished. Anything that was rationed or price controlled was likely to be traded on the black market, and – as we have seen – this meant that money could talk very loudly. There was a flourishing exchange system in the countryside, none of which was available to city-dwellers because of restrictions on travel.

Nancy Jackman was cook for a large family in Norfolk during the war. She recalled that 'the family I worked for fiddled the system shamelessly. You see they thought they had been born with an entitlement to a certain standard of living and they really thought that poorer people were better equipped to live on less – even during the war. I don't think there was any nastiness in it.' She first noticed when 'extra eggs began to be delivered to the kitchen door now and then – and I mean a lot of extra eggs – and large parcels of meat would come pretty regularly. Then the penny dropped. It was all black market stuff. The meat and eggs and butter were all delivered by a man I'd never seen before and there were never any bills – or at least none that came to me. He would just drop everything on the big kitchen table and leave without saying a word. The amounts were pre-war quantities – huge joints, and butter by the pound.' It all came from a relative of her employer who owned a large estate in Suffolk. Nancy was horrified to be told in a note that the servants' meal should continue to reflect the current rationing situation. 'The mean old devil wanted me to continue to cook spuds and cabbage for the servers while the family enjoyed all the black market stuff.' She ignored it. She considered informing the authorities, but knew that it would mean losing her job.[84]

By 1955, with rationing over, the English were eating four eggs a day, rising to five in 1970. Despite famous campaigns, such as 'Go to Work on an Egg', launched by the British Egg Marketing Board in 1954, attributed to novelist Fay Weldon and starring comedian Tony Hancock, consumption had dropped to two by 2000. One reason was health advice about avoiding cholesterol in eggs, a misunderstanding since eggs are not a main source of the kind of cholesterol that can contribute to heart disease. Another was the salmonella scare provoked in 1988 when health minister Edwina Currie claimed that most of Britain's egg production was infected with the salmonella bacterium.[85]

Bacon and egg flan, eggs in onion sauce, kedgeree, eggs baked in potatoes: the food of the poor, according to Jocasta Innes, whose *Pauper's Cookbook* of 1971 offered to tell the less well-off how to eat well. Besides eggs, there was the inevitable chicken Maryland, but also the boiled chicken and chicken legs of cheap mass-produced chicken.

The first chapter of Delia Smith's 1978 book was about eggs, and now quality had become an issue. She mentioned free-range eggs, and suggested that these would have richer-coloured yolks, due to the hens' ability to browse on grasses. Recipes are given for the most obvious kinds of eggs, including boiled eggs. These are mostly overtly French in character, significantly adapted to the English public. A cheese soufflé, for example, can be made with 'any hard cheese', while the hollandaise can be made in a blender. Smith represents a new compromise between the old-fashioned kind of French haute cuisine, modern agriculture, modern supermarkets and British family circumstances. Her recipes are accounts of how to do familiar things. Later, Smith reissued her *How to Cook* course, with a first book entirely devoted to eggs, which provoked much negative comment. It is however an illustration of how far she felt the nation had drifted from cooking and understanding ingredients at all.

By the second decade of the twenty-first century, Innes' replacement Jack Monroe is much less interested in eggs as staples, and much more interested in pulses. She does have a recipe for 'Majorly' curried eggs, which she clearly sees as an ironic comment on Empire. Monroe is a social justice warrior in the best sense, who has toyed with vegetarianism and veganism, and her recipe specifies free-range eggs despite their extra cost. Her recipes are about vegetables, and her egg recipe of choice is chachouka.

Until the twentieth century, elaborate chicken recipes were relatively unusual. Florence White's comprehensive *Good Things in England*, for example, lists recipes for chicken galantine, chicken pudding and stewed chicken with – perhaps inevitably – a 'Madras chicken curry'. That's it, under chicken. The chicken galantine used an entire chicken, with a veal cutlet and fat bacon; the stewed chicken was the young chicken with lemon peel and lemon juice, and came from eighteenth-century Worcester. The chicken pudding, from the first half of the nineteenth century in Kent, was a whole chicken baked in a basin lined with suet crust, with ham and parsley. White pointed out that it could have been baked in a cloth before the coming of the basin.[86] The assumption was that all chicken is whole. It is not until chicken is sold in pieces that recipes for those pieces really proliferate.

The pre-eminent gourmet of his time was Auguste Escoffier, the man who separated meat and sauce, and who brought to fruition the trends set in motion by La Varenne. Escoffier had an enormous influence on restaurant cuisine everywhere. Thoroughly French, he revolutionised restaurant kitchens and made them disciplined, ordered places through his work at the London Savoy, Ritz and Carlton Hotels from 1890 to 1920 and his creation of the brigade system. His *Le Guide Culinaire* is still in print in English. Escoffier's book begins with Sauces, forty-one pages of them – and his recipes are on the skimpy side. He starts with stock, then moves to glazes, simple reductions of stock, and then to the roux. Only then does he begin on sauces proper. These too are an Enlightenment encyclopedia, divided into small compound brown sauces, small compound white sauces (which include sauce Béarnaise), hot English sauces, in their own special section, full of mustard and horseradish, gooseberries and oysters, and above all, Reform sauce, which to a modern palate is very odd (sauce espagnole, a beef-stock gravy, turned into sauce poivrade, then reduced with added chopped ham and tongue and chopped gherkins, with sliced egg white). The separation of gravy from roast meat might be seen as an adaptation of Escoffier's method to English cooking. Escoffier gave dozens of recipes for chicken supremes, or breasts. Most are called after English noble families or regions of France. In his introduction, he commented on the different cuts of supremes, such as cutlets (supremes with the bone in). It is very clear that it is in the lengthy section of his cookbook covering this particular cut that its popularity originates.[87]

Agnes Jekyll's 1922 *Kitchen Essays* also anticipated the enormous post-war move to jointed chicken. Jekyll, the sister of gardening guru Gertrude Jekyll, certainly did not represent popular taste. But she did give a recipe for chicken Maryland as a remedy for those who were too thin – it seemed you could be too thin in 1922, whatever the Duchess of Windsor said. You had to joint the chicken yourself into what are mysteriously called slices and joints. The chicken was fried in butter, and then placed in a stew pan with a pint of cream.[88] This was close to Escoffier's recipe, though he does not try to make the sauce in the same pan as the chicken. Jekyll also had a recipe for chicken pilaf, in a section of her book called 'Cottage Hospitality': onions fried in butter to pale brown, then a pinch of saffron and two cups of rice. So far, so authentically risotto. Then two ounces of stoned raisins. Then a braised pheasant or chicken, with the rice heaped at the other end with well-fried onion rings and a few split almonds. She also noted that children's tastes are simple and instinctive, like their religion, and adds that 'chicking, please' is still their birthday choice. Since the chicken comes with bread sauce, it is probably roasted.[89]

During the interwar period, the British public's enthusiasm for chicken grew even more, documented particularly in a number of mass observation studies. D. M. Bates, a thirty-one-year-old inspector of taxes, was typical of those who enjoyed chicken for Christmas dinner: '[his] mother cooked the chicken with stuffing ... [they had] roast chicken, sausage, potatoes, sprouts from the garden, Christmas pudding (which he delighted in because it was set alight, tea, and biscuits'. His tastes were widely shared. Describing dinner in November 1937, 'the menu,' reported another mass observer, 'was some hors d'oeuvres, sole bonne femme, chicken, and a sweet'.[90] In 1938, a twenty-four-year-old architectural assistant in Liverpool reported on an Easter Sunday lunch that followed the same lines – grapefruit, roast chicken, baked apple pudding, coffee and chocolate biscuits. Roast chicken had pushed out roast pig and roast beef and become associated with major festivals and particular pleasure. Chickens were ordered in advance for Christmas Day, though deliveries could go wrong: one unlucky customer in 1937 ordered his chicken and Christmas cake from the Army and Navy stores, but they were not delivered in time.[91]

There were no recipes for chicken in wartime cookbooks. Other poultry could be imitated. There are recipes for mock duck, mock soups. But no effort was made to impersonate chicken, and that was one reason why it was missed. Contra Elizabeth David, who moaned about bowls of collected fat and its likely rancidity, wartime cook-books gave detailed directions on how to clarify fat to enable it to keep and to be used for cake-making or pastry. The result would be a mixture of lard and beef dripping, very much the kind of fat already used in regional baking. Before mass production, chicken was virtually fat-free, and therefore not very amenable to this kind of reuse.

While turning off your tastebuds had become a patriotic act, there was still memory. English people remained devoted to their memories of chicken as a festive dinner. The wartime diary of a teacher in Surrey reports that in November 1943 'we had a gala festivity! One of the aged ladies from the poultry run at school, guillotined and boiled with white sauce! A red letter day and a whole wing for each of us! The moment we sat down to eat it the siren blew.' She was on fire watch, but she ignored it until she had finished the chicken.

The austerity of the post-war era was if anything harder to bear than wartime rationing. The black market continued to flourish. Attitudes to it softened as the rationale for fair shares for all faded. Efforts to shore up national morale with films like *Here Come the Huggetts*, in which the Huggetts went abroad and complained that there weren't any queues, could not stave off the sense of bleakness. Nationalised food is always a problematic concept; we may eat at a table, but we also eat as individuals. Food remained in short and often poor-quality supply. Many of the chickens available, Marguerite Patten recalled of 1946, were elderly boiling fowls who had given good service in laying eggs, and were killed and sold for meat. They needed prolonged cooking to make them tender. If the birds were simmered, not boiled, the result was tender chicken, plus excellent stock with a thin layer of precious fat on top which could be used in cooking.[92] By 1947, however, she was suggesting chicken roll for entertaining. This required only a small chicken, eked out with breadcrumbs into a steamed pudding with hard-boiled eggs, which might even be powdered egg reconstituted. It could be served hot or cold. The point was that it claimed to serve eight people with just one chicken; portions would clearly not have been large.[93] In 1949, Patten recommended chicken pudding, with a suet crust pastry and a filling made of diced chicken and sliced onions. It was designed to be cooked in one of the new pressure cookers.

Three years later, Patton presented the far more French and high-culture quenelles, made with minced raw chicken and either real or reconstituted dried egg. These may well have been a fair distance from the extravagant French version made with choux pastry. Cooks could make bacon and chicken toast to use up leftover cooked chicken as a kind of open sandwich. The chicken could be extended with the addition of cooked rice, in which case it was a chicken terrapin.[94] Perhaps the grimmest food is that contained in Patten's victory cookbook, which was supposed to feature celebratory meals. Inevitably, they include chicken Maryland, reimagined again for British readers. A chicken mould involved deploying cold chicken from an elderly hen, with dried egg, turnip, carrots and dried mixed herbs. More interesting and probably considerably better tasting were the black pudding casserole and the sheepshead roll, offering a way to manage a sheep's head for those who had never cooked it before, with vegetables, garlic, cloves and mace, and herbs. It advocated using the brains. It would have been nourishing. It would have been interesting. It did not pass into English cooking. Though to be fair, nor did the chicken chop. This appeared to be a curry, made with chilli pepper, lemon, cayenne pepper, turmeric, fresh ginger, cinnamon and dates. It is advertised in Patten's cookbook as one of her favourite meals from West Africa.[95] All this food is dispiriting in the same way. It relies on making a bland meat even more bland.

Remembered with deep affection by many post-war Britons, the *Constance Spry Cookery Book* first appeared in 1956, just as rationing had finally come to an end. For many people, Constance Spry meant more than Elizabeth David as a way out of the greyness of rationing, back into a modified and modernised version of what they had loved before the war. The twentieth chapter, on poultry and game, was written at the very moment when industrial chicken-rearing methods were changing the basis of chicken cookery. Spry more or less ignored that.

Her twenty pages of chicken recipes focused on roasting birds and their leftovers. She still thought it was worthwhile to give details of how to use an old and spent hen. Most of the recipes had French names, or French and English combinations rubbing shoulders awkwardly: chicken with orange, chicken with apple and bacon (à la normande), chicken bonne femme, but also boiled chicken. The recipes were reliable, sensible, and based on French hotel cooking between the wars. French methods were central to Spry's creations; she was especially committed to French methods of saucing and garnishing. It would be wrong to describe this food as inedible, but there is no doubt that it is unlikely to appeal to most diners under the age of sixty in the 2020s. It is stodgy and solid.

A special chapter, the Winkfield chapter, was directed at those ambitious cooks, cordon bleu graduates. Perhaps depressingly, the recipes in this section for chicken, taking up around ten pages, were largely about new ingredients, such as mango. Here surely is the embryonic coronation chicken.[96] Spry was said to have invented it with chef Rosemary Hume, also of the Cordon Bleu Cookery School in London. Preparing the food for the banquet at the coronation of Queen Elizabeth II in 1953, Spry proposed the recipe of cold chicken, curry cream sauce and dressing that would later become known as coronation chicken.[97] Food historian James McIntosh suggests that the original was an attempt by Spry tactfully to mix appropriate coronation splendour with the thrifty use of available ingredients, such as curry powder rather than fresh spices, which were not available.[98] The sauce was more complex than it is in modern versions. Spry included it in her 1956 cookbook as Poulet Reine Elizabeth. However, the original recipe did not contain mango or mango chutney, so it looks as if at some point the two chicken recipes were spliced together. Patten also gave a recipe called Coronation chicken, containing mayonnaise, halved apricots, fruit syrup and blanched almonds. She suggested adding chopped spring onions 'to give a more savoury taste'.[99] This version may not have particularly worried Spry, who was enthusiastic about exactly the kind of food on which Britain was to turn its back in the 1990s. However, her ways with chicken stretched into the world of the ready meal, with a recipe for chicken Kiev.

It's impossible to pinpoint an exact date when chicken in parts took over from whole chicken, because it was always possible to ask a butcher to take the breast fillets or supremes from a chicken. Some gourmet recipes fashionable in the interwar period use supremes of chicken – chicken marengo, chicken cacciatore. What made the use of chicken divided into parts normal was probably the popularity of American chicken Maryland – liked by Winston Churchill – and then, later, southern fried chicken in the form of Colonel Sanders and his fast food brand.

But the pre-jointed chicken also arose naturally from intensive chicken farming. This was the creation of a Californian businessman called John Kimber, who in 1934 realised that it would be more profitable to breed chickens to lay eggs, separately from breeding chickens for meat, and to rear the birds differently. The result was that chicken breasts in particular took over from chops, steak and sausages as the fast-cooking weekday meal. The white meat added a touch of luxury, but could withstand virtually any kind of sauce, so that it became a vehicle for food fashion. An undated cookbook from the early 1980s gives a good indication of the kind of chicken dish enjoyed when chicken breasts became widely available: chicken with mushrooms, rustic chicken casserole, chicken with honey glaze, saucy chicken and bacon casserole, lemon chicken – meant to be Chinese in style – with basil sauce, and creamy tarragon chicken. There is also a recipe for something called chicken risotto which is not a risotto at all and which illustrates the gulf between cooking in the early 1980s and cooking in the late 1990s. There is no Parmesan, everything is simply added to the pan together and boiled. I suppose a kind person might call it a pilaf; faux-Indian rather than faux-Italian.

I've been writing as though English enthusiasm for bland flavours is social. But it's possible that it may be innate. Studies of taste illustrate the fact there are super-tasters, whose abilities are genetically inherited.

There are normal tasters, and there are also people who barely taste at all. A turning point between these groups is bitter tastes; some people detect the bitter taste in tonic water – quinine – far more strongly than others, and similarly, there is a separate tongue receptor for the bitter flavours in broccoli and Brussels sprouts. Sensory scientists have additionally divided people into two groups. The first are food adventurers and the second are picky eaters, eaters who don't like things too sweet, too hot, too fatty or too spicy. By contrast, food adventurers are willing to be surprised even by intense flavours. Oddly, they resemble non-tasters in their food choices.[100]

This perhaps helps to explain Fanny Cradock. Marguerite Patten described Cradock as the saviour of British cooking after the war, and Delia Smith and Jamie Oliver have both cited her as an inspiration. Others were less complimentary; in the episode of the BBC series *The Way We Cooked* dedicated to Cradock and Graham Kerr, Keith Floyd and Hugh Fearnley-Whittingstall, among others, disparaged her methods and cooking skill. Despite their extravagant appearance and eccentricity, her recipes were extremely widely used and her cookery books sold in record numbers. English food has always been more about Fanny Cradock than about Elizabeth David.

She was as artificial as it was possible to be. One writer, who remembered being terrified of her as a child, described her as follows: 'with her imperious manner, heavily painted face, supercilious pencilled eyebrows and coiffed hair, she looked like a cross between Danny La Rue and Edna Everage'.[101] Despite claims to enjoy plain English fare, she espoused food colourings, piping bags and recipes like Jelly à la Zizi (layers of different-coloured jelly) and Green Cheese Ice Cream (her invention): ice cream with Gruyère cheese, dyed green. She added cream or flambéed brandy to everything. Journalist Simon Swift tried eating nothing but Fanny Cradock recipes for a week. They included Maypole Chicken – a roasted bird staked with a kebab skewer with peeled oranges hanging off – and the Green Cheese Ice Cream. Swift concluded that 'Cradock couldn't cook. Her food, like her own persona, is about disguise. Fanny wasn't her real name; she didn't grow up in a French chateau but in Leytonstone; she wasn't married to

Johnnie until two years after her cookery show ended.' The nation tolerated Cradock because rationing had already broken it in to disguising food as something other than what it was. It was ready to believe that the food was authentically glamorous because it used ingredients lavishly that had been hard to obtain during the war. Its intense preparation was aimed at the women who had flooded or been driven back into the home with the coming of peace and prosperity.[102] What Cradock promised was a try at restaurant food served at home. It didn't matter how it tasted. And she was followed by a series of television chefs, exactly at the time when fewer people were cooking for themselves: Keith Floyd, Delia Smith, Nigella Lawson, Jamie Oliver … Different styles appeared to offer people a choice.

In her 1978 cookery course, Delia Smith lamented the rise of the battery chicken, complaining that 'they are threaded onto rotisseries in shop windows in every High Street, there are chains of takeaway chicken shops, freezer centres are full of them. Any part or portion of a chicken can be bought separately.' She then added, 'it is a credit to our farmers that they put chicken within the reach of everyone at what, in these days, is a very reasonable price'.[103] Laboriously, she explained the reason that cheap chicken was flavourless, and particularly why frozen chicken lacked any kind of taste: it was slaughtered too young. She commended the large roaster as the best-flavoured bird available, specifying one of 6lb (2.75 kg) – far bigger than most birds from earlier eras for roast chicken; the breast should be covered with bacon, as with pheasant, and the body cavity stuffed with a mixture of pork sausage meat, breadcrumbs, onion and sage. She also gave recipes for older birds, though explaining that she had adapted them to modern birds: *coq au vin*, and also chicken in the pot.

―――――――

In food consumption, the new often has a hard time ousting tradition, including fairly recent tradition. In deepest, darkest Gloucestershire, each small town has a curry house. Always on the menu is chicken tikka masala, a mongrel dish where tinned soup meets real authentic spicing to lubricate and soothe. At Rafu's in Highworth, you can also have lamb or duck tikka. Or you can just get a ready meal out of the fridge; M&S do an individual portion of chicken tikka masala, with 400 calories.

Medieval and early modern doctors subscribed to a set of beliefs about the need for a diet that balanced the body with its environment. Like Ayurvedic Hindu medicine, medieval medicine saw pepper as warming, and as a preventative for fevers and colds. So a good peppery dish of chicken was not only itself in balance, but balanced the body too. Sugar was warm, more temperately warm than pepper, and so could be used to treat the same illnesses as pepper. In chilly weather, a mix of warm spices – one of which was sugar – could be combined with chicken because chicken was an easily digestible invalid food. So a chicken tikka masala is health food ... for the year 1500. It is this idea of dietetics which makes for the apparent overlap between the constituent parts of chicken tikka masala and the medieval chicken recipes we saw earlier.

Here are the ingredients from a modern recipe:

4 free-range skinless chicken breasts, cut into ½/1 cm cubes
2½ cm fresh ginger, peeled and grated
1 garlic clove, finely diced
Salt and pepper
½ cup/small handful fresh coriander, finely chopped, plus extra
    for garnish
Juice and zest of 1 lime
3 tbsp vegetable oil
1 tsp chilli powder
1 red onion, roughly chopped
1 tsp ground turmeric
1 tsp ground cumin
10 fl oz/250ml light/single cream or plain yoghurt
1 dessertspoon tomato puree
Juice of ½ lemon

Note the chilli powder, which is a New World food; the tomato purée, ditto, and the skinless chicken breasts. These are modernisations. Westernisations, even. This is traditional in the sense that it is a huge bodge job, ravaging many cuisines in the quest for ease.

Labour Foreign Secretary Robin Cook once announced chicken tikka masala as the new national dish of Great Britain. Food critics immediately responded by condemning it as merely a British invention. Chicken tikka masala, they sneered, was not a shining example of British multiculturalism but a demonstration of the British facility for reducing all foreign foods to their most unappetising and inedible forms. Rather than the inspired invention of an enterprising Indian chef, this offensive dish was dismissed as the result of an ignorant customer's complaint that his chicken tikka was too dry. When the chef whipped together a can of Campbell's tomato soup, some cream, and a few spices to provide gravy for the offending chicken, he produced a mongrel dish of which Britons now eat at least eighteen tons a week.[104] Cook's idea was based on the claim by Ahmed Aslam Ali to have invented the dish at his Shish Mahal restaurant in Glasgow: 'We used to make chicken tikka and one day a customer said "I'd take some sauce with that, this is a bit dry" so we cooked chicken tikka with the sauce which contains yoghurt, cream, spices.'

Although his claim has been dismissed as 'preposterous' by Delhi's leading food historians, the exact origins of the dish remain unclear. Zaeemuddin Ahmad, a chef at Delhi's Karim Hotel, which was established by the last chef of the last Mughal emperor Bahadur Shah Zafar, said the recipe had been passed down through the generations in his family: 'Chicken tikka masala is an authentic Mughlai recipe prepared by our forefathers who were royal chefs in the Mughal period. Mughals were avid trekkers and used to spend months altogether in jungles and far off places. They liked roasted forms of chickens with spices.'

Rahul Verma, Delhi's most authoritative expert on street food, said he first tasted the dish in 1971 and that its origins were in the Punjab. 'It's basically a Punjabi dish not more than forty to fifty years old and must be an accidental discovery which has had periodical improvisations,' he said. This sensible remark shows how pointless it is to claim ownership of any dish: they migrate and as they do so they shift. Hemanshu Kumar, the founder of Eating Out in Delhi, a food group which celebrates Delhi's culinary heritage, also ridiculed Glasgow's claim: 'Patenting the name chicken tikka masala is out of the question. It has been prepared in India for generations. You can't patent the name, it's preposterous.'[105]

This is really about two things. One is the resetting of the national palate to something amazingly close to the default settings of the later, post-Crusading Middle Ages, where spices and richness combined to make for an intensity of flavour that could be 'carried' best by gamey meat, but could be reasonably deftly mapped on to the elderly boiler or richly fed capon. The second is the equation between chicken tikka and a 'new' British identity of multiculturalism, where to be British is no longer to crave well-done roast beef or flour-based gravy, but dishes and ingredients from the (former) Empire. Adding tomato and cream – wherever it was first done – changes the dish's texture so that it becomes more familiar to an English diner, moister and also both sweeter and tarter; moreover, it mitigates the spice flavours and reduces them to something milder. Similar changes will occur in the dish's aroma. The dish is therefore partially naturalised and made acceptable. Because English diners deal constantly with cold and damp, the warmth and fattiness of the spiced food are themselves appealing. Reducing the spices' warming impact will create greater appetite bounce-back.

At the same time there's something novel here, something unusual. 'What do we know of England, who only England know?' Here are the balti houses, the kebab vans. Now that we no longer have an empire, we can at least eat the world. But strong tastes have come to correlate with masculinity, too, as Lizzie Collingham notes: the lager-drinking lads' culture is also the culture of tikka and vindaloo – perhaps with chips. But while Collingham sees chip shops as immigrant-led, and as a respite from boring British food, this ignores the extent to which this kind of food was always the food of the very poor, especially the cracklings, fragments of batter denuded of fish: its mating with curry is an unusual transgression of class as well as ethnic bounds. The medieval spiced chicken dish would have been eaten only by the prosperous. Chicken tikka masala is barely middle class, and middle-class Britons, including those of Indian origin, tend to shake it off in favour of something more 'authentic' (which means more expensive, usually). And the old wrong idea that foreigners or medieval people used spices to disguise rotten meat has at last come true, in a way. The meat in chicken tikka masala isn't rotten, but it's unlikely to be premium organic free-range chicken either. The watery, easily desiccated flesh of the battery chicken is made more palatable by the addition of a creamy sauce and spices.

For the upper classes, pheasant has always been preferable to chicken. The birds are about the same size, with the same dry breast meat. But the social slaughter of pheasant shooting is valued rather than the meat it provides. The season begins on 1 October and ends on 1 February. Early twentieth-century gamekeepers used to try to lay on a big shoot with a bag of twelve hundred birds killed in one day; this still happens at Sandringham every Boxing Day, where thousands of birds can be killed. Wounded birds drop out of the sky into the gardens of local people. Pheasant can be eaten as is, with anchovy sauce, Harvey's sauce, Worcestershire sauce, mushroom ketchup and mango chutney, turning it into a mass of powerful yet indistinct flavours.[106]

———————

A different British love affair with food is perhaps the passion for the cooking of Heston Blumenthal. Britain, and especially British men, took to Heston's scientific research, his insistence on 'deconstruction', his ingenious DIY approach, dismantling his backyard barbecue to make a pizza oven. His declared aim 'to make us feel like kids again' is to say the least only shared by some. (Some of us eat at restaurants in order to feel like adults. This group might include children.) Heston's dream seems less a little kid than an older kid in a fraternity, hence his giant boiled egg made using a condom. He has his own fan site.

When the *Daily Mail* compared his way with roast chicken to Delia Smith's, Heston lost out. His way was classic modernism: cook the chicken for three to four hours in a very low oven (90°C) until the internal temperature reaches 60°C on a digital thermometer, with lemon and thyme inside the carcass and half a pack of butter smeared over the skin. Put six to twelve chicken wings or thighs in the pan to roast with it. Then leave it to rest for forty-five minutes while you make gravy with the wings or thighs and wine and stock, and put it in a very hot oven (230°C) for ten minutes to crisp the skin. This is very deconstructed. It involves expensive equipment, retailed by Heston. It's more expensive than usual because of the wings; you need to tear apart two extra birds to accompany your roast. It's more labour-intensive and suited to the leisured or those who work from home because of the long cooking time. It's higher in fat because of the butter. It bears all the hallmarks of a dish that sets out to improve on the old-fashioned Delia, who simply suggests stuffing the chicken's cavity with garlic, tarragon and lemon slices, then seasoning it and rubbing with olive oil and sticking it in a hot oven (230°C) uncovered for forty-five minutes, resting it for twenty minutes on a board while you make gravy with the juices by adding white wine and simmering to reduce.[107] Delia's chicken had wrinkled skin, suggesting it had lost water. Nonetheless, it was quicker and easier.

It has long been part of British recipe writing to insist that recipes are easy, or simple, or quick, or all three. Nigel Slater and Jamie Oliver have also built careers on Heston-like can-do blokeishness, but in a hurry. Part of this is a kind of can't-be-doing-with-all-that, life's-too-short attitude to food. The converse has been to have someone else do the work; this is what French haute cuisine is all about. But the modernist movement is immensely attractive because it does more than anyone since Escoffier to organise, systematise and masculinise food, taking it firmly out of the hands of women, drawing it into the realm of science. The cult of Heston pales beside the devotion inspired by Spaniard Ferran Adrià. These too are in part dwarfed by the overall enterprise that is modernist cuisine. It may not matter to you yet, but it probably will. Modernist cuisine is what your mother *didn't* make. In the movement's bible, *Modernist Cuisine*, mothers are criticised for their erroneous 'commonsense', and for their limited repertoire and audience, 'only' cooking for themselves and their families.[108] We can compare this to the vindication of *la vraie cuisine de maman*, still important in France and Italy, by Elizabeth David, Alice Waters and Michel Bras, among others.

This is food writer Russ Parsons' summary of how to roast a chicken according to Nathan Myhrvold's *Modernist Cuisine at Home*:

> Remove the wishbone and French the drumsticks; make a brine and inject it into the breasts, legs and thighs; blanch the chicken in boiling water for 20 seconds, then plunge it into an ice water bath for 20 seconds, repeat twice more; pat it dry, season it with soy sauce and refrigerate it overnight; roast at precisely 205 degrees to a core temperature of 140 degrees; rest for 45 minutes (the bird, not you); brush with oil and place under the broiler, turning once, until the skin is crisp.

The recipe 'takes the better part of two days, with at least a couple of hours of busy fussing'. It 'incorporates ingredients that once were found only in laboratories or food factories, such as starches and gums that thicken liquids more efficiently than old-fashioned flour and gelatin'. Myhrvold, a former chief technology officer at Microsoft, has become 'a kind of guru of the molecular gastronomy movement, having built a laboratory kitchen and spent more than four years working with a team to publish the original *Modernist Cuisine*', at a stonking price and in five volumes, for eager geeks who are tired of rebuilding their hard disks and breaking into their iPhones.[109] With a mere six-figure budget for equipment, this can be yours, so you can do sous-vide – a method of cooking food in a water-bath at very precise temperatures – at home, and then you too can enjoy the sous-vide slime with the fake crunchy top achieved by later toasting. All of it tastes just like every other piece of sous-vide meat; it's meant to taste like chicken, but unless your palate is very sensitive, it will remind you of sous-vide pork, sous-vide veal and sous-vide turkey.

Every day Britons consume 2.2 million chickens. Around a billion chickens every year. And an additional 400 million are imported. Of the total of UK chicken production, free range accounts for 5 per cent and organic 1 per cent. The independent poultry trade disappeared during the Second World War. Before the war, chickens were primarily laying hens for egg production; when rationing was lifted in 1954, production of chickens for meat grew. Retailers, not the government, pressed British poultry farmers to follow American methods and exploit economies of scale and to drive down prices. The chickens are slaughtered at thirty-five days. And prices are low, on average £3.45 per bird. Less than the average pint of beer.

Watery breasts that slice like butter, weak bones that bear no resistance, and meat with little or no flavour. These sacrifices to taste, quality and flavour are a direct result of intensive farming. And yet the British still see themselves as less brutally intensive chicken farmers than Americans. The debate surrounding a fresh independent trade deal with a United States led by Donald Trump has turned on anxieties about chlorinated chicken meat, which is banned here and in the European Union, but permitted in America. The chlorination is an effort to kill the germs that abound in meat because of the intensive way in which it is raised and the way in which it is killed. Food poisoning bugs such as *E. coli* or campylobacter, many of which are becoming resistant to antibiotics, can spread quickly through a flock. Some 63 per cent of supermarket chickens are now infected with campylobacter, a side effect of mass production.[110]

Is it accurate to portray English farming as pastoral and caring? Intensive farming has grown in the UK, which now has 800 'mega-farms', huge industrial units mimicking the feedlots of California or Texas. The biggest can house more than a million chickens, 20,000 pigs or 2,000 cattle.[111] This growth is mainly due to Britain's insatiable appetite for chicken, elite and cheap at once. There isn't enough land, farmers claim, to raise this number of chickens in traditional ways.[112] Five companies – two of which are owned by multinationals – control most of the poultry production in the UK.

So, like industrial bread, industrial chicken has become a reliably tasteless staple. A famous study in 2000 illustrated this. A dish, chicken à la king and rice, prepared from identical ingredients and to a standard recipe, was served to consumers in a variety of settings ranging from a residential home for the elderly to a four-star restaurant. Diners were asked to rate its acceptability. Results showed that location contributed significantly to overall acceptability. 'A hierarchy of locations emerge with upscale restaurants receiving higher scores than institutional settings.'[113] And some people like that easy associativeness, unimpaired by flavour. The people who just don't care what they eat, who think all this fuss about food has gone much too far, who want to cry that you eat to live, you don't live to eat. They might be the ones who absent-mindedly eat the same tuna sandwich every day for lunch because they know it's safe. They stay slim, or they balloon, but they are the super-tasters, in all likelihood, for whom many foods are intolerably bitter.

The gold-and-white of chicken is what makes it desirable as a food, but what makes it good for farmers is the ease with which it puts on weight. But chicken too easily becomes what the industry calls PSE, which stands for pale, soft and exudative. The massive muscle contractions that occur at the moment of slaughter squeeze lactic acid into the muscles, exacerbated in intensively reared chickens because their immense breasts are not properly or fully formed. The lactic acid denatures the protein and the meat turns pale, loses its ability to retain moisture (which is why you find blood in the bottom of your cheap chicken breast pack) and can become so soft that it falls apart when cooked. To treat the problem, chicken meat is often injected with salts and phosphates to force it to retain water after death. This can increase selling weight by up to 30 per cent. The extra weight is not meat, but water.

Texture is big business, and the science of food structure even has its own ology: food rheology. And yet in our everyday enjoyment of eating, texture is often considered the poor relation of taste and smell (US research found that textural awareness is often subconscious). But food professionals know all too well that, while flavour is the focus when we're savouring a mouthful, get the texture wrong and the food will be rejected. Not only does texture have a casting vote over a food's acceptability, it is also essential in identification. When foods are pureed and strained, we can recognise less than half of them. We are incredibly sensitive to texture. Touch is of course the primary sense we use to determine it, but kinaesthetics (the sense of movement and position), sound (crunch: good; squeak: bad) and sight are also involved. People can detect ice crystals in ice cream measuring 1/25th of a millimetre. Food technologist Malcolm Bourne says the three most relished texture notes are crispy, creamy and chewy. And food with more bite has become more popular in recent decades, because dental health improvements have meant that many people keep their own teeth for most of their lives. While food aversions are generally subjective, there are definitely trends in unpopular textures. To the western palate, sliminess is often greeted with suspicion and associated with decay; this in part explains the aversion to offal, dark meat, seafood, and some other gourmet foods. The most extreme textural revulsion occurs when we encounter an unexpected combination – a small lump of ice in ice cream, a piece of grit in spinach, a fragment of bone in a fillet.[114]

But despite the mass production, despite the water injection, chicken appears on virtually all weight-loss regimes as an acceptable food. The NHS website says 'Lean white meat such as chicken and turkey breast' can be 'eaten regularly'. Chicken and turkey are categorised as healthy, like fruit, walnuts, whole grains. As an example of the amazing ignorance displayed on the whole site, there is an utter lack of awareness of the impact of the chicken's own diet on its body. For the first time since records began in 1870, a typical chicken (*not* a posh pricey organic bird) now has more fat than protein, according to a London University study, and a single serving has up to 50 per cent more calories than it did in the 1970s. Even a typical organic chicken had 17.1 grams of fat per 100 grams, although it contained more protein than fat. The couch potato poultry of the factory farm might now be contributing to obesity among consumers. 'Chickens used to roam free and eat herbs and seeds; they are now fed with high energy foods and even most organic chickens don't have to walk any distance to eat.'[115] The chicken has become intrinsically a trick, a virtual pie, disguising its own buttery unctuousness under a thin veneer of rhetoric.

Some fears go even further:

> So, ok, there was, like, a wife who didn't have anything
> prepared for her husband's dinner. So she quickly got a basket
> of takeaway chicken, and then she tried to make her dinner
> look classy by turning down the lights, and putting candles on
> the table, and they ate by candlelight. When she and her
> husband started eating the chicken, they thought it tasted
> funny. They finally noticed it was not a chicken, but a rat.

The details vary, but the story remains the same over a hundred, a thousand such retellings. The name of the outlet varies, but it is always a fast-food chain, usually KFC. The chicken is consumed in a dark place, usually a car, but sometimes by candlelight. The presence of the rat is not usually explained, but is sometimes attributed to insanitary conditions. The rat eater usually becomes sick, and sometimes dies.

A key element is that – as we saw with pies – the breaded coating disguises the disgusting object. Fried chicken is the endlessly returning subject of urban myth. Urban myths, as they are called, are recently created stories, sometimes reported as news, which show social rules and shibboleths being violated in exciting ways. The rat is crucial both for plausibility – it's the right size – and for its opposition to the chicken, its status as black, diseased vermin as opposed to the chicken's white-and-gold symbolism. And yet the rat may embody a concealed truth about the chicken. As we saw earlier, the two are not intrinsically dissimilar. The chicken is bony and flavourless. The chicken is a scavenger, like the rat. The rat is also a foodstuff of dystopia; virtually all dystopias feature the eating of rats. If the housewife can't or won't cook, dystopian eating is upon us.

People were shocked to discover that chicken nuggets were made of recovered meat, and especially skin: 'If you knew about the high percentage of skin, the water, and the pulped carcasses that go into some of them, would you be so keen to reach into the freezer for chicken nuggets?'[116] Journalist Felicity Lawrence learned that 'you need some skin to keep the nuggets succulent; 15% is about right … Mixed in that proportion with breast and dark meat, it matches what you would get if you were eating a whole bird'. And yet once coated in its crunchy crumbs, anything might be in there: 'recycled pet food, breasts injected with pig and cattle proteins, banned carcinogenic antibiotics – they've all been found by the authorities recently in chicken destined for processing'.[117] The gold-and-white nugget references wealth and rarity – it is, after all, a *nugget*. But what if this is the wrong kind of gold, the wrong kind of white? Prized for both its flexibility and its reassuring pallor, chicken in this form can now be re-viewed as the epitome of bad food. And yet nuggets do conform to a desirable taste-and-texture pattern, though here the balance between added fat and added cutting tastes has swung to the exact opposite of the Apicius way. The nugget adds only salt. The ketchup which may accompany it is usually very low in vinegar and spice, and largely sugary. But salt and sugar together do make for weak cutting power.

Because the food of the rich is actually unaffordable, the poor – and those who cater for them – are forced to fake it, and this makes for an uneasy, uncanny likeness between the transgressive disgust deliberately evoked by gourmet food and the far less deliberate revelation that the food of the poor is not what it pretends to be. As we have seen, when Trimalchio revealed that his embryo chickens were a fake, that was cute; the revelation that chicken nuggets might contain more water and skin than white meat is significantly less cute, and so is the revelation of horsemeat in cheap burgers and who-knows-what in pies and sausages.

The urban legends might contain another inconvenient truth. It has been argued that chicken farming is destroying the environment. Philip Lymbery, chief executive of Compassion in World Farming and author of *Farmageddon* and more recently *Deadzone*, claims that factory farming is not an efficient, space-saving way to produce the world's food but a method in which the invisible costs are actually far higher than the savings:

Taking farm animals off the land and cramming them into
cages and confinement looks space-saving; you are putting an
awful lot of animals into a small space. But what is overlooked
in that equation is you are then having to dedicate vast acreages
of relatively scarce arable land to growing the feed … The crops
fed to industrially reared animals worldwide could feed an extra
four billion [people] on the planet.

As the global demand for cheap meat grows, the expansion of agricultural land is putting more and pressure on our forests, rivers and
oceans, contributing to deforestation, soil erosion, marine pollution
zones and the global biodiversity crisis: 'The mixed farm habitats of
once common farmland birds such as barn owls, turtle doves and
skylarks are being stripped away.' Antibiotic use is another red flag
area, leading to the rise of antibiotic-resistant superbugs.[118] A further
issue is the enormous amount of water consumed by industrial farming, especially in growing feed for industrially reared animals.[119]

And yet it is not easy for the lone consumer to work out what
action to take. The sad case of Swaddles Organic shows the danger. Its
CEO Neil Stansfield was given a 27-month prison sentence in 2009.
He had been buying perfectly ordinary food (pork pies, salmon, and
of course chickens) from high-street supermarkets, repackaging it in
reassuringly expensive wrapping, calling it organic, and selling it on at
inflated prices to other retailers and via mail order. He had built up a
massive client base that, intoxicatingly, included Fortnum & Mason.[120]
The Swaddles disaster showed that people could not tell organic food
from the rest by taste. As with the chicken à la king experiment, they
were buying something else: the dream, the delicious dream of the
organic, with happy and healthy animals flowing into our bodies and
making us happy and healthy too. Here is Stansfield earlier in his
career: 'We're impassioned by supplying natural, ethical and unadulterated food and we're here to help educate consumers about the
well-being that comes from choosing British-grown organic meat.'[121]

Ironically, what the dream of self-sufficiency suggests to most of us
is the chance to choose, rather than to be dictated to by others, perhaps

most of all by supermarket buyers. While trolley rage is a known syndrome, its origins may lie not just in rising prices and declining manners, but in the way in which supermarkets constantly choose for us. Germaine Greer comments that 'if the vendor decides that only a minority of people is buying a particular line, and it is not moving off the shelf fast enough, it will be deleted … The individual shopper has no recourse.'[122] The shopper, atomised in the aisles, a single integer in a spreadsheet, has never had much recourse; money gives the illusion of choice, in that one can then forego the obligation to buy the cheapest chicken and instead betake oneself to … Swaddles, who pretended to offer choice but who actually offered exactly, precisely what was obtainable in the supermarket.

Bland, moderately priced, easy-to-raise chicken is – literally – everywhere, but its very amenability makes it both ubiquitous and quiet. 'It's the skinless, boneless breast,' says Niki Segnit, 'especially from intensively farmed birds, that has earned chicken its pale reputation. It's like a sort of dry tofu for carnivores.'[123] So it acts as a cover for other, more delectable and exceptional foods. Caviar, or lime, or oysters, or gruyere and ginger, or strong-tasting herbs, or nuts. Usually the addition of something to add unctuousness is de rigueur. Butter, or cream, or olive oil or mayonnaise or coconut milk. And on top of that, cutting edges, sharpness – lemon, ginger, sage – pepper, wine. Fat plus cutting edge plus white background. Most recipes across time work on this basis, and their variability depends less on the chicken than on the other strong flavours that are fashionable and available. The chicken is a backdrop. White rice or good white bread would do as well. Except that chicken also adds a different – even if problematic – texture.

In England, chicken remains boring, and is valued *as* boring. American fried chicken is everywhere, and nowhere. Here is restaurant critic Jay Rayner on eating at Lanes of London: 'a piece of fried chicken, coated in a bright orange breadcrumb case that flakes off like scabs to reveal pallid-skinned hen. It looks like a boulder that has been badly coloured in by a child. It may be half a very small bird; it's hard to tell.'[124] Either way, it's well understood that only boring people order chicken. It is so mainstream, so bland, that it is a way of making a statement without making a statement.

Perhaps it is not surprising, therefore, that chicken appears in dystopias as the food of the future. In Frederik Pohl's *The Space Merchants* (1952) the whole world is fed from the flesh of Chicken Little, a giant blob of flesh (with a beating heart) who lives underground and is endlessly carved to make meat products while still alive.[125] Also in *The Space Merchants* is the idea of addictive junk food. When someone drinks Popsie (a soft drink), they will crave Starr cigarettes. The cigarettes will spark a craving for a kind of confectionery, which will make you long for Popsie. Morgan Spurlock argued in his documentary film *Super Size Me* that fast food is addictive, and there has been some support for this claim from the scientific community.[126] Generally, however, the addictiveness is simply a sugar response – even 'savoury' fast food contains sugar.[127] One riposte might be a vegetarian or a vegan diet, with no chicken at all.

The English hate to admit this, but if I have learned one thing, it is that our assessment of ourselves is usually tinctured by America's response to us. One reason might be the influx of Austrian and northern Italian immigrants to the US, and their quest for their original food cultures in absentia. The British culinary ways of the eighteenth century were ossified as pioneer food, and it was in nobody's interests to relearn them or to open restaurants based on them or present them as novelties. So it is that the golden British roast chicken hovers just at the edge of the gaze, object of love, nostalgia and longing, but still quite incapable of chic.

———

Ostensibly, the chicken is cute and innocent and vulnerable, as on a Hallmark Easter card. This is a delusion, as all henkeepers know. Chickens are not fluffy and stupid and pure. We seek knowledge of farms and their environs, but shun knowledge of animals as individuals. An animal you know well becomes inedible, a pet. I've come to know that my chickens are not 'chicken', but as individual and emotional and capable as dogs and cats.

Ginger is the most solitary and individual of the thirty or so hens we have owned and come to know. After our second big flock had settled in, we noticed that Ginger kept finding ways to escape from her enclosure. We searched our acre or so of chaotic land, but we could never find her. One day, however, we learned she had made herself a secret lair in an abandoned coop, and was using it to lay her eggs in. She had fourteen of them stored up in a nest warm with down from her belly. Each egg was golden-brown. They would never hatch, because Ginger is a hybrid and we don't have a rooster. But she didn't know that. We took the eggs and ate them, and I don't think she ever forgave us. She never went back to that old coop again, but she still wanders. She's been searching ever since for a place safe from us.

The egg is so potent a symbol, so culturally powerful, that I can understand Ginger's crazy faith in it. The egg is so magical in some traditions that it is the best of all secret hiding places, the site of golden treasure. And the equally golden-breasted chicken is also a symbol of wealth, its sheeny skin and white flesh signifying health, hope and domestic joys. Moreover, Ginger is a chicken that seeks out new life and new worlds. After the egg incident, she escaped daily from the garden and set out determinedly for the nearest market town. She was like a character in a Beatrix Potter book. What did she want? We kept having to improve the fencing; she could locate gaps far smaller than her own body and squirm through them. She wasn't foraging; she went the same way every day, at her best speed, always sticking to the pavement.

If chickens are people, is it wrong to eat them? Part of eating is defining food as what we are not. When there is cannibalism, as there was in the Ukrainian famine in the early 1930s, and as there probably was during some English famines in the past, the act itself bespeaks the lack of alternatives. If we think of animals as having personalities, we are less likely to ill-treat them. Less likely to kill and eat them (though not always, as we saw in Pigs). Yet if we do still eat them, we might see ourselves as communing with their natures. This is not necessarily a Palaeolithic notion. As recently as the Middle Ages, nobles saw themselves as eating the wildness and strength of the stag and boar. Perhaps the subtler ferocity of chicken is part of an equation of power not with acres of wild land (the medieval noble) but with vaults of gold (the modern model).

As Ginger treasured her eggs, so I too treasure my power to buy a bird like Ginger, white and gold. But … I have stopped eating chicken almost completely. I could never kill one of *my* chickens. Therefore, it seems wrong to eat chickens killed by others. Okay, not all our chickens are as strongly individuated as Ginger, but now I seem troublingly close to saying that I am willing to eat less charming individuals, or those who have been too shy to make an impression on me, or those I simply haven't met. Chickens are far from 'bird-brained': studies have shown they have cognitive abilities comparable to those used by primates.[128] Siobhan Abeyesinghe and colleagues published a seminal study 'Do hens have friends?' They concluded:

> Chickens certainly have more capabilities than people are aware
> of. I do think they are unjustly maligned. It suits us to do so
> because we have something invested in farming them in large
> numbers. We have this psychological shielding to devalue
> animals we use for meat so we feel less concern about them.
> Work like this is great to make us stop and think: yes, chickens
> are smarter than we thought, but also we should use that
> information to enrich their environment in a biologically
> relevant way and think about welfare implications.[129]

The trouble is that such research ignores the darker side of chicken character. It is utterly incongruous that the ferocious chicken came to be linked with purity. The ancient Hebrews knew something that would shock most modern people: if I died, my hens would eat me. The Hebrews thought that chickens that have tasted human flesh were unclean. It was acceptable if they had merely tasted human blood, but if any 'tear and eat the corpses of the dead their flesh may not be eaten until they become feeble and weak and until a year has elapsed'. Chickens are not just gentle vegetarian foragers; they are omnivores who will defend their territory aggressively and will seek out and eat carrion and live prey. As Annie Potts points out, the domestic hen may well be the nearest living relative of *Tyrannosaurus rex* still to roam the earth, a possibility well understood by many chicken owners.[130] Analysis shows that *T. rex*'s collagen makeup was almost identical to that of a modern chicken.[131]

Just as some palaeontologists hypothesise that *T. rex* was both a hunter and a scavenger, so too 'free-range' hens may range in unexpected ways. Introducing new hens to an existing flock is a bloody nightmare. Nobody warned us about how violent they could be to strangers, and we got it badly wrong. One of our new pullets was pecked so savagely by the others that her brain was exposed at the base of the neck, and she died. Hens have to be introduced very slowly, with a good thickness of wire between them, allowed to see each other but not to touch for several days, then allowed a few minutes together, resegregated, allowed back together – and even then they will peck and peck at the weakest one. Twenty-first-century chicken breast may look pale and pretty, but chickens are fast-moving two-legged omnivores, and they act as such creatures do. Sentiment clouds us when we think about how best to look after our dependents. When we eat chicken, we are doing what they would do to us if we were their size and they ours.

My first flock diminished over time, from other predators and in pursuit of roadkill, and eventually there was only one left, one of the very first pair I'd had with my Eglu. I was terribly sorry for her. She was three years old, which is old for a chicken. I thought a lot about how lonely she must be. Having learned by then how properly to introduce new hens, I held off restocking for a few weeks. Lucky I did, because the lone hen turned out to be utterly, entirely happy. She started laying eggs every day, her feathers grew sheeny, and she enjoyed the dog's food whenever the dog didn't fancy it. A whole year and a half went by before she lost a battle with the fox, or the badger, or the red kite; we could trace the signs all around the driveway, in the little piles of her feathers. So she was probably eaten, though not by us.

Tinned food

Enid Blyton's food is now almost better known than any other aspect of her books.[1] The Famous Five are mainly famous for eating – but they eat in a comically conservative fashion. The same foods recur again and again. Part of that conservatism is a surprising fondness for tinned food:

> They opened a tin of meat, cut huge slices of bread and made sandwiches. Then they opened a tin of pineapple chunks and ate those, spooning them out of the tin, full of sweetness and juice. After that they still felt hungry, so they opened two tins of sardines and dug them out with biscuits. It made a grand meal.[2]

Tinned food meets all the needs of the Five: '"Golly," said Dick, his eyes gleaming. 'Soup-tins of meat – tins of fruit – tinned milk – sardines – tinned butter – biscuits – tinned vegetables! There's everything we want here.'"

Though never uttering the words 'lashings of ginger beer' often attributed to them, the Five do like food in lavish quantities and in a manageable form. An ecstatic scene sees Anne arranging tinned foods: 'Anne had a very happy morning. She arranged everything beautifully on the shelf … tins of meat next, tins of soup together, tins of fruit neatly piled on top of one another.'[3] Anne is entirely in control here, something that doesn't happen often. Like a small uncomprehending Andy Warhol, she piles up tins as riches.

The tins that Blyton's children love so devotedly represent a kind of food which even in her own day was problematic. Developed and redeveloped as an instrument for feeding an army or a navy, tinned foods made for a worrying autonomy. They cut their owners proudly free of the annoyances of parents, communities, cooks, servants, even of one another. Blyton's frighteningly competent children are powered by tinned food; they are conservative empire builders, foot-soldiers and radical typists in miniature.

The tinning process was the invention of Frenchman Nicholas Appert. Appert had tried out just about every possible food trade. He had been a hotelier, a brewer, a chef, a sweet maker and a jam maker, until he discovered that any food hermetically sealed in bottles and sterilised by boiling in an autoclave would keep for months, even years, and would still taste very nearly identical to freshly cooked food, unlike smoking, drying and salting. Or so Appert claimed. (Yes, yes; tinned food doesn't really taste like freshly cooked food, but it tastes more like fresh food than, say, salt cod tastes like fresh.[4]) Appert published his *Art de conserver* in 1810, and claimed a prize from the French government for making the best contribution to supplying the army and navy with food. Years before Pasteur, his work demonstrated the role of heating in the prevention of food spoilage. He couldn't explain it, but it worked.

The entire process was time-consuming, taking about five hours to transform fresh food into long-lasting preserves. It involved placing the food in glass bottles, loosely stopped with corks, and immersing them in hot water. Once the bottles were heated, they were removed and the corks sealed tightly with sealing wax, then reinforced with wire. Appert demonstrated that this process would keep food from spoiling for extended periods of time, provided the seals were not broken. It was used to preserve soups, meats, vegetables, juices, various dairy products, jams, jellies and syrups. He also invented the stock cube.

Appert's factory switched from jars to tin-plated cans in 1822 because they were more robust and easier to transport. With the shift from jars, there were tins, no end of tins. But it was almost fifty years before an Englishman named Warner invented the tin *opener* ... Till then, a hammer and chisel were needed to open cans. But eventually a good can-opener followed, and key-style openers were the first innovation.[5] The tinning or canning of food was a decisive moment for the globalisation of food, the moment when the local and the seasonal were trumped by the permanent, the available and the pre-prepared. Safe, secure, easily stored, portion-controlled tins. The food inside tasted uniformly dull because tins had to reach quite a high temperature to stave off all risk of botulism. Peas would be squishy by the time non-acidic vegetables reached that temperature.

It is no coincidence that tinned food arose as European empires expanded. Imperialism meant tins could be a staple of expatriate communities, and meant new markets for Western staples. Canned and powdered milk made its way to the farthest tip of south-east Asia, while in Belize, British settlers could eat what they were used to.[6] Tinned foods linked the settlers of the Empire with 'home', and allowed their food culture independence from the foods of the cultures they sought to colonise.[7] Dinner in Bombay could be a near-exact replica of dinner in London. Curries, mulligatawny soup and kedgeree were joined by vegetables, including the potato, with tinned foods – salmon, asparagus, jam, even cheese – on hand from European stores at hugely inflated prices. Tinned foods allowed Raj meals to have appearance of 'home' foods, though the actual contents of the tins could be disappointing. Some maharajahs also served tinned food to the English, in an effort to play the host. When this went wrong, it provided agreeable proof that the Indians could not truly be like the English. (Indians in London meanwhile struggled to find vegetarian fare; the young Mohandas K. Gandhi was driven to write a guide book to vegetarian London for students like himself.)[8]

Just as the Famous Five ransacked shops for prepared food while at large in alien lands, English memsahibs patronised the Army and Navy stores in Bombay for mail-order tinned foods. From Victorian times, 'native' food had been seen as inadequate and even unhealthy. Adventurousness was halted by the easy familiarity of tinned foods. Before tins, the invaders had no choice but to swallow local foods.

Tins let them choose what they knew. And what they knew was a mix of French haute cuisine and English cuisine bourgeoise. Bad imitations of French cuisine followed apace. The Raj ate Indian food at breakfast and lunch, reserving expensive imported tins for dinner and especially for entertaining. Jam found its way into a good many recipes, such as a Sri Lankan Christmas cake with pineapple jam as an ingredient.

Under the influence of writers like 'Wyvern', and Steel and Gardiner, a lot of the dinner parties which kept the creaking social wheels of the Raj moving involved the use of tinned foods from England, with whole townships behaving as though they were marooned in the Flanders trenches *avant la lettre*. As tinned food became better in quality, the premier wine and provisions store in Calcutta provided the following for just one subdivisional officer in September 1936: Polson's butter, Cadbury's chocolate, Pascall's Creme de Menthe sweets, Cooper's Oxford marmalade, Nestlé's thick cream, Lipton's pure Empire coffee, Del Monte's large white asparagus, and McVitie and Price's round Scottish shortbread.[9]

Admittedly, 'Wyvern' himself did not always like the result. He describes 'people giving a dinner party' garnishing one *entrée* with tinned mushrooms 'made of white leather', and he grumbled about 'dinners of ceremony' that often involved tinned food – 'dish of preserved salmon *hot*, and sodden; the *entrées* were spoilt by the introduction of terrible sausages, and mushrooms; and the tinned vegetables were ruined by being wrongly treated by the cook'; though here it is once more the (Indian) cook's fault. But he also lists many essential food items you *must* have in the storeroom:

> pickles, sauces, jams, bacon, cheese, macaroni vermicelli, vinegars, flavouring essences, the invaluable truffle, tart fruits, biscuits, isinglass (a collagen gel), arrowroot, oatmeal, pearl barley, cornflour, olives, capers, dried herbs, and so on … and no storeroom should be without tarragon vinegar, anchovy vinegar, French vinegar, and white wine vinegar.

He also urges bottled Parmesan cheese sold by Crosse & Blackwell, and even reviews various brands of bottled sauce: 'Jams, jellies, currants, raisins, ginger must all have room in the house-keeper's cupboard.' Should the memsahib really have brought all this out with her? 'She should have; it's impossible to get it here.'[10]

Tins were also involved in a new kind of creolisation; it wasn't just in India that tins could be used to bolster an unfamiliar diet. While Raj wives ate savouries of tinned sardines at maharajahs' palaces, Indian emigrants to Britain were also eating tinned sardines spiced with a range of their own flavourings. The tin was the British contribution.[11]

But colonisers could also learn preservation methods – gingerly, often desperately, hungrily – from the foods of those they colonised, and one such learned food was pemmican. Pemmican is what the children in the *Swallows and Amazons* books call tinned corned beef: 'On the hunks of bread and butter they put hunks of pemmican, and washed them down with deep draughts of Rio grog out of stone bottles.'[12] Like the Five, the Swallows and the Amazons are fiercely independent, and their independence is fostered by tinned foods. They speak of the adults who supply them as 'natives'; they themselves are explorers. But in calling their tinned corned beef 'pemmican', the Swallows are echoing a very old form of preservation learned by European fur traders from the Native Americans who sold it to them. Pemmican derives from a word in the Cree Indian language, *pimîh-kân*, or fat. To make pemmican Native Americans began by cutting meat into thin slices or strips and drying it either in the sun or over a fire. After the meat was dried, it was spread out on stone-headed implements and then pounded. The pounded meat was called 'beat meat'. 'Beat meat' was then mixed with melted fat and marrow; this was crucial to the preservation. Sometimes a paste made of fruits or berries was added.

Pemmican was stored in folded rawhide containers called parfleches, greased along their seams to keep out air and moisture. In this way, it could be kept fresh for years. Three-quarters of a pound (340g) of pemmican a day was a sufficient ration, although a hard-working traveller might eat more. The meat used could be bison, moose, elk or deer. The African equivalent of pemmican was and is biltong, although in the Second Boer War (1899–1902), British troops were given an iron ration of four ounces of pemmican instead, and four ounces of chocolate and sugar. The iron ration was prepared in two small tins (soldered together) which were fastened inside the soldiers' belts. A man could march on this for thirty-six hours before he began to drop from hunger.[13]

The Swallows references draw attention to the long and honourable association between preserved food and survival, a situation for which the Swallows and the Five seem almost to be in training. Pemmican was used by explorers including Robert Falcon Scott and his rival Roald Amundsen, and by Burke and Wills (who seem to have got the wrong kind which did not keep well, so that they succumbed to scurvy).[14] The Swallows are admirers of Nansen, neuroscientist and polar explorer, whose ship *Fram* was frozen in the ice for months on end. Nansen himself recounts making a meal out of pemmican: 'This [breakfast] generally consisted of "lobscouse" … made of pemmican and dried potatoes.'[15] Lobscouse is a kind of sailor's stew, in which mixed preserved meat is combined with crumbed ship's biscuit and spices, with onions, potatoes and leeks. The earliest reference is from 1706. The name seems to derive from a Scandinavian word meaning hodgepodge.[16]

The British in South Africa thought pemmican was superior to biltong, and so they used it rather than the local product, perhaps because they had become accustomed to selecting food from right across the globe rather than integrating their own eating into that of the peoples they sought to rule. Blyton's children do not forage, and they do not even go blackberrying; the Swallows do not augment their pemmican with local berries or leaves. Instead, like any colonising explorer, these children are dependent on people they do not see; their independence is an illusion, as is any autonomy dependent on the labour of other unseen hands.

Perhaps this explains why Blyton at any rate was very ambivalent about tinned foods, despite her frequent references to them. Her ideal women are housewives keen to make food from scratch. The word 'homemade' occurs repeatedly. Blyton was in favour of homemade food as a sign of the active rural housewife, enthusiastic about feeding hungry children in a motherly fashion:

> There were *homemade* scones with new honey. There were slices of bread thickly spread with butter, and new-made cream cheese to go with it. There was sticky brown gingerbread, *hot from the oven*, and a big solid fruit cake that looked almost like a plum pudding when it was cut, it was so black.[17]

Tellingly, Blyton also provides a commentary herself on the value of homemade foods, using George as her mouthpiece:

> 'Why is it that people on farms always have the most delicious food? I mean, *surely people in towns can bottle raspberries and pickle onions and make cream cheese?*'
> 'Well either they can't, or they don't,' said George. 'My mother does all those things – and even when she lived in a town she did. Anyway, I'm going to when I'm grown up. It must be so wonderful to offer homemade things by the score when people come to a meal!'[18]

The oddity is that for Blyton, tinned baked beans and home-grown raspberries were compatible, not opposites. Yet in setting out this notion of a feast, she flew in the face of the rigid class significance of food in the post-war era. For while the Raj and other colonies relied on tinned foods as a touch of 'home', the English had learned to despise them as a convenience. To understand this, we need to go back to an era immediately before Blyton, an era in which girls were pioneers and explorers of a brave new world of female independence and autonomy. Girls as independent and tough as Blyton's heroines were beginning to move into jobs, even careers, in particular as typists. The typist, independent, in her maisonette or flat, without family responsibilities, represented a kind of nightmare to traditionalists. But such a girl often had no choice but to eat 'convenience' food. *That* she had no choice was scandalous to her critics.

The hapless, hopeless typist in T. S. Eliot's *The Waste Land* of 1922 is plainly one of the lost. She 'lays out food in tins' prior to the visit of the house agent's clerk, 'one of the low, on whom assurance sits/ As a silk hat on a Bradford millionaire/... The meal is ended, she is bored and tired'. So he finds his caresses 'unreproved', and he doesn't care if they are undesired. Everything about the typist is indifferent, and the tins most of all. In Eliot's eyes tinned food is akin to prostitution.[19] Tinned food is a sign of rejection of the 'female' role, of divorce and anti-marriage movements, of feminism. Typists themselves are dubious enough. Eliot was following in the wake of the 'fallen woman' novels which depicted the independent flat-dwelling typist sinking into extramarital sexual pleasure. If she no longer had to cook, what else might she do with her time? The dread of the new and independent woman was exacerbated by the horror of tinned food.

Modernist literature documents a startling outbreak of rage and anxiety about tinned food, seen as the thin end of a wedge of mass production, a sign of the inauthentic rather than the 'real'. In E. M. Forster's *Howards End*, Leonard Bast eats tinned food, which shows why he can never really be a man of culture. Knut Hamsun objected to tinned food, while John Betjeman complained of 'tinned fruit, tinned meat, tinned milk, tinned beans'. Tinned salmon seemed especially troubling, and of course it is not very much like fresh salmon in either taste or texture (later, Graham Greene was to describe tinned salmon as a feature of lower-class cuisine). H. G. Wells's Mr Polly buys a 'ruddily decorated tin of a brightly pink fishlike substance known as "Deep Sea Salmon"', and the same writer's Lucas Holderness is a tinned salmon addict too. George Orwell claimed that the First World War could never have happened if tinned food had not been invented: 'tinned food is a deadlier weapon than the machine gun'.[20] 'I think it could plausibly be argued that changes of diet are more important than changes of dynasty or even of religion.' The working-class eagerness for tinned food horrified him:

The English palate, especially the working-class palate, now rejects good food almost automatically. The number of people who prefer tinned peas and tinned fish to real peas and real fish must be increasing every year, and plenty of people who could afford real milk in their tea would much sooner have tinned milk – even that dreadful milk which is unfit for babies.[21]

Thanks, he thinks, to tinned food, cold storage, synthetic flavouring, the palate is 'almost a dead organ':

Look at the factory-made, foil-wrapped cheese and 'blended' butter in any grocer's; look at the hideous rows of tins which usurp more and more of the space in any food shop, even a dairy; look at a sixpenny Swiss roll or a twopenny ice cream; look at the filthy chemical byproduct that people will pour down their throats in the name of beer.[22]

For Orwell this maladaptation was caused by the entry of machines and machine-made values into life: 'In a healthy world, there would be no demand for tinned food, aspirins, gramophones, gas-pipe chairs, machineguns, daily newspapers, telephones, motor-cars etc.' But this was naive. Orwell in fact saw all food as sinister; fresh food generated horrifying washing-up.[23]

It's hard to side with any part of Orwell's tirade. His only saving grace is that he knew how unreasonable he was being. 'In some districts,' he wrote doubtfully, 'efforts are being made to teach the unemployed more about food values,' and he saw the cheek of condemning families to inadequate incomes and then nagging about their diet. Yet he also thought it a pity that 'merely for the lack of a proper tradition people should pour muck like tinned milk down their throats and not even know that it is inferior to the product of the cow.'[24] He was, like every other reformer, agog to adjudicate between one person on benefits and another. The miner's family spent only 10d a week on green vegetables and 10½d on milk, but they wasted money on tea and sugar, just because they wanted 'something tasty'. He felt sure that the French were not as wasteful as the English: 'I have pointed out elsewhere how civilised is a French navvy's idea of a meal compared with an Englishman's.'

It was exactly this kind of meal that Orwell and Elizabeth David tried to bring to people who already knew how to bake bread and how to make good use of a sheep's head and whitebait. Or rather, not those people at all, but people of their own class who found they had to live like common people because of the war and rationing. Underlying Orwell's sympathy was the fear of the devitalisation of the poor which underlies *1984*; can skinny people be capable of revolution? Hence the notion that the tin and the machine gun are allied in destroying them.

Orwellian sneering at 'food in tins' is not yet dead. Most food manifestos, including the doom-laden ones, are one long turning-up of the nose at them. For some, Nigel Slater is a god, a national treasure, but for others he is the man who grumbles that at Harvest Festival 'pensioners now insist on bringing tins of Heinz beans. A marrow would be much more pleasing, though presumably a bugger for the old dears to fit in their handbags.'[25] My bet is that if they did bring a marrow, Slater would wonder aloud why the old dears had let it grow so big when they could have curtailed its ambitions at the posh little courgette stage. A long list of People Who Get it Wrong occupies Slater's book *Eating for England*, with tinned food users the leading losers. The economical cook is 'willing to take a punt on the can with no label on it. The chances are it will be baked beans, but what the hell, you never know, it could be tinned peaches.' Both are clearly equally unwelcome to Slater, though the Famous Five would have enjoyed them. The Neat and Tidy Cook is a villain for Slater too, because she buys everything ready-made, disliking getting her hands dirty. Slater's favoured shopper is a figure oddly like himself. The Cool Modern Shopper Cook is knowledgeable about rice varieties, and while all the others are female, his ideal is referred to as 'they' or 'this person'. Tinned food is linked with sloth and misguidedness. Compare Jack Monroe, *The Guardian*'s recessionista, who endorses tinned food, even the derided tinned tomatoes and tinned potatoes: 'A tin of branded tomatoes can cost you £1.20. A tin of value ones costs 35p. If you are cooking food from scratch those are just building blocks in your meal anyway. Nobody's going to notice if they are handpicked, vine ripened tomatoes'.[26] Because her whole approach is to save money, she actively advocates tins. Perhaps this might help explain the aversion of some; is it actually simple snobbery?

Tinned foods came from the grocer. My own grandfather was a grocer in a small Australian town called Bathurst. As the grocer, he had what he felt to be a responsibility for the health of the town. Food historians tend not to like grocers. Grocers, we too often learn, were grim cheats. But my grandfather could sell you exactly the amount of flour you wanted – not only 1 lb or 2 lb, but 9 oz or 11 oz. He'd then wrap it in a single sheet of paper – no bags – with cunningly tucked-in ends; he wrapped Christmas presents the same way all his life. He said a grocer had to be utterly trustworthy. You had to know where everything came from, ham and cheese and flour and sugar. If people stopped trusting you, they wouldn't buy from you. He knew all about tinned food. He didn't eat it, but he knew about it. He had to know about what he sold. Oddly, the army of defenders of proper butchers, greengrocers and bakers have little to say in favour of the grocer, who is usually seen as a stationary Ocado van full of manufactured goods, but being a good grocer also involved expertise. My grandfather was good at giving food its true value. Broken biscuits, the end of hams or bacon, the end of cheese or its rind; he knew people would buy them and find a use for them.

The Worshipful Company of Grocers of the City of London, which ranks second among the City Livery Companies, was originally not a source of boring sameness in tins, but of the exotic. Responsible for introducing strangeness to the English palate, it had to be trusted to wean people off the familiar. Originally it was known as the Guild of Pepperers, whose earliest records date from 1180. The company was formed as a religious and social fraternity of merchants trading in spices, gold and other luxury goods from Byzantium and the Mediterranean. Livery companies, or guilds as they were also known, began in medieval times to protect the interests of particular trades and the practitioners of those trades. Perhaps if we thought of the grocer as an Anglophone delicatessen we would treasure him more.

Tinned food worried my grandfather because of what was then known as ptomaine poisoning. We tend to see food poisoning as the result of the hypermodern industrial food industry, but tinned food also had its plagues. Ptomaine poisoning was the old name for food poisoning that came from a jar or tin. It could be caused by salmonella bacteria or listeria and usually developed a day to three days after consumption. But the real nightmare was botulism. Tinned food has to be heated for three minutes to kill botulism bacteria. Botulism used to be the scourge of preserved vegetables.[27]

Tinned food was part of my childhood too, albeit an unloved part. I remember tinned ravioli as the worst of it. Rubbery, rubbishy, with saccharine tomato sauce. A thousand pineapple rings, slick with sugar, in a country where fresh pineapple was common. Peaches, where the tinning seemed to slice off a shaving of the sharp acid flavour, though tinned peaches differ very little from home-poached ones. Like most snobbish food writers, like novelist Michael Ondaatje, I retain an affection for condensed milk and baked beans.[28] I also recall powdered milk in huge tins, which I link with the panic buying that followed the 1968 Tet Offensive, a huge tin of it, spilling its yellowish contents all over the Coles supermarket aisle. There used to be no salmon other than tinned salmon, no asparagus other than tinned, no fresh new potatoes. My mother said there was real asparagus in the twenties and thirties, when she was a child, but she disliked it; she preferred the tinned variety, which could be transmogrified into asparagus mousse, or the faux-posh asparagus rolls – you had to roll out slices of sliced brown bread, butter them – or use margarine, it spreads better and taste is clearly not the point – and then roll it around a limp khaki stalk of asparagus, and secure with a toothpick.

Convenience food of this kind had its own class politics, as we have seen. And as with T. S. Eliot's typist, it also acquired a gender politics, which it retains to this day. Food, and convenience food, was part of what was to be known in the fifties as 'the problem that has no name'.

Each suburban wife struggled with it alone. 'As she made the beds, shopped for groceries … she was afraid to ask even of herself the silent question – "Is this all?"' When Betty Friedan wrote *The Feminine Mystique* in 1963, one of the matters which concerned her in defining 'the problem that has no name' was the way in which the role of the housewife had shifted from production to consumption. Homemaking had become largely a matter of shopping, and housewives had become the powerless, passive targets of marketing initiatives. In the past, advertisers reasoned, tinned and pre-packaged foods made women feel guilty, but Madison Avenue worked out that they could now be presented as a luxury, better than anything the woman could make from scratch. Friedan cited a campaign for one of the baked-goods mixes common in the 1950s:

> Every effort must be made to sell X Mix as a base upon which the woman's creative effort is used. The appeal should emphasise the fact that X Mix aids the woman in expressing her creativity because it takes the drudgery away. At the same time, stress should be laid upon the cooking manipulations, the fun that goes with them, permitting you to feel that X Mix baking is real baking … A transfer of guilt might be achieved. Rather than feeling guilty about using X Mix for dessert food, the woman would be made to feel guilty if she doesn't take advantage of this opportunity to give her family 12 different and delicious treats.[29]

Clearly, the idea is that the choice of *product* is the only way in which the hapless housewife can exercise her power. But what was the product? According to General Mills, the baking mix Bisquick was born when one of their sales executives met a train dining-car chef in 1930 who mixed lard and the dry ingredients for biscuits ahead of time. The recipe was adapted using hydrogenated oil, thus eliminating the need for refrigeration. Originally intended for making biscuits very quickly (hence its name), Bisquick can be used to make a wide variety of baked goods. The basis for every cake mix is much the same. This faux food was marketed and sold by Betty Crocker, a kind of Delia Smith – except that unlike Delia, Betty didn't exist. A faux woman, she lived on faux food. 'Betty Crocker' is in British shops now, she and her brown glossy hair and her smile and her strawberry cake mix and her brownies. The great thing about Betty is that she has no investment in her own food. Unlike the post-war housewife in Michael Cunningham's *The Hours*, Laura Brown, Betty is not jeopardised by a failed cake. She has no feelings to bruise.

There is nonetheless a movement that wants to endow homemaking with prestige, called the radical homemaking movement. Shannon Hayes, one of its leading voices, argues compellingly along Friedmanesque lines that homemaking became a problem when housewives became the mere destinations of consumer goods. All kinds of food identities have been lost to the twin behemoths of work and marketing-driven convenience foods, with families owned in equal parts by employers and manufacturers. When housewives were producers, and especially when they were producers of food, their role had dignity and an identity which made sense. The process of food preparation involves the rewarding business of frugality, taking the worthless and making it valuable to the family. For Hayes, the old paradigm was that women had to choose between the gilded cage of homemaking and the glass ceiling of the workplace.[30] The people she calls 'radical homemakers' are rejecting those choices and instead investing themselves 'in the support of family, community, and environmental stewardship, so that those things, in return, will pay them lifelong dividends'. They are doing this by giving up conventional employment and instead, embracing the domestic arts and a sustainable home life. These women are not really living like housewives in the 1950s, but like pioneer women in the 1770s. Men and women both do household chores, thrift is highly valued, and many food and services are obtained through barter. What is fascinating is that food and its decline into convenience has become the biggest and most generally agreed sign that society isn't working and cannot continue to work in the way it currently does. Hayes writes, 'What's an economy for? Isn't it supposed to serve everyone? Are families really served by an economy where employees are overworked, where families do not have time to eat meals together, an economy that relentlessly gnaws at our dwindling ecological resources?'[31]

Hayes illustrates her thesis with a description of food preservation at home, 'tomato canning feminists'. Home preserving is reviving after a long sleep, the antithesis of canned convenience foods. Hayes, and Sharon Astyk, in her introduction to a book on food preservation at home, fit the model of 'crunchy cons', American conservatives who have embraced not so much environmentalism as the idea of Inconvenient Food – not fast, not takeaway, not ready, but natural, unadulterated, not well-travelled but local.[32]

Michael Pollan's recent book *Food Rules* could be summarised as follows: Only eat it if great-grandma would have. The trouble is … well, there are a lot of troubles. Do we really want to live like great-grandma, and if we can't how do we have the cheek to think we can reproduce her culinary standards? Pollan rather impertinently suggests that if your own great-grandma was a rotten cook, you should create an alternate ideal great-grandma from France or Italy. But if we have to decide in advance what sort of great-grandmother we want to emulate, then we are not recovering but *inventing* tradition. Pollan is only echoing the ideas of every food writer from Elizabeth David through to Alice Waters. Like the crunchy cons, they are desperate to recover a skill set and a mindset lost by their parents. The people who knocked down Euston Station and devastated the inner cities have wrecked food creation, avid as they were to have modernity and not much else. Yet they were not lazy; they were diligent, to learn other things than jam-making. Their aesthetics were unlike ours. Shabbiness and age were signs of poverty and ignorance. Bright squares were modern and prosperous. With the battered chintzes they threw out the jam pots. But why? Probably not because they were thinking so much as reacting to marketing ploys, about which they were significantly less savvy than people are now. Feminists are less guilty than Madison Avenue in this respect, for it was Nescafé and Betty Crocker who allied to teach women that food was a lot of work. But this is one of those unfortunate moments when it turns out that feminism itself looks very like a dance to the music of business.

So the tinned food which once liberated women has become a weapon against them, just as it was in the hands of Enid Blyton. While nestling down cosily around the jars of homemade jam, we might shift at least a little in our seats as we see how movements against ready-rolled pastry uncannily echo Eliot and Forster and Blyton. Food reform movements nearly always take as their starting point some kind of notion of food history, cooking from scratch, naturalness, tradition. On this page of the hymnal are school lunch reform; the campaign for animal rights and welfare; the campaign against genetically modified crops; the rise of organic and locally produced food, farmers' markets and local box schemes; efforts to combat obesity and Type 2 diabetes; the slow food movement and the Food Ark; efforts to promote urban agriculture and ensure that communities have access to healthy food; initiatives to create gardens and cooking classes in schools; nutrition labelling and the traffic light system.

Here food reform tends to collapse under the weight of its own contradictions. Yes, the 'American' and increasingly the British diet of highly processed food laced with added fats and sugars is responsible for a range of theoretically preventable diseases linked to diet: heart disease, stroke, Type 2 diabetes, and at least a third of all cancers. However, dietetics doesn't really know for sure how to treat these disorders; it can't even help people lose weight and keep it off for more than twelve months. Frankly, history teaches that legislation is the arch-enemy of local food, and also that efforts to re-educate the poor to spend their food pound nutritiously have *never* worked, not once in the whole of history, because the strictures of poverty make meeting daily calorie needs on a low income the main 'rule'.

And the constant evocations of tradition are very selective. Just as great-grandma might have balked at stinky cheese and courgettes, so she might have disliked the food miles they have undergone. Nor is it easy to discard modern agriculture with abandon. Hunger activists like Joel Berg, in *All You Can Eat: How Hungry Is America?*, point out that there are too many food-insecure families even in Western countries, while criticising supporters of 'sustainable' agriculture – i.e., the production of food in ways that do not harm the environment – for advocating reforms that threaten to raise the cost of food to the poor. And in *The End of Food*, by Paul Roberts, the impossibility of sustaining the current plethora of food is grimly highlighted, dependent as it is on unsustainable water use, oil-based fertilisers, and increasingly limited strains and varieties of food crops. Further scientific miracles in the form of GM crops may make things better – or worse.

A differently challenging reading of our disintegrating food cultures comes from Janet Flammang. 'Significant social and political costs have resulted from fast food and convenience foods,' she writes, 'grazing and snacking instead of sitting down for leisurely meals, watching television during mealtimes instead of conversing.' 'Viewing food as fuel rather than sustenance, discarding family recipes and foodways, and denying that eating has social and political dimensions' all have frightening implications. Food is also about the rituals of eating. The setting, the surroundings, the constraint of manners. It is at what Flammang calls 'the temporary democracy of the table' that children learn the art of conversation and acquire the habits of civility – sharing, listening, taking turns, navigating differences, and above all waiting patiently – and it is these habits that are lost when we eat alone and on the run. The very autonomy that tinned food gave to the Famous Five, the freedom to eat when they like, has now been identified as the problem.

Never mind that this confuses two things, cooking and serving. You could serve fish and chips at a family dining table on fine china and with the kind of salt you have to pass. The point of cooking, Flammang suggests, is that it symbolises giving and generosity. Love, in fact. But does it symbolise this for the recipients of the meal, or only for its creator? There is now a risk of an approach to food that is more or less fictive and dependent on an inner lie about what food poverty really meant to great-grandma and her generation. Call me an oddity, but I doubt if most people associate family meals with democracy. I myself think family meals, to which I have been subjected, and over which I have bossily presided, are a tyranny, a pre-feminist maternal tyranny.

Eat your vegetables; if you haven't finished that salad you can't be hungry for pudding; elbows off the table; use the napkin; hold your fork properly. They have become unfashionable because many parents dislike giving orders to their children, and because they themselves remember family mealtimes as torment. But it is true that as they go they take with them whole categories of food. Roast dinner with many vegetables is hard to simulate in cook-chill form, even to the most undiscerning palate. It has become endangered.

While food appears to offer us one of the shortest and most prim-rose-strewn paths out of the corporate-controlled world, a way to be autonomous and independent, this seduction costs somebody something. Carlo Petrini, founder and president of the Italian-born organisation Slow Food (founded in 1986 as a protest against the arrival of McDonald's in Rome), urges eaters and food producers to join together in 'food communities', in which eaters in the affluent West support nomad fisher folk in Mauritania by creating a market for their bottarga, or dried mullet roe.[33] But this is a very limited solution; limited, in fact, to the affluent eaters in the West who prop up the poverty foods of abroad.

I note the Slow Food Ark for Britain does not include sheep's head soup, pluck, tripe or any of the other past foods of the very poor. Nor does it include bread, a rasher of bacon and a good cup of sugary tea. Nor 'bread-and-cheese' or sloes. So this is a quite selective – meaning selected by the prosperous – view of the food past. Part of what is selected is feast food for all, and part is posh food for the few. But the result is to idealise an utterly unrealistic food past which never really belonged to anybody – and cannot be re-created in the present. All of us in the Anglophone world are fighting to preserve French and Italian food cultures as experienced on holiday – privileged holiday – just as they were experienced by David, and by Evelyn and May, and also the bits of our food culture that most obviously resemble them. I love and yearn for those foods as much as anyone, but it seems highly unlikely that imported bottarga can stem the tide of Type 2 diabetes or decrease food miles, and to keep on implying that it can is just to say that the poor ought to eat like the rich.

The fact is that a kitchen now costs far more than the food cooked in it. In 2008 *The Guardian* reported that 'The proportion of a UK household's budget that goes on keeping a roof over the family's head has more than doubled in the past 50 years,' according to official figures, and this trend has continued in the years since. Housing costs such as mortgage interest and rent now take up the biggest slice of the weekly budget. Meanwhile, spending on food and non-alcoholic drinks has dropped sharply from 33 per cent of a weekly household budget in 1957 to around 11 per cent by 2010, and has hovered around that figure since, reaching 10.8% in 2019/20. This does not represent a 'free' choice – let's buy the industrially made bottarga from Aldi instead of the artisanal cheese, and spend the money we save on the house. This represents the power of the strongest force in the universe, the compound interest-like effect of mortgages and soaring house prices. In 2019–20 food and non-alcoholic drink purchases contributed £40.58 to average weekly household expenditure, of which £6.39 went on meat, £1.46 on fish, £1.98 on fresh vegetables and £1.85 on fresh fruit.[34] Yes, these are grim figures. No, they probably don't suggest a food renaissance of the kind often claimed for the UK of late. Like other renaissances, food renaissances are only for the few.

A dilemma forms around the inelastic limits of time and space. I have made my own jam – including delightful hedgerow jam, and free jam made from Mirabelle plums, which seem to be everywhere in Oxfordshire, ignored and unrecognised. And my husband and I both make bread and never buy supermarket bread, and make our own granola. I make my own pizza dough and the sauce to go on it. I can furrow my brow with the best of the foodies, and wonder aloud why anyone would ever buy cereal or bread or pastry when a few minutes of effort will always yield a superior result. I know that it is impossible to say this without sounding moralistic. In that sense perhaps I too am a radical homemaker, more radical than my mother was, although she never worked outside the home. But she was much, much better at cleaning than I am. Her bathrooms were snowy and you could literally have eaten dinner from her floors. No mould dared to invade the shower. My house is deeply untidy. You *can't* have it all.

And my own past is by no means as pure. For three months, while our kitchen was sluggishly installed, we ate takeaway burgers. I once spent three nights every week in Norfolk, where I dined exclusively on ready meals. I remember dinner parties when I was an undergraduate, for which I'd make an avocado quiche with bought ready-rolled short-crust pastry. Why? Because I lacked confidence, and money. Which leads to a reluctance to take a risk with dinner. Bad food culture is driven by the dread of not eating. To cook from scratch, you have to be willing to risk failure, and the waste it implies – and you have to be able to afford it, emotionally and financially. What I've learned is that children won't die even if dinner is a bit of a failure, that bread, cheese and fruit is okay if it's a disaster. That food doesn't matter as much to children as it does to parents, that they are perfectly willing to miss the odd meal – or to eat junk if junk is all that you can provide that day.

Sometimes food is what we want or need to forget. For something else. The whole point of eating out, for some women especially, is that *they* don't need to think about preparing or serving it. Manners. Friendliness. Sociability. Love. Family. Which are sometimes now sacrificed to food shibboleths and rectitudes.

ENVOI

'Oh, my mother never had any authority.'

I remembered my grandmother darting imperiously around the kitchen, preparing Sunday lunch with a huge mix of vegetables and a pudding – poking, prodding, commanding, swift and sure as a spring bird. The food was always awesome and simple; a plain roast chicken, skin gleaming and thin, like a silk scarf.

'What about when she cooked?'

'Oh, well, then, yes. I suppose. But she never had any real say. She didn't make any of the big decisions about money, or anything. Just took the housekeeping money and spent it.'

So what matters is not domestic work. That's drudgery. Cooking is drudgery. But balancing the chequebook is proper. Men's work. Powerful work.

My mother is the speaker. In her cupboard, we found foods my grandmother would never have seen. Or liked. Tins. Each tin full of flavourings. Tinned tuna with pineapple and sugar. Nothing plain; plain is boring. Packets. Packet sauces. Packet cheese sauce. All laden with additives, the ingredients labels dense with unfamiliar names. 'Why do you have this? I could make cheese sauce when I was four. You taught me.'

'It's a novelty, I suppose.' Said without any stigma attaching to the word. It's a novelty like the cheese flavoured with wasabi I found in the fridge. It's a novelty that has driven basics out of her life. 'I haven't roasted anything for years. I don't know how to make stock. I don't know how to make custard.' I showed her both, as she had once shown me. As my grandmother had once shown me. Refinding a lost knowledge? It might be comforting to imagine so. But I thought at the time, cynically, that she'd turn back to the smart packets. The ones that liberated her from the 'drudgery' and stress of getting it right.

At the time we had these conversations, she was dying of liver cancer, though neither of us knew that. I don't think anything tasted good to her, though she still enjoyed eating out. I think the wasabi cheese was a search for something that might taste good when all the simple things had come to taste wrong.

NOTES

Introduction

1. Virginia Woolf, *A Room of One's Own* (1929; Oxford: Oxford University Press, 2000), pp. 8–9.
2. Woolf, *A Room of One's Own*, p. 14.
3. Juliet Gardiner, *The Thirties: An Intimate History* (London: HarperPress, 2011), p. 67.
4. Roger Deakin, *Wildwood*, (London: Penguin, 2008), pp. 283ff.; Caroline Eden and Eleanor Ford, *Samarkand: Recipes & Stories from Central Asia & the Caucasus* (London: Kyle Books, 2016), p. 199.
5. John Clare, 'August', *The Shepherd's Calendar* (London, John Taylor, 1827), p. 70.
6. Jonathan Bate, *John Clare* (London: Picador, 2003), p. 438.
7. Hermione Lee, *Virginia Woolf* (London: Vintage, 1997), pp. 182–85.

On breakfast: an essay

1. Ken Albala. *Food in Early Modern Europe* (Westport, CT: Greenwood Press, 2003), p. 232.
2. Ian Mortimer, *The Time Traveller's Guide to Elizabethan England* (London: Random House, 2012), p. 246; *Robert Laneham's Letter*, ed. Dr. Furnivall (London: Ballad Society, 1890), cit. R.B. Morgan, ed., *Readings in English Social History from Contemporary Literature, Vol.III. 1485–1603* (Cambridge: Cambridge University Press, 1921), p.78.
3. *Henry IV Part I*, Act 2, Scene 1, and see also Act 1, Scene 2.
4. Andrea Broomfield, *Food and Cooking in Victorian Britain* (Westport, CT: Greenwood Press, 2007), p. 24; Andrew Boorde, *A compendyous regyment or a dyetary of healthe made in Mountpyllyer* (1567), p. 251; White, in *Eating with the Victorians*, new edn., ed. C. Anne Wilson (Stroud: Alan Sutton, 2004), p. 3; however, she takes seriously the satirical *Court and Kitchin*.

5. Pepys' *Diary* from https://www.pepysdiary.com/diary/ [Accessed on March 25, 2022].

6. Frances Burney, *Cecilia: Memoirs of an Heiress* (1782; Oxford: Oxford University Press, 1988), pp. 191–92; 743–45.

7. Charles Dickens, *Oliver Twist* (London: Richard Bentley, 1838), vol. I, p. 28.

8. Charlotte Bronte, *Jane Eyre* (1847; Oxford: Oxford University Press, 1986), p. 344.

9. Morton P. Shand, *A Book of Food* (London: Jonathan Cape, 1927), p. 44.

10. Broomfield, *Food and Cooking*, p. 36; cit. Alexis Soyer, *A Shilling Cookery for the People* (London: Geo. Routledge & Co, 1854); 'Wyvern' aka Arthur Kenney-Herbert, *Culinary Jottings for Madras* (Madras: Higginbotham & Co, 1878); P. J. Burnett, *Useful Toil: Autobiographies of Working People from the 1820s to the 1920s* (London: Routledge, 2013), pp. 216–17.

11. Elizabeth David, *English Bread and Yeast Cookery* (Harmondsworth: Penguin, 1979), p. 542.

12. Lucy Lethbridge, *Servants* (London: Bloomsbury, 2013), p. 244, cit. Zoe Josephs, *Survivors: Jewish Refugees in Birmingham 1933–1945* (Oldbury: Meridian, 1988), p. 139.

13. Sir Walter Scott, *Waverley* (1814; Oxford: Oxford University Press, 2015), p. 56.

14. C. Anne Wilson, *The Book of Marmalade* (London: Prospect Books, 2010), pp. 33ff.

15. The *Compleat Cook or Accomplished Servant Maids Necessary Companion* (London: Printed for J. Deacon, n.d.), 'Introduction'; *History and Material Culture: A Student's Guide to Approaching Alternative Sources*, ed. Karen Harvey (Aldershot: Routledge, 2009), p. 185.

16. Peter Brears, *Cooking and Dining in Tudor and Early Stuart England* (Totnes: Prospect Books, 2008), p. 543; recipe for sucade in John Partridge, *The Treasurie of Commodious Conceits, and Hidden Secrets* (1573, repr. 1584).

17. Partridge, *The Treasurie*, chap. 302, B3r.

18. William Macintosh, *An Essay on Ways and Means for Inclosing, Fallowing, Planting, &c. Scotland*, no. 6 (London, 1729), p. 230.

19. Charles Dickens, *Our Mutual Friend* (1865; London: Penguin, 1997), p. 80.

20. Charles Dickens, *Bleak House* (1853; London: Penguin, 2003), p. 418; Dickens, *Our Mutual Friend*, p. 267; Dickens, *Bleak House*, p. 673; he says they remind him of the sun.

21. Henry James, *The Middle Years* (1917), cit. Andrew Dalby, *The Breakfast Book* (London: Reaktion, 2013), p. 178.

22. Thomas Forester, *Norway in 1848 and 1849* (London: Longman, 1850), p. 76.

23. Agatha Christie, *The Secret of Chimneys* (London: Bodley Head, 1925), p. 49.

24. B. S. Rowntree, *Poverty: A study of town life*, 2nd edn. (London: Macmillan, 1902); Wilson, *Eating with the Victorians*, pp. 20–21.

25. Gabriel Tschumi, *Royal Chef: recollections of life in royal households from Queen Victoria to Queen Mary* (London: W. Kimber, 1954), pp 47–48.

26. Dalby, *Breakfast*, p. 143; Gwen Raverat, *Period Piece: A Cambridge Childhood* (London: Faber & Faber, 1952), pp. 40, 53.

27. Raverat, *Period Piece*, p. 54.

28. P. G. Wodehouse, *Thank You, Jeeves* (1934; London: Arrow, 2008), pp. 215; 219.

29. C. S. Lewis, *The Horse and His Boy* (London: Geoffrey Bles, 1954), pp. 146–47.

30. https://www.nutrition.org.uk [Accessed on March 25, 2022].

31. Richard Adams, 'Majority of teachers in survey know pupils who arrive at school hungry', *The Guardian* 15 January 2016, https://www.theguardian.com/education/2016/jan/15/hungry-pupils-breakfast-teachers-survey [Accessed on March 25, 2022].

Loaves

1. Thomas S. Willan, *Elizabethan Manchester* (Manchester: Manchester University Press for the Chetham Society, 1980), p. 7.

2. Jérôme Assire, *The Book of Bread* (Paris: Flammarion, 1996), p. 26.

3. Scott C. Shershow, *Bread* (London: Bloomsbury, 2016), p. 88.

4. Sylvia Thrupp, *The Worshipful Company of Bakers: A Short History* [London: Worshipful Company of Bakers, 1933], plates following p. 208. This incarnation of the Hall was destroyed in the Blitz.

5. Shershow, *Bread*, p. 88; Bernard Dupaigne, *The History of Bread*, trans. Antonio and Sylvie Roder (New York: Abrams, 1999), p. 39.

6. Jean-Michel Lecat, *La grande histoire du pain et des boulangers* (Paris, Editions de Lodi, 2006), pp. 28, 58; Dupaigne, *History of Bread*, pp. 24–25.

7. Hilary E. M. Cool, *Eating and Drinking in Roman Britain* (Cambridge: Cambridge University Press, 2007), p. 76

8. Cool, *Eating and Drinking*. p. 77.

9. Martial. *Epigrams*, Book 14. 223.1.

10. Cool, *Eating and Drinking*, pp. 78–79.

11. For the role of trees in Anglo-Saxon heathenism and Christianity, see Michael D. J. Bintley, *Trees in the Religions of Early Medieval England* (Woodbridge: The Boydell Press. 2015); Clive Tolley, 'What is a "World Tree", and Should We Expect to Find One Growing in Anglo-Saxon England?', in *Trees and Timber in the Anglo-Saxon World*, ed. Michael D. J. Bintley and Michael G. Shapland (Oxford: Oxford University Press, 2013), pp. 177–85; and John Blair, 'Holy Beams: Anglo-Saxon Cult Sites and the Place-Name Element Bēam', in *Trees and Timber*, pp. 186–210.

12. Delia Hooke, 'Pre-Conquest Woodland: Its Distribution and Usage', *Agricultural History Review* 37 (1989), 113–29.

13. Ann Hagen, *A Handbook of Anglo-Saxon Food & Drink: Processing and Consumption* (Norfolk: Anglo Saxon Books, 1992).

14. Francis Pryor suggests that 'they [Anglo-Saxons] liked the food of the people they overran so much that they went to the trouble of imitating a Roman mortar in their own pottery workshops': *Britain AD* (London, HarperCollins, 2004), p. 94.

15. Ælfric, *Colloquy*, ed. G. N. Garmonsway (Exeter: Exeter University Press, 1978), 36 (Ælfric, Abbot of Eynsham, died circa 1012).

16. *A Collection of Poems by John Lydgate*, London, British Library, MS Harley 2255, fol. 157.

17. Alexander Luders and John Raithby, eds., *The Statutes of the Realm*, 11 vols. (London: Record Commission, 1810–1828), Vol. I, pp. 199–200.

18. Rudyard Kipling, 'Below the Mill Dam', *Traffics and Discoveries* (London: Macmillan, 1908), pp. 369–70, 376; David Gilmour, *The Long Recessional* (London: Pimlico, 2003), p. 168.

19. Ann Rycraft, 'Can We Tell What People Ate in Late Medieval York?', in *Feeding a City: York*, ed. Eileen White (Totnes: Prospect Books, 2000), pp. 63–64.

20. Rycraft, 'York', p. 64.

21. Geoffrey Chaucer, 'The Tale of Sir Topas', 14, and 'General Prologue', 147, from *The Canterbury Tales*, in *Chaucer's Poetry*, ed. E.T. Donaldson (New York: Ronald Press, 1958), pp. 10, 351.

22. William Harrison, *The Description of England*, ed. George Edelen (Washington; New York: Folger Shakespeare Library; Dover, 1994), pp. 133–34; Shershow, *Bread*, pp. 38–39.

23. C. Anne Wilson, *Food & Drink in Britain* (Chicago: Academy Chicago Publishers, 2003), p. 241.

24. 'Medieval Sourcebook: The Assizes of Bread, Beer, & Lucrum Pistoris': http://legacy.fordham.edu/halsall/source/breadbeer.asp [Accessed on March 25, 2022].

25. Rycraft, 'York', p. 63; Michael Prestwich, *York Civic Ordinances, 1301* (York: Borthwick Institute of Historical Research, 1976).

26. Eileen White, 'The Daily Exercise: The Housewife in Elizabethan and Jacobean York', in *Feeding a City*, pp. 103–5.

27. Thomas Tusser, *Five Hundred Points of good Husbandry*, ed. William Mavor (London: Lackington, Allen, and Co., 1812), p. 17.

28. From Henry Best's farming and account books, published by the Surtees Society in 1857; cit. G. E. Fussell, *The English Rural Labourer* (London: Batchworth Press, 1949), pp. 30–31.

29. Joseph Arch, *The Story of His Life By Himself* (London: Hutchinson, 1898); W. H. Hudson, *A Shepherd's Life: Impressions of the South Wiltshire Downs* (New York: Dutton, 1921), p. 147; Fussell, *English Rural Labourer*, p. 31.

30. Fussell, *English Rural Labourer*, p. 31.

31. Richard Carew, *The Survey of Cornwall* (1602; reprinted London, 1811); Fussell, *English Rural Labourer*, p. 31.

32. William Langland, *Piers Plowman* (1377), trans. Aubrey Schmidt (Oxford: Oxford University Press, 200), Passus VI, p. 73.

33. Fussell, *English Rural Labourer*, p. 29.

34. Fussell, *English Rural Labourer*, pp. 29–30.

35. Gregori Galofré-Vilà, Andrew Hinde and Aravinda Guntupalli, 'Heights Across the Last 2,000 Years in England', *Oxford University Discussion Papers in Economic and Social History* 151 (2017), https://ora.ox.ac.uk/objects/uuid:7a2abc40-b986-47b0-8e5a-b30ff738eb5b/download_file?safe_filename=Galofre-Vila_et_al_2017_Heights_across_the.pdf&file_format=pdf&type_of_work=Working+paper [Accessed on June 19, 2022].

36. P. Stuart-Macadam, 'Anemia in Roman Britain: Poundbury Camp', in *Health in Past Societies*, ed. H. Bush and M. Zvelebil, British Archaeological Reports International Series 567 (Oxford: Tempus Reparatum, 1991), pp. 110–13; Charlotte Roberts and Keith Manchester, *The Archaeology of Disease* (Ithaca: Cornell University Press, 2007), p. 23.

37. Karen Hess, ed., *Martha Washington's Booke of Cookery and Booke of Sweetmeats* (New York: Columbia University Press, 1981), pp. 118–19.

38. *A Good Huswife's Handmaide for the Kitchen* (London, 1594) 51r–51v.

39. Tusser, *Five Hundred Points*, p. 79.

40. Gervase Markham, *Countrey Contentments or The English Hus-wife* (1615), ed. Michael R. Best as *The English Housewife* (Montreal: McGill-Queen's University Press, 1986).

41. Kate Bennett, 'Introduction', in *John Aubrey: Brief Lives with An Apparatus for the Lives of our English Mathematical Writers* (Oxford: Oxford University Press, 2015).

42. Mary Davies, *Collection of Medical and Cookery Recipes* (1684), New York Public Library, Whitney Cookery Collection 5, p. 80. Inscription on verso on first leaf: 'Mary Davies her booke 1684'. The recipes are in several hands.

43. Elizabeth Raffald, *The Experienced English Housekeeper* (1769; Lewes: Southover Press, 1997), pp. 140–41.

44. George Bryan, *Chelsea in the Olden & Present Times* (Chelsea: published by the author, 1869), p. 201, quoted in *The London Encyclopaedia*, ed. Christopher Hibbert et al. 3rd edn. (London: Pan Macmillan, 2011), p. 155; Mary-Anne Boermans, *Great British Bakes: Forgotten Treasures for Modern Bakers* (London: Square Peg, 2013), pp. 266–77; Boermans gives four near-contemporary descriptions of the product.

45. Henry Mayhew, *London Labour and the London Poor* (London: Griffin, Bohn, and company: 1861), p. 202.

46. Boermans, *Great British Bakes*, pp. 62–63.

47. Jane Austen, Letter to Cassandra, 3 January 1801, in *Letters of Jane Austen* (London: Forgotten Books, 2013), vol. 1, pp. 250–51.

46. Chronicler John Stow said in 1598 that the puddings were 'voided' down the lane to their 'dung boats' on the Thames, *A Survey of London* (London: J. M. Dent & Sons, 1842); Adrian Tinniswood, *By Permission of Heaven: The Story of the Great Fire of London* (London: Jonathan Cape, 2003), p. 42.

47. John Evelyn, *A character of England as it was lately presented in a letter to a noble man of France* (London, 1659).

50. *The Diary of Ralph Josselin, 1616–1683*, ed. Alan Macfarlane (London: Oxford University Press for the British Academy, 1976), 9 September 1666.

51. Clifford Geertz, *The Religion of Java* (Chicago: University of Chicago Press, 1960), p. 11.

52. *Sarum Manuale*, Arthur Jefferies Collins, ed., *Manuale ad usum percelebris ecclesia Sarisburiensis* (Chichester: Henry Bradshaw Society, 1960), p. 4, cit. Keith Thomas, *Religion and the Decline of Magic* (London: Weidenfeld and Nicholson, 1971). p. 32.

53. Thomas, *Religion*, p. 56.

54. Miri Rubin, *Gentile Tales: The Narrative Assault on Late Medieval Jews* (New Haven: Yale University Press, 1999).

55. Rubin, *Gentile Tales*, p. 26.

56. Walter Gregor, 'Bread', *The Folk-Lore Journal* 7 (1889), 195–98.

57. John Aubrey, *Remaines of Gentilisme and Judaisme 1686–87*, ed. James Britten (London: W. Satchell Peyton for the Folklore Society, 1881), p. 163.

58. Esther Copley, *The Complete Cottage Cookery* (London: Groombridge & Sons, 1859); David Davies, *The Case of the Labourers in Husbandry* (Fairfield, NJ: Augustus M. Kelley, 1795), p. 175.

59. Charles Vancouver, *General View of the Agriculture of Hampshire* (London: Sherwood, Neely & Jones, 1808); R. W. Bushaway, 'Custom, Crime and Conflict in the English Woodland', *History Today*, 31 (1981), 37–43, p. 37.

60. William Cobbett, *Cottage Economy* (London, 1821, reprinted 1828), no. III, par. 82, p. 46; Burnett, *Useful Toil*, p. 18.

61. Cobbett, *Cottage Economy*, no. III, par. 106, p. 62.

62. Eliza Acton, 'Preface', *The English Bread Book* (London: Longman, 1857), pp. v-vi.

63. Copley, *Cottage Cookery*, pp. 86–87; Acton, *English Bread*, p. 107.

64. Burnett, *Useful Toil*, p. 39.

65. Davies, *The Case of the Labourers*, p. 118, my emphasis.

66. Bee Wilson, *Swindled: The Dark History of Food Fraud, from Poisoned Candy to Counterfeit Coffee* (London: John Murray, 2009), p. 76.

67. From the anonymous *Poison Detected or Frightful Truths* (1757), in Wilson, *Swindled*, p. 79.

68. Jane Cobden Unwin, *The Hungry Forties: Life under the Bread Tax* (Shannon: Irish University Press, 1971), pp. 14, 61.

69. 'Charles Robinson Woodman, Heyshott Village', in Unwin, *The Hungry Forties*, pp. 21–23; Burnett, *Useful Toil*, pp. 11–12, 26, 41.

70. 'Mr and Mrs Jenner, Heyshott Village', in Unwin, *The Hungry Forties*, pp. 48–52.

71. Washington, *Booke of Cookery*, p. 104.

72. Quoted in C. R. Fay, 'The Miller and the Baker: A Note on Commercial Transition 1770–1837', *Cambridge Historical Journal* 1 (1923), 85–91, p. 91.

73. Wilson, *Swindled*, pp. 107–8.

74. Cyrus Edson, 'Some Sanitary Aspects of Bread Making', *The Cosmopolitan* 15 (1893), cit. Shershow, *Bread*, pp. 60–61.

75. David, *English Bread*, p. 106.

76. *Cottage Loaves and Plain Bricks: Memories of Bread and Baking in Waltham Forest 1913–1950* (Waltham Forest Oral History Workshop, 1981), p. 11.

77. Shershow, *Bread*, p. 60.

78. *Cottage Loaves and Plain Bricks*, p. 19.

79. Linda Gross, 'The History of Making Toast', 19 June, 2017, https://www.hagley.org/librarynews/history-making-toast#:~:text=It%20wasn't%20until%201919,the%20automatic%20pop-up%20toaster.Crompton [Accessed on May 8, 2022].

80. 'Tracing the origins of Britain's sliced bread', *The Telegraph* 4 July 2011, http://www.telegraph.co.uk/comment/letters/8614081/Tracing-the-origins-of-Britains-sliced-bread.html [Accessed on March 25, 2022].

81. Peter Laslett, ed., *John Locke, Two Treatises of Government* (Cambridge: Cambridge University Press, 1988), p. 298; Shershow, *Bread*, p. 28.

82. Oliver Rackham, *The Illustrated History of the Countryside* (London: Weidenfeld and Nicholson, 1994), p. 21.

83. Rackham, *Illustrated History*, p. 26.

84. Rackham, *Illustrated History*, p. 79.

85. John Wright, *A Natural History of the Hedgerow* (London: Profile Books, 2016), p. 54.

86. Wright, *Hedgerow*, p. 55. And see David Underdown's theory about independent wood pasture villages and more orderly champaign villages, in *Revel, Riot and Rebellion* (Oxford: Clarendon, 1985).

87. Ruth Goodman, *How to be a Tudor: A Dawn-to-dusk Guide to Tudor Life* (New York: Norton, 2016), p. 151.

88. Dorothy Hartley, *The Land of England: English Country Customs Through the Ages* (London: MacDonald, 1979), pp. 77–83.

89. Hartley, *Land of England*, p. 57.

90. Hartley, *Land of England*, pp. 125; 60.

91. Andrew Dalby, *The Treatise (Le Tretiz) of Walter of Bibbesworth* (Totnes: Prospect Books, 2012), pp. 75–77.

92. M. W. Barley, 'Plough Plays in the East Midlands', *Journal of the English Folk Dance and Song Society* 7 (1953), 68–95; Alex Helm, 'The Cheshire Soul-Caking Play', *Journal of the English Folk Dance and Song Society* 6 (1950), 45–50, p. 48.

93. George E. Evans with P. Barkham and D. Gentleman, *The Pattern Under the Plough: Aspects of the Folk Life of East Anglia* (1966; Beaminster: Little Toller Books, 2013).

94. Evans, *Pattern*. pp. 122, 131, 133.

95. Alexandra Harris, *Weatherland: Writers and Artists under English Skies* (London: Thames & Hudson, 2015), pp. 64–66.

96. Nicholas Crane, *The Making of the British Landscape: From the Ice Age to the Present* (London: Weidenfeld and Nicolson, 2016), pp. 326–28.

97. Wolfgang Behringer, *A Cultural History of Climate* (Cambridge: Polity Press, 2009), pp. 93–94.

98. Goodman, *How to be a Tudor*, p. 146.

99. John Wildman, *Truths Triumph* (London, 1648). pp. 5–6, and Robert Sibbald, *Provision for the poor in the time of death and scarcity* (Edinburgh, 1699), cit. Geoffrey Parker, *Global Crisis: War, Climate Change and Catastrophe in the Seventeenth Century* (New Haven, CT: Yale University Press, 2014). p. 55.

100. Parker, *Global Crisis*, p. 59.

101. E. P. Thompson, 'The Moral Economy of the Crowd in the Eighteenth Century', in *Customs in Common: Studies in Traditional Popular Culture* (Harmondsworth: Penguin, 1993), p. 188.

102. William Shakespeare, *Coriolanus*, Act 1, Scene 1, 15–23.

103. Crane, *British Landscape*, p. 330.

104. Josh Sutton, *Food Worth Fighting For: From Food Riots to Food Banks* (Totnes: Prospect Books, 2016), p. 27.

105. Henry Lord Norris to Sir William Knollys, 1596, cit. Mary H. A. Dolman (Mrs. Bryan Stapleton), *Three Oxfordshire Parishes: A History of Kidlington, Yarnton and Begbroke* (Oxford: Clarendon Press, 1893), p. 61.

106. Katherine Halliday, 'New light on "the commotion time" of 1549: The Oxfordshire rising', *Historical Research* 82 (2009), 655–676.

107. Maurice Beresford, *Lost Villages of England* (Stroud: Sutton, 1998), p. 323.

108. John Walter and Keith Wrightson, 'Dearth and the Social Order in Early Modern England', *Past and Present* 71 (1976), 22–42, pp. 22–4; John Walter, 'The Geography of Food Riots', in *Crowd and Popular Politics in Early Modern England* (Manchester and New York: Manchester University Press, 2013), pp. 67–72.

109. John Walter, 'Grain Riots and Popular Attitudes to the Law: Maldon and the Crisis of 1629', in *Crowd and Popular Politics*, p. 49.

110. Pat Rogers, 'The Waltham Blacks and the Black Act', *The Historical Journal* 17 (1974), 465–86.

111. Quoted in Sutton, *Food Worth Fighting For*, pp. 25–26.

112. Sutton, *Food Worth Fighting For*, p. 57.

113. 'What shocking hard times', ci. Roy E. Palmer, *A Touch of the Times: Songs of Social Change 1774–1918* (Harmondsworth: Penguin, 1974), pp. 223–24.

114. Jonathan Bate, *John Clare: A Biography* (London: Picador, 2003), pp. 398–410.

115. Stephen Hussey, '"The Last Survivor of An Ancient Race": The Changing Face of Essex Gleaning', *The Agricultural History Review*, 45 (1997), 61–72.

116. Sutton, *Food Worth Fighting For*, pp. 31–32.

117. John Beckett, 'Swing riots', in *The Oxford Companion to British History*, ed. John Cannon (Oxford: Oxford University Press, 2009), https://www.oxfordreference.com/view/10.1093/acref/9780199567638.001.0001/acref-9780199567638-e-4117 [Accessed on March 25, 2022].

118. Sutton, *Food Worth Fighting For*, p. 71.

119. J. L. Hammond and Barbara Hammond, *The Village Labourer: 1760–1832* (London: Longmans, Green & Co., 1936), pp. 183–85.

120. Eric Hobsbawm and George Rudé, *Captain Swing: A Social History of the Great English Agricultural Uprising of 1830* (New York: Norton, 1973); Carl J. Griffin, *The Rural War: Captain Swing and the politics of protest* (Manchester: Manchester University Press, 2012).

121. Shershow, *Bread*, p. 102.

122. Jeremy Burchardt, *The Allotment Movement in England 1793–1873* (Woodbridge: The Boydell Press: 2002).

123. Sutton, *Food Worth Fighting For*, pp. 81–84.

124. Sutton, *Food Worth Fighting For*, p. 76.

125. Dalby, *Walter of Bibbesworth*, p. 55.

126. Samuel Richardson, *Pamela or Virtue Rewarded* (1740; Oxford: Oxford University Press, 2008), p. 15

127. Richardson, *Pamela*, pp. 41, 81; my emphasis.

128. Charles Dickens, *Hard Times* (1854; Harmondsworth: Penguin, 1969), p. 148.

129. Charles Dickens, *Barnaby Rudge: A Tale of the Riots of 'Eighty* (1841; London: Penguin, 2003), p. 665.

130. Details of the diets of the rural poor are drawn from John Burnett, *Plenty and Want: A Social History of Diet in England from 1815 to the present day* (London: Taylor & Francis, 2013); Edwin Grey, *Cottage Life in a Hertfordshire Village* (St Albans: Fisher, Knight, 1935); B. Seebohm Rowntree and May Kendall, *How the Labourer Lives. A Study of the Rural Labour Problem*

(London: Thomas Nelson & Sons, 1913); William Tuckwell, *Reminiscences of a Radical Parson* (London: Cassell, 1905).

131. Reports of the Poor Law Commissioners, 1843, cit. Burnett, *Plenty and Want*, p. 27.

132. Ellen Ross, *Love and Toil: Motherhood in Outcast London, 1870–1918* (Oxford: Oxford University Press, 1993), p. 55; see also Nickie Charles and Marion Kerr, *Women, Food and Families* (Manchester: Manchester University Press, 1988).

133. Richard Hoggart, *The Uses of Literacy* (Harmondsworth: Pelican, 1958), p. 38.

Liquid foods

1. Paul Henzner, in Jack C. Drummond, *The Englishman's Food: a history of five centuries of English diet* (London: Jonathan Cape, 1939), p. 44.

2. Edward Bury, *England's Bane, or the Deadly danger of drunkenness* (London, 1677); Mark Hailwood, *Alehouses and Good Fellowship in Early Modern England* (Woodbridge: Boydell Press, 2014).

3. Peter Clark, *The English Alehouse: A Social History 1200–1830* (London: Longman, 1983); Mark Hailwood, *Alehouses and Good Fellowship in early modern England* (Woodbridge: The Boydell Press, 2014).

4. Hailwood, *Alehouses*, p. 5.

5. Stewart Lee Allen, *The Devil's Cup: Coffee, the driving force in history* (Edinburgh: Canongate, 2001), p. 12.

6. Sophie D. Coe and Michael D. Coe, *The True History of Chocolate* (London: Thames and Hudson, 2013), p. 157.

7. John Burnett, *Liquid Pleasure: A Social History of Drinks in Modern Britain* (London and New York: Routledge, 1999), p. 71.

8. Burnett, *Liquid Pleasure*, p. 73.

9. 'Literature in Coffeehouses', https://sites.google.com/a/umich.edu/eighteenth-century-coffeehouses1/literature-in-coffeehouses [Accessed on April 2, 2022]; James Salter, 'A catalogue of the rarities to be seen at Don Saltero's Coffee-house in Chelsea' (1729), in *Eighteenth-century Coffee-house Culture*, ed. Markman Ellis, vol. 3 (London: Pickering & Chatto, 2006).

10. Richard Ames, *The character of a bigotted prince* (London, 1693).

11. Richard Ames, *Chuse which you will, liberty or slavery* (London, 1692); see also Brian Cowan, 'What was Masculine about the Public Sphere?: Gender and the Coffeehouse Milieu in Post Restoration England', *History Workshop Journal* 51 (2001), 127–57.

12. *Coffee-house Culture*, pp. 89–90.

13. Richard Steele, *The Spectator: No. 49*, Thursday, April 26, 1711, [Steele on Coffeehouse Society]' in *The Commerce of Everyday Life: Selections from the*

Tatler and the Spectator, ed. Erin Mackie (London: Palgrave Macmillan, 1998), p. 91.

14. Matthew Green, *The Lost World of the London Coffeehouse* (London: Idler Books, 2013).

15. The most expensive teas in the world are typically very small estate China teas, like Da-Hong Pao Tea.

16. Burnett, *Liquid Pleasure*, p. 57.

17. Friedrich Engels, *The Condition of the Working Class in England*, trans. Florence Kelley Wischnewetzky (New York: John W. Lovell, 1844), p. 107.

18. John Griffiths, *Tea: The Drink That Changed the World* (London: Deutsch, 2007), pp. 32–37

19. Shashi Tharoor, *Inglorious Empire: What the British Did to India* (London: Hurst & Company, 2017), p. 230; Sarah Rose, *For All the Tea in China: How England Stole the World's Favorite Drink and Changed History* (New York: Viking, 2010).

20. Rebecca Smithers, 'UK tea sales fall by more than 6% over past five years' in *The Guardian* 5 August, 2015, https://www.theguardian.com/ lifeandstyle/2015/aug/05/uk-tea-sales-fall-teabags-coffee [Accessed on April 2, 2022].

21. *OED2, Oxford English Dictionary Online* (1989) https://www.oed.com/ oed2/00094688 [Accessed on April 2, 2022].

22. Jessica Warner, *Craze: Gin and Debauchery in an Age of Reason* (London: Random House, 2003), p. 11.

23. Patrick Dillon, *Gin: The Much-Lamented Death of Madam Geneva* (London: Justin, Charles & Co., 2003), p. 14.

24. Bernard Mandeville, *The Fable of the Bees* (London, 1714), p. 86.

25. Warner, *Craze*, p. 16.

26. Emily Vikre, 'Where does alcohol come from anyway?', 13 August 2015, https://food52.com/blog/13777-where-does-alcohol-come-from-anyway [Accessed on May 23, 2022].

27. Thomas Wilson, *Distilled spirituous liquors the bane of the nation* (London, 1736), p. 10.

28. Thomas Birch, ed., *A Collection of the Yearly Bills of Mortality from 1657 to 1758 inclusive* (London, 1759), supplement, 13.

29. Warner, *Craze*, p. 49.

30. Stephen Hales, *A Friendly Admonition to the Drinkers of Gin, Brandy, and other distilled spirituous liquors* (London: Dod, 1751), pp. 11–12.

31. Daniel Defoe, *Augusta Triumphans* (London: Roberts, 1728), p. 45.

32. Wilson, *Distilled spirituous liquors*, pp. 8; 34.

33. Derek Jarrett, *England in the Age of Hogarth* (London: Hart-Davis and MacGibbon, 1974).

34. Jarrett, *Age of Hogarth*, p. 98.

35. Quoted in Valerie Fildes, *Breasts, Bottles and Babies: A History of Infant Feeding* (Edinburgh: Edinburgh University Press, 1986). p. 236.

36. Mary Dorothy George, *London Life in the Eighteenth Century* (London: Penguin, 1966), p. 68.

37. Wilson, *Distilled spirituous liquors*, p. 37.

38. Fielding, *An Enquiry into the Causes of the Late Increase of Robbers* (London: Millar, 1751), p. 30. The *Enquiry* does not, however, include the passage beginning 'Gin shops are undoubtedly the nurseries of all manner of vice and wickedness', attributed to Fielding by a number of modern works on gin, including Warner, *Craze*, and Richard Barnett, *The Dedalus Book of Gin* (London: Dedalus, 2011); it is in fact from an 1814 work by lawyer and polemicist Basil Montagu, *Some Enquiries into the effects of Fermented Liquors* (London, 1814, 3rd edn., 1841), p. 48, showing how these concerns and panics persisted.

39. Jessica Warner and Frank Ivis, 'Gin and gender in early eighteenth-century'. *Eighteenth-Century Life 24* (2000), 85–105, p. 91.

40. Jonathan White, *Luxury and labour: ideas of labouring-class consumption in eighteenth-century England*, PhD thesis, University of Warwick, 2001, p. 104.

41. Warner and Ivis, 'Gin and gender', p. 13.

42. Warner and Ivis, 'Gin and gender', p. 86.

43. Charles Dickens, *Sketches by Boz: Illustrative of Every-Day Life and Every-Day People* (1836; London: Penguin, 1995), pp. 217–18.

44. *Illustrated London News*, May 6, 1848, p. 298.

45. Kal Raustiala, 'The Imperial Cocktail: How the Gin and Tonic became the British Empire's Secret Weapon' *slate.com*, 28 August, 2013, http://www.slate.com/articles/health_and_science/foreigners/2013/08/gin_and_tonic_kept_the_british_empire_healthy_the_drink_s_quinine_powder.single.html [Accessed on April 2, 2022].

46. John A. West, 'A Brief History and Botany of Cacao', in *Chilies to Chocolate: Food the Americas Gave the World*, ed. Nelson Foster and Linda S. Cordell (Tucson: University of Arizona Press, 1992), pp.105–22, pp. 113–14.

47. Anonymous poem, 1792.

48. Percy Bysshe Shelley, *A Vindication of Natural Diet* (1813), http://www.animal-rights-library.com/texts-c/shelley01.htm [Accessed on April 2, 2022].

Fishes

1. Michael Alexander, *Old English Riddles from the Exeter Book*, 2nd edn. (London: Anvil Press, 2007), p. 74.

2. William Butler Yeats, *Fairy and folktales of the Irish peasantry* (London: Walter Scott Publishing Co., 1888), p. 35.

3. Yeats, *Fairy and folktales*, p. 37.

4. Janet Bord and Colin Bord, *Sacred water: holy wells and well lore in Britain and Ireland* (London: Paladin, 1985).

5. James Owen, *Trout* (London: Reaktion Books, 2012), p. 43.

6. Owen, *Trout*, p. 41.

7. *Geoponika*, ed. and trans. Andrew Dalby (Totnes: Prospect Books, 2011), XX, 46; 'Roman fish sauce', https://coquinaria.nl/en/roman-fish-sauce/#bibliografie [Accessed on May 9, 2022].

8. Henry C. Darby, *Domesday England* (Cambridge: Cambridge University Press, 1977), p. 280.

9. Ida L. Gordon, ed., *The Seafarer* (New York: Appleton Country Crofts, 1960).

10. Gustav Milne, *The Medieval Port of London* (Stroud: Tempus, 2003); Ellen W. Moore, *The fairs of medieval England: an introductory study* (Toronto: Pontifical Institute of Medieval Studies, 1985); *Counties and Communities: Essays on East Anglian History presented to Hassell Smith*, ed. A. Hassell Smith et al. (Norwich: Centre of East Anglian Studies, University of East Anglia, 1996).

11. J. R. R. Tolkien. *Sir Gawain and the Green Knight* (London: HarperCollins, 1995), II.37, lines 16–18, p. 43.

12. Harleian MS. 4016; Constance B. Hieatt and Sharon Butler, eds., *Curye on Inglysch: English Culinary Manuscripts of The Fourteenth Century* (Oxford: Oxford University Press for the Early English Text Society, 1985), p. 114; pp. 61–62.

13. Peter Macardle, *Confabulations: Cologne Life and Humanism in Hermann Schotten's Confabulationes Tironum Litterariorum of 1525* (Manchester: Manchester University Press, 2009), p. 66. Another saint also saved a child from choking on a fishbone in Northern England, in Shannon Lewis-Simpson, *Youth and age in the Medieval North* (Leiden, Boston: Brill, 2008), p. 113; Steve Roud, *London Lore: The Legends and traditions of world's most vibrant city* (London: Arrow, 2010), p. 212.

14. See Martha Carlin and Joel. T. Rosenthal, eds., *Food and Eating in Medieval Europe* (London: Bloomsbury, 1988); also Paul S. Lloyd, *Food and Identity in England, 1540–1640: Eating to Impress* (London: Bloomsbury, 2016), p. 41.

15. Frederick J. Furnivall, *Early English Meals and Manners* (Oxford: Oxford University Press for the Early English Text Society, 1868); Peter Brears, *Cooking and Dining*, p. 250.

16. Philip Hoare, *The Sea Inside* (London: Fourth Estate, 2013), pp. 70–71.

17. Christopher Dyer, *Everyday Life in Medieval England* (London: The Hambledon Press, 1994), p. 110, from *Calendar of Liberate Rolls*, iv, pp. 346–415.

18. Brears, *Cooking and Dining*, p. 143.

19. Desiderius Erasmus, 'A Fish Diet', *Colloquies*, trans. Craig Thompson (Toronto: University of Toronto Press, 2016), p. 678.

20. Quoted in Bridget A. Henisch, *The Medieval Cook* (Woodbridge: The Boydell Press, 2009), p. 59.

21. Jules Michelet, *La Mer*, cit. Mark Kurlansky, *Salt: A World History* (London: Vintage Books, 2002), p. 130.

22. Langland, *Piers Plowman*, trans. George Economou (Philadelphia: University of Pennsylvania Press, 1996), Passus IX, lines 94–95, p. 82.

23. See also Richard C. Hoffmann, 'Economic Development and Aquatic Ecosystems in Medieval Europe', *American Historical Review* 101 (1996), 631–69.

24. John Taverner, *Certaine experiments concerning fish and fruite* (1600), http://quod.lib.umich.edu/e/eebo/A13396.0001.001/1:4.1.1?rgn=div3;view=fulltext 11–12] [Accessed on April 2, 2022].

25. C. F. Hickling, 'Prior More's fishponds', *Medieval Archaeology* XV (1971), 118–23; C. K. Currie, *Medieval Fishponds: aspects of their origin, function, management and development*, unpublished MPhil thesis, University College, London, 1988, pp. 183–88; E. K. Balon, *The domestication of carp* (Toronto: Royal Ontario Museum Life Sciences Miscellaneous Publications, 1974).

26. Mark Dawson, *Plenti and Grase: Food and Drink in a Sixteenth-Century Household* (Totnes: Prospect Books, 2009), p. 131.

27. Andrew Jotischky, *A Hermit's Cookbook: Monks, Food and Fasting in the Middle Ages* (London: Continuum, 2011).

28. Mortimer, *Elizabethan England*, p. 208.

29. Mortimer, *Elizabethan England*, pp. 209–11.

30. Quoted in G. L. Alward, *The Sea Fisheries of Great Britain and Ireland* (Grimsby: Albert Gait, 1932).

31. Erasmus, *Colloquies*, p. 679.

32. Mortimer, *Elizabethan England*, p. 309.

33. Wilson, *Food & Drink in Britain*, pp. 27–32.

34. Callum Roberts, *The Unnatural History of the Sea* (London: Gaia Books, 2007), pp. 124–25.

35. Oliver Goldsmith, *An History of the Earth and Animated Nature* (London: R. Edwards, 1976), pp. 125–29.

36. Peter Heath, 'North Sea Fishing in the Fifteenth Century: The Scarborough Fleet', *Northern History* 3 (1968), 53–69.

37. D. B. Quinn, *England and the discovery of America, 1481–1620* (London: Allen & Unwin, 1973).

38. Hoare, *Sea Inside*, p. 94.

39. James G. Bertram, *The Harvest of the Sea* (London: John Murray, 1873), p. 190.

40. Alan Davidson, *North Atlantic Seafood: A Comprehensive Guide with Recipes*, 3rd edn. (Berkeley: Ten Speed Press, 2003), pp. 38–39.

41. *The West Briton* 31 July, 1818, cit. John McWilliams, *The Cornish Fishing Industry: An Illustrated History* (Stroud, Amberley Press, 2014), p. 17.

42. Davidson, *North Atlantic Seafood*, p. 39.

43. Quinn, *England and the Discovery of North America*.

44. John McWilliams, *The Cornish Fishing Industry*, p. 47.

45. Brian Fagan, *The Little Ice Age* (New York: Basic Books, 2003), p. 77.

46. James Evans. *Emigrants: Why the English Sailed to the New World* (London: Weidenfeld & Nicolson, 2017), pp. 15–17.

47. Quoted in Mark Kurlansky, *Cod: A biography of the Fish That Changed the World* (London: Vintage Books, 1997), pp. 48–49.

48. Heather Dalton, *Merchants and Explorers: Roger Barlow, Sebastian Cabot, & Networks of Atlantic Exchange 1500–1560* (Oxford: Oxford University Press, 2016); Evan T. Jones and Margaret M. Condon, *Cabot and Bristol's Age of Discovery: The Bristol Discovery Voyages 1480–1508* (Bristol: Cabot Project Publications, 2016); this short book provides an up-to-date account of the voyages, based on the research of the Cabot Project (University of Bristol), aimed at a general audience. Chapter 7, 'Bristol and the "New Found Land": 1499–1508 voyages', pp. 57–70, includes a discussion of Sebastian's involvement in Bristol exploration at this time.

49. William F. Hutchinson, et al., 'The globalization of naval provisioning: ancient DNA and stable isotope analyses of stored cod from the wreck of the Mary Rose, AD 1545', *Royal Society Open Science* 2 (2015), https://royalsocietypublishing.org/doi/10.1098/rsos.150199; Julie Gardiner, *Before the Mast: Life and Death aboard the Mary Rose, The Archaeology of the Mary Rose*, vol. 4 (Portsmouth: Oxbow Books for the Mary Rose Trust, 2005); Lizzie Collingham, *The Hungry Empire: how Britain's quest for food shaped the modern world* (New York: Basic Books, 2017).

50. Interspersed from Hutchinson et al., 'Globalization', and see F. P. Bennema and A. D. Rijnsdorp, 'Fish abundance, fisheries, fish trade and consumption in sixteenth-century Netherlands as described by Adriaen Coenen', *Fisheries Research* 161 (2015), 384–399; J. E. Candow, 'Migrants and residents: the interplay between European and domestic fisheries in northeast North America, 1502–1854', in *A history of the North Atlantic Fisheries Vol. 1: From early times to the mid-nineteenth century*, ed. D. J. Starkey, J. Th. Thór, I. Heidbrink (Bremen, Germany: H. M. Hauschild, 2009), pp. 416–52.

51. Mark Kurlansky, *Cod*, pp. 53–55.

52. John McGurk, *The Elizabethan conquest of Ireland: the 1590s crisis* (Manchester: Manchester University Press, 1997), p. 2; Harold A. Innis, *The Cod Fisheries: the history of international economy* (New Haven, CT: Yale University Press, 1940); E. F. L. Poynter, *The Journal of James Yonge* (London: Longmans, 1963).

53. Kurlansky, *Cod*, p. 56.

54. Hannah Glasse, *The Art of Cookery, made plain and easy*, 5th edn. (London, 1755), pp. 225–26; there were numerous eighteenth-century editions following the first publication in 1747.

55. Kurlansky, *Salt*, p. 129.

56. Simon Cooper, *Life of a chalk stream* (London: William Collins, 2014), p. 205.

57. Tag Barnes, *Waterside Companions* (London: Arco Publications, 1963), esp. pp. 67; 43–45; 71–72.

58. Cooper, *Chalk stream*, p. 83.

59. Ian Whitelaw, *The History of Fly Fishing in Fifty Flies* (London: Aurum Press, 2015), p. 12.

60. Izaak Walton, *The compleat angler* (1676; Menston: Scolar Press, 1971).

61. Walton, *Compleat angler*, p. 99.

62. According to Bevan, Walton simply cites and compiles other angling books – including Wynkyn de Worde, *A Treatise of Fysshynge Wyth an Angle* (1496), Leonard Mascall, *A Booke of Fishing – With Hooke and Line* (1590), William Samuels, *The Arte of Angling* (1577), and Gervase Markham, *The Pleasures of Princes or Good Mens Recreations* (1614).

63. Richard Franck, *Northern Memoirs* (London, 1694), p. 150.

64. Franck, *Northern Memoirs*, p. 95.

65. William O. Hassall, Molly Harrison and Asa Briggs, *How They Lived* (Oxford: Basil Blackwell, 1962), p. 140.

66. Ian Niall, *The Poacher's Handbook* (Ludlow: Merlin Unwin Books, 1950), pp. 1–4.

67. Niall, *Poacher's Handbook*, p. 107.

68. Keith Thomas, *Man and the Natural World* (London: Penguin, 1984), p. 177.

69. Guy Pocock, ed. *The Letters of Charles Lamb*, vol. 1 (London: J. M. Dent & Sons, 1904), pp. 116–17; George G. Byron, *Don Juan* (1824; London: Penguin, 2004), canto XIII, stanza 106, p. 469.

70. 'To a Fish of the Brooke', in *Humorous Poems*, ed. W. M. Rossetti (London, 1872), pp. 230–31.

71. Jonathan Balcombe, *What a Fish Knows: The Inner Lives of Our Underwater Cousins* (New York: Scientific American/Farrar, Straus and Giroux, 2016).

72. Harrison, *Description*, pp. 419–20; see also Peter Ackroyd, *Thames: Sacred River* (London: Vintage Books, 2008), p. 276.

73. Laura Mason and Catherine Brown, *Traditional Foods of Britain: An Inventory* (Totnes: Prospect Books, 1999), pp. 92–3.

74. Peter Coates, *Salmon* (London: Reaktion, 2006), pp. 72–73; see also T. S. Eliot's commentary on tinned foods in *The Wasteland*, published the year before the election, 1922.

75. Coates, *Salmon*, p. 75.

76. David J. Starkey, Chris Reid and Neil Ashcroft, *England's Sea Fisheries* (London: Chatham, 2000), p. 63.

77. Peter Frank, *Yorkshire Fisherfolk: A Social History of the Yorkshire inshore fishing community* (London: Phillimore, 2002), p. 2.

78. Frank, *Yorkshire Fisherfolk*, p. 189.

79. Philip Hoare, *Leviathan or The Whale* (London: Fourth Estate, 2009), pp. 230–31; 283–87; 289–93.

80. Anne Addison, 'Strange Things on the Dinner Table', *WW2 People's War*, *The BBC*, http://www.bbc.co.uk/history/ww2peopleswar/stories/92/a1110592. shtml [Accessed on April 2, 2022].

81. Callum Roberts, *Unnatural History*, p. 46.

82. Maggie Lane, *Jane Austen and Food* (London: Bloomsbury, 1995), p. 109.

83. Maggie Lane, *Jane Austen*, p. 144.

84. Isabella Beeton, *The Book of Household Management* (1861; London: Jonathan Cape, 1968), p. 117.

85. Roberts, *Unnatural History*, pp. 144–46.

86. Paul R. Thompson, *Living the Fishing* (London: Routledge & Kegan Paul, 1983), p. 123.

87. Thompson, *Living the Fishing*, p. 129.

88. Marc A. Jones, *The Grimsby Fisher Lads: The Story of Humber Fishing Apprentices* (Epsom: Bretwalda Books, 2015).

89. Wilson, *Eating with the Victorians*, p. xvi.

90. Peter Cunningham, *Hand-Book of London: Past and Present* (London: J. Murray, 1850).

91. Sarah Freeman, *Mutton and Oysters* (London: Victor Gollancz, 1989), p. 278.

92. Tim Jepson and Larry Porges, *National Geographic London Book of Lists: The City's Best, Worst, Oldest, Greatest, and Quirkiest* (2014), p. 66.

93. Florence White, *Good Things in England* (1932; London: Jonathan Cape, 1951), p. 129.

94. George Sala, *Twice Round-the-Clock on the Hours of the Day and Night in London* (London: Houston and Wright, 1862), p. 139.

95. Broomfield, *Food and Cooking*, pp. 88–89.

96. Sala, *Twice Round-the-Clock*, p. 12.

97. Nathaniel Hawthorne, *Passages from English Note-Books*, vol. 2 (Boston: James R. Osgood and Company, 1875), 15 November 1857.

98. Mayhew, *London Labour*, p. 65.

99. *Bailey's English Dictionary* (1736).

100. Steve Roud, *The English Year* (London: Penguin, 2008), p. 420. The festival continues to this day.

101. Charles Dickens, Jr., *Dickens's Dictionary of the Thames: From its source to the Nore* (London: Macmillan & Co, 1885).

102. David Burton, *The Raj at Table: A Culinary History of the British in India* (London: Faber, 1993), p. 108.

103. Navroji Framji, *Indian Cookery for Young House Keepers: Containing Numerous Local Indian Recipes both Useful and Original* (Bombay: Thacker & Co., 1883), p. 105.

104. Mrs J. Bartley, *Indian cookery 'general' for young housekeepers* (Bombay: Thacker & Co, 1903).

105. Burton, *The Raj at Table*, p. 109.

106. Burton, *The Raj at Table*, p. 101.

107. Flora Annie Steel and Grace Gardiner, *The Complete Indian Housekeeper and Cook*, ed. R. Crane and A. Johnston (Oxford: Oxford University Press, 2010), p. 240.

108. Jennifer Brennan, *Curries and Bugles* (London: Viking, 1990), p. 62.

109. Ruth Goodman, *How to be a Victorian* (London: Penguin, 2014), p. 376.

110. Jepson and Porges, *London Book of Lists*, p. 51.

111. Carlin and Rosenthal, *Food and Eating*, p. 29.

112. Glasse, *Art of Cookery*, p. 118; Eliza Acton, *Modern Cookery in all its branches*, 2nd edn. (London: Longman, 1845), p. 67; Dickens, *Oliver Twist*, vol. II, p. 92.

113. John K. Walton, *Fish and Chips and the British working class 1870 to 1940* (Leicester: Leicester University Press, 1992), p. 33.

114. Walton, *Fish and Chips*, p. 6.

115. Walton, *Fish and Chips*, p. 12

116. Francie Nichol and Joe Robinson, *The Life and Times of Francie Nichol of South Shields* (London: Allen & Unwin, 1975), cit. Walton, *Fish and Chips*, p. 57.

117. Walton, *Fish and Chips*, p. 16.

118. Walton, *Fish and Chips*, p. 89.

119. Walton, *Fish and Chips*, p. 107.

120. Walton, *Fish and Chips*, p. 158.

121. Jane Grigson, *English Food* (London: MacMillan, 1974), p. 77.

122. Virginia Woolf, *The Years* (1937; Oxford: Oxford University Press, 2009), Appendix, p. 458.

123. Virginia Woolf, *A Room of One's Own* (London: Hogarth Press, 1929), p. 10.

124. Letter to Lady Robert (Eleanor Cecil), in Virginia Woolf, *Letters Vol. 1: The Flight of the Mind 1888–1912*, ed. Nigel Nicolson and Joanne Trautmann (London: Hogarth Press, 1975), p. 278.

125. Harold McGee, *On Food and Cooking: The Science and Lore of the Kitchen* (New York: Scribner, 1984), pp. 208–9.

On lunch: an essay

1. Goodman, *How to be a Tudor*, p. 252.
2. Mary (Mamie) Dickens, *My Father as I Recall Him* (London: Roxburghe Press, 1896), p. 64.
3. Charles Dickens, *The Posthumous Papers of the Pickwick Club* (1836; London: Penguin, 2000), p. 727.
4. Wilson, *Eating with the Victorians*, p. 50.
5. Broomfield, *Food and Cooking*, p. 51.
6. Flora Thompson, *Lark Rise to Candleford: A Trilogy* (London, Oxford: Oxford University Press, 1945), p. 44.
7. Arnold Palmer, *Movable Feasts: A Reconnaissance of the Origins and Consequences of Fluctuations in Meal-times* (Oxford: Oxford University Press, 1952), p. 80.
8. John Betjeman, *Summoned by Bells* (London: John Murray, 1960), p. 94.
9. Elizabeth David, *An Omelette and a Glass of Wine* (New York: Lyons and Burford, 1984), p. 21.
10. Elizabeth David, *French Provincial Cooking* (London: Penguin, 1960).
11. Elizabeth David, *A Book of Mediterranean Food* (London: John Lehmann, 1950), Introduction, p. 5.
12. Ambrose Heath, *Good Food: Month by Month Recipes* (London: Faber & Faber, 1932), pp. 185–86.
13. David, *Omelette*, p. 24.
14. David, *Omelette*, p. 19.
15. David, *Omelette*, p. 21.
16. David, *Mediterranean Food*, p. 132.
17. David, *Mediterranean Food*, p. 103.
18. Katherine Whitehorn, quoted in Christina Hardyment, *Slice of Life: The British Way of Eating since 1945* (London: BBC Books, 1995), p. 91.
19. Claire Tomlin, quoted in Lisa Chaney, *Elizabeth David: A Mediterranean Passion* (London: MacMillan, 1998), p. 426.
20. Elizabeth David, *Summer Cooking* (London: Penguin, 1955), p. 210.
21. Betjeman, *Summoned by Bells*, pp. 93, 103; Judith Priestman, 'The dilettante and the dons', *Oxford Today* 18 (2006), https://web.archive.org/web/20090417002131/http:/www.oxfordtoday.ox.ac.uk/2005-06/v18n3/05.shtml [Accessed on May 31, 2022].

Foraging

1. John Webster, *The displaying of supposed witchcraft* (London, 1677), p. 347.
2. Webster, *The displaying*.

3. For the folklore of plants, see Steve Roud and Jacqueline Simpson, *A Dictionary of English Folklore* (Oxford: Oxford University Press, 2000), and Roy Vickery, *A Dictionary of Plant-Lore* (Oxford: Oxford University Press, 1995), which contains Vickery's otherwise unpublished folklore materials on memories of foraging. Steve Roud's *The Penguin Guide to the superstitions of Britain and Ireland* (London: Penguin, 2006) also contains many nuggets of information.

4. Vickery, *Dictionary of Plant-Lore*, p. 404.

5. John Gerard, *The Herball, or, Generall Historie of plantes*, enlarged edition (1633), p. 46.

6. Peter V. Glob, *The Bog People: Iron-Age Man Preserved* (London: HarperCollins, 1971), p. 33.

7. Don Brothwell, *The Bogman and the Archaeology of People* (London: British Museum Publications, 1986); T. G. Holden, 'The Last Meals of the Lindow Bog Men', in *Bog Bodies: New Discoveries and New Perspectives*, ed. R. C. Turner and R. G. Scaife (London: British Museum Press, 1995), pp. 76–82.

8. Richard Wrangham, *Catching Fire: How Cooking Made Us Human* (London: Profile, 2009).

9. Mark Porter, 'Girls are maturing faster but puberty at 7 is not the norm', *The Times* 17 August 2010, https://www.thetimes.co.uk/article/girls-are-maturing-faster-but-puberty-at-7-is-not-the-norm-mcvwx5hv0b2 [Accessed on June 19, 2022].

10. Stephanie V. W. Lucianovic, *Suffering Succotash: A Picky Eater's Quest to Understand Why We Hate the Foods We Hate* (London: Penguin, 2012).

11. On honey, see Bee Wilson, *The Hive: The Story of the Honeybee and Us* (London: John Murray, 2005).

12. Greg Critser, *Fat Land: How Americans became the Fattest People in the World* (London: Penguin, 2004), pp. 129–30.

13. John Evelyn, *Acetaria: A Book of Sallets* (London: 1699); and see also Joan Thirsk, *Food in Early Modern England: Phases, Fads, Fashions 1500–1760* (London, Hambledon Continuum, 2006).

14. Dock pudding recipes: Alexis Soyer, *A Shilling Cookery for the People* (London: Routledge, 1854), p. 114, and see The Foods of England Project, http://www.foodsofengland.co.uk/dockpudding.htm. [Accessed on April 7, 2022]. While still eaten in West Yorkshire, it may once have been more widespread, since it closely resembles the recipe in *The Forme of Cury*, compiled 'by the Master-Cooks of King Richard II', c.1390: see *The Forme of Cury, a roll of ancient English cookery*, ed. Samuel Pegge (1780; Cambridge: Cambridge University Press, 2015), and also http://www.foodsofengland.co.uk/book1390cury.htm. [Accessed on April 7, 2022].

15. *John Evelyn, Cook*, ed. Christopher Driver (Totnes: Prospect Books, 1997); and see Rachael Field, 'sorrel, bedstraw, nettles, and many other hedgerow

herbs were used to make cheese at almost any time of the year, without the sacrifice of calf, lamb, or piglet' (*Irons in the Fire: A History of Cooking Equipment* (Marlborough: Crowood Press, 1984). Thanks to Emily Van Evera.

16. Jane Grigson, *Jane Grigson's Vegetable Book* (Harmondsworth: Penguin, 1978), pp. 154–55.

17. See Jennifer McLagan, *Bitter: A Taste of the World's Most Dangerous Flavor* (Berkeley: Ten Speed Press, 2014) and Lucianovic, *Suffering Succotash*.

18. Both Kenelm Digby and Robert May advise sparing use.

19. M. Hampton and Q. O. N. Kay, '*Sorbus domestica L.*, new to Wales and the British Isles', *Watsonia* 20 (1995), 379–84.

20. *Le Menagier de Paris*, trans. Janet Hinson from original by Jerome Pichon (1846), http://www.daviddfriedman.com/Medieval/Cookbooks/Menagier/Menagier.html. [Accessed on April 7, 2022].

21. Andrew Boorde, *The Breviary of Halthe, for all manner or sicknesses and diseases the whiche may be in man or woman doth folowe* (c.1547).

22. Roud and Simpson, *Dictionary of English Folklore*.

23. Richard Mabey, *Food for Free* (London: HarperCollins, 2012), pp. 59–60.

24. Roud and Simpson, *Dictionary of English Folklore*; Patrick Roper, 'Rowans, Whitebeams and Service Trees', http://rowanswhitebeamsandservicetrees.blogspot.co.uk/2010/03/descriptive-list-of-sorbus-drinks.html [Accessed on April 7, 2022]; Charles Roeder, 'Notes on food and drink in Lancashire and other northern counties', *Transactions of the Lancashire and Cheshire Antiquarian Society* XX (1902), pp 41–104.

25. Lucy Yates, *The Country Housewife's Book: How to Make the most of Country Produce and Country Fare* (1934; London: Persephone, 2008).

26. Esther Copley, *Cottage Comforts* (London: Simpkin and Marshall, 1829), p. 48.

27. https://en.wikipedia.org/wiki/2004_Morecambe_Bay_cockling_disaster [Accessed on April 7, 2022].

28. Charles Maclean, *Island on the Edge of the World: The Story of St. Kilda* (Edinburgh: Canongate, 1977), p. 26.

29. Vicomte de Mauduit, *They Can't Ration These* (1940; London: Persephone, 2004), p. 45.

30. See Keith Murray, *History of the Second World War* (London: HMSO, 1955).

31. Derek J. Oddy, *From Plain Fare to Fusion Food: British Diet from the 1890s to the 1990s* (Woodbridge: Boydell Press: 2003); Carolyn Ekins, 'The 1940s Experiment', https://1940sexperiment.wordpress.com/rationing-diet-sheets/. [Accessed on April 7, 2022].

32. David Everitt-Matthias, *Essence: Recipes from Le Champignon Sauvage* (Bath: Absolute, 2006) and *Beyond Essence: New Recipes from Le Champignon Sauvage* (Bath: Absolute, 2013). Among others, recent cookbooks focusing on

flowers include Frances Bissell, *The Scented Kitchen: Cooking with Flowers* (London: Serif, 2006); Jekka McVicar, *Cooking with Flowers* (London: Kyle Cathie, 2003); Sharon Shipley, *The Lavender Cookbook* (Philadelphia, PA:, Running Books Publishers Ltd, 2004).

33. William Lawson, *A new orchard and garden; with, The Country Housewife's Garden* (1618; Totnes: Prospect Books, 2003), pp. 15, 91; John Murrell, *Murrell's Two Books of Cookery and Carving* (1638), ed. Stuart Peachey (Bristol: Stuart Press, 1993).

34. 'In the spring they make of them excellent minnow-tansies; for being well washed in salt, and their heads and tails cut off, and their guts taken out, and not washed after, they prove excellent for that use; that is, being fried with yolks of eggs, the flowers of cowslips, and of primroses, and a little tansy; thus used they make a dainty dish of meat.', Walton, *Compleat angler*, chapter 18, p. 197.

35. *The Receipt Book of Joseph Cooper*, cook to Charles I, in Eleanor Sinclair Rohde, *A Garden of Herbs* (1922; Bedford, Mass.: Applewood Books, 2007), p. 54.

36. Thomas Austin, ed., *Two fifteenth-century cookery-books* (London: Oxford University Press, 1964), p. 20.

37. The tradition is attributed to the Irish saint, Boethius, by the early nineteenth-century poet and scholar John Leyden; James Johnston quotes and expands on Leyden: James F. Johnston, *The Chemistry of Common Life* (Edinburgh and London: William Blackwood and Sons, 1879), p. 385.

38. Gerard, *Herball*, pp. 132–3.

39. Glasse, *Art of Cookery*, pp. 116–17.

40. Auguste Escoffier, *Le Guide Culinaire: Aide-memoire de cuisine Practique* (Paris: Flammarion, 1903), p.141.

41. Murrell, *Cookery and Carving*; see also W. M., *The Queen's Closet Opened*, London, 1695–98), which has you putting them up in fresh vinegar and salt with a piece of alum.

42. White, *Good Things*, p. 105.

43. Francis Bacon, 'Sylva sylvarum', in *The Works of Francis Bacon*, ed. J. Spedding, R. Ellis, D. Heath (Boston: Houghton, Mifflin and Company: 1753), vol. IV, p. 167.

44. *A Proper Newe Booke of Cokerye*, ed. Catherine F. Frere (1545; Cambridge: W. Heffer, 1913), in White, *Good Things*, p. 232.

45. This myth has been adopted by, among others, *The Economist*, and also by botanical.com's *A Modern Herbal* (http://botanical.com/botanical/mgmh/mgmh.html [Accessed on April 7, 2022], which provides an electronic version of *A Modern Herbal* (London: Jonathan Cape, 1931) by Mrs Maud Grieve which 'continues to be one of the most popular resources for herbal information, written in the early part of the last century'. The entry under

Glasswort/Marsh Samphire quotes the (fake) More passage: (http://www.
botanical.com/botanical/mgmh/g/glassw18.html [Accessed on April 7,
2022]). http://www.saudiaramcoworld.com/issue/199406/samphire-from.sea.
to.shining.seed.htm [Accessed on April 7, 2022] is an account of a project in
Saudi Arabia to plant samphire in the desert (!). The author, Arthur Clark, in
a section at the end called 'Advice to Herbivores', has the following: 'In a
1991 story about the plant, *The Economist* noted that, though it's a gourmet
food today, samphire's older name in the British Isles – somewhat ironically –
is "poor man's asparagus". Indeed, Sir Thomas More wrote almost 500 years
ago that samphire improved "many a poor knave's pottage", affording him a
relish to accompany "his mouthful of salt meat"', and he goes on to quote
Gerard and Sophie Grigson among others. The *Wiccan Herbal Encyclopedia*
duly has under glasswort Sir Thomas More, enumerating the useful native
plants that would improve 'many a poor knave's pottage' if he were skilled in
their properties, says that 'Glasswort might afford him a pickle for his
mouthful of salt meat' (http://www.magicspells.in/magical_herbal_
enclyclopedia_g.htm [Accessed on April 7, 2022]. Similarly see: *Viable Health*
(http://www.viablehealth.com/botanical/mgmh/g/glassw18.html [Accessed
on April 7, 2022]; *The Family Doctor* (http://www.the-family-doctor.com/a-
modern-herbal/g/Glassworts.htm [Accessed on April 7, 2022]; *Mystic Ways
Pagan Knowledgebase* (http://mysticways.wiki.zoho.com/Herbal-
Encyclopedia---G.html [Accessed on April 7, 2022]. The trouble with
praiseworthy autodidacticism is that it leads to fakelore if the creator is more
interested in the legend than in truth.

46. Charlotte Mason, *The Ladies' Assistant for regulating and supplying the table:
being a complete system of cookery*, 6th edn. (London: J. Walter, 1787),
p. 340.
47. *Adam's Luxury, and Eve's Cookery: or the kitchen garden display'd* (1744;
London: Prospect Books, 1983), p. 144.
48. Auguste Escoffier, *A guide to modern cookery* (London: William Heinemann,
1907), pp. 630–31.
49. Evelyn, *Acetaria*, pp. 149–53.
50. Roger Phillips et al., *Wild Food* (London: Pan, 1983); Everitt-Matthias,
Essence and *Beyond Essence*; Richard Mabey, *Food for Free*, and *Weeds: The
Story of Outlaw Plants* (London: Profile Books, 2010).
51. Piero Camporesi, *Bread of Dreams: food and fantasy in early modern Europe*,
trans. David Gentilcore (Cambridge: Polity, 1989).
52. W. Rubel and D. Arora, 'A Study of Cultural Bias in Field Guide
Determinations of Mushroom Edibility Using the Iconic Mushroom,
Amanita Muscaria, as an Example', *Economic Botany* 62 (2008), 223–43.
53. Mark Boyle, 'Moneyless man reveals how to live a cashless life without
starving', *The Guardian*, 2 June 2010, http://www.theguardian.com/

environment/blog/2010/jun/02/mark-boyle-moneyless-man-food-for-free [Accessed on April 7, 2022].

54. Rebecca Kessler, 'Urban Gardening: Managing the Risks of Contaminated Soil', *Environmental Health Perspectives* 121 (2013), A326-33, http://ehp.niehs.nih.gov/121-a326/ [Accessed on April 7, 2022]; Metals_urban_garden_veg_synopsis.pdf (cornell.edu) [Accessed on April 27, 2022].

55. Boyle, 'Moneyless man'.

56. *Jamie's School Dinners*, DVD, Fremantle, 2005.

57. John Vidal, 'More than 30% of our food is thrown away', *The Guardian*, 15 April, 2005, http://www.theguardian.com/uk_news/story/0,,1460183,00.html [Accessed on April 7, 2022]. Most retailers say they have significantly reduced the amount of food wasted each year since 2000.

58. Sarah Bentley, 'Who's to blame for supermarket rejection of "ugly" fruit and vegetables?', *The Ecologist*, 29 December 2011, http://www.theecologist.org/News/news_analysis/1174157/whos_to_blame_for_supermarket_rejection_of_ugly_fruit_and_vegetables.html [Accessed on April 7, 2022].

59. Nigel Slater often refers to the grim English food of the 1960s; see Slater, *Eating for England: The Delights and Eccentricities of the British at Table* (London: Harper Perennial, 2008).

Apples

1. *OED2*.

2. Craig Taylor, *Return to Akenfield* (London: Granta, 2007), p. 25. The title refers to the original *Akenfield*, by Ronald Blythe, first printed in 1969.

3. Ronald Blythe, *Akenfield* (London: Penguin, 2005), p. 187. See also Joan Morgan and Alison Richards, *The New Book of Apples* (London: Ebury Publishing, 2002), and Sue Clifford and Angela King with Philippa Davenport, *The Apple Source Book: particular uses for diverse apples* (London: Hodder & Stoughton, 2007).

4. Taylor, *Return*, pp. 189–90.

5. Michael Pollan, *The Botany of Desire: A Plant's-eye View of the World* (London: Bloomsbury, 2003), p. 47.

6. http://gloucestershireorchardtrust.org.uk/ [Accessed on April 15, 2022].

7. Alan Davidson, *The Oxford Companion to Food*, 2nd edn. (Oxford: Oxford University Press, 2006), pp. 26–29.

8. John Parkinson, *Paradisi in sole paradisus terrestris* (1629; London: Methuen, 1904), p. 588.

9. *OED2*; William Rabisha, *The Whole Body of Cookery Dissected* (1661; Totnes: Prospect Books, 2003), p. 104; William Cavendish, *The Country Captain* (1649; Oxford: Oxford University Press, 1999), IV. ii, 379.

10. William Shakespeare, *Twelfth Night*, I. v. 167; John Kersey, *Dictionarium Anglo-Britannicum*, 2nd edn. (London: J. Wilde, 1715); William Somerville, *Hobbinol or the rural games* (1740: London: J. Stagg, 1773), III, 46–7, p. 60; Samuel Pepys, *Diary*, 27 July, 1663.

11. Gerard, *Herball*, ch. 101, 'Of the Apple-Tree', p. 1459; Philip Miller, *The Gardeners Dictionary*, abridged 4th edn. (London: John & James Rivington, 1754), vol. 2, 'MALUS, The Apple-Tree'.

12. 'Parishes: Willington', in *The Victoria History of the County of Bedford: Volume 3*, ed. William Page and Herbert Arthur (London: Constable, 1912), pp. 262–66, *British History Online*, http://www.british-history.ac.uk/vch/beds/vol3/pp262-266. [Accessed on April 15, 2022].

13. 'Parishes: Hutton Conyers', in *The Victoria History of the County of York: North Riding, Volume 1*, ed. William Page (London: Constable, 1914), pp. 403–5, *British History Online*, http://www.british-history.ac.uk/vch/yorks/north/vol1/pp403-405. [Accessed on April 15, 2022].

14. Daniel Lysons, *Magna Britannia* (London: Thomas Cadell, 1822), p. ccliv.

15. John Brand, *Observations on Popular Antiquities*, revised by Sir Henry Ellis (London: Chatto & Windus, 1853–55), vol. 1, p. 346.

16. Elizabeth Lord, *A Detection of damnable driftes* (1579); Jacob and Wilhelm Grimm, 'Hansel and Gretel', in *The Annotated Brothers Grimm*, ed. and trans. Maria Tatar (New York: Norton, 2012), p. 81; 'Jane Watson', in *Depositions from York Castle*, ed. James Raine (Durham: Published for the Surtees Society, 1861), p. 92. See also Diane Purkiss, *The Witch in History* (London: Routledge, 1996).

17. Anne Sexton, 'Jesus Suckles', line 2, in *The Complete Poems* (Boston: Houghton Mifflin, 1981), pp. 337–38.

18. Morgan and Richards, *Apples*, p. 35.

19. *Le Ménagier de Paris*, http://www.daviddfriedman.com/Medieval/Cookbooks/Menagier/Menagier.html. [Accessed on April 15, 2022]

20. Constance B. Hieatt, Brenda Hosington and Sharon Butler, *Pleyn Delit: Medieval Cookery for Modern Cooks* (Toronto; London: University of Toronto Press, 1996), no. 120.

21. Laud MS 553, in Hieatt, Hosington and Butler, *Pleyn Delit*, no. 116.

22. *Forme of Cury*, p. 87.

23. *Forme of Cury*, p. 32.

24. British Library MS Harleian 4016; see Bridget A. Henisch on wafers in *The Medieval Cook* (Woodbridge: The Boydell Press, 2009), pp. 84ff.

25. Gerard, *Herball*, 3.101, cit. John Evelyn *Silva: or, A discourse of forest-trees* (London: Colburn, 1825), vol. 2, p. 118.

26. 'Queen Mary – Volume 12: January 1558', ed. Robert Lemon, in *Calendar of State Papers Domestic: Edward, Mary and Elizabeth, 1547–80* (London:

Longman et al, 1856), pp. 96–99, *British History Online*: http://www.british-history.ac.uk/cal-state-papers/domestic/edw-eliz/1547-80/pp96-99. [Accessed on April 15, 2022]

27. 'Addenda: Miscellaneous 1571–1572', ed. Arthur John Butler and Sophie Crawford Lomas, in *Calendar of State Papers Foreign, Elizabeth, Volume 17, January-June 1583 and Addenda* (London: J. Frances, 1913), pp. 438–98, *British History Online*: http://www.british-history.ac.uk/cal-state-papers/foreign/vol17/pp438-498. [Accessed on April 15, 2022]

28. Lawson, *New orchard and garden*, pp. 25–26.

29. Edward Hasted, 'Parishes: Tenham', in *The History and Topographical Survey of the County of Kent: Volume 6* (Canterbury: W. Bristow, 1798), pp. 284–96, *British History Online*: http://www.british-history.ac.uk/survey-kent/vol6/pp284-296. [Accessed on April 15, 2022]

30. Lawson, *New orchard and garden*, p. 37.

31. John Evelyn, *Pomona: or An appendix concerning fruit-trees in relation to cider* (London: John Martyn and James Allestry, 1670), p. 3.

32. Thomas Dawson, *The Good Huswife's Jewell* (London, 1587), 38v; compare the slightly earlier 'To make an Apple Moye' from *A good Huswifes Handmaide*, 43v: 'Take Apples, and cut them in two or foure peeces, boyle them till they be soft, and bruise them in a morter, and put thereto the yolkes of two Egs, and a little sweet butter, set them on a chafingdish of coales, and boyle them a litle, and put thereto a litle Sugar, synamon and Ginger, and so serue them in.'

33. Robert May, *The Accomplisht Cook: the art & mystery of cookery* (1660; London: N. Brooke, 1685), p. 300.

34. Markham, *English Housewife*, p. 109.

35. Elinor Fettiplace, *Elinor Fettiplace's Receipt Book*, ed. Hilary Spurling (London: Viking, 1986), p. 167.

36. Kenelm Digby, *The Closet of the Eminently Learned Sir Kenelme Digbie Kt., Opened*, 1669, ed. Jane Stevenson and Peter Davidson (Totnes: Prospect Books, 1997), p. 197.

37. Rabisha, *Body of Cookery*, p. 38.

38. Hess, *Martha Washington*, p. 3.

39. Hannah Woolley, *The Gentlewomans Companion* (1675; Totnes, Prospect Books, 2001), pp. 189–90: 'Take half a score green Pippins from the Tree, pare them, and boil them in a Pottle of water till they are like a pulp, strain them from the cores, then take two pound of Sugar, and mingle it with the Liquor or pulp so strained, then set it on the fire, and as soon as it boyleth put in the Pippins you intend to preserve, so let them boil leasurely till they be enough, when they are preserved they will be green.'

40. Hess, *Martha Washington*, pp. 299–300.

41. Raffald, *English Housekeeper*, p. 108.

42. C. Anne Wilson, *Food & Drink in Britain from the Stone Age to the 19th Century* (Chicago: Academy Chicago, 2003), p. 349; Raffald, *English Housekeeper*, pp. 107–8; 177.

43. Maria Rundell, *A New System of Domestic Cookery* (London: John Murray, 1808), p. 217.

44. White, *Good Things*, pp. 228–9.

45. Markham, *English Housewife*, p. 104; Sir Hugh Plat, *Delightes for Ladies* (London, 1602).

46. Lady Anne Morton, *Receipt Book*, 1693, New York Public Library, Whitney Cookery Collection MS4.

47. Maggie Black and Deidre Le Fay, *The Jane Austen Cookbook* (Toronto: McClelland & Stewart, 2002).

48. Rundell, *Domestic Cookery*, esp. pp. 154–60, 169; Fergus Henderson and Justin Piers Gellatly, *Beyond Nose to Tail: A Kind of British Cooking* (London: Bloomsbury, 2007), pp. 146–47.

49. Acton, *Modern Cookery*, p. 354.

50. Jane Grigson, *Jane Grigson's British Cookery* (London: Atheneum, 1985); Elizabeth David, *Spices, Salt and Aromatics in the English Kitchen* (Harmondsworth: Penguin, 1981), p. 103; see also 'Apple', in Jane Grigson, *Jane Grigson's Fruit Book* (London: Penguin, 1983), pp. 1–27.

51. J. C. Loudon, *An encyclopædia of agriculture*, 3nd edn. (1825; London: Longman, Rees, Orme, Brown, and Green, 1835), p. 667.

52. Henry John Drewal, 'Performing the Other: Mami Wata Worship in Africa', *The Drama Review* 32 (1988), 160–85.

Pigs

1. Laurence Andrew, *The noble lyfe & natures of man of bestes, serpentys, fowles & fisshes* (Antwerp, 1523).

2. Marie-Louise Sjoestedt, *Celtic Gods and Heroes* (Mineola, NY: Dover, 2000), p. 35; Miranda J. Green, *Dictionary of Celtic Myth and Legend* (London: Thames & Hudson, 1997), pp. 44–45

3. Joan Thirsk, *Food in Early Modern England* (New York and Hambledon: Continuum Press, 2007), pp. 195–228, esp. p. 201.

4. 'Pleas and evidences: The Abbey rental (c.1334)', in *The Ledger Book of Vale Royal Abbey*, ed. John Brownbill (Edinburgh: Record Society, 1914), pp. 92–113, http://www.british-history.ac.uk/report.aspx?compid=52594&strquery=pig [Accessed on April 17, 2022].

5. 'Plea Rolls for Staffordshire: 3 Edward I', *Staffordshire Historical Collections, vol. 6 part 1*, ed. George Wrottesley (London: Harrison & Sons, 1885), pp. 66–72, http://www.british-history.ac.uk/report.aspx?compid=52422&strquery=pig [Accessed on April 17, 2022].

6. 'Boxgrove', in *A History of the County of Sussex: Volume 4: The Rape of Chichester*, ed. L. F. Salzman (London: Oxford University Press, 1953), pp. 140–50, http://www.british-history.ac.uk/report. aspx?compid=41725&strquery=pig [Accessed on April 17, 2022].

7. 'Market Privileges 1351–1370', *Borough Market Privileges: The hinterland of medieval London, c.1400*, ed. Hannes Kleineke (London: Centre for Metropolitan History, 2006), http://www.british-history. ac.uk/report.aspx?compid=51626&strquery=pig [Accessed on April 17, 2022].

8. 'Misc. Roll DD: 16 Nov 1319 – 5 Aug 1328 (nos 252–298)', *London Assize of Nuisance 1301–1431: A Calendar*, ed. Helena M. Chew and William Kellaway (London: London Record Society, 1973), pp. 54–69, http://www. british-history.ac.uk/report.aspx?compid=35974&strquery=pig [Accessed on April 17, 2022].

9. 'Spelthorne Hundred: Feltham', in *A History of the County of Middlesex: Volume 2: General; Ashford, East Bedfont with Hatton, Feltham, Hampton with Hampton Wick, Hanworth, Laleham, Littleton* London: Victoria County History, 1911), pp. 314–39, http://www.british-history.ac.uk/report. aspx?compid=22203&strquery=pig [Accessed on April 17, 2022].

10. 'Folios 110b-135b', in *Calendar of letter-books of the city of London: A: 1275–1298*, ed. Reginald R. Sharpe (London: J. Frances, 1899), pp. 207–30, http://www.british-history.ac.uk/report.aspx?compid=33031&strquery=pig [Accessed on April 17, 2022].

11. 'Alien Houses: Hospital of St Anthony', in *A History of the County of London: Volume 1: London within the Bars, Westminster and Southwark*, ed. William Page (London: Victoria County History, 1909), pp. 581–84, http://www. british-history.ac.uk/report.aspx?compid=35395&strquery=pig [Accessed on April 17, 2022].

12. 'Parishes: Chesterton', in *A History of the County of Oxford: Volume 6*, ed. Mary D. Lobel (London: Victoria County History, 1959), pp. 92–103, http://www.british-history.ac.uk/report.aspx?compid=63728&strquery=pig [Accessed on April 17, 2022].

13. Edward III. A.D. 1353. Letter-Book G. fol. vi. (Latin.), in 'Memorials: 1353', in *Memorials of London and London Life: In the 13th, 14th and 15th centuries*, ed. H.T. Riley (London: Longmans, Green, 1868), pp. 270–73, http://www.british-history.ac.uk/report.aspx?compid=57694&strquery=pig [Accessed on April 17, 2022].

14. E.g. Pierpont Morgan Library, MS H.8 fol. 15R, Hours of Henry VIII.

15. Henisch, *Medieval Cook*, p. 53.

16. Máire MacNeill, *The Festival of Lughnasa: A study of the survival of the Celtic festival of the beginning of harvest* (Dublin: Irish Folklore Commission, 1962), p. 43.

17. 'Parishes: St Paul's Walden', in *A History of the County of Hertford: volume 2*, ed. William Page (London: Victoria County History, 1908), pp. 405–11, http://www.british-history.ac.uk/report.aspx?compid=43301&strquery=pig [Accessed on April 17, 2022].

18. 'Parishes: Rickmansworth', in *County of Hertford*, pp. 371–86, http://www.british-history.ac.uk/report.aspx?compid=43298&strquery=pig [Accessed on April 17, 2022].

19. '*Fragmentum*, 97', in *Poetae Latini Minores*, ed. Emil Baehrens, vol. 4 (Leipzig: Teubner, 1882), p. 98.

20. Claudine Fabre-Vassas, *The Singular Beast: Jews, Christian and the Pig* (New York: Columbia University Press, 1997), p. 133.

21. R. Po-chia Hsia, *The Myth of Ritual Murder* (New Haven, CT: Yale University Press, 1988), p. 9.

22. See Cecil Roth, *A Jewish Book of Days* (London: E. Goldston, 1931), p. 313.

23. Though the young Karl Marx ate roast paschal pork and also red-dyed eggs with matzohs: Venetia Newell, *An Egg at Easter* (Bloomington: Indiana University Press, 1971), p. 159.

24. Herman Pleij and Diane Webb, *Dreaming of Cockaigne: Medieval Fantasies of the Perfect Life* (New York: Columbia University Press, 2001).

25. Ben Jonson, *Bartholomew Fair* (1614), II. v, 68–70.

26. Jonson, *Bartholomew Fair*, II. v, 147–50; William Shakespeare, *Henry IV Part 2*, II. iv, 250.

27. Jonson, *Bartholomew Fair*, II. ii, 9–10.

28. Dawson, *Plenti and Grase*, p. 102.

29. Rabisha, *Body of Cookery*, pp. 10–11; Harrison, *Description*, pp. 313–14; 126; Tusser, *Five Hundred Points*, p. 86.

30. Charles Kingsley, *Hereward the Wake* (London: J. M. Dent & Sons, 1866), vol. II, p. 106.

31. Mark Grant, *Galen on Food and Diet* (London and New York: Routledge, 2000), p. 154.

32. Thomas Cogan, *The Haven of Health* (London, 1636), R2v.

33. William Bullein, *Bulleins bulwarke of defence* (1579), fols. 74v-75r.

34. Ben Norman, *A History of Death in 17th Century England* (Barnsley: Pen & Sword Books, 2020), p. 38.

35. Jeffrey Masson, *The Pig Who Sang to the Moon* (London: Jonathan Cape, 2004).

36. Jonathan Swift, *A Modest Proposal*, in *The Restoration and Eighteenth Century*, ed. Ian McGowan (Basingstoke: Macmillan, 1989), pp. 137–44, p. 143.

37. E. B. White, 'Death of a Pig, an Essay', *The Atlantic* (1948), http://www.theatlantic.com/ideastour/animals/white-full.html [Accessed on April 17, 2022].

38. William Youatt, *The Pig* (1860), cit. Masson, *The Pig Who Sang*, p. 31.

39. Lena Cowen Orlin, *Material London, ca 1600* (Philadelphia: University of Pennsylvania Press, 2000); Emily Cockayne, *Hubbub* (New Haven, CT: Yale University Press, 2010), pp. 192–4.

40. William Cobbett, *Rural Rides* (London: Reeves and Turner, 1885), p. 75.

41. Cobbett, *Rural Rides*, pp. 168, 481.

42. Charles Lamb, 'London Fogs', in Charles and Mary Lamb, *Essays and Sketches*, ed. William MacDonald (London: J. M. Dent, 1903), p. 246; *The Life, Letters and Writing of Charles Lamb*, ed. Percy Fitzgerald (London: E. Moxon & Co., 1876), vol. 1, p. 260; Charles Lamb, Letter to Wordsworth, 30 January, 1801, *The Letters of Charles Lamb*, ed. Thomas Talfourd (London: Edward Moxon, 1849), p. 129; Denise Gigante, *Taste* (New Haven, CT: Yale University Press, 2010), p. 89

43. Percy Bysshe Shelley, 'A Vindication of Natural Diet', in *The Selected Poetry and Prose of Shelley* (Ware: Wordsworth, 2002), p. 581; Joseph Ritson, *An Essay on Abstinence from Animal Food* (London: Richard Phillips, 1802), p. 124; Charles Lamb, 'Edax on Appetite', in *The Works of Charles Lamb* (London: Edward Moxon, 1850), vol. 4, pp. 166–74; and see Gigante, *Taste*, pp. 94–110.

44. Charles Lamb, 'A Dissertation upon Roast Pig', in *The Works*, vol. 3, pp. 161–68.

45. Ritson, *Essay on Abstinence*, pp. 103–5.

46. Lamb, 'Roast Pig', pp. 165–66.

47. Charles Lamb, Letter to Coleridge, *Letters*, p. 248.

48. Lamb, 'Roast Pig', p. 165.

49. Constance Spry and Rosemary Hume, *The Constance Spry Cookery Book* (London: J. M. Dent and Sons, 1956), p. 574

50. Lane, *Jane Austen*, pp. 61–62.

51. Markham, *English Housewife*, p. 72.

52. Joanne Yate's Receipt Book, 1688, 'Jane Yeate her booke', New York Public Library, Whitney Cookery Collection, MSS Col 3318, vol. 3.

53. May, *Accomplisht Cook*, p. 145.

54. May, *Accomplisht Cook*, p. 168.

55. Dawson, *Good Huswife's Jewell*, p. 54.

56. Hieatt, Hosington and Butler, *Pleyn Delit*, nos. 6; 77; 100 and 101.

57. Hess, *Martha Washington*, pp. 58, 89.

58. Fettiplace, *Receipt Book*, p. 33.

59. Glasse, *Art of Cookery*, pp. 138; 196ff.; 256.

60. Cobbett, *Rural Rides*, p. 152.

61. Terence Scully, *The Art of Cookery in the Middle Ages* (Rochester, NY: Boydell, 1995), p. 107.

62. Lucy Yates, *The Country Housewife's Book: how to make the most of country produce and country fare* (London: Persephone Books, 2008), p. 203.

63. Copley, *Cottage Cookery*, p. 80.

64. Charles E. Francatelli, *A plain cookery book for the working classes* (1861; Whitstable and Walsall: Pryor Publications, 1993), pp. 24–25.

65. Copley, *Cottage Comforts*, pp. 80–81.

66. Copley, *Cottage Comforts*, p. 81.

67. James Greenwood, 'Veiled Mysteries', in *Odd People in Odd Places: The Great Residuum* (1883), http://www.victorianlondon.org/publications7/odd-00.htm [Accessed on April 17, 2022].

68. Greenwood, 'Veiled Mysteries'.

69. Maria Kniazeva and Russell W. Belk, 'Packaging as Vehicle for Mythologizing the Brand', *Consumption Markets & Culture* 10 (2007), 51–69.

On tea: an essay

1. Oscar Wilde, *The Importance of Being Earnest*, in *Plays, Prose Writings and Poems* (London: J. M. Dent, 1996), pp. 419–81, pp. 423; 461; 465; 429.

2. Maya-Rose Nash, *Tea-Ology* (Bloomington: AuthorHouse, 2010), p. 15; see also Jane Pettigrew, *A Social History of Tea* (London: National Trust, 2001).

3. George van Driem, *The Tale of Tea* (Leiden; Boston: Brill, 2019), p. 440; Jillian Azevedo, *Tastes of the Empire* (Jefferson, NC: McFarland, 2017), p. 63; Alexander Pope, *The Rape of the Lock*, in *The Rape of the Lock and other major writings*, ed. Leo Damrosch (London, Penguin, 2011), p. 47.

4. Ross W. Jamieson, 'The Essence of Commodification: Caffeine Dependencies in the Early Modern World', *Journal of Social History* 35 (2001), 269–94.

5. '1738 SWIFT Pol. Conversat. Introd. 2 Whether they meet … at Meals, Tea, or Visits. 1778 F. BURNEY Evelina (1791) I. xxvi. 144, I was relieved by a summons to tea. 1789 WESLEY Wks. (1872) IV. 453 At breakfast and at tea, on these two days, I met all the Society.' *OED2*.

6. Hannah More, 'Bas Bleu: Or, Conversation', https://www.eighteenthcenturypoetry.org/works/o3982-w0020.shtml [Accessed on April 14, 2022].

7. Saberi, *Teatimes*, p. 20.

8. Saberi, *Teatimes*, p. 21.

9. Cit. Pettigrew, *Social History of Tea*, p. 107–8.

10. Palmer, *Movable Feasts*, pp. 97–101.

11. *Dinner at Buckingham Palace*, ed. Paul Fishman and Fiorella Busoni (London: Metro Publishing Ltd., 2003), p. 20.

12. Pettigrew, *Social History of Tea*, pp. 102–5.

13. Dickens, *Sketches by Boz*, p. 276.

14. Daphne Du Maurier, *Rebecca* (1938; London: Virago, 2003), p. 8.

Milk

1. Dorothy Hartley, *Food in England* (London: Little, Brown, 1996), pp. 469ff.
2. Markham, *English Housewife*, p. 171.
3. Thomas Ady, *A candle in the dark* (London, 1655), p. 59.
4. W. W., *A true and iust recorde, of the information, examination and confession of all the witches, taken at S. Ofes in the countie of Essex* (1582), reprinted in *Witchcraft in England 1558–1618*, ed. Barbara Rosen (Amherst: University of Massachusetts Press, 1991), pp. 103–57, p. 143.
5. http://www.catholicculture.org/culture/liturgicalyear/activities/view.cfm?id=1185 [Accessed on April 18, 2022].
6. Rosen, *Witchcraft*, p. 112.
7. Kenneth J. Tiller, 'The Rise of Sir Gareth and the Hermeneutics of Heraldry', *Arthuriana* 17 (2007), 74–91; I am grateful to Anna Caughey for this reference.
8. *London in miniature: being a concise and comprehensive description of the cities of London and Westminster, and parts adjacent, for forty miles round* (London: Corbett, 1755).
9. French visitor to London, 1765 cit. *London Encyclopedia*, p. 769.
10. Tim Knox, 'Duck Island Cottage', *The London Gardener* 1 (1995), https://www.londongardenstrust.org/features/dicframe.htm [Accessed on June 19, 2022]; David Jacques, *Gardens of Court and Country* (New Haven, CT: Yale University Press, 2017), p. 49.
11. Mayhew, *London Labour*, p. 191.
12. Francis Bacon, *Sylva Sylvarum* (1626), §354, *The Works of Francis Bacon*, ed. Basil Montague (London: William Pickering, 1826), vol. IV, p. 176.
13. 'Elizabeth … hearing … a certeine milkemayde singing pleasauntly, wished her self to be a milkemayde as she was', in John Foxe, *Actes & Monumentes*, rev. edn. (London: 1570), II. 2294/2.
14. Robin Ganev, 'Milkmaids, Ploughmen, and Sex in Eighteenth-Century Britain', *Journal of History of Sexuality* 16 (2007), 40–67.
15. Otherwise known as 'Dabbling in the Dew': *The New Penguin Book of English Folk Songs*, ed. Steve Roud and Julia Bishop (London: Penguin, 2014), pp. 162–63.
16. Boorde, *Compendyous regyment*, p. 267.
17. Ann Yearsley, 'Clifton Hill', *Poems on several occasions* (London: G. G. J & J. Robinson, 1786), p. 84. She is described on the title page as 'a milkwoman of Bristol'.
18. Woolley, *Gentlewomans Companion*, p. 129.
19. Cockayne, *Hubbub*, p. 100.
20. Paul S. Kindstedt, *Cheese and Culture: A History of Cheese and Its place in Western Civilisation* (Vermont: Chelsea Green Publishing, 2012), pp. 117–18.

21. Kindstedt, *Cheese and Culture*, pp. 162–63.

22. Trevor Hickman, *The History of Stilton Cheese* (Stroud: Sutton, 1995), p. 171.

23. William Fordyce Mavor, *General view of the agriculture of Berkshire* (London: Sherwood, Neely and Jones, 1813), p. 375.

24. Richard Blundel and Angela Tregear, 'From artisans to "factories": the interpenetration of craft and industry in English cheese-making, c.1650–1950', *Enterprise & Society* 7 (2006), 705–39.

25. Thomas B. Macaulay, *The History of England from the Accession of James II* (London: J. M. Dent & Sons, 1848), vol. 1, p. 222: 'Something had been put into his broth. Something had been put into his favourite dish of eggs and ambergrease. The Duchess of Portsmouth had poisoned him in a cup of chocolate. The Queen had poisoned him in a jar of dried pears. Such tales ought to be preserved; for they furnish us with a measure of the intelligence and virtue of the generation which eagerly devoured them.'

26. Raffald, *English Housekeeper*, p.126; Nutt's masquerade as Glasse has been documented by Elizabeth David in her book on ices, *Harvest of the Cold Months: the social history of Ice and Ices* (London: Michael Joseph, 1994), pp. 312–13.

27. Mayhew, *London Labour*, p. 207.

28. Andrew W. Tuer, *London Cries* (London: Field & Tuer, 1883), p. 21.

29. P. Michaels, *Ices and Soda Fountain Drinks: A treatise on the Subject of Ices, Sundaes, Wholesale Ice Cream, Cordials and Soda Fountain Drinks*, London: Maclaren, 1923).

30. George R. Sims, *Living London: Its Work and Its Play, Its Humour and Its Pathos. Its Sights and Its Scenes* (London: Cassell & Co., 1902–03).

31. Report of *The Lancet* Special Commission on 'The Sanitary Condition of the Italian Quarter', *The Lancet*, 18 October 1879, p. 590.

32. *The Lancet* 146 (1895), p. 472.

33. *The Lancet* 248 (1946), p. 277.

34. David, *Harvest of the Cold Months*, p. 352.

35. William A. Jarrin, *The Italian Confectioner, or Complete economy of desserts* (London: William H. Ainsworth, 1827); William Gunter, *Gunter's Confectioner's Oracle Containing Receipts for Dessrts on the most economical plan for private families* (London: Alfred Miller, 1830); William Jeanes, *The Modern Confectioner* (London: Oxford University Press, 1861).

36. Elizabeth David, *Is there a Nutmeg in the House?* (London: Penguin, 2001), p. 274; David, *Harvest of the Cold Months*, pp. 316–22.

37. Robin Weir, John Deith, Peter Brears, et al., *Mrs Marshall, the Greatest Victorian Ice Cream Maker* (W. Yorkshire: Syon House, 1998).

38. Read more: 'The Chilling Truth about Ice Cream', *The Daily Mail* 11 December 2014, http://www.dailymail.co.uk/health/article-393432/The-chilling-truth-ice-cream.html#ixzz1YDLd8MZE [Accessed on April 18,

2022]; 'Cold Comfort Food', *The Independent* 6 August 1994, http://www.independent.co.uk/arts-entertainment/food--drink--cold-comfort-food-robin-weir-is-dedicated-to-icecream-the-real-thing-not-the-frozen-froth-were-often-sold-michael-bateman-meets-him-1374963.html [Accessed on April 18, 2022].

39. Sian Henley, 'Inside scoop: Britain's best ice cream makers', *The Daily Telegraph* 24 May 2014, https://www.telegraph.co.uk/foodanddrink/10849825/Inside-scoop-Britains-best-ice-cream-makers.html [Accessed on April 18, 2022].

40. Steve Shapin, 'Down to the Last Creampuff: The end of Haute Cuisine,' *London Review of Books* 5 August 2010, and see Michael Steinberger, *Au Revoir to All That: the rise and fall of French Cuisine* (London: Bloomsbury, 2009).

Cake

1. Thomas Tryon, *The way of health, long life and happiness* (London: A. Sowle, 1683), p. 233.

2. Glasse, *Art of Cookery*, pp. 276–77.

3. For instance, Samuel's morsel of bread (King James) is a 'cake' in John Wycliffe's 1382 translation, 1 Samuel 2. 36.

4. Bartholomaeus Anglicus, *De Proprietatibus Rerum*, trans John Trevisa (1398; 1495), xvii. ixvii, 643.

5. Brian Branston, *The Lost Gods of England* (London: Thames and Hudson, 1957).

6. Thomas Blount, *Glossographia* (London, 1674).

7. John Aubrey, *Remaines of Gentilisme*, p. 23.

8. Brand, *Observations on Popular Antiquities*, vol. 2, pp. 484–85.

9. *A Book of Characters, selected from the writings of Overbury, Earle, and Butler* (Edinburgh: William Nimmo, 1865), p. 25.

10. Meera Lester, *Why Does Santa Wear Red?: And 100 Other Christmas Curiosities Unwrapped* (London: Adams Media, 2007), p. 146.

11. *Wiltshire Notes and Queries* I (Devizes: G. Simpson, 1893–94), pp. 150–51.

12. Asterius, *Oratio 4: Adversus Kalendarum Festum*, trans. Galusha Anderson and Edgar Goodspeed (New York: Pilgrim Press, 1904), https://www.tertullian.org/fathers/asterius_04_sermon4.htm [Accessed on April 20, 2022].

13. Henisch, *Medieval Cook*, pp. 84–85.

14. 'Thou sall accept the sacrifice of rightwisnes, obles and offrandis', Richard Rolle, *The Psalter*, ed. H. R. Bramley (Oxford: Clarendon Press, 1884), p. 187.

15. Joseph Addison, *The Tatler* no. 220 (1710), 8.

16. Dawson, *Good Huswife's Jewell*, pp. 80–81.

17. Aubrey, *Remaines of Gentilisme*, p. 167.

18. Bob Bushaway, *By Rite: Custom, Ceremony and Community in England 1700–1880* (London: Junction, 1982), pp. 157–58; Wilson, *Eating with the Victorians*, p. 27.

19. Henisch, *Medieval Cook*, p. 133.

20. Henisch, *Medieval Cook*, pp. 18 ff.

21. Aubrey, *Remaines of Gentilisme*, p. 40.

22. Rev. Thomas Fosbroke, 6 January 1817, in William Hone, *The Every-Day Book*, ed. Kyle Grimes, http://honearchive.org/etexts/edb/day-pages/006-january06.html [Accessed on April 20, 2022].

23. Letter from Sir Thomas Randolph to the Earl of Leicester, 15 January 1563, in John Pinkerton, *Ancient Scottish Poems*, cit. *Satirical Poems of the Time of the Reformation*, ed. James Cranstoun (Edinburgh and London: William Blackwood and Sons, 1891–93), vol. II, p. 103.

24. Brand, *Observations on Popular Antiquities*, vol. 1, pp. 23, 30.

25. Digby, *Closet*, p. 181.

26. Thomas Naogeorgus and Barnabe Googe, *The popish kingdome, or reigne of Antichrist* (London, 1570).

27. Brand, *Observations on Popular Antiquities*, vol. 1, 526ff.

28. Pepys, January 6, 1659/1660, Pepysdiary.com/diary/1660/01/06/ [Accessed on April 20, 2022].

29. Charles Lamb, *Elia* (London: Carey, Lea & Carey, 1828), p. 23.

30. Edmund Gayton, *Festivous Notes on the History and adventures of the Renowned Don Quixote* (London, 1654), p. 17.

31. Henri de Valbourg Misson, *M. Misson's Memoirs and observations in his travels over England*, trans. John Ozell (London: D. Browne, 1719), pp. 35, 71.

32. Aubrey, *Remaines of Gentilisme*, p. 65.

33. Thomas Speght, *The workes of our antient and lerned English poet, Geffrey Chaucer* (London, 1598).

34. Brand, *Observations on Popular Antiquities*, vol. 2, p. 101; See also John Leland and Thomas Hearne, *Joannis Lelandi Antiquarii de rebus britannicis collectanea* (London: Richardson, 1770), vol. iv. p. 400.

35. Aubrey, *Remaines of Gentilisme*, p. 22.

36. Aubrey, *Remaines of Gentilisme*, p. 65.

37. 'Memorials, Introduction', in *Wills: 20 Edward I (1291–2), Calendar of wills proved and enrolled in the Court of Husting, London, Part 1*, ed. R. R. Sharpe (London: J. Frances, 1889), pp. 103–7, p. xxi, http://www.british-history.ac.uk/report.aspx?compid=66828&strquery=cake [Accessed on April 20, 2022].

38. Wellcome MS 1127; D. Wujastyk, *A handlist of Sanskrit and Prakrit manuscripts in the library of the Wellcome Institute for the History of Medicine* (London: WIHM, 1985).

39. Wellcome MS 1127.

40. White, *Good Things*, p. 292.

41. Wellcome MS 1127.

42. Harleian MS. 279, Thomas Austin, *Two Fifteenth-Century Cookery-Books* (London: N. Trübner & Co. for The Early English Text Society, 1888), p. 35; spelling modernised.

43. Hester Denbigh, New York Public Library, Whitney Cookery Collection MS 11.

44. Abigail Rand, *Abigail Rand Her Book*, New York Public Library, Whitney Cookery Collection MS 7.

45. The most fearsome examples of these are the baby shower cakes depicting actual birth: http://www.cakewrecks.com/home/2013/4/18/10-hilariously-inappropriate-baby-shower-cakes.html; http://www.cakewrecks.com/home/2013/10/25/you-want-vagina-cakes-ill-give-you-vagina-cakes.html [Accessed on April 20, 2022].

46. Raffald, *English Housekeeper*, pp. 132, 273.

47. Annie Gray, *The Greedy Queen: Eating with Victoria* (London: Profile Books, 2017), pp. 102–3.

48. Anonymous, *The Private Life of the Queen by a Member of the Royal Household* (New York: D. Appleton and Company, 1901).

49. Gray, *Greedy Queen*, p. 171.

50. Spry and Hume, *Constance Spry Cookery Book*, p. 814.

On dinner: an essay

1. Frances Burney, *Evelina* (Oxford: Oxford University Press, 2008), p. 320.

2. Leland, *Antiquarii*, pp. 4–6.

3. Leland, *Antiquarii*, p. 2; The list of provisions is reprinted in various forms by numerous writers, e.g. William Wheater, *The History of the Parishes of Sherburn and Cawood* (Selby: W. B. Bellerby, 1865), p. 101. Modern discussions include Michael Shrub, *Feasting, Fowling and Feathers* (London: T. & A. D. Poyser, 2013), pp. 22–23.

4. Gardiner, *Before the Mast*.

5. Pepys, *Diary*, https://www.pepysdiary.com/diary/ [Accessed on June 16, 2022].

6. Palmer, *Movable Feasts*, p. 8.

7. Thomas de Quincey, 'The Casuistry of Roman Meals', *The Collected Writings of Thomas de Quincey*, ed. David Masson (Edinburgh: Adam and Charles Black, 1890), Vol. VII, pp. 11–43, pp. 38–39; James Woodforde, *The Diary of a Country Parson 1758–1802*, ed. John Beresford (Norwich: Canterbury Press, 1999), p. 49.

8. *The Letters of Samuel Johnson*, ed. Robert W. Chapman (Oxford: Clarendon Press, 1952), vol. 3, p. 41.

9. James Boswell, *Life of Samuel Johnson* (London, Chicago, Toronto: William Benton, 1791), 5 August 1763, p. 134.

10. Boswell, *Life of Johnson*, 3 June 1784, p. 535.

11. James Boswell, *Journal of a Tour to the Hebrides* (London: T. Cadell and W. Davies, 1812).

12. Peter Brears, *Cooking and Dining with the Wordsworths* (London: Excellent Press, 2011); Stephen Gill, *William Wordsworth: a Life* (Oxford: Oxford University Press, 1989), p. 245.

13. Dorothy Wordsworth, *The Grasmere and Alfoxden Journals*, ed. Pamela Woof (Oxford: Oxford University Press, 2002), pp. 59; 108; 54, and numerous entries on pies.

14. Joseph Budworth, *A Fortnight's Ramble to the Lakes in Westmoreland, Lancashire, and Cumberland* (London: Hookham & Carpenter, 1792), p. 101.

15. Lady Charlotte Campbell Bury, 'General Rules for a Good Dinner', *The Lady's Own Cookery Book*, 3rd edn. (London: Henry Colburn, 1844), p. 13.

16. De Quincey, 'Roman Meals', pp. 24; 36.

17. Bronte, *Jane Eyre*, p. 13; Brears, Dining with the Wordsworths.

18. Cedric Dickens, *Drinking with Dickens* (London: Mears Caldwell Hacker, 1980), p. 15; Dickens, *Our Mutual Friend*, p. 132.

19. Dickens, *Drinking*, p. 59; Charles Dickens, *The Life and Adventures of Martin Chuzzlewit* (1843–44; London: Penguin, 1999), pp. 195–96.

20. Dickens, *Bleak House*, p. 327.

21. Lady Maria Clutterbuck [Charles Dickens], *What shall we have for dinner?* (London: Bradbury & Evans, 1852), p. vi.

22. Penelope Vogler, 'Rereading: What Shall We Have for Dinner?', *The Guardian* 16 December 2011, https://www.theguardian.com/books/2011/dec/16/rereading-charles-dickens-dinner [Accessed on April 22, 2022].

23. Jennifer Davies, *The Victorian Kitchen* (London: BBC Books, 1989), p. 97; Susan M Rossi-Wilcox, *Dinner for Dickens* (Totnes: Prospect Books, 2005).

24. Daniel Pool, *What Jane Austen Ate and Charles Dickens Knew* (New York: Touchstone Books, 1993), citing *London at Dinner; or, where to dine* (London, 1858), p. 75.

25. John Ruskin, *Fors Clavigera: Letters to the workmen and labourers of Great Britain* (Orpington: Kent G. Allen, 1871–74), Letter 31, 1 July 1873.

26. William Makepeace Thackeray, 'A Little Dinner at Timmins's', *The Works of William Makepeace Thackeray* (London: Smith, Elder & Co., 1884), vol. XII, pp. 160–61.

27. Woolf, *Room of One's Own*, p. 23.

28. Betjeman, *Summoned by Bells*, pp. 101–2, 93.

29. Virginia Woolf, *Mrs. Dalloway* (1925), in *The Annotated Mrs. Dalloway*, ed. Merve Emre (New York; London: Liveright, 2021), pp. 140; 207.

30. Letter to Jacques Raverat, in Virginia Woolf, *Letters Vol. 3: A Change of Perspective 1923–1928*, ed. Nigel Nicolson and Joanne Trautmann (London: Chatto & Windus, 1981), p. 164.

31. Daisy Dunn, *Not Far from Brideshead* (London: Weidenfeld & Nicholson, 2022), pp. 108–9; 94–95.

32. Palmer, *Movable Feasts*, p. 15.

33. Juliet Gardiner, *Wartime: Britain 1939–1945* (London: Headline, 2004), p. 74.

34. Nigel Gray, *The worst of times: an oral history of the Great Depression in Britain* (London: Wildwood House, 1995), pp. 28, 35.

35. Adrian Tinniswood, *The Long Weekend: Life in the English Country House, 1918–1939* (London: Jonathan Cape, 2016), p. 278.

36. Georgina Landemare, *Churchill's Cookbook* (London: Imperial War Museums, 2015).

37. Marguerite Patten, *We'll Eat Again: A collection of recipes from the war years* (London: Hamlyn, 2004).

38. 'Relever d'une pointe de Cayenne, et completer avec une julienne composée de: 70 grammes de jambon maigre et de langue écarlate, 50 grammes de champignons, et 30 grammes de truffe': Escoffier, *Guide Culinaire*, p. 34; for the commercial sauce, see https://en.wikipedia.org/wiki/%C3%80_la_zingara.

39. Fiona McCarthy, *Last Curtsey: The End of The Debutantes* (London: Faber and Faber, 2006), p. 101.

40. McCarthy, *Last Curtsey*, p. 62.

41. George Sayer, *Jack: a life of C. S. Lewis* (Wheaton, IL: Crossway Books, 2005), p. 342.

Chicken, and a few rarer birds

1. Andrew Lawler, *Why did the chicken cross the world? The epic saga of the bird that powers the civilisation* (New York: Atria Books, 2014), p. 7.

2. Peter W. Hammond, *Food & Feast in Medieval England* (Dover: Alan Sutton, 1993).

3. 'The Beefsteak Club', https://janeausten.co.uk/blogs/extended-reading/the-beefsteak-club [Accessed on April 26, 2022].

4. Columella, *De Re Rustica* 8.2.13; 8.2.7 (London: Loeb Classical Library, 1941).

5. Joan P. Alcock, *Food in Roman Britain* (Stroud: Tempus, 2001), p. 45.

6. Cool, *Eating and Drinking*, p. 102.

7. Rosemary Luff, *Colchester Archaeological Report 12: Animal bones from excavations in Colchester, 1971–85* (Colchester: Colchester Archaeological Trust Ltd, 1993), pp. 97–98.

8. Cool, *Eating and Drinking*, p. 102.

9. Nina Crummy, Philip Crummy and Carl Crossan, *Colchester. Archaeological. Report 9: Excavations of Roman and later cemeteries, churches and monastic sites in Colchester, 1971–88* (Colchester: Colchester Archaeological Trust Ltd, 1993), pp. 178–80.

10. Joseph D. Vehling, *Cookery and Dining in Imperial Rome* (New York: Dover, 1977), 6, 9, 13.

11. Seneca, *To Helvia on Consolation*, X. 8–9.

12. *Historia Augusta*, XX. 5–7, cit. 'Apicius', http://penelope.uchicago. edu/~grout/encyclopaedia_romana/wine/apicius.html [Accessed on May 6, 2022].

13. Cit. *Forme of Cury*, and repeated and modernised in Hieatt, Hosington and Butler, *Pleyn Delit*, no. 69.

14. Dalby, *Walter of Bibbesworth*, lines 280–87, p. 65.

15. Jotischky, *Hermit's Cookbook*, p. 175.

16. Roger Virgoe, *Private Life in the Fifteenth Century: Illustrated letters of the Pastons Family* (London: Macmillan, 1989), p. 72; John Russell, *The Boke of Nurture*, in *Early English Meals and Manners*, ed. Frederick J. Furnivall (Oxford: Oxford University Press for the Early English Text Society, 1868), pp. 54–55, https://www.gutenberg.org/files/24790/24790-h/nurture.html [Accessed on May 6, 2022].

17. William Shakespeare. *As You Like It*, II. vii. 154.

18. In the twenty-first century, only Vietnamese Pho Soup uses sandalwood, and even that is dying out; if overused, it can be indigestible.

19. Harleian MS. 4016.

20. Paget to Petre, 11 December 1645, 'Henry VIII: December 1545, 6–15', in *Letters and Papers, Foreign and Domestic, Henry VIII, Volume 20 Part 2: August-December 1545*, ed. James Gairdner and R. H. Brodie (London: HMSO, 1907), pp. 471–88, http://www.british-history.ac.uk/report. aspx?compid=80435&strquery=chicken [Accessed on May 6, 2022].

21. 'Randolph to Killigrew. [Jun. 21–22.] Elizabeth: June 1560', *Calendar of State Papers, Scotland: volume 1: 1547–63, ed. Joseph Bain (1898)*, pp. 417–38, http://www.british-history.ac.uk/report.aspx?compid=44060& strquery=chicken [Accessed on May 6, 2022].

22. Action Desk Sheffield, 'Horsemeat, A Wedding Treat', *WW2 People's War*, http://www.bbc.co.uk/history/ww2peopleswar/stories/25/a7269825.shtml [Accessed on May 6, 2022].

23. A reflection of the folk belief that running water cannot be charmed.

24. John Stow, *A Survey of London* (1603; Oxford: Clarendon Press, 1908), pp. 216–23.

25. 'Memorials: 1351', in *Memorials of London and London Life: In the 13th, 14th and 15th centuries*, ed. H. T. Riley (London: Longmans and Green, 1868), pp. 266–69.

26. Cockayne, *Hubbub*, pp. 82, 96.
27. 'Parishes: South Stoke', in *A History of the County of Oxford: Volume 7: Dorchester and Thame hundreds*, ed. Mary Lobel (London: Oxford University Press, 1962), pp. 93–112, http://www.british-history.ac.uk/report.aspx?compid=63771&strquery=chicken [Accessed on May 6, 2022].
28. Edward Hasted, 'Parishes: Brookland', in *The History and Topographical Survey of the County of Kent: Volume 8* (Canterbury: W. Bristow, 1799), pp. 382–88, http://www.british-history.ac.uk/report.aspx?compid=63502&strquery=chicken [Accessed on May 6, 2022]; my emphasis.
29. 'Cucklington', in *A History of the County of Somerset: Volume 7: Bruton, Horethorne and Norton Ferris Hundreds*, ed. A. P. Baggs et al. (London: Victoria County History, 1999), pp. 177–84, http://www.british-history.ac.uk/report.aspx?compid=18751&strquery=chicken [Accessed on May 6, 2022].
30. Thirsk, *Food in Early Modern England*, p. 251.
31. Thirsk, *Food in Early Modern England*, p. 254.
32. Markham, *English Housewife*, pp. 100–3.
33. John Murrell, *A New Booke of Cookerie* (London, 1615), http://www.uni-giessen.de/gloning/tx/1615murr.htm [Accessed on May 6, 2022].
34. Markham, *English Housewife*, pp. 89–90.
35. Fettiplace, *Receipt Book*, p. 119.
36. Rabisha, *Body of Cookery*, p. 129.
37. May, *Accomplisht Cook*, p. 11.
38. Anne W. Blencowe, *The Receipt book of Mrs. Anne Blencowe* (London: G. Chapman, 1925), p. 73.
39. Raffald, *English Housekeeper*, p. 32.
40. *Calendar of State Papers Domestic: William and Mary, 1689–90, ed. William John Hardy (London: Her Majesty's Stationery Office, 1895)*, pp. 172–205, http://www.british-history.ac.uk/report.aspx?compid=57541&strquery=chicken [Accessed on April 26, 2022].
41. Jane Austen, *Pride and Prejudice* (1813; Oxford: Oxford University Press, 1985), p. 192.
42. Austen, *Pride and Prejudice*, p. 146.
43. 'Letters of Timothy Tickler, esquire', *Blackwood's Edinburgh Magazine* (1823), p. 14.
44. Mary Elizabeth Braddon, *The Doctor's Wife* (London: J. Maxwell, 1864), vol. 1, p. 260.
45. Patricia Bunning Stevens, *Rare Bits: Unusual Origins of Popular Recipes* (Athens, OH: Ohio University Press, 1998), p. 93.
46. Beeton, *Household Management*, p. 464; Beeton omits the white wine.
47. Victorian Table Etiquette' in *Lone Hand Western: Reliving History*, http://lonehand.com/victorian_table_etiquette.htm [Accessed on May 6, 2022].

48. Harrietta Oxnard Ward, *Sensible etiquette of the best society, customs, manners, morals, and home culture* (Philadelphia: Porter & Coates, 1878), p. 162.

49. David Gilmour, *The British in India: three centuries of ambition and experience* (London: Allen Lane, 2018), p. 351.

50. Glasse, *Art of Cookery*, 1st edn. (London, 1747), p. 101; by the fifth edition the 'two Fowls or Rabbits' had become 'two small Chickens', p. 101.

51. Michael Axworthy, *The Sword of Persia: Nader Shah, from Tribal Warrior to Conquering Tyrant* (London: I.B. Tauris, 2006).

52. Mary Randolph, *The Virginia Housewife* (1824; Bedford, MA., Applewood Books, 2007), pp. 164; 80.

53. William Makepeace Thackeray, 'Kitchen Melodies – Curry', *The Oxford Thackeray* (London: H. Frewds, 1908), p. 198.

54. Beeton, *Household Management*, pp. 215, 174, 259, 336, 487.

55. Mike Paterson, 'The Hindoostane Coffee House, *The London Historians' Blog*, https://londonhistorians.wordpress.com/2011/09/05/the-hindoostane-coffee-house/ [Accessed on May 6, 2022]; Elizabeth Buettner, '"Going for an Indian": South Asian Restaurants and the Limits of Multiculturalism in Britain', *The Journal of Modern History* 80 (2008), 865–901.

56. Jeremy Macclancy, *Consuming Culture: why you eat what you eat* (New York: Henry Holt, 1993), pp. 204–5.

57. Charles Allen, *Plain Tales from the Raj: Images of British India in the Twentieth Century* (London: Deutsch, 1974), pp. 94, 126–27.

58. Steel and Gardiner, *Complete Indian Housekeeper*, p. 305.

59. Steel and Gardiner, *Complete Indian Housekeeper*, p. 250.

60. Kim Wagner, *Rumours and Rebels: A New History of the Indian uprising of 1857* (Oxford: Peter Lang, 2017), pp. 62–69; see also Andrew J. Rotter, *Empires of the Senses: Bodily Encounters in Imperial India and the Philippines* (Oxford: Oxford University Press, 2019), p. 228. Rotter points out that the infected item was meant to be offered to a deity.

61. Richard Collier, *The Sound of Fury: An Account of the Indian Mutiny* (London: Collins, 1963), p. 114.

62. Donald Richards, *Cawnpore and Lucknow: A Tale of Two Sieges* (Barnsley, Pen & Sword, 2007), p. 45.

63. Saul David, *The Indian Mutiny: 1857* (London: Penguin, 2003), p. 528; P. J. O. Taylor, *What really happened during the mutiny: a day-by-day account of the major events of 1857–1859 in India* (New Delhi: Oxford University Press, 1997), p. 323.

64. *An Englishwoman in India: the memoirs of Harriet Tytler*, ed. Anthony Sattin (Oxford: Oxford University Press, 1986).

65. David Burton, *The Raj at Table*, p. 113; Henrietta A. Hervey, *Anglo-Indian cookery at home: a short treatise for returned exiles/ by the wife of a retired Indian officer* (London: 1895), https://wellcomecollection.org/works/zdv3tfgq

[Accessed on May 6, 2022]. See also David Burnett and Helen Saberi, *The road to Vindaloo: Curry Cooks & Curry Books* (Totnes: Prospect Books, 2008).

66. Rudyard Kipling, *Kim* (1901; Oxford: Oxford University Press, 1987), p. 196.

67. Mauser, *How to live in England on a Pension* (Oxford: Oxford University Press, 1934), p. 18; Elizabeth Buettner, *Empire Families: Briton and Late Imperial India* (Oxford: Oxford University Press, 2004). p. 203.

68. *Englishman*, 17 May 1926, p. 29; Marjorie Grant Cook and Frank Fox, *The British Empire Exhibition, 1924. Official Guide* (London: Fleetway Press, 1924).

69. 'An Indian Dinner Origin of Mulligatawny Soup', *The Times* 10 February 1939.

70. Vicky Bhogle, *Cooking like Mummyji: Real British Asian Cooking* (London: Simon and Schuster, 2006), pp. 104–7.

71. Bhogle, *Cooking like Mummyji*, pp. 16–17.

72. Lewis Wright, *The New Book of Poultry* (London: J. Frances, 1902), p. 166.

73. Massimo Montanari, *Medieval tastes: Food, Cooking, and the Table* (New York: Columbia University Press, 2015), pp. 83, 163.

74. Rachel Duffett, *The Stomach for Fighting: Food and the Soldiers of the Great War* (Manchester: Manchester University Press, 2012), p. 28; Wright, *Poultry*, p.166.

75. Duffett, *Stomach for Fighting*, p. 216.

76. Duffett, *Stomach for Fighting*, p. 217.

77. Duffett, *Stomach for Fighting*, p. 219.

78. Duffett, *Stomach for Fighting*, p. 198.

79. John Lewis-Stempel, *Six Weeks: The Short and Gallant Life of the British Officer in the First World War* (London: Weidenfeld & Nicolson, 2010), p. 132.

80. Lewis-Stempel, *Six Weeks*, p.133.

81. Avner Offer, *The First World War, an agrarian interpretation* (Oxford: Clarendon Press, 1989), pp.51–52; Lizzie Collingham, *The Taste of War: World War Two and the battle for food* (London: Allen Lane, 2011), p. 13.

82. Jill Beattie's wartime memories, cit. Collingham, *Taste of War*, p. 100.

83. Mrs O. Smith, Diarist 5427, pp. 25–33, *Mass Observation*, https://www.massobservation.amdigital.co.uk/ [Accessed on June 19, 2022].

84. Nancy Jackman with Tom Quinn, *The Cook's Tale: Life below Stairs as it really was* (London: Coronet, 2012), pp. 191–94.

85. 'Egg industry fury over salmonella claim', BBC 3 December 1988, http://news.bbc.co.uk/onthisday/hi/dates/stories/december/3/newsid_2519000/2519451.stm [Accessed on May 6, 2022].

86. White, *Good Things*, pp. 173, 188.

87. Escoffier, *Guide Culinaire*, pp. 377–81.

88. Agnes Jekyll, *Kitchen Essays, with recipes and their occasions* (New York: T. Nelson & Sons, 1922), p. 189.

89. Jekyll, *Kitchen Essays*, p. 48.

90. Major Frederic Newhouse, D.S. 426, *Mass Observation*.

91. Adrienne Williamson, D.S. 186, *Mass Observation*.

92. Marguerite Patten, *Marguerite Patten's Century of British Cooking* (London: Grub Street, 2015), p. 23.

93. Patten, *Century of British Cooking*, p. 39.

94. Patten, *Century of British Cooking*, p. 89.

95. Patten, *Century of British Cooking*, pp. 78, 252.

96. Spry and Hume, *Constance Spry Cookery Book*, p. 1005.

97. Eagerly endorsing it, Prue Leith gives a different version: 'Whole chickens (not tasteless breasts) are slowly poached in stock and wine, and the sauce contains sweated onion, curry spices, tomato puree, red wine, bay leaf, lemon, apricot puree, homemade mayo, cream and seasoning': Prue Leith, 'Prue Leith on Constance Spry: The coronation chicken is still on the menu, *The Guardian*, 2 November 2018, https://www.theguardian.com/food/2018/nov/02/prue-leith-on-constance-spry-the-cooks-cook [Accessed on May 6, 2022].

98. 'The history behind the Coronation Chicken recipe', https://www.cordonbleu.edu/london/coronation-chicken/en [Accessed on May 6, 2022].

99. Patten, *Century of British Cooking*, p. 95.

100. Bob Holmes, *Flavour: A User's Guide to Our Most Neglected Sense* (London: W H. Allen, 2017), pp. 40–41.

101. Fiona Duncan, '"The dust was as thick as the breakfast tea, the chamber as chilly as our toast" – In the footsteps of Fanny Cradock, the Bon Viveur', *The Telegraph* 31 March 2018, https://www.telegraph.co.uk/travel/hotels/articles/from-the-archives-fanny-cradock-bon-viveur-hotels/ [Accessed on May 6, 2022].

102. Simon Swift, 'To Diet For', *The Guardian* 14 October 2006, https://www.theguardian.com/culture/2006/oct/14/foodanddrink.features16 [Accessed on May 6, 2022].

103. Delia Smith, *Delia Smith's Cookery Course* (London: BBC, 1978), p. 179.

104. Elizabeth M. Collingham, *Curry: A Tale of Cooks and Conquerors* (London: Vintage Books, 2006), pp. 2–3.

105. Dean Nelson and Jalees Andrabi, '*Chicken tikka masala row grows as Indian chefs reprimand Scottish MPs over culinary origins*', *The Telegraph* 4 August 2009, http://www.telegraph.co.uk/foodanddrink/5972643/Chicken-tikka-masala-row-grows-as-Indian-chefs-reprimand-Scottish-MPs-over-culinary-origins.html [Accessed on May 6, 2022]; 'Scots lay claim to Chicken Tikka Masala, Indians fume', *The Times of India* 6 August 2009, https://timesofindia.indiatimes.com/world/uk/scots-lay-claim-to-chicken-tikka-masala-indians-fume/articleshow/4861329.cms [Accessed on May 6, 2022].

106. Ann Barr and Peter York, *The Official Sloane Ranger diary: the first guide to the Sloane Year* (London: Ebury, 1983), p. 116.

107. Read more: Anne Shooter, 'Delia Vs Heston', *The Daily Mail* 12 January 2013, http://www.dailymail.co.uk/femail/food/article-2261172/Delia-smith-Vs-Heston-Blumenthal-Waitrose-end-unlikely-double-act-recipes-actually-work-best.html#ixzz2KKWAmbGt [Accessed on May 6, 2022].

108. Bee Wilson, *Consider the Fork* (London: Penguin, 2012), p. 338.

109. Russ Parsons, 'The California Cook: Squinting into the future of cooking', *Los Angeles Times* 29 September 2012, https://www.latimes.com/food/la-xpm-2012-sep-29-la-fo-calcook-20120929-story.html [Accessed on June 15, 2022]; Nathan Myhrvold, *Modernist Cuisine at Home* (Bellevue, WA: The Cooking Lab, 2012).

110. Richard Griffiths, 'You can't Polish a Chlorinated Chicken', 12 January 2018, *The British Poultry Council*, https://www.britishpoultry.org.uk/you-cant-polish-a-chlorinated-chicken/ [Accessed on May 6, 2022].

111. Madlen Davies, 'The reason chicken is a popular British food? Because we started factory farming', *The New Statesman* 26 July 2017, https://www.newstatesman.com/culture/food-drink/2017/07/reason-chicken-popular-british-food-because-we-started-factory-farming [Accessed on May 6, 2022].

112. Steve Hawkes, 'Britain is running out of space to farm chickens, warns poultry industry', *The Telegraph* 13 October 2013, https://www.telegraph.co.uk/news/earth/agriculture/10375738/Britain-is-running-out-of-space-to-farm-chickens-warns-poultry-industry.html [Accessed on May 6, 2022].

113. John S. A. Edwards, et al., 'The Influence of Eating Location on the acceptability of identically prepared foods', *Food Quality and Preference*,14 (2003), 647–52.

114. Amy Fleming, 'Food Texture: How Important is it?', *The Guardian* 2 July 2013, http://www.guardian.co.uk/lifeandstyle/wordofmouth/2013/jul/02/food-texture-how-important [Accessed on May 6, 2022].

115. The study by the Institute of Brain Chemistry and Human Nutrition at London Metropolitan University compared samples of chicken analysed over the past 35 years. They found that a chicken contained 8.6 grams of fat per 100 grams in 1970, compared with 22.8 grams in a supermarket bird in 2004. Over the same period, the amount of protein fell by more than 30% from 24.3 grams per 100 grams to 16.5: Yiqun Wang, et al., 'Modern organic and broiler chickens sold for human consumption provide more energy from fat than protein', *Public Health Nutrition* 13 (2009), https://www.cambridge.org/core/journals/public-health-nutrition/article/modern-organic-and-broiler-chickens-sold-for-human-consumption-provide-more-energy-from-fat-than-protein/01F274E25955E7263FEC19F3BAA64B2E [Accessed on June 15, 2022].

116. Felicity Lawrence, 'Fowl Play', *The Guardian* 8 July 2002, http://www. guardian.co.uk/uk/2002/jul/08/bse.foodanddrink [Accessed on May 6,2022].

117. Benjamin Weiser, 'Word for Word/Fast-Food Fracas', *The New York Times*, 26 January 2003, http://www.nytimes.com/2003/01/26/weekinreview/word-for-word-fast-food-fracas-your-honor-we-call-our-next-witness. html?pagewanted=3&src=pm [Accessed on May 6, 2022].

118. Bibi van der Zee, 'Why factory farming is not just cruel – but also a threat to all life on the planet', *The Guardian* 4 October 2017, https://www. theguardian.com/environment/2017/oct/04/factory-farming-destructive-wasteful-cruel-says-philip-lymbery-farmageddon-author [Accessed on May 6, 2022].

119. 'Freshwater use and farm animal welfare', *Compassion in World Farming*, https://www.ciwf.org.uk/media/3758866/Freshwater-use-and-farm-animal-welfare-4-page.pdf [Accessed on May 6, 2022].

120. Zoe Williams, 'Did you fall for Swaddles organic swindle', *The Guardian* 26 September 2009, http://www.guardian.co.uk/environment/2009/sep/26/ organics-fooddrinks [Accessed on May 6, 2022]; 'Organic food company guilty of selling non-organic food', *The Telegraph* 22 July 2009, http://www. telegraph.co.uk/news/uknews/law-and-order/5888811/Organic-food-companly-guilty-of-selling-non-organic-food.html [Accessed on May 6, 2022].

121. 'Company director jailed for re-selling cheap supermarket food as expensive organic produce', *The Daily Mail* 23 September 2009, http://www.dailymail. co.uk/news/article-1215622/Company-director-jailed-selling-fake-organic-food-served-Buckingham-Palace.html#ixzz2GviyUuB4 [Accessed on May 6, 2022].

122. Germaine Greer, *The Whole Woman* (London: Doubleday, 1999), p. 147.

123. Niki Segnit, *The Flavour Thesaurus: Pairings, Recipes and Ideas for The Creative Cook* (London: Bloomsbury, 2010), p. 27.

124. Jay Rayner, *Wasted Calories and Ruined Nights: A Journey Deeper into Dining Hell* (London: Faber & Faber, 2018), p. 4.

125. Frederik Pohl and Cyril M. Kornbluth, *The Space Merchants* (London: Heinemann, 1955).

126. Jeremy Laurance, 'Fast food is addictive in same way as drugs, say scientists', *The Independent* 30 January 2003, https://www.independent.co.uk/news/ science/fast-food-is-addictive-in-same-way-as-drugs-say-scientists-131374. html [Accessed on May 6, 2022]; 'Fast food "as addictive as heroin"' BBC News 30 January 2003, http://news.bbc.co.uk/1/hi/health/2707143.stm [Accessed on May 6, 2022].

127. Jay Rayner, 'Sure, it might be cruel, but intensive farming saves lives', *The Guardian* 13 January 2008, http://www.theguardian.com/commentisfree/ 2008/jan/13/lifeandhealth.ruralaffairs [Accessed on May 6, 2022].

128. Andy Cawthray, 'Food for thought, or thoughts for food?' *The Guardian* 14 March 2013, http://www.guardian.co.uk/lifeandstyle/gardening-blog/2013/mar/14/keeping-chickens-personality [Accessed on May 6, 2022].

129. Siobhan Abeyesinghe et al., 'Do hens have friends?', *Applied Animal Behaviour Science* 143 (2013), 61–66.

130. Annie Potts, *Chicken* (London: Reaktion Books, 2012).

131. Alok Jha, 'Who are you calling chicken? T. rex's closest loving relative found on the farm', *The Guardian* 13 April 2007, http://www.guardian.co.uk/science/2007/apr/13/uknews.taxonomy [Accessed on May 6, 2022]; Potts, *Chicken*.

Tinned food

1. Jane Brocket, *Cherry Cake and Ginger Beer: A Golden Treasury of Classic Treats* (London: Hodder & Stoughton, 2008).

2. Enid Blyton, *Five Run Away Together* (1944; London: Hodder, 1991), p. 94.

3. Blyton, *Five Run Away Together*, p. 100.

4. Jean-Paul Barbier, *Nicolas Appert inventeur et humaniste* (Paris: Royer, 1994); Gordon L. Robertson, *Food Packaging: Principles and Practice* (New York: Marcel Dekker Inc., 1998), p. 187.

5. Scott, 'The can opener wasn't invented until 48 years after the invention of the can', *todayifoundout.com* 4 June 2012, https://www.todayifoundout.com/index.php/2012/06/the-can-opener-wasnt-invented-until-48-years-after-the-invention-of-the-can/ [Accessed on April 24, 2022].

6. *Food Nations: Selling Taste in Consumer Societies*, ed. Warren Belasco and Phillip Scranton (New York: Routledge, 2002).

7. Steel and Gardiner, *Complete Indian Housekeeper*, and for more on this topic: E. M. Collingham, *Curry*; Burton, *Raj at Table*; Pat Barr, *The Memsahibs: The Women of Victorian India* (London: Martin Secker & Warburg Ltd., 1976).

8. M. K. Gandhi (1999), *The Collected Works of Mahatma Gandhi*, vol. 1 (New Delhi: Publications Division, Government of India, 1999).

9. David Gilmour, *The British in India: three centuries of ambition and experience* (London: Allen Lane, 2018), p. 354.

10. 'Wyvern', *Culinary Jottings*, pp. 25–29.

11. Bhogle, *Cooking like Mummyji*.

12. Arthur Ransome, *Swallows and Amazons* (1930; London: Red Fox, 2001), p. 100.

13. Vilhjalmur Stefansson, *Not by Bread Alone* (New York: MacMillan, 1946), pp. 263–4, 270.

14. Royal Society of Victoria Exploration Committee account book 1858–1873, http://www.burkeandwills.net.au/Stores/provisions.htm [Accessed on April 24, 2022].

15. Fridtjof Nansen, *Farthest North* (New York and London: Harper and Brothers, 1897), vol. 2, p. 121.

16. Anne Chotzinoff Grossman and Lisa Grossman Thomas, *Lobscouse and Spotted Dog* (New York; London: W.W. Norton, 1997).

17. Enid Blyton, *Five Go Off to Camp* (1948; London: Hodder, 1991), p. 70, emphasis mine

18. Enid Blyton, *Five on a Hike Together* (1951; London: Hodder, 1991), p. 73, emphasis mine.

19. T. S. Eliot, *The Waste Land*, lines 223–38 (1922; New York; London: Norton, 2001).

20. John Carey, *The Intellectuals and the Masses* (London: Faber, 1992); George Orwell, *The Road to Wigan Pier* (1937; Oxford: Oxford University Press, 2021), p. 68.

21. Orwell, *Wigan Pier*, p. 69.

22. Orwell, *Wigan Pier*, p. 140.

23. Orwell, *Wigan Pier*, p. 141; George Orwell, *Down and out in Paris and London* (1933; Oxford: Oxford University Press, 2021), pp. 54–55; 84ff; 155.

24. Orwell, *Wigan Pier*, p. 69.

25. Slater, *Eating for England*, p. 4.

26. Xanthe Clay, 'My 49p lunch with a girl called Jack', *The Telegraph* 4 March 2013, http://www.telegraph.co.uk/foodanddrink/9900773/My-49p-lunch-with-a-girl-called-Jack.html [Accessed on April 24, 2022].

27. Marler Clark, 'Florida: Botulism Risk from Canned Products', *Food Poison Journal* 18 December 2007, http://www.foodpoisonjournal.com/tags/canned-food/ [Accessed on April 24, 2022].

28. Michael Ondaatje, *The English Patient* (Toronto: McClelland and Stewart, 1992).

29. Betty Friedan, *The Feminine Mystique* (London; New York: W.W. Norton, 1963), p. 186.

30. Shannon Hayes, *Radical Homemakers* (Left to Write Press, 2010). See also 'The Radical Homemaker', http://theradicalhomemaker.net/ [Accessed on April 24, 2022], but for a response see Madeline Holler, 'I am Radical Homemaker Failure', *salon.com* 30 June 2010, http://www.salon.com/2010/06/30/radical_homemaker_failure/ [Accessed on April 24, 2022].

31. Shannon Hayes, *Radical Homemakers*, Kindle edition, loc. 465.

32. See Sharon Astyk, http://www.resilience.org/author-detail/1007660-sharon-astyk [Accessed on April 24, 2022]; Sharon Astyk, *Independence Days: A Guide to Sustainable Food Storage and Preservation* (Gabriola Island, BC: New Society Publishers, 2009); Rod Dreher, *Crunchy Cons: The New Conservative Counterculture and Its Return to Roots* (New York: Three Rivers Press, 2006).

33. Carlo Petrini (2009) *Terra Madre: Forging a New Global Network of Sustainable Food Communities* (White River Junction, VT: Chelsea Green Publishing, 2009).

34. 'Housing costs dominate family expenditure', *The Guardian*, 28 January 2008, https://www.theguardian.com/money/2008/jan/28/familyfinance. consumeraffairs [Accessed on May 24, 2022]; Department for Environment, Food & Rural Affairs, 'Family Food 2019/20', 27 January 2022, https://www. gov.uk/government/statistics/family-food-201920/family-food-201920 [Accessed on May 24, 2022].

ACKNOWLEDGEMENTS

As we all know, memories of food are often sharper and emotion-ally more profound than the first experience of it, and this book is laden with the delight I have taken in eating during its creation. This book has been longer in the making than any banquet has a right to be. It would be appropriate for these acknowledgements to list every-one who has eaten with me over the past 15 years, everyone who has made me a drink, everyone who has handed me a plate – and I don't want to omit the people who wash the dishes. The list of those who should graciously be thanked for the food they have served to me and the thinking they have done about it, however, would be longer than the book itself, so that try as I might, the acknowledgements evidently participate in the process the book seeks to undermine, of concealing the labour of food.

Nevertheless, an attempt must be made. I'm enormously grateful to audiences at the Institute of Historical Research, London, Williams College, the Shakespeare Association of America conference, York Festival, Bradford Festival, the Renaissance Association of America conference, the Williams alumni touring group, and a variety of re-en-actment societies, especially the Beaufort Society, for their responses to my ideas. There is no more stringent or exacting group of scholars anywhere than food historians, and I know that many of them know more than I do about specific subjects. I am grateful to them all. The undergraduates whom I have taught have been an endless source of inspiration. Many of them have worked on and thought about food and eating with me, and helped me to refine my ideas. Perhaps it is invidious, but I would single out Charlie Cao, a man so in love with food history that he recreated the earliest pound cake recipe with only a fork to help him do the beating, and Caleb Bompas, who first alerted me to the extent to which Elizabeth David is a modernist fiction writer. Successive graduate students have borne with my obsession and offered thoughts and observations. Librarians at a range of archives have helped enormously as well: the New York Public Library manuscript archive and the Wellcome Collection particularly. Both Keble College and Oxford University have made the research for this book possible by generously giving me research leave. The encouragement of colleagues is especially vital to a long-term project like this one.

This book was sparked by a conversation with Arabella Pike, whose commitment to this project has never wavered; I thank her, and I'm also very grateful to Alex Gingell, and to the peerless and patient copy-editing of Steve Gove. My agent Catherine Clarke has as always been a stay and support. Many people have helped me to pull the mass of research into shape, most of all Fran Fabricki and Debanjali Biswas. I owe a particular debt of gratitude to the members of the London History Salon, especially Sarah Dunant, Stella Tillyard, and Philippa Gregory for warmth and intelligent listening ears. I am especially grateful to Hermione Dowling for her invaluable research on food in children's books. Colleagues at Oxford have been generous, and I am hugely thankful to Matthew Bevis for holding the fort during my research leave, and to Rupert Christiansen for his warm and kind support.

At the same time, this book has taken me far from libraries and into conversations with the manager of Shipton Mill, the apple sellers at Stroud farmers' market, cheesemongers and fishmongers in Marylebone High Street, fishermen on the upper Thames, chefs, bakers, jam makers, and farmers, as well as waiters everywhere who have been willing to answer questions and chat about food with me.

There have been some changes around my own family table. My parents both died in the years while I was working on this book, but I have my memories of the meals we shared and the talks that flowed around our dinner table. My children have grown up in that same decade, and have contributed their own passions and loathings to it, forging our family history into food memories.

Ivan Dowling has sat across from me at many tables, including our own, from local pubs to starred places, and tolerated my insatiable curiosity about what we ate and why while calmly enjoying his own choices. This book is for him, and I can only apologise for the fact that it is a poor recompense for his company.

LIST OF ILLUSTRATIONS

'Milk Below Maids (Cries of London)' (*Hulton Archive/Getty*)
Poultry merchants (*The Print Collector/Alamy*)
Workers preparing cans of fruit and vegetables (*Popperfoto/Getty*)

INDEX